drawn by Roger Cheney

Concepts and Mechanisms of Perception

CONCEPTS AND MECHANISMS OF PERCEPTION

R. L. Gregory

*Professor of Neuropsychology and Director
of the Brain and Perception Laboratory,
University of Bristol*

DUCKWORTH

First published in 1974 by
Gerald Duckworth & Co. Ltd.
The Old Piano Factory
43 Gloucester Crescent, London NW1

ISBN 0 7156 0556 9

Filmset by Keyspools Ltd, Golborne, Lancs
Printed in Great Britain by
Unwin Brothers Ltd, Old Woking, Surrey

Contents

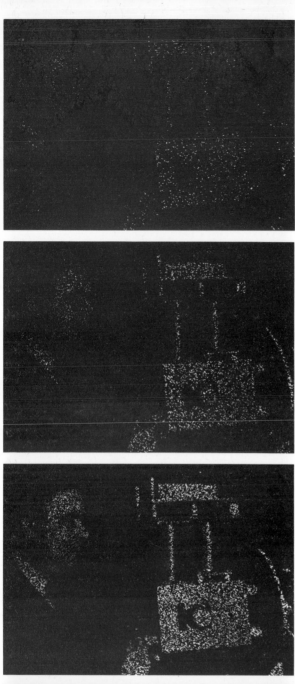

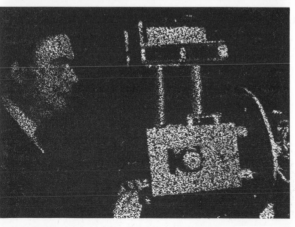

The author, and his disturbance-rejecting camera, are revealed by increasing data. Data points are given by a new video sampling technique, developed in the Brain and Perception Laboratory.

Preface

This book contains the papers written, some with colleagues, over the last twenty years that still seem to me to be of interest. Most of them have appeared widely scattered, in scientific and philosophical journals, but some have been written specially for this book. They fall into three categories: first, experiments, mainly on visual perception; secondly, the design of various instruments, including data recorders, a device for improving photographs taken with astronomical telescopes through the atmosphere, and a machine for drawing pictures in three dimensions. The third category is philosophy, dealing mainly with difficulties of interpreting experimental data to discover processes of perception and aspects of brain function. All the published papers are given here in full. The diagrams and graphs have been redrawn, mainly by Mr Vincent Joyce. In the text occasional improvements in grammar and expression have been made; but I thought it best to make no essential changes in the content.

Included here also in full is the case study – now, I am told, difficult to obtain – of the recovery of vision in a man effectively blind since early infancy, who received corneal grafts to his eyes when he was over fifty years of age. The study of his recovery of vision, following the operations, was carried out with Miss Jean Wallace, who was my first research assistant and to whom I owe special thanks as a colleague.

Thanks are due also to Professor Violet Cane, for her mathematical skill and generous expenditure of time, energy and ideas, especially on problems of neural 'noise' limiting sensory discrimination, and associating this with ageing; and to Mr Stephen Salter for his most expert work on designing and building many of the instruments and devices – especially the image-improving camera. His skill as an engineer shows up my failings as a 'gadgeteer'. Technicians are vital to any laboratory. I was unusually fortunate in my first technician,

Mr William Matthews, now Chief Technician of the Cambridge Psychology Department. Life was never quite the same after he left my laboratory. Thanks are also due to Mr Philip Clark, my photographic assistant over the last ten years, who started working with me at the age of fifteen. He is responsible for many of the photographs in this book.

The papers are linked with extensive newly written passages, which give the background to each project, and in many cases introduce fresh arguments or additional data. There is a full index and bibliography; and when I have had co-authors they are acknowledged. Much that is in this book would have been impossible without their work – for which I express great thanks.

I am grateful also to the various Research Foundations which have supported our work. We have not always managed to produce what was required, or expected: so additional thanks are due for their unfailing tolerance. I would not have started without the encouragement and support of the late Sir Frederic Bartlett, F.R.S., and Dr Norman H. Mackworth, then Director of the Medical Research Council's Applied Psychology Unit, at Cambridge. This support was continued by Professor Oliver Zangwill, Head of the Department of Psychology in the University of Cambridge, under whom I was a Demonstrator and later a Lecturer. He allowed me the facilities to accept grants to organize a group for developing instruments, in addition to the more usual running of experiments, and teaching of undergraduates and research students, in his Department.

In 1967 I left Cambridge, to help to found the Department of Machine Intelligence and Perception, in the University of Edinburgh. Christopher Longuet-Higgins, F.R.S., a distinguished Fellow of Corpus Christi College, of which I was also a Fellow, gave up the Chair of Theoretical Chemistry at Cambridge, while a leader in his field, to become a 'new boy' in a new subject. We joined Donald Michie, who a few years before had started the Experimental Programming Unit at Edinburgh. Donald Michie had also changed subjects, being at one time Reader in Experimental Surgery at Oxford. All three of us, in our mid-forties, switched our allegiances to the computer and the dream of building Robots. So we found ourselves out on an artificial limb, partly of our own creation. Most of the people in my Cambridge Laboratory moved to Edinburgh. Jim Howe became a major force in the administration of the new Department. The Bionics Unit, which I ran, was launched by a generous grant from the Nuffield Foundation. The Department was financed mainly by the Science Research Council.

The University, under the Principal and Vice Chancellor, Sir Michael Swann, F.R.S., created three Research Professorships and several other posts, as well as a building, which, however (because pre-adaptation cannot be expected to be as appropriate as Natural Selection) fell somewhat short of the ideal. The imagination of the University in founding the Department was not always matched by our limited tolerance of vicissitudes.

In 1970 I left Edinburgh to set up the Brain and Perception Laboratory in the Department of Anatomy of the University of Bristol. This owes its existence to the generosity of the Medical Research Council; to the University, under the Vice Chancellorship of Dr Alec Merrison, F.R.S., and to Professor Barry Cross who gave it generous space in his Department in the Medical School. Here we are trying to alloy our experience from Cambridge and Edinburgh, as well as from the several American Departments from which I have received vital stimulation, especially M.I.T., U.C.L.A. and N.Y.U. It is impossible to do justice to the generosity of my American friends.

Secretaries in our Universities tend to be undervalued people. They are paid less than junior technicians carrying far less responsibility and often showing less initiative. From my first secretary, Mrs Olive Faircloth, to my present, Mrs Moyra Goodban, my secretaries have been trusted friends, who share jokes and crises. I cannot thank them sufficiently for their tolerance, loyalty and intelligence.

This book owes its existence to my publisher and close friend, Colin Haycraft, who ten years ago commissioned my first book, *Eye and Brain*; and to his staff, especially Miss Emma Fisher. Finally I should like to thank my wife, Freja, who has done the proof correcting, and preparation of the bibliography and index, as well as undertaking that most difficult of jobs: being my wife.

Brain and Perception Laboratory, Bristol, 1973. R.L.G.

Pretext

Much of research is a kind of play activity: a game against Nature and sometimes a game against one's colleagues and rivals. It is a game with many sets of only partly formulated or understood rules, making 'progress' and a 'step forward' difficult to evaluate. Individually, people rely very much on that most curious and exciting sense of dawning insight—the 'Aha!' sensation. It is perhaps the goal and chief reward of trying to solve problems. The problem can be trivial; I once had an *aha*, at full strength, when stopping a lampshade slipping down its wire, by using a bent hairpin as a toggle so that the heavier the weight the more strongly the hairpin gripped the wire. This is a typical example. It arose from irritation, with useless attempts with sticky tape, and there was a certain economy and neatness in the solution—though of course it was not essentially new. In fact, one must have used the same toggle principle on the running rigging of model sailing boats, as a child. This again is typical; the idea, an 'invention' even, only has limited novelty. It is little more, perhaps never more than a reshuffling of the pack of one's concepts, to draw a new combination which shows promise. Perhaps the *aha* experience is a gasp of recognition, that the novel draw of concept cards fits surprisingly with features from the past to improve some aspect of the future. For a full-strength *aha*, it must be (or at least seem to be) one's own novelty: a reshuffle of one's own pack of cards. There is then the primitive pleasure of owning, for a time, this unique secret: then to divulge it to the poised ear of a friend; who must assume the right expression of appreciating your *aha*, almost as though it had been his own, and yet recognizing it as yours. This is the supreme test and sign of friendship in a laboratory, and too rare. But of course one man's *aha* may be another's yawn. Or worse: he thought of it days, or months, before and dropped it as useless. Then he comes up with *his* stunning new *aha*, which you are supposed to see and admire as the Ultimate

Thought. There is of course a lot of serious, sometimes tragic, rivalry and farcical play-acting in all this. People seek approval; but if given too easily it counts for nothing, so approval is continually sought where it is least likely to be found. Universities and laboratories vary greatly in their rewards by approval, and their maintenance of standards by challenge and criticism. The problem is to live with criticism and use it—even accept much of it as just—while keeping one's own individual approach. No doubt some of the eccentricity found in astringent places, such as Cambridge, is a defense against criticism; so that individual originality may not be quite defeated by tradition.

Protective eccentricity gives such charmed places as Cambridge colour and amusement; and it protects not only individual optimism, but also the shared game-playing activity essential to the generation of ideas. It is surely possible to be too serious where seeking truth is concerned. It would be interesting to know how many ideas arise directly from jokes—and why humour is regarded as a threat—and why so little research has been done on what is funny and why. Of course jokes, and games, can be at least as serious and important as 'real' things, as shown by the man playing chess who broke his leg as it was twined round the leg of the chess table. Most labs have their own private jokes, and in America one can buy jokes to stick on one's door. Jean Wallace, my first assistant, and I had a joke we tended with care. It started as a splendid hyacinth, living in solitary state in a glass beaker. Then we got another, which we called the lowercinth. Finally, a third joined the hyacinth and the lowercinth —our cynthesis. To visitors they were simply three plants in a row, in beakers.

A disturbing aspect of ideas is how they are geographically located. In talking philosophy to an Oxford man there are subtle but distinct differences of aims and beliefs. Similarly, religions and (perhaps more understandably) political ideas are geographically located. So, depending upon where you are born, or live, you accept the surrounding *zeitgeist* as generally true, but without any *aha*. The *aha* comes only with a jolt, with sudden change. But suppose there is a 'brain centre' giving the *aha* experience: should we really expect our 'aha brain centre' to be latched to the truth? Why should we take *ahas* more seriously than hiccoughs? Yet, do philosophers or mathematicians have any other sign that they have arrived at a truth—that they can stop thinking and start talking? If one man's *aha* is another's yawn, or if *ahas* are contradictory (as they can be), why should we accept them? If they correlate highly with the place where one lives, or (positively or negatively) with one's teacher's ideas, then surely all philosophies, religions and politics are suspect when judged by *ahas*. This, surely, is partly why 'hard' experimental fact and behaviourist accounts in psychology have such power. It is the triumph of the hard physical sciences that new observation and theories can sweep across geographical and cultural boundaries, sometimes within weeks, to change all educated human thought. Psychology is not like this. It is only a few 'hard' ideas (nearly always taken from other sciences) such as Shannon's Mathematical Theory of Information, which break through the barriers between 'schools' of psychology.

The theories which have something of this 'hard' power describe man as a system already essentially familiar in physics or engineering. This is a sign of the weakness of psychological experiments—they seldom reveal anything very surprising. Concepts are chosen which are already familiar within the physical sciences. So the originality of ideas in psychology is far less than the ideas in quantum mechanics, or fundamental particle theory. It is indeed extraordinary that matter is described in fantastic terms in physics, while in psychology mind is described by analogy with discarded 'common sense' accounts of matter. But the outstanding fact is that we are clearly very different from other lumps of matter: if only because we think and find things frightening or funny. This at once brings out the factual inadequacy of Behaviourism—espoused with most force recently by B. F. Skinner—as a philosophy. It must be admitted that it has inspired many important experiments; but can we believe it as an account of ourselves? Can we believe that 'consciousness' is an empty word? that seeing red is no more than responding in certain ways to photic stimulation, with no inner state of a 'red' sensation?

It is surprisingly easy to use the verbal techniques of philosophy to show Behaviourism as paradoxical and self-defeating. For example if knowing, considering, and so on are rejected and if all words are mere noises (though associated with actions), then why should I consider Behaviourists' reports or comments as significant? More specifically, why should I accept such a statement as 'There is no such thing as feeling' as more than empty noises? Here we are reminded of the poignant postcard received by Bertrand Russell, saying: 'I am a solipsist—why are there so few other philosophers like me?'

In practice, Behaviourist psychologists are far from consistent. In the laboratory there is no pain; but at home, tread on the toe of their dog, or their wife, and the Behaviourists are as upset as the rest of us. In fact, they do pay more attention to words—including words such as 'pain' and 'red'—than they do, say, to sneezes. It is very hard to believe that Behaviourists do not, like other men, believe that words can somehow represent internal states. Surely they should try to discover more about these states rather than deny them. But if there are such obvious inconsistencies and rejections of fact, why does Behaviourism exert its seductive influence on experimental psychologists? Why do clever men, for example, deny individual memory—though like the rest of us they expect us to remember what is in their books or that we have met before? I shall hazard some guesses.

Behaviourism attempts to limit its descriptions to 'stimuli' and 'responses'. Now both stimuli and responses are *physical events* (flashes of light, limb movements, and so on), which can be recorded and measured with the standard techniques of the physical sciences, and described without extending the usual concepts of established science. So Behaviourist psychology may look like physics or engineering, and so be accepted as 'hard' science. By contrast, the *experience* of red, or pain, or seeing a joke seems very different—not part of physics or engineering, not part of science—even a little spooky. The aim and hope of Behaviourism is to exorcise the 'ghost in the machine', by denying all but physical stimuli and responses.

It is possible to believe that as a philosophy Behaviourism misleads devastatingly, while also holding that it is useful—for concentrating the attention of experimentalists on problems which can be readily tackled in the laboratory. Certainly much has been discovered with experiments relating stimuli to responses, by people who apparently reject experience and the problems it imposes. This rejection of what most of us would take as basic facts, may have helped them—perhaps in much the same way that a horse may run a race better when wearing blinkers. But blinkered horses run races at the cost of missing much that goes on around them.

We may generalize this with a further analogy—not from running to a goal but from building a building. Like scaffolding—necessary to support the builders and parts of an incomplete building—so scientists need, at certain stages of theory-construction, a temporary scaffolding of concepts, to support their enthusiasm and their half-formed arguments. The danger is confusing the 'building' with the 'scaffolding' and getting so used to living on the scaffolding that the building never is finished, or is abandoned as unnecessary. This may indeed go some way to explaining the present apparent distrust of science; for scientists are, perhaps, apt to describe the conceptual scaffolding, erected for temporary support, when the public wish to be shown the building emerging within. The scaffolding may hide parts of the building, at least from some points of view, so the builder may not be the best person to describe the architecture of what we know. Here philosophers and the popularisers of science may be surer guides.

Is the discovery of facts or the development of theories the main aim of science? If we had an indefinitely large number of facts about the brain, but without linking concepts, would we understand brains? Facts serve theories. Facts alone cannot predict, control, or give the *aha* of understanding. But to hold a theory does imply limitations of view. One cannot hold that planets move in ellipses and in circular epicycles at the same time. The sensation of insight might come by merely shielding the mind from alternative views. This can avoid distraction, but it might hide essential facts, or places or ways to find them. One can be sympathetic to Skinner's rejection of psychological theories, if one suspects that the theories hide what may be important. The predictive power of psychological theories is, by and large, low; so why should one have confidence in them? On the other hand, should one reject endeavours to develop theories of brain function as being inevitably useless or misleading? Personally, I think that a point of view is necessary for guiding research; and it should be based on as general considerations as possible. Philosophy has its place here, allowing the mind to range beyond available facts and yet imposing a discipline; and keeping communication open with its subtly special use of words. For what seem to be very general reasons (rather than specific experiments) I now consider that to understand perception we should develop certain concepts not to be found in physiology. The new concepts are closer to computer 'software' statements than to physics, or physiology. This implies a judgement (or bias) as to what is important, and where we are likely to find significant new facts. These alternative views, these 'paradigms', to use T. S. Kuhn's term, are vitally important in directing research and thinking. They must be appreciated if we are to understand what the other man is trying to do, or say. For this reason I shall include in this Pretext my present conclusions on the science and philosophy of perception.

An adequate theory of perception should include not only the favoured sense of sight but also: hearing, touch, hot and cold, taste, smell, balance and position of the limbs, the various kinds of pain; and tickle, from its irritation to sensuous pleasure and delirious laugh-making. To the philosopher and the experimental scientist it is how we see that offers the most exciting questions, with hearing the runner-up, for sight dominates by seeming directly to give reality. By simply looking we seem to understand what we see. This close association between seeing and knowing makes the sense of vision attractive not only to philosophers, but also to experimental psychologists and physiologists who hope to discover, in the brain, mechanisms serving our experience and knowledge of the world. By coming to understand how we see, might we not at one stroke discover also how we think, remember, formulate hypotheses, appreciate beauty and—most mysterious—accept pictures and words as symbols conveying not merely present reality, but other realities distant in space and time? But if seeing involves all this, surely the net of understanding must be cast wide.

Perceptual theories form a spectrum: from 'Passive' to 'Active' theories. Passive theories suppose that perception is essentially camera-like, conveying selected aspects of objects quite directly, as though the eyes and brain are undistorting windows. The baby, it is supposed, comes to see not by using cues and hints to infer the world of objects from sensory data, but by selecting useful features of objects available to it directly; without effort, or information processing, or inference. Active theories, taking a very different view, suppose that perceptions are constructed, by complex brain processes, from fleeting fragmentary scraps of data signalled by the senses and drawn from the brain's memory banks—themselves constructions from snippets from the past. On this view, normal everyday perceptions are not part of—or so directly related to—the world of external objects as we believe by common sense. On this view all perceptions are essentially fictions: fictions based on past experience selected by present sensory data. Here we should not equate 'fiction' with 'falsity'. Even the most fanciful fiction as written is very largely true, or we would not understand it. Fictional characters in novels generally have the right number of heads and noses, and even many of the opinions of people we know. Science fiction characters may have green hair and an exoskeleton—but is this novelty not a mere reshuffling of the pack of our experiences? It is doubtful if a new 'card', suddenly introduced, could be meaningfully described or seen.

The Passive paradigm may, at least initially, seem more acceptable as a scientific theory. It fits well with—and indeed essentially is—the familiar 'stimulus/response' notion in which behaviour is described as controlled directly by prevailing conditions. This is also familiar in engineering: in most devices 'input' directly controls 'output'; and much emphasis is put on measuring input and output, and relating them by transfer functions or something equivalent, to describe the system. Skinner claims to do much the same—to give at least a statistical account of the relationship between stimulus (input) and behaviour (output) in animals and men. An engineer would go on to suggest 'models' of what the internal mechanisms might be which transform inputs into outputs. But, rather curiously, Skinner does not attempt to make this further step, and apparently distrusts it. His description is purely in terms of input-output relations, with emphasis on how the probability of certain kinds of behaviour is changed by environmental changes, especially 'reinforcers'. Skinner himself has little interest specifically in perception, but Passive theories of perception are in many ways similar. They have the same initial scientific credibility, but are (I believe) essentially inadequate. They deny that perception is an active combining of features stored from the past, building and selecting hypotheses of what is indicated by sensory data. On the Active account we regard perceptions as essentially fictional. Though generally predictive, and so essentially correct, cognitive fictions may be wrong—to drive us into error. On this Active view, both veridical (correct-predictive) and illusory (false-predictive) perceptions are equally fictions. To perceive is to read the present in terms of the past to predict and control the future.

Why should one want to push all this about 'brain fictions' (as I do) when stimuli and responses are so easily observed, and so like the usual stuff of science? The essential reason is (I believe) very easily demonstrated, by common observation and by experiment. Current sensory data (or 'stimuli') are simply not adequate to control behaviour directly in familiar situations. Behaviour may continue through quite long gaps in sensory data, and remain appropriate though there is no sensory input. But how can 'output' be controlled by 'input' when there is no input? The fact is that sensory inputs are not continuously required, or available, and so we cannot be dealing with a pure input-output system. Further, when we consider any common action, such as placing a book on a table (a favourite example of philosophers), we cannot test from retinal images the table's solidity and general book-supporting capabilities. In engineering terminology, we cannot monitor directly the characteristics of objects which must be known for behaviour to be appropriate. This implies that these characteristics are inferred, from the past. The related highly suggestive—indeed dominating—fact is that perception is predictive. In skills, there may be zero delay between sensory input and behaviour. But how could there be zero delay, except by acting upon a predictive hypothesis? Surely J. J. Gibson's description of perceptions as selections from the available 'ambient array' will not do: it would have to be a selection from a *future* 'ambient array' for the Passive account to work: but this evokes a metaphysics we cannot welcome or accept.

The significance of prediction in perception has too long been almost totally ignored. The kind of laboratory data which show the predictive power, and limitations and errors, of the sensory-motor system most clearly, are data from human tracking. In experiments in my laboratory we use a large oscilloscope screen, to display a (circular) target, which is tracked with a joy stick, positioning a marker spot to be kept within the target circle as it follows some function. In addition, the target is made to disappear (by z-modulation of the oscilloscope) at intervals—the subject being required to continue tracking it, though it is not visible. Success indicates clearly the subject's internal model, or hypothesis, of the function the target is following though it is invisible. Fig. 0.1(a) shows the tracking of a simple sine wave track, which is continually visible. Note that there is *no delay* between the target and the marker. Fig. 0.1(b) shows the effect of data gaps on this track: they have little or no effect when the track is simple and familiar to the subject. Figs. 0.2(a) and 0.2(b) show a more complicated course, also familiar to the subject. The 'kink' is predicted, with no reaction-time, and the data gaps still have little effect. Figs. 0.3(a) and 0.3(b) show the effects of a 'noise' track. Here prediction is impossible; errors occur during the data gaps; and false predictions may generate very large errors. Here we see dramatically the essential power of prediction. In spite of the physiological delay between sensory input and motor output, there is no delay where prediction is possible. In spite of absence of input, during the data gaps performance continues appropriately where prediction is possible. A simple input-output view of this situation does not cover the facts even of this case, where the available data are directly relevant to the task (see Vince 1948). In most situations, sensory data are only indirectly related to the perception or the performance.

It is the fact that behaviour does not need continuous, directly appropriate sensory data that forces upon us the notion of inference from available sensory and brain-stored data. This account is very much in the tradition of the nineteenth-century polymath physicist and physiologist Hermann von Helmholtz, who described perceptions as 'unconscious inferences'. This notion was unpalatable to later generations of psychologists, who were over-influenced by philosophers in their role—sometimes useful but in this case disastrous—of guardians of semantic inertia: objecting to inference without consciousness. But with further data on animal perception, and computers capable of inference, this essentially semantic inhibition has gone. Curiously, though, the kinds of inference required for perception are remarkably difficult to compute. The recent engineering-science of Machine Intelligence is finding it surprisingly difficult to design computer programs to identify objects from TV camera pictures. The reason seems to be (apart from the very large and fast

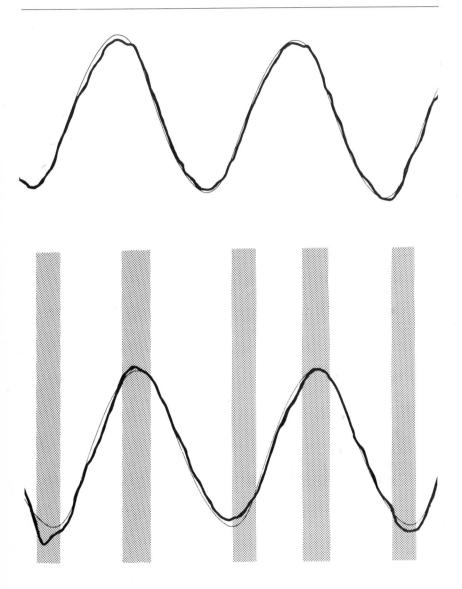

Fig. 0.1 (a and b)

(a) *The motion of a target (a small circle) moving up and down on the screen of a large oscilloscope is shown. The subject steers a marker spot with a joy stick, aiming to keep the spot within the circle. The target course is shown by the thin line, the subject's track by the thick line. After some practice with this simple repeating course there are few errors, and no systematic delay — so the subject is evidently basing his performance on his running prediction of the course, rather than on the course itself.*

(b) *the same as (a) above, except that the target is frequently removed (by Z-modulation of one beam of the oscilloscope) for one-second periods, without warning. Performance continues through the data gaps, without serious error, after practice. This shows the power of prediction to interpolate through data gaps (shown by grey bars).*

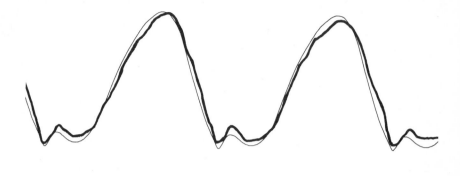

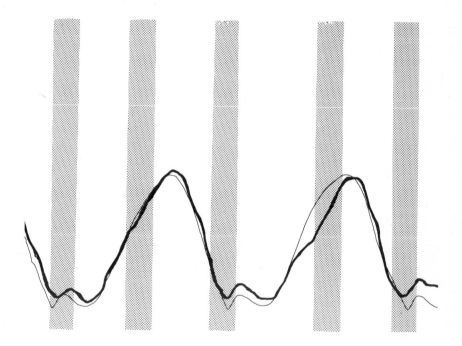

Fig. 0.2 (a and b)
(a) *A more complicated, but still a repeating and predictable track. There may still be no delay time between the target and tracking courses – so the subject can predict complex courses. A stimulus/response analysis of this situation is evidently not adequate—for he is following a prediction of the stimulus, not the stimulus itself.*
(b) *The same as (a) above, but with the one-second data gaps. Performance can still continue through the data gaps – so it cannot be controlled by input, as there is no input during the data-gaps.*

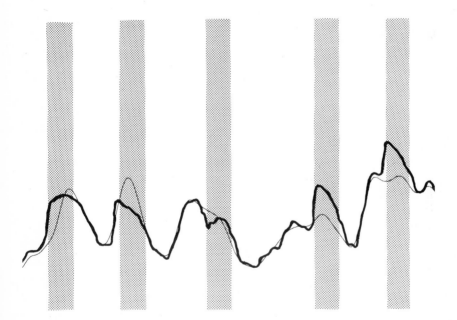

Fig. 0.3 (a and b)
(a) *A random ('noise') track. Here tracking is quite accurate, when slow, though delayed. Some errors are probably due to unfortunate anticipations. ('Trends' tend to be continued after they could have been corrected: so this does not look like 'neutral' servo following).*
(b) *The same as* (a) *above, but with the one-second data gaps. Here very large errors are generated. They are generated not by the subject ceasing to 'respond', but by following unfortunate predictions of the course, when the target is invisible.*

computers required to perform the operations serially) that the computer requires a vast amount of stored data of common object properties, with ready and rapid access. It needs what we have called 'fictions' to augment and make use of data monitored from the world by its camera eye and—in machines dealing with real objects—its touch probes. In short, we may think of perception as an engineering problem, but it is a highly atypical problem even for advanced computer engineering, and it requires a special philosophy which is unfamiliar in science, because only brains and to a limited extent computers are cognitive.

The notion that interpreting objects from patterns is a 'passive' business must strike the computer programmer engaged on this problem, in Machine Intelligence, as an extremely non-funny joke. His problem is to devise Active programs adequate even for perceptual problems of embarrassing simplicity, solved by simple creatures long before man came on the scene.

The notion of perceptions as predictive hypotheses going beyond available data is alien and suspect to many physiologists. Cognitive concepts appear unnecessary, even metaphysical—to be explained away by physiological data. Certainly more physiological data are needed: but will they tell us by what mechanisms the brain's hypotheses are mediated, or will the 'brain fiction' notion drop out as unnecessary? Prediction is dangerous, but there are surely strong reasons for believing cognitive concepts to be necessary. In the first place, it is not surprising that special concepts should be required for brain research, because the brain is unique, in nature, as an information-handling system. (Or at least it is on an Active theory of brain function.) With the development of computers, we now have other information-handling systems to consider: it is interesting to note that to describe computers, 'software' concepts are adopted, similar to cognitive concepts.

More basically, what are essentially cognitive concepts are very familiar in all the sciences, but hidden under a different guise—the *method* of science. Generalisations and hypotheses are vital to organised science, for the same reasons that they are essential for brains handling data in terms of external objects. Science is itself not 'Passive' in this sense: it puts up hypotheses for testing, and acts on hypotheses rather than directly on available data. Cognitive concepts are surely not alien to science, when seen as the brain's (relatively crude) strategies for discovering the world from limited data—which is very much the basic problem of all science. Scientific 'observations' without hypotheses are surely powerless, as an eye is powerless without a brain's ability to relate data to possible realities—effectively blind.

The full power of human brain fiction is apparent when we consider how little current sensory information is needed, or is available, in typical situations. Here we do not need initially to consider particular experiments; and indeed the intentional simplifications and restrictions of the laboratory environment can make the point less obvious—that behaviour is generally appropriate to features of the world which are not continually available to the senses. When you trust your weight to the floor, or your mouth to the spoonful of food, you have not monitored the ground's strength or the food's palatability: you have acted on trust, on the basis of the past. You have acted according to probabilities, based on generalisations from past events—and neither generalisations nor probabilities exist, except in brains; for they are not properties of the world of events; though they may be derived from events. Although they are not properties of the world (and so cannot be 'stimuli') yet generalisations and probabilities—derived from events by brains—are the basis of decisions and behaviour. Behaviour is guided not by stimuli, but rather by guesses. Suppose, now, that you were able to give up acting on informed guesses, and demanded continuous direct selections of reality. How would you get on? Would you never make mistakes—never fall through rotten floor boards, never be upset by bad food, never be misled by going beyond the evidence? No, indeed, if there were sufficient evidence available. But the fact is that there is frequently no possibility, or time, for testing floor boards or food. They must be taken on trust—trust based on the past, as stored in the brain to deal with the future.

We have arrived at questions which may be answered by experiment. We can measure performance, in the partial or total absence of sensory data, and establish whether and how far perception and behaviour continue to remain appropriate. We find that we can continue to drive, or walk, or perform laboratory eye-hand tracking experiments, through gaps in sensory data: and not merely inertially, for we can make decisions and change our actions appropriately during data-gaps. We must then be relying on internal data. This requires an internal 'fiction' of the world—which in unusual situations may be false. If the situation is unfamiliar, or changes in unpredictable ways, then we should expect systematic errors, generated by false predictions. Errors and illusions thus have great importance for Active theorists: they become obsessively-used tools, for discovering the underlying assumptions and strategies of the perceptual 'computer' by which we infer—not always correctly—external objects from sensory data.

Comparing books written by Passive and Active theorists, we find an amusing difference between their indexes. Passive books devote much space to stimulus patterns and very little space to the *phenomena* of perception: spontaneous reversals in depth; changes into other objects; distortions; paradoxes, in which the mind reels by being apparently confronted by a logically impossible object. Active theorists fill their books with examples of phenomena, interpreting them in various ways, while the Passive theorist ignores them or dismisses them as too trivial for his concern. But neither uncertainty nor ambiguity, neither distortion nor paradox, can be properties of objects: so how can we *perceive* uncertainties, ambiguities, distortions or paradoxes if perception is but a passive acceptance of reality? This simple, though surely powerful, argument is not raised or answered by Passive theorists who hold that perceptions are selections of external reality.

By playing down even the obvious and dramatic phenomena of perception (such as the kinds of illusions found in children's puzzle books) treatments of perception written by Passive theorists may look academically safe (because they do not look like children's books), but the cost is leaving out the phenomena, and the exciting theoretical issues, of perception. Puzzles are puzzling only when we lack understanding: to refuse to consider visual puzzles because they appear childish is surely to be childish—in not accepting our ignorance concerning puzzling facts. The problem is how to explain the puzzles: we shall not succeed by writing them off as unworthy of consideration.

Perceptual phenomena are essentially illusory. Illusions are discrepancies from physical reality. We can hardly expect sciences concerned with physical objects to give us a way of thinking about *discrepancies* from physical reality. Certainly we can learn a great deal about perception from physics and physiology: but in my view perception is a very odd subject requiring for some aspects its own concepts. Let me try to illustrate this, by considering *physical restraints* and their significance for carrying out logical processes.

In physics and engineering, we think of stable states and transformations, occurring according to physical restraints which are vital for understanding the system. This is, for example, obvious in billiards; or in the bearings and pivots and guides of an engine, which we understand by considering the physical restraints which set limits to what can happen and make control and prediction possible once appreciated. But now consider the arrangement of letters, or words, on this page. Or consider the pieces of a game, say chessmen on a board. We may at once note two curious features about the page of print, or the chessmen. In the first place, they are *representing* a state of affairs, as well as themselves *being* a state of affairs. The pieces are representing a state or stage of a game; the letters a state of part of an argument or a description. Secondly, although the pieces or letters are themselves physically stable (and may remain in the same position for a very long time: as in an ancient book, or game found in an Egyptian tomb) we do not understand their positions by considering physical restraints. They are not like an engine, stopped in a certain position; for to understand the arrangement of the letters or the game's pieces, we must know not merely the *physical restraints* but also the *conventional restraints*, of the game or the language which the pieces or letters are representing. And this is only so while they are serving as symbols: as soon as the chessmen are captured, or returned to their box, they are just like any other lumps of matter. (They are then, in a sense, dead.) Now the question is: should we regard brain cells purely as ordinary lumps of matter—or more like chess pieces or words—capable of representing abstract situations, and other objects? This may seem fanciful, a too-philosophical problem to worry a scientist: but I wish to suggest that the implications of either answer have immediate consequences, which affect not only how we think, but also the kinds of experiments we wish to perform in our scientific research.

Accounts of brain function in which we have not considered formal as well as physical restraints are, in my view, inadequate and misleading: just as misleading as to describe the moves in a game of chess in terms only of the physical restraints of the men on their board. To understand the brain (I submit) we must know not only its physics and physiology (which do set 'end stop' restraints) but also the restraints imposed upon its states by the rules of its symbolic game. The brain game is played to win against the physical world; brain states representing more or less abstract selected versions of reality. Cognitive psychology is the attempt to learn the brain game and its rules.

Sometimes, of course, the game is against thinking objects—other brains. Then the special features of zoology, and later sociology and politics, are generated. These have their own symbolic restraints; and then the brain game must be played in their terms.

Because strategy is hardly a subject matter of science, the importance of cognitive strategy, in perception, is easily ignored, or dismissed as not properly part of science. For this reason, I am trying to emphasise its importance in understanding brain function. The cognitive strategy carried out by brains is not so like what physics *describes* as it is like the *methods* of physics. More specifically, it is surely scientific *method* which is the best paradigm we have of how data can be used for discovering the nature of things and predicting from past experience—by building and selecting predictive hypotheses. It is suggestive that discrepancies from the truth can be generated in science not only by loss of the calibration of instruments but also by applying inappropriate strategies to problems. This, I believe, is like many kinds of illusions, which cannot be understood from physiology alone. We must know the brain's cognitive strategies —and how they can generate not only knowledge but also, when the strategies are inappropriate, dramatic errors (Gregory, 1973).

There are, however, many theories of perception which hold that physics and physiology are sufficient to understand perception. A clear example is the celebrated (and I believe essentially misleading) Gestalt theory of perception which postulated physiological restraints to explain visual phenomena, such as preference for and distortion towards figures of 'simple' and 'closed' form. Visual forms were supposed to be represented in the brain by similarly shaped electrical brain fields—circles by circular brain traces, presumably houses by house-shaped brain traces. These 'brain traces' were supposed to tend to form simple and closed shapes, because of their physical properties; much as bubbles tend to become spheres, as this form has minimum potential energy (Kohler, 1920). Now this implies that visual 'organizations' and distortions are due to physical restraints and forces which will not in general be relevant to the logical problems the brain must solve to infer objects from sensory patterns and stored data. This is quite different from a cognitive account of perceptual distortions, and other such phenomena supposed to arise from mis-application of strategies, quite apart from the physiology involved. In using a slide rule, an error may be due to physical errors in the rule itself, or to misapplication of the rule for the problem in hand. This is exactly the distinction involved here, between 'physiological' and 'cognitive' errors.

We should expect physiological restraints to produce the same effects for any object situation (for example after-images, due to retinal fatigue from any bright light). Misplaced strategy errors should on the other hand be related to the kind of perceptual in-ference, from sensory pattern to object, being carried out. So the point is that the physiology should only produce errors when it is exerting *general* restraints. We should not expect this except in abnormal situations, such as when the physiological 'components' are driven beyond their dynamic range. Considering phenomena of perception, such as ambiguous, distorting or paradoxical figures: do these figures upset the *physiology*, or select inappropriate *strategies* to generate errors? In these cases, it seems to be the object significance of the figures which is relevant. So these phenomena seem quite un-like after-images—here it is not so much the physiology as the cognitive strategies which we need to discover. This needs a different (but still a 'scientific') way of thinking, and powerful experimental techniques to discover cognitive strategies and how they can mislead.

Separating errors due to physiological restraints from errors due to misplaced strategies has importance beyond understanding perceptual errors. The same distinction (between physiological restraints and cognitive rules, and how either can go wrong) might be important for understanding mental illness. If schizophrenia is errors in the brain's strategies for developing hypotheses of external states of affairs, this should be understood not only in terms of biochemistry and physiology, but also in terms of the rules and strategies by which we normally cope with things. Perhaps this matter of strategies is hidden by the apparent ease with which we continually solve problems of the utmost difficulty to computer programmers. To see a table as something to support a book upon, is to solve a problem so difficult that it challenges the most advanced computer technology, and yet to us it is so simple that a Passive theory of perception may seem plausible. This shows that Passive theories may be so misleading as to hide aspects of brain function we must see clearly, to understand not only perception but all mental processes and how they can go wrong.

Recent discoveries by physiologists, especially by electrical recording from single brain cells during controlled stimuli to the eyes, are so clearly important that they tend to dominate much current thinking about perception. The problem of how sensory patterns are interpreted in terms of objects tends to be ignored. The important physiological discovery is that certain stimulus patterns (lines of certain orientation, or movement, etc.) produce repeatable activity in specific brain cells. This discovery came as an unpalatable shock to Passive theorists, who tend to ignore brain function. To Active theorists, it gives a clue to the kinds of data accepted for building object-hypotheses. One might think from this that Passive theories would drop out, leaving the field to physiologists and Active cognitive psychologists to work together in blissful harmony. Actually things are not quite like this: the physiological advance is so concrete, and clearly important, that many physiologists and cognitive psychologists feel that finding more feature detectors, and object detectors, is the sole path we need to follow to understand vision. But is it? These psychological mechanisms relate only to currently sensed features of stimulus patterns, which is but a part of object perception. The physiological account thus remains Passive, and so essentially inadequate, for the same reasons that cognitive Passive accounts are inadequate. The task ahead is to relate physiological processes not only to direct input-output links, as in reflexes, but also to the brain's logical and correlating activity endowing it with the power to predict. Some of the most interesting clues are at present coming from studies of development of perception in babies. Early changes of the nervous system as a result of experience are now being discovered which will perhaps help to tie up, or relate, physiology and cognition. Possibly the most fundamental and rigorous ideas are coming not from biology, but from attempts to program computers to 'see' and handle objects. It proves necessary to make the computers develop hypotheses, and select the most likely, given the data from its glass eye. Some computer programs designed to give 'scene analysis' (recognising objects from pictures by computer) assign alternative object probabilities to selected features in the picture; and then change these probabilities, according to probabilities initially assigned to other features of the scene. For example, a given shape may be a box or a building. If what is taken to be a hand is above it, then the probability of the box hypothesis will be increased and the building hypothesis decreased—for hands are generally too small and too low to be above buildings, but not to be above boxes (Guzman, 1971). Now this gives interactions, due to conditional probabilities, which may generate visual effects—in computers or brains—quite like the old Gestalt phenomena, but for an entirely different reason. The reason is to be understood in terms of cognitive strategies for making effective use of data for deciding what objects are probably present in the scene.

In Machine Intelligence, only precisely formulated theories are adequate: gaps or errors in the theory show up as errors in the machine. At present, machines perform only the simplest tasks and are confused by shadows or small changes we scarcely notice. Although the difficulties in Machine Intelligence demonstrate all too well how little we understand, it now seems that we are beginning to understand ourselves—the inference-mechanisms of our humanity—by inventing adequate concepts for machines to infer objects from data: to receive our world with their metal brains and human-devised programs. Is this science fiction? Yes—but like all fiction it may be very largely true.

Returning to phenomena of perception: a particularly relevant phenomenon is 'subjective contours', though surprisingly little is known about these effects. Are they caused by physiological activity *directly activated* by the stimulus patterns, or are they *logical constructs* from sensory and stored data: to be regarded as *cognitive* contours, *mediated by* physiological processes? Perhaps the following discussion and figures will make this, surely vital, distinction clearer.

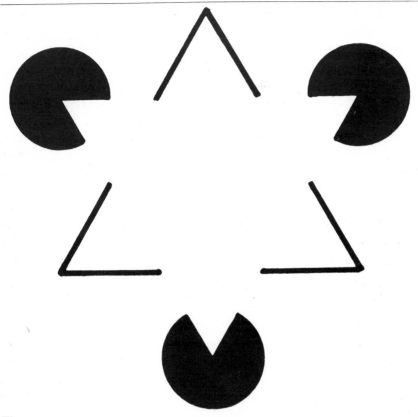

Fig. 0.4

A figure showing created features—a triangular area of enhanced brightness with sharp contours (after Kanizsa, 1955).

It is surprisingly easy to devise simple line figures which evoke marked illusory contours. Unlike the well-known brightness contrast effects, these illusory contours can occur in regions far removed from regions of physical intensity difference; and they can be oriented at any angle physically to present contours. Fig. 0.4 is the figure described by Kanizsa (1955). An illusory triangle is observed whose apices are determined by the blank sectors of the three disks. The 'created' object appears to have sharp contours which bound a large region of enhanced brightness.

We may discover what features are necessary for producing this effect by removing parts of this figure. Figs. 0.5, 0.6, 0.7, show such a sequence. Three dots spaced as the apices of an equilateral triangle (Fig. 0.5) give no created contours, although they are readily seen as indicating a triangle. The broken triangle (Fig. 0.6) does not evoke the figure (except perhaps slightly after the effect has been observed in Fig. 0.4): but combining the equilaterally spaced dots with the broken

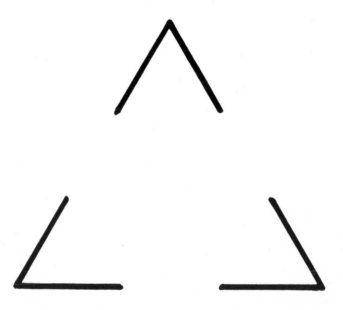

Fig. 0.5
Three dots are seen intellectually *as forming a triangle, but there are no created contours.*

Fig. 0.6
This is seen as a triangle with gaps—but the gaps do not have visible created contours.

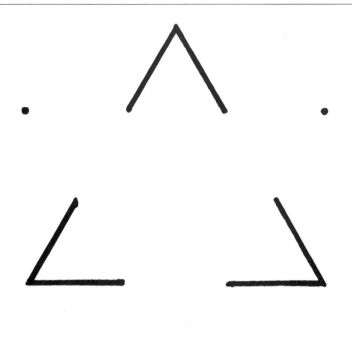

Fig. 0.7
Combining the equilaterally spaced dots with the broken triangle evokes the illusory object, though less markedly than with the sectored disks.

triangle (Fig. 0.7) does evoke the illusory object, though less markedly than with the sectored disks of Fig. 0.4. It might be described in physiological or in cognitive terms. The physiological paradigm would be satisfied with the supposition that feature detector cells of the striate cortex (Hubel and Wiesel, 1962) are activated by the disk sectors (or less effectively by the dots) to give the appearance of continuous lines, though only their ends are given by stimulation. The cognitive paradigm of perception, in which perceptions are regarded as hypotheses selected by sensory data, but going beyond available data, would be satisfied by supposing that the illusory object is 'postulated', as hiding the unlikely sectors and the breaks in the triangle. As these features are removed from the figure, the hypothesis becomes weaker, until the 'postulated' masking object is no longer seen.

The effects occur equally in stabilised retinal images (flashed after-images) and so the effects cannot be due to eye movements. By adopting the technique devised in 1899 by Witasek of sharing parts of the figures between the two eyes, with a stereoscope, it is easy to show that the effect is not retinal in origin but must be after the level of binocular fusion. This follows because the effect holds when the sectored disks are viewed with one eye and the interrupted line triangle with the other eye, when they are stereoscopically fused. The illusory triangle may, on the second paradigm, be called a cognitive fiction—likely to be true but in this case false.

By changing the angle of the disk sectors, so that they no longer meet by straight line interpolation, we find that the effect still occurs. The created form is now changed, to give interpolation with a curved fictional contour. This may be seen in Fig. 0.8. This new effect seems to increase the plausibility of the cognitive fiction notion, for it seems unlikely that 'curved edge' detectors would be selected by the misaligned sectors. This might be answered by direct electrophysiology.

Fig. 0.8
The angles of the sectors are reduced, so that they no longer meet by linear interpolation. The result is a curved *illusory created figure. (This has concave sides, which would not be expected on a Gestalt interpretation).*

The black-line-on-white-background figures give a homogeneous whiter-than-white fictional region. The corresponding negative white-line-on-black background gives a blacker-than-black region. The illusory intensity can be measured, in either case, with a reference light spot as in a matching photometer. The enhancement is 5–10 per cent of the background brightness. The whiter-than-white and the blacker-than-black enhancements change when the figures are viewed as after-images, as the after-image changes from positive to negative, and vice versa. Both the black and white illusory triangles are reported as appearing somewhat in front of the rest of the figures, which is compatible with this 'postulated masking object' notion.

Not only contours but large homogeneous areas of different brightness are created—but are such areas of different brightness created by line detectors? Consider Fig. o.6. We have lines with gaps; but there is no observed difference in brightness between the inside and the outside of this triangle, and no contours between the gaps. So why should there be contours and a brightness difference with the illusory triangle, if both it and the normal line triangle are neurally signalled in the same way? The lack of contour in the gaps of Fig. o.6 and the absence of enhanced brightness in such figures show that aligned features are not sufficient for producing these effects. What seems to be needed is a high probability of an over-lying object, giving gaps by masking. This would require processes of a logical sophistication beyond those believed to occur at the primary visual projection region of the cortex, the striate area. If these effects should indeed be described in terms of 'cognitively postulated objects' (or other such logical constructs), created to maintain a hypothesis that breaks in a figure are due to partial masking by a nearer object, itself unsensed, then we are committed to concepts beyond those of classical physiology for even 'elementary' sensory processes.

If cognitive constructs are an essential part of such elementary visual phenomena as contours and brightness, then we must be careful in assigning to recorded physiological activity a specific direct function in sensation. If we are not dealing with a direct input-output system, then we should not expect physiological activity occurring early in the system to be directly related to the output, or to sensation. These phenomena suggest that retinal patterns (and so the early stages of physiological activity) are contributing to perceptual hypotheses, which are far richer than sensory inputs.

Another phenomenon showing how even apparently elementary sensation is modified by likely object properties is the Size-Weight illusion. A small dense object of the same weight as a larger object of the same weight feels, and is judged to be, the heavier. Even the elementary sensation of weight is, then, greatly affected by the *probable* weight of the object. To generalise this: elementary sensation is bound up with, or if you like contaminated by, object perception.

A related Weight illusion is experienced dramatically with the 'empty suitcase effect'—an empty suitcase flying up in the air, ridiculously, as it is lifted when assumed to be full. This at once shows that the physiology of weight estimation and sensation involves reference to a *likely* weight: again we come back to the hypothesis

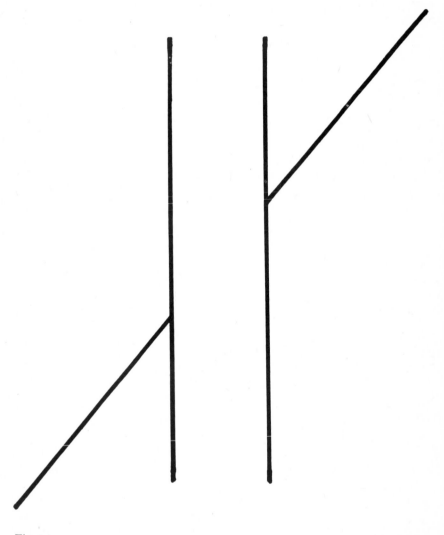

Fig. 0.9
The obliques actually line up, but appear displaced. This is a typical visual distortion illusion. It can only be explained in terms of a theory of perception. Should the explanation be in terms of interactive physiological processes; or in terms of a misplaced strategy, in the cognitive use of sensory data to infer objects?

notion; with the clear advantages of perceptual hypotheses, of being able to set and control muscles to perform tasks without need of continuous sensory monitoring: in this case of weight (see pp. 240 ff.). Although useful when appropriate, an inappropriate hypothesis, or part of a hypothesis, must generate corresponding sensory errors: as in the 'cognitive contours', which are *created* illusions, and the weight errors, which are *scale* distortions.

Can visual distortion illusions be generated by cognitively created features? If so, we would have to take seriously the notion that some visual distortion illusions should be explained as cognitive, rather than physiological phenomena. We find that at least some of the classical visual distortion illusions (Fig. 0.9) can be generated by cognitive features. Fig. 0.10 shows a kind of Poggendorff figure, in which the usual parallel lines are physically absent but are generated by four sectored disks placed well away from the interrupted oblique figure. Figures such as Fig. 0.11 also evoke cognitive contours and they also produce distortion illusions. Such distortions in the absence of physical contours show that these illusions must, if the above inter-pretation is correct, have their origin at a cognitive level, which is—probably anatomically, presumably physiologically and certainly logically—distant from primary feature detection.

So here we have phenomena, easily seen and investigated, which seem relevant for deciding between two very different paradigms of perception. Is physiology sufficient, or do we need this additional, philosophically tacked-on, set of cognitive concepts? Will they come to be regarded as unnecessary as physiology advances along its chosen highly successful path? Or will cognitive concepts become absorbed by physiology, to become part of physiology with no natural break? At present it would seem that logical information-handling processes should be regarded very differently from the mechanisms mediating them. (As it is, similarly, necessary to have both the 'hardware' and the 'software' languages for computers.) The kinds of concepts and the kinds of activity involved in research into these aspects of brain function are so different, that it is more than convenient to separate cognitive from physiological processes—though we suppose them to be totally dependent on each other for the brain to be perceptive.

The developments of Instruments and Devices has not so far been mentioned. Did they result from displacement activity, due to lack of an adequate paradigm or a plausible idea for investigating percep-tion? Perhaps, but surely the future lies not only in recording data from brains but also in inventing machines capable of recognising and handling objects. If our view of perception is approximately correct perceiving is, itself, inventing a plausible reality for coping with the

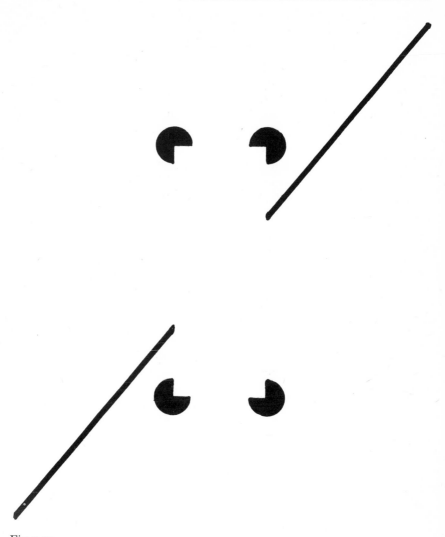

Fig. 0.10
The sectored disks produce a cognitive rectangle which, though having no physical contours, produces a distortion (displacement) illusion.

immediate future. So inventing machines is, like painting pictures, an extension of perception and a new way of seeing.

Some of the devices described in this book were intended as practical solutions, mainly to research problems; especially those concerned with recording data, and limitations of optical instruments. Others arose from considering how the brain might (in certain limited respects) function. The best example of this is the method for improving pictures through disturbance: especially astronomical telescope photographs through atmospheric disturbance. This device

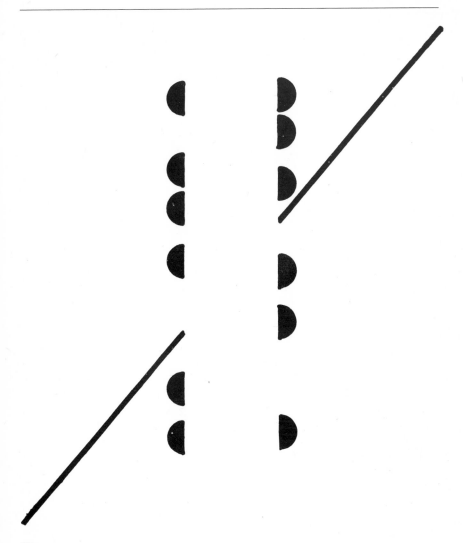

Fig. 0.11
A further cognitive created region, producing a dramatic displacement illusion. (The implication is that distortion (or displacement) illusions can be generated by cognitive processes.)

shows how very important is even a crude internal representation (not necessarily a picture) of the external situation for using limited sensory (or optical) data effectively. This machine has a kind of very limited intelligence, for it makes its own decisions as to when to accept its disturbed image as useful data. This may well be a strategy adopted by extremely primitive organisms; so it is strange that only now is it coming into human technology. Indeed, the present state of Artificial (Machine) Intelligence has deep within it a strange biological paradox. It is just those aspects of control and selection of relevant from irrelevant data which are the most difficult to mechanise —though they were the first problems to be solved by organisms. Only man (and then with the aid of symbols) can carry out numerical calculations, or derive solutions by explicit logic from premises. Yet this is very easy to mechanise, as visualised by Leibnitz three centuries ago. Simple geared calculating machines can, with human or even super-human ability, perform computations or derive deductive conclusions never accomplished by sub-human brains. The strange thing is that although machines can perform wonders of logic and computation, the full power of present technology cannot rival or simulate the ability of even a simple organism to see. Until we have invented machines capable of recognising objects and their potentialities, we should not claim to have in our understanding adequate Concepts and Mechanisms of Perception.

PART ONE EXPERIMENTS

1 *Sensory processes*

[In order to introduce problems of perception, to be taken up in detail later, we will start with two general though fairly technical reviews of accepted facts.

The first was written as a chapter in a book, *Psychology Through Experiment*, edited by the late Professor George Humphrey. George Humphrey spent much of his life at Queen's University, Ontario; ending his career as the first Professor of Psychology in the University of Oxford.

The paper is an introduction to the physiology of the senses of vision and hearing.]

★   ★   ★

WE may think of perception as the end result, the output, of physiological systems adapted to handle information originating from the environment. When we see a table, hear the sound of a chair dragged across the floor, feel the cold hardness of the wood or the softness of the cushion, highly complex mechanisms are involved. It might be said that as we come to understand these mechanisms we *explain* perception. There may be other kinds of explanation of perceptual phenomena, but certainly one important approach is to discover the sensory processes involved. This is no simple task.

To study sensory processes in man we make use of intact people who respond in some agreed manner to various stimuli, or signals provided by the experimenter. The data from an experiment will consist of the physical values of stimuli, such as the brightness, colour and area of spots of light, and the recorded responses of the subject. The subject is not expected to report on his own sensory processes, and yet his reports are used to discover what sensory processes are involved. How is this possible? The answer is that the experimenter

3

has in mind some sort of theoretical model, or set of models, of what might be going on. Many psychological experiments on sensory processes are attempts to provide evidence for or against predictions which are made from hypothetical models of the system. Some experiments are, however, purely exploratory. Curiosity or practical need may suggest some situations as worthy of investigation.

Appropriate models may be suggested by thinking about instruments, or devices for handling information, or purely mathematical or statistical models may serve. When it became possible to measure the electrical activity in nerve fibres during controlled stimulus conditions (Adrian, 1928, 1932) a new world was opened up. Although immensely important, it should be realized that only a minute part of the total activity can be detected and recorded at any one time. The physiologist does not escape the necessity of thinking in terms of models just because his data are taken from inside the system. He must decide whether a given effect is important or a mere artifact; and if it is important just what its significance is. This can only be done in terms of some conceptual model of the system.

Verbal reports have some advantages over the various physiological records we can obtain from animal preparations or from human subjects. In particular, when an investigator tries something out on himself he has a unique opportunity to note unexpected effects.

The theory of information, due to Shannon (1949), has opened up the possibility of obtaining quantitative measures where only a few years ago this was impossible. It has been clear for a very long time that the nervous system conveys information from the sense organs to the brain, via afferent fibres, and that the brain may command the muscles, via efferent nerves. These nerve fibres clearly carry messages. Adrian (1928) discovered the key to the physical form of the messages when he discovered that all nerves transmit trains of electrical impulses, the rate of these impulses increasing with stimulus intensity. Information theory enables us to say just how much information such systems could represent, or transmit, in a given time.

Science has so far primarily concerned itself with energy systems, but the problems of the *control* of energy – involving information – are now receiving detailed attention. The distinction between energy and information can be puzzling, for any information system requires energy in order to function. Energy is required to produce speech sounds, radio signals or nervous messages. Such systems cannot, however, be understood simply in terms of energy. The eye must have sufficient light energy to function, but the organization of this energy into temporal and spatial patterns is also vital, and requires information concepts for its understanding. It is the particular form of the activity of groups of nerve cells under various conditions of stimulation which is important. The organism must function as an efficient energy system to allow the processes to take place which give us thought and perception, but an important part of our understanding of these processes is not in terms of energy but rather in terms of the flow and handling of information.

THE STRUCTURE OF THE EYE

The eye is often compared with a camera. Like a camera it has a (nearly) light-tight box, the sclerotic coat with its black choroid lining. The light enters the circular pupil through the transparent cornea which forms a bulge of about 8 mm radius, the radius of the eye-ball being about 12 mm. The size of the pupil is controlled by the iris, as in a camera lens. The lens of the eye lies behind the cornea, the space between them being filled with a lymph-like fluid which is renewed about once every four hours. 'Spots before the eyes' may

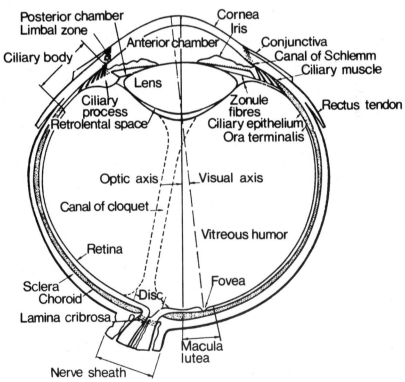

FIG. 1.1 *Diagrammatic cross-section of the human eye.*

be caused by particles floating in this aqueous humour. The lens of the human eye is quite unlike a camera lens for it is flexible, and kept under tension. Its radius of curvature, and thus its focal length, is modified during accommodation changes, by the ciliary body.

The image is formed primarily by the air/cornea surface, for it is here that the light is bent most, since the difference between the refractive index of air and that of the aqueous humour is greater than between the aqueous (or vitreous) humour and the lens. A man who has had a diseased lens removed can see tolerably well. The fish does not have the advantage of a low refractive index in its external medium. Its lens is denser than that of man, and nearly spherical in shape. It is not flexible and moves bodily in the eye to achieve accommodation.

Examining the Purkinje images during accommodation changes. It is just possible to do this with no apparatus beyond a lighted candle; but a cocoa tin with an arrow pierced in its side, and containing a frosted electric bulb, is more suitable. If this is placed in a dark room and so arranged that the illuminated arrow may be seen reflected in the subject's eye, three images of the arrow can be seen, the images being produced by reflection from the convex surface of the cornea and by the front and back faces of the lens. By requesting the subject to accommodate to objects at various distances, the relative changes in size of the images may be noted. This is best done by viewing them through a small telescope clamped in a retort stand, but this is not essential. The following images should be noted:

The Purkinje images. With the eye accommodated to infinity ('emmetropic') the following images should be visible:

1st image: right way up, bright: from the convex surface of cornea.

2nd image: right way up, large, dim: from the front surface of lens.

3rd image: inverted, small, bright: from the back, posterior surface of the lens.

If the subject now accommodates to a near object only the 3rd image (from the posterior surface of the lens) changes in size to any marked extent. It becomes smaller, approximating to the first image in size but inverted. This shows that in accommodation to near vision the radius of curvature of the posterior surface of the lens is reduced. The mechanism of accommodation was discovered by Helmholtz,[1]

---

[1] Hermann Ludwig Ferdinand von Helmholtz (1821–94), as a physicist, contributed to the theory of the conservation of energy, as a physiologist to the so-called law of specific energies and to the determination of the rate of conduction of nerve activity, as a psychologist, to the study of vision and hearing, where his work is outstanding. The *Handbuch der physiologischen Optik* (first volume 1856, last 1866, tr: 1924) and the *Tonempfindungen* (1863) are classics, and remain important works of reference.

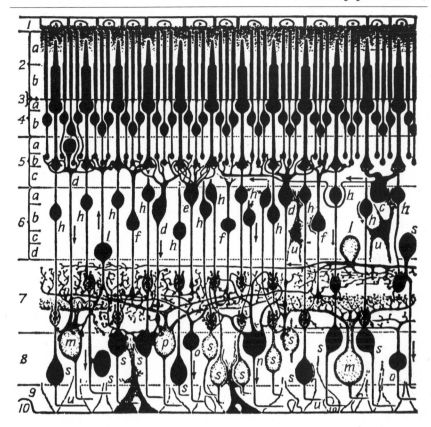

FIG. 1.2 *Schematic diagram showing the neural microstructure of the retina of the monkey, based on Golgi impregnations. The layers are:*

1. *Pigment epithelium*
2a *Outer segment of rods and cones*
2b *Inner segment of rods and cones*
3. *Outer limiting membrane*
4. *Outer nuclear layer*
5. *Outer plexiform layer (cone-pedicles and rod spherules)*
6. *Inner nuclear layer*
7. *Inner plexiform layers*
8. *Ganglion cells (origin of primary visual projections)*
9. *Layer of optic nerve fibres*
10. *Inner limiting membrane*
    c, horizontal cells; d, e, f, g, bipolar cells; i, l, amacrine cells; m, n, o, p, r, s, ganglion cells.

and is described clearly in Fulton, 1955, pp. 430–3.

The retina. The light-sensitive layer, the retina, at the back of the eye has been described as 'an outgrowth of the brain'. It is a complicated arrangement of receptor cells (the 'rods' and the 'cones') and various other kinds of cells, some of which provide cross connections between the receptors. Both excitatory or inhibitory interactions may occur across the receptors, due to cross connection. The structure is described by Polyak (1941); evidence of interaction is derived from recording activity at the ganglion cells, Kuffler (1953), Barlow (1953), Hartline (1940a).

The receptors. These are of at least two kinds: the rods and the cones. They are so named from their appearance, but Willmer (1946) has pointed out that in the central foveal region the cells are very tightly packed, and the 'cones' in the fovea look similar to the rods of the peripheral regions. Although the foveal receptor cells look like rods they are believed to be, functionally, cones.

The rod cells are highly sensitive, and provide 'scotopic' vision in dim light. They do not provide colour vision. The cones give 'photopic' colour vision, but require more light than do the rods. The spectral sensitivity curves of the rods and cones are different, as may be seen in Fig. 1.3. The change in the wavelength for peak sensitivity changes over a rather critical range of intensity. The change in wavelength of the peak sensitivity is known as the Purkinje shift.

Osterberg (1935) counted the rods and cones across the retina and found that the ratio of rods to cones increases from the centre to the periphery. In the fovea there are, probably, only cones and in the extreme periphery virtually only rods. There are, in a single retina, about 125,000,000 rods and 6,500,000 cones. There is a marked convergence of the receptors on to fibres, particularly for the rods. The foveal cones seem to have one–one connection with their fibres.

The sensitive receptor cells lie at the back of the retina, behind layers of nerve fibres, blood vessels and various supporting cells. The light has to pass through all these obstructions before it reaches the receptors, though the obstructions are minimal in the central foveal region. We do not normally see these obstructions, and at first sight this is surprising. The slightest speck of dust, or a fine hair, lying on a camera film will produce a clear shadow image. The reason we do not see such shadow images from the blood vessels is that light always reaches the retina from precisely the same direction – down the optical path. Consider a receptor lying behind an obstruction; it will always be in shadow, and it adapts so that its sensitivity is higher than neighbouring receptors free of obstruction. This selective adaptation is thought to prevent the fixed obstructions being visible. If it were possible to shift the direction of the light reaching the retina these obstructions should become visible. A beautiful and well-known demonstration makes this possible.

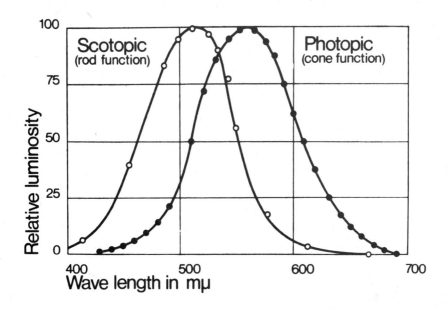

FIG. 1.3 *Relative luminosity curves for human rod and cone vision.*

Demonstration to see one's own retinal blood vessels. The only apparatus required is a small torch. The naked bulb of an ophthalmoscope
is ideal for this, as it gives a small source of adjustable brightness.

The experiment is best done entirely on one's self, or the eye may
be hurt. First remain in a dark room for at least five minutes, then
place the lighted bulb in close contact with the shut lid of the eye,
near the temporal margin of the orbit. If now the bulb is moved with
regular oscillation, a startling tree-like pattern will emerge and
remain visible while the light is in motion. The pattern will die away
rapidly when the movement is stopped – evidently because selective
adaptation again occurs – but during the movement the shadow
pattern will be displaced across the retina so that new receptors are
affected. This never occurs in nature.

It is worth thinking out just why, normally, light always reaches
the retina from the same direction, and noting also that this is why
the pupil appears black. It is impossible to see into someone's eye
because light would have to come precisely from the direction of the
observer's eye to illuminate the part of the retina observed. The
secret of the ophthalmoscope is that it sends in a beam of light on the
path along which the observer looks.

The blind spot, where the optic nerve leaves the eye, is readily
demonstrated. It may be 'seen' by fixating the left-hand dot with the

right eye only (or the right-hand dot with the left eye), holding the
page vertically,

.   .

at a distance of about 9 inches. The peripheral dot will disappear as
it falls on the blind region.

If a homogeneous field, such as a sheet of white paper, is fixated
we do not see a black patch. The visual system tends to extrapolate
whatever is seen across the blind spot. This is a remarkable thing;
and it warns us how 'high level' perceptual processes may complicate
the simplest observation, and may confuse theoretical issues.

EYE MOVEMENTS

Eye movements were studied in detail by Dodge, early in this century.
He found, using photographic techniques, two main types of eye
movements, and these occurred under different conditions. When
the eye is swept across the field it moves in a series of small jerks,
called saccades. These occur about four times per second. Barlow
(1952) says: 'There is general agreement that the most usual type of
movement is a rapid jerk, followed by a period of 0·1–0·3 seconds
during which the eye is relatively stationary, and terminated by
another quick movement bringing the eye to a new fixation position.
When the eye is following a moving object it moves smoothly, once it
has (found) the object and is able to follow it.' These two types of
movement seem to be quite distinct, and actuated by physically
separate brain systems. Holmes (1938) finds that some patients with
certain lesions simply cannot take their eyes off whatever is fixated,
sometimes whether the object fixated is stationary or moving, without
recourse to deliberate blinking, or some other such trick to break the
visual contact.

We may demonstrate quite convincingly the saccadic voluntary
movements and smooth following movements with only simple
apparatus.

Demonstration of eye movements. A small neon lamp, of the type
used as indicators in electronic equipment, is placed in an otherwise
dark room and viewed from any convenient distance, of the order of
6–10 feet. The neon is arranged to flicker at a rate of 20–30
flashes/second. (This may be obtained by feeding it from an A.F.
oscillator, by increasing the output voltage with a suitable step-up
transformer.)

The flicker rate is adjusted so that when the neon is fixated its light appears continuous, but if the neon is moved steadily across the field it will be seen to flicker. The steady light is seen when the flicker rate is above what is called the critical flicker fusion frequency (c.f.f.) and this is lower for a fixed than for a moving image. (The value of c.f.f. is a function of the brightness, and area of the light and the level of adaptation of the eye. It is of the order of 30 flashes/second.)

If the image moves smoothly across the retina the flicker is seen as a train of luminous dashes, and the limited recovery time of the retinal receptors does not limit the ability of the system to distinguish flicker because successive sets of receptors are brought into play with each flash.

If the eye is swept slowly across the field, flicker is not seen. The jerky movements of the eyes prevent the smooth sweep of the image which is necessary to see the flicker. If, now, the eye follows the movement of a small self-luminous object the regular flicker *is* seen, provided the eye is accurately tracking the object. This situation enables us to verify a new and rather surprising finding about what may be called the 'smooth eye movement' system.

Eye movements and proprioception. If the observer's hand is held before the eyes and tracked, although the hand is completely invisible in the dark, the neon being feeble, the flicker may be seen, indicating that smooth eye movements can be mediated by proprioceptor information. Evidently the tracking need not be visual for smooth eye movements to take place (Gregory, 1958*a* [No. 14]).

It seems that the eyes move in saccadic jerks, except when following moving objects, in order to prevent images effectively fading as selective adaptation occurs.

THE PERCEPTION OF DEPTH

The images on the retina are on a curved surface, but it is not misleading to call them 'two-dimensional'. The visual world, on the other hand, is three-dimensional – we see things in depth. The processes giving depth perception are complicated, many being 'perceptual' in that we discuss them in terms of properties of the stimulus field rather than of the visual system. Such factors as apparent size, texture gradients and perspective will not be discussed here – we shall consider only some of the specific sensory processes involved in depth perception.

Demonstration that the use of both eyes is important for depth perception. This may be shown in many ways. Hering's Fall is a standard method; here small beads are dropped at various distances from a vertical wire placed about one foot from the subject. He reports whether the beads pass in front of or behind the wire. Another method is to place two (or sometimes three) vertical rods some distance from the subject and so screened that the top and bottom of the rods are hidden: they are thus seen in a horizontal slit perhaps a few inches in width. The centre rod is placed at various distances while judgements of 'in front' or 'behind' the comparison rods are made. The difference between one and two eyes is very great. This experiment might be done for various distances from the display, to show that the advantage of binocular vision falls off with distance.

It is worth obtaining not only estimates of the limits of discrimination of distance, but also some observations of perceptual changes experienced when occluding one eye. The following is very striking. Place an unmarked white china tea-cup, say, 10 feet from the observer, so that he looks almost directly into it. The illumination should be even, and originating from behind the observer from a single source. There must be no shadows cast into the cup. If this is viewed with two eyes nothing odd will occur, but when viewed with one eye it will be seen to be a reversible visual situation, like the well known Necker cube, only here we are looking at a real object. It is an odd effect, difficult to describe but simple to set up and examine.

When a near object is viewed binocularly two factors should be considered. (1) The eyes will converge upon the object and, like a range finder (the 'base' between the eyes being about $2\frac{1}{2}$ inches), the angle of convergence can provide information as to the distance of the object. (2) The retinal images will be disparate, that is, they will differ according to the two positions from which the object is viewed. These two views are fused centrally to give one perception having depth.

These factors may be isolated quite simply, and so investigated and assessed individually (Sloan and Altman, 1954).

Convergence (1) The light entering the eye may be bent. This may be done by interposing prisms having small angles (5–10 degrees) between the object and the eye. This changes the effective distance of objects while retaining the same retinal disparity.

Disparity (2) May be artificially increased or decreased with four mirrors[1] arranged as shown in Fig. 1.4(*a*) and (*b*), or reversed,

[1] Ordinary back-silvered looking-glass mirrors may be used. The mirrors may be mounted for ready adjustment on photographic tripod ball-and-socket heads. They may be attached to these by brass plates to which the heads are fitted with a tapped hole, and which are stuck to the back of the mirrors with 'Bostik' rubber glue. The plates are necessary to give sufficient area for the glue, but need not be larger than about 4 inches square. The mirrors can be positioned by simply pushing them, once the tripod heads are set to correct friction with the screw adjustment. This is a useful dodge, having many applications. The heads themselves can be mounted on a wooden or 'handy angle' frame.

so that the right eye is effectively in the left socket and vice versa as in Fig. 1.4(c).

Disparity can effectively be removed simply by viewing an object which gives the same image from any view point. Evenly lit spheres, or vertically orientated cylinders, may be used.

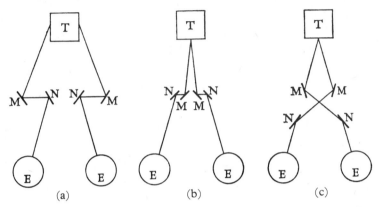

FIG. 1.4 (a) *The telestereoscope. This increases the disparity.*
(b) *The iconoscope. This reduces the disparity.*
(c) *The mirror pseudoscope. This reverses the two eyes.*

DISCRIMINATION

A. Intensity discrimination. A distinction is often made between the absolute and the differential sensitivity of the eye. This is certainly convenient experimentally, for the stimulus conditions are different for the two cases, but it is not so clear how these conditions differ from the 'point of view' of the brain.

For determining an absolute threshold, the eye is stimulated with a spot of light viewed against complete darkness. The 'stimulus' or 'signal' may be of any size, colour, shape or duration, and in any position with respect to the eye's fixation.

For determining a differential intensity threshold, a background field is added, the subject being required to discriminate the signal field from the background. The absolute case always has an implicit background, however, for the light from the test field will scatter in the eye, stimulating surrounding receptors. Further, the retina is not entirely 'silent' even in complete darkness, as has been shown with electrophysiological recording by Kuffler, Fitzhugh and Barlow (1957) for the cat, and no doubt this is true also for the human eye although we have no such direct evidence. Random background activity, 'noise', is present in all sensitive communication systems, and tends to set a limit to sensitivity. This is probably true also for the senses.

1. Weber's Law for intensity. Consider a single candle in an otherwise dark room. If a second candle is now lighted, the room is perceptibly brighter, but if a candle is lighted in a room filled with daylight its added light, although the same as before, will not be perceptible. In the first case the illumination was increased by 100 per cent, but in the second the candle represents but a small percentage increase in the total illumination. Now Weber's Law states that the just detectable difference in intensity is a constant proportion of the background intensity. If the increase is ΔI and the background I, this may be written

$$\frac{\Delta I}{I} = \text{constant}$$

The constant is known as Weber's Constant, C, this being about one per cent. (Its value is different for each sense and depends on many factors such as adaptation of the sense organ and, in the case of vision, the area of test background fields).

Weber's Law does not hold true for small values of background intensity. When I is small a relatively greater change (ΔI) is required for detection. Weber's Law may be extended to cover very small values of I by adding a small constant to the denominator, thus:

$$\frac{\Delta I}{I+k} = C$$

The value of this hidden constant, k, can be determined graphically by plotting ΔI against I and extrapolating back past the origin along the I-axis. The constant might originate from the 'dark light of the retina' or the random 'noise' background of the neural system.

The absolute threshold may be thought of as $\Delta I/k$. This added effective light, 'noise', would become insignificant for all but low values of I, which would explain the breakdown of Weber's Law. Indeed, we may be rather more confident as to why the Law breaks down at low intensities than why it holds in the first place. We may say that constant proportional sensitivity is a useful characteristic of most measuring instruments, and so argue that Weber's Law is useful for the senses. A rather different suggestion has been made by Barlow (1957*a*) in discussing the idea of sensory discrimination as limited by the random noise level of the system. Barlow regards Weber's Law as a puzzling special case holding only for large areas.

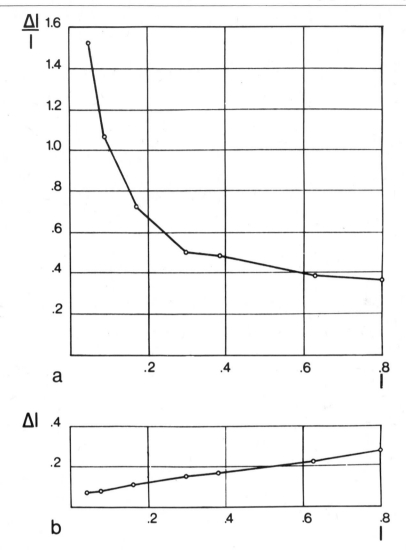

FIG. 1.5 (a) *Shows experimental points for* ΔI/I *against I for low intensities where Weber's Law breaks down.*
(b) *Shows the same data as in* (a), *but plotted as* ΔI *against I.*

He considers the case of small areas, and finds that a square root relation holds. Now this square root relation is attractive, because it would be expected if the eye were like a photocell discriminating 'signal' from random 'noise' in the cell. The whole question of the status of Weber's Law, and the conditions under which it holds, is still open to debate although it has been studied continuously since the birth of experimental psychology.

Duration in secs

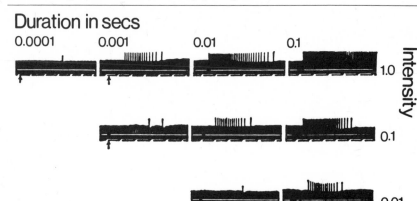

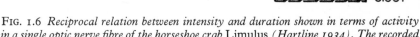

FIG. 1.6 *Reciprocal relation between intensity and duration shown in terms of activity in a single optic nerve fibre of the horseshoe crab* Limulus *(Hartline 1934). The recorded activity in mammalian optic nerves is much more complicated because of the intervening retinal cells which are not present in the Limulus eye.*

2. *The effect of flash duration.* For either the absolute or differential threshold this is given by the Bunsen-Roscoe Law, which is:

$I \times t$ = constant (where I is the intensity and t the duration)

for durations less than about ·02 second.

3. *The effect of test field size.* For either absolute or differential this is given by *Piper's Law* which is:

$I \times \sqrt{A}$ = constant (where A is the area of the field)

providing A is not greater than about 15–20 degrees or less than about 6 minutes of arc. For very small fields *Ricco's Law* holds. This is:

$$I \times A = \text{constant}$$

4. *The effect of position on the retina.* For the absolute threshold with dark adapted eye, the greatest sensitivity is 15–20 degrees from central vision. This is where the density of rods is greatest. Measures of absolute sensitivity are made in this region, and it is an old trick of astronomers and mariners, looking at faint objects, to use this region by 'looking off' the position of interest.

B. *Spatial discrimination – acuity.* The problem of what sets the minimum size limit below which we cannot see a gap in a line, a dot in a clear field, or the texture of a surface, is more complicated than the factors limiting intensity discrimination. But acuity is probably limited (for the normal young eye) by intensity discrimination.

When we speak of the size of an object in this context we speak loosely: we mean the angle subtended at the eye by the test object.

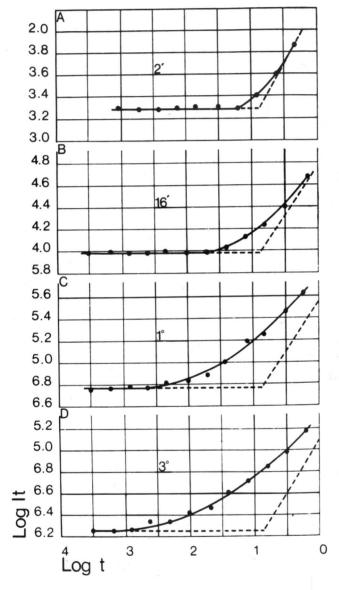

FIG. 1.7 *Intensity-time curves for four areas for the human eye. For short durations the relation I × t = constant holds. It may be seen that the breakdown for longer times occurs earlier for large than for small areas. The reason for this is not known, but it is difficult to see how the explanation could be in terms of the photochemistry of the retina. (Areas increased progressively from top to bottom.)*

Acuity is expressed as the subtended angle, in minutes or seconds of arc (where 1 minute of arc = 1/60 degree, and 1 second of arc = 1/60 minute, or 1/3600 degree). In addition to giving the subtended angle, however, the distance of the observer from the object should always be stated, since his acuity may be affected by the amount of accommodation required to bring the test object into focus.

It is an important optical fact that images are never perfectly sharp. Consider the image of a point of light against a perfectly black background – say a single star on a black night. If this were a point source (which is true of a star), the image is never a point but more like a disk of finite size. The size of the image will increase with the brightness of the source. The finite size of the image is due to a number of factors, in particular to aberrations of the lens, spread of light through and across the retina and to diffraction.

The intensity gradients across the retinal image will in general be less steep than those of the object. Hecht and Mintz (1939) have

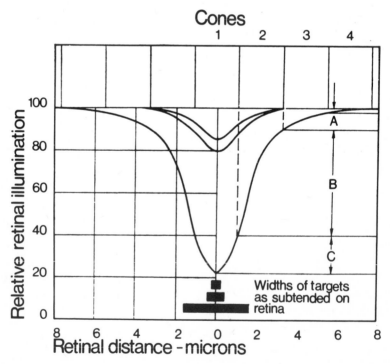

FIG. 1.8 *Light intensity distribution in diffracted images produced by the fine wires whose geometrical images are shown as three lines in the lower part of the figure. The scale on top of the figure represents the retinal mosaic, consisting of cones whose diameters are 2.3 μ, this being the average size of foveal cones.*

considered the importance of this in acuity, and give the following diagram relating the spread of photic energy to the density of the cone receptors. (The scale at the top of the figure represents a mosaic of cones of 2·3 μ diameter, this being the average size of the central foveal cones (Fig. 1.8)).

It is clear that the image will spread across several cones, in two dimensions, of course. If we try to resolve a double star we have the following situation, for each star will produce its own diffraction pattern and these will overlap if the angle subtended by the stars is sufficiently small.

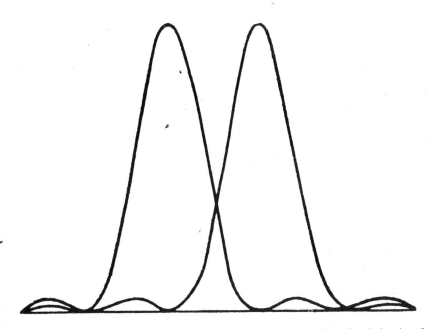

FIG. 1.9 *Light intensity distribution from two points or wires. For discrimination the two peaks must be detected from the trough between them.*

The problem confronting the visual system is to discern the fall in intensity between the two peaks. Thus acuity becomes ultimately a matter of intensity discrimination.

If this is so we should expect area to be important, for we have seen (Ricco's and Piper's Laws) that smaller intensity differences may be distinguished with larger than with small areas. This has been confirmed for acuity: Anderson and Weymouth (1923) showed that the visibility of a fine line increases with its length. For fine lines, acuity is so high that the geometrical image may be smaller than the diameter of a single cone: in fact the image may be but 1/60 of a cone diameter. Evidently the intensity gradient information may be summed across many receptors, each contributing some information.

Hecht and Mintz (1939) found that a long fine wire subtending 0·5 second of arc could be distinguished against a bright homogeneous background. In the vicinity of borders, discrimination thresholds are raised (Fry and Bartley 1935).

EXPERIMENTS ON ACUITY

1. Acuity as a function of intensity. Acuity increases with intensity as shown in Fig. 1.10.

Many attempts have been made to give some simple explanation of this curve. In particular, Hecht suggested that this is the integral of a normal statistical distribution curve, representing the thresholds

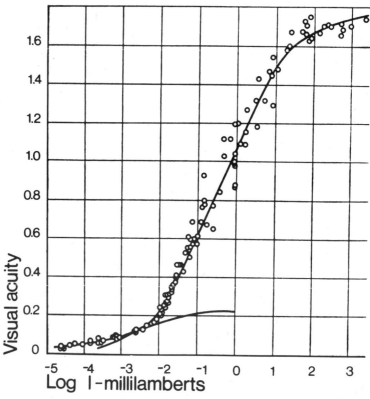

Fig. 1.10 *Curves showing relationship between visual acuity and level of illumination (I). Circles show König's data. The two solid lines show (lower) rods and (upper) cones, the success with which a normal probability integral can be fitted to the data.*

of the retinal receptors. With increasing intensity more receptors would become functional and so the effective retinal 'grain' would become finer, giving higher acuity. This theory has many objections; in particular we know from electrophysiological and other evidence that the variance of receptor thresholds is not nearly great enough; if it were, about half the receptors would never normally be effective, as acuity goes on increasing at very high intensities. This would mean that half the receptors are virtually useless, which is unlikely.

Although the curve looks simple, there is probably no one simple explanation.

2. Acuity for one and both eyes. Acuity may be compared for one and both eyes. It is better for both eyes; and the same is also true for intensity discrimination, though brightness remains the same.

3. Acuity as a function of the number of possibilities. This experiment involves a most important theoretical point. It is possible to think of sense organs in two ways: as receivers of energy, or as transducers of information. In either case energy is involved, but if we think of the eye (or ear) as conveying information then concepts beyond pure energy considerations become important. One might think of *energy* from the gap in a test ring stimulating the retina and causing (after a lot of neural activity in the brain, etc.) a response. Alternatively, one might think of the retinal activity serving as *information* to increase the probability that the gap is at one rather than another of the possible positions in which it could be. On the former view the number of positions in which the gap *might* be found is irrelevant, but on the informational analysis it is very important. The question is: does the number of positions in which the gap might be found affect acuity? We leave it as an exercise to design an experiment to answer this question.

TEMPORAL DISCRIMINATION – FLICKER FUSION

Temporal discrimination would seem to be limited by intensity discrimination – in much the same way as for spatial acuity. In spatial discrimination the gradual falling off in intensity of the borders of images produces overlap of the images from adjacent objects: the difference in intensity between the 'trough' and the centre of the images must be distinguished. In flicker the 'trough' lies in time rather than space. The time-constants of the eye are important in determining the 'temporal troughs' for given stimulus conditions.

The eye integrates energy over time. The Bunsen-Roscoe (or more correctly Bloch's) law states that, for time intervals up to about 0·02 second, the eye is a perfect integrator. For detection a flash can be indefinitely short provided it is sufficiently intense: it is the product of time and intensity that matters. The same law holds (very nearly) for photographic emulsions, and in both cases it has a photo-chemical basis, though for emulsions there is an effective loss of speed for very short flashes, but this is because two processes are involved.

For the eye there is also summation of information in time. A very important question is how far the perceptual phenomena found for pattern recognition in a tachistoscope follow the Time × Energy relation which holds for the energy required to detect a flash. We might expect a quite different relation to hold for tachistoscopic experiments involving pattern recognition.

Flicker itself is of comparatively little interest in normal life, but if we consider an image travelling across the retina, due to the movement of an object in the visual field, then it is clear that the rate at which each part of the retina can respond to differences in intensity may be important for the detection of the movement. The Time × Intensity relation is found to hold for the threshold for seen movement (Leibowitz, 1955).

An eye which adopted a longer integrating time would, other things being equal, be more sensitive, but its temporal discrimination would be worse. There is evidence to suggest that in dark adaptation the eye sacrifices temporal discrimination for sensitivity, the integration line becoming longer (Gregory, 1955a [No. 10]).

Experiment to estimate critical flicker fusion frequency (c.f.f.). For measuring c.f.f. it is important to have an arrangement which main-

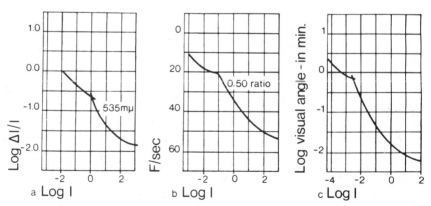

Fig. 1.11 *Three similar functions where intensity is a variable:* (a) *brightness discrimination,* (b) *c.f.f.,* (c) *acuity.*

tains the intensity of the source constant for all rates of flash. The simplest method is a sector wheel (episcotister) revolving at controlled rates and arranged to interrupt the light from a small source.

It will be found that c.f.f. increases with increase in (*a*) brightness, (*b*) area of flickering light, (*c*) area of background.

Discrimination – conclusions. A number of types of discrimination have been considered. Speaking generally, sensory discrimination seems to be limited by the ability of the nervous systems involved to detect small intensity differences. This is even true of acuity and colour vision. Thus intensity discrimination becomes of cardinal importance to the study of sensory processes.

ADAPTATION TO INTENSITY OF LIGHT

The eye can function over a range of intensities of the order of 100,000:1. We are, however, temporarily dazzled and almost blind if we emerge suddenly from near darkness into bright light. This would seem to be a weakness of the system. Adaptation to dim light takes place comparatively slowly: sensitivity may increase for up to one hour in darkness. It is difficult to imagine that this long time course is of any biological advantage.

Since the work of Hecht (1934) it has been rather generally supposed that the retinal basis of adaptation is the density of the photochemical rhodopsin. It has recently been shown by W. H. Rushton and co-workers, with unusually beautiful experiments, in which the concentration is measured directly in the living eye, that the change in rhodopsin concentration with normal levels of incident light is very small. This implies either that rhodopsin concentration is unimportant for adaptation, or that the small changes which do occur have a surprisingly large effect on the quantum capture and thus on sensitivity of the eye (Rushton, 1952; Rushton and Campbell 1954; Rushton, 1956). Rushton's experiments give the first direct information on this matter, but that other factors influence sensitivity can be readily demonstrated. Not all of these are retinal in origin.

1. The diameter of the pupil increases in dim light, giving a 10:1 variation in the eye's light-gathering power.

2. The retinal *area* over which summation takes place in the retina increases in the dark, this being due to decreased lateral inhibition (Barlow, Fitzhugh and Kuffler 1957).

3. The *duration* over which integration of energy takes place increases with dark adaptation (Gregory, 1955*a* [No. 10]).

It would seem that many mechanisms are involved. These are

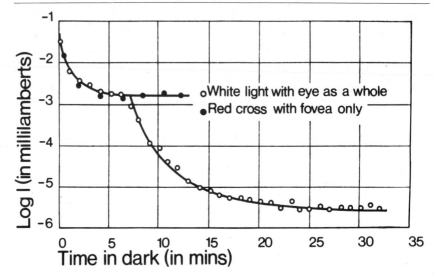

FIG. 1.12 *Dark adaptation of the human eye, showing the increase in sensitivity with time in darkness for cones (solid dots: fovea only) and rods (circles: white light, eye as a whole).*

very imperfectly understood, and until they are understood we are confronted with challenging fundamental problems. At the present time adaptation is still largely a mystery; until it is solved many other visual processes remain mysterious.

THE PERCEPTION OF MOVEMENT

If we consider the perception of the movement of a small self-luminous object viewed in an otherwise dark room, it is clear that there must be at least two distinct neurological systems, or 'channels', for the perception of movement. The movement of the light may be seen (*a*) if the eye is held still, the image travelling across the retina as the object moves across the field, or (*b*) if the eyes follow the object, in which case the image will remain stationary upon the retina, (except for small tracking errors). We may call the first system – depending upon shift of the image across the retina – the image/retina system, and the second – depending upon tracking of the eye – the eye/head system.

A similar distinction may be made for tactile movement perception – if the skin of the hand is stroked by an object, movement is experienced: it is also experienced if the hand is allowed to move with the object. Clearly, quite different neural systems are involved in these two cases.

Stability of the visual world during eye movements. The problem may be stated quite simply. If the eyes are moved (i.e. rotated) the images of objects in the field will be displaced across the retinae. Movement of images normally gives information of movement: why then, does not the visual world apparently move during eye movements?

It has been thought that the stability of the visual world during voluntary eye movements is produced by proprioceptive feedback from the extrinsic muscles of the eye. These proprioceptive feedback signals would be used by some central mechanism to cancel the movement signals from shifts of the image across the retina. There are, however, serious objections to this 'inflow theory': (1) Neural feedback loops are almost certainly too slow, so that the cancelling signals would not arrive in time to prevent perceptual instability. (2) Passive eye movements (such as by pressure with the finger) would be expected to produce signals from the stretch receptors. These should have some discernible effect, but none has been detected in perception (though Cooper and Daniel and Whitteridge (1953) have recorded activity, in the goat). (3) Helmholtz pointed out that patients suffering from paralysis of some of the extrinsic eye muscles experienced movement of the visual field when they tried to move their eyes, though in fact the eyes remained stationary. The experienced movement was always in the direction the eyes should have moved. It was this observation – which Kornmüller (1930) has repeated by anaesthetizing the muscles with cocaine – which led Helmholtz to suggest the 'outflow theory', which is that the eye movement command signals are utilized for stabilization, presumably by an internal monitoring loop. (4) It is easy to show that passive eye movements do not shift after-images. This provides evidence against proprioception playing a part in stabilization, for some stretch receptor activity should be produced, and this should produce movement of the after-image.[1]

After-images move with the eyes even when viewed in complete darkness, during voluntary eye movement. Stability, therefore, does not hold for after-images: why should this be? The most probable answer is that under normal conditions perceptual stability is achieved by a cancelling of opposed signals from (*a*) an internal loop monitoring the command signals to the eye, and (*b*) from the shift of images across the retina. There should be equal and opposite signals from these during eye movements: if these were arranged to

[1] The best way of obtaining the after-image for this type of observation is to fixate an electronic flash tube, giving say 110 joule flash in about 1/1000 second, as used for photography. This is a very useful tool for visual experiments.

cancel stabilization could thus be achieved during normal voluntary eye movements (Gregory, 1958 a [No. 14]).

APPARENT MOVEMENT

1. The 'waterfall effect'. Probably all the sense modalities can be fooled. A flickering white light may appear strongly coloured – because of the different time-constants of the physiological colour systems – and coloured lights will be observed if the eye-ball is pressed fairly hard with the finger: this stimulates the so-called pressure phosphenes. Any sense organ may be stimulated faradically, that is, with a weak electric current. The sense organs also tend to be fatigued, or adapted, by strong stimulation. The after-effects of a strong stimulus are perhaps most striking in the case of movement, though it is surprising how few people notice these effects until they are pointed out.

Demonstration of the 'waterfall effect'. An endless belt of transverse black and white stripes may be driven continuously and fixated for say 10 to 30 seconds. The belt is then stopped, and it will be found that it appears to *drift backwards* in a marked but rather odd manner. It moves, and yet it does not change its position. Quantitative measurements can be obtained most easily by timing the duration of the effect.

This effect is most marked if the eyes are kept fixed upon the belt using a fixation spot which may be projected upon it. If the eyes are allowed to follow the belt the *real* movement is still seen (by the 'retina/head' system) but the *after-effect* is absent. This suggests that it is not the perception of movement *per se*, but the stimulation of the image/retina system which produces the effect.

2. The phi-phenomenon. This is historically important in Gestalt Theory. The effect is familiar from the apparent movement experienced in illuminated signs. The conditions required for this apparent movement concern primarily the distance of the flashing lights and the interval between the first light going off and the coming on of the second light.

Wertheimer (1912) argued that this form of apparent movement is due to spread of activity in the cortex, a view suggested by the Gestalt theory of isomorphism. This theory is now generally abandoned, and the origin of the phi-phenomenon would be looked for first at the retinal level. It seems likely that what we have called the image/retina movement system is activated by flashes of light occurring within appropriate intervals and distances, much as when the movement is continuous.

3. The autokinetic effect. This also is historically important in Gestalt Theory. It is the apparent movement of a small dim spot of light observed in an otherwise dark room, or any small spot against a homogeneous field. Koffka (1935) says of it:

> These 'autokinetic' movements, then, prove that no fixed retinal values belong to retinal points; they produce localization within a framework, but do so no longer when the framework is lost. . . The autokinetic movements are the most impressive demonstration of the existence and functional effectiveness of the general spatial framework, but the operation of this framework pervades our whole experience.

Koffka stressed the importance of perceptual 'reference frames' in stabilizing the field, in this special case where the framework could only be conceptual, because it had been shown that the autokinetic movements were not, as had previously been thought, due to eye movements. Guilford and Dallenbach (1928) showed, photographically, that suitable eye movements do not occur under these conditions. We may check this in a simple manner.

Experiment to discover whether the eye moves during the autokinetic effect. The fovea is blind to dim blue light (Willmer, 1946). If we view a small dim blue patch of light it disappears when it is fixated. This effect may therefore be used to detect eye movements.

A set of Ilford Narrow Cut Spectral Filters is obtained, and a hole punched in the centre of the Blue filter. With the same punch, a disk of the same size is obtained from the Red filter, mounted in the hole in the Blue filter and bound between glass slide covers. The outer Blue filter is then masked with a hole of about 1 inch diameter. This arrangement is mounted in the side of a light-tight box fitted with a dim light (Gregory, 1959 [No. 15]).

If this arrangement is viewed in the dark, nothing but a red disk of light will be seen with central regard, but if the eye is moved slightly, a bluish-white halo will appear round the red spot, as the blue field becomes visible. With dark adaptation this effect becomes quite marked. The subject is required to note whether this halo appears during autokinetic movements of the red spot.

The answer is, it does not. Thus the effect cannot be due to slow movements of the eyes.

Experiment to produce induced 'autokinetic' movements. If the eyes are held hard over to one side, or up or down, for from 10 to 30 seconds before viewing the red spot, it will be found that, generally, there is a very fast drift of the spot in the opposite direction from the previous eye movement. Evidently the muscular imbalance sets up a related apparent movement. (The same thing happens with tension applied to the neck muscles, as may be shown by pushing the head backwards or forwards, or rotating it on a vertical axis right or left.) It may be suggested that in these cases we have upset the neural movement channels which normally, in the absence of external movement, cancel out during eye movements. We seem to have upset the stability system which is so important for distinguishing between the movements of the body or eye and movement of external objects. The usual autokinetic effect may be due to small random disturbances of these very complicated and delicately balanced systems (Gregory and Zangwill 1963 [No. 16]).

COLOUR VISION

The eye is sensitive over a range of wavelengths from about 400 mμ to about 700 mμ. The photopic sensitivity curve shows the sensitivity of the eye to wavelengths along the spectrum, but in addition different colours are seen as wavelength is changed, though this does not appear from the luminosity curve, which ignores colour, being concerned only with sensitivity and wavelength.

The seven spectral colour names – Red, Orange, Yellow, Green, Blue, Indigo and Violet – were given by Newton.[1] He originally adopted five, adding Orange and Indigo because he liked the magic number seven.

It is not practical, in experiments on colour vision, to require the subject to name each colour he sees, because it is quite impossible to name the several hundred discernible hues consistently. Colour experiments – apart from certain demonstrations – generally involve matching a field composed of a monochromatic or mixture of lights with some other mixture, (or under some other condition), and requiring the subject to state when the fields appear identical. The data are then in terms of the various mixture components, or other conditions required to give a match.

Thomas Young (1807) made the most important single discovery after Newton's work on light. Young found that any spectral hue may be produced (and matched by) a suitable mixture of three and only three coloured lights. Further, the choice of these three colours (wavelengths) was found to be not critical. Young wrote:

As it is almost impossible to conceive of each sensitive point of the retina to contain an infinite number of particles, each capable

[1] These may be memorized with the mnemonic: 'Richard Of York Gained Battles In Vain'.

of vibrating in unison with every possible undulation, it becomes necessary to suppose the number limited, for instance, to the three principal colours, red, yellow and blue . . . and each sensitive filament of the nerve may consist of three portions, one for each principal colour. (1802)

Young later changed his 'principal colours' (1807) to red, green and violet.

Helmholtz's modification of Young's hypothesis gives us three types of receptor (cones, each type having its own spectral sensitivity curve). The colour seen depends on the relative activity of the three systems. Since the sensitivity curves must overlap, it is not possible to stimulate one curve at a time (except perhaps for far blue or far red light) and so the problem of discovering the form and spectral position of these hypothetical curves turns out to be very difficult. Four principal techniques have been adopted: (1) recording the activity from single receptors with micro-electrodes placed on the giant ganglion cells at the front of the excised retina, the optic nerve or selected regions of the brain, (2) selectively fatiguing the eye with bright coloured lights applied to one eye and making binocular matches under special mixture conditions, (3) studying colour vision in cases of colour anomaly, (4) measurements of hue discrimination.

The reader is referred to Granit (1947) or to Morgan and Stellar (1950) for a summary of Granit's work on the electrophysiology of the retina. The adaptation work was mainly undertaken by, and is described by, Wright (1946), where the colour anomaly evidence is also given. This is reviewed by Brindley (1957).

In addition to colour the receptors also transmit information of brightness and saturation. A colour is desaturated by the addition of white light: if brightness were given by special cones having roughly the overall photopic sensitivity curve of the eye, then saturation might be given by the relative activity of this brightness receptor and the colour cone systems. If white light were then added to a monochromatic light this would produce desaturation of the colour by adding brightness with only slight increase of activity in the colour systems being stimulated by the monochromatic light. The evidence for such a brightness receptor is, however, not conclusive.

Demonstration of colour mixture with three coloured lights. If three slide projectors are available, with some form of intensity control, they may be fitted with aperture stops and their lights combined on a screen, giving three overlapping disks of light. A different colour filter is then placed in each beam. The Red, Green and Blue Ilford Spectral Filters are ideal.

It will be found that with suitable adjustments of relative intensity the portion where all three beams overlap can be made white. Change in the intensity of the colours will change the mixture to any desired spectral hue. Brown and black (which are not present in the spectrum) cannot be produced.

If a Yellow filter is placed in one lantern, and the Red and Green in the remaining lanterns, it will be found that the monochromatic yellow can be matched with these two (red and green) lanterns. This turns out to be important.

This finding that spectral hues can be produced with only three (but a minimum of three for the normal eye) lights does *suggest* that all colours are seen by the combined activity of three basic colour systems, but it does not *follow* that there are only three colour systems. How can we find out whether there are more than three systems?

Three is the minimum possible number. The maximum number would be one colour system for each discriminable hue: that is, any given monochromatic light would stimulate only one set of receptors which would be unaffected by all other wavelengths. This would require several hundred sets of receptors, or colour systems: one for each hue. It is quite clear that the eye is not like this. If it were, visual acuity in monochromatic light should be extremely poor – impaired by a factor of at least 100 – if no receptors but those sensitive to a given narrow band of wavelengths were functional. It would have to be a narrow band because of the several hundred hues we can distinguish without – on this hypothesis – allowing combined activity from different systems to play a part in colour vision. Visual acuity in monochromatic light is very nearly equal to acuity in white light of comparable brightness; except for the case of blue light when acuity is poor, but this is due to the blue-blindness of the fovea (Willmer, 1946).

It is clear that there must be at least three systems but there cannot be very many more than three, or acuity in monochromatic light would be very poor due to the effective coarsening of the retinal 'grain'. The main problem in colour vision is to determine how many colour systems there are, and what their spectral sensitivity curves may be.

Hering postulated a special yellow receptor, largely because yellow seems to be a unique experience. This is no argument: the simplicity or uniqueness of an experience is no guide to the degree of complexity of the physiological processes subserving it. In any case, we know that yellow *can* be produced by red and green mixture. There would thus have to be *two ways* of seeing yellow: by the special yellow receptor and by the systems primarily serving red and green. We can show in a simple experiment that there are not two ways of seeing yellow and this is a matter of considerable importance.

Experiments to discover whether there is a special yellow receptor. We require some form of anomaloscope. (This does not have to be of high class, or accurately calibrated.) An anomaloscope is an instrument designed to measure the relative intensities of red and green light required to match yellow light. It provides two adjacent comparison fields, one of these fields being produced by monochromatic yellow light, and the other by a mixture of red + green light in adjustable proportions. The situation is thus exactly like that of the three lanterns described above, but with a yellow filter in one lantern providing one field and a red and a green filter in the others to give the second comparison mixture field. The instrument is normally used as a test for colour anomaly, the common kinds of colour anomalous (or 'colour blind') eyes requiring unusual proportions of red and green to match the yellow, as discovered by Lord Rayleigh in 1881.

All that we require beyond the anomaloscope is a bright source of light, and a red and a green filter. The subject first carefully adjusts the relative intensities of the red and green lights so that the mixture field matches the monochromatic yellow field. The whole display will then look the *same* yellow. He then looks at a bright source of light through, say, a red filter. This fatigues, or adapts, the eye to red. If he now looks back at the anomaloscope fields, they should appear green. Now the question is: with this selective colour adaptation, do the two fields still look alike? Is the match retained?

If the monochromatic yellow stimulates a special yellow receptor, the pre-adaptation to red should not produce a change of colour of the yellow field. If, however, yellow is always seen effectively by mixture of the red and green systems, then the monochromatic yellow field should change in colour. Both fields should appear green after red stimulation, red after green stimulation—the match remaining unchanged by the adapting red or green light.

The answer is that both fields *are* equally affected, suggesting that monochromatic yellow and red + green light stimulate the same retinal systems. For extremely bright adapting light, there is some shift but this is too small to affect the argument; and the shift is always in the same direction, towards red (Wright, 1936; Brindley, 1953; Gregory, 1955 *b* [No. 6]).

It is possible to see a fairly good yellow by stimulating one eye with red and the other with green light. If the intensities are suitably balanced, at least some observers will occasionally see yellow; though there is a great deal of retinal rivalry, producing alternating red and

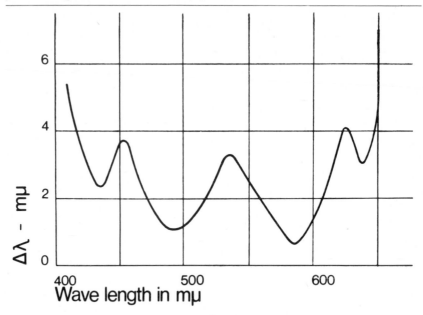

FIG. 1.13 *Hue discrimination. This shows by how much wavelength must be changed (Δλ) for a detectable difference in hue for each position along the visible spectrum (λ). This curve gives perhaps the most fundamental information obtainable by psychophysical means for discovering the response systems giving colour vision.*

green. When yellow is seen this must be due to central fusion of activity from red and green systems from the two eyes.

Hue discrimination. Hue discrimination is of practical importance in the dyeing and paint industries, as well as for the theory of colour vision. It is measured by changing the spectral wavelength, and recording the change in wavelength required for a difference in hue to be seen, brightness being kept constant.

Fig. 1.13 shows a hue discrimination curve determined by Steindler (1906) for normal vision. It will be noted that $\Delta\lambda$ (the difference in wavelength required to detect a difference in hue) is plotted against λ (wavelength). In this curve there are four minima: 440, 485, 575 and 625 mμ. These are the spectral positions where hue discrimination is best.

Given that there are several cone systems, each having its own sensitivity curve, the hue discrimination curve should correspond to these primary response curves in the following way. Consider first the high values of $\Delta\lambda$ at the extreme red and blue ends; at either end only one colour system will be functional, and change of wavelength should produce only a change in brightness. This is the case for red over quite a wide range. As wavelength is reduced towards yellow, the next receptor system (green) will become stimulated, and the hue will depend on the balance of outputs from these two systems. Now $\Delta\lambda$ will depend upon the *relative* slopes of the fundamental response curves for each value of λ. Thus, there should be a relation between the hue discrimination curve and the fundamental response curves. It is important to note that hue discrimination is limited by the minimum intensity difference which can be detected between the fundamental colour systems. Intensity discrimination again turns out to be of basic importance.

Colour anomaly. More usually, though misleadingly, referred to as 'colour blindness', colour anomaly is essentially an inability to distinguish certain colours which are readily distinguished by the majority of observers under the same conditions. The most common form of confusion is between red and green. Its discovery is usually attributed to the chemist John Dalton, in 1794.

Lord Rayleigh (1881) discovered that people who are apt to confuse red and green require unusual amounts of red or green in a red + green mixture field to match a monochromatic yellow light. It was this finding which led Nagel, in 1907, to develop the anomaloscope, used as a test of anomaly. Those observers requiring unusual matches are known as anomalous Trichromats. This means that they, like normal observers, require three lights to match the spectral hues, but that the proportions of red and green required to match yellow are unusual. Some observers require only two lights to match all the spectral hues they can discern: these are called Dichromats. Occasionally Monochromats are found who have no ability to distinguish colours apart from their intensity differences. Their world is like a black and white film.

The following classification may prove helpful:

I. TRICHROMATS	II. DICHROMATS	III. MONOCHROMATS
1. Normal colour vision	1. Protonopia	
2. Protonomaly	2. Deuteronopia	
3. Deuteronomaly	3. Tritonopia	

Now what does this mean? Section I observers (Trichromats) all require three mixture lights to match the spectral hues, but protonomalous observers require more red, and deuteronomalous observers more green, to match yellow. In Section II (Dichromats) only two mixture lights are required. Protonopes do not require red, deuteronopes green, and tritonopes (rare) blue. Monochromats are of only one kind – no colour vision.

HEARING

The physics of sound. A vibrating diaphragm or string, or a column of air as in an organ pipe or the larynx, alternately compresses and rarefies the air round it.

When the increase in pressure is replaced by a local decrease, a pressure wave is replaced by a 'trough'. A diaphragm, such as the drum of the ear, may be displaced back and forth with the alternating pressure waves. When this is suitably attached to the mechanism of the middle ear, and to the neural mechanism of the cochlea and the brain, rapidly alternating pressure changes may be heard as sound.

The ear can signal tones over a frequency range from about 30 c/s–20,000 c/s. Frequencies below 30 c/s are heard as vibration rather than tone. The upper limit of 20,000 c/s is reached only by children and young adults. There is a continual falling off in the upper frequency limit of hearing with age (presbyacusia). The useful upper limit might be put at 16,000 c/s.

The energy in a simple (sinusoidal) sound wave. The energy of sine waves can be measured in terms of peak amplitude, or in terms of root-mean-square amplitude. The latter (*rms*) is generally used, because it is a more stable value for complex waves, and we require to measure energies in complex as well as sine waves. In the case of sine waves, there is a very simple relation between these two measures. Where P is the pressure:

$$P_{rms} = \frac{P_{max}}{\sqrt{2}} = 0 \cdot 707 P_{max}$$

No simple relation holds for complex waves.

We shall use *rms* values, and this is standard practice. The intensity range of the human ear is extremely large; it covers a range of about $10^{12}:1$. (This is, of course, 1,000,000,000,000:1.) The threshold of detection is only 10^{-16} watt. If the ear were more sensitive, we would hear the random movement of air molecules.

Relative intensities are given in decibels (db). This is a very useful measure, and is defined as:

$$N(\text{decibels}) = 10 \log_{10}\frac{P^2}{P^2_r} = N = 20 \log_{10}\frac{P}{P}$$

or
$$N = \frac{\log E_2}{\log E_1}$$

What does this mean? N refers to the number of decibels (where 1 decibel = 0·1 bel); P is the pressure of the tone being measured, and

P_r the pressure of some standard reference tone. E is energy, or P^2. It should be particularly noted that the decibel unit is not an *absolute* unit, such as the metre, the second, or the gramme. The decibel is a *relative* measure. Any decibel value (e.g. 30 db) always means '30 db above, or below, some other intensity'. In hearing, we frequently find that no reference value is given explicitly. Thus we may read: 'a 30 db tone of 100 c/s was presented to the left ear'. This can be said, although the decibel is only a relative measure, because there is a generally agreed conventional origin (or P_r) to the scale. This is the absolute threshold for the average human ear for young adults. The value of this threshold has been determined, and is conventionally accepted as 0·0002 dyne/sq. cm for a 1000 c/s tone.

Complex waves – harmonics, beats. To get a feel for the physics of sound it is almost essential to have the use of two or three audio-frequency oscillators and a suitable oscilloscope. Arrangements should be provided for mixing the signals from the oscillators. In addition, a tape recorder with microphone (preferably a twin-channel stereophonic recorder), and various musical instruments, such as tuning forks, organ pipes, and a stringed instrument, are extremely useful.

The use of an oscilloscope. A cathode ray oscilloscope is an instrument similar to a television receiver. A beam of electrons appears as a spot on a fluorescent screen at the end of the tube. This spot is repeatedly deflected at constant rate across the tube, from left to right, and is very rapidly returned. It is swept across by the time-base, the return being known as the fly-back. In the absence of incoming signals, a horizontal line is seen traced out on the tube face by the scanning spot. It is seen as a line because of persistence of vision, and because of the time constant of the 'phosphor', i.e. the fluorescent substance. Incoming signals are in the form of voltages, which are generally amplified by internal amplifiers whose gain must be suitably controlled. A change in the input signal voltage causes the spot to move up or down, and as it is carried along at constant rate (hence the expression 'time-base') a wavy line is seen which represents the changes of the signal voltage in time. The amplitude of the wave is linearly related to the voltage. If a microphone is attached, pressure changes in the air may be seen as waves – a dynamic graph – on the screen. A tuning fork, or the output from a single oscillator, will give a sine wave. What is actually seen is a number of sine waves, or perhaps part of one, depending on the setting of the time-base frequency control. Suppose we wish to look at a 1000 c/s wave: if the repetition rate of the time-base is 1000/second, we shall see one sine wave, minus the bit missing during the fly-back time. With a repetition rate of 500/second, we shall see two sine waves, and so on. If the time-base repetition rate is not equal to, or a submultiple of, the signal frequency, then the display will run across the screen – an endless chain of sine waves chasing each other, but never catching and never caught.

If the outputs from two oscillators are mixed, and the result viewed on the 'scope', different patterns are produced as the intervals between the tones are changed. At any moment when they are in phase they will add together producing a greater deflection of the spot; when out of phase the spot will tend to return to the centre line of the screen. Two waves of the same form and amplitude but opposite phase would produce a straight line, and silence. Zero amplitude (and silence) is produced at regular intervals by two waves of different frequency but the same amplitude, at those moments when they have equal and opposite values. If we set one oscillator to 1000 c/s and the other to 1010 c/s, we shall hear this happening ten times a second, and the result is a 'beat' which in this case will be heard as a throb rather than a tone.

A vibrating string, organ pipe or other instrument, gives a fundamental frequency and overtones, or harmonics, which are always multiples of the fundamental. The different timbre of musical instruments is due to the various relative amplitudes (or energies) of the harmonics. Instruments such as oboes and stringed instruments are rich in harmonics, while tuning forks and flutes are not; they give almost pure sine waves. Pipe organs can synthesize the various timbres of instruments by providing the appropriate harmonics from their range of pipes. These are controlled by the stops. Any wave, however complex, can be built up out of a set of sine waves of various amplitudes and frequencies. Similarly, any complex wave can be analysed into a set of simple sine waves.

The structure and function of the ear. Pressure changes enter the ear through the auditory canal (*meatus auditorius*) and reach the ear drum (*tympanum*) (Fig. 1.14). This is an oval membrane placed obliquely in the meatus. It vibrates with the pressure changes reaching it from the sound source. Attached to the inner side of the tympanum is the first of three tiny bones or ossicles. These are (*a*) the hammer (*malleus*), (*b*) the anvil (*incus*), (*c*) the stirrup (*stapes*). These form a set of levers which reduce the amplitude of vibration of the drum. The further end of the stirrup (the footplate) is attached to a second membrane, the oval window. This forms the boundary between the middle ear (containing the ossicles) and the inner ear in which lies the cochlea. The cochlea is a snail-shaped cavity in the temporal bone. If we take a cross section of one of the turns of the cochlea (Fig. 1.15)

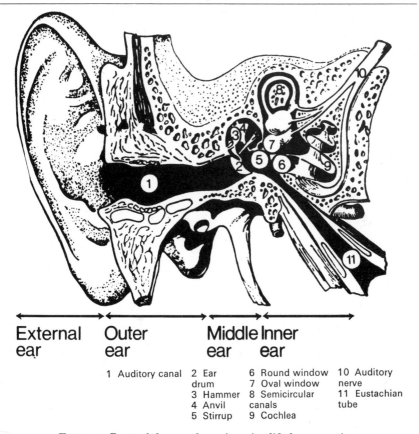

External ear	**Outer ear**	**Middle ear**	**Inner ear**

1 Auditory canal 2 Ear drum 6 Round window 10 Auditory nerve
3 Hammer 7 Oval window 11 Eustachian tube
4 Anvil 8 Semicircular canals
5 Stirrup 9 Cochlea

FIG. 1.14 *Parts of the ear, shown in a simplified cross-section.*

we see three chambers divided by two membranes: Reissner's membrane and the basilar membrane. The three divisions, or tubes, running along the inside of the cochlea are the *scala vestibuli*, the *scala tympani* and the *cochlear duct*. The cochlear duct lies between the vestibular and tympanic scalae. Within it, and lying on the basilar membrane, are the receptor hair cells. They lie in rows in the Organ of Corti, deep in the densest bone of the body, surrounded and nourished by fluid, protected from mechanical damage and from the fluctuations of the blood supply. No blood vessels are found here. The hair cells lie bathed in endolymph fluid, from which they are nourished. The freedom this gives them from pulsatory disturbance is no doubt an important factor in the extremely high sensitivity of the ear – we are not deafened by our own pulse.

The scalae vestibuli and tympani are joined by an opening, the *helicotrema*, at the apical end of the cochlea. We shall see the significance of these tubes (which are filled with a fluid, the perilymph) with their common opening, and the significance of the reduction in amplitude of airborne vibrations from the drum to the oval window by the ossicle lever system.

The manner of vibration of the drum is important theoretically, Its amplitude of movement is small – only about 0·54 mm peak amplitude for the extremely high pressure of 1000 dynes/sq. cm at 100 c/s. This amplitude will fall off nearly linearly with increase in frequency, until at 10,000 c/s it will be only 0·00054 mm.

The ossicles as a mechanical matching transformer. The function and movements of the ossicles are discussed in detail by Wever and Lawrence (1954). The ratio of input to output amplitude for the cat ossicles turns out to be 2·5 : 1, but owing to the different areas of the drum and the oval window, the effective ratio is 60·7 : 1. For the

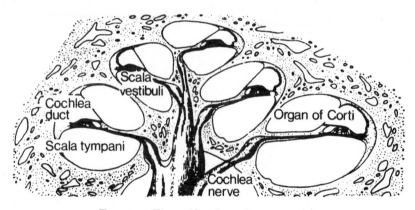

FIG. 1.15 *The cochlea shown in cross-section.*

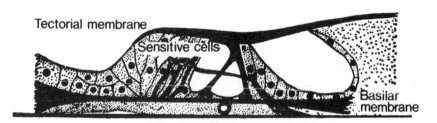

FIG. 1.16 *The Organ of Corti.*

human ear the ratio of the ossicle input–output movement is 1·31 : 1 and the total effective impedance ratio is 18·3 : 1. Now why is this matter of importance? The reason is that the sound energy is converted from vibrations in air to vibrations in a comparatively dense fluid, the perilymph, and for high efficiency of energy transfer some kind of *transformer* is needed to *match* the two impedances. (The problem is exactly the same as that of matching the loudspeaker of a radio set to the output valve, though in this case the transformer is electrical, while in the ear it is mechanical.)

The impedance of the cochlear fluid changes with frequency, so that the optimum matching ratio will depend on the frequency. The ear is most sensitive at about 1500 c/s; at this frequency the acoustic efficiency is 38 per cent (a loss of 4·2 db). At 100 c/s the efficiency is only 3·5 per cent (a loss of 14·6 db). It appears that the effective mismatch of the middle ear system at low frequencies is largely responsible for the falling off in sensitivity below 1000 c/s.

The transmission of sound in the cochlea. Sound is no longer airborne after the oval window; it is a series of pressure waves in the perilymph. These travel up the scala tympani, through the helicotrema and down the scala vestibuli, which terminates in a membrane at the

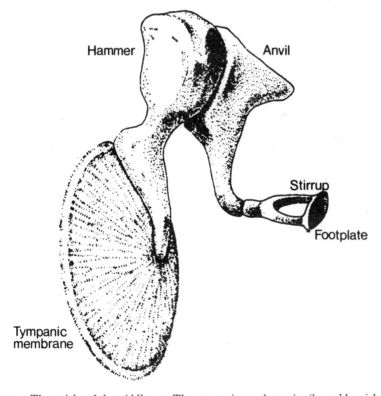

FIG. 1.17 *The ossicles of the middle ear. The tympanic membrane is vibrated by airborne sound; these vibrations are passed through the lever system of the ossicles to the footplate of the stirrup, which is surrounded by a narrow membrane enclosing the perilymph fluid which carries the energy to the Organ of Corti.*

Hammer

Anvil

Stirrup

Footplate

Tympanic membrane

round window. (A frequency diagram of a schematic cochlea is shown in Fig. 1.18). The pressure waves produce vibration of the basilar membrane which probably sets up a shearing force in the Organ of Corti, between the basilar membrane and the tectorial membrane (Békésy, 1956). This shearing would serve to provide greater force (with a sacrifice of amplitude) to deflect the hair cells, the mechanical stimulation of which initiates impulses in the auditory nerve. From this point on, the sound waves are represented in terms of neural activity; the Organ of Corti may thus be thought of as a transducer changing the sound waves into a form which can be handled by the nervous system.

We can isolate the separate tones in a chord – unlike colour vision, where the eye cannot provide any information of the component lights producing a colour mixture. It appears that the various frequencies are represented in different regions of the basilar membrane, as shown diagrammatically for the guinea-pig ear in Fig. 1.18. This spatial representation of frequencies has been established by a

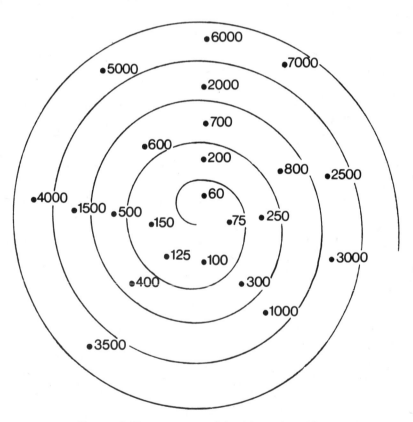

FIG. 1.18 *Frequency map of the guinea-pig cochlea.*

number of techniques including: (1) damaging regions of the cochlea with fine drill holes, and testing for specific deafness, (2) subjecting the ear to extremely loud pure tones over long periods and looking for related local damage, and (3) recording from different regions while the ear is stimulated with tones of various frequencies. These studies show that middle- and high-frequency tones are localized spatially, but that there is considerable spread of activity around any locus of primary stimulation. The physics of the cochlea as a system which localizes frequencies to specific regions is still open to doubt. Helmholtz suggested that it works by the principle of resonance. (This can most easily be demonstrated with a piano. If the dampers are removed from the strings, by holding the loud pedal down, a piano will 'answer' any loud tone by sympathetic vibration of those strings which gave the same tone when struck.) Helmholtz suggested that the basilar membrane is tuned to different frequencies along its length, much as the piano is tuned to different frequencies from bass to treble. Békésy has, however, provided strong evidence against this view: he cut the membrane, while observing it under a microscope, and found that the cut ends did not fly apart. It thus appears that the membrane is not under tension, and so it could hardly be 'tuned' in the manner of a stretched string, or system of strings. He also found, by direct observation, that there could be a phase lag up the cochlea greater than one cycle; this could not occur with a resonant system.

Several attempts have been made to construct models of the cochlea. Békésy (1956) has considered the problem in terms of a travelling wave in a system of varying stiffness. He used a set of pendulums mounted on a rod which was periodically rotated through a small angle and investigated the properties of such a system under various conditions of coupling between the pendulums. (This is a good example of the physical model approach to physiological problems; the actual arrangement used is quite simple, and makes an interesting demonstration.)

The finding that there is considerable spread of activity either side of the central locus of vibration of the basilar membrane raises the question: why does a loud pure tone not sound like a cluster of neighbouring tones? A possible answer is that the ear adopts neural gradient sharpening, as does the retina. This indeed is a general property of sensory networks. If a matchstick is pressed into the skin of the hand or arm, until a marked depression is produced, the sensation is of a point. But since the surrounding skin has been pressed inwards, the surrounding touch receptors must be stimulated; so it appears that activity from the peripheral receptors is rejected (inhibited). This is typical *lateral inhibition*. On this view of suppression of activity from less stimulated neighbouring receptors, we should expect that a tone might suppress, or mask, a neighbouring weaker tone – this is indeed so.

MASKING EXPERIMENTS

1. Masking by tones. This experiment requires an audiometer and a separate audio oscillator. The signals from these are mixed into a common earphone.

The oscillator is set to a frequency which is not a multiple of any of the spot frequencies given by the audiometer, for we want to avoid the harmonics. A frequency of 800 c/s is convenient. Its intensity is set rather high, say 80 db. (This may be found with sufficient accuracy by comparison with the audiometer. To do this, connect the outputs into separate 'phones, place one 'phone against each ear, and with the audiometer set the nearest frequency to the desired masking tone, and giving an 80 db output, adjust the oscillator until the intensities balance. It may be advisable to reverse the earphones in order to check that the observer's ears are roughly equivalent.)

An audiogram is then obtained while the 80 db 800 c/s tone from the oscillator is mixed with the audiometer signal. If this is repeated with various intensities of masking tone, a family of curves such as those shown in Fig. 1.19 should be obtained.

It will be noted that (*a*) the only masking *below* the frequency of the masking tone is very close to that tone, and (*b*) there is a marked rise in the threshold for several octaves *above* it, with a depression at each octave.

If now the same procedure is adopted, but for binaural masking, where the audiogram is obtained from one ear while the masking tone is applied to the other, very little masking will be found. It is generally thought that any effect which may be discovered is due to sound crossing the head by bone conduction. It appears that masking takes place *in* the ear and not *across* the ears.

The reason for masking being almost entirely upwards in frequency may be due to some property of the cochlea, or it may be due to distortion in the ear producing harmonics (which are always upwards) from the fundamental masking tone.

2. Masking by 'white noise'. The same procedure may be adopted, but using in place of the masking tone a source of 'white noise'. (The curious term 'white noise' is taken over from optics, for

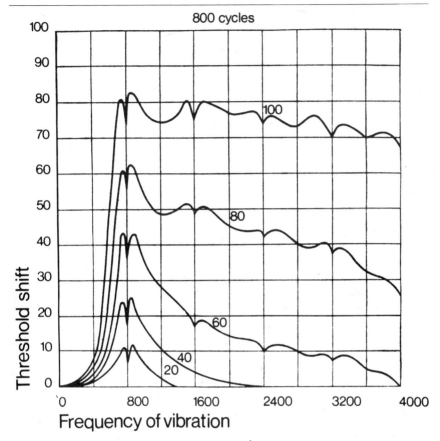

FIG. 1.19 *Masking effects of an 800 c/s tone.*

normally white light consists of all frequencies in the spectrum. A monochromatic coloured light is analogous to a pure tone in this respect. White noise sounds like a hiss.) (See Egan *et al.* 1956.)

The results for noise masking are similar to tone masking, in that masking increases with frequency, though continuously.

Localization of sound. People who are totally deaf in one ear are handicapped in their ability to localize the position in space of a source of sound. If a sound originates from one side of the head, it will provide more energy to the nearer ear – provided the frequency is fairly high. The reason for the difference in energy (and so of loudness) is that the head shadows the sound to the further ear. Long wavelengths of sound get round the head; there is hardly any shadowing for long, low-frequency waves.

Demonstration of the frequency-selective effect of the head shadowing sounds. If a noise source placed to one side of the head is heard, (*a*) with the nearer ear occluded, say by the palm of the hand, and then (*b*) with the further ear similarly occluded, it will be found that the noise sounds higher (i.e. with greater energy of high-frequency components) in the nearer ear. This demonstrates that the shadowing is frequency-selective, the higher frequencies being shadowed by the head and so lost to the further ear.

It may seem to follow that sound localization should be relatively poor for low-frequency sounds, but this is not the case. At low frequencies the ears make use of the phase difference between the ears due to their different distances from the source. Any given change in pressure reaches the nearer ear first, and throughout a wave this time difference will remain constant, while the direction of the source from the head is maintained. The simplest way of investigating binaural time discrimination is by applying pairs of clicks separated by various time intervals, one to each ear. Wallach, Newman and Rosenzweig (1949) found that time differences as small as 30–40 μ/second provided information of direction, and only one click is heard. With intervals greater than 2–3 m/seconds a double click was heard, and localization lost.

The best way of experimenting with these effects is with a twin channel tape recorder. Clicks at any desired time intervals may be produced on the two channels, by using two microphones so placed that the one to give the later click is the correct distance further from the sound source than the other microphone. If a single click is now produced, this will be recorded as one click on each channel, spaced in distance along the tape and in time when played back separately to the two ears.

It is found that phase difference is used for sound localization for frequencies below about 1500 c/s. Localization is rather poor for intermediate frequencies where, in other respects, hearing is most efficient.

Marler (1955) has provided evidence that in animals warning cries tend to lie in the range where localization is poor, thus the location of the 'sentry' is not given away. But mating calls are in the region where localization is good: thus the position of the suitor is discovered; so the mate is not frustrated, at any rate for auditory reasons.

Experiments on the localization of sound. (1) The subject should sit in the centre of the room with his eyes covered. The experimenter makes various kinds of sound, each of short duration, from various positions round the subject, who indicates by pointing where he thinks each sound originates.

For demonstration purposes clicks may be produced with coins. Tones may be produced with an oscillator (or audiometer) and an

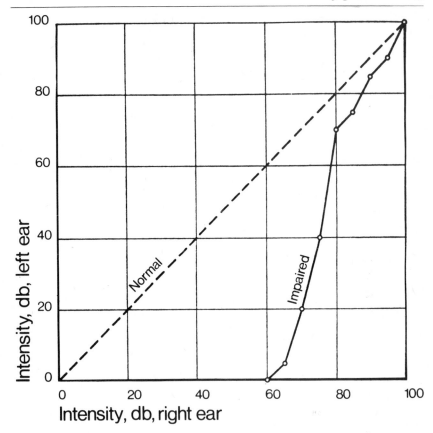

FIG. 1.20 *Recruitment. The broken line shows how a normal person will make a binaural loudness match; the solid curve shows how a nerve-deaf ear 'catches up' with the normal ear at high intensities. Data for a patient deafened to 2048 c/s in the right ear. (Loudness recruitment is taken up again later on p. 196.)*

earphone which may be moved from place to place silently. The best system, perhaps, is to mount small 'speakers or 'phones round the subject and to switch the various tones or other sounds to these in random order.

(2) The ears may effectively be reversed, with a pseudophone. This consists of two horns, one placed in each ear and bent round the head so that the sound reaches each ear from the opposite side of the head. Or microphones and earphones may be used.

These experiments may be combined. It is interesting to locate sounds with the pseudophone both with and without vision. The information from the auditory sense tends to be ignored when vision is available. This has been investigated by Jackson (1953) in an amusing experiment in which spurious visual indications of sound sources were used. Held (1955) got his subjects to wear a pseudophone for several hours continuously and found that this produced a systematic shift in sound localization.

Information in speech waves. A central and difficult problem is to discover which characteristics of the complex waves of speech are important for carrying information. These experiments take the form of destroying or modifying some features of the speech wave, and finding the effect upon intelligibility tests. One of the most striking findings is due to Licklider (1946), who showed that if the peaks of speech waves are cut off (this is quite simply done with two backed diodes) speech is still intelligible. Under conditions of noise masking, a small percentage of clipping may actually improve intelligibility. Important information is evidently carried by the time intervals of the cross-over points on the zero-energy axis. It looks as though it is the ear's remarkable ability to discriminate very small time intervals – which was noted for binaural hearing when we discussed localization – which is vital to the recognition of speech.

The concepts of Information Theory, first stated systematically by Shannon (1949), have proved of great use in quantifying the information transmitted in speech under various conditions. It is also important to the general problem of sensory discrimination. 'Information' is used in a special technical sense which does not involve meaning. 'Information' is defined in terms of the selection of items from a set of possible items. The larger the set the greater the number of decisions required, and the more 'information' is needed. The simplest possible case, and the case requiring least 'information', is a choice of one out of a set of two possible items. The unit of 'information' – the 'bit' – is defined as a choice between two possibilities. Morse code is a very simple code containing only two kinds of events, a dot and a dash. It requires only a very simple receiving apparatus to distinguish between two kinds of possibilities, and mistakes are unlikely, but it requires a large number of these binary choices to represent a lot of information in a message. In a language containing a large number of characters (such as Chinese) a lot of information may be carried by each symbol, and then fewer symbols are needed for any given message. Thus the message will be shorter, but the apparatus required to discriminate the symbols from each other must be more complicated. Information is defined as the logarithm of the number of alternatives. Thus a choice of 1 out of 10 alternatives carries half the information carried by a choice of 1 out of 100 alternatives, and a third as much as 1 out of 1000 alternatives. The alternatives may be anything – playing cards, voltages, intensities, speech sounds. In practice logarithms to the base 2 are used. We may take an example: suppose that the ear can distinguish with equal ease (i.e. with equal probability of error) 16 things, no matter what these may be; this situation is characterized by 4 bits of information, since $\log_2 16 = 4$.

We should consider the case of a continuous scale, such as intensity or frequency. Suppose we have a measuring instrument, say a loudness or a frequency meter, graduated in divisions. Each division represents one of a number of possible values the variable might take. Now the greater the number of divisions on the instrument the greater the amount of information it can represent. To represent a continuous variable perfectly the instrument would need an infinite number of divisions, and its 'differential threshold' would have to be zero. It is thus in practice impossible to represent a continuous variable perfectly – it would require an infinite amount of information.

An important feature of all communication channels is 'noise'. This is random disturbance of the signal. The effect of noise upon channel capacity, which is the rate of transmission of information, has been formulated in the Hartley-Shannon Law. If the band width (or frequency range) of the system is W, the mean signal power S, and the mean noise power N, then the Law states that the channel capacity is:

$$W = \log_2 (1 + \frac{S}{N}) \text{ bits/second}$$

It may be seen from this that by suitably 'trading' the variables it is possible to describe an infinite number of different systems having identical channel capacities, or information rates. Thus if there is plenty of time available, low band width and low signal/noise ratio may be adequate. But to transmit the same amount of information in a short time the band width and power must be increased, or the noise level must be reduced. Here the essential problem of sensory discrimination is formulated in a manner allowing quantified data to be obtained by experiment. Although the importance of discrimination has been stressed throughout, discussion of the formulation given by Shannon has been postponed until now, because speech is so familiar, and yet so baffling, that the formulation may seem of immediate use. Having thought this out, it might be worth our while to think again about the general problem of discrimination by the senses.

If a signal is masked by noise the moment to moment value of the noise will add to or subtract from the value of the signal energy. If the value of the signal plus the noise at this moment should happen to represent say another symbol, then an error will generally occur unless the redundancy of the code is sufficient to allow rejection of the error. Redundancy is the use of more symbols than would be necessary for the transmission of the message in a noise-free system. The larger the physical intervals between signals the less probable it is that noise will distort a symbol so that it is mistaken for another symbol. Thus to reduce the probability of errors: (*a*) The number of kinds of symbols, or number of steps should be small by comparison with the total range over which the receiver works. (*b*) The code should be redundant. Repetition is one form of redundancy. (*c*) Each symbol may be transmitted over a long time interval, the receiver incorporating some form of integrator. The signal/noise ratio increases with time, given integration. If the integrator is perfect, S/N increases with the $\sqrt{t}$, or with $\sqrt{N}$, where N is the number of repetitions of the message.

Many experiments have been done on recognizing words chosen at random from restricted vocabularies of various sizes under noise masking conditions. In general, intelligibility falls as the number of words in the vocabulary is increased. This is similar to the experiment in visual acuity mentioned in a previous section, in which the number of possible positions of the gap is changed. If either the number of words in the vocabulary or the number of speech symbols is increased, the chances of confusion and error through noise is increased.

The recognition of speech. The ear can distinguish tones best when they are about 50 db above threshold, and in the frequency range 500–4000 c/s (Miller, 1951). The ear can thus handle, in the technical sense, most information in this region, because it can make most discriminations. There are about 1600 distinguishable tones and about 300 intensity levels (cf. Miller, 1951, pp. 49–50). We cannot recognize so many, but they can be distinguished. The number of distinguishable pure sounds should thus be 300^{1600}. Comparatively few sounds are used as phonemes for speech, and there are fairly clear reasons for this. Individual voices are different; and yet all use the 'same' phonemes or set of phonemes; the speaker may be at various distances, and speak at various energy levels. The auditory system is capable of very much finer discrimination than is required for speech recognitions; this will tend to provide a safety factor against wrong identifications. The transmitted information is largely redundant, and this reduces errors.

The amount of information in a sound wave is given by

$$\text{Amount of information} = 2\,TW \log\frac{S+N}{N}$$

where $\log(S+N)/N$ can be regarded as the signal/noise ratio in decibels, W is the width of the frequency band, and T the duration of the message, or in words: *the amount of information in a speech wave is proportional to duration of the speech, to the range of frequency components involved, and to the logarithm of the number of discriminable steps in amplitude.*

In English only about 50 speech sounds (phonemes) are used out of all the possible combinations of frequencies and amplitudes. This is no doubt a concession to the noisiness of the world and of our nervous systems. Any masking noise will tend to reduce the information in the message; redundancy serves to preserve the message against noise or, to make this more explicit, to reduce the probability that any disturbance sufficiently important to cause an error will occur. In addition, language itself is redundant. In English 'q' is always followed by 'u', and so if 'u' were missing the word could still be read with certainty. Thus 'q een' can be read almost without hesitation. A gap such as 'b ead' can generally be filled in with a reasonable probability that no error will occur in a context. The same is true of spoken language, both in the physical characteristics of the speech sounds and in the statistical structure of the language.

2 Human perception

[The *British Medical Bulletin* produced its first collection of papers on Experimental Psychology in 1964. The following was written for this collection, and is a brief account of 'higher' perceptual processes. It is included here, like the previous paper, to serve as an initial summary of basic generally accepted facts.]

★   ★   ★

SPECULATIONS on how we perceive objects go back to the beginning of human thought, and remain central to the discussions of philosophers concerned with how we come to know the physical world. We have come a long way since Plato's theory – which he could have disproved with a few simple psychological experiments – that we see by spraying surrounding objects with particles shot out of the eyes. Understanding of perceptual processes comes not only from the techniques of experimental psychology, but also from physiology, and by the use of analogies from computer and communications engineering. Psychological experiments are of particular value in showing what kinds of information are used to judge the shape, size, distance and rate of movement of objects, and carefully designed experiments can sometimes suggest the kind of central neural systems involved in making these judgements. It remains most important to try to get direct physiological evidence, and this is now becoming available.

The retinas receive flat mosaic patterns of light, the ears ever-changing patterns of frequency and amplitude of vibration; but what we see are solid objects lying in three-dimensional space, and in speech what we hear are separate words and phrases, although an unfamiliar language sounds a continuous babble – expressed by the Greeks with the apt onomatopoeic 'barbarous'.

THE 'INNATE VERSUS LEARNING' CONTROVERSY

Traditionally the central problem in perception is how far the organization is innate, and how far it is dependent upon early learning. The great emphasis placed on the 'innate versus learning' issue is a somewhat unfortunate heritage from the philosophical controversy: does all our knowledge of the world come from the senses, or do we know some things *a priori*? It is this question which marks off philosophical empiricism from idealism, but although of first importance to philosophers, it is not so clearly a vital distinction for psychological theory. Psychology as an academic subject was nurtured in, and developed from, departments of philosophy, and it is no accident that emphasis on innate perception is stressed by the Gestalt school, which arose from German metaphysics, while British and American psychologists took their stand from the British empiricists, who hoped to get evidence to settle this controversy especially from the rare cases of adult recovery of sight following congenital blindness.

The reported cases of arrested vision in man were collected by von Senden in 1932 and there is a new case (Gregory and Wallace 1963 [No. 3]). The idea (first put forward by Molyneux in a letter to Locke, 1690) that these cases should tell us much about the development of human perception now looks forlorn, although it has been seriously discussed by Hebb (1949), and several studies have been made on animals reared in darkness (Riesen, 1947, 1950) with this problem in mind. The difficulty is that whatever is found can be interpreted without reference to the innate versus learning controversy. Lack of perception following blindess could be due to many factors – including loss of critical periods for maturation, continued reliance upon the previously available senses, and associated emotional disturbance – while rapidly developing perception could be due to cross-modal transfer, or to communication with sighted individuals. In short, it is difficult to discuss normal perceptual development on the basis of these cases of arrested vision, for adults who have recovered sight are not living fossils of normal infants.

Evidence of very early selection of certain kinds of pattern – and so of some perception – is provided in human babies, by the work of Fantz (1961), who recorded the eye movements of babies presented with pairs of patterns: for example, a simple representation of the human face and beside this a random pattern made up of the same individual lines (Fig. 2.1). The babies are found to fixate the face-like pattern (*a*) longer than the random pattern (*b*), and the same technique gives some evidence for innate appreciation of depth, a solid object

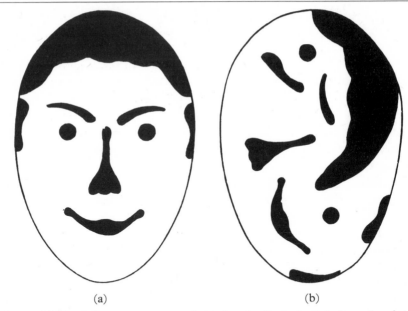

(a)   (b)

FIG. 2.1(a) *Simple face pattern presented to infants by Fantz (1961). It was found that babies looked longer at (a) than at (b), a random face pattern. This indicates some innate recognition of faces in human infants.*

being preferred to a flat representation of the same object. This is not evidence against philosophical empiricism, however, for some selection of sensory input and immediate recognition of biologically important objects could have developed by natural selection, and be available from birth. It is extremely difficult to establish just what is inherited and what has to be learned, but perhaps no *basic* psychological issue is at stake, though the problem is interesting and does have importance, especially for sociologists.

THE RETINAL IMAGE AND PERCEPTION

We have already pointed out that the mosaic for retinal stimulation gives rise to something quite different – perception of separate solid objects lying in three-dimensional space. This involves separating objects; and so it is of no account that normal retinal images are inverted or systematically distorted, or even that they are to some extent blurred. The retinal images do not represent simple geometrical projections of external objects, for the retina is not a simple shape, and images passing over it go through various transformations, though these are not generally perceived. Further, the perception given by an image is modified by the apparent distance of the object, though perceptions may be little affected.

Although constant distortion of the image is of no account, since it provides information but is not itself seen, it is certainly of interest to know if the perceptual system can adjust itself to a change, say, in the orientation of retinal images. Stratton (1896, 1897*a*, 1897*b*) was the first to consider this problem: he wore an inverting optical system for a period of eight days; and found that although at first the world appeared upside down, after several days he could behave almost normally and things would appear right side up. More recently Erismann and Kohler, at Innsbruck (Kohler, 1962; Werner and Wapner 1955) have made a detailed study of perceptual adaptation to optical modifications of the retinal image. They found that after a few days of wearing inverting prisms continuously, the world begins to switch from inverted to normal orientation. The change generally starts either when an object is touched or when something is seen which looks impossible in its inverted position, like a candle flame. Some of the phenomena occurring at this stage are difficult to describe, for they may be logically paradoxical: if two faces are presented together, one the right way up and the other inverted, they may be reported as both appearing the normal way up

FIG. 2.2 *A 'figure-ground' ambiguous figure (after Rubin 1915). The black silhouette may be seen, as 'figure', against a white ground, or the white profile against the black ground. With prolonged observation the two aspects alternate: the retinal image remains constant but the perception changes.*

and yet one as inverted with respect to the other! Finally the world appears much as normal, and the subject can ride a bicycle and lead a normal life.

It is now technically possible, using glass fibre optics, to produce transformations more complicated than up-down and right-left reversals. Present experiments are difficult to evaluate, because we do have experience of the retinal image tilting with head movements, and right-left reversals with mirrors. Held and Hein (1958) have shown that adaptation to the simple transformations requires simultaneous active touch. Recent experiments have investigated disturbance of time rather than space. Smith and Smith (1962) have employed a television camera and monitor, with a video tape loop to give a delay, so that movements of the hand are seen after a fixed time interval. They find that disturbance of the normal time relations between touch and vision upsets tasks such as writing and drawing, which remain extremely difficult, little or no adaptation being possible for time shifts.

PERCEPTUAL CONSTANCY AND DISTORTIONS OF VISUAL SPACE

The perceptual system transforms retinal images in systematic ways according to the perceived distance and orientation of objects. In general these transformations tend to maintain perceived size and shape more or less constant, in spite of changes in the size and shape of images with changes in viewing position. The end result is known as 'visual constancy'. It has also been called by Thouless (1931, 1932*a*, 1932*b*) 'phenomenal regression to the real object', but this phrase is now little used, though his experiments are classical. Thouless measured size constancy by comparing a cardboard shape of, say, a circular disk, placed at a given distance, with a series of disks of different sizes at some other distance. By selecting a nearer disk appearing the same size as the more distant one, and establishing by simple geometry the difference in the retinal projections of the two disks, an estimate of constancy is obtained. It can be expressed as a ratio, with perfect constancy giving a ratio of one, and no constancy giving zero. Constancy may also be measured during movement (Anstis, Shopland and Gregory 1961 [No. 23]). The amount of constancy is a function of the amount of information indicating distance and orientation, and also of personality variables, and training in perspective drawing. As would be expected, size constancy correlates with accuracy of judgements of apparent distance, that is, of distances which seem to an observer to intervene between him and an object; but the correlations are not always very high (Rump, 1961). This finding allows the possibility that the 'scaling', of which perceptual constancy is the result, may depend on neural systems which are different from those that mediate judgements of apparent distance. This possibility is important, as we may now see.

Some simple patterns upset the perceptual system and give distortions of visual space, so that lines may look too long, too short or bent. Examples are given in Fig. 2.3. Now, if the illusion figures are examined, it will be seen that they are all typical flat projections of objects lying in three dimensions. (For example, the Müller-Lyer figure with the out-going fins is the same as the retinal image of the corner of a room: with the in-going fins, the outside corner of, say, a building or a box). Further, in every case the features which correspond to features of more distant objects are expanded in the flat illusion figures (Tausch, 1954). It seems likely that the observer's scale of size (and shape) constancy can be determined by general features which indicate distance. When these features are inappropriate – as when perspective features occur in a flat display or drawing – we should expect the scale to become inappropriate, to produce systematic distortions in size and shape (Gregory, 1963*b* [No. 28]).

Figures which spontaneously fluctuate, generally in depth, show something of how the central perceptual system can give very different

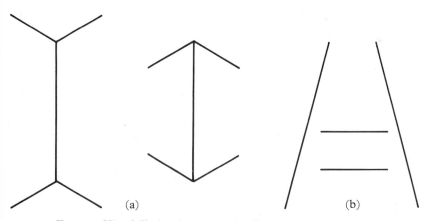

(a)   (b)

FIG. 2.3 *Visual illusion figures showing distortions of visual space.*
(a) *The Müller-Lyer figure, in which the diverging arrows lengthen the vertical line, while the converging arrows shorten it.*
(b) *The Ponzo illusion: the upper horizontal line appears longer than the lower. This may be because the converging lines, being typical perspective lines, give depth information and set the scaling for size accordingly; the effect would be to enlarge the upper horizontal line which would normally be farther away and so give a smaller retinal image. But here the figure is flat and the result is distortion.*

perceptions from the same image. The best-known example is the 'Necker cube' (Fig. 2.4) which spontaneously alternates in depth, and this can occur even when the image is optically stabilized on the retina (Pritchard, 1958). The faces of the Necker cube shown drawn on a paper background do not appreciably change size upon reversal; evidently distortion of the scale for constancy does not occur even though in a sense the faces appear in depth. But the figure can be viewed as a transparency, illuminated from the back; or as a luminous,

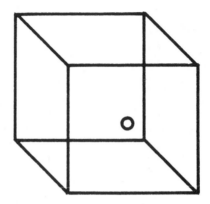

FIG. 2.4 *Necker Cube. This figure shows reversal in depth (the point 'o' may be seen as either the near or the far corner of the cube), and yet it seems to lie on the plane of the paper and so is paradoxical.*

two-dimensional, flat wire model in a dark room (Fig. 2.5*a*). If the figure is given *no background* in one of these ways, one may see one's own scaling system at work, for the apparently nearer face now looks smaller than the apparently farther face, whichever this may be. If a luminous three-dimensional skeleton cube (Fig. 2.5*b*) is viewed in darkness with one eye, it will also reverse in depth, and when reversed it looks like a truncated pyramid, with the apparently nearer face the smaller (Fig. 2.5*c*). This demonstration shows that size constancy can be mediated on the basis of apparent depth. It seems therefore that the scaling of constancy can be determined either: (i) by features which are typical indicators of depth – particularly perspective – or (ii) directly by apparent distance. An error in either scaling system produces distortion of visual space. By studying these distortions, we may learn something of the principles underlying the scaling which gives constancy of size and shape, as well as the origins of the illusions (Gregory, 1963*b* [No. 28]).

Ames and his colleagues (Ittelson, 1952) have devised a number of

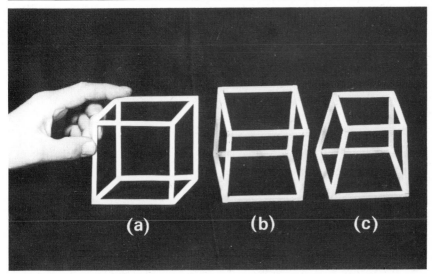

FIG. 2.5 *Photographs of wire models of skeleton shapes in two and three dimensions. These models are viewed glowing in the dark.*

(a) *This model is flat, like the cube in Fig. 2.4, but it appears as though in true depth, and the apparently farther face looks larger than the apparently nearer face. Thus constancy scaling is evidently evoked.*

(b) *A true cube model: this looks like a cube when seen correctly, but when reversed it looks like a truncated pyramid, the farther face being larger than the nearer. This distortion is not simply due to constancy being inoperative, but to constancy working backwards, as shown by model (c).*

(c) *This is a true truncated pyramid. It may be viewed from the small end so that the retinal images are equalized; then the apparently more distant face always appears the larger.*

significant demonstrations. The best known is the 'distorted room'. This demonstration depends on the fact of projective geometry that the correspondence between a given plane projection, in two dimensions, and a configuration in three dimensions is indeterminate; there is an infinite set of three-dimensional configurations which can give a particular plane projection. A monocular retinal image is effectively a single plane projection. The Ames room is non-rectangular but is so shaped that at a particular viewing point the monocular retinal image is the same as that given by a rectangular room. Clearly it must look like a normal room, for there is nothing to distinguish the two; but if objects are now placed in the Ames room, their distances and sizes are distorted, while the room itself still looks rectangular. This shows that the usual squareness of rooms is an important reference for perceiving the distance and size of objects (Segall, Campbell and Herskovits 1963) (see Fig. 2.6).

FIG. 2.6 *Three people of about the same height seem to be of radically different sizes in a large Ames room. The person on the left is actually nearly twice as far from the camera as the one on the right, but the unusual perspective of the room conceals this fact.*

PERCEPTION OF MOVEMENT

The study of perception has been mainly concerned with static situations, although movement perception is biologically primary. Its study does present considerable technical difficulties which are only beginning to be tackled seriously.

Data on thresholds for movement detection are sparse, but some data are given by J. F. Brown (1931) and R. H. Brown (1961), and for difference thresholds by Leibowitz (1955). The periphery of the retina provides nothing but movement information (and so is biologically primitive), while the extreme periphery mediates only an unconscious fixation reflex, (which can be lost to motor-cyclists wearing goggles).

Several experimental techniques have been developed for stabilizing images on the retina. Ditchburn and Ginsborg (1952) and Ratliff and Riggs (1950) used a contact lens with an attached mirror so that the image moves precisely with the eye. It is also possible to fix the object itself to the eye (Pritchard, 1961). Very accurate measurement of small eye movements can be made from the attached mirror, and this has been used by Cornsweet (1956) to investigate what initiates the eye movements, which are evidently of great importance in perception though it is no longer thought that they serve to increase spatial acuity (Ratliff and Riggs 1950).

If forms such as squares, letters or faces are observed with the image stabilized, meaningful parts disappear and reappear spontaneously as units (Fig. 2.7), and this has been attributed to central factors (Pritchard, Heron and Hebb 1960); but it might be because it is difficult for subjects to report random loss of images, and because of the general tendency to fill in gaps in familiar redundant patterns.

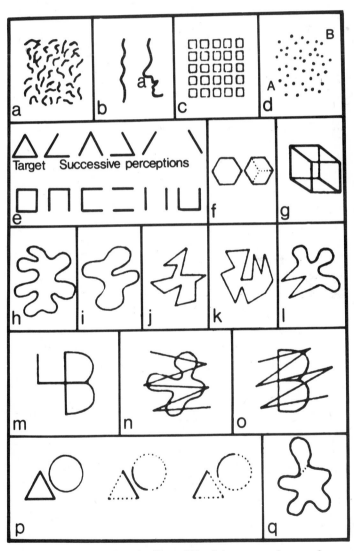

FIG. 2.7 *Forms studied with retinally stabilized images. e, f, p, q show successive perceptions with stabilized retinal image.*

Possibility of slippage of the contact lens should not be overlooked (Barlow, 1963).

An interesting question is: why, when the eyes are moved, does the visual world remain stable? We shall describe some observations which indicate the answer to this question, as an example of the way quite simple observations in perception can sometimes illuminate neurological problems:

(i) The visual world is stable during voluntary eye movements.

(ii) With passive movements of the eyes (produced for example by pressure with the finger), the world is not stable, but swings round in a direction opposite to the eye movements.

(iii) An after-image viewed in darkness (giving a retinally stabilized image) is seen to move with the eye during voluntary eye movements.

(iv) An after-image viewed in darkness does not move with passive eye movements.

(v) If, because of some neurological abnormality, the eyes do not move following command, then the entire visual world swings round in the direction the eyes should have moved. This also results from anaesthetizing the eye muscles (Kornmüller, 1931).

(vi) When a moving object is followed with the eyes, the fixed background swings round against the direction of movement.

(vii) When the illumination is provided by a stroboscope set to a low flash rate (say 10 flashes/sec.), the visual world may swing round with the eyes (Gregory, 1958a [No. 14]).

These observations are not compatible with Sherrington's view (Sherrington, 1906) that stability is given by proprioceptive feedback from the extrinsic eye muscles (although stretch receptors have been found), for not only should proprioception give some stability during passive eye movements but, more crucial, the stretch receptor activity should produce shift of after-images viewed in darkness during passive eye movements; and this is not the case. The observations favour a suggestion essentially due to Helmholtz (1856–66) that stability is normally given by monitoring of the eye movement command signals, these being used to cancel movement signals from the retina. After-images would be shifted by the monitored signals, for these will go uncancelled. A theory has been proposed by MacKay (1958, 1961) who suggests that movement is only seen when there is sufficient information available to overcome a small hypothesis of stability.

There is evidence that movement is directly coded in the peripheral nervous system, rather than computed, as a function of change of position with time. Velocity seems to be signalled without use of a clock (as in the speedometer of a car). It seems that this velocity system is disrupted by stroboscopic light. This is illustrated by a curious illusion pointed out by MacKay: when an object, part of which is self-luminous (e.g. a lighted cigarette) is illuminated with a stroboscope and moved about, the lighted portion apparently floats free of the object, returning to its rightful position when the movement ceases. This may be owing to the two movement systems giving different 'answers' under the special conditions. The observation (Gregory, 1958a [No. 14]) that a stroboscopically illuminated background can behave like an after-image, moving with the eye, suggests that it is signals of velocity rather than of position which normally give stability.

Further evidence for two movement systems is provided by the paradoxical appearance of the after-effect of seen movement which follows looking at moving water, (it is often called the 'waterfall effect'), or fixating a rotating wheel or spiral. This after-effect is an illusory appearance of movement in the opposite direction to the stimulus (Wohlgemuth, 1911). This phenomenon is interesting as an example of a probably partly central adaptation. It also illustrates a perceptual paradox, for in the after-effect the (actually stationary) object seems to move and yet not to change position. This could be owing to adaptation of only one of two systems mediating movement perception – probably the velocity but not the positional system.

A further well-known illusion of movement – the 'autokinetic effect' – is seen when a small dim light is viewed in total darkness: it appears to move about. This is generally attributed to eye movements; but this is not so, as was shown fairly conclusively by Guilford and Dallenbach (1928), and as may be easily checked (Gregory, 1959 [No. 15]) by surrounding the light with a dim blue halo which is not visible in central fixation (Willmer, 1946), but is seen whenever the eyes move so that the blue light ceases to fall on the *fovea centralis*. The result is: the autokinetic effect occurs without the blue halo becoming visible, and so the eyes cannot have moved. A theory has been proposed (Gregory and Zangwill 1963 [No. 16]) based on the idea that the visual stabilizing system described in Gregory, 1958a [No. 14] is labile, as may be demonstrated by differentially fatiguing the extrinsic eye muscles, whereupon a large autokinetic movement occurs in the direction of fatigue, or in the opposite direction, but not in other directions.

The autokinetic movements are probably the direct result of the command signals required to maintain fixation in spite of momentary changes in the efficiency of the musculature. This theory is an example of the current move away from mentalistic explanations. The auto-kinetic effect was discussed by the Gestalt writers (Koffka, 1935) in terms of supposed internal 'reference frames' believed to be unstable under these conditions, and to produce illusory movement by analogy with induced movement (Duncker, 1938). Indeed, the autokinetic effect was regarded by Koffka as strong evidence for mentalistic reference frames, but this kind of argument is now generally abandoned.

SENSORY DISCRIMINATION – CONCEPT OF THRESHOLD AS LIMITED BY 'SIGNAL-TO-NOISE' RATIO

The simple 'stimulus-response' kind of psychological model has largely given way to a picture of dynamic decision-taking on available information. Rather than calling the sensory input a 'stimulus', the terms 'information source' or 'signal' are often preferred; the distinction is not purely verbal, but represents a new way of thinking about sensory processes, in which energy becomes of secondary importance, and information, given a technical definition in terms of probability (Shannon and Weaver 1949), takes pride of place, even though energy considerations cannot be ignored. The sensory system is thought of as subject to the same kind of limitations as any man-made instrument, and we seek the kind of knowledge about them that engineers use in describing communication or telemetering systems. Thus, measures of neural band width and noise level become important, and give a new look to psycho-physics. It was a television engineer (Rose, 1942) who first suggested that the intensity discrimination of the eye might be limited by noise, as a television camera or any other detector is limited by random, ultimately thermal, activity. This suggestion went unnoticed, and several workers put forward the same suggestion some years later, though developing it in somewhat different ways.

The best-known treatment is due to Tanner and Swets (1954). Barlow, Fitzhugh and Kuffler (1957) obtained direct recording of residual noise in the cat's optic nerve, and Barlow (1957a) applied psychological methods to the problem of estimating the noise level. Cane and I have tried to develop a statistical model for distinguishing one distribution of neural activity from another (Gregory and Cane 1955 [No. 7]; Gregory, 1956) and to relate noise level to loss of sensory discrimination in human ageing (Gregory, 1957b). We should expect impairment in sensory discrimination if the afferent system should become noisy as a result of ageing or trauma. A dramatic example may be nerve deafness; I have suggested that noise level may explain presbyacusia, tinnitus, recruitment and other characteristics of nerve deafness, because it appears to be due to random neural activity, (associated with damage to the hair cells), rather than to simple attenuation of auditory signals, as in conduction deafness. Evidence for this view has been obtained by subjecting the normal ear to external 'white noise' and comparing it with the nerve-deaf ear; they then appear to have very similar characteristics (Gregory and Wallace 1958 [No. 9]). This suggests that hearing aids for this type of deafness should be designed to minimize the masking effect of internal neural noise rather than to increase the signal level by amplification only.

Energy is significant for vision in a number of fundamental ways. The quantum fluctuation of light itself affects sensitivity. It has been shown, by most elegant experiments, that the fully dark-adapted eye is sensitive to about 200 quanta at the cornea, corresponding to only 5–8 quanta absorbed by the rods (Hecht, Shlaer and Pirenne 1942). It also turns out that a single rod is sensitive to one quantum (the theoretical minimum energy), and the need for several neighbouring rods to be stimulated points to the neural analogue of a 'coincidence gate' as one mechanism tending to facilitate discrimination between signals and noise in the visual system.

The general picture of sensory discrimination is of a continuous background of random neural activity tending to mask all neural signals. Neural activity is accepted as representing a signal only when it is large enough, or characteristic enough, to be reliably distinguished from background neural noise. The central nervous system is thus continuously discriminating between activity which may be merely spontaneous noise or which may be a genuine signal.

We end with the fundamental problem: how does the perceptual system discriminate between objects? Experimental work on this problem is mainly on animals and is only briefly treated here. It takes three main forms: (i) discovering pairs of patterns which animals find difficulty in distinguishing, and using these data to suggest or to test models which might be applicable (Sutherland, 1961); (ii) ablation of parts of the brain, following special training of the animal, mainly octopus (J. Z. Young, 1961); (iii) recording from the occipital cortex in the cat, while presenting the unanaesthetized or lightly anaesthetized animal with various simple displays, such as bars of light which may be stationary or moving (Hubel and Wiesel 1962). Related work on the frog's retina is described by Lettvin, Maturana, McCulloch and Pitts (1959). This important work shows that orientation of lines, velocity and direction of movement, and the angles of corners, are separately coded and represented in the brain, as shown by individual cells responding only to specific stimuli, such as movement in a given direction or lines at a certain angle. Since any object can be described by the presence or absence of certain 'defining' characteristics – angles, corners and so on – it seems that at last we have clear and direct evidence of neural systems capable of discriminating between and recognizing features of objects, and so providing the basis for perception of the world.

3 Recovery from early blindness: a case study

[We come now to a human drama: the story of a man who lived a philosopher's dream. When a few months old he became effectively blind, and had to wear bandages round his eyes until the age of eight. He lived an unusually active life for a blind person, continually trying to make and do things almost, sometimes quite, beyond what was possible. Through the years he tried to persuade doctors and eye surgeons to graft fresh corneas but the operation was regarded as so unlikely to be useful in his case that it did not justify the use of precious corneas, which until the introduction of corneal banks were in short supply and so only used on cases likely to be successful. Then, when he was over fifty years of age, he did receive corneal grafts and the operations were successful. At last he could see. Or could he? Could he open his eyes upon our world, and see as we see?

My colleague Jean Wallace, who investigated the development of S.B.'s perception with me, was my first research assistant. She brought useful experience from her previous work on human ageing, as she had been a member of the Nuffield Research Unit on Ageing, directed by Alan Welford. Her experience in dealing with older and handicapped people was invaluable. We worked together throughout, discussing each detail. Our most grateful thanks are due to the surgeon, Mr A. Hirtenstein, F.R.C.S. He gave us every facility and every encouragement. The staff, and especially the matron, of the Royal Birmingham Eye Hospital were also most helpful.

We described the case in a monograph supplement of the *Quarterly Journal of Psychology*: R. L. Gregory and Jean G. Wallace, *Recovery from Early Blindness: A Case Study*, 1963. The study was made during 1959, while we were at the Cambridge Department of Psychology. It is given here in full.

The principal theoretical interest of the case is that it gives strong evidence of cross-modal transfer, from touch to vision. It appeared that visually given information could select 'models' or 'hypotheses' from his previous touch world. The ability to relate information across the senses is vital if objects are to attain symbolic meaning.

65

Language may depend on it. Evidence that other higher animals do not show cross-modal transfer is provided by Ettlinger (1960), and Burton and Ettlinger (1960).

The series of drawings made by S.B. while still in the hospital are part of the evidence for his inability to see objects, or parts of objects unknown to him through his previous touch experience. The sequence of drawings of buses also show that he would sometimes add typical touch features from his early experience though these features were no longer present or appropriate. This occurs in the spokes he drew on the wheels of his first bus drawing – although modern buses do not have spoked wheels. Figure 3.1 shows a typical bus of the period when he as a boy would have first explored and discovered wheels – when all bus wheels had spokes.

The finding that visual distortion illusion figures gave little or no distortion is paralleled by the similar lack of distortions reported in people living in 'non-carpentered' worlds, where perspective convergence at the retina is a less reliable index of distance than in our world of many parallel features. This is summarized and discussed best by Segall, Campbell and Herskovits (1963 and 1966).

The most dramatic example of touch/vision transfer is the claim

FIG. 3.1 *Spoke-wheeled bus*

of Paul Bach-y-Rita and his colleagues that touch 'images', applied to a large area of skin, can be accepted by the brain as representing external objects (1967). The technique employs a television camera: its optical image is made to provide a corresponding touch 'image', with a mosaic of electrically actuated probes placed on the tactile viewer's back. It is claimed that after some five hours of practice – and provided the TV camera is actively moved around by the subject – he begins to recognize objects, from their touch patterns. The sensation of the probes on the skin is lost as the patterns come to represent external objects. This 'tactile vision' is available to congenitally blind people – though it will be a long time before this becomes a practical blind aid, if ever. The processes of coming to 'see' tactually are reported as similar to the stages by which S.B. came to develop his visual perception of the world, when light entered his eyes to give images after a lifetime of blindness.

The study of the case of S.B. had a deep effect upon how I came to think about perception. It made me think about the origin of illusions for the first time and directed my attention to their connection with perceptual learning and their significance in epistemology, which I am still engaged in working out. More generally, it forced me to think about the relation between objects, images, pictures and perceptions; something of which is discussed in *The Intelligent Eye*. I was remarkably fortunate to have the opportunity to make this study, which is the first of its kind since 1904.

Recently (1971) some new cases of adult recovery from early blindness have been reported, from Italy, by Dr Alberto Valvo of the S. Giovanni Hospital, Rome. Valvo studied and reports the development of vision following cases of long-term blindness due to such severe corneal conditions that previous grafting techniques could not be used. The new technique – due to Professor Benedetto Strampelli – is truly remarkable. Strampelli grafts an artificial, acrylic, lens into the cornea – preventing rejection by isolating the lens with a specially prepared tooth. The point is that teeth accept foreign substances (as in dental stoppings), and dentine is not rejected by the corneal tissues. So Strampelli places the acrylic lens in a hole bored in a tooth, and transplants the tooth into the eye. The result is a good quality retinal image, having a small angle of view and no accommodation but with a large depth of field as the optical aperture is small. The improvement in optical quality is immediate (unlike removal of the lens for cataract and to a lesser extent the usual corneal graft procedure). The new technique, termed osteo-odonto-keroprosthesis, makes it possible for some previously hopeless cases to receive sight, and may provide still further cases for study. The first cases, studied and described by Valvo, confirm several of our findings with the case of S.B. In particular, Valvo has confirmed that upper-case letters, previously learned by touch, can be read immediately visually; while lower-case letters, not previously known by touch, require extensive visual learning before they can be read by eye when sight is restored. This evidence of immediate transfer from touch to vision in man is of unusual interest. There seems to be no evidence for touch-vision transfer in sub-human species, and as suggested by the American neurologist Norman Geschwind (1964), it may be a crucial factor in man's unique ability to use symbols and develop language.]

★   ★   ★

THIS is the case history of a man born in 1906 who lost effective sight in both eyes at about ten months of age, and after fifty years as a blind person received corneal grafts to restore his sight. Such cases are rare, and few have been investigated in any detail, or have available pre-operative records giving their early history. Since cases of recovery from congenital or early blindness have been discussed by philosophers for over three hundred years, and have more recently attracted the interest of experimental psychologists, we feel justified in presenting in full everything which might be regarded as relevant to the case.

René Descartes (1596–1650) in a famous passage in his *Dioptrics* (1637), considers how a blind man might build up a perceptual world by tapping objects round him with a stick. He first considers a sighted person using a stick in darkness, and says '. . . without long practice this kind of sensation is rather confused and dim; but if you take men born blind, who have made use of such sensations all their life, you will find they feel things with such perfect exactness that one might almost say that they see with their hands. . . .' Descartes goes on to argue that normal vision resembles a blind man exploring and building up his sense world by successive probes with his stick.

John Locke (1632–1704) once received a letter from Molyneux in which was posed the now celebrated question: 'Suppose a man born blind, and now adult, and taught by his touch to distinguish between a cube and a sphere of the same metal. Suppose then the cube and sphere were placed on a table, and the blind man made to see: query, whether by his sight, before he touched them, could he distinguish and tell which was the globe and which the cube? . . . . The acute and judicious proposer answers: not. For though he has obtained the experience of how the globe, how the cube, affects his touch, yet he has not yet attained the experience that what affects his touch so or so, must affect his sight, so or so. . . .' In the *Essay Concerning Human Understanding*, 1690, (Book II, Chapt. 9, Sect. 8) Locke comments as follows:—'I agree with this thinking gentleman, whom I am proud to call my friend, in his answer to this his problem; and am of the opinion that the blind man, at first, would not be able with certainty to say which was the globe, which the cube. . . .'

Bishop George Berkeley, (1685–1753) in his *A New Theory of Vision* (1709) distinguished carefully between sight and touch as ways of perceiving and knowing, and took the hypothetical case of recovery from blindness in the following way: 'In order to disentangle our minds from whatever prejudices we may entertain with the relation to the subject in hand nothing is more apposite than the taking into our thoughts the case of one born blind, and afterwards, when grown up, made to see. And though perhaps it may not be an easy task to divest ourselves entirely of the experience received from sight so as to be able to put our thoughts exactly in the posture as such a one's: we must nevertheless, as far as possible, endeavour to frame true conceptions of what might reasonably be supposed to pass in his mind' (op. cit. Sect. XCII). Berkeley goes on to say that we should expect such a man not to know whether anything was 'high or low, erect or inverted . . . for the objects to which he had hitherto used to apply the terms up and down, high and low, were such only as affected or were some way perceived by his touch; but the proper objects of vision make a new set of ideas, perfectly distinct and different from the former, and which can in no sort make themselves perceived by touch' (op. cit. XCV). He goes on to say that it would take some time to learn to associate the two.

In 1728 Cheselden presented the celebrated case of a boy of thirteen who gained his sight after removal of the lenses rendered opaque by cataract from birth, but this was not by any means the first successful operation of its kind: the earliest reported dates from A.D. 1020, of a man of thirty operated upon in Arabia. Other cases were reported in 1668, 1695, 1704 and 1709.[1] After the Cheselden case of 1728, we find some fifty cases up to the present day, one of the most recent being that of Latta, 1904.

The evidence provided by the famous Cheselden case was discussed by Julien Offray de la Mettrie (1709–1851) in his *Natural History of the Soul* (1746)[2]. De la Mettrie argues that only education received through the senses makes man man, and gives him what we

---

[1] For a summary review of these cases, see von Senden, 1960, pp. 326–35.

[2] A description of de la Mettrie's comparatively little known but remarkable work is to be found in *The History of Materialism* by F. A. Lange, Eng. tr. London, 1925.

call the soul, while no development of the mind outwards ever takes place.

The published cases have been collected and described by Herr M. von Senden in his book: *Raum- und Gestaltauffassung bei operierten Blindgeborenen* (1932), which was virtually unobtainable in this country before the recent and most welcome translation, arranged by Miss Sylvia Schweppe and undertaken by Mr. Peter Heath, entitled *Space and Sight* (1960).

The importance of these cases has been stressed by many classical writers, including Hume and Helmholtz, and most recently by the psychologist D. O. Hebb, in his influential book *The Organization of Behaviour* (1949). Hebb cites the von Senden collection of cases, and makes a great deal of use of them in developing a theory of the development of perception. We shall later consider Hebb's arguments and conclusions.

Operable cases of blindness – strictly *near-blindness* for the retina must be functional and eye tissues are never entirely opaque – are of two kinds: cataract of the lenses and opacity of the corneas. The former was treated from early times by slitting the eye ball and removing the lens; treatment of corneal opacity is recent and involves highly skilled grafting of a donated cornea. All the earlier cases are therefore cases of cataract, while some of the more recent – including the one to be described here – were rendered blind, or nearly blind, by opacity of the corneas.

With improvement in operative technique, and also a more ready supply of corneas, it has become extremely rare to find a case of very early blindness which remains untreated after the first few years of life. The case to be described – that of S.B. – is exceptional because he was regarded for many years as inoperable, until finally an attempt, and a successful attempt, was made when he was fifty-two years of age. We can hardly expect such a case to recur in the near future, and so it is unfortunate that no experimental psychologist was informed of the case until after the corneal grafting took place. If another such case should occur, we hope that it may be possible for an investigation to be initiated some time before the operation is undertaken. A later investigator may be able to learn something from our evident mistakes.

It is unfortunate that very few of the published accounts of recovery from early blindness describe any detailed observations or tests made on the patients. It is also far from clear how much residual vision they had prior to the operation. At the time we undertook the enquiry, we had but the most sketchy knowledge of the literature. We knew of von Senden's work from summaries and accounts, but had not seen the original, which was not then readily available in this country. We did, however, set out to try some reasonably objective tests, though these we had to prepare with only a few days' notice as we were anxious to see the patient as soon as possible.

THE CASE OF S.B.

(1) *First considerations*

S.B. was born in 1906, of poor parents, and was one of a family of seven, there being three brothers and three sisters. He spent his youth as a resident pupil of the Birmingham Blind School, being admitted in 1915 and leaving in 1923, with a training in boot repairing sufficient for his livelihood, and a fair general education.

It is important to note that S.B. received far more education prior to operation than did the previously published cases, with the possible exception of one described by Latta (1904). There is reason to believe that this may be important in evaluating the case. At the time of the corneal grafting – most of the previous cases were for removal of the lens – he was aged 52. We saw him in hospital shortly after the graft operation on the second eye. It is unfortunate that we did not see him earlier, but we did not hear of the case until it was reported in a daily newspaper after the first operation. We were, however, able to get first-hand reports from the hospital staff, who were generous with their time and help, and the surgeon, Mr A. Hirtenstein, F.R.C.S., gave us a first-hand report of his observations.

It was from the first clearly of the utmost importance to establish the amount of vision present before the operation, and back to as early an age as possible. The label 'congenital cataract' should not be taken to mean that there has been virtually no visual experience preceding operation, or that vision was as limited in the first months or years of life as it was later, when perhaps fuller tests were carried out. A cataract may well increase in opacity during the first months or years, and whether this has happened can hardly be established. There is in fact remarkably little evidence about the extent of early vision in the previously published cases, but it is noteworthy that many of the patients cited by von Senden clearly had appreciable visual capacity immediately prior to operation, and yet still made slow progress in the use of vision after operation.

S.B. was admitted to the blind school not technically as 'blind' but as 'partially sighted'. The word 'blind' signifies to the ophthalmologist 'insensitive to light', though its lay use is rather an absence of *useful* vision. Cases of strict blindness are inoperable, the retina being non-functional, and so we should expect any case such as this to be technically 'partially sighted'. The question – a difficult one – is whether S.B. had *useful* vision, or more vision than the earlier cases described by von Senden.

It is most important to be clear that where blindness is literally complete surgery is always out of the question. The retina must be functional, and since the tissues and media of the eyes are never opaque, some effective retinal stimulation must always be expected. This point cannot be over-stressed. The word 'blindness' may in normal usage cover cases with sensitivity to light, providing appreciation of form is too poor to be of significant use, but to the ophthalmic surgeon (as became clear to us during discussions) 'blindness' is used to denote *total insensitivity to light*. In this sense there are *no cases of recovery from blindness*. This should be borne in mind when these cases are compared with the findings of experiments in which animals are reared in darkness, for then, and then alone, visual experience has been truly absent.

The most that should be claimed for any of these human cases is that vision has been dramatically improved upon operation, but as anyone can verify by practising 'seeing' with the eyes closed, under some conditions – particularly bright sunlight – quite a lot of visual experience is possible under conditions similar to the worst lens cataract or corneal opacity. The direction of bright lights can be seen, as can the movement across the eyes of shadows. It could well be that this minimal vision, which we must suppose even the 'best' cases to have had, makes them very different from the strictly blind – those whose retinas are dead – and we know nothing of what would happen if *they* could be made to see.

In order to test for retinal function in cases of cataract or corneal opacity, use is made of what are called entoptic phenomena. The entoptic perception of the retinal blood vessels can be readily produced in normal subjects by holding a small light source, such as the naked lamp of an ophthalmoscope, in contact with the closed lid near to one corner of the orbit, and moving it rapidly back and forth with a quite small movement, the eye being dark-adapted. The retinal vessels will be seen as a livid red tree-like pattern, which will fade as soon as the agitation of the light is stopped. They appear because the light entering the side of the eye, through the choroid coat, reaches the light sensitive cells (the rods and cones) *after* travelling through the layers of vessels and nerve fibres, which lie to the *front* of the retina. Under normal conditions they are not seen because they form an image – a shadow image – upon the sensory cells which moves precisely with them as the eyes move, and selective adaptation cancels out the non-uniformities of intensity. Similarly, an optically stabilised image fades out and becomes invisible within a few seconds. The shadow images do shift across the retina with movement of the light source, however, and this stimulates fresh receptors, and so the image is made visible so long as the light source is kept moving. This technique is used in testing the retinas in order to establish whether an operation is worth attempting. An operation is not attempted unless the patient is able to give satisfactory reports on his entoptically observed retinal vessels.

A study of these entoptic phenomena in cases of congenital 'blindness' could prove rewarding, for the study should reveal perception of form where there has been the least possible previous visual experience. Should it be technically possible, it might be of interest to stimulate the central visual system of a totally blind person. We know from the work of Penfield that visual experience can be elicited by electrical stimulation of the occipital cortex, in the course of certain brain operations. Would it be possible to stimulate the visual mechanisms of the totally blind? The effect of hallucinogenic drugs might also be of interest in this connection, for they may stimulate directly the central components of the visual system, and in the case of the totally blind this might perhaps be accomplished for the first time in an individual's life. [The visual cortex of a blind subject has now been stimulated electrically (Brindley and Lewin 1968).]

(2) *Amount of pre-operative vision*

It will be appreciated that on admission to the blind school, S.B. would have seemed no exceptional case, since his vision at that time was evidently insufficient to be of use to him. As we shall see, we find no reference to useful vision anywhere in the school reports.

Since the matter of degree of sight is now so important to us, we shall give all the evidence at length, and try to assess it. It falls into four classes.

(A) The testimony of S.B. with particular regard to his visual memories.

(B) The testimony of S.B.'s older and surviving sister.

(C) The medical and school reports of the blind school he attended.

(D) The expert opinion of the surgeon, based on the observed state of the eyes at the time of operation.

The available evidence will be given under these headings, and an attempt will then be made to assess it.

A. *The testimony of S.B.* We questioned him on his early visual experience on several occasions, but particularly at our first interview, (on 26th January, 1959) while he was still a patient in hospital. We asked him to describe just how much vision he had before the first operation. He told us, *first*, that he believed he became blind at the age of ten months – the age given in the records of the blind school – and, *secondly*, that the only visual memories he had before the operation were of three colours – red, white and black. He claimed, then, and later, that he remembered no other visual phenomena.

We ascertained that he was able to name these three colours immediately after the operation, but that he tended to be confused over other colours. It is possible that he would have had experience of these three colours as an adult suffering from undoubtedly extremely severe corneal opacity, for some awareness of light and dark would be expected and very brilliant red is, as described above, seen entoptically during the standard ophthalmological examinations. No doubt the ophthalmologists would tend to use the word 'red' in trying to communicate under these conditions. This does not, of course diminish the probability that he also experienced these colours as a small child, as he thinks he did, but this might be overlaid by later experience.

How far can we trust S.B.'s testimony? It may be appropriate to say here a word or two on his character as it appeared to his teachers, and much later, to us.

The school character reports indicate that S.B. was bright and intelligent, if sometimes lazy. There are criticisms of his sense of the truth; thus for *Midsummer 1920*: 'Unreliable and unstable in character. Sometimes works v. hard (mainly to please!) and then has slack periods. Plausible manner and a clever excuser . . . has no fixed purpose, and seems bent on doing things with a minimum amount of work attached'. By *Xmas 1920:* 'Has improved in conduct and school work. Character more stable'. *July 1921:* '. . . Appears to be trying to overcome instability but has a crooked streak which "wangles" out of things'. And finally: *Xmas 1921:* '. . . Has worked hard for he is anxious to get into the shops. Strong, sturdy, and pleasant. Plausible and not thoroughly trustworthy'.

We do not know what correlation there may be between school reports of 'untrustworthiness' and the ability to tell the truth over important matters in later life. Any estimate we may make for normal children and adults might well be misplaced for the specially handicapped.

So far as we could judge, when talking with S.B. or when giving him the various perceptual tests to be described, he was trustworthy.

He made his perceptual judgments with unusual care, and was perfectly co-operative in every way. Our tests were performed in the hospital which had just given him sight: he appeared to identify us to some extent with that hospital and the people who had helped him. He seemed to us to be remarkably stable and balanced in his opinions, in his attitude to his experience, and in the interest that was being taken in him. On no occasion did we find that he had told us an untruth (except by omission on one personal matter of no importance to our enquiry) and his remarks or reports seemed not to be biased towards or against what he might have thought we desired from him. Such judgements are bound to be subjective but we state them for what they may be worth. We believe him to be entirely honest in stating that he had no visual memory of form.

B. *The testimony of S.B.'s elder sister.* We did not for some months know that any friend or relation who might be able to provide evidence on S.B.'s vision as a small child was still living. Finally, S.B. informed us that he had an elder sister, but that as she wished to avoid the publicity the case was attracting in the Press, he had not told us about her. (It might be added that he probably did not realise the importance we attached to finding such witnesses, and it became quite clear that the sister did in fact wish to avoid publicity for a personal reason). It must suffice that S.B.'s sister is some four years older than S.B., that she is married and has a considerably higher standard of living than he had, and that she seemed to us a sensible, forthright and honest person. We could see no motive for any deception or exaggeration especially as she was anxious to remain anonymous. We spent an evening at her home, during which she gave us the following details:—

She remembered him clearly as a small child. She used to take him weekly to the clinic, to have his eyes washed. She emphasized that his eyes were in a shocking state, and that there was a severe running discharge. She remembers his head covered by a large bandage, under which the discharge used to seep. Apparently he wore a bandage more or less continuously as a small child.

The family used in effect to test S.B.'s vision, when the bandages were removed, as a game. Her recollection is that as a small child he could 'point roughly to large white objects'. She thinks that his vision was limited to appreciation of fairly bright large surfaces, apparently without any appreciation of colour. She is confident that his vision was too rudimentary to be useful when the bandages were removed, and he was blind-folded throughout his young childhood, so that what vision he had was generally not available. There seems no doubt, from her statements, but that he led the life of a blind child.

This story of the bandages is born out by the report of the Matron of the Blind School for Xmas 1915, which reads:—

'Admitted this year – eyes in shocking state of discharge. With care and treatment they soon begin to appear quite normal. The condition of his eyes gets much worse during the holiday, and on his return make one feel sick to look at him. . . .'

And also her report for July 1916: '. . . Eyes always look exceedingly bad after a holiday'. This is strong language for a Matron of an institution devoted to diseases of the eyes; discharge from the keratitis must have been unusually severe. It is worth adding that the testimony of S.B.'s sister is independent of the medical report, since she had not access to it.

On the cause of S.B.'s blindness, she thought that he went blind at the age of ten months as the result of an infection following vaccination. This was also the belief given in the two medical reports (almost certainly not independent) at admission, but the cause is not known with certainty. According to the Medical Officer's report for 1st June 1915, the mother had poor sight, and this was confirmed by S.B.'s sister. It is possible that there was some hereditary factor, but we have no further evidence on the matter.

C. *The medical and school reports of the Birmingham Royal School for the Blind.* We are very fortunate in having full medical and school records, in the original handwriting, for the period 1915–1923, when S.B. was at the Birmingham Blind School as a full time student.

We now quote from the Progress Book of the Birmingham Royal Institution for the Blind, by kind permission of the Superintendent.

Date of Birth: 30.5.06.
Date of Admission: 2.6.15.
Condition of Blindness
  (partial or total)　.　.　.　Partial
Cause of blindness as certified
  by the Institution's Oph-
  thalmic Surgeon　.　.　.　Keratitis.
Position in school on
  admission　.　.　.　.　.　Placed in lowest class
Estimate of attainments on
  admission　.　.　.　.　.　Has never attended school before; knows practically nothing.
Mental condition.　.　.　.　Appears to be a bright intelligent lad.

Physical condition . . . Normal but for sight.

Medical Officer's Reports

Admitted 1st June, 1915.

Family History:	Parents living and healthy; father, good sight. Mother, not good. 3 brothers in Army. 3 sisters healthy.
Personal History:	Measles and chickenpox. Eyes bad since 10 months old.
On examination:	Heart and lungs negative. Submaxillary glands enlarged. Skin rough.

Feb. 1918

Complains of pain over front of chest.

Heart – *irregular* (tachycardia). No history of rheumatism. No cardiac murmur.

26th Feb. 1918

Two days ago went out with friends – had more exercise – was followed by an attack of pain in precordia for 36 hours. There is now a definite mitral systolic bruit – increased when lying down. Slight irregularity, but tachycardia better.

8th March 1918

Again complained of pain over heart – now no tachycardia, but heart irregular.

Restrictions :

Feb. 1918.	Gym and drill suspended. Walking outside school boundary suspended.
March 1918.	Piano exercises stopped also.
May 1918.	Allowed walking in moderation, and renewal of piano exercises.

1st July, 1918

Influenza – 8th July, convalescent. 20th July. General health much better.

3rd Sept., 1918

Returned looking well – eyes much clearer and cleaner.

6th Sept., 1918

To have drill included now, and to be carefully watched for symptoms of previous attacks.

Headmistress informed.

Ophthalmic Surgeon's Reports

3rd June, 1915 :	Keratitis.
	Eyes bad since 10 months old. ? after

vaccination. O/E: Diffuse dense nebulae each eye. Some vascularisation and epithelial xerosis.
Conjunctivitis with slight discharging. Dacryocystitis. Some scarring of upper tarsus.
Vision: fingers at one metre.

2nd Sept., 1915: Eczema of face and forehead. Ectropion of lids. Keratitis.

27th Jan., 1916: Left cornea vascularised and fleshy.

18th Sept., 1916: Vision 3/60. Eyes much cleaner and quieter.

22nd Jan., 1917: Rt. and Lt. vascular keratitis.
No regurgitation from lac. sacs.

11th Oct., 1917: Left mucopurulent discharge from lac. sac.

22nd Oct., 1919: Keratitis and xerosis I.S.Q.
Regurgitation from lac. sacs.

14th Oct., 1920: Eyes quieter and cleaner: no regurg. from lac sacs. Vision: 2/60. Illiterate.

13th Feb., 1922: Eyes quiet. Xerosis conj. Vision 2/60?

19th Feb., 1923: Xerosis I.S.Q. Vision: fingers at 9 inches.

From these reports it seems that at that time he had some ('finger') vision when his eyes were free from discharge which, it appears from the sister's testimony and the Matron's report quoted above, was not generally the case at home. We may gain further information from the reports of his school progress, which will also be given in full.

School Reports:

July 1915

Elementary education: has only been in school a few weeks, so no report is possible at this stage.

Conduct: good   *Signed:* S. Robinson.

Xmas 1915

BRAILLE: Reading: Failed to learn anything for some time, but is making some progress now.

Writing: Too careless to obtain any result.

Arithmetic: Working of sums, slow; but very quick at mental arithmetic.

Composition: Fair.

Literature and recitation: Very good progress made.

History, geography, nature, etc.: This boy is very interested in his work and answers well.

Handwork: Works well and has shown great improvement.

Conduct: Very good. *Signed :* J. I. Falconer

July 1916

BRAILLE: Making satisfactory progress in infant reader. *Writes* Grade 1. Has mastered the signs and can now write them perfectly.

Has done excellent work this term, and now sets his *sums* down nicely too, in the Taylor Frame.

Composition: Has done excellent work.

History, geography, nature: Answers splendidly and does good work. He takes a keen interest in these subjects.

Handwork: A good little handworker – a careful boy.

Conduct: This boy has gained the class prize this year. A most polite well-mannered boy, and an excellent worker.

Height: 4 ft. 2¾ ins.

Weight: 4 st. 8¾ lbs. *Signed :* J. I. Falconer.

19th December, 1916

BRAILLE: Reading: Making satisfactory progress – sometimes gets somewhat 'mixed'.

Writing: Writes Grade 2 to the 6th line.

Arithmetic: Tables to 12 times. Pence tables. Long measures reduction.

Composition: Tells a story well.

Recitation: A most marked improvement to this subject. Enunciation and pronunciation specially improved.

History, geography, nature: Answers well – tries very hard.

Handwork: A good worker.

Cane-seating – little progress.

Conduct: This pupil's conduct continues to be excellent.

Height: 4 ft. 3½ ins.

Weight: 4 st. 9½ lbs. *Signed :* J. I. Falconer.

25th July, 1917

BRAILLE: Reading: Prep. Temple Reader 1; could do better, but sometimes careless. Out of class two mornings for music.

Writing: Fairly good.

Arithmetic: Has not mastered Long Division; finds a difficulty in 'setting down'. Two sums right, out of four, in exam.

Composition (Oral): Tells a story well, also retells his lessons well.

Recitation: Excellent.

History, geography and nature: Answers well in all oral lessons. History not so good as other subjects.

Handwork: Cane seating: started double frame. Carpentry: good.

Conduct: This boy still is very little trouble. A good little boy.

Height: 4 ft. 4½ ins.

Weight: 4 st. 10¾ lbs. *Signed:* J. I. Falconer.

Xmas 1917

BRAILLE: Reading: 'Guy of Warwick'. S. has improved much this term.

Writing: A marked improvement shown.

Arithmetic: Seems to have more idea of 'setting down' now. Factors and their uses learnt. Multiple of £.s.d. factors.

Composition (Oral): Still very good.

Recitation: Excellent.

History, geography and nature: Answers intelligently and thoughtfully.

Handwork: Satisfactory progress shown.

Conduct: A good boy in school, but he sometimes has to be checked for talking too much. *Signed:* J. I. Falconer.

July 1918

BRAILLE: Reading: Reads nicely – just a little inclined to guess sometimes.

Writing: Quite good. Grade 11, with a few abbreviations.

Arithmetic: Has done v. good work; all four rules and reduction of money.

Handwork: V. Good. A steady worker. Chair-seating: 6th row patt. Knitting: plain and purl on fine needles: has also made sev. bags and small purses.

Conduct: A useful boy with plenty of 'esprit de corps'. Works well. Has not been v. strong this Term (see med. report). Rather disobedient over small rules, otherwise a good boy. *Signed:* J. I. Falconer and L. H. Best.

Xmas 1918

BRAILLE: Reading: Oxford Reader 4. Has done very satisfactory work.

Writing: Writes Grade 2 with fair amount of accuracy; more contractions used.

Arithmetic: Has done excellent work. Difficult examples with four rules in money, length and weight.

English subjects: Shows much thought and interest in these subjects; has a good fund of information regarding present day affairs. Greatly interested in machinery.

Handwork: Does v. good work in knitting and chair-seating when care is taken; needs to be checked occasionally for hurrying too much.

General: A very helpful and smart boy.

Signed: J. Falconer and L. H. Best.

July 1919

BRAILLE: Reading: Shows slight improvement, but is still far from being good.

Writing: Fair: improving. Composition: plenty of ideas, but cannot express them. Spelling weak.

Arithmetic: Mental, fair; has made some progress with fractions, practice and areas.

English subjects: Interested in these subjects, and satisfactory progress has been made. Literature: inclined to be lazy, and not sufficiently interested.

Handwork: Plasticine, v. good. Cane work, good. Chairseating, v. good.

General: Good. A smart lad in appearance, and v. anxious to help. *Signed:* J. Falconer and G. W. Bloomfield.

Midsummer 1920

BRAILLE: Reading: Not much progress: touch poor.

Writing: Revising all Braille rules, as written work is v. poor.

Composition: Mainly oral. Anxious to give a good impression – usually shallow.

Arithmetic: Good work done. Improved in fractions. Fairly strong in Unitary Method.

Literature: Has shown interest. Recitation, has made more effort; nice voice.

History and Geography: At times v. good. Lack sustained effort. Sometimes unusually thoughtful.

Xmas 1920

Writing: Has revised all contractions in Braille to abbreviated words.

Composition: Memory much improved.

Arithmetic: Very pleasing progress. Fractions, percentages, etc.

Midsummer 1920

General Comments:

Boot-repairing: good work for a beginner.

V. active at all sport – a good footballer.

Unreliable and unstable in character. Sometimes works v. hard, (mainly to please!) and then has slack periods. Plausible manner and a clever excuser.

Nice mannered boy, and affectionate but has no fixed purpose, and seems bent on doing things with a minimum amount of work attached.

Signed: J. Falconer.

Xmas 1920

Medium progress – should do well, if more attention were expended.

Still v. keen over games – v. active and alert.

Has improved in conduct and school work. Character more stable.

Is improved in general behaviour and has made decided effort in class work.

Signed: J. Falconer.

July 1921

BRAILLE: Continues to improve, but slow touch. Not yet fully contracted, but still works steadily. Spelling fair. Mental and practical arithmetic fair. Has shown a fair grip of decimals.

Other subjects. Has developed a keen interest in books, but must read more for himself. Concentration improved, but not much activity in class work.

Boot-repairing and making: Work is developing in quality and speed.

A thorough boy where games and mischief are concerned. Rather too talkative and self-opinionated. Appears to be trying to overcome instability but has a crooked streak which 'wangles' out of things. Helpful, obliging, observant. Upright in physique.

Signed: J. Falconer.

Xmas 1921

BRAILLE: Reading: Good – deliberate. Writing: Improving; spelling fair. Composition: Needs developing. Arithmetic: V. good – quick and accurate.

Other subjects: Pays attention, and is anxious to show that he has understood a lesson. Science: Good.

Boot-repairing and making: V. good progress.

Rather aggressive in manner, but has worked well.

Less noisy but still self-opinionated. Has worked hard for he is anxious to get into the shops. Strong, sturdy, and pleasant. Plausible and not thoroughly trustworthy.

Signed: J. Falconer.

It may be noted that there is no mention of any useful vision. It is only Braille reading which is mentioned, and his aptitude for manual skills does not suggest the help of residual vision. This is confirmed by technical training reports for the final year at the blind school when he was taught boot repairing and making as a trade by which to make a living.

Technical Training: (Full-Time – resident pupil)
July 1923
Boot-repairing and Boot-making:
Started full-time training in January, 1922. Training proceeding satisfactorily, and may be completed by Xmas 1923.
Independence: 4
Quality: $\frac{3}{4}$
Speed: $\frac{1}{2}$
Assessment: 14/– per week (rate of an average sighted worker £2.10.0).
Conduct: Fairly satisfactory. Rather boisterous at times, and over-assertive.

Signed: J. Falconer.

Xmas 1923
Boot-making and repairing
Training now completed. To become a home-worker under our auspices, at Burton-on-Trent. Shed and equipment to be provided.
Quality: $\frac{7}{8}$
Speed:
Independence: $\frac{7}{8}$.
Character: Noisy. Self-opinionated. Active. Showy in appearance – loves finery. Difficult to convince, and will rarely make the 'amende honorable'. Likes to be first, but has not sufficient self-control or balance to be a good leader.

Signed: J. Falconer.

The assessment of 14/– per week against the rate of £2 10s. for an average sighted worker is evidence that his vision was not of an order to be useful even in this comparatively simple trade. This is a point which may be made with some confidence when it is remembered that he was undoubtedly an intelligent boy, and certainly as an adult he has always taken great pride in making things with his hands, as was very clear to us when we visited his workshop and his garden.

D. *Expert opinion on the immediately pre-operative condition of the eyes.* We now quote from a letter written to us by Mr Hirtenstein dated 24 November 1959.

'When I first examined him in November 1957 both corneas were completely opaque with heavy superficial and deep vascularisation; in addition there was bilateral band-shaped keratinisation in the inter-palpebral areas. He had thickened lid margins, with poliosis; the eye movements were full. There was no nystagmus (either before or after the operations.) The iris and pupil could not be visualised on slit-lamp examination nor could the depth of the anterior chamber be estimated. Trans-scleral retinal stimulation produced a normal pattern of retinal vessels in the left eye and this was the main reason I decided to try the operation. The vision in the right eye was reduced to hand movements in front of the eye. The left eye had accurate projection of light only.'

(3) *Assessment of the evidence for early blindness*

It is clear that S.B. as a child was not blind in the strict sense of being entirely insensitive to light, and this we should expect, given that a successful operation was possible. There is strong evidence to suggest that he wore bandages entirely covering his eyes during most, and possibly virtually all, of his childhood. There is evidence that his vision was not sufficiently good to be of any material use to him for orientation or recognition of objects. He appears from all accounts to have led the life of a blind person throughout his life.

Can we conclude that the case of S.B. may be taken as an example of 'recovery from blindness' in the sense used by von Senden or Hebb? It cannot be claimed that this is equivalent to a previous life of total lack of retinal stimulation, as in the case of Riesen's chimpanzees, but was S.B.'s vision at all times after about the tenth month too rudimentary to be his dominant sense, and too rudimentary to aid him appreciably in any task or skill?

We want to know how S.B.'s early vision compared with that of the previously reported patients, but this is difficult to discover as the earlier case reports tend to be exceedingly sketchy and often non-existent, and little trouble seems to have been taken to form any estimate using more indirect evidence. There are plenty of indications that in some cases there was considerable residual vision immediately prior to the operation, and yet progress in using vision was often slow. In his chapter 'The significance of residual vision in cataract patients for their consciousness of space' von Senden (1960, pp. 71–86) refers to patients having prior to operation awareness of (1) brightness; (2) brightness and colours; (3) brightness, colour and shape. He says (pp. 71–2) 'Unfortunately the details as to the vision of the patients before and after operation are extremely fragmentary ...' and considers that there are only four cases which can definitely be classed as having only brightness vision prior to operation. (These are: Wardrop II (1826); Nunneley (1858); Ahlström (1895): Latta (1904).) Thus von Senden thinks that only four out of nearly seventy cases can be said to have had only brightness vision before operations (and at least one of these (Latta, 1904) developed useful vision comparatively fast, being comparable with the case of S.B.).

There are several cases in which pre-operative vision was clearly superior to S.B.'s and yet vision was extremely slow to develop after operation. Von Senden attributes this to 'their intelligence and will to live ... since they were accustomed to make use of everything and had thereby already acquired extensive schematic notions of space, they also made use of their visual capacity and tried experiments on their own account. ... This may indeed have been partly a game at first, as with Ware and Home; but the important thing was that they thought about impressions gathered from this game, and did not merely enjoy them as qualitative stimuli and accept them as such' (op. cit. p. 85, considerably condensed). We see nothing to disagree with in von Senden's view of the matter (though we might not wish to follow his arguments concerning the essential difference between tactual and visual space, with which he is concerned in this section of his book) and we feel that too little weight has been given to the probable importance for visual development of making *effective* use of the information available through the impaired visual channel. To disagree with this, one would have to argue that visual learning is very different from the other kinds of learning we know something about; where progress depends upon use, reward, and relating things – building up, in Sir Frederic Bartlett's word, schemata. This involves active processes of selecting and relating and depends largely upon intelligent interest. It is a tragic fact that blind people (particularly before there were good schools for the blind), tend to be generally lacking in intelligent interest. To take a striking illustrative example, the case of a seven year old boy:—'The boy appears initially to be devoid of all concepts relating to knowledge of objects, mathematical figures, etc. He cannot even tell by feeling whether a thing is round, square or triangular; here too it is primarily a deficiency in his mental upbringing.' (Uhthoff 1, 1890, quoted by von Senden, 1960, p. 112).

We consider that although S.B. was once reported as having finger vision in early boyhood, his residual vision was certainly less than in the cases described by von Senden, including many which took months to gain useful vision. Our main reason for this conclusion is that although S.B. was of at least average intelligence and education he did not, according to the available records, get any assistance from residual vision. This we believe for two reasons: (1) The absence of any comment in the school report of any help from vision in reading, crafts or other skills, combined with the rather low final assessment; (2) The fact that throughout his life he lived the life of a blind man, and developed the special skills, such as orientating himself by echoes, which are necessary to those who lack effective sight if they are to live active lives. S.B.'s residual vision was apparently insufficient, even for a man of his intelligence and training, to serve him in any simple or complex task, and so we conclude that the case of S.B. may be considered with the classical cases.

The following differences from most of von Senden's cases should be noted.

1. The operation was for opacity of the cornea and not for cataract of the lens, as in most of the earlier cases.
2. So far as we know, S.B.'s vision was entirely normal up to the age of ten months.[1]
3. S.B. had the advantage over almost all the previously reported patients in that he received specialised and careful education, including the reading and writing of Braille.
4. So far as we can judge, S.B.'s general level of intelligence, and also his sense of curiosity were above average.
5. A most unusual feature was absence of nystagmus, both before and after operation. No reason is advanced for this, unless it be his visual experience as a baby, though this seems unlikely. Nystagmus is an almost invariable feature in these patients, though occasionally it is absent.

We shall now describe our observations on the case.

OBSERVATIONS AT THE WOLVERHAMPTON AND MIDLAND COUNTIES EYE INFIRMARY (JANUARY 1959)

(1) *Introduction to the case*

We first heard of the case of S.B. through a short report in a daily

---

[1] This may not be very different from the earlier cases, for the state of the eyes in infancy has not previously been recorded. We should expect opacity in lens or cornea to increase in infancy, and it is unlikely that vision is ever absent in the early weeks or months in operable cases of blindness.

paper, which stated that a man blind from birth, had upon operation immediately recovered his sight. Having read something of earlier cases of recovery from congenital blindness, and being impressed by their significance for contemporary perceptual theory (in particular D. O. Hebb's writing on the subject) we determined to try to investigate this case. We wrote immediately to the Hospital Secretary (the name of the surgeon was not given in the press) and received the following picture of the case, and invitation to investigate it, from the surgeon, Mr A. Hirtenstein, F.R.C.S.

16 January 1959

Dear Mr Gregory,

Thank you for the letter regarding a patient of mine, who, as you know, underwent a corneal graft operation a month ago.

I have myself been very interested to note how quickly he readjusted himself to the vision he gained after operation. Prior to the operation he only had light perception in the first operated eye; in the other eye he could perceive vague hand movements close to his face. He lost his sight at the age of ten months after smallpox vaccination, and was trained as a blind person from the age of seven to eighteen years, at the Birmingham Blind Institute. I am contacting the Secretary of the Institute to find what records they have of his early years.

After the operation he seemed to have absolutely no difficulty with spatial perception, and he could recognise faces and ordinary objects (i.e. chairs, bed, table, etc.) immediately. He learned the names of colours very quickly, and seemed to have no difficulty in recognising cars, windows, doors, etc. His explanation is that, though he could not see any of these things before, he had a definite and accurate mental image of all things he was able to touch; in the case of a car, for instance, he used to wash his brother-in-law's car, and thus he had a good idea of its shape. He was working as a boiler-scraper, and although he hasn't yet seen a boiler, he assures me that he would be able to recognise one immediately, as his mental picture of its shape is very accurate.

As you know I operated on his second eye a fortnight ago, and I hope the visual result will be equally satisfactory for him. His present vision is, of course, not very good yet, but I hope it will improve after further operations, as the first ones were only preparatory ones.

He will probably be staying another week or so in the Wolverhampton Eye Infirmary, and if you would like to see him yourself, and carry out any tests you might wish to do, you would be more than welcome. Do let me know if you are able to come up, as I would very much like to meet you if possible. Thank you very much for enclosing the two interesting articles of yours. I look forward to discussing Mr B.'s case with you.

Signed : A. Hirtenstein (F.R.C.S.)

We are most grateful to Mr Hirtenstein, and the Matron and staff of the Wolverhampton and Midland Counties Eye Infirmary, who gave us all the facilities we requested, and helped in every way possible. We were given the use of a quiet and well lighted room for our investigations, and were left entirely undisturbed.

It is unfortunate that this case was not examined earlier from the psychological point of view, but it is understandable that it seemed to be of no very special interest to those who were involved in eye operations every working day of their lives. Special investigations take time, and time is obviously a precious commodity in a busy hospital geared to treatment rather than to research. We saw S.B. while still in the hospital, and interviewed members of the staff to obtain details about what had happened before we saw him. These were trained and careful people, and indeed had far more experience in dealing with, and observing, blind people than we had.

S.B. received a corneal graft on his left eye on 9 December, 1958, and on the right eye on 1 January, 1959. We first examined him on 26 January – 48 days after the first operation. The first examination was carried out in a quiet private room in the hospital, lit by winter daylight, and lasted about $3\frac{1}{2}$ hours.

We first saw S.B. walking confidently along a corridor. He guided himself through a door without the use of touch, and he struck us immediately as a cheerful, rather extrovert and confident, middle-aged individual. At first impression he seemed like a normally sighted person, though differences soon became obvious. When he sat down he would not look round or scan the room with his eyes; indeed he would generally pay no attention to visual objects unless his attention were called to them, when he would peer at whatever it was with extreme concentration and care, finally making some almost oracular comment. He never said anything silly or hysterical, and answered every question with unusual care. He never evaded a question, and showed an intelligence and sense of curiosity very much higher than a sighted man of his trade would be expected to show. He displayed an unusual dislike of being surprised by anything. He had a matter-of-fact attitude to his situation and his experience, and disliked not knowing things known as a matter of course to sighted people. At no

time did he dramatize his situation, or exaggerate his lack of knowledge, as one might have expected if he were trying to impress us with
his past blindness. He was proud of his independence as a blind man,
and indeed he was unusual in his independence. He would go for
long cycle rides, holding the shoulder of a friend, and he was fond
of gardening, and making things in his garden shed, provided by the
blind school for his trade as a cobbler.

He had no nystagmus. Searching eye movements were minimal,
and when they did move over a large amplitude, they did so in larger
than normal saccadic jerks, which were plainly visible. No records
were taken of his eye movements.

It was very soon apparent that his vision was far from rudimentary:
he could name almost any object in the room. Much to our surprise,
he could even tell the time by means of a large clock on the wall.
We were so surprised at this that we did not at first believe that he
could have been in any sense blind before the operation. However
he proceeded to show us a large hunter watch with no glass, and he
demonstrated his ability to tell the time very quickly and accurately
by touching the hands. It appears that he always used this method of
telling the time before the operation.

We were even more surprised when he named correctly a magazine
we had with us. It was in fact *Everybody's* (for 17 January, 1959),
and had a large picture of two musicians dressed in striped pullovers.
Although he named the magazine correctly, he could make nothing
of the picture. We at once asked him how he knew which magazine
it was, and he said that although he could not read the name, he could
recognize the first two letters, though not the rest, and he guessed that
the *Ev* belonged to *Everybody's*. Further questioning revealed that he
could recognize any letter in upper case, though not in lower case,
and it so happens that the title of the magazine was written with only
the first two letters in upper case, thus:

He then told us that he had learned capital letters by touch, these
being inscribed on blocks and taught at the blind school. Lower case
letters were not taught.[1] This was particularly interesting, for it

[1] The upper case letters were taught since they often occur embossed on name plates, and
they are useful to the blind, whereas lower case letters are seldom used in embossed form and
so were not taught.

suggested direct transfer from touch experience. It also showed how he could guess correctly from comparatively little evidence. We were, after this early experience, continuously on our guard for intelligent guessing covering up perceptual abnormality.

His colour naming was not at that time by any means perfect. He told us that his only visual memories were of red, white and black. He could name these correctly, and apparently could do so very shortly after the operation. When we saw him he was uncertain about yellow, complaining of the large number of kinds of yellow. Latta's patient responded with great displeasure to yellow. S.B. did not show *dislike* for any colour, but seemed to prefer greens and blues, for example when seen in kodachrome projections, even when he could not name the objects. He liked bright colours, and later often expressed disappointment when things were 'dingy'.

When we established that he could distinguish upper case letters, cars from lorries as seen in the distance through the window, and name such objects as trees and tables, we realized that more sophisticated tests were called for. Fortunately we had brought everything we could think of in the time available, including the tests to be described.

(2) *First visual experiences after operation*

S.B.'s first visual experience, when the bandages were removed, was of the surgeon's face. He described the experience as follows:—

He heard a voice coming from in front of him and to one side: he turned to the source of the sound, and saw a 'blur'. He realized that this must be a face. Upon careful questioning, he seemed to think that he would not have known that this was a face if he had not previously heard the voice and known that voices came from faces.

At the time we first saw him, he did not find faces 'easy' objects. He did not look at a speaker's face, and made nothing of facial expressions. On the other hand, he very rapidly (apparently within a couple of days) distinguished between passing lorries and cars, and would get up at six each morning to look at them some way off. He 'collected' different types of lorry, and took much pleasure recognizing vans, articulated lorries, and so on. His particular interest in cars and lorries may have been in part that they made familiar sounds, which helped in identification; that they could only be driven by sighted people, and so held out particular promise to him. He had spent many hours trying to visualize the shape of cars while washing them, particularly his brother-in-law's car, which he frequently washed down.

He told us that he did not suffer particularly from giddiness when he first opened his eyes.

As in previous cases (Latta, 1904), he experienced marked scale distortion when looking down from a high window. In the famous Cheselden case, objects were at first reported to be touching the eye;[1] this was not true for S.B. but he found that when looking down from a high window (about 30–40 feet above the ground) he thought he could safely lower himself down by his hands. When later he saw the same window from outside, he realized that this would be impossible.

On the whole, his early estimates of the size of objects seem to have been quite accurate providing they were objects already familiar to him by touch. Thus buses seemed to him to be too high but the right length. This may well have been because he was used to walking their length, but not feeling their height; adding the separate tactile sensations of the height of each step and adding enough above the stair-case would be a comparatively difficult and unfamiliar task. In drawings of buses, to be given later, he emphasized the features familiar to touch but ignored the bonnet, which would not easily have been explored by touch, by a blind boy.

He may well have made many mistakes of identification of objects which we did not hear about, but from the beginning he was proud of his ability to name objects correctly, and took no pleasure in allowing others to find out that he made mistakes.

It was very soon obvious (as we had to some extent anticipated) that merely to ask questions about what he saw would not give us much information about his visual capacity. In fact the only example of a curious and interesting mistake was described to us by the Matron, who said that about three days after the operation he saw the moon for the first time. At first he thought it a reflection in the window, but when he realized, or was told, it was the moon, he expressed surprise at its crescent shape, expecting a 'quarter moon' to look like a quarter piece of cake! It is noteworthy that this is the only clear instance of an expression of surprise, or of a clear error of this sort. That it should occur with an object he could not have touched is perhaps significant. It also shows – when it is remembered that the full moon only subtends $0.5°$ – that his visual acuity must have been reasonably good at that time, a few days after the first operation.

It is also worth noting that reflections fascinated him and continued to do so for at least a year after the operation.

---

[1] Although this is often quoted at its face value, it is worth remembering that normally a strong light, particularly if painful, is not regarded so much as 'out there' as in the eye itself. The same is true for intense (and unusual?) stimuli in any sense modality. E.g. a very loud sound is a sensation *in the ear*.

(3) *Perceptual tests*

One of the difficulties about trying to discover the perceptual world of the blind is that they use the normal words of the sighted, even though they cannot always have the meanings we attach to them. Thus a blind man will say, 'I saw in the paper to-day . . .' when he read it by touch in Braille. When S.B. named an object correctly (say a chair or a vase of flowers) we could not discover what special features he used to decide what object it was. It was obvious that facial expressions meant nothing to him, and that he could not recognize people by their faces, though he could immediately do so by their voices, but we could learn little more.

We tried to get some insight into his previous world by getting him to say what surprised him when vision returned. The attempt failed almost completely, as he seldom admitted to any surprises.

We would have liked to obtain accurate measures of such things beloved by the experimental psychologist as the visual constancies, but this was not practicable, for he tired easily, and we were anxious not to upset either him or the hospital staff. We decided to get him to look at various well-known visual illusions, about which a great deal is known for normal observers, even though explanations for many of them are lacking. The lack of explanation of these illusions did not worry us greatly, for with more knowledge, which is bound to come with further research in perception, they will surely be explained, and then any findings should be relatable to general perceptual issues.[1] It seemed to us that this would be the best way of getting some reasonably objective information as to his perceptual capacities and peculiarities.

The first three tests to be described here were given on the morning of 26 January, 1959, and the remainder on the same afternoon, when the first three were repeated.

Test 1. The Hering illusion. This is shown in Fig. 3.2a, where it will be seen that although the heavy vertical lines are in fact straight and parallel, they appear to diverge in the middle. This figure was presented to S.B. printed in heavy black lines on a white card of size

---

[1] Since undertaking this investigation, we have made an intensive investigation of the geometrical illusions, and have come to the conclusion that they arise from discrepancy between estimated distance and degree of constancy evoked by such perceptual features as perspective lines. The illusion figures presented here seem to produce distortion of visual space by evoking constancy which is inappropriate to the flat plane (visible as a textured surface) on which the figures lie. On this view, we might say that the anomalous results obtained for S.B. show that these figures did not serve to evoke constancy scaling for him, and thus the illusions were absent.

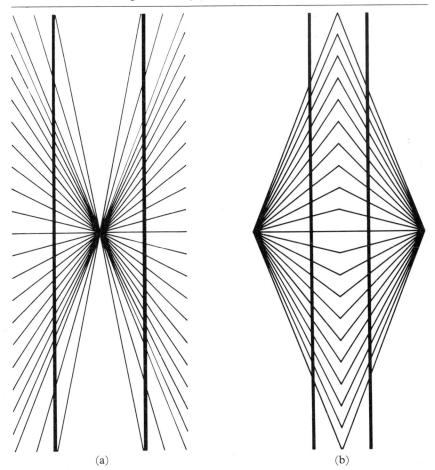

(a)   (b)

FIG. 3.2 *The Hering illusion.* (a) *First form.* (b) *Second form (Wundt).*

$10\frac{1}{2}'' \times 4''$. He held it close to his eye, and studied it very carefully in silence.

Result First he said the lines were straight. He then became doubtful, and thought that they might be further apart at the top and middle. When shown the figures again, in the afternoon, he first said: 'One goes out in the middle' and ended by saying that both were straight. We may conclude that the illusion was, if present, considerably less marked than in normal observers. Fig. 3.2*b* gave a similar result.

Test 2. The Zöllner illusion. Normally, the verticals look non-parallel and may fluctuate in their positions (Fig. 3.3*a*).

Result He reported the verticals, after careful study, as all parallel, and after questioning about variation he said it was 'all calm'.

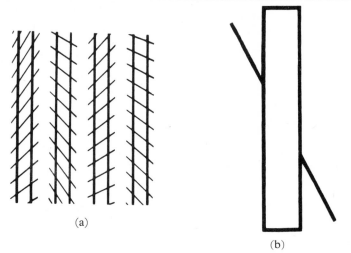

(a)

(b)

FIG. 3.3 (a) *The Zöllner illusion.*   (b) *The Poggendorff illusion.*

Test 3. The Poggendorff illusion. Normally, the right-hand section of the slanting line appears to lie below the continuation of the left-hand section. (Fig. 3.3*b*).

Result S.B. reported it as: 'all one line'.

Test 4. Ambiguous depth illusions (reversing figures). (a) The Necker Cube. This also is a very well-known illusion: it was shown as presented in Fig. 3.4*a*. It was displayed on a card 10 cm. × 15 cm. the figure being 5·2 cm. × 8·0 cm. Normally, this figure is seen to reverse at intervals, the side representing the front being ambiguous.

Result This gave a most unusual, possibly unique, result. The figure was evidently *not seen in depth* and it *did not reverse*.

We took the greatest possible care to ensure that he understood what we meant by 'depth' and 'reversal', after he asked us 'What is depth?' We did this by showing him (after first obtaining negative answers to our question as to whether it reversed or was seen in depth) a child's wooden brick we had brought along, and pointed out that it receded from him, by pointing out the depth with a finger, and getting him to touch it while looking at it. When he looked again at the picture cube he said that he could not see depth, and that 'it looks quite different [from the brick].' He tried, rather unsuccessfully, to draw a cube, but unfortunately this drawing is lost.

(b) The staircase illusion. This is similar to the Necker cube in that it also is a figure reversible in depth. It was presented on a card. (Fig. 3.4*b*).

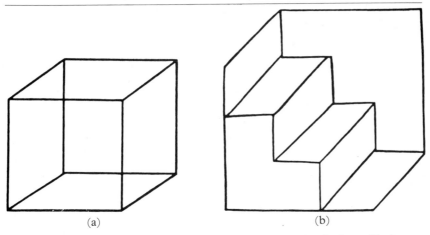

(a)   (b)

FIG. 3.4 *Ambiguous depth illusions.* (a) *Necker cube* (b) *Staircase illusion.*

Result The result was the same; evidently no depth, and no ambiguity was observed.

Test 5. The Müller-Lyer illusion. This famous illusion is shown in Fig. 3.5. When the shafts of the arrows are in fact of equal length, the arrow with diverging fins is seen as longer than that having converging fins. This was presented to S.B. as two arrows end to end, and was so arranged that it could be varied, and continuously adjusted by the observer, who holds the device in his hand. The length of the fixed arrow was 74 cm., and the movable arrow is normally observed to be *shorter* than this. S.B. adjusted the arrow for apparent equality of length four times, each time with great care.

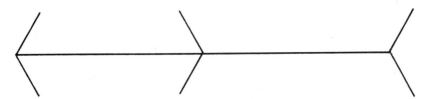

FIG. 3.5 *Müller-Lyer illusion.*

Result His estimate of length on the four successive readings were as follows :

1.	10·0
2.	16·5
3.	17·0
4.	16·0

These figures meaning the *under-estimation of length* from the standard of 74 cm. His average illusion is thus 14·12 cm, in the normal direction. This may be compared with the mean obtained on ten normal observers on the same apparatus of 20 cm. The extent of the illusion as measured for S.B. is unusually small, though some 'normal' observers can be found with a similar degree of illusion.

Test 6. Perspective size changes. Figure 3.6 shows four men, all actually the same size, but normally appearing of increasing size as the apparent distance, due to perspective, increases.

Result S.B. reported: 'They don't look far away, it's just as though the men were standing underneath (? the buildings). The first man looks smaller, but the last three look the same.' It should be made clear that these comments were in answer to a request for a description of the relative sizes of the men, and we had to state that the objects depicted *were* men. As will be seen later he was hardly able to identify drawings of such objects as men.

FIG. 3.6 *Perspective size illusion.*

Test 7. Figure and ground. One of the classical problems in the study of perception is how 'figure' is distinguished from 'ground' and whether the distinction is innate or learned. Normally objects stand out against a hardly perceived background, for example the objects in a room against the walls, even when highly decorated, but this can be perceptually ambiguous, as when at dusk the sky is sometimes seen as 'object', with the black roofline as unimportant 'background'. Similarly, looking at a map, the land or the sea can be seen as 'object' or 'background'.

The only example given to S.B. was Fig. 3.7.

FIG. 3.7 *Figure and ground effect.*

Result S.B. made little of it; after some time he said, of the black curved part: 'Is it the case of a fan – a turbine fan?' He meant by this, as questioning elicited, part of the boiler equipment on which he worked. This is particularly interesting, for he had not at that time seen this equipment; he was however certain that he knew what it would look like, from his experience with touch plus his recent visual experience. He gave no response indicating figure–ground fluctuation, and could make nothing of the white part, even when the 'face' was pointed out in detail.

Test 8. The Ames distorting room. The Ames distorting rooms are of importance for studies on 'visual framework'. They emphasize that many judgements of size, shape or distance which may seem to be absolute are relative in the sense that they depend on other features in the visual field.

The rooms are non-rectangular, but are so made that they give, from a chosen viewing position, a retinal image corresponding to a rectangular room. Clearly they *must* appear rectangular from the chosen position, since no information is available to indicate otherwise, but they become interesting when objects are introduced into the rooms, for objects in fact at different distances may appear to be the same distance from the observer. When this is so, objects of the same size and the same *apparent* distance will give different sized retinal images. To the normal observer the objects will appear of different sizes even when this is quite contrary to all their past experience. For example, a child can be made to look larger than an adult. It would seem that, at least in a Western culture, where most rooms are rectangular, the walls serve as a reference frame for deciding the ever-present perceptual question: is it a large object far away or a small near object giving this size of retinal image?

We should expect S.B. to see an Ames room as rectangular – or at any rate he should not find its shape surprising – but it was an open question what he would see when identical objects were placed in such a room, at actually different distances though at apparently the same distance.

To test S.B.'s reactions to this special situation, we used a small model Ames room, into which he looked, using one eye.

Result He reported the room to be rectangular (in fact the rear wall receded from him to the right), and this result in no way surprised us since the resulting retinal image would be the same as for a truly rectangular room, or box. We then held a half-penny in each of the two windows in the back wall, one window being in fact further from the observer than the other, this distance not being apparent. S.B. reported that the right hand coin looked smaller than the left. When the right hand coin was replaced by a penny piece, and this compared with a half-penny in the left window, he reported that they were of the same size. This response is quite normal for observers using the particular model Ames room we used for this test. We were, rightly or wrongly, considerably surprised by the result.

Test 9. After-effects of movement. The well-known after-effect of perceived movement, often called the 'waterfall effect', is a marked apparent movement of stationary objects viewed immediately after exposure of the retina to moving stimuli. A familiar example is the apparent movement of the bank of a river when seen after the moving water has been viewed for half a minute or so. The effect may most readily be observed by fixating the centre of a gramophone record while it is rotating, and then stopping the turntable. It will be seen to rotate in the opposite direction, the effect lasting for up to at least twenty seconds.

We tested S.B. for this effect using in place of a simple rotating display, a large spiral mounted on a turntable. Normally after this is viewed, rotating slowly, a marked after-expansion or contraction is seen. This is a particularly good display to use because the effect cannot be due to eye movements, since the after-effect is symmetrical round the centre of rotation of the spiral.

Result First we switched on the motor and asked S.B. to tell us what he saw. He was unable to say, and we discovered that he did not understand or appear to know the words 'contract' or 'expand'. After several exploratory trials we got him to watch carefully for 30 seconds, and to tell us what he saw when the disc was stopped. He reported: 'stationary'. He appeared to get no after-effect under conditions when a normal observer would experience an expansion lasting 15–20 seconds. This was probably not due to lack of acuity, for he did appear to see real movement of the spiral. Language was, however, inadequate for this bizarre situation, and we may have been mistaken in thinking that he obtained no after-effect of any kind, though this appeared to be the case.

Test 10. Rorschach ink blots. We showed S.B. cards I and X of the Rorschach test. Our purpose was not to test his personality, but rather to see whether vague and quite unfamiliar shapes would evoke any interesting response.

   Result

Card I (no colour). He said: 'It is just a design – I can't see what.' We asked him: 'Does *part* of it show something?' He answered: 'I haven't the slightest idea.' Even after the most leading questions he was quite unable to make anything of it.

Card X (coloured). This time he said, 'Is this a wallpaper design, or a cushion cover? It looks like a design for something. I can see colours but not what they are – there aren't any flowers are there? I thought it was something of a plant, but there are no flowers, so I thought it was a design.' This response is interesting in being one of the few cases where he is evidently thinking aloud. Colour always stimulated him: his greater interest in the coloured card is typical.

Test 11. Kodachrome projections of scenery. We showed S.B. several kodachrome transparencies of objects and scenes familiar to sighted people but never seen by him. They were shown by projection.

Slide 1. The Interior of a Cathedral (Hereford). He said: 'Is it a building with lights in it? What's all that gold, is it the sun?' (The lighting was in fact rather gold-coloured sunlight). He took a stained glass window to be a door in a church. (This might have been from the common gothic carving to be found in Victorian churches and school doors.) He was rather puzzled by what he thought was a door, and asked: 'Why should it have lines down it?'

Slide 2. The Cambridge 'Backs' showing the River and Kings' Bridge. He made nothing of this. He did not realize that the scene was of a river, and did not recognize water or bridge. We named the water and the bridge to him, pointing them out.

Slide 3. Evening Scene of Malvern Hills. 'This is a landscape is it? I can only tell fields by the colour. What's this gold colour?' He liked the green, but could name nothing on the picture.

Slide 4. The Cambridge 'Backs' showing Trinity Bridge. This time he immediately, though with a trace of uncertainty, identified the water as water, and pointing to the double arched bridge said: 'Are those bridges again?'

So far as we could tell S.B. had no idea which objects lay in front of or behind other objects in any of the colour pictures. He showed pleasure at green foliage, but could make very little of buildings or other objects. We formed the impression that he saw little more than patches of colour.

Test 12. The Ishihara Colour Vision Test. We gave S.B. the whole of the standard Ishihara Colour Vision Test. That we had it with us turned out to be peculiarly fortunate, for the result was remarkable.

Result We presented the book of test cards in the normal order, and asked him to try to make out any numbers or letters among the coloured dots. To our extreme surprise he read *every single number correctly, as for normal colour vision.* That his colour vision would thus appear nearly normal is of secondary importance here, what amazed us was that he was able to make out figures without the aid of any high-contrast outlines. He made only one correction, from a 1 to a 7, which are normally found rather difficult to distinguish.

He also succeeded, quite easily, in tracing out the 'mazes' on the final test cards, after we showed him what was required, using the small paint brush provided as a pointer which does not harm the cards.

It seems very difficult to avoid the inference that he used earlier tactile experience of number shapes. He had never had this or any similar test administered, as we established from the hospital staff.

The fact that he succeeded in reading these numbers is of particular interest as they have no contours, in the ordinary sense, but consist of dots coloured slightly differently from other dots which are of various colours. It would seem impossible for him to have followed outlines with his eyes, since he could not know which colour was relevant until *after* he had recognized each figure. We noted that he did not attempt to follow the figures with his finger, or make any related movements with his hands or fingers. He read the numbers out quite confidently and quickly, without apparent unusual mental effort.

This observation that he was able to read the characters even though masked in the coloured dots of the Ishihara test displays, seems to provide very strong evidence for transfer from earlier tactile experience. This is surprising in view of Riesen's findings that trans-modal transfer does not seem to occur in chimpanzees kept while young in the dark. [Later work confirms this.]

(4) *The patient's first drawings*

We asked S.B., on the same day that the visual tests already described were administered, whether he would try to draw for us. He said that he had not so far tried to draw, though he had tried to write, and indeed he produced a laboured but just legible version of his own name, which he produced with great pride. (His wife had recently given him a ball point pen – his first writing instrument – and he had written his name to show to Mr Hirtenstein.)

(A) *A Hammer* (Fig. 3.8) was a subject of his own choosing – *a cobbler's chipping hammer*. This seems to be the first drawing that he ever made. He was most doubtful of his ability to draw, but once started, he enjoyed it, and attacked it with great concentration. He placed his head very close to the paper, using only his preferred (right) eye, and checking the results from time to time holding the paper further away.

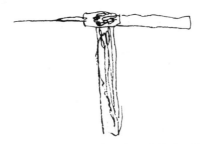

FIG. 3.8 *S.B.'s first drawing. This drawing of a cobbler's chipping hammer was made in our presence on the 48th day after the first operation.*

(B) *A Bus* (Fig. 3.9). This was a subject which we suggested to him. We chose it because he was familiar with buses as a blind man, and all transport interested him. We also had some evidence that at first buses seemed to him too tall, though of the correct length, and this seemed a matter of some interest. He had seen several buses since his operation – also cars and lorries – and it was clear that he thought this an interesting task.

FIG. 3.9 *Drawing of a bus, 48 days after the first operation (cf. Fig. 3.1).*

He expressed dissatisfaction with his drawing – because he found himself quite unable to draw the bonnet, or radiator. This is striking, for it would be the principal part that he would hardly have touched when blind. The rather exaggerated windows might well represent his tactual conception of them, perhaps as felt from the inside. The wheels, it may be noted, are shown as having spokes. We questioned him on this and he replied that he knew that buses had hub wheels, but that he was more familiar (apparently as a boy) with the feel of cart wheels. Evidently the more striking tactile impression would be of a wheel having spokes, and this seemed to mean 'wheel' for him. He also said that he did not know how to draw hub wheels, without spokes, so he 'made them simply like cart wheels'. He said that he knew the shape of hubs quite well, for he often washed his brother-in-law's car, and then he tried to picture it as it seems by sight. He drew buses later (Fig. 3.13*a* and *b*) and these we discuss below.

When he had drawn the bus and had discussed it, we left him to choose his own subject.

(C) *A Farm House* (Fig. 3.10). He said that this was meant to be the gable end of a farm house, with a path leading up to the house from a gate. It represented his idea of the Archers' house in the radio serial, to which he listened regularly.

Fig. 3.10 *Drawing of farm house.*

(D) *S.B.'s House* (Fig. 3.11). This was also his own choice. The archway at the right hand side represents the entry to a passage round the side to the back of the house. He was worried by his inability to represent the pavement.

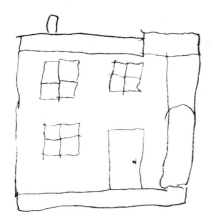

Fig. 3.11 *S.B.'s drawing of his own house.*

(E) *A Man* (Fig. 3.12). (No man in particular). He first drew the head, spending a long time on the mouth. We asked him to add the body, so any distortion of scale between the head and body should not be taken as important. When he had finished the body he said 'I'm afraid I forgot to put him any knees'.

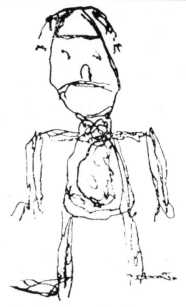

FIG. 3.12 *Drawing of a man (48 days after the first operation).*

(5) *Discussion of S.B.'s drawings*

It is well known that some blind people are capable of drawing objects familiar to them by touch.[1] Typically, the characteristic tactile features appear to us exaggerated; and perhaps they can give us some information as to how objects appear to the blind. It is interesting that S.B.'s early drawings are all typical of drawings of the blind. He introduces no features which he had not known previously by touch, although at that time (48 days after the first operation) he could name these objects confidently from vision alone. Thus although he could use vision to recognize objects, he seemed incapable of recalling the specifically visual information and representing it in his drawings.

The hammer (his first drawing) was quite certainly drawn from touch memory as he had never seen it. The first drawing of a bus (Fig. 3.9) is revealing in showing importation of a characteristic tactile feature, which was not in fact present in the buses he saw in the period after the operation: the spokes of the wheels. The buses he had seen had disc wheels; but to him a wheel characteristically had spokes and he imported these and added them to his bus, which he drew, as with the other drawings, sitting in the hospital room without having the object present to draw from.

[1] See Revesz, 1950, and Lowenfeld, 1952.

The farm house (Fig. 3.10) represents his imagined house in a radio serial (the Archers) and incorporates only features known to him by touch. It may be noticed that the window is identical with drawings of the windows of his own house (Fig. 3.11). It may seem surprising that he should have a touch image of an object as large as a house, but in fact he painted his own house, using a ladder, and feeling the brush along the woodwork, which he did fairly competently. It may be noted that the roof is ambiguously represented.

He took longer to draw the man (Fig. 3.12) finding it difficult, and was dissatisfied with the result. Blind people like exploring other people's faces with their fingers, and at that time he knew that his previous conception of faces was highly inadequate, for his vision did not serve to give him recognition of individuals from their faces, or the significance of facial expression. He seemed to have a feeling of inadequacy and disappointment over this. After doing this drawing he looked worried and apparently could make little of his own drawing. He ended by saying: 'I'm afraid I forgot to put him any knees', and relinquished it with a sigh.

(6) Addendum : later drawings

The later drawings of a bus (Figs 3.13 *a* and *b*) were done six months and a year later, respectively. They give some indication of the patient's increasing ability to use specifically visual information. There are several points of interest. In all cases the radiator is omitted, and this would not have been known by touch as the front of a bus is a position of danger to a blind man. The mirror is shown in all three drawings and mirrors always fascinated him. One suspects that he is representing the windows as he knew them by touch from the inside. The spokes, imported from touch in the first drawing, are absent in

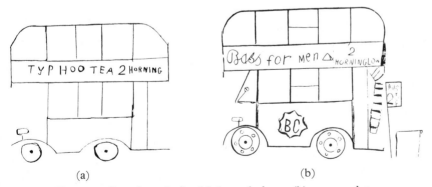

(a)   (b)

FIG. 3.13 *Drawings of a bus* (a) *6 months later ;* (b) *one year later.*

the second and a much more sophisticated version of the wheels is given in the third. There is no writing present in the first drawing. This appears in the second but is only upper case lettering, which he already knew by touch, while in the third drawing lower case lettering is beginning to appear: this he learned only after he gained his sight.

Finally, it will be noticed that in all three cases the buses are shown in profile and facing to the left. As a blind man he would only touch buses when they presented this aspect to him (since traffic is on the left-hand side of the road in this country), and he retains this aspect even in the last drawing.

These drawings illustrate the general finding that although S.B. came to use vision, his ideas of the world arose from touch. His general way of life as a blind man remained with him until his death.

OBSERVATIONS MADE IMMEDIATELY
AFTER DISCHARGE FROM HOSPITAL

Before leaving hospital, S.B. had been out for short periods and we were not with him on these occasions. He had spent Christmas at home after the first operation (on the less successful eye) and had been out for one or two walks in Wolverhampton. He was driven to London from the hospital by Mr Merrick Winn, with whom we stayed with S.B. and his wife at a London hotel.

S.B. was very tired when he arrived, and his eyes were painful. Mr Winn told us that on the drive down S.B. had been almost completely unresponsive, accepting quite calmly what must have been unfamiliar visual scenes. He complained that the world seemed a drab place, though when the sun appeared he could see more clearly, and he was disappointed when it set. The one spontaneous comment S.B. made to us that evening was to describe the colours in the sky at sunset, to end sadly: '. . . then we came down a hill and it all disappeared'. When questioned about his general lack of interest in the journey, he said that the speed was too great for him to see very much; this was probably not the whole story, as later observation shows. He seemed dispirited, and indeed he never again seemed the cheerful, rather extrovert, man he was at the hospital when we first saw him.

Next morning, at breakfast, he sat for preference facing a very large wall mirror in which the room was reflected. This fascinated him, and mirrors continued to be chosen objects. (At his 'local', a year later, his favourite place was opposite a mirror from which he could see the street, through a window.)

We took him round London, and showed him several of the 'sights', but he was almost uniformly bored. He found all buildings dull, of no interest. His only signs of appreciation were to moving objects, particularly the pigeons in Trafalgar Square (Fig. 3.14). He took great interest in them and liked to touch them while he watched. He described how as a blind man he often felt isolated and sought sounds of activity and movement.

He found the traffic frightening, and would not attempt to cross even a comparatively small street by himself. This was in marked contrast to his former behaviour, as described to us by his wife, when he would cross any street in his own town by himself. In London, and later in his home town, he would show evident fear, even when led by a companion whom he trusted, and it was many months before he would venture alone. We heard that before the operation he would sometimes injure himself by walking briskly into a parked vehicle, or other unexpected obstruction, and he generally did not carry a white stick. As a blind man he was unusually active and aggressive. We began to see that this assurance had at least temporarily left him; he seemed to lack confidence and interest in his surroundings.

We were disappointed in his lack of interest and response to the everyday sights, and so we suggested that we take him to the Science Museum, in South Kensington, with a view to showing him things, particularly tools, which he would have heard about and wished he could have used when blind.

FIG. 3.14 *S.B. in Trafalgar Square.*

(1) *Visit to the Science Museum, South Kensington*

S.B. had a long-standing interest in tools and machinery; we were thus particularly interested to discover whether the sight of these things would serve to stimulate him, and dispel the lethargy into which he had fallen.

We took him to the large Watt's beam engine in the main ground floor gallery. This certainly interested him, especially when we arranged to have it run (by compressed air) for his special benefit. But he understood little or nothing of its function, and was finally disappointed.

A model windmill he at first described as: 'It's a sort of cross – is it a windmill?' Upon questioning, it appeared that he had made simple windmills for children, and this enabled him to guess its identity. He made nothing of the rest of the model, only the cross-like sails.

We showed him a large stone-cutting bow-saw, which had large clearly defined teeth. At first he made nothing of it: it took perhaps 30 seconds for him to identify it as a saw.

The most interesting episode was his reaction to the fine Maudeslay screw cutting lathe which is housed in a special glass case. This is a large and fairly simple example. We chose this object because a lathe would be a tool that he must often have wished to use.

We led him to the glass case, which was closed, and asked him to tell us what was in it. He was quite unable to say anything about it, except that he thought the nearest part was a handle. (He pointed to the handle of the transverse feed.) He complained that he could not see the cutting edge, or the metal being worked, or anything else about it, and appeared rather agitated. We then asked a museum attendant (as previously arranged) for the case to be opened, and S.B. was allowed to touch the lathe. The result was startling; he ran his hands deftly over the machine, touching first the transverse feed handle and confidently naming it as 'a handle', and then on to the saddle, the bed and the head-stock. He ran his hands eagerly over the lathe, with his eyes tight shut. Then he stood back a little and opened his eyes, and said: 'Now that I've felt it I can see'. He then named many of the parts correctly and explained how they would work, though he could not understand the chain of four gears driving the lead screw.

The episode with the lathe was extraordinarily interesting to watch: it is a great pity that a film record was not made.

(2) *Visit to the Zoo, Regent's Park*

The officials of the Zoological Society Gardens very kindly arranged a special visit in which we were allowed to enter many of the cages, normally closed to visitors.

Before he saw the animals, we asked S.B. to draw an elephant, as he imagined it would look. (Fig. 3.15).

FIG. 3.15 *Drawing of an elephant.*

It may be noted that this is a very poor drawing of an elephant; and yet when he saw the real thing, for the first time, later that day, he recognized it and expressed no surprise. This brings out the extreme difficulty we had trying to understand his world.

S.B. had no difficulty in identifying the giraffe, elephant, monkey, lion, snakes or giant tortoises. He appeared to identify the tiger at once, though he was surprised to see that it was striped. However, after several cages of leopards, panthers, etc. there was another tiger and he did not recognize it as such. (As the first tiger was in the next cage to the lion, recognition of it may have been due to an association between the two.) He could not identify bears, seals, rhino, hippopotamus, crocodiles, or a gazelle. He was given a mongoose to hold, and thought that it might be a ferret, then a badger, then a stoat. He had never heard of a mongoose. He was amused by the elephants and giraffes, and particularly amused when he saw two giraffe heads looking at him from high up over the top of an adjacent cage. This was the only visual situation noted which ever made him laugh. He was allowed to throw cabbages into the mouths of the hippopotamus and his aim was good. We obtained a film record of this. When allowed to handle the animals, he did so with pleasure, and showed no fear or revulsion when snakes were hung round his neck. This also was filmed.

(3) *Visual skill – a game of darts*

At S.B.'s request, we played a game of darts with him. He had played when he was blind, by touching the board and walking backwards until he was told to stop. He would then be told the result of each throw. He now tried, for the first time, with sight. He occasionally scored accurately but was on the whole inaccurate, with a marked tendency to aim too low. He then tried with his eyes shut, and there was little difference in his performance. There was, perhaps, some evidence that with sight he tended to underestimate the distance.

We made several general observations during the two days that we were with him at this time:—

He walked downstairs with complete confidence, with no hand on the rail; but on two occasions when there were three or four steps only, he stepped straight off the top one and had to be saved from falling. He would walk past objects (cages of animals in the zoo for instance) without seeing them, when a normally sighted person would have reacted to them at once. On the other hand, when we asked him, outside Buckingham Palace, if he could see Big Ben, he said that he could see 'that sort of tower if that was what we meant', and whenever his attention was drawn to animals in the zoo he would react at once. He said again that he did not recognize people by their faces but by their clothes – the colour – and that he was unable to understand expression on faces. He only looked at faces when spoken to and then in a rather 'blind' fashion, though there was some evidence on the second day that he was beginning to look at faces with more curiosity. At a meal, one would look up and find him rather tentatively studying one's face. One would have given a lot to know what he saw.

OBSERVATIONS MADE SIX MONTHS AFTER OPERATION

We visited S.B. at his home six months after the operation and spent a day with him in his familiar surroundings.

At his house we saw his shed, in which were hand tools for cobbling and woodwork and a new circular saw which he had recently installed and which he demonstrated with great pride. He apparently used it only for cutting up fire wood, but he operated the machine with frightening confidence.

The shed was fitted with a coke stove, and he informed us that he had installed this himself while blind, a statement confirmed by his wife, though he may of course have had some help. He was a keen gardener before his operation, growing mainly vegetables and setting them out in rows with strings. He described how he used to try to picture the plants, and particularly liked them for their smell.

S.B. was clearly proud of his ability to deal with the tasks of making and mending: he was an aggressive man determined to tackle all that was possible to him with unusual perseverance and on the whole successfully. He used to go for long cycle rides, being guided by a friend's hand on his shoulder, and he took particular pride in the installation of the stove in his shed. But talking to him now he seemed dispirited, and we formed a strong impression that his sight was to him almost entirely disappointing. It enabled him to do a little more, and he had a strong desire to drive a car, but it became clear that the opportunities it afforded him were less than he had imagined. We found a still active middle-aged man of fairly high intelligence, but with a labourer's job and unable to read more than a few simple words. His income and status were obviously lower than they would have been if he had not been so handicapped, and these facts were very clear to him. He described the world as rather drab; he still to a great extent lived the life of a blind man, sometimes not bothering to put on the light at night, and he still made little of the normal visual occupations of the cinema or television. He did not get on well with his neighbours, who regarded him as 'odd', and his workmates played tricks on him and teased him for being unable to read.

At his favourite 'local' he cheered up considerably, and was clearly regarded as a 'character'. He was able to recognize his friends at a distance of at least fifteen feet, from one bar to another, and he would now cross roads with some confidence. He certainly relied a great deal on vision, but we formed the impression that this very reliance cost him his self-respect, for he had been proud of his abilities when the handicap was obvious, but now his previous achievements seemed paltry and his present position almost foolish. He was not a man to talk freely, but was obviously depressed, and we felt that he had lost more than he had gained by recovery of sight.

In view of his depressed state, we felt it best not to undertake formal tests. We did, however, ascertain that he was able to find his way about without the use of his eyes, and that he could detect the presence of houses and doors by the echoes from his footsteps. He was still fascinated by mirrors, and he still noted improvement in his ability to see. In particular, he said that he noted more and more the blemishes in things, and would examine small irregularities and marks in paint-work or wood. Quite recently he had been struck by how objects changed their shape when he walked round them. He would look at a lamp post, walk round it, stand studying it from a different aspect, and wonder why it looked different and yet the same.

THE END OF THE CASE

We find that a common feature of the earlier cases is a psychological crisis following the operation. There are many instances given by von Senden; two examples will serve as illustrations:—

Mesmer (1777)

'In her ill-humour she once complained to her father: "How comes it that I now find myself less happy than before? Everything that I see causes me a disagreeable emotion. Oh, I was much more at ease in my blindness." The father consoled his daughter with the thought that her present agitation was solely due to the sensation of strangeness in the sphere she was now moving in. The new situation she found herself plunged into by the recovery of her sight must necessarily awaken in her an uneasiness never felt before. She would, however, become as calm and contented as others, as soon as she had grown more accustomed to seeing. "I am glad to hear it", she replied, "for if I were always to feel such uneasiness as I do at present at the sight of new things, I would sooner return on the spot to my former blindness".'

(von Senden, pp. 160–1)

Beer (1783–1813)

'Among the most remarkable psychological phenomena presented to my observation in all the patients so far operated upon, is the rapid and complete loss of that striking and wonderful serenity which is characteristic only of those who have never yet seen; for hardly are the first lively sallies of their curiosity satisfied after the operation, than already they evince this striking transformation of their attitude. Gloomy and reserved, they now shun for a time the society of others, which was so indispensable to them while they were blind that they lamented every moment that they were obliged to spend without it.

'Might not the reason for this sudden and striking change of temper, indeed I might say of the whole character, be partly due, perhaps, to the fact that the patients have supposed all objects, which they could only get to know by feeling, when blind, to be quite different from what they subsequently see them to be; and might not also even a sort of injured pride contribute something to this transformation, in that they now suddenly find themselves so far behind other people of their age, even in the most trivial matters of knowledge? I fancy that in some at least, I have found traces of such a thing.'

(von Senden, p. 161)

Now it seems clear that S.B. had a similar crisis, starting at the time he left hospital, and not ending before his death.

Before the operation he was regarded by everybody as a cheerful rather dominant person, and we independently formed this opinion when we first saw him at the hospital. He seemed changed when he came to London; dispirited and bored. It seemed to all of us that he was deeply disturbed; yet too proud to admit or discuss it.

We give now two letters written to us by his wife, which give some insight into his mental condition at this time.

12 January 1959

Dear Mr Gregory,

Sorry to have kept you waiting for the enclosed drawings from my husband, but he is not at all well. He has been at home from work for the last six weeks with internal shingles and nerve pains, mostly in his right arm, hand and shoulder, also all underneath his arm and chest it is swollen with pain.

He has treatment continually from his doctor. It is the reaction no doubt, and he is not well enough to join you as you talked about when you were here.

He is very disappointed about everything. But when he feels better he says he will do more drawings for you when he is able. S. says Mr Hirtenstein is very pleased with the condition of his eyes. And he wishes you a very Happy Christmas and hopes to see you again soon.

Best wishes to Miss J. Wallace and yourself.

Signed : H.B.

The second letter we do not give quite in full because she has described part as confidential. (It does not add a great deal to the picture.)

8 June 1960

Dear Mr Gregory,

I was very sorry that Mr B. was not well enough to be at your lecture [a lecture given at the Christmas meeting of the British Psychological Society in London at which we had hoped he could be present] but he really wasn't fit to undertake the journey. He is not any better. I wish you could help him. His nerves are so bad. I can see his hands trembling, even as he ate porridge this morning, and he could not cut even sausages on his plate. He had a notice from National Health Ins. to see another Doctor, and I have been told it was a Psychiatrist. But instead of seeing him Mr B. signed off and went back to work. I think hospital rest would do him good. If he collapses again, I shall see what his doctor says, He (Mr B.) had been at home weeks, ill, having injections from his doctor and Codines and tablets, and has great pain in his right arm.

We shall be pleased to hear from you. I think it would be well not to mention this letter of mine. Mr B. needs the help, which I think you can give to him, but would not agree to my asking for it. I want to get him well again, as he was a cheerful help to me and lots of people, and he had great faith and patience, which has now gone. It seems to me our world is not grand as we thought and Mr B. did not know the way people acted – until he got his sight. I still think that the physical and mental ill-treatment which we have both endured years ago, before we met each other, have contributed a great deal towards his ill health. Some things best forgotten, but some people can be very cruel. [There follows a paragraph about S.B.'s present state which she describes as confidential] . . . but since last Sunday, he has sat listening to the wireless, in the evenings, content with the dog which makes a great fuss of him, S., as he does not get home until 5.30 p.m. from 7.0 a.m. and I can't imagine S. will manage to keep going at that rate.

Signed : H.B.

On 2 August 1960, S.B. died.

His story is in some ways tragic. He suffered one of the greatest handicaps, and yet he lived with energy and enthusiasm. When his handicap was apparently swept away, as by a miracle, he lost his peace and his self-respect.

We may feel disappointment at a private dream come true: S.B. found disappointment with what he took to be reality.

RELEVANCE TO THE THEORY OF PERCEPTION

The fact that we have attempted to make some sort of a study of a case of recovery from early blindness does not give us the right to attempt an authoritative statement as to the importance of such cases for the theory of perception. In thinking about this single case, however, the whole problem has been much in our minds and has inevitably led us to develop some opinions.

In 1949, Professor D. O. Hebb made a great deal of the cases assembled by von Senden, in his well-known book: *The Organization of Behaviour*. Indeed he regarded them as providing powerful evidence for the slow development of perception in infancy. 'We are not used,' he writes, 'to thinking of a single perception as slowly and painfully learned. . . . but it has already been seen, in the discussion of the congentially blind after operation, that it actually is' (Hebb, 1949, pp. 77–8). In the light of our experience with S.B., this inference strikes us as distinctly questionable. Is it really certain that what applies to perception after recovery of vision in the adult applies in essentially the same way to its normal growth in infancy?

First, what are the reasons for the slow recovery of vision in the adult patient? Hebb evidently believes that the situation of such a patient is essentially that of the child, with its normal perceptual development arrested until the eyes are opened. Although he is evidently aware of the 'emotional crisis' through which such patients commonly pass, he plainly does not regard reduced motivation as the principal cause of slowness in learning. Indeed he draws special attention to the fact that motivation is not disturbed in the first phase after operation, immediately upon beginning to use the eyes. He suggests, further, that the 'crisis of motivation' is due directly to the difficulty in achieving pattern vision, and is thus a direct response to the disheartening slowness with which perceptual skill is acquired.

But is it? In the case of S.B., the patient made extremely rapid progress after operation and very soon found that his vision was useful, as in telling the time. It did in fact change his way of life within a few weeks of the first operation and some progress continued for the next two years, until his death. It is true that he did not learn to read, and for this and many other reasons found himself handicapped in the world of sighted people. It is this sense of overall inadequacy, we suggest, rather than deficiency of pattern vision *per se*, which produced a crisis which lasted until the end.

Further, if emotional crisis is primarily a response to slowness in perceptual learning, why does it not occur in the normal child? It could of course be argued that the process is more difficult for the adult, but throughout Hebb argues that the position in the child is basically similar to that of the adult whose vision is restored at operation. Is this a tenable assumption? The adult, after all, has developed a 'touch world' which has served him well for many years, and which has become accepted as the principal vehicle of his occupational and social adaptation. The child, on the other hand, is concerned to develop a 'visual world' *ab initio*, and although tactile and motor activities contribute in an important way to its evolution, it is difficult to think of the two cases as in any real sense similar.

We find similar difficulties where Hebb tries to show that the perception of form is largely built upon patterns of eye movements (Hebb, 1949, pp. 84–91). Hebb takes as evidence here the reported fact that operated patients count the corners of polygons in order to name them, moving their eyes from corner to corner as a man might move his fingers in active touch. Yet can one really infer that the patient is reproducing the normal visual behaviour of the young child? First, there is no clear evidence that, in the acquisition of form perception, children really do scan the contours of objects or figures in the manner suggested by Hebb. And secondly, it would indeed be surprising if people who had lived for years without vision did not, at least at first, tend to 'touch' the salient features with their eyes – though one must bear in mind that ocular scanning is often severely disturbed by nystagmus. Although further study of the role of eye movements in the growth of form discrimination is evidently needed, it would appear *prima facie* unlikely that cases of the kind described in this study can tell us anything very significant about the normal development of perception in infancy.[1]

It is of course true that in nearly (though not quite) all these cases of recovery of vision after long-standing blindness the development of perceptual skill is very slow, even when considerable sight was present before operation. But this, we suggest, is due not to the fact that visual learning, whether in the child or the adult, is *inevitably* slow but to lack of practice in making appropriate use of the available input. It would seem that the difficulty is not so much in learning *per se* as in *changing perceptual habits and strategies from touching to seeing*. A not dissimilar phenomenon occurs in many cases with gradual loss of a sense or a limb; the patient will, at a certain stage, do better to abandon using the sense or limb altogether; to change his way of life to avoid and ignore it even if it is partly functional. In the event of some recovery of function, great difficulty may be experienced by the patient (and by those concerned with his rehabilitation) in inducing him to revert to the use of the impaired sense or limb. Indeed this may be one of the principal obstacles in the re-education of patients with any type of higher neurological disability.[2]

Another point of some interest in the present case is the relatively good intelligence and education of our patient, in which he resembles the patient reported by Latta (1904). Our patient, like Latta's, was much concerned while blind in trying to *visualize* the world and to know it as other men know it. One might even say that their attempt

---

[1] The same objections apply, *mutatis mutandis*, to arguments from studies such as those of A. H. Riesen (see, e.g., his chapter 'Plasticity of behaviour' in *Biological and Biochemical Bases of Behaviour*, edited by H. F. Harlow and C. N. Woolsey, Wisconsin, 1958) on bringing up animals in darkness and then studying their behaviour as adults after exposure to light. Studies of this kind are of course important in so far as they throw light on arrested development and its *sequelae* but it is doubtful whether inferences regarding normal development can properly be based upon them.

[2] See, e.g., Goldstein (1932).

to see was made long before their eyes were opened to the light, and in this respect they differ not only from most other cases in the literature but also of course from infants.

The findings that S.B.'s visual space was not disturbed by the geometrical–optical illusions, and that apparent depth was not evoked by perspective drawings, show that his spatial organization was far from normal. Since investigating the case, we have devoted considerable thought to the origin of these illusions and have arrived at the tentative view that they depend upon inappropriate scaling by the mechanism which produces size-constancy. If this should prove correct, it may be surmised that the figures failed to evoke constancy size-scaling in our patient, either through lack of early learning or maturational defect. It would seem of some importance, therefore, to devote attention to the study of these illusions in children with special reference to the development of size constancy.

Perhaps the most important outcome of our study is the evidence it provides for *transfer from early touch experience to vision many years later*. The fact that our patient was able, certainly with a minimum of training – and perhaps with none at all – to recognize by vision upper case letters which he had learned by touch, and that he was *unable* to recognize by vision lower case letters which he had *not* learned by touch, provides strong evidence for cross-modal transfer. It will be borne in mind, too, that it took him many months to learn to recognize by vision letters which he had *not* previously learned by touch. One may point out that the 'control' provided by the lower-case letters is vital to the argument, since we can never wholly rule out the possibility of some residual vision (undoubtedly present in this case). The fact that S.B. could recognize the figures in the Ishihara Plates (perhaps the most surprising observation we made) gives evidence of transfer and, incidentally, renders it most unlikely that the *modus operandi* of transfer lies in identity of motor patterns (i.e. patterns of eye-movement corresponding with patterns of active touch). As has been said, gross observation of eye-movements, which consisted in large and apparently uncontrolled jerks resembling exaggerated saccades, made it impossible to believe that the patient could follow outlines of relatively small figures, such as the Ishihara digits, by controlled movements of the eyes.

We may conclude that this case does provide evidence of transfer of perceptual information from the tactual sphere to the visual modality.[1] This seems somewhat at variance with the evidence from

[1] Professor D. O. Hebb has suggested to us that the surprising degree of cross-modal transfer which we ascertained in this case may have been due to the amount of vision available to the patient in early infancy. (Hebb, personal communication, 1961).

studies of cross-modal transfer in animals[1] and we can only speculate as to the reasons for the discrepancy. It may be that language is the decisive factor.

In our view, these cases tell us little about the classical philosophical problems of the nature of perceived space. We cannot sustain the view that these cases provide windows through which we may see the perceptual system of the infant – they are not living fossils in which the past is re-enacted. We studied an adult with a unique past; what we found was the effect of this past on a normal brain. We did not find the brain or the perceptual system of an infant and we learned little or nothing about the normal development of vision. At the same time, we believe that our case has demonstrated the impact of visual experience on a man to all intents and purposes long blind, and the gains and losses which this revelation brought in its wake. We have ascertained that vision, although it may prove genuinely useful to the man long blind, is at the same time a potential source of grievous hurt. We have further ascertained that, in such a case, direct transfer of information from patterns of touch to equivalent visual patterns is almost certainly possible. This may be the basis of the unique power of the human brain to reach truth through symbols.

APPENDIX

Correspondence on the case

A correspondence took place between Mr Hirtenstein, Dr von Senden (who is still interested in the problem though he has not been active in the field for many years)[2], and ourselves. Since quite a number of points arise in the correspondence we include it here, publishing the letters in full except for small passages, of a conventional nature, which would not be of general interest.

First we have a letter from Dr von Senden to Mr Hirtenstein, dated 14 May 1959. This letter has several points of interest. It gives Dr von Senden's reaction to the newspaper accounts of the case. Since Dr von Senden quotes the relevant passages we do not give them separately here.

---

[1] G. Ettlinger (1960), and D. Burton and G. Ettlinger (1960).
[2] At Dr von Senden's request, a few minor alterations in phraseology have been made to improve his already excellent English.

14 May 1959

Dear Dr Hirtenstein,

I still have to thank you for your kind lines of the 3rd February. Some days before Miss Schweppe had already sent to me a copy of your letter to her of the 16th January which was especially important, since you had written to her: 'He had no difficulty in recognising shapes, faces and objects with which he was tactually familiar whilst blind. This he explains by saying that he had a very accurate mental picture of things he could feel.'

If he used the word 'picture' it is the question whether he used it like other blinds do without an idea what this word means to the seeing person, or with an at least partially influenced by visual experiences, conception of space and shape.

With regard to the hand movements which he could perceive prior to operation on the last operated eye, he will have perceived them only as a change of more or less light, without a change of 'direction'. But if you write that he had an accurate light projection on the first operated eye then he must have had to my opinion also a certain idea of a visual 'direction', that a light can change this direction independent of his own behaviour. And if you have moved the light beyond the reach of his arm he could get conscious of the fact that visual objects cause sensations to the visual organ without touching it, that they are remote in a 'space', this otherwise being inconceivable for the blind. He *can* have possessed even a certain ability to discern some colour shades, e.g. the difference of the normal eye-lid grey of a closed eye from some more yellow or brown or even red shades.

In this regard I would like to know (a) whether your patient had a nystagmus ante operation, (b) how he had pointed out before operation the different positions of the light, by following it with the whole head or by showing at it with his arm?

When the journalist of the *Daily Express* interviewed him Mr B. told him with regard to his wife: 'She was just as bonny as I thought she would be. My wife had given me a word picture of what the world was like and I found out that buses I travelled on and cars looked just as I imagined. Lorries seemed very strange.' Here the word 'picture' seems to have no optical component. Therefore, I presume that the 'mental picture' as well as the 'word picture' means what I have called in my book the tactual schema. Mr B. had no doubt compared before operation, e.g. his own rather tall figure with that of his wife by feeling. The result of this feeling act could be with regard to his wife 'long and thin' or 'short and roundish'. I find it not so astonishing that the first visual impression which he got of his wife confirmed in his mind anyhow this gross tactual schema; especially if he has had at this moment already a certain experience in the interpretation of visual impressions, if his wife has not been among the very first 'objects' presented to his new sense.

In the meantime, Mr Merrick Winn of the *Daily Express* has published a series of articles after having spent 10 days with Mr B., together with Mr R. L. Gregory and Miss Jean Wallace of the University of Cambridge, two months after his first act of seeing. I have no idea how Mr Winn has attained his very dissolving pictures which shall adequately show how your patient could really see at this period, according to the physiological status of his eyes. But if he could get indeed no sharper images from the visual things I find therein a confirmation of my standpoint that he *could* get at the first aspect of his wife no more than confirmation of his tactual schema 'long and thin' or 'short and round'.

In virtue of my examination of 66 cases of operated blind-born patients described in the literature I had come to the conclusion that a blindborn – by means of his tactual sensations – can neither get an idea of the deep space nor a conception of the shape of things, which one can reasonably design as such, and that he will get post-operation this spatial idea immediately but the comprehension of shape only after a more or less long lasting learn process. On reading the publications about your case one has the impression as if space *and* shape were (so to say) presented to him without his doing in his first act of vision, in spite of his very distracted vision. If this would be true one could only wonder why Mr B. should show such an antipathy against any practical use of his new sense; if it comes not from an anxiety for eventual consequences for his economical life (e.g. loss of a pension).

Very significant in the report of Mr Winn was the matter with a fork: 'I'd pick up a fork, feel it and remembering how a fork felt when I was blind I could say: 'This is a fork'. Then I had to learn to remember it the next time I saw it.' Without feeling the corresponding visual object before he cannot say what it is. I dare suppose that it was a similar proceeding in your tests with him: a visual aspect, a feeling act for control, say what it is and then impress the visual image upon his mind ('learn to remember it the next time'.) You seem to have wondered how quickly this proceeding had a good success with Mr B. But according to the report of Mr Winn he must have had still infinite difficulties in this later period of his learning to see.

Mr Winn describes your patient as a cheerful, very good-natured and courteous man – which is confirmed by the picture of Mr B. in the *Daily Express* – who likes to do any favour to his fellow-creatures if he can. Since you – and probably some other surgeons – had made all imaginable efforts with him and had to surmount so many obstacles for about 3 years he felt a deep gratitude for you and had the best will not to undeceive you. Therefore he showed during your tests full interest and full energy to support your efforts by his own efforts 'to learn to remember as soon as possible the visual images, and tried to declare to you his success in his regard by his "mental pictures".' When Mr Winn spared no pains with him and was rather disappointed at the end Mr B. was in the same crisis which is reported in nearly all cases and which can be surmounted only by full moral energy of the patient.

After all I have not the impression that it has been really of visual cognising of a former tactually gained 'mental picture' or 'word picture', but a confirmation of a tactual schema after feeling control of the respective visual object.

The first visual object he caught sight of was your face of which he could not have a 'mental picture'. In this regard he has told Mr Winn 'I saw a dark shape with a bump sticking out and heard a voice, so I felt my nose and guessed the bump was a nose. Then I knew if this was a nose I was seeing a face'. I find this description very exact and conclusive. Above all it has been his consciousness of the situation which led him, which generally is highly developed in all blind persons. He knew your voice already before the operation, when he heard it post-operational close to him the situation was quite clear for him. If you use perhaps a well-scented hairwater this would have been a further confirmation for him. The first visual impression which excited his reflection (probably as being the nearest and the lightest object) was the 'bump' in the middle of a darker surface which he called 'shape' as he knew this word pre-operatively from a seeing person. He knew that a nose is 'in the middle of a face', asked himself whether this bump could be a nose, controlled his doubt by feeling his own nose. But even then he felt not quite sure but 'guessed' that it was indeed a nose, and concluded that the whole surface (if his guessing was right) must be your face. Thus the seeing of the 'bump' was not a *recognising* of a 'mental picture' 'nose' but partially a knowledge of the situation, partially a real seeing act, partially a controlling tactual proceeding and for the rest a mental conclusion.

Now Miss Schweppe and the publisher of the English translation mean that there is an essential contrast between the declaration of your patient with regard to the 'mental picture' and the conclusion in my book that a man born blind cannot get any kind of a shape-conception. Therefore she has suggested to me that I should (1) ask Mr B. himself by letter, (2) declare in the Preface of the English edition of my book for which reason the result of your investigations is such a contrast to my own conclusions.

(Ad 1) I cannot image that Mr B. would be delighted to receive a letter from an unknown foreigner or could be encouraged thereby in his efforts to improve his vision. I am afraid indeed to increase by my questions his feeling of embarrassment and misery. And if he would be inclined to reply then I must doubt whether his declarations will have a greater value, since he scarcely can understand the special point of my questions. In this respect it would be a more promising way if you – having his full confidence – would try to elucidate this contrast, if you believe that this would be possible and if you have the time for it.

(Ad 2) I have only tried to evaluate in my book the reports of those who have executed such an operation on a man born blind without having myself an occasion to occupy myself with such a blindborn, neither before nor after an operation. Therefore I feel myself not competent enough to express an opinion with regard to your case of which I know too little, and would do it only if you mean that it would be favourable to mention your case in the Preface.

Nevertheless you will understand that it is my personal interest to clear up this seeming contrast resp. to hear your opinion about it. This is the principal purpose of my letter. Therefore I beg your pardon if I have still some more questions:

1. How long have you occupied yourself with Mr B. before the first operation? Have you had an opportunity to examine whether he has had more than a mere knowledge about space and shape, as communicated to the blind by seeing persons?

2. What has happened in the 3 weeks between the first and the second operation with regard to the training of his seeing? It is mentioned somewhere that your patient has visited other patients within the hospital and has walked about in the hospital garden in this period. Has he made his experiences under control or without it?

3. In your letter to me you write that the psychological aspect following the operation (the second op.?) was investigated by Mr R. L. Gregory of Cambridge University. In this respect I would like to know how long after the operation Mr Gregory has seen your patient the first time. Had you given him information before the operation or was he induced only by the first notice in the *Daily Telegraph*? Was it possible in your opinion to reconstruct at that moment truly the whole development of his learning to see? I have the impression that Mr Gregory cannot say out much more than Mr Winn in his press articles.

I am regretting, dear Mr Hirtenstein that this letter has become so long and that I waste your time immoderately. But I would be very obliged to you for a reply which can be so much shorter. If you want to read the conclusions of my book in English please ask Miss Schweppe to send them to you. For I believe that the contrast is only in the words but not in the real state of your case, as I have tried to explain above.

Signed : M. von Senden.

Secondly, we have Mr Hirtenstein's reply to the letter quoted above, dated 24th November, 1959. This letter gives several details concerning both the eyes and also S.B.'s visual ability as observed by Mr Hirtenstein.

24 November 1959

Dear Dr von Senden,

I apologise for not having written to you sooner, but your letter dated 14 May never reached me, and I have just received a copy of it from Miss Schweppe.[1]

As to your questions :—

1. S.B. had no nystagmus before or after the operation.

2. The light projection before the operation was tested by a pencil-light, and the patient indicated with his hand from which direction the source of light came. This was quite accurate in his case, with both eyes. Moreover, trans-scleral retinal stimulation produced a clear pattern of retinal vessels subjectively, and this was the main reason that I decided to operate on him.

3. S.B. was referred to me by a fellow-ophthalmologist, and

---

[1] Miss Sylvia Schweppe, of the British Museum, was instrumental in arranging for Dr von Senden's book to be translated into English and published. The story of how she managed to find a micro-film copy of the German – the publisher's copies were destroyed by Allied bombing – and how she overcame other difficulties is quite remarkable.

I knew the patient for a few weeks prior to his first operation. I had no means of testing him about space and shape of objects before the operation.

4. As soon as the operated eye was uncovered after the first operation, the patient's ability to assimilate new visual sensations was truly remarkable. He was able to learn colours quickly and recognise simple objects with which he was familiar through tactile sensation, (chairs, tables, doors, etc.). He walked through the Hospital corridors without difficulty, and avoided objects and subjects in his path. It is interesting that his visual re-education still continues; every time I see him in my Out-patient Department he seems to be more confident in his walking and ability to 'get around' generally. He now travels a consider-able distance by train and bus to visit me at the Hospital from his home.

5. Mr Gregory saw the patient only after the second opera-tion; he learnt about the case from the daily newspapers, and I invited him to examine S.B. whilst still in the hospital. He spent a considerable time with the patient, and he is just about to publish his findings. I think it would be perhaps worthwhile for you to get in touch with him, as he would, I'm sure, give you all the information you require about this case.

Signed : A. Hirtenstein.

Thirdly, we give extracts from a letter written by one of us to Dr von Senden. We include it here because it gives an account of our general impression of S.B. at that time (November 1959) before later events had a chance to change and perhaps dull our impressions. (This letter was written before we had read Dr von Senden's book, though we knew of his work and had read accounts of it.)

30 November 1959.

Dear Professor von Senden,

We found that S.B. has a strong personality, and is not suggestible.

He had difficulty in naming some colours, in particular yellow, but could name most objects and judge distances accurately. He made very little from pictures, or large clear colour photo-graphs projected on a screen.

We gave him a large number of perceptual tests, including

reversible figures (the Necker cube for example) and we also gave him the Ishihara colour test. This produced a most interesting result, for he was able to read correctly every one of the numbers represented by the coloured dots seen by normal observers. What struck us was not so much that his colour discrimination was normal on this test, as that he was able to recognise block letters and figures already known tactually, and it is quite clear that this knowledge had transferred to sight without special learning being required. This was the most definite and the most striking finding of our examination.

He did not seem to get any depth from perspective drawings, or to get reversals of Necker cubes, although his visual acuity was probably adequate. (It is worth pointing out that one can get reversals of Necker cubes when the retinal image is degenerated by viewing through highly astigmatic lenses.)

The patient showed no nystagmus at any time I examined him. His eye movements were far from normal, however, for his 'searching' or 'scanning' movements were infrequent. He did not look round to the source of a noise anything like as often as normal, and he did not look at people's faces. He could however recognise people by the way they moved and from their clothes, or so he informed me.

As for the 'psychological' reason why he became upset after the operation, my own opinion is that while blind he had managed exceptionally well. He went for bicycle rides with companions; he tended his garden and was something of a craftsman. Once he regained his sight, he felt, I think, up against the competition of sighted people. Further, he had throughout his life been treated with special consideration by his family and friends. After the operation this became modified. To his workmates he became something extraordinary and they would play small jokes on him. He must feel that by being blind for more than 50 years he has lost a great deal, not only sensory experience, but perhaps more important the chance of holding an interesting and well paid job. One must remember that he is an intelligent man with a strong personality. He would undoubtedly have risen above the social position into which he was born if he had not been handicapped, and he must realise this. I should add that this last point was not made explicitly by him; I give it as a reasonable inference from the evidence which is available to me.

With regard to his first 'perception' of the surgeon: he told me that the newspaper account was wrong. His account is that he heard Mr Hirtenstein's face and looking toward him (by sound) 'saw' a confusion of colours, and knew that this must be Mr Hirtenstein's face. (He may, of course, have been wearing a mask). He was able, within hours, to name many objects correctly, and would get up early in the morning to watch cars passing on the street below.

He tended to misjudge the size of objects he had not been able to touch or walk along. For example, a bus looked too high but the right length.

Signed : R. L. Gregory.

Before replying to this letter, Dr von Senden wrote to the Editor responsible for the English translation of his book *Space and Sight* commenting on a report of our case appearing in the *Daily Express*.

12 December 1959

According to the first short report of the *Daily Express* of the 7th January, 1959, Mr B. had told his interviewer that his wife 'was just as bonny as I thought she would be. My wife had given me a word picture of what the world was like and I found out that buses I travelled on and cars looked just as I imagined' . . . 'When the doctor removed the pad I could see his black hair and his face.'

People who read those lines were glad that learning to see apparently was a rather simple affair. But those who knew my book were surprised, having the impression that these assertions of Mr B. were contradictory to the conclusions which I had drawn from my studying all comparable cases reported in the literature.

The question is how the words of Mr B. must be interpreted, whether the circumstances he tried to express with these words corresponded with the signification which seeing people adjudge to them. A person born blind learns all words of his language from seeing persons but cannot know which sensual or mental content they have for a seeing person. He uses all these words indeed, but as a seeing person cannot explain to a blind one much about things, a blind person cannot explain exactly (by means of the words of the seeing world) to a seeing person what occurs to him in his daily life. The same words have a different sense for these two categories of human creatures.

As Mr Hirtenstein – who has executed the two operations on him – wrote to me he has 'had no means of testing him about space and shape of objects before the operation'. According to him the patient had a very poor vision but could indicate before the operation accurately the direction of a little pencil light with his hand! This fact indicates that Mr B. has had already before operation a certain idea of a visual 'direction'; he had been aware that a light can change this direction independent of his own behaviour, how it is when a light 'moves'. Thus he must (or at least could) have become conscious pre-operatively of the fact that visual objects cause sensations to the visual organ without any participation of the sense of touch, and could conclude that they are remote in a deep 'space'. Therefore we may say that 'space' was nothing fundamentally new to him before operation. As I have shown in my book every operated blindborn has the space immediately post-operatively without any education for this purpose, but B. has had it already earlier.

When Mr Gregory – as he wrote to me the other day – asked him later how it really has been when he used his new sight for the first time after the operation he has answered that the newspaper account was wrong! His own account is that he 'heard Mr Hirtenstein's voice, and looking toward him (by sound) 'saw' a confusion of colours, and knew that this must be Mr Hirtenstein's face' (who may, of course, have been wearing a mask in this moment). This description is quite analogous to all other descriptions in the literature, as mentioned in my book.

This report of Mr Gregory is very interesting indeed also in many other points. But as he intends to publish something about this case I don't want to anticipate him. But as he has accompanied Mr Winn and Mr B. for several days during their stay in London I like to allude to the remark in the very fine report in the *Daily Express* (two months after the operation) where Mr Winn says: 'S.B. was still basically a blind man. He could see but did not care. All this time he had been "seeing" largely not to let us down'; and on another spot: 'He never knew my face properly in all these 10 days we were together but he knew me instantly by my voice, clothes, walk, even breathing'. Therefore I agree with Mr Hirtenstein and do not wonder if he writes that B. 'was able to learn colours quickly and recognise simple objects with which he was familiar through tactile sensation (chairs, tables, doors, etc.)'. But I am sure that in these acts of 'recognising' sight was participating only a very little. A hospital room contains only a small number of furniture objects. An intelligent blind man like Mr B. has no difficulty in building up for his own use the tactual schema of the room within the first 24 hours. He can exactly indicate then where the different objects are, which name they have, etc. And if 'he walked through the Hospital corridors without difficulty and avoided objects and subjects in his path' there is nothing extraordinary in this, especially if we remember that during the $3\frac{1}{2}$ weeks between the two operations he could attain any kind of visual experiences without a scientific control, that he walked alone in the garden and had passed the Christmas days in his own home.

With regard to his assertion that his wife was 'as bonny as I thought she would be' I may remark that this word 'bonny' to my opinion has no component of space or shape. It merely signifies that the aspect as well as the tactile feeling causes agreeable sensations. B. himself declared to Mr Winn: 'I always felt in my own way that women were lovely, but now I can see them I think they're ugly'. Also for this 'lovely feeling' we have parallels in some other cases.

Concerning the bus I can imagine that he has had indeed a certain conception of it pre-operatively. When he awaited (very very often in his long life) on the halting-place of his bus he could *hear* the typical rolling noise of the arriving vehicle and that this noise ceased together with the stopping of the bus; he could *see* that the diffused brightness surrounding his eyes before the arrival of the bus was darkened when it is quite near to him and that the brightness eventually reappeared when the bus had passed his place; and he could *number* how long the light was darkened by the outrolling bus. Having got these three different dates and correlating them to each other he could have got to a certain degree the idea what it means what seeing people call the 'movement' of a vehicle, what seeing people call the 'length' of an object, and that one can measure 'breadth' and 'height' on a similar way. Thus he could imagine already pre-operatively a 'mental picture' of a bus. But it is quite clear that in the forming of this or other 'mental pictures' the visual sense has participated a great deal.

Therefore I am sure that this case is not fundamentally different from the other known cases, and that this case does not alter the conclusions in my book.

Signed : M. von Senden.

The relevant parts of Dr von Senden's reply to my letter of 30.11.59 were as follows :—

14 December 1959

Dear Mr Gregory,

What has equally struck me as yourself is your test with the block letters and numbers. Had anybody punched out them for his personal use in wood or some other material? Block letters and numbers have indeed a very pregnant form and are easily distinguishable from each other. Also in this regard it would be very interesting to ask him anew how he has proceeded to transfer from touch to vision. Have you observed perhaps that he has made some movements with his finger-tips as if he followed out mentally (perhaps with closed eyes) the outlines of the block letters which he saw and recognized their name by controlling the well known tactual sequence of the resp. letter?

Very interesting also are his drawings. What order had he got when he made these drawings? Was he to draw for instance a table out of memory as a proof for the 'word picture' which he had affirmed to possess from touch? Or was he drawing an object he could see in this moment?[1]

In any case I may assure you that I shall be very pleased to read some day your publication about this case, don't forget it please!

Signed : M. von Senden

We have presented all the evidence available at this time, and it is now unlikely that more will ever be learned. We hope that the material has been presented in a form which makes it possible for the reader to form his own opinions as to what, if anything, this and other cases can contribute to our understanding of human perception and its development.

We feel privileged to have had the opportunity of studying this case, and feel grateful to all those – including S.B. – who made it possible.

---

[1] As described above his drawings were from memory, and some were of objects he had never seen, especially the chipping hammer.

4 *Blinking during visual tracking*

[We turn now to other matters. We also turn back in time, to the first experimental papers in which I was involved. In 1950 I became a research worker in the Medical Research Council Applied Psychology Unit, which at that time was housed in the University Department of Psychology at Cambridge. The Director of the M.R.C. Unit was the late Professor Sir Frederic Bartlett, F.R.S. He was a great man, wise and kindly, with the ability to impart importance to ideas, observations and everyday events. He commanded a respect which is undiminished. My immediate boss was Dr N. H. Mackworth, who later became Director of the Unit. Norman Mackworth was – and is – a first-rate experimentalist. Unfortunately I never worked with him directly, but he always gave me every encouragement. He arranged for me to be seconded to the Royal Navy for a year, to work on psychological problems of escaping from submarines. This followed the mysterious disaster of the submarine *Affray* in which all lives were lost.

I worked at the Royal Naval Physiological Laboratory, near Portsmouth, learning about submarine life by practical experience. We carried out tests under controlled atmospheric conditions, with the laboratory's large pressure chamber. This involved building dummy escape gear with all the controls, and led to my designing and building the printing recorder, described on p. 406. The investigation itself will not be described here.

The following paper was essentially the idea and the work of Dr E. C. Poulton. Christopher Poulton is now Assistant Director of the M.R.C. A.P.U. The problem of how often, and when, the eyes blink during a maintained task may seem prosaic. It originated from a purely practical problem connected with pilots possibly missing vital events during blinks, but it turned out to have more general implications and to be surprisingly interesting. It became clear that normal blinking is not initiated by afferent stimuli, such as the corneas drying. Blinking is centrally innervated. Blink rate appeared to be related to general psychological states, especially to degree of concentration, or attention, on a task in hand. This made it possible that blink rate could be used as a useful index of such difficult things to estimate as 'amount of attention' paid to a task, such as flying or driving.]

★   ★   ★

M OST of the previous work upon blinking has been concerned with the effect of various tasks upon the blink rate. They have recently been summarized by Drew (1950). Lawson (1948), however, has produced evidence that blinking can interfere with the performance of tasks requiring constant visual attention, as for example in certain radioactive measurements where small flashes of light are counted. He suggested that blinking may be 'a primary cause of proneness to accident' in driving and flying.

The present experiments were primarily concerned with the effect of blinking upon performance. This required elaborate recording, to determine the exact level of performance immediately after blinking; an analysis of the nature of the task, for it was to be expected that the effect of blinking would be more marked when anticipation was not possible; and an investigation into the nature of the effect. The effect might be purely one of interference with vision, as Lawson assumed (1948); or might be due partly to the blinking response competing with the responses required of the subject by the task; or blinking and poor performance might be associated simply because both were associated with inattention. In the latter case the inattention would be the cause of both the blinking and the poor performance, there being no direct causal association between them.

METHOD

Main blink experiment

This was designed and carried out to determine the effect of blinking upon tracking performance. The blinks were recorded both with an electromyograph and by two observers. The electromyograph consisted of an E.E.G.-type direct-coupled amplifier feeding an electromagnetic ink-writing oscillograph. Electrodes were fixed with adhesive tape above and below the left eye, and a third earthed electrode was clipped to the lobe of the left ear. There was no evidence of irritation from the electrodes, and movements were not hampered. The blinks were also recorded on the same paper record by two observers in the next room who watched the subject through peepholes. The subjects were told that their 'brain waves' were to be measured. No reference to blinking was made in their presence, and they were unaware of the observers.

The subject's task was to follow a track with a ball-pointed pen lying in a slot across a horizontal paper tape moving from left to right in front of them at 1 in. per second. The track was a heavy black line drawn in indian ink by a mechanically-driven pen which described simple or complex harmonic courses. The number of harmonic components was changed by switching four motors situated in the next room.

A continuous record was obtained for each subject. On the same paper tape were recorded the following: (1) the harmonic course line, (2) the line drawn by the subject while following the course – the size and nature of his errors could be determined by measuring the differences between these, (3) blinks as recorded by the electromyograph – from this record the temporal position of the blinks in relation to the course could be accurately determined, (4) blinks as observed by the two observers in the next room – these two records ensured that the electronic equipment was recording blinks and nothing but blinks, and (5) a time-marker – this made a special constant-speed control of the tape-driven motor unnecessary.

The subject was unable to see any of the pens, or the records traced by them, excepting only the course line. The horizontal slit along which he moved his pen while following the course was 3·0 mm wide, and was formed by two perspex bars each 10·0 mm wide. He had a preview of the course for 10.5 seconds right up to his pen. This preview could be screened from him.

Procedure The various experimental conditions were: (1) an almost straight course to be tracked with 10·5 seconds preview, and (2) the same course with no preview – the course was actually a simple harmonic with a periodicity of 2 cycles per minute and an amplitude of 7·5 mm, (3) a predictable simple-harmonic course (periodicity 25 cycles per minute, amplitude 15·0 mm) with no preview, (4) a less predictable complex-harmonic course with 10·5 seconds preview, and (5) the same course with no preview. (The complex-harmonic course was produced by two equal-sized harmonic displacements of 21 and 14 cycles per minute, and a 25-cycle per minute displacement of twice this size. Its total amplitude was 30·0 mm). The five conditions were arranged in Latin Square form with 15 subjects.

The experiment started with a rest period lasting 2·0 minutes, before which the subject was told to relax, 'while the machine is being tested out.' This was followed by a pause during which the experimenter changed the roll of paper and gave the subject his final instructions, namely that he would have to track continuously for 20 minutes, that the course and the length of view ahead would change from time to time, but that he was not to stop for an instant. This latter point was emphasized, for it was found in pilot experiments that if he was allowed to pause every two or three minutes, his blinking was practically confined to these points.

While he waited, pen in hand, to begin tracking, blinks were recorded for half a minute while the course was still kept covered. Blinks were thus recorded while he was expecting the task to begin. The course was then uncovered, and he received five one-minute practice periods without a break between them. In the test proper, which immediately followed the practice periods, he tracked under each of the five conditions already practised, for periods lasting three minutes, again without a break.

At the end of this 20-minute period of continuous tracking, the experimenter covered the course and told the subject to put down his pen and relax. However, his blinks were recorded for a further half-minute. A pause of about one minute followed; there was then a final two-minute rest period in which blinks were recorded.

Scoring The total number of blinks scored was 2,400. Each observer missed about 6 per cent. (Neither observer knew when the other pressed his key, for auditory cues were masked by the noise of the course motors, which were situated in the observers' room). In determining the effect of blinking, only the first eight blinks produced by each subject under each experimental condition were counted. By limiting each subject's contribution, the results of those who blinked relatively infrequently were not swamped by those with high blink rates.

The errors were measured 0·5 seconds before each blink, at the time of the blink, and 0·5 and 1·0 second after it. The errors were classified as 'large' when 4·0 mm or greater, and 'small' when less than 4·0 mm. In each case the number of 'large' errors was compared with the corresponding figure derived from matched control times.

In determining the exact time of each blink with respect to the course, the complex-harmonic course was divided into half-cycles, extending in each case from an apex to the adjoining trough. These half-cycles were classified according to the amplitude of movement as 'large' if greater than 15·0 mm and 'small' if 15·0 mm or less.

Further, each half-cycle of both the simple- and complex-harmonic course was divided into six equal sections of approximately 0·2 seconds each.

The records were also scored to test two hypotheses as to the nature of the subject's decisions during his blink 'blackouts'. The first hypothesis was that he ceased initiating all movement during the 'blackout'. This hypothesis was tested by measuring the error which would have occurred 0·5 seconds after each blink, had he stopped his pen movement one reaction-time (0·25 seconds) after the start of the blink, for the duration of his 'blackout' (a further 0·25 seconds). The second hypothesis was that he ceased initiating any new movement during the 'blackout', and that he consequently maintained the same speed of movement for a period of 0·25 seconds, beginning one reaction-time after the start of the blink.

Subsidiary blink experiment

This was to determine the length of time for which the subject had to track before his blink rate rose to a more or less constant level. The experimental layout and procedure were the same as those described above, except for two modifications. First there were two experimenters in the room with the subject and no other observers. One of the two experimenters watched him while he was tracking, and recorded his blinks behind a screen in pencil upon the graphic record. This was the only check upon the electromyograph. There was no suggestion that any subject was aware that his blinks were being recorded while he was tracking.

The second difference was that the same rapid complex-harmonic course, and the same length of preview (0·1 seconds) were used throughout the experiment. The course was produced by three electric motors in the same room as the subject (which gave equal-sized harmonic displacements of 50, 14 and 6 cycles per minute). There were 11 subjects.

Mechanical 'blackout' and voluntary-blink experiment

This was designed to determine the effect upon tracking of interference with vision of about the same duration as the blink 'blackout', and to compare this effect with the effect of voluntary blinks. The experimental apparatus was the same as that used in the 'blackout' tracking method described by Poulton (1952b). The subject had to keep a pointer, operated by a positional control, in line with a 'stimulus' pointer which moved in a single vertical dimension in a simple-harmonic or complex-harmonic course. The display was viewed through a screened rotating clear disc. Over this, segments of black paper could be placed, so that the display could be occluded for intermittent short periods.

The mean size of the error when the subject tracked with a clear view of the display was compared with his mean error when the display was 'blacked out' about 50 times per minute for 0·05, 0·25, 0·40 and 0·55 seconds respectively. In a further experimental period he had to track while blinking voluntarily at the same rate per minute. (These high rates were chosen in order to exaggerate the effects). The experiment was divided into two halves. Half the subjects started with the simple-harmonic course (of 25 cycles per minute). The rest started with the complex-harmonic course (produced by three equal-sized harmonic displacements of 14, 22·5 and 25 cycles per minute). The six experimental periods in each half were arranged in Latin Square form, with 12 subjects. Each period lasted one minute, but only the second half of it was scored.

Practice periods were given before each half. From these the rate of voluntary blinking was determined. The mechanical 'blackout' rate was equated with it, except in cases where it corresponded closely to the periodicity of the simple-harmonic course, when a slightly lower or higher rate was chosen. The subjects averaged 24·9 blinks in the second half-minute of the experimental blinking period with the simple-harmonic course, as against a mean mechanical 'blackout' rate of 25·0. With the complex-harmonic course they averaged 23·0 blinks as against a mean 23·3. The greatest individual discrepancy between blink rate and 'blackout' rate per half-minute was seven.

Subsidiary voluntary-blink experiment

This was carried out upon five comparable subjects, in order to relate the length of voluntary- and normal-blink 'blackouts'. None of the subjects knew the aim of the experiment, which was performed out of doors. One or two 30-second close-up ciné shots were taken of each of them separately, depending upon his rate of blinking, while the experimenter and photographer looked away and conversed. The subject looked into the near distance.

The subject was then given the same instructions about voluntary blinking as the subjects in the tracking experiment, and told to practice a few voluntary blinks. A further 30-second close-up ciné shot followed, while he blinked about once every 1·5 seconds, in time with the experimenter's conducting. The ciné camera was set at 16 frames-per-second throughout. The average number of frames per blink in which the experimenter judged that vision was completely obscured by the eyelids was then calculated for the normal- and voluntary-blink periods and compared.

INCIDENCE OF BLINKS

Expectancy

The mean number of blinks per minute before, during and after tracking in the main blink experiment was as follows:—

'Resting' before experiment..	17·6
Immediately before tracking	23·5
Tracking straight course	8·6
Tracking curved course	2·7
Immediately after tracking	41·6
'Resting' after experiment	21·6

All the means are significantly different at the 5 per cent point, some at the 0·1 per cent point.

The blink rate immediately before tracking was determined under conditions identical with the 'resting' blink rate, except that the subject held a pen in his hand, and knew he was about to start the experiment. Under these conditions the mean blink rate rose by about one-third.

It seems likely that many people show this more or less involuntary increase in blink rate when they are about to start a fairly arduous unfamiliar task. Changes in blink rate may thus give some indication of 'anticipatory tension'.

Initial 'shock'

In the subsidiary blink experiment the mean number of blinks per minute for the first minute of tracking was 0·6. For the next three minutes it averaged 2·2, and from the fifth minute onward it averaged 3·3. These differences are significant at the 5 per cent point.

The initial low blink rate corresponds to the 'initial spurt' of many laboratory work-curves. A similar inverse association between blink rate and level of work as shown by the number of missed signals in successive half-hour periods of the Clock Test, will be seen to be present when a comparison is made between the work of Carpenter (1948) and Mackworth (1950), for the blink rate was relatively low in the first half-hour, when few signals are usually missed, and higher in the succeeding half-hours, when more signals are missed. Yet blinks never apparently coincided with missed signals. It seems likely therefore that the blink rate is inversely associated with the degree of 'concentration' or 'attention'. It may be possible to use it as an index of attention.

Level of work

It will be seen from the results reported above that as compared with the 'resting' blink rate before the experiment, the blink rate was halved while tracking an almost straight-line course. It was further reduced by a factor of 3 while tracking a curved course. Drew's (1950) findings were in general similar. This suggests that, in estimating the amount of time for which vision is obscured in visual tasks, it is misleading to use 'resting' blink rates, as has been done by Lawson (1948). In the present instance such a procedure would clearly be quite invalid.

It was also found that when the initial 'resting' blink rate of each subject was compared with his mean tracking blink rate, the product-moment correlation coefficient was only $+0.13$. This shows the small value of each subject's true 'resting' blink rate in predicting how much he will blink while tracking.

The corresponding correlation coefficient calculated from Drew's results was $+0.73$. This high value was associated with a rather low 'resting' blink rate, as compared with that found by us. This was probably because in Drew's experiment the 'resting' blink rate was estimated by an experimenter in the same room. We found that when observed under such conditions, subjects tended to fixate objects for rather longer than they would have done otherwise, and so to blink rather less frequently. Some constraint was clearly being placed upon them. The 'resting' and tracking conditions were thus not so different. Drew's results suggest that a better prediction of the tracking blink rate could be made from the 'resting' blink rate if measured while subjects were aware that they were being observed, although not, of course, aware that blink rate was being measured.

Temporary restraint

With the complex-harmonic course 62 per cent of the blinks occurred during small amplitude half-cycles and only 38 per cent during large. The expected values were 48 and 52 per cent respectively, the difference being highly significant. Further, for all three conditions of curved courses combined, 42 per cent of blinks occurred during the

0·4 seconds immediately preceding the apices and troughs (the points of zero speed of displacement) and only 25 per cent during the 0·4 seconds immediately following them. The expected frequency was in both cases 33 per cent, the difference being again highly significant.

Clearly subjects concentrated their blinks during or immediately before the easy parts of the course and tended to avoid blinking during or immediately before the more difficult parts.

Recovery

The mean blink rate immediately after tracking was two and one-third times as great as the 'resting' blink rate before the experiment. Over two minutes later the blink rate was still slightly but significantly raised.

The blink rates of the individual subjects after tracking correlated about $+0.80$ by the product-moment method with their initial resting rates. (Any value above $+0.51$ shows a significant correlation at the 5 per cent level of significance). Further, estimates of their 'blink deficits' accumulated while tracking correlated only about $+0.10$ with estimates of the rate at which these deficits were made good after tracking had been completed. Thus after tracking subjects merely showed an exaggeration of their initial 'resting' blink rate pattern. There was no straightforward relationship to the degree of blink deprivation.

EFFECT OF BLINKS

Nature of task

With the almost straight-line courses blinking had no effect upon tracking. This was so both when the subject was given a preview of the course of 10·5 seconds, and when he had no preview. However, with the curved courses, blinking did affect tracking. Fig. 4.1 shows the distributions of errors with the curved courses 0·5 seconds after blinking.

There was no difference between the error distribution 0·5 seconds before blinking and the control distributions, nor between the distributions at the time of blinking and the controls. Further, by 1·0 seconds after blinking the distributions of errors had returned to the control form, except in the case of the complex-harmonic course without preview, where there was still a predominance of errors of 6·0 mm and greater, which was significant at the 5 per cent point.

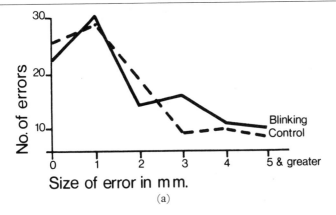

(a)

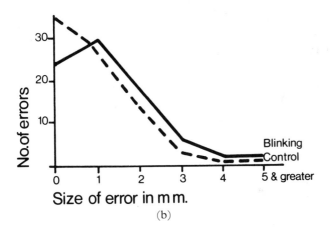

(b)

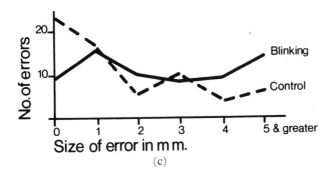

(c)

FIG. 4.1 *Errors following blinking grouped according to size. (a) Simple-harmonic course without preview. (b) Complex-harmonic course with preview. (c) Complex-harmonic course without preview. Continuous lines: errors 0·5 seconds after blinks. Broken lines: errors at comparable control times. The amplitude of movement of the simple-harmonic course was 15·0 mm, the total amplitude of the complex course 30·0 mm. The distributions in (a) and (b) are not significantly different. However those in (c) are significantly different at well beyond the 1 per cent point.*

Under all three conditions of curved courses, there were rather fewer small errors, and rather more large errors, 0·5 seconds after blinking than at the control times. However the difference was only significant for the complex-harmonic course without preview, when anticipation was reduced to a minimum. Where the subject was allowed a preview, and where the course was simple-harmonic and consequently completely predictable, anticipation was possible (Poulton, 1952a). It was only with the complex-harmonic course without preview that the subject had little idea of what the course was about to do next.

Several conclusions follow from these results. Blinking can have a detrimental effect upon a task such as tracking. However, it has no effect when the course is almost a straight line. It has a detrimental effect only upon a proportion of occasions even when the course is curved. And this effect is considerably reduced when either kind of anticipation is possible.

Timing of blinks

When the subject did not blink, he performed significantly less accurately during the 0·4 second period covering the point of inflexion of the course than during the 0·4 second periods on either side of the apex or trough. The criterion used in obtaining this result was the number of large errors (4 mm or greater) found in samples from all three conditions of curved courses combined. The result corresponds to the finding of previous experiments that within reasonable limits the tracking error varied directly with the speed of displacement (Poulton, 1952a), for the maximum speed of displacement occurs at the point of inflexion.

In contrast, 0·5 seconds after blinking the subject was found to be performing least accurately during the 0·4 second period immediately before the apex or the trough. Large errors following blinks were thus distributed in a significantly different way from those at the control times. When he did not blink, the 0·2 second period of the course showing the highest number of large errors was the period immediately beyond this.

This was to have been expected. The short but most difficult section of course on either side of the point of inflexion will normally result in a maximal error about one reaction time later, i.e. just before the subject is able to make a correction. Whereas a blink, depriving him of vital information at such a time, will delay his correction for a further period corresponding to the duration of his 'blackout', so that his maximal error will occur this much later. Thus the distribution of large errors following blinking will have its maximum rather later than the control distribution of large errors.

THE NATURE OF THE EFFECT

Interference with vision

The mean tracking error with different lengths of mechanical 'blackouts' is shown in Table 4.1, which shows also the effect of voluntary blinking at the same average rate per minute. It will be seen that the greater the length of the 'blackouts', the greater was the deterioration in performance with the complex-harmonic course. With the simple-harmonic course no deterioration was shown with mechanical 'blackouts', in this experiment. However, in a previous experiment on 12 subjects, a significant deterioration was found with this course also, although it was significantly less than with the complex-harmonic course.

These results with mechanical 'blackouts' correspond to the results following blinks described above. Both blinks and mechanical 'blackouts' of the same length produced deterioration in tracking moving courses. But in both cases the effect was less with simple-harmonic courses, which allow perceptual anticipation. This strongly suggests that at least part of the deterioration in tracking associated with blinking is due to interference with vision.

Competition between responses

Table 4.1 also shows the mean tracking error in the second part of the experiment, when subjects blinked voluntarily at the same rate per minute as the mechanical 'blackout' rate. It will be noted that these results are for voluntary blinks. Close-up ciné photographs suggested that in most subjects the voluntary blink 'blackout' is about 20 per cent longer than the normal 'blackout', a difference significant at the 5 per cent point.

With the simple-harmonic course the mean error with voluntary blinks was significantly greater than the error with mechanical 'blackouts' of 0·55 seconds. Yet this is the maximum average duration of the interference with vision caused by normal blinking (the sum of 'blackout' time and 'mobile vision' time – Lawson, 1948). The difference does not appear to be explicable simply upon the grounds that voluntary-blink 'blackouts' are generally of about 20 per cent longer duration than normal-blink 'blackouts'.

TABLE 4.1
EFFECT OF MECHANICAL 'BLACKOUTS' AND VOLUNTARY BLINKS
WHILE TRACKING

| | | *Mean error for* | |
		Simple-harmonic course	*Complex-harmonic course*
Duration of mechanical 'blackouts' (in seconds)	0·0	23	26
,,	0·05	19	24
,,	0·25	25	31
,,	0·40	22	35
,,	0·55	23	45
Voluntary blinks .. .. .. —		32	39

For 5 per cent significance, differences must be about 5. The level of error which would have occurred if the subject had not responded at all has been taken as 100.

It seems likely therefore that voluntary blinks can have an additional detrimental effect upon performance. This is presumably because attention is distracted from the task. Where normal blinking is a nervous habit, it may also have this distracting effect.

Inattention

As described above, the complex-harmonic course without preview, the experimental condition which showed the most marked deterioration 0·5 seconds after blinking, still showed a significant deterioration 1·0 second after blinking. This was due to 15 per cent of errors of 6 mm and greater. All these very large errors actually increased in size between 0·5 and 1·0 second after blinking.

On the assumption that the detrimental effect of blinking was due to interference with vision, and possibly competition between responses, it is to be expected that by 0·5 seconds after blinking the subjects would have been starting to correct the misalignment caused by blinking; and that by 1·0 second after blinking much of this correction would have occurred. That in these cases the error actually increased in size during this time suggests that blinking was accompanied by a lapse of attention.

This lapse of attention may in fact have been in some sense the cause of the blinking. However, there was no significant increase in error between 0·5 seconds before blinks and the times of the blinks themselves, as would be expected if attention had lapsed sometime before blinking occurred. It follows that in a task such as tracking, blinking may be the earliest sign of inattention.

On this view, the significant deterioration in tracking found 0·5 seconds after blinking could have been caused partly by the blinking, and partly by the inattention of which blinking was the earliest sign. The sequence of events would thus be as follows:—

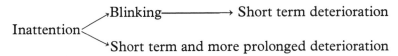

Inattention → Blinking ————→ Short term deterioration

Inattention → Short term and more prolonged deterioration

PERFORMANCE WHILE BLINKING

In order to throw light upon the nature of the subject's decisions during normal blink 'blackouts', theoretical errors were estimated for the three conditions under which he tracked curved courses, on two assumptions. These assumptions were: (1) that the subject ceased initiating all movement during the 'blackout' period, and (2) that he ceased initiating any new movement during this period, maintaining instead his initial speed of movement. In all cases the theoretical errors were much greater than the subject's actual errors. The constant-speed-of-movement hypothesis gave the less inaccurate approximation.

It seems clear that the subject must have been responding to an acceleration component of the course during his blink 'blackouts', as well as to a velocity component. He must in fact have been tracking an expected course during his 'blackouts'.

5 *Variations in blink rate during non-visual tasks*

[It seems that blink rate is related to attention in visual tasks. Is it, then, related to attention also in non-visual tasks? Could it, indeed, be used as an index for measuring general attention? Certainly this would be useful. It is important to know whether pilots lose attention during long flights, and perhaps warn them by a buzzer sounding when their attention fails. Actually this is not so simple a matter, even given a physiological index serving as a signal of lost attention – for he may be thinking, day-dreaming, perhaps, of other things and so defeat the index. Still, it seemed worth while to discover whether blink rate varied in non-visual tasks, including tasks similar to Poulton's visual tracking situation; so I repeated essentially the same experiment with *audio* tracking, and various other non-visual tasks requiring varying degrees of attention.]

★ ★ ★

IT has been found by a number of experimenters, for example, Ponder and Kennedy (1928), Carpenter (1948) and Drew (1950), that blink rate tends to vary with changing experimental conditions. This has suggested the possibility that blink rate might be used as an index of some general psychological unobservable, such as Attention or Effort.

Ponder and Kennedy were the first to deny that blinking is reflex; they showed that no afferent stimuli are necessary for normal blinking, and argue that it is probably innervated from the region of the basal ganglia. This suggests that subtle modifications of blink rate with changing task conditions are at least plausible on physiological grounds.

Most previous work has investigated blinking in relation to visual tasks. It has been regarded as important for studies on reading (Luckeish and Moss 1942), and as a possible cause of accidents

144

through loss of information (Lawson, 1948). Drew showed that blink rate decreases as the necessity for detailed control of movement increases; he found this both for a laboratory tracking task and for driving a car in various traffic conditions. A reduction in blink rate associated with increase in difficulty of a tracking task was also found by Poulton and Gregory (1952 [No. 4]).

This present series of experiments was undertaken in an attempt to discover whether blink rate is associated with changes in the conditions of non-visual tasks.

CHANGES IN BLINK RATE WHILE LEARNING A STYLUS MAZE

The task was the learning of a small stylus maze which was hidden from the subject by a screen. The maze had a groove cut in a wooden board 10 in long by 5 in wide. It had nine culs-de-sac, each 1 in. in length and regularly spaced along the maze; five were on the right, and four on the left. All the turns were right angles; there were no curves in the maze. It was placed horizontally on a table; the subjects put their right arm round a small screen which hid the maze but did not otherwise restrict their field of view.

Blinks were recorded with an electromyograph consisting of a direct-coupled E.E.G.-type amplifier feeding an ink-writing oscillograph. Electrodes were placed above and to the side of the left eye.

Errors were recorded on the same record as the blinks. The experimenter depressed a key when the subject's stylus touched the end of a cul-de-sac, a record thus being made of errors which could be directly related to the blink record. The beginning and end of each trial were also recorded.

In this and the other experiments to be described, the experimenter resorted to a trick in order to reduce the risk of the subjects realizing that blinks were being recorded. The subjects were told that their brain activity was being electrically recorded. The subject did not at any time see the maze; he was told that he must not see it because, if he did, the task would be absurdly easy. No reference to blinking or to the eyes was made at any time.

Twenty naval ratings served as subjects; their ages ranged from 19 to 25, except for one who was 35 years of age. They had various ground-crew jobs on aircraft.

Procedure

When the electrodes were placed in position, and the recorder was operating satisfactorily, the subjects were told to relax for a 2-minute period. A similar period followed the learning of the maze to a criterion of three correct runs. These two periods provided some measure of the normal rest rate for the subject. There were ½-minute pauses between each trial; this had the advantage that these 'pause rates' could be compared with the beginning and end 'rest rates'. It also had the advantage over the vigilance type of experiment that changes in blink rate during the course of the experiment, perhaps related to such variables as boredom or fatigue, could be ignored or separately studied.

The records were scored by dividing the learning trials and the pauses into ¼-minute periods which were averaged separately. This was done partly because the first half of the maze was learned very quickly; it was only the second half which seemed to present difficulty after the first two or three trials.

Results

The pause rate was markedly higher than the rest rate, the trial rate was below the rest rate. Blink rate decreased during each trial, and it also decreased during each pause between the trials.

The difference between the trial rate and the rest rate (the smallest difference) is significant at the 0·05 level. When the second half of the trial periods is considered, the difference is significant at the 0·001 level. The difference between the pause and the trial rates is highly significant at the 0·001 level. The figures are given in Table 5.1.

An attempt was made to find a relation between blink rate and errors. The method adopted was to rank the twenty subjects in order of the difference between trial (T) and pause (P) blink rate, and also in order of the number of errors made per trial. The correlation between these ranks was then assessed using Kendall's τ test. Clearly, a correlation coefficient of nearly zero would indicate that there was no relation between errors and the difference between pause and trial

TABLE 5.1
STYLUS MAZE EXPERIMENT

		PAUSES			TRIALS			
	Rest 1	*1st* ¼ *min.*	*2nd* ¼ *min.*	*1st and 2nd* ¼ *min.*	*1st* ¼ *min.*	*2nd* ¼ *min.*	*1st and 2nd* ¼ *min.*	*Rest 2*
Means:	21·52	33·04	27·36	30·2	22·32	15·00	18·66	20·24
S.D...	2·49	3·68	2·99	3·08	4·12	4·97	6·05	5·39

blink rate for each subject, while a correlation of 1 would indicate that in each case the subject with fewest errors per trial had the greatest reduction in blink rate.

It was found that, when P–T was ranked and correlated with mean errors per trial for each subject, τ was 0·37.

When only the first ¼-minute period of the trials was taken for T, τ was 0·48. The difference between the rest rate and the mean trial rate was also ranked for each subject. This gave a τ of 0·24.

CHANGES IN BLINK RATE WHILE ADDING NUMBERS

This experiment was undertaken partly to find out whether the motor activity present in learning the stylus maze was an important factor in modifying the blink rate; although this seemed unlikely, it was a possibility. A further reason for varying the task was that some subjects learned the maze by building up a visual picture; it seemed just possible that to these subjects the task might be in a sense 'psychologically visual', even though information was not lost through blinking.

Procedure

Single digit numbers chosen randomly were recorded on a magnetic tape-recorder in four series of twenty digits each. The subjects were asked to add each series mentally, and to give the answer verbally at the end of each series.

A further twenty naval ratings took part in this experiment. The same blink recorder was used, but electrodes were developed which, instead of being fixed with sticking plaster as in the stylus maze experiment, were held in place with suction.

The suction electrodes

A special electrode was designed for this purpose; it consisted of a small hollow copper cylinder across the open top of which was stretched a thin rubber diaphragm. When the electrode was attached, this diaphragm was pushed into the hollow electrode with the finger so that the air was expelled through a small hole in the centre of the electrode face. The diaphragm was released when the electrode was in place, and the resulting vacuum held it firmly to the skin. A sticky electrode jelly was used which besides ensuring adequate electrical contact also sealed the vacuum inside the electrode. The advantage of this method over the use of sticking plaster is that it is less unpleasant for the subject; also the electrode may be readily transferred from one place to another without coating the skin with gum, which is annoying since it increases the electrode resistance. Most important, it improves the quality of the records because the electrode is held firmly at its centre, whereas if it is held with plaster it tends to work loose.

Results

The blink rates (number of blinks per minute) were calculated for four experimental conditions. These were: (1) a 2-minute Rest period at the commencement of the experiment; (2) the same period at the end of the experiment; (3) the average of the Trial periods for each subject; (4) the average of the Pause periods for each subject. The Means for the twenty subjects in these four conditions are: (1) $R_1 = 17\cdot84$; (2) $R_2 = 22\cdot88$; (3) $T = 20\cdot62$; (4) $P = 25\cdot06$.

An analysis of variance showed that the difference between the means of (3) and (4) were highly significant at the $0\cdot001$ level. The results of the analysis are shown in Table 5.2.

TABLE 5.2
NUMBER ADDING EXPERIMENT

Item			d.f.	S.S.	M.S.	F. ratio	p.
Subjects	..	..	19	1406·27	74·01	10·11	< 0·001
Conditions	..	..	3	143·75	47·92	6·55	< 0·001
Error ..	..	..	57	417·49	7·32		
Total	..	..	79	1967·51			
S.D. 2·7							

CHANGES IN BLINK RATE DURING AUDIO-TRACKING

This experiment was undertaken in an attempt to discover whether blinking is related to the rate-of-change of a non-visual tracking course.

Apparatus

Two audio-frequency oscillators were built, employing the Wein

Bridge frequency selective network principle. This allowed the frequency of each oscillator to be varied by mechanical rotation of a single potentiometer. Each oscillator fed a high quality 5 in. speaker; these were mounted on boards one at each side of the subject's head. The two notes could thus be recognized from their direction.

The oscillator feeding the right-hand speaker was continuously varied in frequency, its frequency-control potentiometer being connected by a string drive to a crank-driven variable gear to set the period of the simple harmonic course produced by the crank driving the potentiometer.

Both the course and the subject's response to it were recorded by ball-pointed pens in slides mounted across the record paper and in line with the blink-recording pen. The ball pens were mounted at an angle of about 40° from the vertical, so that their points almost touched when they passed each other. One of the pens was mechanically connected to the crank driving the frequency-control potentiometer of the course oscillator, the other pen was connected to the corresponding potentiometer of the response oscillator, which was controlled by the subject with a 2 in. control knob connected through a reduction gear. This gear was introduced to make it impossible for the subject to develop a stereotyped hand movement; the knob had to be turned through rather more than 360° to follow the course oscillator.

The subject's task was to follow the simple-harmonic changes in frequency of the right-hand speaker by producing corresponding changes in the left-hand speaker by rotating the control knob. All the moving parts of the apparatus were screened from the subject in order to avoid visual cues.

Results

The blink record was related to the tracking course by dividing each sine-wave drawn by the course pen into eight equal sections. The number of blinks falling in each section was determined for each sine-wave in turn, and these were totalled for each record and expressed as a percentage of the total number of blinks for each subject.

Fig. 5.1 shows the average of the results obtained in this way for fifteen subjects. This was obtained by expressing their contributions as a percentage of their tracking time to the total.

Each subject is given an equal weight, although both the average blink rate and the tracking time have between-subject variation.

From Fig. 5.1 it is clear that where the rate-of-change of frequency

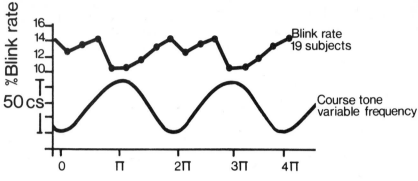

FIG. 5.1 *Blink rate during audio tracking.*

of the tracking course is maximum at the high frequency end of the range, the blink rate is at its minimum. But the corresponding point at the low frequency end is not so clear. This asymmetry may be due to the fact that the task was actually different at the two ends, the 'beat notes' being clearer at the high than at the low end of the frequency range. The 'beat notes' served as a zero error signal provided the tracking rate demanded of the subject was not too high, when he had not time to use them.

The mean blink rate for all the fifteen subjects during the audio-tracking was also determined, and was found to be 18·49 blinks per minute. The Rest rates for these subjects were not determined, but this Mean may be compared with the average Rest rate of the forty subjects of the previous experiments, which is 20·62 blinks per minute.

The blink rate during audio-tracking was thus almost the same as the rate during maze learning. These means are markedly below the rate during trials of the number-adding experiment, which is not significantly different from the Rest rate. The reason for this exception in the case of the number-adding is not clear; it might be suggested from the result of this audio-tracking experiment that the trial mean is related to the degree of continuity of the task.

Any attempt to use blink rate as an index should take into account the degree of continuity of the task. Quantitative data should be found for the parameters of the rate-of-change of blink rate with changing conditions. The Audio Tracking experiment might provide a technique for studying the characteristics of the blink mechanism in following changing task conditions.

6 Colour anomaly, the Rayleigh equation and selective adaptation

[The next short paper represents my sole contribution to problems of colour vision (though there is a discussion of colour vision in *Eye and Brain*, with comments on the points made here in relation to the Land Phenomenon – that surprisingly realistic colour can be obtained with but two lights, in certain conditions, though three lights are generally required to mix all the spectral colours, and white). The ideas in this paper are due almost entirely to G. C. Brindley. Giles Brindley was then at the Cambridge Physiological Laboratory doing most distinguished work in visual physiology. He has the most powerful deductive-type brain I have met; and is a dedicated scientist, willing to suffer pain for his experiments when necessary. He is now engaged on transplanting electronic circuits into the skulls of blind people, working towards artificial eyes for the blind.

The study of colour vision has a peculiar fascination. Like many students, I was drawn to it as a research topic in spite of – or because of – the fundamental and brilliant work produced in this field by the neighbouring Physiological Laboratory: especially W. H. Rushton, G. C. Brindley and E. N. Willmer. At that time theories of colour vision were legion. C. Grindley, of the Cambridge Psychological Laboratory, told me the story of a conference on colour vision held in London with fifty contributors: fifty-one theories were expounded – one contributor putting forward two theories!]

★   ★   ★

As long ago as 1878, von Kries reported that adapting lights fail to upset colour matches. This observation was modified in 1934 by Prof. W. D. Wright, who showed that lights of very high intensity, above about 15,000 Trolands, do upset colour matches. Wright considers the breakdown at glare intensities to be due to radical photochemical changes. G. S. Brindley has recently reported a detailed investigation of this breakdown at high intensities. It might be suggested that the original findings of von Kries – that matches do not break down after adaptation with intensities within the normal range – has important implications for theories of colour vision, and in particular for the explanation of the Rayleigh equation.

I have confirmed the finding for thirty normal and four anomalous observers, using a Nagel spectrographic anomaloscope, and Ilford Spectral Red and Spectral Green Filters for the adapting lights. After adaptation to red light, both the monochromatic yellow field and the red + green mixture field of the anomaloscope appeared green, the match remaining true. After adaptation to green light, both fields appeared red, the match again remaining true. In the case of two protanomalous and two deuteranomalous subjects, it was found that their matches also held after selective adaptation, though their red + green mixtures were, of course, different from the normal observer's mixture, as was found to be the case by Lord Rayleigh, in 1891.

Now since matches hold after adaptation, although subjects with defective colour vision require abnormal mixture intensities to make their match, it appears that the mechanism of colour anomaly must be different from that of selective colour adaptation. But this difference is not generally made evident in discussions on colour vision.

On a trichromatic theory in which no special yellow receptor system is postulated – yellow perception being attributed to combined activity of red and green systems – we should expect the match to hold after adaptation, since the perception of yellow is supposed to be the result of red + green mixture whatever the spectral composition of the stimulus light. Not only is the finding that matches do hold after selective adaptation compatible with a trichromatic theory, but also it may be regarded as evidence against the supposition that there is a special yellow receptor system functional in the foveal region of the retina. A special yellow receptor would be stimulated by the monochromatic yellow field, but would be comparatively unaffected by the adapting light, if this red or green. If it were affected, it could scarcely be supposed to produce a shift towards red or green, but only a reduced sensitivity to yellow light, which again would not allow the match to hold after adaptation.

The stability of colour matches with selective adaptation up to high intensities thus provides at least *prima facie* evidence against a foveal yellow receptor system. This is strengthened by Brindley's finding that when the match does break down with very high adapting intensities, increase in red light is always required to restore the match, no matter what the colour of the adapting light. If selective adaptation is supposed to depress the sensitivity of the stimulated systems (for which there is a great deal of evidence) whereas anomaly is attributed to abnormal spectral *positions* of the response systems, then there is no longer any paradox in the fact that colour adaptation does not produce a change in colour matches while the anomalous eye requires abnormal mixture intensities to make the match.

We may tentatively conclude that these facts (*a*) provide evidence against a foveal yellow receptor system, and (*b*) suggest that colour anomaly is due to abnormal spectral positions of the fundamental response curves, rather than to abnormal sensitivities, or to neural 'leakage' across receptor systems.

7 *A statistical information theory of visual thresholds*

[The next paper represents the start of a great deal of hard work which, looking back on it, probably did not really pay off. But it was exciting at the time and may still hold some interest.

Having tea, on a Cambridge blue day, in the garden of the Garden House Hotel overlooking the river, my colleague Violet Cane and I had the idea that thresholds should be regarded in terms of signal/noise ratios. We suddenly realized that the very word 'threshold', traditionally used in psychophysics, is misleading in suggesting that a given stimulus energy is – or is not – sufficient to get over a fixed step to enter the nervous system. Thinking about electronic devices, and the inevitable randomness of detector systems, we realized that the 'threshold' could hardly be a fixed step, but must involve a probability of detection for a given stimulus energy. We also realized that 'false-positives' would inevitably occur; and that the proportion of false-positives might be of great interest. This, at any rate, is how I remember it. In fact several other people in Cambridge – especially H. B. Barlow in the Physiology Laboratory, and E. R. F. W. Crossman in the Psychology Laboratory – were also thinking along these lines at about that time. Tanner and Swetts, in America, published their now celebrated signal detection theory of sensory discrimination before we did. Unknown to any of us, a television engineer, A. J. Rose, had published the essential idea in a paper ten years before (Rose, 1948). While we were working on this, H. B. Barlow produced a brilliant series of papers on the measurement of the noise level of the retina; and E. R. F. W. Crossman used related concepts to good effect in analysis of tracking and card sorting tasks. Our theory received some interesting critical comment, but was never accepted as particularly useful. This work has not so far as I know been followed up. Some of the ideas might still be worth developing – especially, perhaps, the notion that nerve deafness may be regarded as noise masking, while conduction deafness is signal attenuation. There are surely implications here for the design of hearing aids;

which we started to explore. At the time this was all-engrossing; we felt that we were at the forefront of a revolution in how to think about psychophysics. Looking back at it, perhaps we hardly saw the leaders for the dust in front. In any case, my mathematics were inadequate; anything of value is due to Violet Cane. She is a mathematical statistician who enjoys handling data and initiating and clarifying ideas, with the patience to work with non-mathematical colleagues such as myself. She is now a professor of mathematics at the University of Manchester.]

★   ★   ★

IT is well known that, for constant stimulus duration, the visual threshold intensity, I, is a function of the stimulus area A. In the case of absolute thresholds it has been generally accepted that: (i) for areas up to about 6′, $AI =$ constant (Ricco's law); (ii) for areas between about 6′ and perhaps 20°, $\sqrt{A}.I =$ constant (Piper's law).

It seems reasonable to regard the absolute threshold as a special case of the differential threshold. It is then important to discover whether these relations in fact hold for the differential case. Brindley has shown that Piper's law holds for differential thresholds where the test field is discriminated against a large field of constant area. Ricco's law is also found to hold for blue light, optical effects making it difficult to test for other colours. Piper's law for differential threshold where the background area is large and fixed has been formulated:

$$\frac{\Delta I}{I} = \text{const.} \sqrt{\frac{I}{A}} \qquad (1)$$

We find, by using various small background areas, that the more general case where either area is variable may be written, at least approximately,

$$\frac{\Delta I}{I} = \text{const.} \sqrt{\left(\frac{I}{A_1} + \frac{I}{A_2}\right)} + C \qquad (2)$$

This would give the Weber-Fechner law, $\Delta I/I = C$, for very large areas A_1 and A_2, which would make $\left(\frac{I}{A_1} + \frac{I}{A_2}\right)$ negligibly small.

We also find that this may be further generalized to cover low intensities in the region of breakdown of the Weber-Fechner law by adding a small constant thus:

$$\frac{\Delta I}{I+k} = \text{const.} \ \sqrt{\left(\frac{1}{A_1}+\frac{1}{A_2}\right)} + C \qquad (3)$$

The value of k in terms of equivalent intensity we estimate at about 0·04 ft. l. For the absolute threshold, when $I = 0$, we should then have $\Delta I/k = C$ when the areas are large.

It appears that these, and perhaps other threshold and summation phenomena, may be described in terms of statistical information available in neural information channels. If we suppose that the area A inspected is to be regarded as a set of n independent observations, where n is approximately proportional to A, and that each of these observations is subject to random variation through noise in the system, then for ΔI to be detected against I, in some fixed proportion of the number of trials (for example, an 80 per cent experimental criterion), we must have

$$\frac{[(r+\Delta r)-r]-C}{\sqrt{\left(\frac{1}{A_1}+\frac{1}{A_2}\right)}V} = \text{constant} \qquad (4)$$

where $(r+\Delta r)$, r, are the mean neural pulse-rates corresponding to intensities $I+\Delta I$, I, and V is the variance of neural pulse-rate over the sample.

We have introduced the constant C to explain the fact that few false positives occur in threshold experiments. Without some criterion of difference greater than zero, we should expect about 50 per cent false positives. The proportion of false positives may change with the observer's attitude, or 'set', indicating that C may vary within limits. It is tempting to regard k as arising from the internal noise present in the system, and to think of the absolute threshold as the case where the signal is to be distinguished against noise background.

If, as seems possible from electrophysiological data, r is proportional to $\log(I+k)$, (4) reduces to (3) above for ΔI somewhat less than $I+k$, and we expect this to hold for relatively small values of ΔI even when $I = 0$, that is, for absolute thresholds. In the latter case, as the test area diminishes, however, and the value of ΔI consequently increases, the approximation $\Delta I/k$ used for $[(r+\Delta r)-r]$ is no longer valid, and the more accurate expression $[\log(k+\Delta I)-\log k]$ is required. For A_2 large, (4) can then be written

$$1+\frac{\Delta I}{k} = \exp\left(C+\alpha\sqrt{1/A}\right),$$

writing A for A_1 and denoting the constant involved by α.

For very large A, the terms containing A are negligible; therefore

$$1 + \frac{\Delta I}{k} = \text{const., or } \Delta I = \text{const.} \tag{5}$$

For smaller A:

$$1 + \frac{\Delta I}{k} = \exp C \left(1 + \alpha / \sqrt{A} \right)$$

or

$$\sqrt{A} \, \Delta I = \text{const.} + \text{const.} \, \sqrt{A} \tag{6}$$

For even smaller A:

$$1 + \frac{\Delta I}{k} = \exp C \left(1 + \frac{\alpha}{\sqrt{A}} + \frac{\alpha^2}{2A} + \ldots \right) \tag{7}$$

It thus appears that Ricco's and Piper's laws might be regarded as the different approximations to the logarithmic equation which can be used at different levels. The expression (7) appears to fit Willmer's data satisfactorily. We are undertaking experiments to determine the various constants involved.

[Some of the more interesting discussion of this theory, appearing at the time in *Nature*, will now be given.]

NOTE BY F. H. C. MARRIOTT

Gregory and Cane (1955) have proposed a statistical information theory of visual thresholds which derives the empirical laws governing absolute and differential visual thresholds from certain plausible assumptions about the properties of the eye as a detector of visible radiation. An essentially similar theory was restated and elaborated by Cane (1956) in a later paper.

The basic theoretical equation defining the threshold is:

$$\frac{[(r + \Delta r) - r] - C}{\sqrt{\dfrac{1}{A_1} + \dfrac{1}{A_2}} \; V} \tag{1}$$

where r, $r + \Delta r$ are the mean neural pulse-rates in the areas A_1 and A_2, illuminated by intensities I and $I + \Delta I$ respectively, V is the variance of neural pulse rates over the sample, and C is a constant sufficiently large to ensure only a small proportion of false positives.

This equation may be interpreted by saying that a positive response is given whenever the increment in pulse-rate exceeds C. The constant on the right, which I shall call β, depends on the statistical definition of threshold. The distribution of δr, the actual increment in pulse-rate, is not known, but if it is assumed that it is roughly normal, and if the areas are measured in suitable units, then β will take the values $+1$, 0 and -1 for definitions of threshold, corresponding roughly to 80, 50 and 20 per cent positives.

Assuming that $r \propto \log(I+k)$, where k is a positive constant, possibly related to the noise background, the authors deduce the equation:

$$1 + \frac{\Delta I}{k} = \exp\left(C + \alpha\sqrt{1/A}\right) \qquad (2)$$

for the absolute threshold ΔI for an area A. In this equation the constant α is a positive multiple of β, the constant on the right of equation (1).

The authors proceed to derive Ricco's law for small fields and Piper's law for larger fields from equation (2). But their derivations involve implicitly the assumption that α is positive; this is true when the threshold is defined by 80 per cent positive responses, but for about 50 per cent positive responses α is zero, and for lower values it becomes negative.

Equation (2), in fact, implies that for some definition of threshold for which $\alpha = 0$ (about 50 per cent positive responses), ΔI, the absolute threshold in terms of illumination, is independent of area. The variations with area for other definitions of the threshold are due to the frequency of seeing curves plotted against ΔI for large areas being steeper than those for small. For 80 per cent positive responses ΔI increases as the area diminishes, as the authors conclude; but for 20 per cent positive responses, ΔI diminishes as the area diminishes, becoming negative for very small areas.

The fallacy lies in deriving an equation for the threshold applicable only to the particular areas A_1 and A_2 considered, and then varying the area without considering which of the other quantities in the equation remain invariant under this treatment. In equation (1), C is defined for the areas A_1 and A_2; there is no reason for supposing that in equation (2) C will remain constant while A is varied. Further, the relationship $r \propto \log(I+k)$ is certainly not true for small areas if the area is varied. Hartline's experiments (1940b,c) showed that in the eye of the frog over a wide range of intensities and areas r depends on the total flux IA. The human retina is also composed of a mosaic of functional units, and there is every reason for believing that in the present respect these units behave like the functional units of the frog. Further, diffraction and optical defects may make the images of very small areas virtually identical. These facts provide the simple and generally accepted explanation of Ricco's law – and certainly a theory which seeks to explain the law without taking them into consideration must be regarded with the gravest suspicion.

The authors' assumptions thus do not lead to reasonable conclusions about visual thresholds, and considerable modifications to their theory are required before it can be regarded as a useful approach to the problems of visual excitation.

REPLY BY R. L. GREGORY AND VIOLET CANE

In our first communication on this subject we did not consider the effect of changing shape of the distribution of the neural impulse-rate, r, with consequent change in variance, as the photic intensity, I, decreases. We have, however, considered this in later papers. Marriott's prediction from our original formulation that ΔI would become negative for stimulus conditions giving a sufficiently small percentage of positive responses depends on the distribution being normal. It is quite clear, however, that the distribution must change at low intensities, for a negative pulse-rate is impossible, and so it must become asymmetrical for low values of r. Now when we consider threshold conditions for various areas of stimulation, the pulse-rate for a given fibre must rise as the area, A, is reduced, if the threshold is to be maintained. But since fewer fibres are stimulated, the *total* number of impulses in unit time might not rise. We are inclined to think that for human central vision, at least, detection is based on the *average* pulse-rate. One of our reasons for holding this view is that in detecting a signal, ΔI, against a background, I, increases in the area of the background produce a lower threshold for discriminating the ΔI field. It should be noted that this result does not hold for short flashes of ΔI. In this case (and most threshold determinations are made using short flashes) the background area has no effect, suggesting that the discrimination for short flashes of the signal, as opposed to continuous viewing, is a matter of detecting changes over time rather than over space. The experimental finding, that increase in background area, for continuous viewing, produces a reduction in the signal intensity (ΔI) required, suggests to us that no mechanism such as retinal facilitation will account for areal summation. It looks as though perception involves selecting relevant areas in the stimulus field. For example, if a narrow black ring is added to the background in the differential threshold situation, so that the signal lies at its centre, the threshold rises, and is the same as though the part of the background lying outside the ring were not there.

A further reason for thinking that average pulse-rates are used is that, for intensities well above absolute threshold, a larger area does not appear brighter than a smaller one of the same intensity, as would be expected if the total pulse-rate were being used as criterion. It is also the case that objects do not appear brighter when viewed with both eyes rather than one, though the threshold falls.

Although we would defend our general approach, there is the difficulty, pointed out by Dr Marriott, that the threshold should not change when it is determined by 50 per cent positive responses. We do not ourselves know what the result for thresholds defined by 50 per cent or fewer correct responses would be, using the frequency-of-seeing method. Other methods produce a positive bias at low intensities, because there are fewer possible readings below the 50 per cent point than above it. Published frequency-of-seeing curves relate to flashes and do not give the information required.

NOTE BY M. G. BULMER AND C. I. HOWARTH

There have been two interesting recent attempts to treat the visual threshold as a problem of discriminating a signal from a noisy background (Barlow, 1956, 1957a, Gregory and Cane 1955, Gregory, 1956). It is known from neurophysiological studies (Granit, 1955) that there is a variable resting discharge in the completely unstimulated eye. This 'retinal noise', together with any noise that may be added more centrally, forms the 'dark noise' which, on this theory, limits the sensitivity of the eye at absolute threshold. If there were no dark noise, there would be no reason why a single absorbed quantum of light should not be seen; if, however, the threshold of vision were set as low as this in the presence of dark noise, there would be a 'false-alarm rate', since the threshold criterion would be exceeded by the dark noise in the absence of external stimulation: thus the greater the variability of the resting discharge, the higher must the threshold be set to keep the false-alarm rate low. It is therefore important to know what is the average value and, more especially, the variability of the resting discharge.

The mean and variance of the resting discharge of single fibres can be obtained from direct electrophysiological studies. It would, however, be difficult to relate these figures to psychophysical thresholds and it would be useful to obtain estimates of the properties of the resting discharge from the psychophysical experiments themselves. Barlow (1956, 1957a) tried to estimate simultaneously the variance of the resting discharge and the number of quanta necessary for vision from the shape of the frequency of seeing curve. His method is very ingenious but is also, unfortunately, rather insensitive and he was unable to estimate either of these quantities with any precision.

It is therefore very interesting that Gregory (Gregory and Cane 1955, Gregory 1956) has attempted to tackle this problem in another way. He has found that in differential threshold experiments, Weber's law:

$$\Delta I/I = C \tag{1}$$

where C is a constant, does not hold exactly, but that when I is not too small, a much better fit is obtained by the relationship:

$$\Delta I/(I+k) = C \tag{2}$$

where k is about 0·03 ft. lambert. In order to explain this, he supposes that r, the mean neural impulse-rate (using this term in a loose sense) corresponding to incident light of intensity I, is proportional to $\log(I+k)$. He also supposes that 'the brain demands a constant fixed difference between impulse-rates arising from the comparison fields to make an intensity discrimination to a given fixed criterion'. The difference between the mean neural impulse-rates is proportional to $\log(I+\Delta I+k)-\log(I+k)$, which when I is not too small is approximately $\Delta I/(I+k)$ (this can be shown by expansion in a Taylor series). Setting this equal to a constant, the observed relationship (2) is obtained.

This explanation of the empirical relationship (2) is the same as Fechner's explanation of Weber's law (1), except that r is supposed to be proportional to $\log(I+k)$ rather than $\log I$. It seems to us, however, that Gregory attaches a significance to the actual value of the constant k which it does not possess. For he says that 'it is tempting to regard k as arising from the internal noise present in the system', and again that 'We are tempted to regard this constant as arising from the mean internal noise in the system'. The meaning of this statement is not very clear, but he seems to be arguing that, since r is proportional to $\log(I+k)$, then setting $I = 0$, k is the equivalent, in light units, of the mean resting discharge. This interpretation of k is, however, incorrect, since equation (2) can be derived from any relationship of the form:

$$r = a+b\log(I+k) \tag{3}$$

where a and b are any constants; for the constant a drops out when the difference between the two impulse-rates is taken. Gregory's interpretation of k rests on the implicit assumption that $a = 0$, which there is no reason to suppose true.

A further criticism of Gregory's model is that he does not consider the variance of r. In any treatment of the threshold as a signal to noise discrimination, the variance of the response is obviously far more important than the mean. It might be possible to interpret the slope of the regression of ΔI on I in connexion with the variance in the same way as the Weber fraction, $\Delta I/I$, can be interpreted when the line passes through the origin.

REPLY BY R. L. GREGORY AND VIOLET CANE

We are inclined to agree with the model 3 proposed by Bulmer and Howarth, at least as an approximation, though we feel that to be useful it requires further interpretation. At the British Association meeting in 1956 (Section 1) we put forward the following:

$$r = \eta + b \log(aI + \varepsilon)$$

$$[E(\eta) = m, E(\varepsilon) = k, \text{var } \eta = \tau^2, \text{var } \varepsilon = \sigma^2]$$

where r is the neural pulse-rate, I is the incident light intensity, of which a proportion, aI, is effective. It appears that nerve impulse-rate is an approximate logarithmic function of light intensity (we include the constant b since we do not know the logarithmic base). It seems to

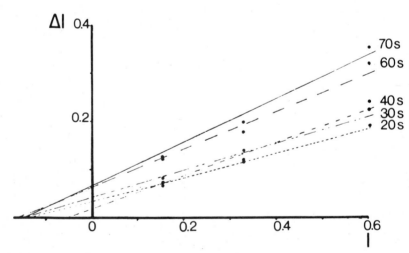

FIG. 7.1 *Relation between ΔI and I, fitted by the method of least squares, for various age-groups. (12 subjects aged 20–30, 11 aged 30–40, 7 aged 40–50, 6 aged 70–80). White light was used, the intensity units being foot-lamberts. The background field (I) subtended 15°, the test field ($\Delta I + I$) subtended 5°. The adjustment method of obtaining thresholds was used. Similar results have been obtained with a frequency method, employing flashes for ΔI.*

us important to distinguish between the addition of noise to the system before and after the logarithmic transform. We distinguish between 'retinal noise' (ε) which will include quantum fluctuation, and 'neural noise' (η) which will be variation in the impulse-rate due to random factors added *after* the logarithmic transform. We have introduced rather a large number of constants, some of which may not be easy to determine, because we do not want to limit our thinking to noise of retinal or 'quantal' origin. On general grounds we should expect noise throughout the nervous system, and we should like to be allowed to consider its effect. We may consider some implications of this model. The pulse-rate when I increases to $I + \Delta I$ is $r + \Delta r = \eta' + b \log(aI + a\Delta I + \varepsilon')(\eta', \varepsilon'$ from the same distribution as η, ε) and

$$\Delta r = \eta' - \eta + b \log(aI + a\Delta I + \varepsilon') - b \log(aI + \varepsilon)$$

The distribution of Δr has a mean of approximately $b \log\{1 + (a\Delta I/aI + k)\}$, that is, $\{b\Delta I/I + (k/a)\}$, if I is not too small, and a variance V equal to

$$2\tau^2 + \frac{b^2\sigma^2}{(I + \Delta I + k/a)^2} + \frac{b^2\sigma^2}{(I + k/a)^2}$$

If we take this distribution as roughly normal, and assume that a difference is reported by the subject when $\Delta r \geqslant c$ (c being constant for a given subject in a given experiment), the value of ΔI which is recognized as different 50 per cent of the time is given by:

$$\frac{b\Delta I}{I + k/a} = c; \text{ that is, } \Delta I = \frac{c}{b}(I + k/a) \ldots \ldots (A)$$

Similarly, the $2\frac{1}{2}$ and $97\frac{1}{2}$ per cent values of ΔI will be given respectively by:

$$\frac{b\Delta I}{I + k/a} + 2\sqrt{V} = C \text{ and} \frac{b\Delta I}{I + k/a} - 2\sqrt{V} = C$$

The standard deviation of the frequency-of-seeing curve will thus be approximately:

$$\frac{I}{b}(I + k/a)\left[2\tau^2 + \frac{2\sigma^2}{(I + k/a)^2}\right]^{1/2}$$

and will increase with I.

Considering retinal noise, we assume this to be spontaneous breakdown of photochemical molecules, and the effect of the quantum fluctuation of light. At low intensities the receptors may be regarded as quantum counters, and the count as Poisson. At high intensities – and it is with these we are primarily interested – the receptors could not be expected to count individual quanta. Further, the probability of an individual receptor being stimulated is no longer small and the Poisson approximation cannot hold. The relation between σ and I could be found by considering the standard deviations of frequency-of-seeing curves obtained for differential thresholds using large I.

Equation A fits our results provided I is not too small. Not only will the approximations no longer hold for small I, but also the rod system of the retina which then becomes functional may be expected to have different constants. From such equations, retinal noise-levels may be estimated in terms of an equivalent external stimulus, k/a being given by the intercept on the I-axis.

To estimate neural noise is more difficult. An indirect method which may indicate a change in its value is the following. We take C as a fixed difference in pulse-rates, as in our previous communication, the difference being set by the number of acceptable false-positives. In the absence of an external stimulus there will be sporadic pulses, the count-rate increasing with increase in m or k. Thus the slope of ΔI against I will increase with any increase in noise. On general grounds, it seemed likely that older people might have a higher noise-level in their nervous system. We have undertaken a series of auditory and visual discrimination experiments to investigate this possibility. We find that, for vision, the slope of the line ΔI against I increases with age, whereas there is no consistent change in the intercept. Some of our results are given in Fig. 7.1. This suggests that neural noise (m) increases with age, whereas retinal noise (k) does not. It is interesting to consider functional losses associated with ageing as due in part to increase in neural noise. This may be supposed to affect memory storage and recall mechanisms (producing errors or delay) and also motor control, producing tremor and increase in decision or reaction time.

This at least is a crude and inadequate model; in particular, it takes no account of the level of adaptation of the eye.

We wish to acknowledge help given, at various times, by members of the Nuffield Unit for Research on Ageing, particularly Dr J. Szafran, and also by R. T. Leslie, E. R. F. W. Crossmann, A. Kendon and Miss J. Wallace, who is in receipt of a grant from the Medical Research Council, which has also made us a grant for apparatus.

NOTE BY H. B. BARLOW

Both Bulmer and Howarth and Cane and Gregory accept the logarithmic relation between impulse frequency (r) and light intensity

(I) expressed in the formula $r = \eta + b \log(aI + \varepsilon)$ (a, b, constants; η, ε, random variables representing neural and retinal noise), but it does not appear to be generally true in the vertebrate retina. Hartline (1932) showed that it was approximately true for the compound eye of *Limulus*, and also, under more restricted conditions, in the frog (1938). These results were avidly absorbed by psychologists, because they fitted so well the logarithmic relation between sensation-level and stimulus intensity which Fechner derived by integration of the Weber law; but the maintained discharge of retinal ganglion cells in the cat does not show any such simple relation (Kuffler, Fitzhugh and Barlow, 1957), and Fitzhugh's results (1957) suggest an almost linear relation between the number of extra impulses evoked and the quantity of light delivered in near-threshold flashes superimposed on a steady background. There may be other types of ganglion cell, not readily isolated by present techniques, which behave in a different way, but it seems rash to use the logarithmic relation in formulating a theory of visual noise.

There are two further criticisms of the formulation which Cane and Gregory now put forward. First, it fails to recognize that the variance of ε (the retinal noise which, they say, includes quantum fluctuations) must increase when I is increased. Second, so many hypothetical quantities (m, k, η, ε, c, a, b, and V) are introduced that it would be a formidable, or impossible, task to evaluate them experimentally. The complications introduced by considering a second source of noise do not seem justified until facts are found which cannot be explained by a simpler theory.

These difficulties can be avoided if one does not express noise as variance of impulse frequency. There are other possible units of measurement which can be defined as precisely, which are more easily derived from measurements of visual performance, and which may be more simply related to the cause of noise. In one of the papers (Barlow, 1956) which Bulmer and Howarth discuss, the natural unit arising from the method is the average number (x) of random independent events (such as the spontaneous activation of a rod) which are liable to be confused with the absorption of a quantum of light: the maximum value of x was shown to be related to the number of quanta absorbed from threshold flashes and to the slope of frequency-of-seeing curves. Rushton (1956) estimated that $1/10$ of the quanta (507 mμ) incident at the pupil are absorbed in the rods; using this figure, and previous results on absolute threshold, the method shows that x cannot exceed 10.

One might hope to compare this figure with estimates of noise obtained by different methods, and this can be done, though the comparison is not at all exact. If plausible assumptions are made (Barlow, 1957a) about the area and time within which stimulus and noise events are liable to be confused, one can calculate the intensity of a steady light which would lead to the absorption of 10 quanta, on the average, in such an area and time. This light would send about 1,000 quanta/sec. deg. (Hartline, 1938) into the eye, and it can be looked upon as a 'dark light' which causes noise at the absolute threshold. It should have the same value as the *Augenschwarz* of Fechner (1860), the *Eigenlicht* of Helmholtz (1856), and Gregory and Cane's k, or k/a. It is, in fact, lower than any of them, but measurements of the difference threshold similar to those upon which the above quantities were based have been made (Barlow, 1957a, Aguilar and Stiles, 1954) under conditions where rods alone are active, and these yield values for the dark light which fall in the range 200–3,000 quanta (507 mμ)/sec. deg. (Hartline, 1938) entering the eye. It can also be shown that the mean and the variance of frequency of the maintained discharge of ganglion cells of the cat's retina are probably compatible with such a dark light, though, as Bulmer and Howarth point out, there are difficulties in relating the two.

These three otherwise unrelated results could all be explained by a dark light of the order of magnitude of 1,000 quanta (507 mμ)/sec. deg. (Hartline, 1938), and this approximate agreement provides some experimental justification for the concept of retinal noise. Furthermore, if a large part of it is caused by thermal decomposition of photosensitive pigments, one can relate the higher dark light and reduced sensitivity of cones to the shift to the red of their spectral sensitivity curves (Barlow, 1957a). Thus the difficulties raised by Bulmer and Howarth, and the complexity which Gregory and Cane's formulation requires, are avoided if visual noise is measured as dark light, not as variance of impulse frequency. There will, however, be plenty of room for argument until the source, or sources, of visual noise are known with greater certainty.

[There is no doubt much in these cricisims, but I still think (in 1973) that the variance of neural frequency is important to considering the limits of discrimination. Possibly the next chapter will justify this view; and the view that R. A. Fisher's 't' test for statistical significance can provide the basis for an appropriate model of sensory discrimination – and how it may be impaired with ageing. Loss of information through variance increasing with age is the basic concept here; with suggestions on the nature of nerve deafness, and other clinical matters.]

8 Increase in 'neurological noise' as a factor in sensory impairment associated with ageing

[The following thesis, not previously published, was written with Violet Cane and Jean Wallace, and received a Senior International C.I.B.A. Foundation prize for work on ageing in 1959. We are very grateful to the Foundation for its encouragement; and to Mr A. S. H. Walford, F.R.C.S., who kindly arranged for patients from the Hearing Clinic, Addenbrooke's Hospital, Cambridge, to serve as subjects for our experiments.

I would like to express my appreciation to Alan Welford (now Professor of Psychology at Adelaide), who was at that time Director of the Nuffield Foundation Unit for research on ageing. It is likely that we would not have considered applying our ideas on discrimination to the ageing problem but for him and his colleagues.]

★   ★   ★

THIS thesis will be concerned with experimental work on human visual and auditory discrimination. The work is being undertaken in an attempt to develop a general theory of sensory discrimination, from the point of view of the efficiency of the nervous system in transmitting information. Some of the behavioural changes associated with ageing are regarded as due to reduction in the efficiency of information transmission in neural channels. The experiments are designed to test a general theory of sensory thresholds, (based on statistical information considerations), and to relate ageing decrements in sensory discrimination to variables which are important within the context of the theory. The experiments are largely preliminary and none have yet been published in detail, though some account has been given of the work on vision in two papers; the first delivered to the Third London Information Theory Symposium at the Royal Institution, in September 1955, published by Wiley (by Gregory), the second in *Nature*, 176, 4496 (1955) by Gregory and Cane, on the general theory of discrimination for the case of vision [No. 7]. The work on hearing has not yet been published; this is concerned with deafness associated with ageing; it is hoped that it may be of some use for the design of better hearing aids for cases of nerve deafness [No. 9].

The basic idea behind the thesis is that much of the deterioration in speed and accuracy of response, and in sensory discrimination associated with ageing, is due to reduction in the rate that the nervous system can transmit information. It will be suggested that the level of random neural activity, or 'noise', increases with age, tending to reduce the 'channel capacity' of the nervous system. It is considered that increase in noise level may be an important factor in ageing.

We shall now define some of the concepts to be used.

The concept of *channel capacity* has been precisely defined by Shannon (1949), as *the rate at which information can be transmitted*. 'Information' is defined in a special way appropriate to communication engineering: the definition takes no account of *meaning*, and does not attempt to define semantic information. Shannon argues that 'the semantic aspects of communication are irrelevant to the engineering aspects', and it seems to us that it is the engineering aspects which are appropriate when we consider the function of the nervous system. An end result of high level neural function may be meaning, but nerve fibres do not convey meaning in the semantic sense; they convey information in Shannon's communication engineering use of the word.

A number of recent writers have used Information Theory to describe aspects of human behaviour, perhaps particularly in multiple choice selection tasks: examples are Garner and Hake (1951), Hick (1952), Munson and Karlin (1954). 'Information' is defined in terms of the number of choices or selections which can be made. The smallest possible amount of information is conveyed by a two-choice selection; this *unit of information* is known as the *binary digit*, or '*bit*'. In the simplest case, where each choice has equal probability, the *amount of information* is defined as the *logarithm of the number of available choices*. Logarithms to the base 2 are used for convenience. Suppose that it is possible to distinguish with equal facility between 16 possibilities (colours, shapes, intensities, people, anything), then the situation is characterized by 4 bits of information, since $\log_2 16 = 4$.

Suppose that we have a measuring instrument, say a thermometer, graduated into divisions. Each division of the scale represents one of a number of possible values of the continuous variable (temperature) which may be read with the instrument. Now it would be said that the greater the number of distinguishable divisions on the scale the more *information* the instrument conveys, or transmits. To represent a continuous variable perfectly the instrument would require an infinite number of distinguishable divisions; thus it is impossible to represent a continuous variable perfectly – it would require an infinite amount of information.

All information systems are subject to some degree of random disturbance, or 'noise'. Ultimately this is thermal in origin. The presence of 'noise' prevents perfect reproduction of a continuous variable, and it introduces the probability of error, through confusion, for discrete messages. The effect of noise upon channel capacity – the rate of transmission of information – has been formulated by Shannon as what is generally known as the Hartley-Shannon Law. If the band width of the system is W, the mean signal power S, and the mean noise power N, then the Hartley-Shannon Law states that the channel capacity is

$$W \log_2 \left(1 + \frac{S}{N}\right) \text{ bits per second} \qquad \dots (1)$$

It may be seen from this that by suitably 'trading' the variables it is possible to describe an infinite number of different systems having identical channel capacities, or information rates. Thus, if there is plenty of time available, low band width and a low S/N may be adequate. But to transmit the same amount of information in a short time the band width and power must be increased, or the noise level must be reduced. (An example here is the difference between transmitting pictures by photo-telegraphy, where it may take 30 minutes to transmit one picture, and the transmission of a single television picture within a fraction of a second but requiring a band width of megacycles to do it. The photo-telegraphy apparatus here is like an aged person!)

Now these basic principles should apply to neurally transmitted information, including the sensory and motor cortex, and activities of thinking and memory. But if the nervous system is seen as an information system, and we can define and measure 'information', it appears sensible to look at age changes in terms of rates of transmission of information in the nervous system. The general slowing down associated with old age is a clue to this and evidence for it.

It has been known since the early work of Adrian (1928) that neural information is coded in terms of the frequency (or rather rate) of action potentials in nerve fibres. A high intensity light stimulus, for example, is coded in terms of a high rate of action potentials travelling up afferent fibres. This fundamental discovery has recently been considered in relation to the types of coding used by communication engineers: MacKay and McCulloch (1952) have estimated the probable efficiency in engineering terms of the neural channel. They compare the neural case with Pulse Interval and Frequency Modulation systems, and tentatively conclude that the nervous system is a Pulse Interval Modulation system, this being very similar to the more familiar Frequency Modulation.

It is known that the impulse rate in nerves is subject to some variance (noise) for constant stimulus, (Barlow *et al.* 1954), though surprisingly little work has been done on this. On the theory of discrimination to be developed here, the importance of the variance of the pulse rates cannot be overstressed. Since the stimulus intensities to be discriminated are in terms of impulse rate, it is clear that variance in the rate must tend to produce confusion when the difference between the stimulus intensities to be discriminated is small. Indeed, the variance of impulse rates may be the primary factor limiting sensory discrimination. It might also, on the afferent side, limit the precision of motor control.

The present work is not concerned with direct measures of the rate of information flow through the human channel. What we are doing is trying to find (statistical) mechanisms behind the input-output relations generally described as 'stimulus' and 'response', and to relate ageing changes to features of this information system, in particular to its noise level.

VISUAL DISCRIMINATION AND AGEING

These eyes, like lamps whose wasting oil is spent. . . . .
Shakespeare

Discussion

Perhaps the most clearly established decrement in human performance associated with ageing is impairment in visual acuity. The cause is not clear from the literature; but it has been established that deterioration in the optical properties of the eye – opacity of the lens, pitting of the cornea, loss of accommodation, astigmatism – are not sufficient to explain the loss of acuity associated with ageing.

Weston (1949), in an excellent paper, concludes that the loss must be due largely to some unknown central changes. Important evidence for this is provided by the fact that the acuity/age differential is greatest for dim lights; in bright lights the acuity of the older groups may be equal, or very nearly equal, to the younger group and this cannot readily be explained in terms of simple optical defects of the eye. This is shown in Fig. 8.1, from Ferree, Rand and Lewis, cited by Weston (1949). What, then, sets the limit to the resolving power of the eye?

It is often stated that the limit is set by the 'retinal grain', the receptor density, in a manner analogous to the limit to photographic definition imposed by the 'grain' of the sensitive emulsion. But this statement requires some qualification, as becomes clear when we examine the published figures for visual resolution and the receptor density for the foveal region of the retina. It is possible to resolve double stars subtending only 60 seconds of arc, while vernier acuity can be as high as 8–10 seconds of arc (Hering, confirmed by Hartridge, 1950). Hecht and Mintz (1939) using a long black line on a white background obtained values as low as 0·5 seconds of arc. But the diameter of a cone in the extreme centre of the fovea is about 3·2 (av. of 10 independent reports) and this diameter at the retina corresponds to a subtended angle of 44 seconds of arc. Thus, it is possible to resolve angular sizes less than even the diameter of a single cone.

The intensity-acuity curve is somewhat mysterious. Hecht's well-known explanation in terms of 'functional retinal grain' (where it is supposed that the thresholds of the individual receptors are randomly distributed so that in dim light only a few receptors are functional) is open to serious objection.

It implies that only a small proportion of the total receptors are in fact functional at normal intensity levels, since acuity increases right up to glare intensities, and this is most unlikely since it would be inefficient and aggravates the receptor density problem. Secondly, Hecht's test of the theory is clearly mistaken. Hecht (1935) compares the observed acuity-intensity curve with the theoretical integral of the Gaussian normal probability curve, but, strangely, he plots log I where his theory demands I. (This curve was given in *A Handbook of Experimental Psychology*, C. Murchison, ed. Worcester 1934, and has been repeated ever since, most recently in Fulton's *Physiology*, 17th Edition (1955) p. 460). Hecht also assumes that each receptor works in an all-or-none manner, which is known to be incorrect (Granit, 1947). It might be thought that saccadic eye movements could, by scanning of the image across the retina, allow resolution to

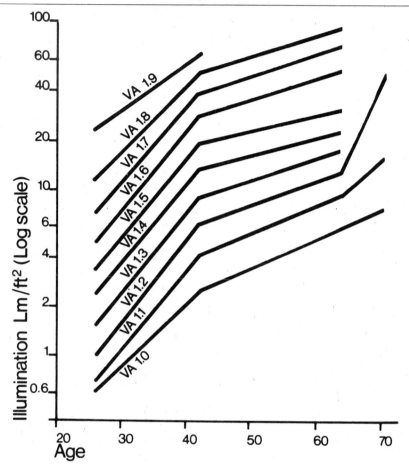

FIG. 8.1 *Showing reduction in visual acuity associated with chronological age for various intensity levels.*

exceed the value to be expected from the known retinal grain; small eye movements might be expected at least to sharpen intensity gradients by stimulation of the specialized 'on' and 'off' receptors (Barlow, 1953) at the borders of areas of equal intensity. But the ingenious work of Ratliff and Riggs (1950), with stabilized retinal images, suggests that eye movements do not in fact contribute to human acuity, though it should be emphasized that saccadic eye movement does prevent loss of acuity through local retinal adaptation, which would effectively reduce contrast.

As Hecht and Mintz (1939) have pointed out, what does seem important here is the spread of the image across the retina, due largely to interference effects. In any practical optical system the image is larger than the ideal 'geometrical image', defined by the

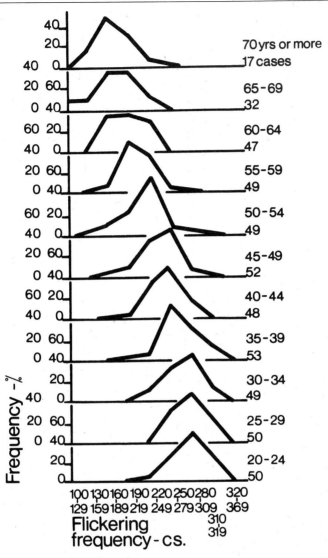

FIG. 8.2 *Showing frequency relationship between critical flicker fusion frequency and chronological age.*

angle subtended by the object; optical interference produces bands of gradually reduced intensity surrounding each image: resolving power is determined ultimately by ability to detect intensity differences between neighbouring sets of interference patterns.

Thus it appears that visual acuity must ultimately be limited by intensity discrimination. This is borne out by Ratliff and Riggs' finding, that with the perfect fixation given by a stabilized retinal image, acuity falls with the fall in contrast. This might well provide a basis from which to start an enquiry into the acuity-age relation:— Is the ageing effect basically due to impairment in intensity discrimination? If this is to explain Weston's finding that acuity is particularly poor at low intensities in the older age groups, then we should expect that intensity discrimination will also be especially poor at low values of I. We should also expect other intensity discrimination determined functions to be related to age – such as flicker fusion frequency (c.f.f.) (see Fig. 8.2). This has been found by Oshima *et al.* (1954).

We have measured the differential threshold $(\Delta I/I)$ for subjects of various ages, using the apparatus and method described in Appendix 1, this experiment will now be briefly described.

Experiment 1

Purpose It was decided to determine the differential brightness threshold $(\Delta I/I)$ for various values of I, and to compare the results for various age-groups, in order to test the hypothesis that differential brightness discrimination is impaired during middle age.

Method The apparatus described in Appendix 1 was used. Flashes of 25 m/second duration were used throughout; the areas of the test and background fields were also held constant. The stimulus light was projected on a white circular screen 3 metres distant from the subject. The reason for using projected light, rather than the more usual Maxwellian view, was that the position of the subject's eye is very much less critical; indeed with the distance used small head movements were second order. In all cases thresholds were determined in descending order of brightness, the value of ΔI being adjusted to give a 80% criterion of correct responses, these being recorded on electromechanical counters actuated by the subject's two response keys. About 20% 'dummy flashes' were introduced into each run, by introducing a silent shutter into the ΔI beam; this shutter was fitted with contacts which routed the subject's signals to counters which recorded his 'dummy' responses separately from the responses to genuine flashes.

Results It may be seen from Table 8.1 – in which the values of $\Delta I/I$ for each value of I may be compared for various ages – that the ratio increases with advancing age, particularly for the lower I-values. This result is compatible with the hypothesis that the deterioration in acuity associated with ageing is in part due to impairment of intensity discrimination. The fact that the age differential is in both cases greatest at low intensities is *prima facie* evidence for this interpretation.

TABLE 8.1

<small>DATA FROM EXPERIMENT I, SHOWING VALUES OF ΔI/I FOR VARIOUS AGES. IT MAY BE SEEN THAT THE INCREASE IN THE ΔI/I WITH AGE IS GREATER FOR SMALL VALUES OF I.</small>

	$\Delta I/I$ for small values of I related to age of subjects (25 m sec. Flash; Intensities in ft. lamberts.)			
Age	$I = 0.234$	$I = 0.117$	$I = 0.0646$	$I = 0.0126$
18	0·086	0·129	0·171	0·686
26	0·086	0·140	0·203	0·660
32	0·118	0·146	0·246	0·645
34	0·107	0·194	0·299	0·711
42	0·129	0·204	0·277	1·063
43	0·107	0·183	—	1·550
52	0·118	0·205	0·309	1·396

This effect seems to us to support the hypothesis that the age decrement in visual resolving power is due in part to reduction in intensity discrimination expressed by increase in $(\Delta I/I)$. We expect to find this effect on the basic idea that neurological noise increases with age. We shall now attempt to justify this statement by outlining a general theory of discrimination which has suggested experiments to be described.

An attempt to measure the neurological noise in the visual system of man

It is believed that in general the impulse rate is roughly proportional to the log of the stimulus intensity for an afferent sensory fibre. In particular, this has been shown by Hartline (1934) for a simple eye (*Limulus*, the horse-shoe crab) in which there are no synaptic cross connections between the receptors, each of which has its own optic nerve fibre. Almost all other eyes are complicated by the sharing of nerve fibres by several receptors, and by cross connections between the receptors occurring at synaptic layers in the retina. The mammalian optic nerve record is highly complex, but it appears reasonable to assume that the receptor cells themselves behave much like those of *Limulus*. It is also possible, as Rushton has suggested (1953), that the human fovea may be like the *Limulus* eye in being free of interconnections, but this is not as yet established.

Now if we assume that it is true of human retinal receptor cells that, at least approximately, r is proportional to $\log(I+n)$ where r is impulse rate and n is random noise, then Weber's Law, $(\Delta I/I = C)$ must be represented in terms of impulse rates by $(r+\Delta r)-r$. We may write, neglecting n for I large:

$$\Delta r = \log(I+\Delta I) - \log I$$

$$= \log(I + \frac{\Delta I}{I}).$$

and since $\dfrac{\Delta I}{I} = C$

$$\Delta r = \log(I+C) \text{ which is const.} \qquad \dots\,(2)$$

Thus we may suggest: *The brain demands a constant fixed difference between impulse rates arising from the comparison fields to make an intensity discrimination.*

It is well known that Weber's Law breaks down at low intensities: the ratio $\Delta I/I$ becomes greater for low values of I. Now suppose that Weber's Law breaks down because the mean noise becomes relatively important as I becomes small. If this is so, the extent of the Weber breakdown might be used to derive a measure of the noise in the visual system: different noise levels should give different breakdown curves. Thus the type of ageing data given in Table 8.1 takes on a new interest: it might indicate changes in neural noise level with ageing.

We have tried to test the hypotheses, (1) that the Weber breakdown is due to a constant in the denominator, as would be expected if the neural pulse rate is not proportional to $\log I$ but rather to $\log(I+n)$, where n is mean noise power, and (2) that the value of n tends to increase with chronological age, as sensory discrimination declines. The following experiment is a test of the first hypothesis.

Experiment 2

A determination of the breakdown of Weber's Law at low intensities to discover whether this may be expressed by a constant added to the denominator of the $\Delta I/I$ ratio

Purpose We expect that the breakdown of the Weber Law could be described by adding a constant to the denominator of the $\Delta I/I$ ratio if, as we suppose, the breakdown is due to noise in the discriminatory system, for this will come in as an additive constant, if r is proportional to $\log(I+n)$.

Method Foveal fixation was used, the circular background field subtending 8°, the test field 2° 20'. The display test field was not flashed upon the background for this experiment; it was continuously increased or reduced in intensity, the threshold being determined by the method of limits. This method was used rather than the more usual short flash technique, which is adopted in the later experiments, because (*a*) it was desired to avoid extra information from the 'on' and 'off' retinal mechanisms, and (*b*) we wanted the subjects to adopt their own threshold criteria rather than have a criterion imposed by the experimenter which is necessary with a normal Frequency psychophysical method. Lastly, (*c*) we wanted a long exposure (beyond the limit of the reciprocity relation) in order to discover the smallest possible value for the constant involved.

The subjects were allowed about twenty minutes for dark adaptation: white light was used for the stimulus display.

The data were examined in the following way: in place of the usual presentation of Weber's Law as a plot of $\Delta I/I$ against I, ΔI was plotted against I on a linear scale. This provides a simple test for the hypothesis that a constant should be added to the denominator to extend Weber's Law to low intensities; for if it is an additive constant which is responsible for the breakdown this method of plotting should give a straight line passing above the origin. (If Weber's Law did not break down the result would be a straight line passing through the origin, the slope being a function of the Weber constant C). Now this method of plotting not only allows us to test this hypothesis, but also allows us to estimate the value of the new constant. This may be done simply by extrapolating back past the origin to cut the I-axis. This value will give a measure of the constant in terms of the intensity units used.

Result The result for one highly trained subject is shown in Fig. 8.3. The values shown are the Means of six trials. It may be seen that a straight line fit is given for the experimental points down to very low intensities, when the curve drops until when $I = 0$, ΔI is a very small value indeed, representing the absolute threshold. Thus the hypothesis to be tested is confirmed up to a point. A constant may be added to the denominator to extend the Weber Law into the breakdown region, but this will not cover the entire range to $I = 0$.

It may further be seen, from the extrapolation, that the value of k in equivalent intensity units is, for this subject, in the region of 0·03 ft. 1.

We propose to write Weber's Law as

$$\frac{\Delta I}{I+k} = C \qquad \qquad \cdots (3)$$

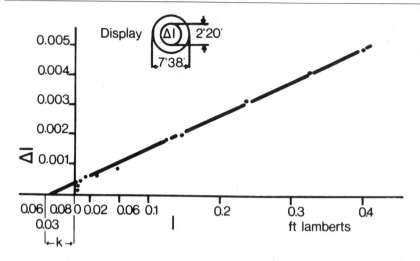

FIG. 8.3 *Data from Experiment 2. This is a typical curve averaged from six trials with one practised subject, aged 30, male. It shows $\Delta I / I$ for continuous viewing with foveal fixation. Extrapolation gives a value of k of about 0·03 ft l.*

which formulation extends the usual law to lower intensities. We shall regard the constant k as some function of the pulse rate variance, or noise, of the system.

The precise relation between k and internal noise remains at present somewhat mysterious, it must be confessed. The values obtained appear too large to be accepted simply as the mean noise power,[1] when we consider the high sensitivity of the eye and the quantal nature of light, which set an upper limit to the possible noise in the the system, if we assume a likely value for the signal/noise ratio of the visual system. It has been established that the eye responds to a light intensity of 50–100 quanta incident at the cornea, (Hecht, Shlaer and Pirenne 1942), the number of quanta actually absorbed by the rods being 5–8, estimated from frequency-of-seeing curves. It appears that a single quantum (the theoretical minimum) is sufficient to activate one rod (Bouman and van der Velden 1947) but as several rods must be stimulated for this activity to be accepted as a signal, it must be allowed that there may be appreciable noise in the system; but this cannot be large owing to the basic limitation imposed by (*a*) indivisibility of quanta, and (*b*) the small number of

---

[1] The experimental points depart from the straight line fit at very low intensities. It seems that the scotopic (rod) function will be different, or have a different slope and intersect, from the photopic (cone) function. We are concerned here only with photopic vision – the high value of 0·03 ft. l. for k evidently applies only to photopic vision.

quanta necessary. The suggestion that there is appreciable noise does, however, provide a reasonable explanation of the finding that more than one rod must be stimulated for the stimulus to reach consciousness or be acted upon, since this requirement will no doubt serve as a 'coincidence gate', reducing errors and false positives.

At present, although we might claim that k appears to be a function of noise, it probably is not a simple measure of noise power. A great deal of work remains to clear this up; in particular the value of k should be estimated for various levels of adaptation. It now seems possible, in view of Rushton and Campbell's (1954) finding that dark adaptation is not due primarily to regeneration of rhodopsin, that variation in noise level may be a function of neural gain in adaptation. Variation in summation time (Gregory, 1955a [No. 10]) could be another factor. Our value for k is too high to represent mean noise power at threshold, but it might perhaps represent the noise level for the incompletely dark adapted eye, or it might possibly represent the noise level for the cone system associated with photopic vision. It is important to establish these points, and this should not be too difficult, but for the moment we shall regard k as some function of visual noise and consider it as such in relation to ageing.

The relation between noise in the visual system and chronological age

Although the precise relation between k and mean noise level is not yet clear, we appear to be on fairly safe ground if we assume that it is some function of noise. The relation might be established in a number of ways, but this we have not yet done. We intend to relate it to the slope of frequency-of-seeing curves obtained for the same subjects. The slope of frequency-of-seeing curves allows us to specify the variance of the threshold (due to quantal and physiological variation) and knowing the quantal variation for the conditions used it should be possible to derive a fairly direct measure of threshold variance due to physiological factors. It might be thought that the pursuit of k is a waste of time when we might use frequency-of-seeing curves instead, but unfortunately many hours of testing are necessary to obtain each curve, and this is hardly practicable for older subjects. We do, however, intend to obtain such curves for selected subjects.

For the present we limit our enquiry to the relation to k, regarded as a function of neural noise.

If we plot the data given in Table 8.1 in the manner described above, we should be able to determine approximate values of k for each age group under these conditions. If k is some function of neural noise, this should relate noise level with age for the visual system. The

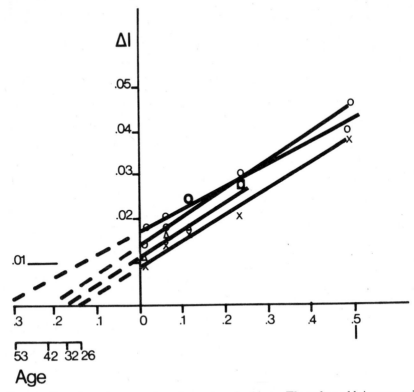

FIG. 8.4 *Data from four experienced age-spaced subjects. The values of k increase with age. (The k values are higher than for Fig. 8.3 because here the stimulus is given as 25 m. second flashes, and not continuously as in Fig. 8.3. Flashes are more convenient experimentally but do raise all k values.)*

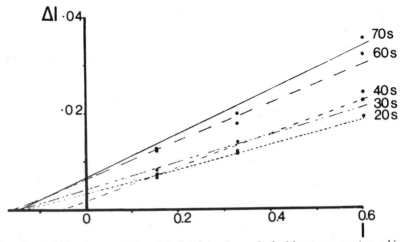

FIG. 8.5 *Relation between ΔI and I, fitted by the method of least squares (12 subjects aged 20–30, 11 aged 30–40, 7 aged 40–50, and 6 aged 70–80). White light was used, the intensity units being foot-lamberts. The background field (I) subtended 15°, the test field (ΔI + I) subtended 5°. The adjustment method of obtaining thresholds was used.*

result of such a plot is given in Fig. 8.4. It may be seen that k tends to increase with age, though it is not easy to fit the best straight line for older subjects owing to increased scatter. This increase in scatter should, however, be expected on the hypothesis that k is a function of noise, if noise level increases with age, since this should produce increased moment-to-moment variation in threshold. This result is regarded as a confirmation of the hypothesis that noise level increases with age. We also find a change in slope, suggesting that the older subjects adopt a *higher criterion* for distinguishing between background and signal. It is important to note that the proportion of false positives does not increase appreciably with ageing. So there must be a correspondingly raised criterion for acceptance of neural activity as representing a signal, if neural noise does increase with age (Fig. 8.5).

The detailed theory: The number of effective fibres and channel capacity

We have to consider not only changes in noise level with age, but the more general concept: change in channel capacity – one cause of which might be change in noise level. Now a further likely cause of reduction in the channel capacity of a neural channel is loss in the number of functional fibres in the nerve trunk. So far we have explicitly mentioned only single fibres carrying pulse modulated signals, but in general the intensity of a given area will be signalled by many fibres, the number being a function of the area of the stimulus and its position on the retina. We may suppose that when the number of fibres is large, the effective sample size from which the mean pulse rate may be estimated centrally is large and so a fine discrimination should be possible. Indeed we should expect the amount of information to be proportional to $\sqrt{N}$, where N is the total number of pulses lying within the area multiplied by the time over which the sample is accepted. If this is true, we may make a number of predictions, some of them being precise numerical predictions.

In the first place, we should expect the resolving power of the eye to be better for long than for short lines, for more receptors and more optic nerve fibres will be providing information for the essential intensity discrimination. This has in fact been found to be the case, as shown by Anderson and Weymouth (1923) and Hecht, Ross and Muelier (1947). Graham and Cook (1937) have demonstrated a reciprocal relation between duration and intensity for constant acuity, and it appears that area and intensity are also reciprocally related for constant acuity (Osgood, 1953, p. 164).

We should also expect absolute and differential threshold to fall with increase in area. In the latter case this should be true of increase in the area of *either the test or the background field*. For a given total field area, we should expect minimum threshold where both fields are equal, as is the case for a statistical significance test between means of two samples S_1 and S_2; the smallest difference may be established to a given criterion when $S_1 = S_2$.

We may now attempt to formulate some of the ideas used so far in the hope that we may know more precisely what to look for in trying to relate neural noise – or loss of channel capacity – to age. We should expect that if individual fibres in nerve trunks tend to degenerate with age, channel capacity may be reduced perhaps without increase in overall noise level in some cases. A study of the importance of area of stimulation of the retina provides a unique opportunity for controlling the effective number of fibres used for discrimination. We shall therefore go into the matter in some detail.

If we include the variance of r in eq. (2), and at the same time suppose that *the area A inspected is to be regarded as a set of N independent observations, where N is at least approximately proportional to A*, then for ΔI to be detected against I in some fixed proportion of the number of trials, (e.g. an 80 per cent criterion set up by the experimenter), we must have

$$\frac{[(r + \Delta r) - r] - C}{\sqrt{\left(\dfrac{1}{A_1} + \dfrac{1}{A_2}\right) V}} = \text{const.} \qquad \ldots \ldots (4)$$

where $(r + \Delta r)$, r are the mean neural pulse rates associated with the intensities $(I + \Delta I)$, I and V is the variance due to noise. If r is proportional to $\log (I + N)$, this reduces to eq. (2) for I somewhat less than $I + N$.

The constant C is introduced here to explain the fact that fewer than 50 per cent 'false positives' occur, and means – given eq. (2) and the variance of impulse rates as expressed in eq. (4) – that some fixed difference between impulse rates is required before discrimination is established, this difference being independent of the intensity I. In other words, Δr must be some fixed finite value at threshold. This is of considerable interest, for it provides an explanation of the Weber Constant, given as C in eq. (3). It may be thought of as a 'gate' to reduce the number of 'false positives' due to noise, to an acceptable level without undue sacrifice of sensitivity. The increasing proportion of 'false positives' associated with long practice may be due to a reduction of C. The value of C may perhaps be affected by psychological 'set' and selective attention.

It has been known for many years that intensity discrimination is affected not only by the value of I, but also by the areas of the fields to be discriminated. Nearly all the experiments on spatial summation have been undertaken with a single stimulus field to be discriminated against complete darkness: the results are generally described by two laws for the absolute-threshold case, these are:

1. For circular fields subtending up to about 6′ for the fovea and 40′ for the periphery

$$A.I = \text{const.} \quad \text{(Ricco's Law)} \qquad \dots (5)$$

2. For circular fields subtending from about 6′ up to about 20°

$$\sqrt{A.I} = \text{const.} \quad \text{(Piper's Law)} \qquad \dots (6)$$

These have been extensively studied, and it has been found that they are consistent with experimental data. Attempts have been made to fit the data with a single function; a function based on the theory to be developed here will be put forward later.

One interesting consideration, which has been invoked to explain spatial summation, is the increased probability of sufficient light quanta striking neighbouring receptors within an interval short enough for photochemical summation to take place – given that this is subject to a decay function in the absence of quanta, as must be supposed. It appears evident that this could only apply for intensities so low that quantum fluctuation is appreciable, but this is not the case for the test fields discriminated against an illuminated background of moderately high intensity since the test field intensity is then above the quantum fluctuation level. Surprisingly, there has been practically no work on spatial summation for differential thresholds, but it has been shown, by Brindley (1954), of red flashes on green background or green on red background that Piper's Law holds when the background is fixed and large, for the test flash between 3′ and 30′ in diameter. For smaller red or green flashes Ricco's Law holds, though for such small areas this may be no more than an expression of the optical defects of the eye; but for blue test flashes Ricco's Law holds up to 12′ diameter and this is certainly not a mere optical phenomenon. Piper's Law may be formulated for differential thresholds in these conditions by

$$\frac{\Delta I}{I} = \text{const.} \sqrt{\frac{1}{A}} \qquad \dots (7)$$

where I is the intensity of the background, ΔI the increment intensity of the test field to be discriminated, and A the area. The fact that the relations hold for the differential case where intensity is above the quantum fluctuation level probably rules this factor out for the differential case. The ageing effect (Fig. 8.5) also provides evidence against a pure quantum explanation and favours some biological factors.

If we are to regard spatial summation as a matter of increase of information with area, we should consider the effect of limiting the

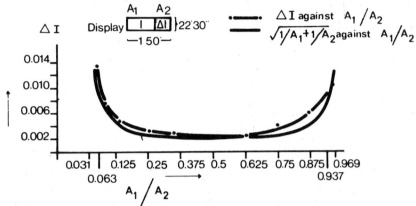

FIG. 8.6 *Data from Experiment 3. The broken lines show ΔI against area of the I field as this is increased to include more and more of the I field. It may be seen that ΔI is the minimum where the areas of the two fields are equal. The continuous line shows the theoretical function* $\sqrt{\dfrac{I}{A_1}+\dfrac{I}{A_2}}$ *fitted at the first middle points. (Average 8 subjects.)*

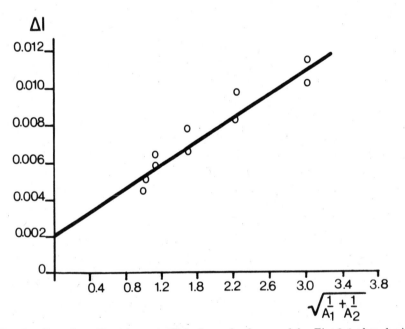

FIG. 8.7 *Data from Experiment 3. This shows the data used for Fig. 8.6 plotted with the theoretical function as abscissa and ΔI as ordinate. The best fit is given by a straight line; the hypothesis is thus satisfied.*

area of the background. The background area should be as important as the test field itself for the discrimination. This can, of course, only be done for the differential case. We should expect the threshold ($\Delta I/I$) to fall as the background area is increased, and we have found experimentally that this is so. The result was somewhat surprising to the subjects, who expected the just discernible test field to be 'swamped' by increase in the area of the surrounding background annulus. And indeed this might be expected if summation is supposed to be due to synaptic facilitation, as has been suggested.

Experiment 3

The effect of varying the background area upon differential intensity thresholds with continuous viewing

Method The screen used was a horizontal rectangle, 10·16 cm long by 2·54 cm in height, and placed at a distance of 3 m from the subject. It was illuminated by a pair of projectors; the projector providing the test field, (ΔI) was fitted with a thin metal slide which could be moved horizontally across the focal plane of the projector so that its vertical edge was focussed upon the screen. In this way it was possible to provide a rectangular test field superimposed upon the rectangular background, and variable in length horizontally. Thus the total area of background plus test field remained constant. The position of the edge of the test field was indicated by a moveable pointer placed immediately beneath the rectangular screen. The subjects were allowed to dark adapt for a period of about 20 minutes prior to the experiment.

Results We find that the general case where *either* field area may be varied can be written at least approximately

$$\frac{\Delta I}{I} = \text{const.} \sqrt{\frac{1}{A_1} + \frac{1}{A_2}} + C \tag{8}$$

where A_1 is the area of the test field, A_2 the area of the background and I and ΔI are as in Eq. (2).

The average results of eight subjects are shown in Fig. 8.6, together with the theoretical curve obtained from eq. (4). The curves are fitted at two points. It should be noted that ΔI is minimal when the areas are equal. Fig. 8.7 shows the same data, but plotted to test the hypothesis that ΔI is linearly related to

$$\sqrt{\frac{1}{A_1} + \frac{1}{A_2}}$$

which should be the case if the basic equation eq. (8) or better its corrected form, eq. (9) is true. This correction is the introduction of k, thus

$$\frac{\Delta I}{I+k} = \text{const.} \sqrt{\frac{I}{A_1} + \frac{I}{A_2}} + C \qquad (9)$$

As the test area is reduced the value of ΔI increases until the approximation $\Delta I/k$ for $(r+\Delta r) - r$ is no longer valid. The more accurate expression, $\log(k+I) - \log k$ should apply. In the absence of a background field A_2 is the whole total noisy visual field apart from the small illuminated test field A_1. As A_1 diminishes ΔI increases until the approximation $\Delta I/k$ used for $(r+r) - r$ is no longer valid and the more accurate expression

$$I + \frac{\Delta I}{k} = \text{exp.}\left(\frac{\alpha}{\sqrt{A}} + C\right)$$

$$= e^C \left(I + \frac{\alpha}{\sqrt{A}} + \frac{\alpha^2}{2A} \right) \qquad (10)$$

should be used, where A_1 is written as A and the constant involved as α. For very large A the terms containing A are negligible, therefore

$$I + \frac{\Delta I}{k} = \text{const., or } I = \text{const.} \qquad (11)$$

For smaller A

$$I + \frac{\Delta I}{k} = e^C\left(I + \frac{\alpha}{\sqrt{A}} \right)$$

or

$$\sqrt{A}\Delta I = \text{const.} + \text{const.} \sqrt{A} \qquad (12)$$

For even smaller A

$$I + \frac{\Delta I}{k} = e^C\left(I + \frac{\alpha}{\sqrt{A}} + \frac{\alpha^2}{2A} \cdots \right)$$

or $A + \Delta I = \text{const.} + \text{const.} \sqrt{A} + \text{const.} A.$ \qquad (13)

It is thus suggested that Ricco's and Piper's Laws may be regarded as approximations to the log equation that can be used at different levels. The constants for Willmer's data (which are given in unusual detail) work out as follows. It should, however, be noted that the thresholds are obtained here by the subject adjusting an intensity control until he is satisfied that he has found threshold; this may affect the result. For Willmer's data the constants are: roughly

$$I + \frac{\Delta I}{3 \cdot 21} = I \cdot 185 \left(I + \frac{4 \cdot 71}{D} + \frac{4 \cdot 71^2}{2D^2} \cdots \cdots \cdots \right) \cdots (14)$$

where D is the angular diameter, $k = 3 \cdot 21$, and $C = 0 \cdot 17$, in the units used, but unfortunately these are arbitrary. It remains to repeat the experiment with the same care using accurately determined intensities in standard units, and with various threshold criteria. The general form of the curve is, however, apparently correct. This development of the theory perhaps provides some confirmation of the basic idea.

Experiment 4

Borders regarded as separating and limiting external information sources: physical objects

Purpose We have argued that when the problem of visual thresholds is considered in terms of available information, rather than energy, the background appears to be as important as the test fields. It provides information for the discrimination to be made. For this reason we find differential thresholds of more interest than absolute thresholds, although these have received more attention. So far we have considered the case where the background is bounded by outer darkness, but this is not a usual state of affairs. If physical objects are to be regarded as independent information sources (and the appearance of an object is generally unaffected by the other objects in the field, though not always), we should expect the borders of objects to limit the area within the total visual field from which information is accepted for a given discrimination. Fortunately it is a very simple matter to test this idea, and this we have done, if crudely.

Method It has been known for some time that if a test field be surrounded by some figure drawn upon an illuminated background, the threshold will be raised. This has been found by Craik and Zangwill (1939), and it is discussed by Bartley (1941). It is perhaps generally accepted by psychologists that the borders produce some sort of retinal interference which raises the threshold. An alternative which we shall put forward here is that borders may serve to limit the area of the field accepted as a single information source. This suggests a quite definite prediction: it should be the case that the area of the background lying outside the figure will not provide information for the discrimination of the central test field, and so will have no effect upon the threshold. This we have tested by comparing the threshold obtained for (*a*) a circular field placed centrally in a large circular background having an inscribed concentric black ring with (*b*) the same central test field but on a plain background limited to the area enclosed by the black ring in the previous display. We have found that, over a wide range of areas for the comparison, the threshold was nearly the same in both cases. This is regarded as evidence that the ring serves to limit the area from which information is accepted for the discrimination. This finding is important if we are to maintain that the previously discussed experimental data and interpretation apply to perception of the world of physical objects.

Results Table 8.2 shows the threshold increment, as the ratio ($\Delta I/I$), of the inner circular field, subtending $0° 21'$ to the observer, to be discriminated against various backgrounds, illuminated with an intensity of $0·45$ ft. 1.

Under the heading 'Test Field', column 'a' gives the values of ΔI for five diameters of a black ring drawn on the background disk. It may be seen that the threshold rises as the diameter of the ring is reduced, although the total area of the background remains practically unchanged. Now these threshold readings are to be compared with those where the total background is reduced to the ring diameters which have been used. Column 'b' shows ($\Delta I/I$) for the corresponding background areas. The prediction is that the thresholds should be

TABLE 8.2
DATA FROM EXPERIMENT 4

	Background Fields (Intensity : 0·45 m l)			Test Field (Area : 3·84 sq. cm)		
	Diam. (cm)	Area (sq. cm)	Angle	(a) (With rings) $\Delta I_a/I_a$	(b) (Without rings) $\Delta I_b/I_b$	(c) $(\Delta I_a/I_a - \Delta I_b/I_b)$
1.	3·81	11·40	0° 44'	0·067	0·095	−0·028
2.	5·08	20·26	0° 58'	0·061	0·063	−0·002
3.	6·35	25·32	1° 14'	0·050	0·055	−0·005
4.	7·62	45·59	1° 28'	0·053	0·045	0·008
5.	8·89	62·06	1° 28'	0·038	0·034	0·004

This table shows the average values of $\Delta I/I$ for four subjects. It may be seen that changing the diameter of the annulus border is comparable to changing the diameter of the background field as a whole. This experiment, though not directly concerned with ageing, is important in answering a possible objection to the general theory put forward: namely, that the previous results may not apply to normal object perception, or practical acuity tests.

the same in the corresponding cases where the areas enclosed by the ring are equal to the total background areas. It may be seen from the difference column, given as (c), that the differences are very small (not significant) except for the case of the smallest area when the 'ring threshold' is lower than predicted.

It appears that the ring does not completely isolate the inner annulus as a separate information source in this case where the angular separation between the ring and the edge of the test field is small. The ring has still less effect on the threshold when closer to the test field. This phenomenon should be investigated further, to discover how far it is retinal and how far central in origin. It would be interesting to employ *C* shaped figures with various gap sizes; we might expect a gradual fall in threshold with increase in gap on a retinal hypothesis, but if cortical it might be a matter of interpreting the figure as a separate object, in which case the effect might be expected to hold until extrapolation across the gap to complete the circle breaks down. There should be a sudden fall in threshold at this gap size.

Comparison of k *for one and for two eyes*

We find that the observed value of k depends on at least the following factors:

1. The duration of the test flash. (Up to the integrating time of the eye.)

2. The area of the test flash.

3. In the case of continuous viewing of the test field, (or if both test and background fields are flashed simultaneously) the area of the background affects k. (It is noteworthy that background area has practically no effect on differential threshold if the test field is projected upon it for a short duration. In fact, the threshold is actually lowest when the two fields are the same area).

It was decided to find out what happens to k when the display is viewed with one eye only. It is often said that the two eyes are quite independent, from the point of view of apparent brightness; Pirenne argues (1948) that the reduction in absolute threshold for two eyes is due purely to increase in probability of quantum capture: he says that the position is the same as if the eyes belonged to different people, each person making independent judgements at each flash. But this argument is unlikely to apply to fairly high intensity differential thresholds. We would expect an improvement in total signal/noise ratio, and so some decrease in differential threshold at all intensities. More precisely, we may suppose that for monocular vision the non-

stimulated eye contributes noise which will be mixed with the signal
and noise from the stimulated eye. Now if we present the stimulus to
corresponding regions of both retinas the signal will be doubled while
the total noise will probably remain constant.

The decrease in signal for one eye should be precisely equivalent
to adding noise to the system, which we suppose occurs with ageing.
Thus the differential threshold for various intensities (and the value
of k) should change from bi- to monocular vision just as from young
to older subjects. This idea has been tested by determining monocular differential thresholds in identical conditions to those employed
in Experiment 2.

Experiment 5

Estimate of k *for monocular vision*

Purpose To compare the value of k for monocular and binocular
vision, for various age groups.

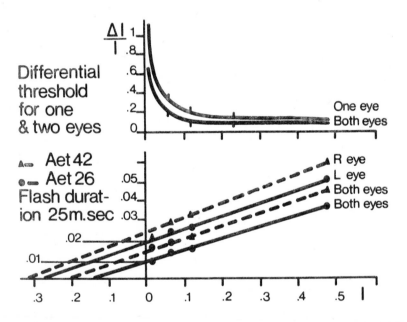

FIG. 8.8 *Data from Experiment 5. The lower graph shows* ΔI *plotted against I for
various values of I for binocular vision (continuous lines) and monocular vision (broken
lines) for two subjects, one aged 26, the other 42. The result is typical of the total data
so far obtained. (a) k increases with age, (b) k is greater for one than for two eyes, (c) the
Weber constant C, given by the tangent of the angle, increases with age and is greater for
monocular vision. The same is true for monocular vision. The same is true for reduced
retinal area with one or two eyes. The upper graph shows* $\Delta I/I$ *against I on the same abscissa
scale to indicate the position of the Weber breakdown as conventionally represented.*

Method Exactly as for Experiment 2, except that the display was viewed monocularly, with the favoured eye.

Results It was found that, for six subjects, differential thresholds were higher for the monocular condition. Fig. 8.8 shows a graphical determination of k for two subjects (*aet.* 26 and 42) for one and two eyes. These subjects are typical, but display rather less random scatter than most. It may be seen that, for these subjects, the increase in age produces the same type of shift that is produced by closing an eye. It also appears (confirmed by the other subjects) that the threshold for two eyes remains lower at high intensities well above the breakdown of the Weber Law. This would be difficult to explain on quantum considerations; it is however to be expected on the present theory of thresholds.

This experiment is of some interest in that very little has been reported on comparison between thresholds for one and two eyes; particularly for differential thresholds. The result indicates that reduction in effective number of fibres transmitting the signal is at least in some respects equivalent to increased noise level. This will assume considerable importance in our treatment of nerve deafness.

HEARING

Introduction

We have been regarding visual discrimination as a matter of incoming signals being detected against internal neurological noise. Within limits, increase in the area or the duration of the photic stimulus – the signal – provides more information and so allows a lower threshold intensity. We have suggested that ageing may be associated with increase in the mean noise power level in the visual system due to neural degeneration. In this section we shall try to apply some of the previous ideas to hearing, and in particular to deafness associated with late middle and old age. This will lead to considerations for the design of suitable hearing aids for old people.

Three types of deafness are generally distinguished, including partial impairment: (1) *Conduction deafness,* where there is loss in the middle ear, often due to thickening of the tympanum or to otosclerosis. (2) *Nerve deafness* (formally known as *Perception deafness*), distinguished by impairment in both air and bone conduction, and associated with degeneration of the sensory cells of the inner ear or other neural damage. This is associated with ageing and will parti-

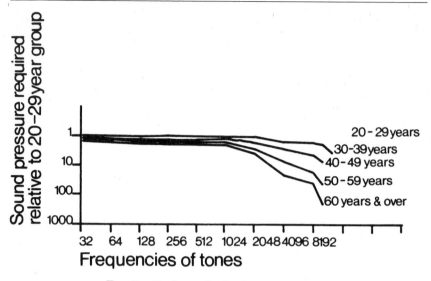

FIG. 8.9 *Presbyacusia, for five age groups.*

cularly concern us here (see Fig. 8.9). (3) *Central deafness*, which is rare and has no known peripheral origin, being regarded as a psychogenic disorder often associated with aphasia, will not concern us here.

There appears to be no mystery to conduction deafness. Otosclerosis, damage to the tympanum or blocking of the auditory meatus would clearly be expected to produce reduction in the amplitude of vibration of the auditory signal at the oval window (and thus of the endolymph in the cochlea) for a given stimulus energy. We may say simply that middle ear deafness is a case of signal attenuation. As we should expect, some suitable external amplifier can make good the deficiency – in fact hearing aids are found to work satisfactorily for cases of conduction deafness.

Nerve deafness, on the other hand, may be a different matter. In the first place it is striking that hearing aids are less satisfactory for cases of nerve deafness than for conduction deafness. It is generally held that nerve deafness is due to attenuation, through reduction in the number of effective auditory nerve fibres. But if this is so, why do not hearing aids make good the loss, as they do for conduction deafness? It seems clear that nerve deafness is characterized by *confusion*, indeed the older term 'perception deafness', which is still often used, indicates this clinical distinction.

Certain definite features are characteristic of nerve deafness: in particular, (i) the deterioration is primarily in the upper end of the frequency spectrum; and often there are sudden dips in the audiogram, (ii) the curious phenomenon of loudness recruitment is common, though not invariable. Middle ear deafness is characterized by a depressed but 'flat' audiogram, and loudness recruitment is never found in pure middle ear deafness. The clinical characteristics are quite distinct: can we explain them in terms of our general information considerations?

It appears clear that middle ear deafness is due simply to attenuation of the auditory signal; the signal/noise ratio for the ear will thus be reduced. But inner ear or nerve deafness is not so simple; it is generally held that this is due to loss in the number of functional fibres of the eighth nerve, often through degeneration or damage of the endings at the Organ of Corti. This is generally supposed to produce attenuation in a manner rather similar to attenuation through middle ear damage. Now this does not appear to us to be correct. The auditory signal is coded by the cochlea and nerve endings so that frequency and intensity are transmitted in terms of pulse rates and number of fibres stimulated. Although the precise manner in which this information is coded is still in dispute, it is at least clear that the nerve does not transmit sound vibrations directly as do the tympanum and stapes: the information is coded and transmitted to the brain in a different form. Now loss of fibres can hardly produce attenuation (as would, for example, damage to the stapes) by reducing signal amplitude, for by this time the signal has been encoded into a different form.[1]

The considerations we have advanced for the case of vision would lead us to suspect that reducing the number of effective fibres might be rather like reducing the area of stimulation of the retina: the number of nerve impulses available for discriminations to be made will be reduced in both cases.

We should also consider the possibility that nerve deafness may in some cases be due to increase in neural noise tending effectively to mask the signal. As for the case of vision, we may suppose that there is a 'gate' tending to reject noise and prevent an undue proportion of false positives and similar errors; thus the noise may not reach consciousness. Actually various types of 'noises in the head' are generally found with hearing impairment, but these should not be regarded as an accurate index of the neurological noise level present.

Although we reject loss of fibres as a case of signal attenuation, we cannot rule out mechanical attenuation in the inner ear as a possible factor in inner ear deafness, as determined by bone conduction. But it does not appear to us that it is likely to be important for a reason

[1] Rasmussen in 1940 counted the number of fibres in the human auditory nerve and found in the cochlear nerve an average of 31,400 fibres with about 2200 less for ages 44 to 60 years. See Covell (1952). Degeneration starts in the embryo (Guild, 1932).

which will be given below in the discussion on loudness recruitment.

Review of the phenomena of nerve deafness in the light of the general theory

If indeed nerve deafness is due to reduction in channel capacity we should expect to find that increase in neural noise has similar effects to reduction in the number of functional fibres. We should therefore enquire whether in both cases the high tone deafness typical of nerve deafness is manifested.

Fletcher (1938) has investigated thermal noise masking very thoroughly, and finds that high tones are more susceptible to masking than low tones. Fig. 8.10 shows a curve due to Fletcher showing the noise spectrum required to give equal masking to tones throughout the sensitivity range of the ear. Thus the addition of white noise does primarily impair high tone response as expected on the hypothesis.

In the case of vision we can control the number of effective fibres by simply increasing or decreasing the stimulus area; we cannot do this for hearing but have to resort to evidence provided by nerve damage as found *post mortem* or produced experimentally. Fortunately it so happens that there is quite a lot of evidence available of the effect upon hearing of loss of nerve fibres in the eighth nerve.

Dandy (1933*a*, *b*, 1935) developed an operative technique for alleviating the symptoms of Ménière's disease by partial sectioning

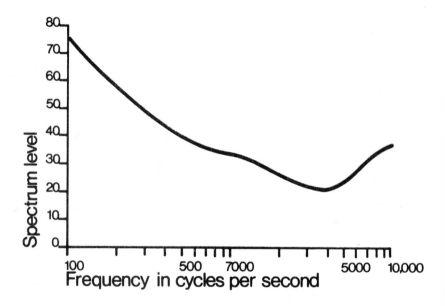

FIG. 8.10 *The thermal noise spectrum producing uniform masking.*

of the eighth nerve on the affected side. Dandy cut into the eighth
nerve from the anterior side in order to cut the labyrinthine fibres;
but there is no observable line of demarcation between the labyrin-

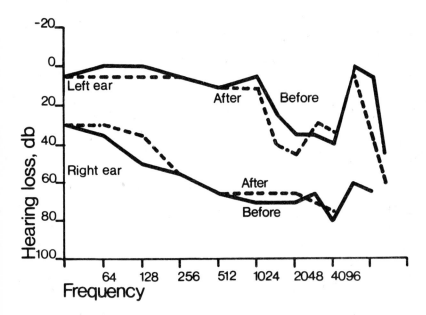

FIG. 8.11 *Effects of eighth-nerve sectioning for Ménière's disease. Results before and after destruction of about one-fourth of cochlear fibres.*

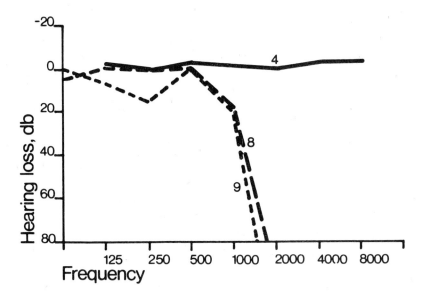

FIG. 8.12 *The effects of partial nerve sectioning upon auditory 'acuity' in cats. Cat 4 remained normal; cats 8 and 9 lost 'acuity' for the high tones.*

thine and cochlear fibres, and so the technique was adopted of cutting across rather more than half the nerve trunk, and thus into the cochlear branch of the nerve. The effects upon hearing were determined by pre- and post-operative audiometry. It was found that in all cases where there was any hearing loss this was for high tones: selective low tone loss never occurred.

Partial section of the eighth nerve has been investigated with animals. Wever and Bray (1937) found that for cats partial sectioning produced high tone loss, and this has been confirmed by Neff (1947), who found no change in cochlear response. The animal studies not only confirm Dandy's finding for the human ear but rule out the possibility that the *direction* of cut into the nerve is important. It appears that the important factor is the proportion of the total number of fibres severed (Fig. 8.11 and 8.12).

The similarity in the effects of added white noise and reduction in number of effective nerve fibres seem to us striking but, although we find the predicted similarity between (a) old age deafness, (b) white noise masking and (c) partial nerve sectioning, we do not know why all these produce *high* tone deafness. We could make a number of guesses: the greater specificity of response to high tones suggests that fewer fibres are responsible for a given band width at high frequencies, which might be one factor, but the situation is clearly complicated by many factors, such as the change over from representation of frequency first by pulse rate in single fibres, then in volleys and finally representation by place. For the moment we shall have to be content to point out the correlation without seeking any more precise explanation. It is interesting that the critical band width for masking, frequency discrimination and intelligibility all display similar functions when plotted against frequency (Licklider, 1951).

Tinnitus and loudness recruitment

Nerve deafness is often, though not always, associated with tinnitus of some kind. This may be an almost pure tone, steady or fluctuating, or it may be a hissing sound. It is usually high pitched. It is known to be generally peripheral in origin. Although we should not equate tinnitus with neural noise, since much noise appears to be 'gated', tinnitus is clear evidence for undue noise of some kind in the system. Where fibres are degenerating we should expect some random activity before they finally become inert. Tinnitus is associated with hearing loss for tones in the neighbourhood of the experienced tinnitus tone, (Davis, 1951). We have also observed this in cases of deafness due to gun fire. We are tempted to regard this as essentially

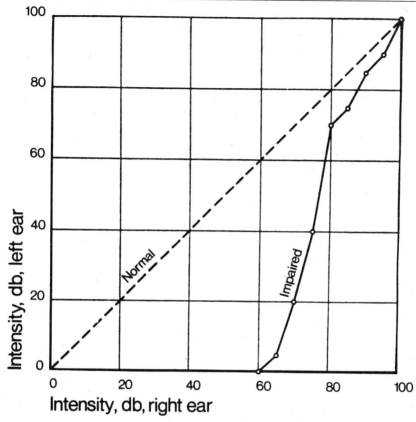

FIG. 8.13 *Loudness recruitment. This shows how for the nerve deaf ear the loudness gradient, determined by matching, is steeper until finally balance is attained.*

pure tone masking, especially as it has been established that masking is neural in origin and not due to the mechanical properties of the basilar membrane. Masking does not show itself in the cochlear potentials, and it does not occur binaurally to any significant extent (Wever, 1949, p. 387) which appears to limit the origin of masking to the auditory nerves afferent to the cochlear nucleus, since Lowy (1945) has found masking though the eighth nerve trunk is severed, which rules out central inhibitory reflex as the cause of masking.

Loudness recruitment (where the subjective loudness scale is unusually steep, as demonstrated by binaural loudness matching when one ear is primarily affected) is found only with nerve deafness. It is associated with damage to the nerve endings at the Organ of Corti, (Dix, Hallpike and Hood 1948) as in Ménière's disease, which appears to be due to abnormal raising of the endolymph pressure or some other condition causing general stimulation of the endings, (Wever, 1949, p. 355). Loudness recruitment is not found when the auditory nerve is injured, as by a tumour in the auditory canal. Dix *et al.* (1948) explain recruitment by suggesting that the auditory elements whose thresholds are high may be less susceptible to injury and degeneration than low-threshold elements, and that they may contribute a proportionately greater share to subjective loudness. It is an important fact that where one ear is primarily affected, so that effective binaural comparison is possible, the apparent intensity of loud sounds is equal for the two ears, though for faint sounds they may be greatly different. This provides strong evidence for the view that mechanical attenuation in the inner ear is unimportant in nerve deafness. It is also perhaps a difficulty for Dix's theory, since some high-threshold fibres would be expected to be damaged, especially as we are dealing with a continuous not a step function (Fig. 8.13).

A suggested explanation of loudness recruitment and auditory fatigue

Recruitment is associated with end organ but not nerve damage as stated above, and it appears likely that recruitment is associated with tinnitus. If we suppose that nerve ending damage tends to produce noise, it appears that recruitment might be associated with raised noise level. This is borne out by Steinberg and Gardner (1937) who find recruitment for the normal ear in the presence of a masking noise.

Increase in intensity produces increase in both the impulse rate and the number of fibres activated. It is generally supposed that loudness is represented by the total neural activity present. But we have postulated a 'gate' rejecting continuous noise activity: it thus appears reasonable to suppose that loudness is represented not by the total neural activity, but by the activity which is above the 'gate' level. Now this suggests an explanation of recruitment: the 'gate' might well restrict the total loudness scale from the lower end. The nerve deaf ear is virtually normal for loud sounds – which we explain by supposing that its essential sensitivity is normal – but the increased noise level and raised 'gate' we suppose reduce the discrimination for low level signals, and perhaps restrict the loudness scale from the lower end, producing recruitment.

It is interesting to consider *auditory fatigue* in this respect. Auditory fatigue is the temporary reduction in sensitivity following continuous stimulation. It is not necessary for the 'fatiguing' sound to be particularly loud; the effect is a function of the duration and loudness of the 'fatiguing' tone. Now we might suppose that auditory fatigue is due not to fatigue or adaptation, in the classical sense, but rather to a

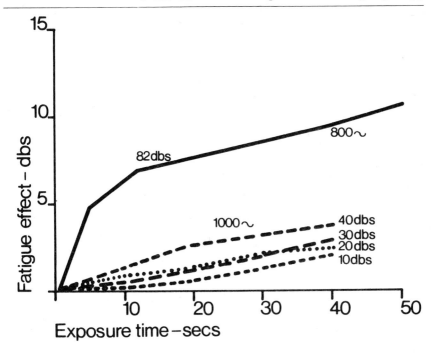

FIG. 8.14 *Fatigue of the ear as a function of tonal duration. The intensity in decibels is indicated on each curve. The fatigue effect, in decibels, is the elevation of the threshold resulting from exposure.*

raising of the 'gate' to reject the continuous 'fatiguing' noise or tone. The neural 'gate' could hardly distinguish between external sound noise or internal neural noise, and so we might expect that it will be raised, provided the time-constant of the 'gate' mechanism is of the right order. We cannot predict an upper limit for the time-constant (it is *a priori* possible even that years of raised noise might be required to shift the 'gate') but we might suppose on general grounds that the low limit will be above the amplitude modulation frequencies which can be readily distinguished. If the 'gate' followed intensity changes of wanted signals it would clearly reject useful information.

We may now suppose that auditory fatigue is due to a raising of the 'gate' tending to reject the continuous external noise or tone: what predictions could we make to test this hypothesis? Clearly auditory fatigue should display the essential characteristics of nerve deafness: in particular recruitment should occur with auditory fatigue as it does with the type of nerve deafness we believe to be associated with raised neural noise. Interestingly enough this is in fact the case. Békésy and Davis (Wever, 1949, p. 324) have observed that auditory fatigue does not affect high intensity tones. It is thus quite different from classical adaptation or fatigue, and unlike attenuation as we predict. Further, auditory fatigue is produced only by high tones, and its neural origin appears to be the same as for nerve deafness – between the electro-cochlear activity and the binaural localization process (Wever, 1949, p. 324). We thus differ from Hood (1950) who regards auditory fatigue as similar to peripheral adaptation as described by Matthews (1931) (Fig. 8.14).

Experiment 6

Purpose This experiment is as nearly as possible a repetition of the visual experiment where the breakdown of the Weber Law was measured and a constant k estimated from the curve. By translating this experiment into sound, we may not only obtain some check on the original results (which is particularly important because quantum fluctuation cannot be a factor here) but further, the method should give at least a relative measure of neural noise which might be related to degree of deafness, for various frequencies as determined by standard audiometric techniques.

Method Differential thresholds for various pure tones were deter-mined: bone conduction being used throughout. A steady tone was suddenly increased in amplitude (the phase remaining constant) for a duration of 25 m. seconds, at intervals of one second. Thus pure tone pips were heard against a background of the same tone. If we call the background intensity I and the increment pip intensity ΔI, then by obtaining threshold values of ΔI for various values of I in the region of the Weber Law breakdown it should be possible virtually to repeat the visual experiment for the case of hearing.

The apparatus used is described in Appendix 2. Thresholds were determined to the nearest one db throughout, in order of increasing intensity. The criterion adopted was to be able to hear *all* the tone pips; it was not possible to adopt a criterion such as the 80% criterion used for the vision experiments, because of the limitation imposed by one db steps. If smaller steps had been used it would have been difficult to obtain enough readings in each experimental run to obtain a series of curves under the various conditions for comparison. It was essential to adopt a technique which yielded a lot of data for it was not always possible to get the nerve deaf subjects on more than one or perhaps two occasions. The aim was to devise a clinical type of test of sufficient accuracy. The consistency was found to be high for each run, re-test differences seldom exceeding one db.

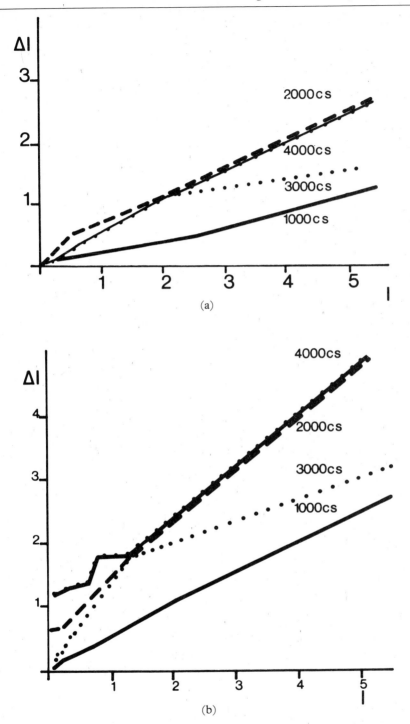

FIG. 8.15 *Differential threshold plotted as ΔI against I for subject A and B on a linear scale, showing the lower end only.*

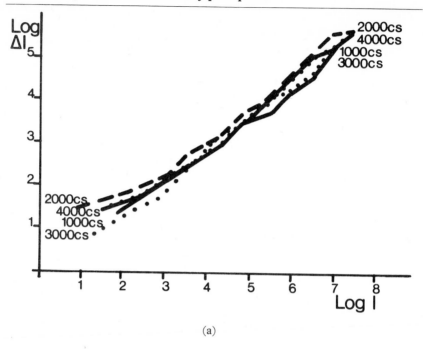

(a)

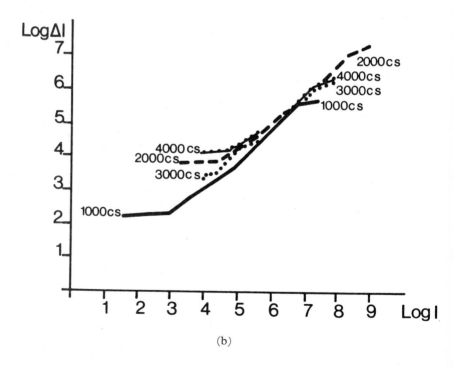

(b)

FIG. 8.16 *The same data as Fig. 8.15 plotted on a two-way log scale.*

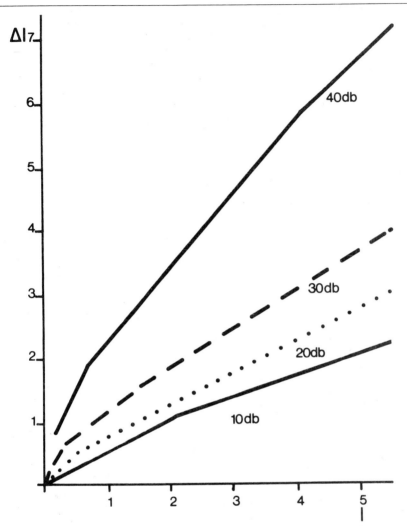

FIG. 8.17 *Differential thresholds* ($\Delta I/I$) *found for various absolute threshold impairments (from 10 db loss to 40 db loss) averaged across subjects, and across frequencies giving the same absolute threshold losses. (Table 8.3 gives the estimated values of* k *and* C *for these data).*

Conclusions We find that with increasing nerve deafness: (*a*) the ΔI against I curve is raised, and (*b*) the slope becomes steeper. This shows that: (i) the value of the constant k increases with nerve deafness, and (ii) the Weber fraction C also increases with nerve deafness.

These findings may be seen in the following figures; further data are given in Table 8.4 (p. 215). Fig. 8.15 shows ΔI plotted against I for two representative subjects: the first is normal, the other has nerve deafness at certain frequencies. These curves are given on a linear scale. Fig. 8.16 shows the same data for these subjects, but given on a log-log scale. The scale in Fig. 8.15 is restricted; this excludes the higher values shown on the 2-way log scale. The ΔI threshold for each value of I for 13 subjects, 3 normal, the remainder with various degrees of nerve deafness, were then grouped according to absolute thresholds (to the nearest 5 dbs) regardless of individuals or test tone frequencies. Means were calculated for each successive 5 dbs of I above the absolute threshold. Fig. 8.17 shows these Means for four different thresholds (10 db, 20 db, 30 db, 40 db).

It is possible to ignore differences between frequencies here, because in all cases the origin of the sensitivity scales (o db) is taken from the absolute threshold for the normal ear for the frequency concerned. This is already built into the audiometer and so requires no special correction.

Values for k and C have been estimated, by extrapolation and by taking the tangent of the slope, respectively. The lower portions of the curves have been ignored for these estimates.

TABLE 8.3

Hearing Impairment (db loss)	k	C
10	0·2	0·30
20	0·6	0·49
30	1·1	0·62
40	1·0	1·10

The data shown in Fig. 8.16 have been used to estimate the values of k and C; shown in this table for impairments of absolute threshold from 10 db to 40 db loss.

It is concluded that:— for small impairment an important cause is neural noise, suggested by increase in k. For severe hearing loss, the main cause is neural degeneration, indicated by steep rise in C without change in k.

Experiment 7

A preliminary investigation of the effect of addition of external white noise upon estimated value of k

Purpose A great advantage of the sound over the visual situation is the possibility of adding physical noise comparable to neural noise. In the case of vision, it is possible to arrange a background of dynamic

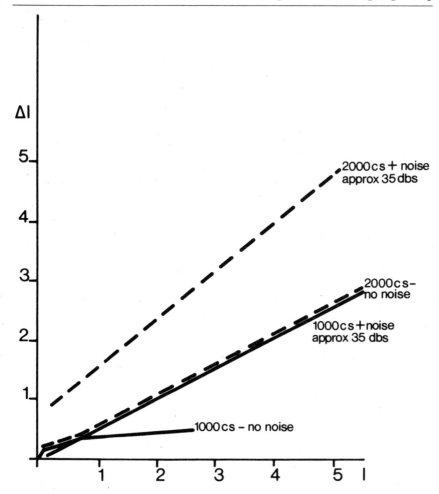

FIG. 8.18 *Differential threshold plotted as* ΔI *against I for one subject, with and without added noise.*

random specks, but it is unlikely that such an arrangement will ever be comparable with neural noise in the visual system. But we should expect that with sound external physical noise should add to neural noise and should increase our estimated value of k. In fact, we should expect that ΔI plotted against I for the nerve deaf ear should look very like the case of the normal ear with the addition of random noise. We should expect that k, as estimated by extrapolation, should increase with increase in the level of added physical noise. By relating the estimated increase in k to the increase in added physical noise, it should be possible to determine how external and internal noises add. Unfortunately we have not yet got sufficient data to say anything definite about this. At present it looks as though the hearing situation may be expressed by

$$\frac{St/a}{\sqrt{N^2+n^2t/a^2}} \qquad \dots (15)$$

where S is signal amplitude, N is noise amplitude, a is the attenuation factor of the ear and t is signal duration within the linear portion of the integrating time of the ear.

Method This experiment was conducted in a manner precisely similar to that of the previous experiment, except that approximately 'white' noise was added continuously during each trial while values of ΔI were determined for increasing values of I. The ΔI tone pips were again of 25 m. secs. duration, repeated at one second intervals.

Results The addition of external physical noise was found to produce the expected changes in the ΔI against I curves. The estimated value of k clearly does increase with added physical noise, and it appears that the increase is of the right order to be compatible with the law of addition suggested in eq. (15) above, though we cannot say anything more definite at present. It may be seen in Fig. 8.18 that addition of approximately 35 dbs of physical noise shifts the 1000 cycles curve so that it fits the 2000 cycles curve: for this subject the absolute threshold at 2000 cycles is raised 25 db above the threshold for 1000 cycles. It is not possible to obtain a reasonably reliable estimate of k from the 1000 cycles curve in the absence of noise since this particular curve is not straight enough; but this does appear possible for the 2000 cycles curves shown. The value of k increases here by about 20 dbs of added physical noise.

It thus appears that addition of external physical noise produces precisely the same effect upon the ΔI against I curves which is produced by nerve deafness. This is compatible with the hypothesis that the nerve deafness is due to raised neural noise: provided external and neural noise add linearly.

Experiment 8

To investigate the effect of masking noise upon absolute threshold for nerve deafness

Purpose Many nerve deaf people appear to be able to hear better in noisy surroundings. The evidence is largely from personal reports and observations from industry where people work in noisy surroundings; obviously this must be accepted with caution for lip reading may take place to some extent, perhaps unconsciously. However, it seemed worth investigating the effect of noise and tone masking in nerve deafness in conditions where extra-auditory information was impossible. This appears to us particularly desirable in view of the interesting finding of Galambos and Davis (1944), working on single auditory nerve fibres, that spontaneous activity may be inhibited by noise.

Method Thresholds were found for pure tone signals against white noise masking.

Results Fig. 8.19 shows the threshold values for the tones of various frequencies for various masking noise levels. The results for two representative subjects are given, one normal, the other displaying nerve deafness over the range 1500–4000 cycles. It may be seen that for the normal subject the threshold intensity rises steadily for all frequencies tested with increasing noise. But that for the nerve deaf subject there is a curious 'kink' for the upper frequencies at low noise levels, though this curve rises steadily where the hearing is normal. Now this kink does appear to be a real effect, though perhaps we have insufficient evidence to be certain. If the effect is genuine, it may well represent the effect upon auditory sensitivity of Galambos and

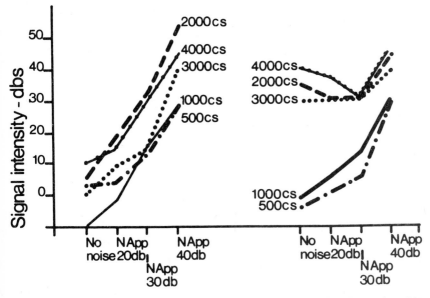

FIG. 8.19 *Thresholds for pure tone signal with varying amounts of background masking noise, for two subjects, (left) normal subject and (right) nerve-deaf subject.*

Davis's (1951) finding that noise inhibits spontaneous neural activity of the auditory nerve, as determined by them electrophysiologically. Is it possible that this is the basis of improvement in hearing with addition of noise which some nerve deaf people seem to experience? If so, it is possible that the deliberate addition of noise in hearing aids may be of advantage in some cases of nerve deafness. We suspect that the addition of noise might well be of some use if introduced with care, but it appears that continuous noise is detrimental in many nerve deaf cases. The most extreme case we have tested, has stated that he is occasionally able to hear an alarm clock ticking in the morning, provided he has not worn his hearing aid for two or three days. He maintains – and he is a highly intelligent man whose testimony is worth quoting – that continuous wearing of a hearing aid is detrimental in his case.[1] This requires serious investigation; it would not surprise us to discover that continuous noise impairs hearing for nerve deafness where this is due to neural noise, though temporary improvement may be afforded by what would normally be noise masking. It appears reasonable to suppose that hearing aids should be designed to filter out those frequencies where the patient displays high internal noise.

Suggestions for the design of hearing aids for the nerve deaf

The following suggestions are essentially preliminary and are intended as an indication of how we hope to apply our studies of thresholds under various conditions to the practical problems of nerve deafness associated with middle and old age. The design of suitable hearing aids for old people is a very real problem and it is not likely to find a simple solution. We believe that the success and simplicity of hearing aids suitable for conduction deafness has somehow drawn attention away from the comparatively unsuccessful application of hearing aids for old people suffering from nerve deafness. The lack of success may be attributed erroneously to personality traits thought to be typical of old people. (See also p. 221.)

1. Where there is primarily high tone loss, as is almost always the case, the aid should correspondingly amplify the high tones. Low tone response may be normal, and high intensity low frequency

---

[1] The following threshold measures were obtained for this subject: first with no, and then with 105 db masking noise. Remarkably, this extremely high noise level did not raise his threshold for the tone detection – it even reduced it somewhat.

	250	500	1500	2500	2000	3000	4000
No noise	45	70	65	85	110	110	110
105 db noise	45	60	60	90	110	85	110

sounds are disagreeable when more or less continuous: especially as they convey very little information for speech.

2. Where there is recruitment, the aid should amplify to bring wanted signals above the internal masking noise; but the volume level from the aid should be restricted to the reduced dynamic range of the ear, by Automatic Gain Control and by Volume Compression.

3. In some circumstances it might be useful to have a noise source available in the aid, to inhibit spontaneous firing of the auditory nerve.

4. In some cases it might be advisable to employ filters to avoid stimulation at frequencies which tend to produce increased neural noise, as by 'stimulation deafness'. Some cases of nerve deafness appear particularly prone to this.

Older people have proved to be, on the whole, considerably slower to learn a new task than younger people, though given time they may perform it at least as well. Thus it is not impossible for them to carry out the necessary actions in the necessary time, but initially the need to learn the unfamiliar slows up their learning. Here, again, it would appear to be central processes which are involved, as stressed by Welford (1951).

We suspect that these typical findings of behaviour studies on ageing may be due to reduction in neural channel capacity, to neural degeneration and to increased 'noise'. If this is so can anything be done about it? If we cannot slow down the degeneration of nerve fibres, a process which appears to start in the embryo, perhaps (with the aid of a drug) we might some day at least reduce random activity in the ageing nervous system.

IMPLICATIONS FOR BEHAVIOUR CHANGES WITH AGEING

It is tempting to consider the probable effects of a general increase in neural noise upon complex perception, motor co-ordination and memory and thinking.

Research in other aspects of ageing has shown that slowing up in motor performance with age appears to be due to a slowing up in central processes; in decision-taking rather than in the actual movements required (Szafran, 1951; Leonard, 1953; Singleton, 1954). In addition, several experimenters have reported that greater difficulty was found by older people where central organization of material was required, and that as the material became more complex the ageing effect became more marked (Clay, 1954; Wallace, 1955).

Older people appear to need more sensory cues than younger ones when carrying out a task, and not only do they need more of one type but they supplement those from one sensory mode by those from another (Szafran, in Welford 1951, and Szafran, 1951). This would suggest that one sensory mode alone was giving inadequate information.

In particular, an increase in 'internal noise' with age might help to account for the increased difficulty found by older people where a choice has to be made from a large number of possibilities, or from unknown or unexpected possibilities rather than familiar ones; in fact, wherever searching takes place. Reaction is then slower and errors more frequent and often of a repetitive nature. Reports have been given of learning tasks, and a task of identification of visual displays under restricted conditions of viewing, where age differences were being investigated. Older people not only found unfamiliar material relatively harder to identify than younger people, but they more often identified objects inaccurately because of a tendency to turn the unfamiliar into something familiar. This may be due to a 'searching' difficulty – the familiar being more readily available – and the same reason may account for the greater tendency of older subjects to repeat the same errors. A response having once been made, even though shown at once to be inaccurate or inadequate, is likely to be repeated several times before the correct response is given, and even then the correct response (e.g. 5) will frequently be in the form of 'not 3 but 5' (3 having been the error) (Kay, 1951; Wallace, 1956).

Appendix 1

Apparatus for the visual experiments

This apparatus was built by Mr R. E. Stonebridge, to the design of Mr R. Leslie and the present author. The optical arrangement is shown in Fig. 8.20.

The lamp source is a 60 watt 12 volt vertical coiled filament lamp, which is supplied with a controlled, voltage metered, D.C. supply. The light is passed through condenser lenses to two aperture stops arranged one above the other in a removable square brass plate. This plate is supplied with four sets of paired stops, and it may be placed in four positions. The stops determine the sizes of the Background and Test fields, which may be varied by changing the position of the alternative plates. Standard lantern slides may be used in place of the plates, when it is desired to project a pattern, or system of borders. The two beams originating from the respective aperture stops pass through one of a series of neutral density filters mounted on

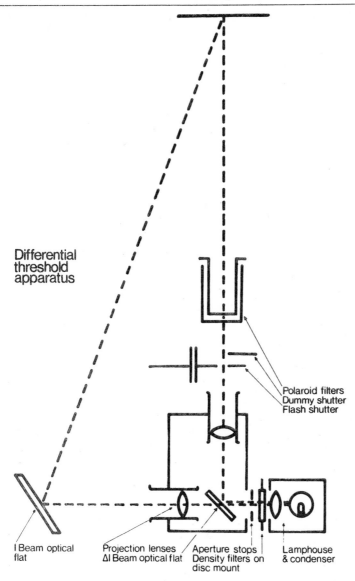

Differential
threshold
apparatus

Polaroid filters
Dummy shutter
Flash shutter

I Beam optical
flat

Projection lenses
ΔI Beam optical flat

Aperture stops
Density filters on
disc mount

Lamphouse
& condenser

FIG. 8.20 *Diagram of optical arrangement.*

a wheel whose position may be controlled by the experimenter. Thus both beams are reduced by the same filter factor. The (lower) Test Field beam passes through a right-angle prism, through a projection lens, through the shutter (to be described) and then through a calibrated crossed-polaroid filter and finally to the screen, which is viewed directly by the subject. The background beam passes directly from its (upper) aperture stop through a second projection lens to a surface-silvered optical flat and to the screen. The optical flat is adjustable so that the relative positions of the two fields on the screen can be placed as desired.

This arrangement is convenient in that Weber's Law is, so to say, built into the instrument: rotating the polaroid filter in the test field beam controls the value of ΔI, while changing the filter mounted on the filter wheel controls I, the $\Delta I/I$ ratio keeping constant, for any setting of the polaroid. A further advantage of combining the two lanterns in this way is that slight variations in the lamp leave the $\Delta I/I$ ratio unchanged. A similar scheme has been used by Mr G. C. Grindley though in his arrangement it was not possible to control the size of the background field.

The shutter was designed by the present author. It consists of a revolving disk with a sector in the Test Field beam. The angular velocity of the sector disk is controlled with an integrator disk driven from a constant speed motor. A secondary, solenoid-operated, shutter is arranged to cut off the beam unless the solenoid is energized; this can only occur when the sector on the revolving wheel has just left the beam, it then remains energized until the sector has completely passed the beam, producing a flash. The secondary shutter immediately closes until another flash is required. The secondary shutter is synchronized to the disk with a commutator contact. A relay circuit provides the initial storage while the sector travels to a position just past the beam, and ensures that only one flash can occur though the operator's key be held down (see p. 454).

The subject's responses are made with two keys which energize counters. Six counters are used to record the number of (*a*) *flashes*, (*b*) *dummy flashes* (in which the shutter is worked normally, but the beam is interrupted by a silent 'flap' shutter fitted with contacts), (*c*) '*seen correct*', (*d*) '*not seen correct*', (*e*) '*false positive*', (*f*) '*missed*'. The first two counters are so arranged that they are not energized until the subject makes his response, this is important for the counters make slightly different noises, so that information of *flash* or *dummy* would be given by auditory cue. As it is, the difference in sound provides knowledge of results but not prior information.

[A great advantage of electronic counters is their perfect silence. Keys and switches are still however a problem. I would like to know how many visual experiments are *in fact* auditory!]

Calibration The absolute intensity levels were determined with an S.E.I comparison spot photometer. The Ilford filter calibrations were used to derive the values of I for each filter. The crossed polaroids filter was calibrated using the photometer and comparing the readings with the $\cos^2$ curve for angle of rotation of the polaroid. This procedure was complicated in the present case by the fact that the emergent ΔI beam was already polarized by the small optical flat (later changed for a right angle prism) in the body of the instrument. This difficulty was overcome by adjusting the fixed polaroid element until it was orientated to the plane of polarization of the emergent beam.

Appendix 2

Apparatus for the hearing experiments

The pure tone signals were provided by a Belelere clinical audiometer. This is equipped with a switched attenuator with a range − 15 to +65 dbs for bone conduction, where 0 dbs refers to the threshold for the average ear. This serves as the reference level throughout. The intensity range of the audiometer was extended, with a Leak high fidelity amplifier. This was chosen for its exceptional stability, 'flatness' and low harmonic distortion.

The white noise was provided by a 2050 thyratron valve placed in a magnetic field.

The tone pips were provided by a mechanical sweeping switch. The problem of switching transients (inherent in this type of work) has not yet been adequately tackled: the 25 millisecond tone pips have rapid rise and fall characteristics, and so transient frequencies are present though their energy is relatively small since it is only the ΔI pip signal which is being switched.

The ratio $\Delta I/I$ is controlled with a one db step attenuator which is shorted out by the pip switch. The arrangement is thus similar to the system of filters used in the vision apparatus: the audiometer attenuator corresponds to the filter wheel, while the second attenuator corresponds to the polaroid filter giving the $\Delta I/I$ ratio. (The difference is that the optical shutter, when open, superimposes the test field upon the background, while the tone pip switch *reduces* the intensity of the continuous 'background' tone. The intensity of the tone pip $(\Delta I + I)$ is thus entirely determined by the audiometer's attenuator, while the 'background' intensity (I) is determined by reduction from this intensity provided by the setting of the second attenuator).

Intensities up to an extreme maximum (only used with one subject) of 100 dbs can be obtained by boosting the audiometer output with the Leak amplifier: this was normally set at zero gain, but its gain was increased when necessary for the Weber Law experiments with nerve deaf subjects. The subjects were placed in the laboratory silent room; the apparatus was in an adjoining room to which two-way communication was possible with microphones and earphones. The microphones were, of course, switched off whenever the subject was listening for signals.

The output waveforms and the levels and 'cleanness' of the tone pips were checked with monitoring oscilloscopes.

Calibration The intensity of the tone signals were determined by the setting of the audiometer attenuator and the gain of the amplifier. The amplifier gain was measured with an oscilloscope, the basic standard being the audiometer. The absolute intensities used for bone conduction are not easy to specify; the bone conduction 'phone is held to the mastoid process by a spring steel band which gives reasonably constant pressure, but the absolute pressure is an important factor in determining the energy transferred to the head.

The audiometer was calibrated for air conduction so that for 1000 c/s, 0 db was the standard 0·0002 dyne/cm^2. (This is approximately 10^{-16} watts.) The other frequencies are so adjusted in the instrument for intensity level that, for any frequency, 0 db on the attenuator refers to the threshold intensity for the standard average ear for that frequency. This is true also for bone conduction. We have measured the relative energies for each frequency used for bone conduction and referred these to the basic level of 0·0002 dyne/cm^2 for 1000 c/s air conduction. The result is given as follows:

250	500	1000	1500	2000	3000	4000	c/s
74	51	49	33	33	50	40	db above 1000 c/s 'air'

Thus, to find approximate absolute levels for the hearing data in energy units, the above factors for each frequency should be used.

Wherever the amplifier gain was changed (it was increased for nerve deaf subjects where high intensities were required), the results were suitably corrected; the data given here is thus in dbs referred to the normal ear for each frequency for bone conduction.

TABLE 8.4

log. I	I	log. (ΔI + I)	(ΔI + I)	ΔI
3	2·0	10	10	8·0
10	10	15	31·0	31·0
17	51	20	100	49
22	160	25	300	140
27	510	30	1,000	490
32	1,600	35	3,000	1,500
38	6,400	40	10,000	3,600
43	20,000	45	31,000	11,000
49	80,000	50	100,000	20,000
54	260,000	55	310,000	50,000
59	800,000	60	1,000,000	200,000
11	13	20	100	87
19	80	25	300	220
25	300	30	1,000	200
31	1,300	35	3,100	1,800
37	5,100	40	10,000	4,900
43	20,000	45	31,000	11,000
48	64,000	50	100,000	36,000
54	260,000	55	310,000	50,000
59	800,000	60	1,000,000	2,000,000
23	200	30	1,000	800
30	1,000	35	3,100	2,100
35	3,100	40	10,000	6,900
42	16,000	45	31,000	15,000
47	21,000	50	100,000	49,000
53	200,000	55	310,000	110,000
59	800,000	60	1,000,000	200,000
32	1,600	40	10,000	8,400
40	10,000	45	31,000	21,000
47	51,000	50	100,000	49,000
53	200,000	55	310,000	110,000
59	800,000	60	1,000,000	200,000

This table shows conversion from logarithmic (decibel) to linear ratio. The absolute values for each tone frequency may be found by applying the factors given in this Appendix.

9 *A theory of nerve deafness*

[The notion that nerve deafness may be regarded as raised internal noise, masking the signal, while conduction is simply attenuation of the signal, still seems reasonable and to have implications for the design of hearing aids. The technique for measuring recruitment binaurally would seem to be useful clinically since nerve deafness may occur in both ears, making the usual binaural comparison unreliable or impossible in some cases. I believe that our method is not used.

The following short paper was published in *The Lancet*, as a summary of our conclusions at that stage on the implications of nerve deafness regarded as neural noise masking.]

★   ★   ★

THREE types of impairment of hearing are generally distinguished:

1. *Conduction deafness* due to loss in the middle ear only, sensitivity for bone conduction being normal. Often caused by thickening of the tympanum or by otosclerosis.

2. *Nerve deafness,* in which there is impairment of both air and bone conduction. Associated with degeneration of the sensory cells of the organ of Corti in the inner ear or with other neural damage, such as a tumour of the eighth nerve.

3. *Central deafness,* which is rare and has no known peripheral origin, being regarded as a central disorder often associated with aphasia. No further mention of this will be made here.

There seems to be no mystery about conduction deafness; the auditory signal is simply attenuated, and this loss may usually be made good with a suitable external amplifier. In nerve deafness, on the other hand, amplification does not make up for the loss, and the defect is not simple attenuation of the signal. The condition has certain rather distinctive features:

(*a*) There is some degree of confusion. The older term 'perception deafness', still sometimes used, indicates this clinical distinction.

(*b*) The deterioration is mainly at the upper end of the frequency spectrum (presbyacusia), hearing for low frequencies often being normal.

(*c*) The audiogram is generally 'peaky', a sudden dip (loss of sensitivity) at about 4000 cycles being particularly common in men.

(*d*) Tinnitus is common, but this may also occur in conduction deafness.

(*e*) The curious phenomenon of loudness recruitment is common.

Recruitment, which is almost certainly found only in nerve deafness, may be roughly described as a shortening of the loudness scale, from the bottom.

In cases of unilateral nerve deafness, it may be demonstrated by applying the same tone to the two ears and asking the patient to balance the intensities for the two ears, over a wide range of intensity. Where there is recruitment, the deaf ear will require higher energies at the lower intensities; but, as the level rises, the difference in intensity for loudness balance decreases and may disappear at high intensities. In conduction deafness, the ratio of the two energies will remain constant for loudness balance, over the working range of hearing.

Previous work on visual discrimination, where thresholds are supposed to be limited by the effective signal-to-noise ratio of the neural systems involved, suggests a possible explanation of nerve deafness. We have regarded visual discrimination as limited by the channel capacity of the system, the channel capacity being a function of the number of fibres available for discrimination and the level of random neural activity, or 'noise', tending to mask the signal. Increase in the amount of noise should raise the threshold and tend to produce confusion. Nerve deafness could be due to loss of channel capacity either through loss of functional fibres or through increased noise. These two possibilities give rather different predictions.

Each of 17 persons used was tested for absolute threshold at the above frequencies and compared with the average ear to assess impairment for each frequency. Subjects with the same absolute thresholds (i.e. the same impairment) are grouped together. This grouping is irrespective of frequency – subjects are combined for any frequency for which their absolute thresholds are equal. Thus

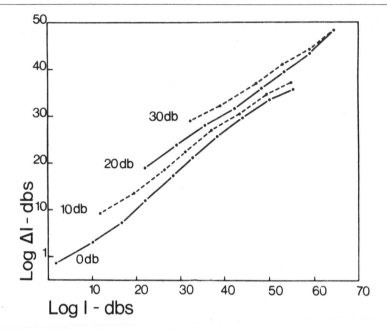

Fig. 9.1 *Intensity discrimination for various degrees of nerve deafness, from o db. to 30 db. absolute threshold loss. Discrimination was of 0·01 sec. tone pips against continuous tone of the same frequency. Frequencies used; 1000, 1500, 2000, 3000, 4000 c/s. Pips were slightly rounded to reduce transients. Bone conduction, to one ear.*

each subject may appear in several of the curves, at various frequencies. Bone conduction to the mastoid process has been used throughout. As in Fig. 9.1 the slope flattens with increasing impairment. It seems possible to estimate effective masking noise for various degrees of nerve deafness by comparing curves in Figs. 9.1 and 9.2 and selecting those giving best fit.

To test the hypothesis that nerve deafness is in some cases due to increased noise masking the auditory signals, we have compared the phenomena of nerve deafness with the effects of noise masking on normal hearing. Their similarity is striking.

Fletcher (1938) found that, when he used thermal noise for masking pure tones, high tones were primarily affected; in other words, he produced presbyacusia in the normal ear by masking with thermal noise. It is well known that partial sectioning of the cochlear nerve produces presbyacusia in cats (Wever and Bray 1937) and also in Ménière's disease patients (Dandy, 1933*a* and *b*). Thus it might be concluded that reduction in channel capacity decreases discrimination

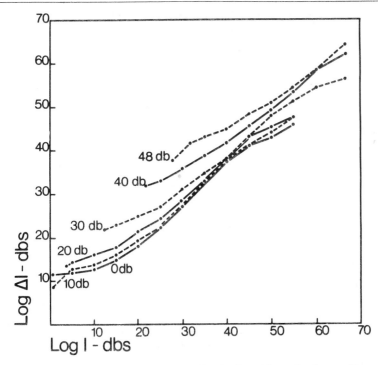

FIG. 9.2 *Intensity discrimination for various levels of masking noise, from 0 db. to 48 db., for subjects with normal hearing. Frequency used: 1000 c/s. Duration of tone pips as for Fig. 9.1; bone conduction, to one ear. A similar change of slope occurs with increasing nerve deafness and with added masking noise for the normal ear.*

of high tones whether this reduction is the result of raised noise or of loss of functional fibres. Steinberg and Gardner (1937) showed that white noise masking produces recruitment in the normal ear. Dix, Hallpike and Hood (1948) found that recruitment appears to be associated with damage to the nerve-endings at the organ of Corti but not with damage to the eighth nerve. This finding is compatible with the hypothesis that neural noise produces recruitment, for disturbance of the nerve-endings (as in Ménière's disease) would be expected to produce random firing, whereas this is not generally found when fibres are sectioned.

When there is marked tinnitus of a particular tone, some loss of hearing is perhaps always found near the corresponding frequency. But although tinnitus is often found with nerve deafness it is not invariably found. We should not expect it if the deafness was due to a tumour of the nerve; but, if the deafness was due to damage of the end-organ, the patient would presumably be aware of his neural noise as some form of tinnitus. If he is not, some explanation is necessary. The normal person is aware of a surprising amount of self-generated sound in a silent room, though he is not normally aware of this internal noise. It is also true that we are not usually aware of irrelevant regular sounds – e.g. the ticking of a clock, and even its chime, when this is familiar though it may be loud. Perhaps in some cases neural noise is rejected in a similar manner, with the result that, although it may tend to mask wanted sounds, there is no awareness of it as tinnitus, at any rate until attention is called to it.

We have found it necessary, on quite other grounds, to postulate a 'gate' in sensory discrimination mechanisms (Gregory and Cane 1955 [No. 7], Gregory, 1956). Perhaps this 'gate' is raised to reject abnormally high residual noise. The idea of a 'gate' is important: it is taken over from electronics where the term denotes a threshold introduced into a circuit so that voltages below the gate threshold are rejected. The gate may be raised or lowered or may be fixed. This suggests a possible connection between auditory fatigue and nerve deafness, and they have many features in common. If a sustained noise or tone tends to raise the gate we should expect recruitment (for only the lower-intensity signals will be affected by the gate) and this is in fact the case. Perhaps some of the results obtained by Hood (1955), who has done much work on auditory fatigue, might be interpreted on this hypothesis. Further, the neural origin appears to be the same for nerve deafness as for auditory fatigue – between the electro-cochlear activity and the binaural localization process, according to Wever (1949).

In examining the possibility that typical nerve deafness is due to raised neural noise we have compared differential intensity discrimination (short-tone pips against a continuous tone of the same frequency) over a wide range of intensities and frequencies in (1) nerve-deaf ears showing various degrees of impairment and (2) the normal ear in the presence of white noise masking. We should expect the curves relating intensity of the tone pip to the continuous tone to be similar for a nerve-deaf ear and a normal ear subject to added masking noise. By determining the level of noise which produces the best fit of these curves, we might hope to estimate the effective level of neurological noise in a nerve-deaf ear showing a given impairment. Preliminary results are encouraging; we find that the curves are similar.

If nerve deafness may be caused by raised neural noise a practical conclusion seems to follow. To attempt to raise the wanted signal above the residual noise with a linear amplifier (such as a standard hearing-aid) is likely to overload the ear, for it seems clear that there is no abnormal attenuation in the system. Now, it has been shown by

Licklider (1949) and discussed by Miller (1951) that almost all the information-content of speech is carried by the zero energy change-over points, and almost none at the energy peaks; it thus appears possible to prevent overloading while retaining the necessary information, by using suitable peak clipping in hearing aids. This has been tried but has produced only slight improvement (Littler, personal communication). Perhaps in addition it may be necessary to filter out those frequencies where impairment is greatest, because continual stimulation appears, at least in some cases, to increase tinnitus and therefore presumably the amount of neural masking noise.

[The idea of regarding nerve deafness as due to raised neural noise masking the available signal still seems to me important, and to have implications for the design of hearing aids. We received an apparatus grant from the M.R.C. to test the idea that hearing for speech in these cases might be improved by 'transposing' the speech frequencies down by, say, an octave. This we did, in two ways:

(i) with a special rotating-head tape recorder, allowing frequency to be varied while keeping playback time constant;
(ii) with a novel circuit we devised, with help from Mr Brian Gaines and Mr Stephen Salter. This first amplitude-clipped the speech waveform, then divided the zero-energy cross-over points by two. This was a long shot.

Four nerve deaf patients from Addenbrooke's Hospital were tested with these devices, by my students Mark Haggard and Malcolm Parlett, over several months. Of the four nerve deaf subjects only one showed evidence of improvement. He was the most intelligent of the sample, and as a professional man, his deafness was a particularly severe handicap. He was the most highly motivated, so it remains possible that given unusual perseverance for learning to understand frequency-transposed speech (and it does sound most odd) this approach could be useful. But on existing evidence I am not optimistic. Selective frequency filtering with some amplitude peak clipping seems a better bet – but it is a nice thought that one might transpose the information-bearing part of the signal to the least impaired region of the ear's response. It would be nice if it worked!]

10 *A note on summation time of the eye indicated by signal/noise discrimination*

[The next short paper follows up a rather obvious characteristic of noise: by integration it increases according to a square root function with the time while a maintained signal increases linearly; so improving the signal/noise ratio with dark adaptation.]

★   ★   ★

RECENT work has shown that the photochemical theory of dark adaptation is inadequate. A number of considerations, such as the effect of vitamin A deficiency upon scotopic sensitivity, suggest that the mechanism of adaptation is at least partly photochemical, but that it is not entirely so is now established apparently beyond doubt. Rose (1948), and other writers, have found that changes in concentration of rhodopsin are probably less during dark adaptation than corresponding changes in sensitivity: this has been directly demonstrated for the living human eye with a technique due to Rushton (1952). The results are reported by Campbell and Rushton (1954), and Rushton and Campbell (1954). It is found that only a small part of adaptation can be photochemical, the rest appears to be neural.

Perhaps a number of neural mechanisms might be suggested: only one will be considered here, namely, the possibility that the summation time of the eye increases with dark adaptation. By 'summation time' or 'storage time' is meant here the interval over which the effect of the stimulus energy is integrated. It is well known that the response time of the eye increases with dark adaptation, as may readily be demonstrated with Pulfrich's pendulum (Pulfrich, 1922) (at least for cone adaptation), as shown by Lythgoe (1938). But although to be expected, this increased delay does not show that storage time increases with dark adaptation. The following observations were made in an attempt to provide more direct evidence.

It appears to be useful, in many respects, to regard the eye as an information source working into a noisy channel. It is generally

222

true of information systems with storage that the signal-to-noise ratio is related to the storage time (see Bell, 1953, p. 50). Where M is the number of repetitions of the signal, S the signal amplitude and N the noise amplitude, noise increases by $(MN^2)^{\frac{1}{2}}$, while S increases linearly with M. Thus S/N improves by $M^{\frac{1}{2}}S/N$. It therefore appears that the ability of the eye to discriminate a signal masked by random 'noise' should give a measure of summation time, and this will be independent of retinal delay. The following experiment was designed to test this idea.

The visual display used was an explicit signal/noise arrangement. A random noise source (a thyratron placed within a magnetic field) was mixed with the output from a 250 c/s. sine wave generator; the resultant noise-modulated sine wave was fed to a C.R.O. whose

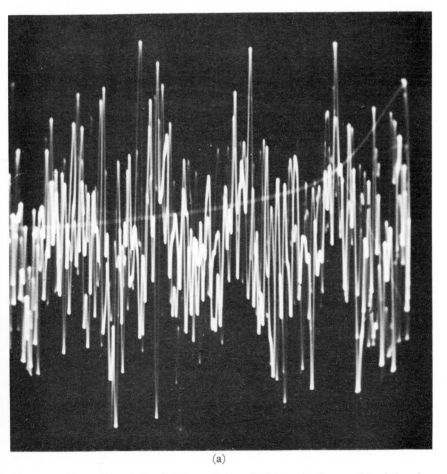

(a)

FIG. 10.1 *Extraction of signal (sine wave) masked by noise improved by increasing summation time.*

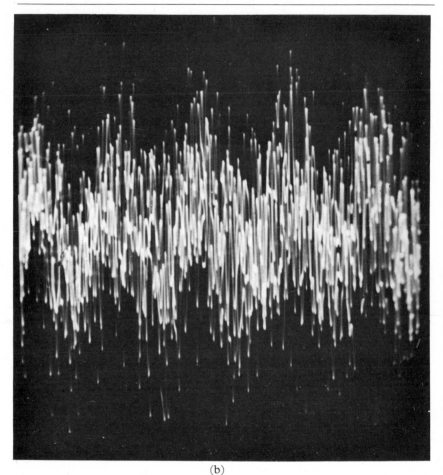

(b)

Fig. 10.1 (cont.).

screen provided the visual display. The C.R.O.'s time-base was set to 50 c/s. and locked to the signal generator. The resulting stationary chain of five sine waves, more or less masked by noise, was viewed by the subject. The C.R.O. tube had a short persistence screen with a green trace.

The expected effect of increase in summation time upon S/N is shown by the series of photographs. Each shows the same value of S/N set up on the C.R.O., but for a longer exposure time in each case. It is to be expected that, if the summation time of the eye increases with dark-adaptation, discrimination of the signal against the noise should improve similarly.

An alternative way of expressing the improvement with increase in summation time with this arrangement is to regard the signal as the statistical Mean of the noise. Increase in the sample size with time

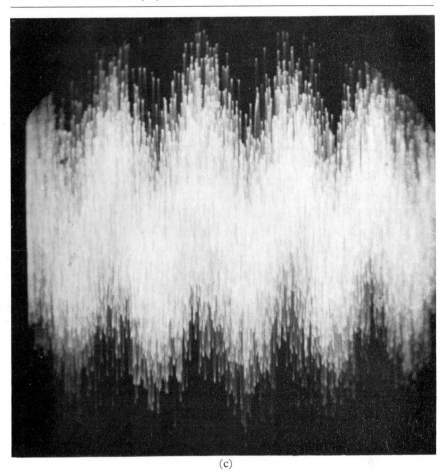

(c)

Fig. 10.1 (cont.).

will increase the accuracy of the position of the Mean, by $\sigma\sqrt{n}$, where σ is Standard Deviation and n the sample size.

The display was viewed monocularly through a calibrated variable-density (crossed polaroids) filter. The signal and noise amplitudes were controlled with switched attenuators, and some control over the noise spectrum was provided by parallel-T filters. Adapting light could be provided by a slide projector illuminating a white screen surrounding the C.R.O. tube, which was itself shielded from the light with an opaque disc placed between glass in the projector's slide holder.

It was found (by switching the signal 'on' or 'off' and asking the subject to report its presence or absence) that signal-to-noise discrimination improved by a factor of 2 when intensity was reduced by 2·5 log units, in the absence of ambient light. That this is not due simply to acuity loss is indicated by the fact that the effect is not appreciable for the (static) photographs; also it does not occur in the presence of ambient light, although this should impair visual acuity in addition to producing general light adaptation.

At low intensities rapid movement of the 'noise' was entirely absent, the display appearing as a steady blur. Rapid movement of the 'noise' was, however, clearly evident in the presence of ambient light even when the trace intensity was adjusted close to differential threshold. Just such a reduction in temporal acuity would be expected if summation time increases with dark adaptation.

It would perhaps be unwise to attribute more than a small part of the increase of the sensitivity of the eye during adaptation to increase in storage time. Its probable importance might be considered in terms of (*a*) increase in the effective number of quanta available to initiate a response, and (*b*) improvement in the signal/noise ratio of the visual system itself, which we should expect for the reason given above.

★   ★   ★

[We turn now to a different and curious problem also involving sensory discrimination. This is not, however, a classical problem; it is not mentioned in any book known to me, and has seldom been considered as a possible issue in sensory processes. The question is: Is differential sensitivity purely a function of the *physical* stimulus intensity (as generally assumed) or is it a function of *apparent* intensity? The question arises because the apparent intensity of a stimulus can be highly variable. It may be systematically varied with different states of adaptation, such as by dark-adaptation of the eye, or more subtly in effects such as the size/weight illusion. This is a large and repeatable effect. If a large tin is partly filled with lead and a smaller tin filled fuller until both are the same scale weight, then the *smaller* tin will feel *heavier* than the larger tin though both are the same weight. This is clearly not an adaptation effect, for the difference appears immediately. It is dependent upon seeing (or just knowing?) the different sizes of the tins. Here, *visually* given information is affecting the judgment of *weight*. This alone is of great interest, for situations demonstrating clear-cut cross-modal effects are rare, although we believe (since Berkeley) that they must be of vital importance. Another and more general example of cross-modal transfer, from touch to vision, is found in the case of recovery from early blindness [No. 3]. This came as a great surprise to us at the time, though it would have pleased Berkeley. Over the last few years there is growing evidence for cross-modal transfer in man and to a lesser extent in the chimpanzee.

The size/weight illusion shows that what may seem a simple matter of afferent signals directly 'reporting' intensity is not so simple: it indicates that these signals far from being accepted directly are referred to internally stored 'expectancies' of the situation. Generally, large objects are heavier than smaller objects. In this case, then, the smaller tin is *probably* lighter than the larger tin. The afferent signals will be the same for each tin, so we must suppose that it is this prior probability, of weight, which affects the perceived weight. After this demonstration it is surely impossible to ignore stored probabilities as important for understanding perception. The demonstration is sufficient to throw out of court purely 'peripheral' explanations, even of the more 'sensory' aspects of perception. It is also sufficient to show how complex are apparently simple 'stimuli'. Most serious, from the point of view of the experimenter, it shows that large changes in the effect of a fixed physical input may occur due to modifications of brain states which may not be under his control, or known. In this case, they can be quite well controlled – because they are set by the visually given size of the object – but this is an all too rare case. It is likely that the same kind of thing occurs continuously in all manner of situations; but because there is no way of controlling the brain's assessed probability it appears merely as variance, or experimental artifacts.

The conceptual move from stimuli as determiners of behaviour, to stored probabilities selected and modified by available sensory data, is surely essential for understanding perception.]

11　Is the Weber fraction a function of physical or perceived input?

[To return to the question of the following papers, using the size/weight illusion: Should Weber's Law be formulated in terms of physical or apparent intensity? Is discrimination impaired if the *apparent* intensity rises, though the physical intensity remains constant? At first we thought this to be so. But we changed our minds: though *not* to saying that there is *no* effect related to apparent intensity.

My colleague in these papers – Helen Ross – made the major contribution. After taking her first degree at Oxford, she worked with me on the U.S.A.F. grant (see p. 316) and then worked for her Ph.D. on this problem as my student. She has since become a Lecturer in the University of Stirling. An enthusiastic skin diver, she has become an expert in vision under water.]

       ★   ★   ★

A BASIC and much studied aspect of sensory processes is the ability of the nervous system to distinguish small differences in the intensity of physical inputs. The Weber fraction $\Delta I / I = C$ is found to hold fairly accurately over a medium range of intensities for most modalities (Woodworth, 1938). Sensory thresholds are now regarded as the distinguishing of signals from noise according to some significance criterion (Tanner and Swets 1954; Gregory and Cane 1955 [No. 7]; Gregory, 1956; Barlow, 1956). Thus we may think of the Weber Constant in terms of detector efficiency. There are many known factors which affect human detector efficiency – such as fatigue, vigilance and sensory adaptation – which are due to changes in the organism.

Estimates of differential thresholds are generally made in terms of the physical input, using physical scales of weight, loudness or photic intensity. This raises problems concerning the relation between physical and psychological measuring scales into which we do not propose to enter here; but the well-known fact that a given physical intensity may give rise to different sensations under various conditions raises a question which seems to demand an experimental treatment. Discrimination is affected by the psychophysical method used (Guilford, 1936), the instructions given to the subject (Fernberger, 1931) and the subjective probability of each decision (Howarth and Bulmer, 1956); but we may also ask whether it is affected by illusions. It is well known that a given intensity of light may produce more or less sensation of brightness as a function of contrast and that a weight may feel light or heavy depending on its size (size-weight illusion). We thus require the idea of *apparent* intensity as well as physical intensity. We say that two weights are apparently equal when they are judged the same weight by a subject. It is found that if one of two physically equal weights is larger in size than the other it will be judged lighter, so in this case physical equality (balancing on weighing scales) is not the same as apparent equality. This difference between physical and apparent equality is what we mean here by an illusion.

The fact that physical and apparent intensities may be systematically different under certain conditions makes it possible to ask whether sensory discrimination is a simple function of physical intensity, or whether it may be affected by changes in the apparent intensity produced by conditions giving illusions.

The size-weight illusion was chosen to investigate this question, as it is large and requires the simplest apparatus. It is only necessary to obtain differential thresholds for weights of different sizes but the same physical weights, to establish whether the threshold is a function of the physical or the apparent weight. This question has been investigated by Seashore (1896) using a similar method to ours, but we cannot place much confidence in his results owing to his method for determining the thresholds, and we find his argument self-contradictory. He suggests that Weber's Law is better fitted by the apparent than the physical weight, and that the Weber fraction should be $\Delta I/$apparent $I = C$. Surprisingly, he concludes that 'all overestimation (of weight) lowers the threshold and all underestimation raises it'. This contradicts his own formulation. Seashore presents two measures of thresholds. Using the limiting method, he accepted the first of three consecutive correctly judged increments; he also gives proportions of incorrect to total number of judgements, though his procedure here is not entirely clear. He gives no indication of the statistical significance of his results, and his two sets of measures go in opposite directions.

We originally intended to perform only one experiment, using the frequency method and presenting the standard before the comparison weight. A second experiment was done with the order of presentation inverted in order to discover what happens to the constant error in these conditions, and finally a third experiment was undertaken lifting the weights simultaneously in order to eliminate constant error. In order to reduce to a minimum the number of readings required for an adequate significance we had to find a method giving a small variance. It turned out that methods 1 and 3 were satisfactory, while the method used for Experiment 2 was unsatisfactory since with this method the variance was high.

The results of all three experiments will be given; it should be understood that they were not designed to give answers to different questions but are attempts to find the best method to answer the original question.

METHOD

Two sets of weights were used: one set 3 in. × 3 in. (Nescafé tins), and the other set 1¼ in. × 1¾ in. (Kodak film tins). All the tins were painted black. Each set was composed of 11 tins which were weighted with lead shot, wrapped in cotton wool, to weigh from 175–225 gm, with 5-gm intervals between them. The 200-gm tin was used as the standard for the tins of the same size.

It was essential for the logic of the experiment that there should be no difference between the series of weights, except for size, which could favour discrimination for either series. It was, therefore, important to standardize the finger-span required to lift the weights, although they were of different diameter in the two series. This was done by fitting the lids of all the tins with identical wire loops, which were grasped by the thumb and forefinger.

Forty-seven subjects were used in the experiments, five of whom served in more than one experiment. They were of both sexes, aged between 17–30 years, and were mainly undergraduates, research students and college entrance candidates.

The subject was seated at a table with one of the standards in front of him. A screen hid all the weights except the pair being compared. The weights were placed in turn beside the standard in a predetermined random order. Each weight appeared 10 times, providing 100 comparisons for each set of weights. The subject was asked to compare each weight with the standard for that series, and judge whether it was heavier or lighter than the standard. If he was not sure, he was asked to guess, thus eliminating the variation in threshold caused by different interpretations of the 'equal' category.

Three experiments were undertaken. The conditions in each

experiment were the same except for the order in which the standard and comparison weights were lifted. In all cases the subjects were required to hold the weights by the wire loops, using the thumb and forefinger, and to lift and lower them smartly and as consistently as possible. The preferred hand was used throughout, except in Experiment 3, when a weight was held in each hand. All subjects were tested on both sets of weights; half being tested first on the large weights and half first on the small weights, although it turned out that order was unimportant.

Experiment 1 (Standard first, comparison second)

Using the procedure described above, the subjects lifted the standard first and the comparison weight second. Sixteen subjects were used.

Results In treating the results non-parametric statistics were used, to avoid assumptions of normality. Unless otherwise stated, the significance of the difference found between the two sets of weights was estimated by the Wilcoxon matched-pairs signed-ranks test (Siegal, 1956, p. 75). The detector efficiency is given by the slope of the probability curve for the response 'heavier' or 'lighter'; it does not matter which. The standard deviation (SD) (i.e. the slope of the probability curve) and the point of subjective equality (PSE) were calculated for the large and small weights using the method of averaged z scores as described by Woodworth and Schlosberg (1955, p. 205). The use of this method results in a slight overestimation of the SD for displaced PSEs. However, the overestimation is small compared to the differences in SD obtained, and we accept the method as sufficiently accurate.

For the large weights the median SD was 11·9 gm, and for the small weights 13·8 gm. The probability of this difference being due to chance was 0·03 (one tail).

It was also found that the median PSE was different for the two series. For the large weights the PSE was 195·2 gm, and for the small weights it was 192·1 gm. This difference in 'time error' is significant at the 0·02 level (two tails).

It seems that this experiment provides evidence that the smaller (apparently heavier) weights are more difficult to distinguish from their standard than are the larger (apparently lighter) weights from theirs. This is a positive result, and suggests that detector efficiency is related to apparent weight. Since this is a somewhat startling conclusion it seemed necessary to obtain additional data.

Experiment 2 was undertaken with the comparison weight

TABLE 11.1
EXPERIMENT 1: STANDARD FIRST, COMPARISON SECOND

Subject	PSE		SD	
	Large	Small	Large	Small
1	192·1	187·6	12·7	11·8
2	201·8	196·3	10·2	8·0
3	193·3	192·8	9·4	10·5
4	198·0	190·2	15·1	19·1
5	190·8	196·0	13·7	13·8
6	207·1	199·8	10·7	14·6
7	195·0	190·7	10·1	12·6
8	192·6	194·3	12·6	13·0
9	196·0	199·0	12·2	16·2
10	202·3	187·6	11·9	13·8
11	194·5	199·5	14·2	12·0
12	196·8	193·8	10·3	14·0
13	190·4	191·5	10·6	22·2
14	195·3	190·4	9·4	14·9
15	190·2	190·0	15·3	13·8
16	203·0	199·3	11·9	10·7
Median	195·2	192·1	11·9	13·8

Significance of difference between PSE, $p = 0.02$ (Wilcoxon).
Significance of difference between SD, $p = 0.03$ (Wilcoxon).

presented before the standard in order to obtain more data on the thresholds but with the time error reversed.

Experiment 2 (Comparison first, standard second)

The procedure was exactly the same as in Experiment 1 except that the comparison weights were presented in each case *before* the standard. Sixteen subjects were used.

Results The subjects found this condition very difficult: they were instructed to reserve their judgement on the comparison weight until they had picked up the standard, but they were unable to refrain from making an immediate judgement using their previous impression of the standard. Their performance was very poor throughout. The direction of the time error was reversed, and the small weights again showed a larger time error than the large weights. For the large weights the PSE was 205·9 gm and for the small weights 208·1 gm. The difference was insignificant ($p = 0.39$ one tail). The standard deviations were larger for both conditions than in Experiment 1, and there was no significant difference between the large and small

TABLE 11.2
EXPERIMENT 2: COMPARISON FIRST, STANDARD SECOND

Subject	PSE		SD	
	Large	Small	Large	Small
1	211·5	220·5	19·5	27·3
2	207·7	201·6	14·0	17·7
3	215·1	208·8	15·2	23·6
4	214·1	211·9	17·9	11·1
5	209·4	207·5	11·7	9·5
6	228·3	216·9	24·0	16·0
7	204·1	203·1	20·1	11·4
8	208·3	204·0	12·2	9·6
9	192·8	209·1	18·6	14·6
10	203·8	209·5	10·3	16·3
11	204·6	202·9	22·0	17·5
12	195·3	190·6	18·1	21·6
13	202·1	206·0	15·9	12·5
14	218·4	215·2	22·7	27·4
15	204·3	217·5	16·1	14·6
16	200·6	198·7	14·3	12·6
Median	205·9	208·1	17·0	15·2

These differences are not significant.

weight conditions: the SD for the large weights was 17·0 gm and for the small weights 15·2 gm. Although this difference is in the opposite direction from that of Experiment 1, it can be dismissed as due to chance ($p = 0.63$ two tails).

Since this experiment gave results which were too variable, Experiment 3 was undertaken. In this experiment it was hoped to eliminate the constant error, by lifting the weights simultaneously. This was found to be a simpler task than Experiment 2 and provided further useful data.

Experiment 3 (Standard and comparison simultaneous)

The procedure was the same as in Experiments 1 and 2, except that the standard and comparison weights were lifted simultaneously, one in each hand. Half the subjects used their dominant and half their non-dominant hand to lift the standard, though hand preference was found to make no difference. It was hoped that if there were no difference in the order of lifting the standard and comparison weights there should be no 'time error'. Twenty subjects were used.

Results This condition gave a result very similar to that of Experiment

1 and gives further evidence that the threshold is higher for the small weights.

The PSE for the large weights was 199·3 gm and for the small weights 196·0 gm. This difference was not quite significant ($p = 0·068$ one tail), but goes in the same direction as in Experiment 1. That is to say, there is some evidence of a larger constant error for the small weights regardless of the time interval between presentation of the standard and comparison weights.

TABLE 11.3
EXPERIMENT 3: SIMULTANEOUS

Subject	PSE		SD	
	Large	Small	Large	Small
1	197·3	199·4	11·3	14·5
2	196·2	190·4	20·1	19·9
3	196·9	197·5	15·2	17·6
4	197·6	202·6	9·7	10·2
5	192·9	198·9	14·2	19·0
6	202·6	195·0	9·7	8·3
7	203·3	193·2	11·4	13·9
8	184·4	177·4	12·6	16·2
9	210·3	201·0	12·7	13·5
10	204·6	208·2	14·5	14·3
11	200·0	204·0	19·4	17·3
12	200·8	199·8	11·2	12·2
13	195·9	192·5	15·8	14·2
14	198·6	189·9	8·5	17·3
15	200·0	191·1	8·5	13·3
16	202·3	195·0	11·6	13·8
17	200·2	188·8	13·9	17·0
18	207·0	199·0	17·6	20·8
19	194·0	202·9	11·3	11·6
20	185·2	195·1	15·0	16·2
median	199·3	196·0	12·6	14·4

The difference between PSE scores is not significant, $p = 0·068$ (Wilcoxon). Significance of difference between SD scores, $p < 0·005$ (Wilcoxon).

The SD for the large weights was 12·6 gm and for the small weights 14·4 gm. The probability of this difference being due to chance was 0·005 (one tail).

DISCUSSION

We feel justified in dismissing the results of Experiment 2 since the SDs obtained were significantly greater than for either Experiment 1 or 3 ($p < 0.02$ on the Kolmogorov-Smirnov test for two independent samples, given in Siegal, 1956, p. 127). Since the SDs and PSEs obtained in Experiment 1 are not significantly different from those obtained in Experiment 3, it seems reasonable to combine the results of these experiments. The combined results give a median SD for the large weights of 12.0 gm and for the small weights of 14.0 gm. The probability of this difference being due to chance is 0.0003 (one tail). The median PSE for the large weights is 197.0 gm and for the small weights 194.8 gm. The probability of this difference being due to chance is 0.005 (one tail).

The difference between the constant error for the large and small weights is interesting since Woodrow (1933) found that the direction and size of the 'time error' is a function of the physical weight of the standard; heavy standards producing a negative 'time error', and light standards a positive one. Our experiment shows that Woodrow's results also apply to the *apparent* weight of the standard; and that constant errors similar to the 'time error' are present even when there is no time interval.

It is tempting to think from the direction and size of the threshold change, that $\Delta I/I$ should be regarded as a function of the apparent and not the physical values of I. The size-weight illusion is of the order of 20 per cent (we cannot give a precise figure, since it fluctuates and tends to lessen during a run) and so, if $\Delta I/I$ were a function of apparent weight, the threshold for the small weights should be raised by about 20 per cent. The observed SD for the large weights was 12.0 gm and for the small weights 14.0 gm. This is an increase of about 17 per cent which is fairly close. To establish that Weber's Law should refer to apparent rather than physical intensities would require the measurement of the illusion and of the differential thresholds for many more values.

It would be interesting to discover whether these findings apply only to thresholds for weights, or whether it is a general finding applying to other and possibly all sensory modalities. The question could be answered whenever a consistent scale distortion is present.

12 *Arm weight, adaptation and weight discrimination*

[A classical explanation of the breakdown of Weber's Law for low intensities (or low weights) is that there is always a hidden constant, which as the stimulus intensity is reduced becomes relatively large. In the case of weight discrimination this hidden constant will be, in part, the weight of the arm itself. Although this is obviously true, in fact the weight of the arm has a remarkably small effect. What happens if the arm changes its weight? We estimated weight discrimination while wearing added weight on the arm – we tried to discover the effect of adapting to added weight, and also the effect of this adaptation after the added weight was removed.

Apart from the intrinsic interest of this situation, it seemed relevant to the performance of astronauts – at blast off, in the weightless conditions of space flight, and during changes in effective gravity as they accelerate, or start re-entry with the braking action of the Earth's atmosphere.]

★ ★ ★

I T is well known that the Weber fraction increases at low stimulus intensities in all modalities (Holway and Pratt 1936). Fechner (1860) suggested that this was due to some additional activity within the sensory system which was negligible in comparison with strong stimuli but which interfered considerably with the perception of weak stimuli. In the case of weight discrimination he suggested that the 'inner stimulation' was caused by the weight of the arm itself and possibly the clothing on the arm. Thus $\Delta I/(I+c) = k$, where c is a constant due to the weight of the arm. That is to say, the difference threshold is proportional not to the intensity of the standard weight alone but to the intensity of the standard plus a constant. Fechner pointed out that the total weight of the arm could not be regarded as the added constant, since the arm is so much heavier than the lightest discriminable weights. One reason he suggested, to overcome this apparent paradox, was that the weight of the arm has no effect upon pressure sensations in the skin, which provide information of external weight. Another suggestion was that the weight of the arm is distributed along its length and so will have less effect than the same weight lifted by the hand with the arm as a lever. Fechner concluded that there were too many unknown factors to estimate the value of the constant due to the weight of the arm.

Should we regard Fechner's concept of the added constant as much the same as 'noise' in the nervous system (Tanner and Swets 1954; Gregory and Cane 1955 [No. 7]; Barlow, 1956; Treisman, 1964)? The concepts may seem similar in the case of the *Augenschwarz*, or 'dark light' of the eye: Fechner recognized this as spontaneous neural activity occurring in the absence of a stimulus. However, in the case of weight discrimination he does not seem to have considered the possibility of *spontaneous* neural activity: he thought the activity was due to a *stimulus*, the weight of the arm. With the advance of statistical thought it is now clear that the addition of a constant (e.g. a weight) need not reduce information; whereas the addition of random activity, 'noise', must impair discrimination.

It is an interesting question whether an additional weight on the arm impairs discrimination. If there is impairment, does discrimination recover when time is allowed for adaptation? These questions were investigated by adding a heavily weighted cuff to the forearm for short and long periods.

METHOD

The test weights were seven grey tins measuring 3·2 cm in diameter and 4·8 cm in height. They were filled with lead shot and wax. The standard weighed 111 gm and the six comparison weights ranged from 103 to 120 gm in 3-gm increments. The lids were fitted with vertical handles (2BA threaded rod). The weighted cuff consisted of pieces of lead sewn into a cloth and weighed 500 gm.

The second author (Helen Ross) served as *S* and was tested by different *Es* for a series of 20 sessions, spread over a two-month period. Each session lasted about 30 min. The DL was measured twice in each session, once with and once without the weighted cuff. In half the sessions the cuff was worn first, and in the other half second. In half the sessions *S* wore the cuff for 30 min before testing was started, in order to allow time for adaptation. There were thus four testing schemes: No prior cuff, cuff first; No prior cuff, cuff second; Prior cuff, cuff first; Prior cuff, cuff second. These four schemes were used in a regular sequence, each scheme being repeated five times.

The difference limen (DL) was measured by the constant method. Each of the comparison weights was judged against the standard 10 times. The comparison weight was lifted equally often before and after the standard, to reduce the effect of time-order errors. The 60 trials for each DL estimate were given in a predetermined random order, a different order being used in each test. *E* presented the weights in pairs, from behind a screen, so that the weight to be lifted first was nearer *S*. *S* lifted the weights once only, in the required order, and judged whether the first or second weight was heavier.

The record sheets were not scored until the end of the final session. The percentage of occasions that each comparison weight was judged heavier than the standard was calculated. The percentages were then changed to probit values, and a straight line fitted by the method of least squares. The DL was taken as the difference in grams between the 50% and 84% intercepts (Woodworth and Schlosberg 1955, p. 206).

RESULTS AND DISCUSSION

The geometric means of the DLs for each of the test conditions are shown in Table 12.1, together with the percentage of correct judgements, and the significance level of the differences. All statistical tests relate to the percentage of correct judgements, since the DLs could not always be reliably estimated from the 60 judgements. Combining the results from all test orders, the geometric mean DL without the cuff was 9·81 gm and with the cuff 11·80 gm. Discrimination was significantly better without the cuff. However, the difference in the DLs was quite small and seems unrelated to Weber's Law. If the weight of the cuff (500 gm) were added to the weight of the standard (111 gm), then the DL would increase by a factor of about 6. Yet, adding the cuff to the arm, this factor was only 1·2.

Is discrimination less impaired if time is allowed for adaptation to the cuff? Table 12.1 shows that with no prior wearing of the cuff the geometric mean DLs were 9·02 gm without the cuff and 12·65 gm with the cuff. After wearing the cuff for 30 min, the DL *with* the cuff was *reduced* to 11·00 gm, and the DL *without* the cuff was *raised* to 10·65 gm. It seems that discrimination is best when *S* has had time to adapt to his effective arm weight. If the arm weight is suddenly changed – whether raised or lowered – discrimination is impaired.

There are similar effects in other modalities: discrimination is finest when *S* is adapted to the test level and deteriorates when he is adapted to some other level. This was found by Craik (1938) for the brightness DL, Békésy (1929) for the loudness DL, and Deutsch (1951) for the pitch DL. Keidel, Keidel and Wigand (1961) presented physiological evidence concerning the process of adaptation in the somesthetic and auditory systems and argued that the resultant changes in neural firing rate can lead to a gain of sensory information for stimuli at the level of adaptation. We have pointed out (Ross and Gregory, 1964 [No. 11]) that changes in apparent weight due to the size-weight illusion can affect discrimination. It now seems that changes in adaptation (which also produce changes in apparent weight) can affect discrimination. Any comprehensive theory of sensory discrimination must take these factors into account.

TABLE 12.1

GEOMETRIC MEANS OF DLs (IN GM) AND PERCENTAGE OF CORRECT JUDGMENTS (IN BRACKETS) FOR DIFFERENT TESTING CONDITIONS

Testing Scheme*	Without Cuff	With Cuff
No prior cuff, cuff first	8·80 (75·0)	16·45 (64·3)
No prior cuff, cuff second	9·26 (73·0)	9·71 (71·3)
Prior cuff, cuff first	10·35 (71·0)	9·53 (71·3)
Prior cuff, cuff second	10·97 (68·7)	12·71 (65·7)
All sessions without prior cuff	9·02 (74·0)	12·65 (67·8)
All sessions with prior cuff	10·65 (69·8)	11·00 (68·5)
All sessions	9·81 (72·0)	11·80 (68·2)

* Significance levels: For all sessions without prior cuff, the 'with cuff' scores were significantly worse than the 'without cuff' scores ($p < 0.005$, Wilcoxon, 1-tail). For all sessions with prior cuff, the difference was not significant. For all sessions combined, the difference was significant ($p = 0.005$). The difference between the 'with cuff' and 'without cuff' scores was significantly greater with prior cuff than without prior cuff ($p = 0.046$, Mann-Whitney U test, 1-tail).

Although in normal environments the weight of the limbs remains nearly constant, there are several special conditions which produce large changes in effective weight. When immersed in water the limbs have nearly zero effective weight, though large forces are required to produce rapid movement. In aerobatic flying there are sudden and violent changes in gravity, which affect weight perception and limb control (Simons and Gardner, 1963). Astronauts in orbital flight have zero limb weight for long periods. We would expect initial impairment under zero-g, followed by rapid improvement. Some studies on the discrimination of the mass of weightless objects (Rees and Copeland 1960; Crawford and Kama 1961) have shown that discrimination deteriorates when gravitational cues are reduced. However, in these space-simulation studies only the objects were weightless. These findings await confirmation when the limbs are also weightless. Is discrimination impaired when a man is adapted to space?

13 Weight illusions and weight discrimination – a revised hypothesis

[We thought originally that Weber's Law might apply to *apparent* rather than true *physical* input intensity. So if there was illusory distortion, such that a weight felt heavier, or a line looked longer or a light brighter, we would have expected a corresponding decrease in ability to discriminate: as though the weight were actually heavier, or the line actually longer or the light actually brighter. When Helen Ross came to look into weight discrimination with *surprisingly light* weights, we got a shock: we found that discrimination did not improve – it was worse than for objects of normal density!

This is compatible with K. J. W. Craik's much earlier finding that brightness discrimination is best when the background field has about the same intensity as the signal field; but we had regarded this as a special property of the dark-adaptation mechanism of the retina. Could it be that this optimum discrimination for average densities is related to Craik's finding for visual discrimination? Could it be that there is a *central* mechanism operating here, related to *expected* values? This could suggest a rather general theory of discrimination; in which input sensory information is related to 'internal models', or 'perceptual hypotheses' of the current state of the external world: that the available sensory information is modifying the model or the hypothesis, or is referred to it and affected by it. It is tempting to think of this as operating with brain circuits equivalent to Wheatstone bridges – for bridge circuits have uniquely favourable properties. They are relatively free of drift though their components drift, and they work over very large ranges of intensity while they are extremely sensitive to small changes of input. All these are appropriate for the biological case. Now it is suggestive that when the internal arm of a bridge (set by expected input value) is set *incorrectly*, the discrimination of the bridge is *impaired*. It is impaired whether it is set to too high or too low a value. Is it possible that the effect discovered by the next experiments reveals the effect of imbalance of 'bridges' in our central discrimination brain circuits? Whether or not this turns out to be the case, surely it is inadequate to think of discrimination simply in terms of differences of input signals. Some kind of reference to what is likely is surely involved – and this takes us beyond a straightforward physiological analysis, into essentially cognitive 'software' processes: even in what is often taken as traditional physiological territory.]

★   ★   ★

THE question has been raised (Seashore, 1896; Koseleff, 1958; Ross and Gregory 1964; Dodwell, Standing and Thio 1969) whether discrimination changes when apparent weight, but not physical weight, changes. If, for example, two objects of identical appearance weighing 100 and 103 gm are just distinguishable in weight, are they equally distinguishable if the size of both objects is changed to the same extent? Koseleff (personal communication) hesitated to perform an experiment, on the grounds that one could never be sure that subjects were experiencing the size-weight illusion while discrimination was being tested. Seashore performed an experiment using three sizes of cylinders; but as his two measures of discrimination gave conflicting trends, it is not clear that he found any reliable differences. He nevertheless maintained that discrimination became poorer as apparent weight increased, and that the differential threshold was proportional to the apparent weight. Ross and Gregory [No. 11], in a similar experiment using two sizes of tins, found that discrimination was poorer for the smaller (apparently heavier) size. They tentatively accepted the same hypothesis as Seashore. However, further experiments by Ross (1965) and Dodwell *et al.* (1969) over a wider range of apparent weights failed to confirm this hypothesis.

The experiments and discussions of these authors were centred around the question of whether the differential threshold was proportional to apparent rather than to physical weight. There are, however, other possible relationships. An alternative is that the threshold is a U-shaped function of apparent weight, with finest discrimination somewhere in the middle of the range of possible apparent weights. Dodwell *et al.* say: 'It . . . seems paradoxical that sensitivity might be increased by an experimental factor, particularly if this involves stimulation of a different modality as in the size-weight illusion'. However, it is not being claimed that the threshold is reduced below the normal limits set by signal/noise discrimination of the nervous system. It is well established that discrimination can be affected by practice, attention, sensory interaction and adaptation. Again, there is no suggestion that the threshold is ever driven below the level of discrimination set by neural noise or other physical limitations.

It has been found in several sense modalities that discrimination is finest when the subject is adapted to the intensity of the test stimuli, and deteriorates when he is adapted to a higher or lower intensity. This was found by Craik (1938), Ranke (1952) and Kern (1952) for light, and Békésy (1929) for sound intensity discrimination. Deutsch (1951) found that pitch discrimination in one ear improves when the other ear is stimulated at the test frequency; and Krauskopf (1954) found that auditory localization in the median plane improved after stimulation by sounds in that plane.

Similar findings have been reported for weight discrimination. Woodrow (1933) found that discrimination was poorer with a varying standard than a fixed standard. Holway, Goldring and Zeigler (1938) plotted the time-course of recovery of discrimination for light weights after adaptation to a heavy weight. Gregory and Ross (1967) [No. 12] found weight-discrimination initially impaired when the arm was weighted with a cuff; but that discrimination returned to normal after wearing the cuff for 30 min. They also found that discrimination was impaired immediately after removal of the cuff, but returned to normal after 30 min. Dinnerstein (1965) found maximal sensitivity in one hand when a weight of a similar intensity was lifted in the other hand, and reduced sensitivity when the weight in the other hand was of a higher or lower intensity. This shows conclusively that there are central components in weight adaptation.

These experiments show finest discrimination when the subject is adapted to the test intensity level. It is not clear whether the adaptation involves only the peripheral sense organs, or only central components, or both. Central and peripheral adaptation mechanisms may well be very different. The size-weight illusion cannot have a peripheral origin (Ross, 1969). It must involve central components, and cannot be due to peripheral sensory adaptation. We might, however, expect a U-shaped function for discrimination-error, since this is found for adaptation situations involving central components.

The problem with weight illusions is to determine the expected weight of an object. Once this is determined it is possible to say whether the apparent weight of an object is veridical, or whether it has an illusion of heaviness or lightness. Ross (1969) argues that weights which are lifted without visual or tactile size-cues are non-illusory, and can be used as a standard for comparison with objects whose size is seen or felt. Objects which have the same apparent weight with and without such cues may be regarded as non-illusory. If objects of various sizes are matched with hidden objects for apparent weight, a linear relationship is found to hold over a wide range of densities between the weight matched and the logarithm of the density of the visible object. The density at which the hidden and visible objects are correctly matched varies with the visible surface material of the object. The average density for the match was found to be about 1·7 for tins, and about 0·14 for blocks of expanded polystyrene, though there was some individual variation between subjects. If these values are typical, most subjects might be expected to show finest discrimination for objects at these densities, and increasingly poorer discrimination for objects which are more or less dense. The following experiment was carried out to test this prediction.

Experiment 1 : Optimum density for polystyrene and tins

Apparatus Four sets of polystyrene blocks and four sets of tins were prepared. Both blocks and tins were painted grey, and their weight was varied by the addition of lead shot. All the weights were lifted by vertical handles of 2BA threaded rod. Each set of blocks contained a standard of 111 gm and six comparison weights ranging from 102 to 120 gm in 3-gm intervals. The volumes of the four sizes of blocks were 4005, 1780, 800 and 550 cc, and the densities of the four standards were 0·0277, 0·0623, 0·1387 and 0·2018, respectively. Each set of tins contained a standard of 200 gm and six comparison weights ranging from 185 to 215 gm in 5-gm intervals. The volumes of the four sizes of tins were 962·7, 326·9, 194·4 and 38·6 cc, and the densities of the four standards were 0·2077, 0·6118, 1·0288 and 5·1813, respectively. The third set of objects is thus in both cases nearest to the density found to be non-illusory by Ross (1969).

Subjects The subjects were 48 undergraduates and research students of both sexes. They were mainly non-psychologists, and all were unaware of the purpose of the experiment.

Method Twenty-four subjects were tested with polystyrene blocks, and 24 with tins. Each subject was tested for two sessions of about an hour, separated by a few days. In each session the subject was tested on all four sets of weights, the order of testing for the different sets being reversed on the second sessions. A different order was used for each subject. The differential threshold (DL) for each set of weights was measured by the constant method. Each of the six comparison weights was compared 8 times with the standard, making 48 judgements for a set, and 192 for a session. The variable weight was presented equally often before and after the standard, but the subject was always asked to judge whether the first or second weight was heavier.

Results The data from the two sessions were combined, giving a total of 96 judgements for each set of weights. The DLs were calculated by probit analysis (Finney, 1952), taking the DL as the difference in grammes between the weights judged heavier than the standard on 50 and 84 per cent of the trials. About a quarter of the DL estimates were a poor fit ($p > 0.05$) to the data points. Changes in the number of correct judgements showed the same trends as changes in the DL, so the former measure was used for assessing the statistical significance of the results.

The geometric means of the DLs for the four sizes of polystyrene blocks were 11·73, 11·70, 10·03 and 10·58 gm, and the corresponding mean numbers of correct judgements (out of 96) were 66·4, 66·7, 70·0 and 67·1. Both measures show the finest discrimination for the third size of block. An analysis of variance showed significant differences due to the size of the block ($p < 0.05$), and also to differences between subjects ($p < 0.001$).

The geometric means of the DLs for the four sizes of tins were 18·33, 17·20, 16·39 and 16·65 gm, and the corresponding mean numbers of correct judgements were 67·4, 67·8, 69·0 and 68·8. Discrimination was again finest for the third size of tin. However, an analysis of variance showed no significant differences between the sizes of tins, though there were significant differences between subjects ($p < 0.01$).

Discussion The results for the polystyrene blocks agree with the hypothesis that the DL is a U-shaped function of apparent weight. The optimum density for discrimination also agrees with the value found by Ross (1969) for another group of subjects for the non-illusory density (0·14). The results for the tins also indicate a U-shaped function, but the failure to find significant differences is disappointing. The tins giving the finest discrimination had a density of about 1·03, and their density was closest in value to the non-illusory value found for another group of subjects (about 1·7). If it is legitimate to assume that the non-illusory density was similar for both groups of subjects, then it can be predicted that discrimination will improve monotonically throughout the first three sizes of tins. This trend was found to be significant on Jonckheere's (1954) test for the order of ranks ($p = 0.035$). It is not possible to predict where the fourth size of tin should lie in relation to the other three, unless unwarranted assumptions are made about the shape of the curve.

Several other experiments with tins were performed, both before and after the U-shaped hypothesis was considered. Though few results were highly significant, all but one (non-significant) were compatible with the hypothesis. A brief summary of these experiments will now be given.

Experiments in which the denser weights should give poorer discrimination

In all these experiments a set of large tins had a density slightly below 1·7, and a corresponding set of smaller tins had a very much greater density. On the U-shaped hypothesis, the smaller weights should give rise to poorer discrimination since they are more illusory.

(1) *Ross and Gregory* (1964, *Exp.* 1). 16 subjects. Black tins with a 200 gm standard. Density of standards: large 0·612, small 5·181. Constant method, with standard presented first, comparison second. Median DLs: large 11·9 gm, small 13·8 gm. Significance level: $p < 0.07$ (Wilcoxon, 2 tails). [No. 11]

(2) *Ross and Gregory* (1964, *Exp.* 2). 16 subjects. Apparatus as above. Constant method. Variable presented before standard, and comparison asked for first weight. (This method produced high variability.) Median DLs: large 17·0 gm, small 15·2 gm. Not significant: $p \simeq 0.63$ (Wilcoxon, 2 tails). [No. 11]

(3) *Ross and Gregory* (1964, *Exp.* 3). 20 subjects. Apparatus as above. Constant method. Standard and comparison lifted simultaneously. Median DLs: large 12·6 gm, small 14·4 gm. Significance level: $p < 0.01$ (Wilcoxon, 2 tails). [No. 11]

(4) *Dodwell et al.* (1969, *Exp.* 3). 20 subjects. Apparatus as above. Median DLs: large 11·8 gm, small 12·1 gm. Not significant: $p \simeq 0.38$ (Wilcoxon, 2 tails). (This result goes in the same direction as nos. 1 and 3, and not in the opposite direction as stated by Dodwell *et al.*)

(5) *Ross* (1965). 14 subjects. Grey tins of 200 and 205 gm. Density of tins at 200 gm: large 1·029, small 10·78 (mercury filling necessary to obtain this density). The tins were lifted in a box described elsewhere (Ross, 1969), and the weights quoted include 10 gm for the lifting apparatus. The tins were lifted successively, and the subject decided whether the first or second was heavier. Pairs of large and small tins were mixed randomly rather than given in two blocks, in the hope of preventing habituation to the illusion. In half the trials both tins were hidden from sight. Mean number of correct judgments (out of 40): visible large 25·7; visible small 23·3, hidden large 25·7, hidden small 26·1. No significant difference was found between the large and small tins when hidden, but the large were significantly better when visible ($p < 0.05$, Wilcoxon, 2 tails). No

significant difference was found between the hidden and visible large weights, but the small weights were significantly worse when visible ($p < 0.05$, Wilcoxon, 2 tails). This experiment shows that the difference between the sizes of tins arises only when they are visible; and that discrimination for hidden weights (which should be non-illusory) is approximately the same as for non-illusory visible weights.

Experiments in which the less dense weights should give poorer discrimination

In all these experiments a set of small tins had a density near 1.7, and a large set had a very much lower density. On the U-shaped hypothesis, the larger weights should give rise to poorer discrimination since they are more illusory.

(6) *Ross* (1964). 8 subjects (few subjects were used, as more were unnecessary for the main purpose of the experiment). Black tins with a 75 gm standard. Density of standards: large 0.229, small 1.943. Constant method, with comparison second. Median DLs: large 5.8 gm, small 5.4 gm. No significant difference.

(7) *Ross* (1965, *Exp.* 2.4). 16 subjects. Grey tins with a 23 gm standard. Density of standards: large 0.596, small 1.241. Constant method, subject judging whether the first or second weight was heavier. Median DLs: large 3.63 gm, small 2.93 gm. Significance level: $p < 0.08$ (Wilcoxon, 2 tails).

(8) *Ross* (1965, *Exp.* 2.5). 20 subjects. Grey tins of 60 and 62 gm. Density of tins at 60 gm: large 0.309, small 1.554. Subject judged whether the first or second weight was heavier. Mean number of correct judgements (out of 60): large 37.7, small 40.5. Significance level: $p < 0.01$ (Wilcoxon, 2 tails).

Experiments in which the prediction is uncertain

In these experiments no tins had a density close to 1.7. Since there are no grounds for assuming a symmetrical U-shaped function for the DL, densities higher and lower than optimum cannot be compared with each other.

(9) *Ross* (1965, *Exp.* 2.1). 20 subjects. Grey tins with a 111 gm standard. Densities of standards: largest 0.340, middle 2.876, smallest 5.987. Constant method, with standard first and comparison second. Median DLs: largest 10.05 gm, middle 7.86 gm, smallest 11.25 gm. On a logarithmic scale, the density of the middle tins is nearest to the non-illusory value. They gave the smallest DL, though this was not significantly different from the other two. It can be firmly predicted

that the smallest tins should give poorer discrimination than the middle tins, as both sets of tins lie on the same side of the U-shaped curve. The significance of the difference between them was $p \simeq 0.17$ (Wilcoxon, 2 tails).

(10) *Dodwell et al.* (1969, *Exp.* 1). 32 subjects for each set of tins. Black tins with a 200 gm standard. Densities of standards: large 0.121, small 4.717. Subjects were tested on one size of tin only. Tins were lifted simultaneously, subjects deciding whether or not there was a difference. Total number of correct judgements: large 2659, small 2698. No significant difference (analysis of variance). On a logarithmic scale the largest tins are furthest removed from the non-illusory density. If a symmetrical U is assumed, they should give rise to poorer discrimination, as found.

(11) *Dodwell et al.* (1969, *Exp.* 2). 16 subjects. Apparatus as above. Constant method, with standard first and comparison second. Median DLs: large 12.85 gm, small 12.75 gm. No significant difference. The result goes in the same direction as the above experiment.

Discussion All the experiments listed above are compatible with the U-shaped hypothesis, except for Ross and Gregory (1964, Exp. 2 [No. 11]) which was non-significant. Out of the eight experiments listed above in which a clear prediction could be made (nine, including part of no. 9), five were significant on a one-tailed test. Three of these were also significant on a two-tailed test. If the hypothesis is not correct, we have to explain why several significant results occurred. Dodwell *et al.* (1969) suggest that the subjects may have known or guessed the hypothesis, and that this may have influenced their performance. On the whole this seems unlikely since the majority of subjects were not psychology students, and the results sometimes disconfirmed the hypothesis which the experimenter held at the time. The only other possible explanation would seem to be that there were slight differences in the ease of discriminability of the tins, unrelated to the size-weight illusion: for example, differences in the centre of gravity, or differences in surface imperfections which might help the subject to recognize individual tins. If this were the case, the difference in discrimination would not arise through chance, but the agreement with the prediction would be fortuitous and correspondingly unlikely.

If the hypothesis is correct, we have to explain why it was difficult to obtain more significant results. The most probable reason is that the effect is small, like most central influences on sensory thresholds. The difficulty may also be increased by the problem raised by Koseleff: we cannot be sure of the degree of illusion that a subject is experiencing at the time that he is being tested for discrimination. Also different individuals have different non-illusory densities. Significance will depend upon obtaining a group of subjects whose non-illusory densities are similar, and remain stable throughout the experiment. Significance would tend to be reduced when subjects are not used as their own controls (e.g. Dodwell *et al.*, 1969, Exp. 1). It would also be reduced when testing is spread over several days, as in Experiment 1 of this paper, and Ross (1965, Exp. 2.1); and when the different sizes are tested in blocks (as in the majority of experiments described here) rather than being randomly mixed (as in the experiment summarized as no. 5 of this paper). Ideally the different sizes of tins should be mixed to prevent adaptation to one density; and the non-illusory density should be measured for each subject. This was attempted in the next experiment.

Experiment 2 : Individual differences

Methods

Apparatus Six sets of tins were prepared for measuring discrimination. The volumes were 962·7, 450·4, 326·9, 194·4, 38·6 and 18·54 cc. They were painted grey, and were weighted with lead shot, apart from the smallest set which was weighted with mercury. For each size of tin six weights were prepared: three of 200 gm and three of 205 gm. The corresponding densities at 200 gm were 0·208, 0·444, 0·612, 1·029, 5·181 and 10·780.

Six sets of tins were also prepared for measuring the illusion. In each of these sets the weights differed by 5 gm intervals. The range of weights covered for these six sets were (1) 190–240 gm, (2) 180–230 gm, (3) 175–230 gm, (4) 165–220 gm, (5) 155–210 gm, (6) 159–190 gm. These values include an additional 10 gm due to the lifting apparatus. These tins were lifted in the box described by Ross (1969).

Subject The subjects were three psychology students, two males and one female, aged between 20 and 25 years. They were paid a small sum for serving as subjects. Though they were familiar with the size–weight illusion, they did not know the purpose of the experiment. Each subject was tested for 11 sessions of about 45 min. over a period of 3 weeks.

Method The value of the non-illusory density was measured on the sixth session, as this was felt to be more representative than the first or last sessions. The subjects were required to match the apparent weight of a visible tin with the apparent weight of a hidden tin of 200 gm. This was done for each size of tin by the method described by Ross (1969). Each size was matched four times, the trials for the different sizes being mixed randomly.

Discrimination was measured on the other ten trials, without using the box. The subjects were presented with a pair of weights of the same size, and were asked to judge whether the second weight was the same or heavier than the first. For each of the six sizes of tins 24 pairs were presented: 12 where both weights were the same, and 12 where the second was heavier. There were thus 144 trials in each session. The pairs of tins were presented in a different order in each session. Pairs of different sizes were interspersed fairly evenly throughout the course of each session to neutralize practice effects.

Results The number of correct judgements was counted for each size of tin over all sessions. The totals are shown as percentages of the total number of judgements in Fig. 13.1. The mean percentage is also shown for all subjects combined. The percentages are plotted as a function of the logarithm of the density of the tins, since the illusion appears to be a linear function on this scale. The data for the strength of the illusion are also shown on the same scale: the means of the visible weights matched with the 200 gm hidden standard are plotted against the log density of the 200 gm visible tin. The lines shown were fitted by least squares. The log density at which a 200 gm visible weight was correctly matched is indicated by a dotted line. The non-illusory log densities for the three subjects were -0.2082 (C.C.), -0.0648 (T.C.), 0.0800 (C.L.); and -0.0775 for all subjects combined. The corresponding ordinary densities were 0.62, 0.86, 1.20 and 0.84, respectively. None of the three subjects gave a perfect inverted U- (or hump-shaped) curve, for discrimination; but all showed maximum discrimination for tins at the density next below the value determined for the non-illusory density. All subjects combined showed an almost perfect humped curve, with a peak for the third size of tin, though the average non-illusory density was minimally nearer the fourth size.

Discussion These results lend support to the hypothesis of a hump-shaped curve for weight discrimination, with maximum discrimination for weights nearest the non-illusory density. The slight discrepancy between the two measures for one subject (T.C.) is probably not important. The weight of the lifting apparatus (10 gm) may perhaps slightly distort the value of the match. There may also be changes of the subjects' non-illusory value throughout the sessions.

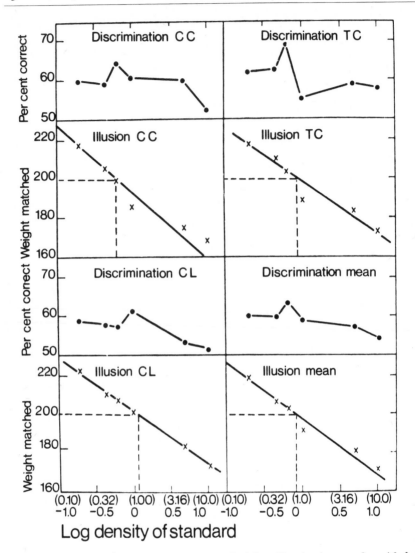

FIG. 13.1 *Percentage of correct judgements as a function of log density, together with data on the illusion showing the log density at which visible and hidden weights were correctly matched at 200 gm. Ordinary densities are shown in brackets beside the corresponding log densities. The data for three subjects are shown separately, together with the group mean.*

It might be preferable to measure the illusion at the beginning and end of the experiment rather than the middle.

It may be queried whether the observed changes in performance were due to changes in response bias rather than in discrimination. Those experiments which were suitable for such analysis were also analysed in terms of Luce's (1959) choice model. The results showed significant changes both in response bias and in discrimination. The differences in bias are hard to interpret, but the differences in discrimination showed exactly the same trends as the differences in the total number of correct judgements or the differences in the DL. It cannot, therefore, be maintained that differences in bias are the cause of the difference in performance.

Discussion

It seems clear that weight estimation is associated with expected weight. This is most dramatically experienced with the 'empty suitcase' effect.

The size-weight illusion is clear evidence that weight estimation involves central factors, for it is most implausible to suppose that visually observed size can directly affect the peripheral weight sensing systems of the limbs. The illusion certainly cannot be due to sensory adaptation of the weight sensing system, for this is obviously not stimulated by visual information.

At this point it seems important to distinguish between effects due to *sensory adaptation* and those due to what we may call the prevailing *perceptual hypothesis* of the weight. In the case of visual size affecting sensed weight, the visual information can only be relevant by previous association of the size and weight of objects. This experience is necessary in order for observed size to set appropriate muscle tensions for lifting weights. It is most reasonable to suppose that the size-weight illusion (where small objects are judged heavier than larger objects of the same physical weight) is due to an inappropriate perceptual hypothesis of the weight of the object. The hypothesis is selected on the basis of visual or other information, which is misleading when the situation is atypical. It remains to consider why differential sensitivity should be affected by an error in the anticipated weight.

Craik (1938) and Keidel, Keidel and Wigand (1961) suggest theories to explain why differential sensitivity to light intensity is maximal when the eye is adapted to the surround intensity and falls off with extra light or dark adaptation. Craik (1938) suggests that adaptation is like a shunt across a galvanometer; the range of the instrument being extended by varying the value of the shunt resistance, so that proportionally more or less current passes through the meter. As the neurological 'shunt' resistance is decreased with light adaptation, so less 'current' would pass through the 'meter', thus generating Weber's Law. We must however disagree with Craik that this model would predict the U-shaped function he found when adaptation is inappropriate to the background intensity. If a shunt is set at too low a resistance value, then too much current is shunted from the meter and sensitivity is lost; but if the shunt is set too high, then the meter becomes overloaded and will cease to operate. Possibly this corresponds to 'dazzle', but the loss of differential sensitivity occurs long before dark adaptation gives dazzle, which could represent gross overloading of any system. Rather than asymmetrical overloading, Craik's curves suggest a gradual loss of sensitivity either side of the match between adaptation and stimulus intensity.

It has been pointed out (Gregory 1968*a* [No. 30]) that a Wheatstone bridge measuring system appears ideal for this physiological situation. It gives a very wide dynamic range; and it is relatively free of drift, though biological components are subject to drift. Now, interestingly enough, a bridge's discrimination falls off either side of normal balance – giving a U-shaped function, very much as Craik found for light adaptation and we find for the weights.

The fact that the size-weight illusion occurs suggests most strongly that weight estimation involves comparison against some central standard, which is set by anticipation (or perhaps directly from the available size-information). In electronic terms (which might be translated into neurological circuits) we may suppose that anticipation, or the visual information generally indicating weight, sets one of the ratio arms of a bridge. The neighbouring arm is set by the directly sensed information of weight from the subject's limb. When these are equal, the bridge balances without special adjustment. When the visual information is misleading, as with an object of atypical density, then the internal (expectancy) arm would be set differently from the external (weight) arm – and the sensitivity of the bridge to differences in the (weight) signal will be reduced.

14 *Eye-movements and the stability of the visual world*

[We turn now to very different issues – to the perception of movement, of size, and the origin of the distortion illusions. Finally, we approach deep cognitive problems of the relation between perception, thinking and language. This represents a rough temporal sequence as it happened: largely, I suspect, due to the impact of the 'recovery from blindness' case study [No. 3]. I have gradually moved away from sensory processes, discrimination, movement detection and so on, towards trying to understand how *objects* are seen from sensory *patterns*. I expect this drift of interest towards the inner 'software' of the brain mediating object-perception, thinking and language, to continue until I get somewhere!

The next paper discusses a classical problem: a favourite of the Master, Hermann Helmholtz. I follow him closely, but there are some added observations perhaps worth considering. In this paper I am rash in questioning a commonly held generalization – that all voluntary searching eye movements are saccadic, and all tracking eye movements are smooth while the target is followed. I report that an after-image viewed in darkness, 'projected' on to the observer's moving hand, may *move smoothly*. The implication seems to be that when one is *set* to follow a visual target the smooth eye movement system is brought into use – although the 'target' does not provide error signals when lost. Perhaps this is not too surprising, but it has a certain interest.

I may have underestimated the importance of Professor MacKay's theory that visual stability may be given not by cancellation of equal and opposite velocity signalling (as argued here), but by a kind of 'null' system in which motion is only observed when surprising according to internal expectancies. Although I believe that this approach is important in many contexts, visual stability during eye movements does not seem to me to exhibit this principle for when velocity information is destroyed, in either the eye movement system or the retina, stability is lost. The experimental trick here is to destroy velocity signals while retaining movement. Retinal velocity signals can be destroyed by illuminating the moving object with short (0·001 sec.) flashes of light with a repetition rate of about 10 flashes per second. What happens when a shift of the image across the retina is *not* signalled as a velocity? What happens when we destroy the image/retina velocity information by illuminating the scene during eye movements with a stroboscope? I found that *stability could be lost*: that when image/retina velocity signals were destroyed by stroboscopic illumination, the visual world would *swing round with the eyes* – like an after-image stuck to the retina – though the image was in fact moving *against* the movement of the eyes. It seems, then, that when either the motor system of the eyes, or the retinal system to signal velocity of the image shift across the retina is impaired, stability is lost – as would be expected on a cancellation theory of stability.

This observation of loss of stability with stroboscopic illumination is curious and well worth experiencing at first hand – or rather first eye! The effect is rather like being under water, with the world swinging in a smooth sickening way, with each movement of the eyes. This apparent movement goes counter to the parallax of the moving fixation spot (the pendulum bob) against the background, which makes the observation all the more surprising. Perhaps because of this contrary evidence, the effect may take a little time; but it is unmistakable when it occurs and it may continue for minutes – apparently until fixation of the moving spot is lost. The relevance to the cancellation *v.* null hypothesis theory issue is that movement *with* eye movements is extremely unlikely – never previously experienced except for after-images. This effect should be predicted on a cancellation theory, (provided the motion parallax of the moving fixation-light against the background does not counter it). I am sure, however, that MacKay's theory has an importance beyond this case. Even if abandoned for stability during eye movements it is important in other contexts.]

⋆   ⋆   ⋆

THE visual perception of movement is generally regarded as of primary biological importance, yet far less work has been done on this subject than on topics such as colour vision, visual acuity and the photic sensitivity of the eye. Further, surprisingly little is reliably known about the neurological mechanisms subserving movement perception. There are many unsettled questions, in particular that of the apparent stability of the visual world during voluntary movements of the eye. Some of the problems raised by the visual perception of movement will be discussed in this article.

Information channels in the perception of movement

The simplest case of movement perception is that given by a moving self-luminous object in a dark room. Perception of its movement may occur under two different sets of conditions: (1) the eyes may follow the object ('tracking'), in which case its image will, ideally, remain stationary upon the retinæ; and (2) the eyes may remain stationary so that the images travel across the retinæ. Since movement is experienced under both conditions, there must be at least two information channels subserving movement perception. The first involves tracking eye movements, and may be called the 'retina/head' system. The second involves shifts of the image across the retina, and may be called the 'image/retina' system. It may be supposed that the two systems are based on essentially different neurological mechanisms.

Movement perceptions may, in special circumstances, be paradoxical. When a fast-flowing river, the view from a moving train, or an endless belt of black-and-white stripes is fixated for several seconds it will be found that if the gaze is transferred to a stationary object it will seem to move in the opposite direction and with corresponding velocities to those of the previously observed real movement. This after-effect of movement is paradoxical, for though movement is clearly observed it may also be seen that nothing is changing in position. Similarly, when a stationary small weak light is observed in total darkness it will seem to move erratically, and yet it may not seem to change its position to any marked extent. Such paradoxical perceptions may be due to incompatible information arriving from the two or more movement channels. Adaptation or random changes in the systems might be the cause.

As is well known, there are two essentially different types of eye movement, first studied systematically by Dodge (1903). When the eye tracks a moving target, once it is 'locked' on to the target it moves smoothly, provided that the target moves in a simple, known manner without excessive changes in direction or velocity. Voluntary movements in the absence of a target take place in small jerks ('saccades') occurring about four times per second, which have been much studied particularly in relation to reading.

It is generally supposed that smooth tracking movements of the eyes occur only in response to retinal cues, that is they form part of what we have called the 'retina/head' system. I have shown that this is not necessarily the case. A small neon lamp is arranged to flash at 25–50 flashes/sec.: the light will appear continuous under conditions of steady fixation, but if, with the eyes remaining still, the lamp is moved steadily across the retina, a regular flicker will be noticed.

This is a well-known effect. If now the eye is swept as smoothly as possible, by voluntary movement without a target this regular flicker is not seen. The lamp seems to move in jerks. Evidently the saccadic movements prevent the smooth travel of the image which is necessary for the observation of the regular flicker. On the other hand, when the eyes follow a moving target the flicker may be observed, as when the lamp is moved across the field with the eyes stationary. Using this technique, I have been able to show that it is not necessary for the observer to track a visual object for the smooth eye movements to occur. The regular flicker indicating smooth eye movements may be seen if the observer tries to track his own hand under conditions of complete darkness apart from the light from the neon lamp, his hand being invisible. That is to say, smooth eye movements may be elicited even in the absence of appropriate retinal stimuli. It follows that the retina/head system may involve a proprioceptive component; information from moving members of the body may suffice to actuate the smooth eye movement system. I have also found that the apparent movements of a stationary small weak light viewed in darkness (the 'autokinetic effect') are influenced by slight unbalanced strains imposed on the eye or neck musculature. The effect may normally be due to randomly occurring imbalance of the musculature or proprioceptive systems of the eye and neck.

Eye movements and perceptual stability

It is a commonplace to state that when the eyes move voluntarily across an extended field (by means of saccadic movements) there is little, if any, change in apparent position of the perceived objects. The visual world does not swing round in the direction opposed to the eye movement. On the other hand, nearly all subjects report that when an object moving across the field is tracked, the stationary background does tend to swing round in the opposed direction. The experience is similar to, though probably less marked than, the movement of the field observed when the eye-ball is moved passively by pressure from the finger. This observation suggests that saccadic eye movements are in some way necessary for the stability of the visual world. It may be that the jerky movements of the eye are themselves important, or that the saccadic mechanism accepts information giving rise to stability which is rejected during smooth tracking movements. Evidence to be given below suggests that the former is the case.

The problem of the stability of the visual world was discussed by Helmholtz (1856–66), and by many later writers, the most recent being MacKay (1958). There have been two main theories. The first, that stabilization is given by proprioceptive information from the extrinsic eye muscles, which has been called the 'inflow' theory, was rejected by Helmholtz, who held that the central command signals (but called by him 'the Will') are monitored by an internal loop which gives appropriate information for providing stability, provided the motor system is functional. This has been called the 'outflow' theory. He pointed out that patients suffering from paralysis of the external recti, and who were therefore unable to execute voluntary eye movements, experience the visual world moving round in the direction in which the eyes should have moved had it been possible to 'execute the command'. This observation has been confirmed under more controlled conditions (Kornmüller, 1930).

A useful technique for investigating many of the phenomena of stabilization and movement perception is provided by observations of after-images (preferably produced by fixating a photographic-type electronic flash tube) under various conditions. It is not always realized that after-images observed in complete darkness move, apparently rather precisely, with the eyes during slow voluntary eye movements though they are not affected by passive movements. We should expect some feed-back from the stretch receptors which are now known to exist in the eye muscles (Cooper, Daniel and Whitteridge 1955), during passive movements, and this should produce some shift of after-images if the inflow theory were true.

We find that if, in total darkness, the drift of an after-image is observed during (a) slow voluntary eye movements, and (b) during the 'proprioceptive tracking' of the observer's hand described above, the after-image shows small saccadic-like jerks in condition (a), but not in condition (b), when it moves smoothly. If the velocity of the hand movement is changed the after-image may seem to lead or lag, and then to 'lock' on to the proprioceptive locus of the hand. The jerks experienced in condition (a) suggest that the stabilizing system has access to information of saccadic movements.

The cancellation theory

Helmholtz does not clearly state how his outflowing command signals are supposed to produce stability. Since stability depends upon the eyes in fact moving, the shift of the retinal image must be important. The term 'outflow' theory is thus misleading, for it ignores this shift of the retinal image and the information it transmits. Passive eye movements produce marked contrary shifts of the visual world: Helmholtz's theory requires these movement signals in conjunction with his command signals to produce stabilization, and this should be stated explicitly. The 'outflow' theory may, in this form, be called the 'cancellation' theory, where signals from the eye/head system are supposed to be cancelled out by signals from the image/retina system. This is similar to the view put forward by von Holst (1954), but is really a natural extension of Helmholtz's theory.

MacKay (1958) has recently made the interesting suggestion that stabilization is not something which is achieved, but rather that things are regarded as stable unless there is sufficient evidence to the contrary. Thus he says: 'what requires informational justification is not the maintenance of stability but the perception of change', and also: 'the retinal changes resulting from voluntary movement evoke no perception of world-motion, because they are not an awkward consequence to be compensated, but part of the goal to be achieved'. He explains the apparent movement of the perceptual world when the eye movements are paralysed by saying that the 'goal' (which is internal and conceptual) shifts with changing expectations. This may be contrasted with the cancellation of the command signals by retinal movement information.

On the 'cancellation' theory the world moves if the eye movement is thwarted because the command signal is not cancelled by the image/retina system, there being no signal. Similarly, after-images move during voluntary eye movements, because there is no shift of the image across the retina to give an image/retina signal.

On the 'cancellation' theory we may predict that if we could destroy movement information in the image/retina system, then the visual world should seem to move with the eye during voluntary eye movements. This may be done simply by illuminating the field with a stroboscope set to 4–5 flashes/sec. Movement is then only seen when the eye follows an object. With the eyes stationary, a moving object is observed to occupy successive positions, but not to move. When it is tracked it does, however, in stroboscopic illumination, appear to move. Voluntary eye movements produce loss of stability; the entire visual field moves in jerks. If now smooth eye movements are produced, by tracking a small self-luminous object held rather close to the eye, the entire visual world may be seen to move with the tracking object, and therefore with the eyes. This is observed best with a faintly glowing filament mounted on a pendulum bob; the visual world then swings with the bob, provided the distance and velocity conditions are appropriate.

This is difficult to reconcile with MacKay's 'null hypothesis' view of the matter, for the expectation of movement can scarcely be supposed to be related to the manner of illumination or to the kind of movement of the eye.

MacKay's observation that a stationary glowing filament moves though the stroboscopically lit field remains relatively stable during passive eye movements, would be expected on the 'cancellation' hypothesis, for the image/retina system should give movement information from the self-luminous filament only, and the eye/head system will give no information. The new observation given here, that the visual world moves with the eyes under these conditions when following a target, seems to be positive evidence for the cancellation hypothesis.

It may be suggested that saccadic movements are important in providing large movement signals which may be readily computed to give cancellation.

15 *A blue filter technique for detecting eye-movements during the autokinetic effect*

[The simple technique described in the next paper allows subjects to know when their eyes have lost fixation of a (generally red) fixation light viewed in darkness. It is included in this Part rather than under Instruments as it is vital for the experiments on the autokinetic effect, described in the paper immediately following this one.]

★   ★   ★

IT IS well known that if a stationary small dim light source placed in a dark room is fixated it will, after a time, appear to move. This apparent movement ('autokinetic sensation') is compelling, it cannot be arrested by the will (as Helmholtz might have put it) and it is seen by all observers in the appropriate conditions. The movement may be erratic or fairly steady, fast or slow. It may cover angles of well over 30°. When large, the effect gives a feeling of paradox – the light moves, yet one does not seem to follow it with the eyes and hence it cannot have moved.

In a recent textbook, Walsh (1957) writes: 'The *autokinetic sensations* . . . are probably produced by slow movements of the eye . . . these sensations represent an imperfection of the visual apparatus, for if the central apparatus had available and successfully dealt with accurate data concerning the position of the eyes, arrangements could be made to "cancel out" the effects of the shift of the image across the retina.'

This seems a surprising statement in view of the now classical paper of Guilford and Dallenbach (1928) who undertook elaborate experiments with a photographic technique to detect and measure eye movements during the autokinetic effect. Guilford and Dallenbach could find neither large slow movements, nor small 'sawtooth' movements which might, by some kind of summation, have produced the autokinetic movement.

The detection of eye movements in the dark is a nasty problem. A convenient method would have many uses, besides serving as a simple check on Guilford and Dallenbach's results. The following method is simple, the apparatus costs very little, and it may be used for at least one nice class demonstration and for various research purposes.

Method

It is fairly well known that the *fovea* of the human retina is blind to weak stimulation by far blue light (Willmer, 1946). The area involved is at the region of central fixation, where acuity is greatest for bright white light. This central blue-blind spot may be demonstrated by placing a blue filter (the Ilford Narrow Cut Spectral Blue is suitable) in front of a small dim light source. If the intensity is suitably adjusted, the blue light will be seen clearly in peripheral vision, as a bluish-white light, but will be invisible to direct fixation. By adjusting the subtended angle of the blue source a small eye movement may be detected, for immediately the eye shifts from direct fixation this bluish-white is seen. After a few minutes dark adaptation the effect is striking. It is even possible, after some practice, to see the edge of the blind area moving about on the blue field with the very small saccadic movements of the eye.

In order to use this method to detect eye movements during the autokinetic effect, a small red filter may be placed in the centre of the blue field. The Ilford Narrow Cut Spectral filters are available as gelatin sheets, for photographic purposes; it is a simple matter to punch a hole in the blue filter and cut out a disk of the same size in the red, using the same punch. This red disk may be mounted in the hole in the blue filter by binding them in 2 in. × 2 in. cover glasses. This may then be mounted in a light box fitted with a torch bulb whose brightness can be controlled with a variable resistance. It will then be found that when the red light in the centre of the blue field is fixated, in a dark room, the usual autokinetic effect will be observed. If the eye is shifted from central fixation, the red light will be immediately surrounded by a bluish-white halo. The question is: when the red light moves during the autokinetic effect does the halo appear? If it does, the eye must have moved; if it does not, then the eye cannot have moved sufficiently to shift the image of the blue from the blue-blind region of the retina. The sensitivity to eye movements may be adjusted by placing a photographic iris diaphragm over the filters and adjusting its aperture, and thus the angle subtended by the blue field, to fill more or less of the retina's blue-blind region (see Fig. 15.1).

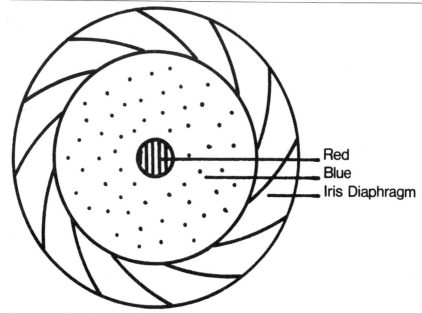

Red
Blue
Iris Diaphragm

FIG. 15.1 *The diameter of the outer photographic iris diaphragm is adjusted so that the blue filter just fills the blue-blind central region of the retina — so that any loss of fixation renders it visible. The inner red filter (inserted in a hole punched in the blue filter) provides a continuously visible fixation. The filters are illuminated from behind, with a dim diffuse light in a light-tight box.*

Results

The autokinetic effect has so far been examined in fifty subjects with this device. None have reported the halo during apparent movements of the red light, though all reported seeing the halo quite distinctly when deliberately fixating a real or imaginary point just displaced from the red light. Thus large slow movements are evidently *not* the cause of the autokinetic effect.

By setting the aperture of the blue field so that its image covers the whole of the blue-blind region (so that sensitivity to eye movements is maximal) it should in principle be possible to examine one's saccadic eye movements while noting the drift of the red spot. When the eye is dark adapted, and the intensity and the angle subtended by the blue field adjusted optimally, the periphery of the blue field is seen to undulate in a curious manner, evidently indicating very small eye movements. These appear to be random rather than directed in any manner related to the direction of apparent movement of the red spot. But the observation is difficult to make.

These results confirm those of Guilford and Dallenbach using the photograph method. It seems quite clear that eye movements are not a necessary feature of the autokinetic effect, as may be very simply demonstrated with this blue filter technique.

16 *The origin of the autokinetic effect*

[This paper, like No. 14, is an attempt to make some rather far-reaching neurological inferences on the basis of self-observable effects, occurring in certain defined conditions. That this kind of experiment can be valid is itself of interest. The inferences made here could be checked with appropriate electrophysiological, or other 'direct and objective', observations, but at present this is technically too difficult.

My colleague was Professor Oliver Zangwill, Head of the Department of Psychology in the University of Cambridge. He is responsible for the historical research in this paper.]

★   ★   ★

IN 1799, A. von Humboldt reported that a stationary point of light when steadily regarded in darkness appears to move (Carr, 1935). This phenomenon ('Sternschwanken') was long thought to be of physical origin and its psychological nature was not appreciated until very much later (Charpentier, 1886; Exner, 1896); we owe the term 'autokinetic' to Aubert (1887). As ordinarily observed, the angular velocity of the apparent motion is from 2° to 3° per sec., and the total movement may amount to at least 30°. The effect is known to be influenced by a number of factors, e.g. the presence of additional lights in the field, an unexpected stimulus in another modality, the prevailing position of the eyes, and fatigue both local and general (Myers, 1925). The time of onset of autokinesis (although subject to marked individual variation) appears to depend on the area and illumination of the light source (though not its colour) and its direction is determined in some measure by the orientation of the shape of the light source (Honeyman, Cowper and Rose, 1946). The effect is also alleged to be sensitive to attitudinal factors affecting perceptual judgements (Sherif, 1936).

It was for long customary to ascribe the autokinetic effect to *eye-movements*; slow, involuntary drifts of the eyes, by causing the image of the light source to traverse the retina, being supposed to give rise to the impression of motion. Indeed, such a view is still upheld by Duke-Elder (1938). Although some individuals seem especially prone to involuntary eye-movement in the dark (Myers, 1925), the work of Guilford and Dallenbach (1928), using a photographic technique, has made clear that slow drifts of the eyes do not necessarily occur when the effect is witnessed and that there is in any case no consistent relation between the direction of such drifts and that of the auto-kinetic motion. This lack of correlation between eye-movements and autokinesis has recently been confirmed by Gregory (1959 [No. 15]).

It was shown by Carr (1910) that the autokinetic effect is markedly influenced by *eye-position*. If, for example, the light source is observed with the eyes strongly deviated to one side, movement is commonly in the same direction as that of the ocular deviation. Further, Carr reported that if the eyes are held for a short time in an extreme position and then returned to the central position to fixate the light source, autokinetic movement tends to be at first in a direction opposite to that of the ocular deviation and to be followed by a movement in the reverse direction. The first phase of this movement may be startlingly rapid and the light has indeed been described as 'moving like a shooting star' (Myers, 1925). Lastly, Carr claimed that a volitionally induced eye-strain without actual deviation of the eyes (e.g. attempting to look to right or left without in fact altering fixation) may also affect the direction of autokinetic movement (Carr, 1910). More recently, Battersby *et al.* (1956) have shown that pro-longed deviation of the head and trunk to one side may constrain apparent movement in the direction opposite to that of the postural shift. Although these various effects seem well attested it is important to note that individual differences are marked.

It is a matter for some surprise that these various effects of postural change on the autokinetic sensation have attracted so little notice. Although given some prominence by Carr (1910, 1935) in his 'innervatory theory' of space perception, they barely find mention in recent texts. This may be due in part to the influence of Gestalt theory, which on principle allowed little part to proprioceptive and 'innervatory' factors in perception and endeavoured to account for autokinesis in terms of the lack of an appropriate 'frame of reference' (Koffka, 1935, pp. 212–3). Although the 'framework' concept has found useful application to the perception of motion both real and apparent (Duncker, 1929), there is reason to believe that the central 'monitoring' of eye-movements plays a vital part in the perception of real motion (Gregory, 1958*a* [No. 14]). If this be the case, it is not unduly fanciful to suppose that this process may undergo temporary derangement under conditions in which the oculomotor musculature is subjected to strain or fatigue. Indeed, Carr (1910, 1935) himself suggested that the autokinetic effect may well depend upon the continual minor 'adjustments of innervation' which he believed necessary to inhibit random eye-movements. Although the explanation which we shall put forward below differs in some respects from that of Carr, we are at one with him in seeking to explain autokinesis in terms of the general properties of the ocular control systems involved in the perception of space and motion.

EXPERIMENTS

Experiment 1: Induction of apparent motion by unbalanced fatigue of the eye muscles

Selective fatigue was induced by requiring the subject to hold his eyes hard over in one of four extreme positions (up, down, right, left) for a period of 30 sec. He was then immediately required to fixate a small, dim, red light for 2 min. with eyes central. This light source was surrounded by a blue annulus to detect shifts of fixation, as described by Gregory (1959 [No. 15]). During this period of fixation, the subject reported the direction of any apparent movement together with some indication of its velocity. For this purpose, he was asked to imagine a clock face with the red light as centre and to report directions of apparent movement in terms of hour numbers. Thus '12' would be a vertical upward movement of the light and '3' a horizontal movement to the right. The experiments were conducted in a sound-proof room and the reports recorded on a tape recorder in an adjacent room.

Results The pooled results for 10 subjects (all young adults) are shown in Figure 16.1. In this 'clock histogram', the twelve sectors represent the reported direction of apparent movement, the distance from the centre in any direction representing time. The central black sections represent the first 30 sec. of apparent movement. The white sectors represent the movement reported during the second 30 sec. of the 2 min. inspection period. The figures in the perimeter show total movement in the various directions over the whole inspection period.

It will be seen from Fig. 16.1 that the direction of movement over the first 30 sec. was commonly in a direction opposed to that of the imposed deviation of the gaze. This is most clearly seen in the case of deviation to the left or right. It is noteworthy that the motion was typically reported as starting *immediately* the light source was fixated and not, as when observed under ordinary conditions, after an interval of 10 sec. or more. It was also said to be very rapid for several seconds; on one occasion, indeed, it continued in the same direction for as long as 93 sec. This initial movement often (though not always)

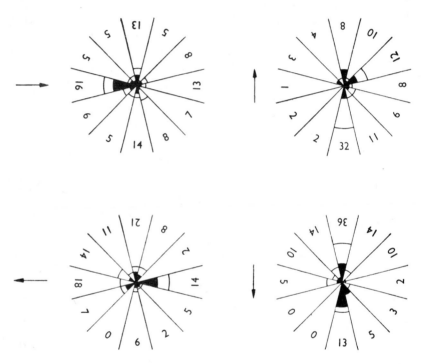

FIG. 16.1 *'Clock histograms' showing durations of apparent movement after eye strain. Direction of strain shown by arrow : duration 30 sec. in each case. The black shading gives direction averaged over all subjects for the first 30 sec., the non-shaded portion over the second 30 sec. after eye strain.*

reversed after a short interval and was succeeded by a relatively prolonged movement in the opposite direction. A typical individual record of the path of the autokinetic movement (as reconstructed from the subject's verbal reports) after deviation of the gaze upwards is shown in Fig. 16.2. In general, it was noteworthy that in spite of these very considerable excursions the light did not appear to change its position in space.

An analysis was made of the initial direction of the movement observed under the four conditions of the experiment. After deviation of the eyes to the right, initial movement was to the left in seven cases (clock position 'nine' in five cases and 'ten' in two cases); after deviation to the left, it was to the right in seven cases (clock position 'three' in six cases and 'two' in one case). In the case of 'upward' and 'downward' deviation, the results were more erratic but there was a comparable tendency for the direction of movement to be at first opposite to that of the ocular deviation.

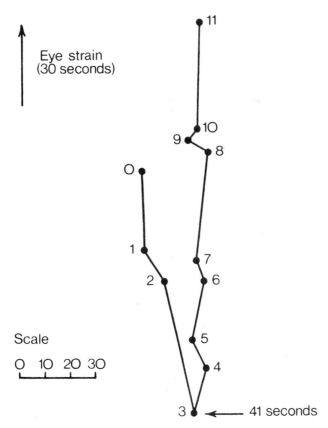

FIG. 16.2 *A typical 'induced-autokinetic' movement after eyestrain. This is derived from the reported directions of movement which were recorded on tape. It illustrates the typical reversal in direction occurring quite suddenly. (The clock histograms show the same type of data but averaged for all subjects. The reversal effect does not appear in the histograms due to variation in time of the reversal. Averaging masks the effect which is shown clearly here, though for one set of observations only.)*

The duration of autokinetic movement *in the same meridian* as that in which the eyes were deviated (i.e. left-right or up-down) was compared with its direction in the remaining meridians. Under all conditions and for every subject, movement in the same meridian was significantly greater than movement in any other meridian. Over the first 30 sec., the movement was predominantly in the same meridian under every condition. (The lowest significance was 0·005, and this occurred only twice). The same effect was still present over the second 30 sec. period, though here the differences were smaller and two conditions were not significant.

Summary

1. After deviation of the eyes to an extreme position (left, right, up or down), fixation of a small light source with the eyes in the central position gives rise to an immediate and well-marked auto-kinetic experience.

2. The direction of autokinetic movement over the first 30 sec. is typically in the same meridian as that in which the eyes had been deviated and is commonly in the direction opposed to that of the deviation. The direction of movement is often, though not always, reversed after a short interval.

Experiment 2 : Induction of apparent motion by unbalanced fatigue of the neck musculature

The procedure was essentially the same as in Experiment 1 except in so far as tension was applied to the neck rather than to the ocular musculature, and the subjects were required to oppose the applied torque with an equal and opposite muscle tension.

A motor cycle crash helmet was modified by attaching to the crown a cross-shaped structure made from two aluminium bars arranged to lie in the sagittal and transverse planes of the head. Each bar projected 13 in. from the centre and 8 oz weight could be hung from the back or front (at a distance of 12 in. from the centre) or from a string attached to one of the transverse arms (also at a distance of 12 in. from the centre) and passing over a pulley so arranged that a rotational torque was applied to the head round a vertical axis, the pulley being placed on a level with and behind the cross. (The torque round the horizontal axis also had a downward vertical component since no attempt was made to balance this by an equal upthrust from the opposite arm of the cross. Similarly, the torque round the vertical axis had a component tending to push the head backwards. These components were regarded as unimportant). Instructions to the subject were as before, except in that he was asked to report on autokinetic movement during application of the torque (1 min.), as well as during a period of 4 min. after the weight had been removed. The same 10 subjects were used.

Results The pooled results for direction of movement *during application of the torque* are shown in Fig. 16.3. There is some slight indication that movement is most commonly in the direction opposite to that in which the torque had been applied.

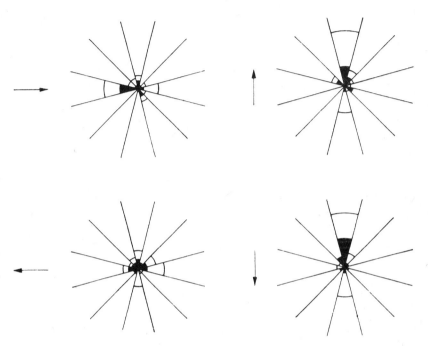

FIG. 16.3 *'Clock histograms' showing directions of apparent movements over 60 sec. periods during torque applied to the head.*

The pooled results (10 subjects) for the first 60 sec. *after removal of the weight* are shown in Fig. 16.4. Again, the shaded portions represent movement during the first 30 sec. and the unshaded portions movement during the second 30 sec. of the total observation period. The figures in the perimeter show total movement in the different sectors over a period of 2 min. after cessation of the torque. It will be seen that movement is predominantly in the same plane as that of application of the torque.

An analysis was made of the *initial direction* of movement observed under the four conditions. In the case of tension to right or left, no very clear tendency was noted for initial movement to be in a direction opposite to the side of tension; in the case of 'upward' or 'downward' tension, on the other hand, there was some tendency for initial movement to be in the direction opposite to that in which the torque had been applied.

The duration of movement *in the same plane* as that in which the torque was applied for the first 30 sec. after removal of the weight was compared with the duration of movement in all other planes. The differences were highly significant for all subjects, the lowest degree of significance being 0·001. For the second 30 sec. period, only one difference failed to attain significance.

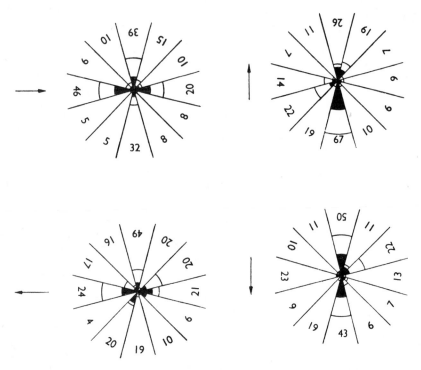

FIG. 16.4 '*Clock histograms*' *showing the apparent movement following removal of the torque applied to the head as shown in Fig. 16.3. (Shaded portion shows movement in first 30 sec., unshaded second 30 sec.) The figures in the perimeter give the total movement in each sector over a 2 min. period following the torque.*

DISCUSSION

These results confirm earlier observations (Carr, 1910; Myers, 1925; Battersby *et al.*, 1956) indicating that the direction (and probably also the rate) of autokinetic movement are significantly affected by constraints imposed upon the oculomotor and neck musculature. As we have seen, the direction of apparent movement is typically in the same plane as that of the induced tension and, in its initial stages at least, most commonly in the opposite direction. It is also note-worthy that, under these conditions, the autokinetic movement begins immediately the light source is fixated and not after a short interval, as is usual under ordinary conditions of observation. This initial movement was reported to be rapid and was often quite extensive. Curiously, it appeared to take place without an apparent shift in locus of the fixated light source, suggesting that the sensation of movement may, under certain circumstances, become divorced from the spatial properties of the environment.

The implications of the last observation appear to us of some importance. Hitherto, movement perception has been held to involve a relational process. 'Movement', writes Carr (1910), 'is relative. The fixed light must move in reference to something. This does not mean that the subject must necessarily be overtly conscious of the basal term and the space relation of the moving object. It does mean that the basal term must be represented at least in the background of experience. Its existence is necessary to indicate the source of motion.' Myers (1925) adopts a very similar view, adducing the concept of 'schema' as put forward by Head and Holmes (1911) to provide a physiological basis for the relational process. For Koffka (1935), on the other hand, the 'framework' with reference to which motion is assessed is normally provided by certain key features of the visual world; if visual stimulation is minimal, no secure framework can be established and autokinesis may result. Yet no precise explanation of the incidence, rate, direction or extent of autokinetic movement is given by any of these theories.

In our view, these earlier authors are guilty of a conceptual confusion. Consider the speedometer of a car – it indicates the velocity of the car with reference to the road, but if it has a zero-error it could indicate an illusory velocity when the car is stationary. In the same way, there is no reason why the neural mechanism which indicates visual movement should not – if deranged – indicate spurious movement in the absence of a moving object. It would therefore seem unnecessary to postulate any 'framework' – external or internal – as a condition for the autokinetic experience. It is necessary only to suppose that signals indicating movement are present in spite of the absence of a moving object in the external world.

We would therefore argue that the autokinetic phenomenon, together with certain other forms of illusional movement such as the 'waterfall effect', are caused by a temporary derangement of the neural systems directly concerned with the visual registration of movement. These illusions should, we submit, be treated as primary illusions of movement and as in no wise due to faulty interpretation of the position of an object with regard to a 'framework', perceptual or conceptual. The signals which engender the experience of motion do not necessarily depend upon movement in the stimuli any more than the experience of colour is necessarily dependent upon the presence of light of an appropriate wavelength. Indeed, illusions of movement are no whit less primary than negative after-images. Such illusions, however, should be sharply distinguished from those involving figure-background relationships, as in the various forms of induced motion (Duncker, 1929), where the concept of a spatial framework is quite properly applicable.

A SPECULATIVE MODEL OF THE OCULAR CONTROL SYSTEM AND SOME PRELIMINARY OBSERVATIONS

An important problem in connection with apparent movement is why it does not occur with voluntary eye-movements, which produce shift of the retinal image without shift of the visual world. The explanation most commonly advanced is that the retinal movement signal arising from the shift of the image is cancelled by a signal indicating that an eye movement has taken place. Although proprioception is now known to play a part in controlling the position of the eye (Brindley and Merton 1960; Merton, 1961), there is little or nothing to suggest that it plays a significant role in the origin of apparent movement or in maintaining the stability of the visual world. The important factor here would seem to be a monitoring of the 'command' signal to the eye-muscles, as originally suggested by Helmholtz (1924 trans., 3, 242–68). His argument has been developed by Gregory (1958*a* [No. 14]) where an 'image/retina' system and an 'eye/head' system are distinguished, both of which are involved in maintaining the stability of the visual world. When the image of a stationary object moves across the retina (as with a voluntary eye-movement), signals from the 'image/retina' system are cancelled by equal and opposite signals from the 'eye/head' system, with resultant stability of the perceived environment. It was further suggested that certain forms of apparent visual motion, in particular the 'waterfall illusion', might be attributed to a process of adaptation within the 'image/retina' system. A more detailed statement of the argument is given elsewhere (Gregory, 1958*a* [No. 14]).

If we accept this position, it may be argued that the autokinetic phenomenon as observed under the experimental conditions described above is due primarily to changes of the nature of adaptation or fatigue located in the 'eye/head' control system. What components of this system may be supposed to become adapted?

The schematic arrangement for eye-movement control suggested by Helmholtz is shown in Fig. 16.5. As will be seen, it is conceived to possess three main components: (1) the oculo-motor system; (2) the monitoring system; (3) the central 'command' system; (4) the cancelling system described in the figure as 'comparator'. The output of this provides the movement signal as a difference between the retinal and command signals. Theoretically at least, adaptation might occur in any of these components and it is pertinent to inquire whether its locus can be defined with greater precision.

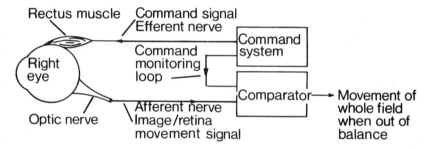

FIG. 16.5 *A diagram of the hypothetical 'outflow' eye movement control system.*

Let us imagine a volitionally imposed strain on the ocular muscles induced by holding the eyes hard over, say to the extreme right. Now if the change is primarily in the musculature itself (e.g. muscular fatigue), it might be argued that stronger 'command' signals would be required to maintain fixation immediately after the eyes have been returned to the central position. Now it is known that an intended but unaccomplished contraction of an eye muscle can effect a change in the localization of objects in the outside world (Myers, 1925; Kornmüller, 1930); hence an increase in 'command' signal would be equivalent to a real movement to the right, i.e. in the same direction as that of the imposed tension. This, however, is not generally found. It would seem, therefore, that the locus of the change is not in the eye muscles themselves.[1]

If the process of adaptation occurs within the 'monitoring' system, it might be expected that the signal indicative of eye-movement would be reduced. This would be equivalent to a real movement to the left, that is to say, in the direction opposite to that in which the eyes

[1] At the same time, we have some evidence that with shorter periods of induced muscle strain (less than 30 sec.) the initial movement tends to be in the *same* direction as that to which the eyes have been deviated. A similar effect was noted under some of the conditions studied by Carr (1910). It is possible, then, that some part of the effect may be attributed to peripheral changes in the oculomotor musculature.

had been deviated. As we have seen, this is the effect most commonly found in our experiments. Although it remains possible that changes might also take place in the 'command' system, it is very difficult to see what form these might take or what effect they would have on the direction of perceived motion. Tentatively, therefore, we may conclude that the main focus of adaptation lies in the system responsible for monitoring eye-movements.

Preliminary observations. By changing the viewing conditions, additional information may be gained relevant to the above considerations. The following observations were made on nine subjects:

(1) If we repeat Experiment 1 using an after-image produced by a bright flash in place of the small light source, *no appreciable autokinetic effect is reported.* At the same time, it is important to bear in mind that the after-image does appear to move with voluntary eye-movements (Gregory, 1958a [No. 14]). This is expected since the monitoring loop will give a signal not cancelled by signals from the 'image/retina' system, no shift of the image on the retina having taken place.

(2) If we now view an after-image together with the light source, the two stimuli occupying different parts of the field, we find – as already reported by Myers (1925) – that the *after-image participates in the movement of the fixated light source.* This shows clearly that for induced autokinesis eye-position must remain constant, and supports the view that the locus of the effect is primarily in the system which monitors the 'command' signals which institute eye-movements.

(3) It is possible to study the effects of previous eye-position (unbalanced strain) by the following very simple method: If the subject is required to keep a small dim blue light in central fixation (Gregory, 1959 [No. 15]) any drifts of the eye in darkness can be noted since the blue patch is invisible when the image is strictly on the *fovea centralis* (Willmer, 1946). We find that (a) fixation cannot be continuously maintained, the blue patch frequently becoming visible as the eye drifts (although a blue annulus surrounding a red light can be kept continuously in central fixation); and (b) after the imposition of unbalanced strain, the eye may move either in the same or in the opposite direction to that of the strain, as judged by whether the blue light appears to the right or left of the centre of the field. Once it has appeared, the blue light may show autokinesis in either the same or the opposite direction to that of the strain, but once again in the same meridian.

These findings are in agreement with our interpretation of autokinesis as being due to fluctuating efficiency of the oculomotor system. Fluctuations in motor efficiency must be corrected by varying command signals in order to maintain fixation. These are wrongly taken to represent movement of the external light. This, we submit, is the origin of the autokinetic effect.

We are left with the following problem: Why do not these small unbalanced signals normally disturb the visual world?

17 The after-effect of seen motion: the role of retinal stimulation and of eye-movements

[I now think that we need not a physiological but a cognitive concept, to explain why the normal world does not shift as the small spot of light shifts, to give the 'autokinetic effect'. The world is *probably* stable. It requires a lot of evidence of movement, before we accept its movement. This is borne out by Duncker's Induced Movement (1912), in which a small stationary spot is seen as moving when its large background is in fact in motion. This *counters* the physiological information from the eyes that it is the background which is moving – but the relative probabilities determine what is seen. Available sensory information is only a small part of perception.

If the apparent movement of the autokinetic effect is due to imbalance of the eye musculature, and of the eye movement command and monitoring systems, what happens if the 'image/retina' movement system is upset? Is the 'waterfall effect' due to adaptation of the image/retina system? Clearly it *can* be due to retinal adaptation to movement, for after-effects of movement can occur in several directions simultaneously though the eye can only move (or be signalled to move), in but one direction at a time. The question remains: Is the waterfall effect due *entirely* to retinal stimulation? The next paper, written with Stuart Anstis (based on an earlier unpublished experiment with Jean Wallace) attempts to answer this question. We believe, as a result, that the waterfall effect is entirely due to image/retina adaptation.]

★   ★   ★

AN experiment is described in which movement after-effects are noted, following presentation of moving stripes under various conditions of eye movement. After-effects only occur when the retinal image moves systematically across the retina, though movement may be observed when this is not the case. The after-effects are due to specifically retinal stimulation, not to perception of movement *per se*.

A moving object can be detected in one of two ways. The object can be tracked by the eyes, keeping its image stationary on the retina, or the eyes can remain fixed on some stationary point, so that the image of the object moves across the retina. These two methods involve what have been termed the 'eye/head' and the 'image/retina' systems (Gregory, 1958a [No. 14]). These two kinds of information are combined in the nervous system to give our subjective perceptions of movement: Teuber (1960) discusses how this may be done.

The well-known after-effect of seen motion represents some modification or adaptation of the movement detection system. In this study the 'eye/head' and the 'image/retina' systems were stimulated separately and together to establish which system mediates the after-effect.

Six subjects, aged 22–27, inspected a field of horizontally moving stripes for 45 sec. After this stimulation, they immediately looked at a randomly patterned surface (a photograph of sandpaper) and reported the presence and direction of any after-effect. Five conditions were used, and the results are shown diagrammatically in Table 17.1.

MOTION AFTER-EFFECT FOLLOWING IMAGE/RETINA AND EYE/HEAD MOTION SIGNALS

TABLE 17.1

Condition	A	B	C	D (E = C + D)
Perceived movements				
Stripes	→	→	×	→
Fixation point	×	→	——→	——→
Stimulation				
Retinal image	→	×	←——	←
Eye movements	×	→	——→	——→
Physical movement	→	→	←--	→
Direction of after-effect	←	×	→	→

The stimulus field was composed of 3 mm black and white stripes, moving to the right at 10 mm/sec. surface speed ($\frac{3}{4}°$ visual angle per sec.). A fixation spot was visually superimposed via a half-silvered mirror: it could be stationary (a bulb filament) or moving (an oscilloscope spot).

The conditions and results were:

Condition A Stationary fixation spot, stripes moving to the right. The images of the stripes thus move across the retina of the stationary eye.

Result : After-effect to the *left* – the opposite direction to the stimulus stripe motion.

Condition B Subject tracked stripes with the eyes, keeping the image, ideally, stationary upon the retina. (This was done by making the fixation spot move along with the stripes.) Here, the eyes move but the retinal image does not shift across the retina.

Result : No after-effect.

Condition C The stripes were stationary, while the eyes tracked smoothly across them, following a fixation point moving to the right at 37·5 mm/sec. Here the eyes move in one direction while the retinal images move in the opposite direction; thus, the eye/head and image/retina systems receive opposite signals.

Result : During the stimulation period the stripes appeared to 'sail' to the left; thus it appears that the image/retina signals dominate during the stimulation. The after-effect was to the *right* – appropriate to retinal stimulation.

Condition D The stripes moved to the right at 10 mm/sec. surface speed, and the fixation spot moved also to the right, but at 37·5 mm/sec., overtaking the stripes. The eyes, tracking the spot, moved to the right but the retinal stimulation was the same as though the stripes were moving to the left. In other words: the eyes move in one direction, with perceived movement in the same direction though the retinal images move in the opposite direction.

Result : After-effect to the *right*. This is appropriate to the retinal stimulation, and not to the perceived direction of the movement.

For simplicity, the inversion of the retinal image has been ignored. Thus an arrow to the right in the 'retinal image' row indicates retinal stimulation appropriate to an object moving to the right past a stationary eye. This does not affect the results.

Note that the after-effect is in the opposite direction to the retinal stimulation in each case. This is not true of any other stimulus parameter. This indicates that the retinal stimulation alone is responsible for the after-effect.

Condition E Here Conditions C and D were combined. The upper third of the striped field was stationary (as in C) while the lower two-thirds moved to the right (as in D). The fixation point, located in the lower two-thirds, moved at 37·5 mm/sec.

Result: An after-effect in the upper part of the field (Condition C) and *no* after-effect – or a very minimal one – in the lower part (Condition D). So the after-effect is much stronger when the stripes are stationary than when they are moving slowly in the same direction as the fixation spot.

It follows from these results that the motion after-effect is determined by the *retinal* stimulation, and is independent of eye movements, or of the subjectively perceived motion which results from a combination of eye/head and image/retina information.

18 *Influence of stroboscopic illumination on the after-effect of seen movement*

[The following note combines what seemed to be a surprising quite general finding with an immediate check to its generality. The finding was made by Stuart Anstis and the present author – that an after-effect of motion (such as that produced by a rotating spiral) immediately ceases under low-frequency stroboscope illumination. Before this paper was published Professor D. M. MacKay and Dr N. de M. Rudolph of the University of Keele discovered that the effect is less general than we had thought. The stroboscope illumination, they found, does not quite abolish the after-effect of motion of a random pattern: though it does where there are strong contours. The following note is written by all four of us. The effect, and its limitation, is worth including here as it can provide a way of quantifying the after-effect of movement under various conditions. It might also tell us more about contours and whether they are primary to vision.]

★   ★   ★

THE after-effect of seen movement (sometimes known as the waterfall effect) is a well-known illusion in which steady viewing of a moving patterned surface is followed, on transfer of one's gaze to a stationary surface, by an apparent motion in the opposite direction. Pickersgill (1959) gives an exhaustive review of the literature.

We have recently investigated the effect of lighting the stationary surface stroboscopically instead of constantly. The stimulus pattern first used (by R. L. G. and S. M. A.) was a rotating Archimedes's spiral which is seen as expanding or contracting, the opposite apparent motion being normally visible as an after-effect. The after-effect was viewed against a similar, stationary spiral. It was found that stroboscopic illumination of the stationary surface abolished the after-effect.

If the stationary spiral is seen by dim steady illumination, the stroboscopic flashes being introduced from the same visual direction via a half-silvered mirror without illuminating the spiral, then the after-effect is not abolished.

If the stationary spiral is illuminated with both steady and stroboscopic light, the after-effect may be made just apparent with a critical balance of their intensities. The after-effect disappears when the stroboscopic illumination is just intense enough to cause apparent instability of the stationary spiral.

In later experiments (by D. M. M. and N. de M. R.) the stimulus was a rotating circular granular black-and-white pattern. In this case, the after-effect of movement was not abolished by stroboscopic illumination of the stationary granular field, but it was briefer than with constant illumination, for flash rates of 4–30/sec. A rotating Archimedes's spiral containing more turns than that used by R. L. G. and S. M. A. and producing a subjectively stronger after-effect, gave results like those obtained with the granular stimulus, except that the after-effect was more readily suppressed by the lowest flash rates (4–10 flashes/sec.)

These findings may have a bearing on the insensitivity to real motion observed in stroboscopic illumination (MacKay, 1958). It now looks as if intermittent illumination of a moving contour not only removes motion-information from the input to the postulated velocity-abstracting system, but also may (at least partially) inhibit its action.

19 The effect of touch on a visually ambiguous three-dimensional figure

[The next two papers are closely related although they concern different modalities – vision and hearing, respectively. Actually, three modalities are involved, for the first paper asks and tries to answer the questions: In the case of a visually ambiguous figure (such as a wire cube) does simultaneous touch information prevent visual reversals? Does touch serve to prevent the visual system from selecting alternative interpretations of the retinal image when this is ambiguous? The answer turned out to be that touch does not prevent, though may reduce the frequency of, visual reversals of visually depth-ambiguous figures.

It is worth experiencing this situation. Particularly odd is the sensation of rotating the cube when visually reversed, for it is seen to rotate in the direction opposite to its true rotation and the direction in which it is *felt* as rotating. The sensation is that one's wrist has broken; or that one's hand belongs to someone else. Although it is vision which is accepted as correct, yet it is vision which fails to give the correct answer and which is, though powerlessly, contradicted by touch.

This experiment was personally important, in making me realize the significance of ambiguous figures: a theme which is developed at length in *The Intelligent Eye*. My colleague was Charmian Shopland.]

★   ★   ★

THE Necker cube is a well-known example of a reversible figure. This simple line drawing (Fig. 19.1*a*) is seen to represent a cube in either of two orientations. If, however, perspective or other cues are added (Figs. 19.1*b* and *c*), the figure reverses less frequently, and there comes a point when it is no longer ambiguous.

Mach (1886) pointed out that solid objects could sometimes be seen reversed. Using a three-dimensional line cube we have confirmed

282

this, provided one eye is kept closed and the subject is experienced. However, when we reduce the depth information more drastically, by painting the cube with self-luminous paint, placing it on a black cloth and viewing it monocularly in a completely dark room lined with black paper, we find that even naïve subjects experience reversals spontaneously.

When the cube is seen reversed the face apparently in front looks considerably smaller than the face apparently behind, and none of the corners square. After a little practice we can introduce head movement parallax without the cube returning to normal and this produces a very curious effect. The cube appears to rotate in the opposite direction from the normal one, the apparently nearer parts now moving *with* the head instead of in the opposite direction. The figure undergoes complex (but systematic) shape transformations, giving one the impression that it is made of an elastic material.

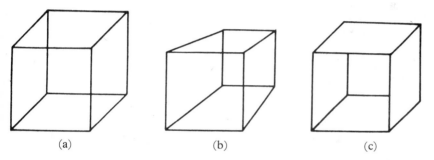

(a)   (b)   (c)

FIG. 19.1 *A simple Necker cube (a) and two examples (b) and (c) of added depth cues (perspective and masking) generally tending to stabilise orientation.*

Touching or holding the cube seems to make it more difficult for a naïve subject to see it reversed in the first place, but having once seen it, touching with the fingers or holding in the hands does not prevent reversal.

These preliminary observations led us to carry out the experiment described in this paper, in which we show some effects of touching and holding the cube. One would not expect touch to have any effect on the reversal of a Necker cube drawn on a piece of paper. If touch gave any information, it would be to the effect that the 'cube' was in fact flat, but merely looking at a two-dimensional Necker cube one is aware that it is flat – it gives the impression both of flatness and of depth. With the three-dimensional figure it is a different matter – the observer is certain that it is in fact a real cube in front of him and that to touch the front and to touch the back he must put his hands at different distances. One might expect haptic information to stabilize to some extent the perception of this cube, as do visual cues. Alternatively one might suggest that haptic information, being in another modality and not specifically attended to, might be ignored altogether; or one might expect that certain subjects would be greatly affected by haptic information, others hardly at all.

Method

The cube used in this experiment was self-luminous and glowed in the dark. Figure 19.2 shows its orientation to the (right-eyed) subject holding it, but in the experiment the hands were only faintly visible by the light coming from it. The cube was made of square section brass and had sides $3\frac{1}{2}$ in. long. The subject could cup it conveniently. in his hands, simultaneously feeling most of the edges and corners while the cube was fixed in position by a grooved wooden support underneath one edge. He was seated at the table to which the support was fixed, with an eyeshade over one eye and his chin on a rest. The table was covered with black cloth and the walls of the room with black paper.

FIG. 19.2 *The orientation of the cube to the (right-eyed) subject holding it. The cube was self-luminous in an otherwise dark room. It was wedged into a support which is not shown. The hands were faintly visible by the light of the cube.*

The depth cues which were available to him were as follows: there was a considerable difference in retinal size of the nearer and further faces; he could tell which of two sides crossed in front of the other; the cube was close enough to him for there to be significant changes in accommodation from front to back of it; he could see his own hands faintly by the light coming from the cube. As he used only one eye and his head was kept still by the chin rest, neither binocular disparity nor head movement parallax were available as cues.

Twelve subjects were used in the experiment, all of them being undergraduate or research students in psychology. The subject was first reminded of the Necker figure (all of them had already experienced the reversal of such a figure) and told that we wanted to know whether the solid 'figure' in front of him would also reverse. He was asked to note at the beginning of each run whether the cube looked as it 'really' was – in which case he was to say 'normal', or whether the front and back corners had changed places – in which case he was to say 'reversed', or whether the cube looked like a plane figure – in which case he was to say 'flat'. If anything else was seen he was to say 'odd' and explain afterwards.

Each run lasted 1 min. and during that time he was asked to report any changes in the appearance of the cube at the time they occurred. Between each run he spent 10 sec. with his eyes closed. There were eight runs, then a pause for comment and re-activating the cube with a bright light, and then eight more runs. The runs were arranged in double alternations between the condition we call 'Vision' and the one we refer to as 'Touch'. During the 'Vision' run the subject sat with his arms resting on the table and simply looked at the cube; during the 'Touch' runs he cupped his hands round the cube and kept both hands moving continuously over its surface. This procedure was explained to him at the beginning of the session and he was told that both active and passive touch were to be used – that is, as well as running his finger tips along the edges of the cube and feeling its lines and corners (trying not to favour any particular lines or corners), he was to feel it with the whole hand (Fig. 19.2).

The reports and comments were recorded on magnetic tape which was played through afterwards so that the times of occurrence of each observation could be obtained.

The total time for which the cube appeared 'normal', 'reversed' or 'flat' during each of the 16 1-min. runs of the experiment were averaged for all subjects. When simply looked at, it appeared normal for an average of 30·8 sec. per min., reversed for an average of 25·5 sec. and flat for an average of 3·1 sec. per min. When explored with the hands as well, the corresponding figures are 40·9, 15·4 and 3·6 sec. per min. respectively.

Results

Fig. 19.3 shows the total time for which the cube appeared 'normal', 'reversed', or 'flat' during each of the 1 min. runs of the experiment,

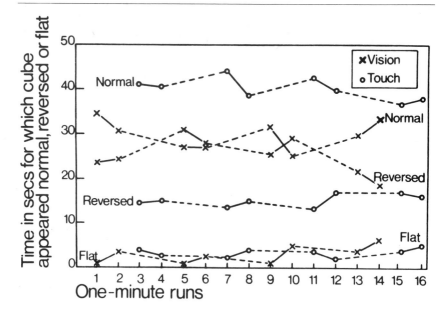

FIG. 19.3 *The total time for which the cube appeared 'normal', 'reversed' or 'flat' during each of the 16 one-minute runs of the experiment, averaged for all subjects. When simply looked at, it appeared normal for an average of 30·8 sec. per min., reversed for an average of 25·5 sec. and flat for an average of 3·1 sec per min. When explored with the hands as well, the corresponding figures are 40·9, 15·4 and 3·6 sec. per min. respectively.*

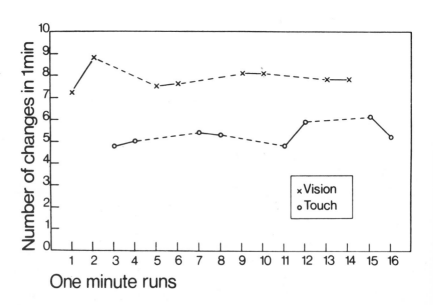

FIG. 19.4 *The number of changes in appearance of the cube during each of the one min. runs of the experiment, averaged for all subjects. It changed appearance an average of 7·9 times when simply looked at, 5·3 times when explored with the hands as well.*

averaged for all subjects. It is clear from inspection alone that when the cube was explored with the hands it looked normal for more of the time and reversed for less of the time than when simply looked at. (Using the Binomial Theorem, $p < 0.004$ in both cases). While exploring with the hands it appeared normal for an average of 40.9 sec. in each 1-min. run and reversed for an average of 15.4 sec. (Binomial Theorem gives $p < 0.004$). The corresponding figures when simply looking at the cube are 30.8 and 25.5 sec. respectively. (These are not significantly different: Wilcoxon 'T' test gives $p > 0.05$). The cube appeared flat for an average of 3.6 sec. on each run when explored with the hands, for 3.1 sec. when simply looked at. This difference is not significant. (Wilcoxon 'T' test gives $p > 0.05$).

The only 'odd' description of the cube was given by subject 5, on one occasion while using vision alone and on three occasions when using touch also. He reported seeing it in the normal orientation and in depth, but with the kind of distortion that typically occurred when the cube was seen reversed, that is, not as a regular cube but with a marked difference in the sizes of the nearer and further faces. This effect had already been observed by one of the authors (C.D.S.), but had not otherwise been reported by the 20 or so people who took part in the preliminary study. This percept seemed to be independent of any change of attitude on the part of the observer.

All the subjects observed that the cube looked distorted this way when reversed. Four subjects commented that fixation seemed to affect reversal (this has previously been observed (Glen, 1940)); one thought that blinks affected reversal, one that the amount of depth in the figure varied; two thought they could will changes (Glen, 1940, has evidence of this also) but said they tried not to do so.

Two subjects thought that touch had no effect at all on what they saw, although they were touching lines they could not see, or failing to find with their hands lines they could see. Two subjects found that touching the front corner in particular seemed to make the cube go back to normal if it were reversed, and two found the same with the back corner. (They were both obscuring this corner with the hand, instead of keeping the hand behind the cube as instructed). One subject found that a corner would sometimes move forward or back with her hand, and another the part she was touching looked normal while the rest of the cube looked reversed.

Several subjects made the comment that touch gave them a clue to the real orientation of the cube at first, but later they 'grew to accept the difference between the visual and the tactile', or found that 'touch lost significance'. We therefore looked for a decrease in the duration of reports of 'normal' from the beginning of the session to the end. Inspection might suggest a very slight trend in the right direction but it is certainly not significant (Friedman Analysis of Variance by Rank gives $p = 0.5$). Looking at the results of each subject separately, we found no more indication of variation with time among those who reported it than among the rest.

For all subjects except one there were more changes when using vision only than when using touch as well. (The probability of this distribution is 0.003 on the Binomial Theorem). The difference in the case of the aberrant subject was nowhere near significant at the 0.05 level (Wilcoxon 'T' test), and in other ways his results were typical. Figure 19.4 shows the number of changes, averaged for all subjects, during each of the 16 1-min. runs of the experiment. Again there is no evidence of any changes with time, nor is there any suggestion of a trend when considering alone the subject who commented that the reversals became more frequent with time.

The reversal rate in our experiment is less in both conditions than is generally reported for two-dimensional Necker cubes, our average rates being 7.9 per min. with vision only and 5.3 with touch also, compared with average rates ranging from 15 to 30 in the literature (e.g. Tussing, 1941; Glen, 1940).

Discussion

This experiment shows that haptic information does not prevent reversals of an ambiguous figure, nor does it prevent the figure from looking like a 'meaningless geometrical pattern'. It could well have been the case that when, say, the front of the cube was located by touch it would always appear to be the front visually, but in fact the cube seemed to split into two objects, one visual, the other tactile.

We may think of the Necker cube as presenting a problem to the perceptual mechanism for which there are only two possible solutions: a Necker cube drawn on a plane surface is usually bi-stable, seeming to lie in either of two orientations. We thought it possible that touch would have an all-or-none effect on the choice of solution, but we find that touch can provide information that guides but does not dominate the perceptual mechanism in its choice. Haptic information cuts down the reversal rate and increases the time during which the cube looks as it 'really' is, but does not prevent reversal.

We might contrast this situation with one in which the perceptual problem is to decide on the values of continuously varying parameters. An example of this is the apparent shape of a distorted room. Here we have walls which may be at any of an infinite number of angles to the line of sight, a floor and a ceiling which may be at any of an infinite number of angles to the horizontal. In this case the perceptual system makes a decision and sticks to it without vacillating. However, given information from touch, the perception is modified in the direction of the true shape of the room, and with more experience the perception corresponds still more with the true shape (Kilpatrick, 1954). With the cube there were some reports of this type – while touching it, it appeared reversed, but not extending as far in space as when seen unreversed. There was, however, no evidence of learning, nor do our results show any effect of haptic experience of the cube on its perception when using vision alone. From the reports of the subjects (but not from the numerical results) we might suggest that they learned not to use but to ignore haptic information as time went on. Perhaps if their task had been to ascertain which way round the cube in fact was, touch would have had more effect.

There were also reports that touching the front or back corner seemed to cause an immediate return to the normal orientation. Witkin *et al.* made a similar finding when putting vision and hearing into conflict: when attempting to judge the direction of a speaker's voice, opening the eyes could make the voice appear to change direction by about 30 degrees instantaneously (Witkin, Wapner and Leventhal 1952). However, in their experiment, the auditory stimulus was unambiguous and a more comparable situation is that of Warren and Gregory (1958 [No. 20]), where a word repeated on a loop of tape was found to change spontaneously to other words or sounds.

20 *An auditory analogue of the visual reversible figure*

[This paper was the work of the American psychologist, Richard Warren. He was visiting Cambridge at the time, and my contribution was little more than to lend him my tape recorder and help with some testing. The idea was entirely his, based on his discovery as a child that when he, or his friends, repeated words several times, they would change not only in meaning but in the way they sounded. By establishing that this occurred with a tape loop, in which the spoken sounds could not physically change, it was established as a genuine auditory effect. Richard Warren went on to investigate the effect fully and he wrote several papers on it, changing however the name of the effect to 'verbal alternation'. He has since abandoned the notion that the effect is essentially similar to spontaneous changes of visual ambiguous figures; but I have not seen an argument to counter this notion.]

★   ★   ★

UNDER the visual conditions normally encountered, reversible figures seldom occur. When certain features of the total situation are abstracted, however, 'ambiguous' figures may be created. Thus, a two-dimensional drawing of a cube produces alternation in apparent perspective with continued inspection. When one looks at an actual cube, reversal of perspective does not occur, for spatial cues fix the orientation of the faces. In speech, ambiguity of sound usually is avoided by the context of other words.

When speech sounds – either words or short phrases – are repeated again and again without pause, then the verbal organization undergoes abrupt transitions into other words or phrases, sometimes accompanied by apparent changes in the component sounds. This *verbal alternation* (as we may call it) is studied best with an endless loop of recording tape, but if the reader would like to experience this effect for himself, all he has to do is to repeat aloud a word such as *say*. It will shift abruptly to *ace* and back again. It is a simple matter to discover dozens of reversible words. A fairly complex example is afforded by *rest*. When this word is repeated over and over, it may shift to *tress*, *stress*, or even to *Esther*, in spite of the fact that a repetition of this last word is not the exact phonetic equivalent of a repetition of the other words.

A preliminary study, with loops of recording tape, has revealed the following four types of change: (1) reorganization of the same speech-sounds to produce different words; (2) change in vowel- or consonant-sounds; (3) hearing a speech sound which is actually absent; and (4) not hearing or suppressing a speech sound actually present. A striking effect, classified best under (1), is that some words heard have an odd pronunciation, often a foreign or regional accent. It is possible to increase the variety of transitions involving changes (2), (3), and (4) by masking with noise, or by using a recording with poor fidelity. Under these conditions, S may hear a single recorded word change to 20 or more different words or phrases.

Some potential applications of the verbal-alternation effect to specific problems suggest themselves. The apparent changes may help in studying speech perception under non-repetitive conditions. Thus, repeating a word or phrase and noting the frequency and variety of shifts may afford a simple measure of the potential ambiguity of the sounds. Another possible use involves listening to repetitive speech under conditions designed to induce great ambiguity, as by the addition of noise. It should be of interest to study and compare the verbal transitions of different Ss.

The verbal effect of alternation seems similar in principle to the reversal of visual figures. Further study may show the same basic perceptual rules to underlie both.

21 *Stereoscopic shadow-images*

[A simple apparatus is described in the next short paper – just a pair of point light sources with cross-polarization – which reveals interesting perceptual effects during observer-motion. This apparatus is well worth setting up and trying out. It is interesting that the effects do not *depend* upon stereoscopically given depth: realistic depth given by monocular vision shows the same effects, if less dramatically: but they are easier to produce with a stereoscopic display. Anaglyphs or projected stereo-photographs can be used in place of this arrangement; but not for the object rotation experiment, in which motion parallax is cancelled perceptually by contrary motion of the observer. The geometry is shown in Fig. 21.1.

A mathematical analysis of this situation has been given by D. N. Lee (1969); and the technique has been used in an interesting way by T. G. R. Bower, to get evidence of object perception in infants – by their surprise at objects presented in this way visually but found absent to their grasp (1971).]

★   ★   ★

THE following simple arrangement makes it possible to project, in stereoscopic depth, three-dimensional objects such as wire models of molecular or crystal structures. Small models may be presented enlarged in three dimensions, magnifications of ten or more times being possible. The optical arrangement consists of nothing but a pair of small bright light sources, separated horizontally by a few inches. The sources are placed behind 'Polaroid' filters, set at orientations differing by 90°. The polarized point sources give a pair of shadow images of an object, such as a wire model, placed between them and a silver screen. Alternatively, back-projection with a ground-glass screen can be used; but the screen must not de-polarize the light. When the shadows are viewed through crossed 'Polaroid' glasses, they are fused by the brain to form a single stereoscopic shadow-image lying in space (Fig. 21.1).

There is no problem in explaining this effect. The point sources cast shadows on the screen which are flat projections from slightly different positions. The shadows have the disparity of retinal images for eyes placed at the sources. The observer's brain fuses the two disparate shadows into a single stereoscopic shadow, looking incredibly like a real, but jet black, object. It lies in space either in front of or behind the screen, depending on which eye accepts which shadow. By using polaroids orientated at 45° from horizontal, the stereo shadow-image may be placed before or behind the screen simply by reversing the spectacles.

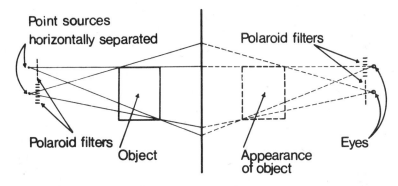

FIG. 21.1 *Geometry of the stereo shadow-projector (with back-projection) for projecting objects (which may be moving or rotating) in stereo depth. They may be enlarged (up to about × 10) and the apparatus may be used to study motion perception in the absence of motion parallax.*

Suitable light sources are miniature filament, 12-V, 100-W tungsten-iodine lamps. The filaments should be orientated vertically, to give maximum horizontal resolution, which is important for giving maximum information of depth through disparity.

Magnification of the normal x- and y-axes is given simply by the ratio of the distance of the object from the lights to the object from the screen. Magnification in depth (z-axis) can be controlled by the horizontal separation of the lamps. In practice a magnification of at least times 10 may be given; but the apparent size of the three-dimensional shadow-image is generally less than might be expected, because of perceptual size constancy.

When the object appears to be in space before the screen it looks smaller than when behind it, though the physical size is of course identical with either orientation of the polaroids. A further perceptual effect is most marked: when the observer moves his head, the stereo shadow-image appears to move with him, to slide across the screen, and rotate to follow the observer as though continuously aimed at him. This is because there is no motion parallax although the image lies perceptually in three dimensions: this corresponds to a normal object rotating to keep the same aspect to the observer though he moves. So he sees movement though his retinal images remain unchanged. When the observer moves away from the screen, the shadow-object does not shrink or lose its depth as might be expected; the reduced angle of convergence of the eyes evidently re-scales the retinal disparity mechanism, so that a given disparity between the retinal images gives greater visual depth. This is indeed fortunate, for the shadow-image appears very similar over a wide range of distance, and so it can be used with effect in a large lecture hall for demonstrating suitable objects. They may be moved or touched by the demonstrator, which makes this a technique having advantages over photographic stereo projection. It is also a useful tool for investigating perception of depth while the observer is moving, and can form the basis of simulators for experiments on the guiding of aircraft and space vehicles.

22 Changes in the size and shape of visual after-images observed in complete darkness during changes of position in space

[The next item, a too short paper with a too long title, reports a series of observations, which changed my view of perception. They provided the basis and the first inkling of the Inappropriate Constancy Scaling theory of distortion illusions, to be developed later.

The first point is that after-images can change in size systematically as the observer moves forwards or backwards, or change shape as he walks round the (invisible) place where they are 'projected' from his eyes. The changes at once appeared to be related to Size and Shape Constancy. If nothing else, this shows that Emmert (1881) was wrong in thinking that after-images only change size when 'projected' on to a visible screen. This extension of Emmert's Law to the case of *no* screen has several consequences which are far from trivial:

(i) The change of size of after-images cannot be due merely to the changing relative areas of the retinal image of the *screen* (or its texture) and the *after-image* on the retina. (This point is generally overlooked in discussions of Emmert's Law. It is still unclear how far Emmert's Law is due merely to the changing relative areas of image and after-image with distance for it could be *partly* due to this.)
(ii) The residual size change could be given by an *active scaling process* giving Size Constancy;
(iii) This is *not always set directly by visual data,* but may be set by the observer's *hypothesis* of distance, which
(iv) May be *wrong,* to generate error.

The reason for trying out the change-of-size-of-after-images-effect in the Farnborough human centrifuge was to discover whether the size changes are given directly by *sensory* data, or whether they are given by the observer's *hypothesis* of how he is moving through space.

It turned out that the hypothesis story was the correct one. This has interesting implications.

It was these observations which gradually made my thinking deviate sharply from the position held, and argued so well, by Professor J. J. Gibson, and his wife, Eleanor. The position adopted here is very different from the Gibsons' 'pick-up of information' theory of perception, in which the perceptual system is regarded as essentially static, but by perceptual learning is tuned to pick up externally available patterns. I regard Helmholtz as right, in arguing for a great deal of 'unconscious inference' – computing – going on to derive perceptions from data, the perceptions being far more than selection of data.

The basic observation was made accidentally, by Jean Wallace and myself, when we were using an electronic flash for quite another reason – attempting to test Donald MacKay's theory of the origin of his ray pattern effects, by stabilizing them on the retina as after-images. We then built a chair on wheels for moving the observer passively. This became the 'train' and 'swing' apparatus, to be described later.

F. W. Campbell is a distinguished visual physiologist of the Physiological Laboratory, Cambridge. The late Professor R. C. Oldfield gave valuable help with the centrifuge observations; he noticed the basic effect quite spontaneously while visiting the laboratory. This independent report was useful confirmation that we were not deluding ourselves, as at that time we had no 'objective' way of measuring the effect. Carolus Oldfield was Professor of Psychology at Reading; then at Oxford, following George Humphrey; he then became Director of the M.R.C. Psycho-linguistics Unit at Edinburgh. I would like to thank Squadron Leader (now Group Captain) Tom Whiteside, for letting us use the Farnborough centrifuge, and being in every way so helpful for what might have looked a way-out experiment – whirling round with a flash gun, looking at nothing!]

★   ★   ★

I T IS well known that if a visual after-image is 'projected' upon a wall, or screen, in a semi-darkened room, the apparent size of the after-image is a function of the distance of the surface upon which it is 'projected'. The size increases with distance, almost in direct proportion to this distance. This is known as Emmert's Law (Emmert, 1881). It is of considerable interest, for it is a convincing demonstration that apparent size is not a simple function of the size of the retinal image, and that many perceptual factors influence the apparent sizes, and distances, of objects. The history of this idea, together with the classical experiments, are described by E. G. Boring (1942).

In carrying out some experiments on after-images produced by a short bright flash of light provided by a 110 joule 1 m.sec. flash tube, a number of curious effects have been observed which would seem to be related to Emmert's effect. It is important to stress that the effects to be described were observed in complete darkness, after the flash, and thus differ in an essential respect from the conditions for Emmert's effect. Since the flash duration was only 1 m.sec. no appreciable movement of the eyeball could occur in the stimulus period. This technique gives after-images of great clarity and detail, which is essential for these new effects.

1. When the head is moved, even by a few centimetres, forward or backwards, the after-image changes in size. It increases in size as the head is moved back, and decreases as it is moved forward. Ten of the subjects were experienced research workers in the psycho-physiology of vision. In addition, the effect has been demonstrated in some 40 relatively naïve subjects, mainly undergraduates. All subjects have observed this effect.

2. A similar effect may be observed with the head stationary. The subject 'projects' the after-image of the flash tube on to his out-stretched hand, still in complete darkness, and slowly moves his hand to and from his eyes. One of two effects may be observed. (*a*) The after-image may seem to remain on the hand, in which case it shrinks as the hand recedes and expands as it approaches. (*b*) The after-image may seem to remain fixed in space and to remain the same size. If the proprioceptive locus of the hand lies between the after-image and observer, the after-image may wholly or partially disappear, as though occluded by an opaque object.

Whether (*a*) or (*b*) occur evidently depends on the 'set' of the observer. Of the ten trained observers, three have reported the 'occlusion' effect on some occasions. All have observed the size change under these conditions.

3. When the observer's hand, or a screen held in his hand, is kept at constant distance, say at arm's length, and the observer moves his head and shoulders and the hand or screen back and forth, then the after-image remains of constant size. It is perceived as an object situated at constant distance.

4. If the flash tube is directed on to the subject's hand, so that an after-image of the hand is produced, some curious phenomena may be observed, but these are difficult to describe briefly. The visual and proprioceptive loci of the hand may separate in a disconcerting manner. Further complex effects occur if the subject attempts to pick up an object viewed as an after-image.

5. When the observer changes his position in space, perspective changes may take place in the after-image. For example, an after-

image may be obtained of a view down a long corridor. With the flash technique this will have unusual clarity. If the observer then walks across the corridor, looking down it, as it were, then his after-image may change in perspective as he moves. These perspective changes are not easy to assess, however, for they vary from time to time.

To observe these effects, it is most important that the eyes be steadily fixated while the after-image is being observed. The short flash technique for producing the after-image ensures that movement of the retina is unimportant during the production of the after-image, which is unusually detailed, but large eye movements after the initial flash temporarily disrupt the after-image and cause it to fade rapidly. The reason for this is not known.

We thought it important to discover whether at least the main effect – the change in size of the after-image with change in position of the observer – is directly related to acceleration forces applied to the observer. To test this, we have examined the effect under conditions of maintained angular acceleration in the Farnborough human centrifuge. Angular accelerations up to 3 g. were used. This was arranged through the kindness of Squadron Leader T. C. D. Whiteside who, with Professor R. C. Oldfield, R. L. G. and F. W. C., acted as observers. The sensation of movement in the centrifuge is marked during deceleration, when the well-known 'tumbling' sensation occurs, the observer apparently falling forward head over heels. In this situation the after-image of the flash tube may expand, as though the observer is falling into it. It seemed clear to all four observers that the magnitude of the effect is not a simple function of 'g', but may be related to the subject's impression of his movement, or the movement of his head, in space.

As a speculation, we may suggest that at least some of these phenomena, and also Emmert's original observation of after-images 'projected' on to a visible screen, may be related to Size Constancy. When an object is viewed normally, decrease in the observer's distance from an object will produce a corresponding increase in the size of the retinal image, but the perceived size of the object may remain almost constant. In the special case of the after-image the image on the retina does not change size as the observer changes his position in space. If the compensation system which normally maintains perceptual size almost constant when the retinal image changes in size were functional in the after-image situation, then we should expect the kind of effects reported here when the observer changes his position in space. If this interpretation is correct, it gives us a technique for studying the Constancies in dynamic situations.

23 *Measuring visual constancy for stationary or moving objects*

[As indicated above (No. 22) these observations were evocative. They were in many ways unsatisfactory, but they raised questions which concern me still. How can a 'subjective' effect, such as size changes of an after-image, be quantified? What corresponds to a 'stimulus' producing the changes in size of an after-image? Does the effect imply that there are active size-scaling mechanisms in the visual system? This last question made me think of traditional size constancy quite differently. This in turn led to the theory of distortion illusions, which invokes the notion that size is set by scaling systems, according to available (real-time) sensory data, and according to (internally stored) hypotheses of the external situation. But this took a long time to arrive. Errors in either the ('primary' or 'secondary') scaling systems evidently give corresponding errors in perceived size – on this theory these are origins of the classical distortion illusions. In fact, although this now seems simple and obvious, to be written down in a minute or less, teasing it out took years. And of course not everyone agrees now that I am right.

After-images are extraordinarily useful, experimentally, for they are precisely stabilized on the retina, move exactly as the eye moves and are unchanging in size as the observer moves through space. Their disadvantage is not so much that they are 'subjective' as that they cannot be modified at the will of the experimenter, once they are established by the stimulus of light, or preferably, flash. Also, they cannot be switched off when desired, and they fade. We had found that Emmert's Law works at least approximately in darkness, with no visible background, but how could we measure *how much* apparent size increases with apparent distance? We needed a new technique.

Null measures are often used in physics, though strangely seldom in psychology. We decided to measure apparent size, and Size and Shape Constancy, using the Null technique described in the next paper: my co-authors were Stuart Anstis and Charmian Shopland.]

★   ★   ★

299

I F two objects of the same size are viewed so that one is twice as far from the eyes as the other, the retinal image of the farther object will be one-half the size of the image of the nearer object, but it does not appear half the size to the observer. They both appear almost the same size and the effect, which is due to perceptual interpretation of the retinal image, is known as size constancy (Thouless, 1931, 1932*a* and *b*; Vernon, 1954).

In this method of measuring constancy of size, the eye is placed close to a small light-source which casts the shadow of an object (such as a flat disk) on a vertical screen. The angle subtended at the eye by the shadow will remain constant for any distance of the screen, but the shadow appears to expand as the screen on which it is projected is moved away from the observer. Other positions of the eye in relation to the source will produce size changes in the retinal image when the screen is moved. With the eye nearer the screen, the retinal image will contract (Fig. 23.1); with the eye behind the source it will expand. The degree of size constancy may be described in terms of the Thouless ratio, which is given by:

$$\log\frac{d_2 l_1}{d_1 l_2}\Big/\log\frac{d_2}{d_1}$$

where d_1 and d_2 are distances of the screen from the eye when the shadow measures l_1 and l_2 respectively, the position of the eye being such that no size change is observed.

One can also measure constancy of shape, this being the tendency for a flat object to have a perceived shape corresponding very nearly to its normal projection ('normal' in the geometrical sense). If the screen is rotated around its vertical axis while the shadow-casting object remains stationary, the shadow appears to enlarge horizontally. Although the shadow on the screen changes shape, the retinal image is unaltered. The shape perceived is nearly that of the shadow viewed normally.

The magnitude of this effect can be measured, again using a null method, by arranging for a compensatory change of shape of the retinal image. This may be done by rotating the (flat) object. The screen and object may be linked to provide simultaneous rotations, their relative angles of rotation being adjustable. The magnitude of the effect may again be stated in terms of the Thouless ratio, which is given by:

$$\frac{\log P - \log S}{\log R - \log S}$$

where R is the ratio of the width of the shadow on the screen to its

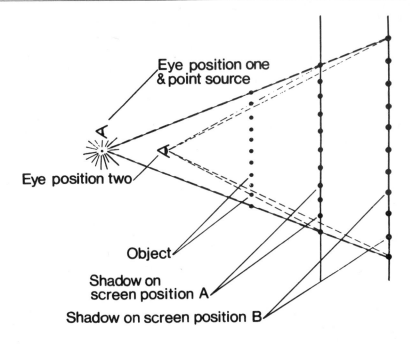

FIG. 23.1 *Angle subtended at eye by shadow with eye in position one is constant for varying positions of screen; with eye in position two, angle subtended decreases as screen moves from position A to position B.*

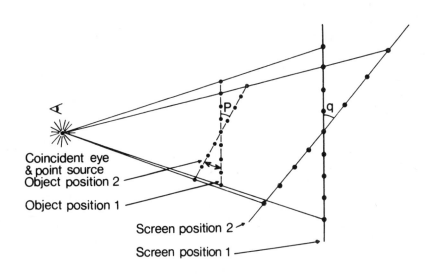

FIG. 23.2 *With eye as close as possible to source, relative angles of rotation are adjusted until no change in shape is observed.*

height, P the ratio of perceived width to perceived height (arranged to be constant and measured when the screen is normal to the observer), and S the ratio of the retinal width of the shadow to the retinal width when the screen is normal. If the angles subtended at the eye are small, the Thouless ratio is given by $\dfrac{\log \cos p}{\log \cos q}$, where p is an angle turned through by the object and q the corresponding angle turned through by the screen (Fig. 23.2), the relative angles of rotation being such that no change of shape is observed.

We are using this shadow method to investigate constancy during movement, which should be important in considering perceptual judgements involved in flying or driving. In particular we have tried to discover whether apparent movement due to constancy can be adapted. It is known that continuous presentation of real movement gives rise to an after-effect of apparent movement in the opposite direction (Wohlgemuth, 1911). The question here is: Can apparent expansion or contraction of the shadow produce an after-effect? By projecting the shadow on a series of screens which move continuously away from the observer and are stopped after 1 min., we find that an after-effect does take place, though the retinal image of the shadow remains unchanged during the movement of the screens. During the movement the shadow appears to expand; in the after-effect, it appears to contract. An after-effect of movement can thus be produced without change of retinal image size. This contraction after-effect does not occur if the shadow is only projected on to the screens after they are stopped, so evidently the after-effect is not merely an induced movement as described by Duncker (1912).

24 Visual constancy during movement: effects of S's forward and backward movement on size constancy

[The next two papers follow directly from this set of observations, and attempt to quantify an essentially 'subjective' effect. They were carried out for practical reasons, associated with possible errors of astronauts in space flight. The later papers develop the theme further, into a general theory of distortion illusions, based on the idea that the constancy scaling systems can be set inappropriately in certain (internal or external) conditions – to generate systematic errors.

For the experiments in the following pair of papers we constructed an amusing and, as it turned out, a useful piece of apparatus. It was a large swing, so arranged that the chair remained horizontal as it swung. The amplitude and the period of the swing were arranged to be comparable to a single step in walking.

The structure was built by my technician Bill Matthews and myself, on one memorable Saturday morning. We used agricultural construction tubing, which turned out to be ideal for a rigid structure which could be easily modified, or dismantled and stored in pieces. In fact it remained set up for years; and was a favourite place for a quiet think, while gently swinging to and fro.

We also built an electric railway with servo-linked visual display, for investigating Size Constancy Scaling during constant velocity motion of the observer. This was used for investigating the errors to be expected in astronauts' docking in space. The carriage and control room (as later set up at Edinburgh) are shown in Fig. 24.1.

We were fortunate in receiving generous support from the U.S. Air Force, allowing us to build elaborate apparatus and to visit space research laboratories in America. This was a case where theoretical and practical issues could be investigated together – and both proved to be unusually interesting. My co-author was Helen Ross.]

★   ★   ★

303

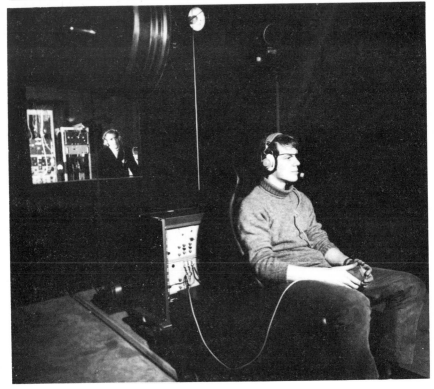

FIG. 24.1 *'Railway' apparatus for investigating illusions in space.*

THIS experiment was undertaken in an attempt to discover whether visual size constancy during movement of an observer is the same whether he is moving forward or backward. The problem, as well as the technique we have developed to try to answer it, arose from the observation that after-images viewed in complete darkness may change their size or shape with movements of the observer, much as they change when projected on a visible screen, according to Emmert's Law (Gregory, Wallace and Campbell 1959 [No. 22]).

The usual method of measuring size constancy – by comparing one shape with another at a different distance and matching them for apparent equality (Thouless, 1931, 1932*a* and *b*) – cannot be used when there is relative movement between *S* and display. We had to devize a different method for measuring constancy under these conditions. The observer (the experimental *S*) is placed in the dark and is moved harmonically backward and forward while viewing a luminous circle which is made to change in size in a manner related to *S*'s movements. The display expands as the distance between the observer and the display increases, and contracts as the distance decreases, thus reducing the normal change in the retinal image. The amount of variation of the display is adjusted by E until S reports no change in size during his movements. If no perceptual constancy were operating, the display would have to be doubled in size for each doubling of its distance and halved for each halving of the distance, while perfect constancy would require no change in the size of the display. In practice it has to be changed by some intermediate amount, which gives a measure of constancy during S's movement. This is a null method; like other null methods it is sensitive, is not too dependent on assumptions of linearity, and it has the particular advantage that the necessary observations can be made in the time available. S's task is the simplest possible: he has only to decide whether or not there is an apparent change for a given setting of the display size variation control.

Method

Apparatus There are many ways in which the size of a display may be varied – mechanical, optical, and electronic are all possible – but here we have used an electronic method. This was very satisfactory for this particular experiment, but optical methods have been found better for some other conditions (Anstis, Shopland and Gregory 1961 [No. 23]).

The apparatus consisted of two parts – a large parallel swinging chair on which S sat and an oscilloscope and associated electronic equipment giving a luminous circle of variable size on the tube face. The oscilloscope used was a standard Cossor double beam model, 1049 Mark IV, with short persistence green phosphor. A photograph of the apparatus is shown in Fig. 24.2.

The display system was connected electrically to the swing by a potentiometer which served to decrease the size of the circle when the swinging chair moved toward it, and to increase its size when the chair swung back. The circle was a lissajous figure traced by the oscilloscope beam and given by a single oscillator with a 90° phase shift between the X and Y plates. The variation in size of the lissajous circle for a given amplitude of swing was controlled by E.

The display (the circular trace on the oscilloscope) was automatically switched off for each half-cycle of the swing, so that it was visible either when S was moving forward or backward, but never both. The display was switched on and off by means of a specially made silent friction switch actuated by the swing. This switch was arranged to bias off the electron beam for one direction of movement, the direction being determined by a reversing switch under E's

FIG. 24.2 *The swing apparatus (with the author seated and Dr J. A. M. Howe pushing) with control equipment at the back. The linear potentiometer for measuring 'awareness of motion' is being operated by the author's right hand.*

control. No after-glow was visible on the tube face after switching or changing the size of the display. The display brightness was controlled by the normal brightness control of the oscilloscope and was set to be clearly visible but not so bright that the surrounding screen was illuminated. It was sometimes necessary to reduce the brightness during the experiment when S became dark-adapted.

The swing structure was built from heavy tubing. The swinging chair was provided with a foot and head rest, and was suspended from three chains and one metal rod. To this metal rod were mechanically connected the position sensing potentiometer and the switch which blacked out the display for one direction of swing. The chair was thus mounted in a parallelogram and remained horizontal throughout its swing. This arrangement was used in order to give horizontal acceleration forces to S, and more particularly, to the balance mechanisms of the inner ear. A normal swing is somewhat ambiguous in this respect, for all the forces merely increase S's effective weight, except for small horizontal forces occurring off the centre of gravity which are somewhat difficult to determine. The parallel arrangement gave acceleration forces similar to those encountered in driving and flying, except for a vertical displacement amounting to 5·5 cm. The period of swing was 1·5 sec. per half-cycle, and the half time of the amplitude of swing was 22 sec. The display was placed 161 cm. from the eye at mid-swing, and the maximum amplitude of swing was 76 cm.

Procedure Ss were 19 research students and undergraduates, 13 male and 6 female, with an age range of 18 to 30.

S was seated in the parallel swing in a completely darkened room. He started the swing by pressing his feet against the floor; he then placed his feet on the rest. While making his judgements, he sat passively on the swing with his head against the back of the chair and his feet on the rest. The size variation control was set initially in the expected range. Half the Ss were given first the condition in which the display was visible only when they moved forward, the other half when they moved backward. The conditions were reversed half way through the experiment, so that all Ss were tested under both conditions.

S reported verbally to E whether the luminous circle appeared to expand or contract. He also reported whether the display appeared to be stationary or to move toward or away from him. The situation was to some extent perceptually ambiguous. The display was not always seen as fixed in space, but would sometimes appear to advance and retreat as well as to expand and shrink (cf. Ittelson, 1952, p. 56).

Occasionally only change in distance was reported. 'Coming nearer' was then treated as equivalent to 'expanding', and *vice versa*. Four *S*s reported only distance changes.

A special difficulty was encountered: *S*s tended to suffer nausea with repeated swinging. This made it undesirable to carry out a lengthy psychophysical procedure for determining *S*'s constancy index. (Our *S*s were volunteers!) The procedure used was as follows. An approximate constancy index for each *S* was first of all found, using trial settings of the size-variation control (SVC). Five SVC settings were then selected, 2 above and 2 below that value, covering the range over which *S* was uncertain. It was not possible to use the same SVC settings for all *S*s, as they differed considerably both in constancy index and in variability of judgement. A typical example is the *S* whose index was estimated at 0·15, and was then tested with SVC settings of 0·03, 0·09, 0·15, 0·22, 0·28. These 5 settings were given in random order until each had been given 4 times. Some *S*s showed high variability; for these, extra SVC settings were used, but only three judgements were made at each setting so as not to increase the length of the experiment. The use of extra settings made it impossible to use a predetermined random order. Extra settings were used for 5 *S*s; the number of extra settings is shown in Table 24.1 by asterisks.

This general procedure allows us to investigate the effect of any perceptual cues of movement on size constancy. Visual cues as well as proprioceptive information of the observer's movement may be controlled at will, their effect being given as a setting of the size variation control. In this first experiment the room was entirely dark – reducing visual cues to the minimum. *S* was passive, and no proprioception was available from the limbs. He viewed the display with only one eye; the effect of using two eyes will be discussed, together with the effect of adding proprioceptive information of movement, in a later paper [No. 25].

Calibration and treatment of data Constancy measures normally fall between zero and one. Zero constancy means that the perceived size follows the retinal size while perfect constancy (one) means that the perceived size remains the same although the retinal image changes with viewing position. In this experiment perfect constancy is given by a ratio of one between the diameters of the display circle at the forward and backward positions of the swing. Zero constancy is given by the ratio at which the retinal image of the object remains of constant size as *S* swings. The constancy value of this ratio is a function of the distance of the swing from the display, and for zero constancy the ratio must be the same as the ratio of the distances of *S*'s eye from the display at the forward and backward positions.

In this case the ratio was $123/199 = 0.618$. Since the ratios indicating zero and perfect constancy are known, any intermediate ratio gives a value of constancy by linear interpolation. The data were treated by a graphical method described by Woodworth and Schlosberg (1955, pp. 202–5). The SVC values for each S were plotted on the x-axis, and on the y-axis the percentage of 'expanding' judgements. A freehand curve (ogive) was drawn through these points. The SVC value on the x-axis at which the curve crossed the 50% point was taken as S's constancy index for that condition. The value at the 84% point was also taken, the difference giving the range of SVC values lying within one standard deviation. This can be taken as a measure of S's variability.

RESULTS AND DISCUSSION

The results for this experiment are given in Table 24.1. It will be seen from Table 24.1 that constancy was greater for forward than backward movement. The median values were 0.18 and 0.14, respectively, the difference being significant at the 1% level by the Wilcoxon test, in which normality is not assumed.

Too few females were used to detect any difference between male and female Ss.

It seems that systematically changing the display size can provide a satisfactory technique for estimating size constancy during move-

TABLE 24.1
MEAN CONSTANCY SCORES AND SDs USING ONE EYE ONLY

S	Sex	Forward	Backward	S	Sex	Forward	Backward
1	M	0.45±0.01	0.24±0.27**	11	M	0.41±0.17	0.0 Off scale
2	M	0.26±0.17	0.14±0.20	12	M	0.05±0.08	0.18±0.07
3	M	0.28±0.17	0.15±0.11	13	F	0.13±0.15	0.00±0.35***
4	F	0.24±0.23	0.25±0.16	14	M	0.13±0.10	0.00±0.25
5	F	0.14±0.15	0.0 Off scale	15	M	0.18±0.10	0.03±0.20
6	M	0.14±0.13	0.14±0.13	16	M	0.18±0.20	0.03±0.15
7	F	0.11±0.28*	0.17±0.31	17	M	0.08±0.25*	0.00±0.25
8	F	0.18±0.13	0.20±0.15	18	M	0.10±0.11	0.10±0.12
9	F	0.41±0.11	0.23±0.15	19	M	0.34±0.11	0.20±0.08
10	M	0.18±0.17	0.24±0.31*	M		0.18±0.15	0.14±0.16

The difference between *SD*s is not significant, but the difference between the constancy scores for forward and backward conditions is significant by Wilcoxon test ($p < 0.01$, 2 tails). Asterisks indicate the number of extra SVC settings used.

ment. There seems to be no reason why this technique should not be extended to measure constancy for shape.

We found considerable differences among Ss in their perceptual interpretation. Although all Ss knew that the display was in fact fixed in space, only a few Ss always saw it as stationary. Some Ss usually saw the display as moving in the opposite direction to themselves, while others were more affected by the size variation of the display, seeing it retreat while shrinking and advance while expanding. As mentioned earlier, there were four Ss who saw only movement and never any size change. A similar variety in perceptual interpretation was found by Ittelson (1952) with S stationary and the display changing in size and position.

This perceptual ambiguity makes it very difficult to find a single setting of size variation which S will accept as giving no change in his visual world. On the other hand, systematic perceptual changes do occur with changes in size variation, and so it is possible to get an estimate for each S's constancy index.

In this present experiment this perceptual ambiguity no doubt produced considerable variance in the estimates, but there is no reason to believe that it produced systematic differences between the two conditions, namely, moving toward or away from the display in total darkness. We may thus assert with some confidence that size constancy is somewhat greater when the observer is carried forward than backward. This could be due to greater experience of forward movement, either individual or ancestral.

25 Visual constancy during movement: size constancy, using one or both eyes or proprioceptive information

[The next paper, written with Helen Ross, describes further experiments along these lines. Here we consider effects of adding binocular vision; and also proprioceptive information signalling the motion of the observer through space.]

★   ★   ★

IT was shown by Gregory and Ross (1964*a* [No. 24]) that, for forward movement on a swing in the dark, visual size constancy was better than during backward movement. In that experiment *S* used only one eye, the other being covered. Further experiments were performed using a similar procedure to determine whether: (1) the use of both eyes gave better size constancy than use of one eye; (2) size constancy was better during forward than backward movement of the observer using both eyes; (3) the addition of a fixation line in the display improved size constancy with both eyes; and (4) the addition of proprioceptive information, by means of swinging on the hands, improved size constancy. It was thus hoped to elucidate further some of the factors involved in size constancy during movement of *S*.

Method

Apparatus and procedure Except where otherwise stated the apparatus and general procedure were the same as those in the preceding paper. For Exps. 2 and 3 a vertical fixation line was added through the centre of the display circle. This was provided by the second oscilloscope trace, so that this fixation line varied in size with the display circle.

For Exp. 4 hand rails were added on both sides of the swing. These were made from rope covered with rubber tubing and tied tightly to the metal supports of the swing. *S* grasped the centres of the ropes and swung himself backward and forward with his hands but without allowing his hands to slip. Care was taken that the amplitude of swing was the same with this method as it was when *S* swung himself by pressing his feet on the ground. Unlike the previous method, *S* never allowed himself to swing passively but always pulled and pushed himself on his hands while making judgements.

Subjects 44 *S*s were research students, undergraduates, and students from the technical college and language schools. They were of both sexes, with an age range between 17 and 30.

Experiment 1

The aim of this experiment was to find out whether the use of both eyes gave better size constancy than the use of one eye only, using the simple circle display, *S* swinging passively in the dark.

Method Seven *S*s were tested under the same general procedure as in Gregory and Ross 1964*a* [No. 24]. They were tested under binocular and monocular viewing. In the monocular condition one eye was covered with a shield. In both conditions only forward movement was used. The orders of testing for the two conditions were alternated between *S*s. The brightness of the display was reduced for the binocular condition in order to keep apparent brightness constant.

Results The results are shown in Table 25.1. It is clear that two eyes give better size constancy than one, the difference being significant

TABLE 25.1
MEAN CONSTANCY SCORES ($\pm SD$) FOR ONE OR BOTH EYES
DURING FORWARD MOVEMENT

S	Sex	One eye	Both eyes	*S*	Sex	One eye	Both eyes
1	F	0·21 ±0·12	0·50 ±0·06	5	M	0·32 ±0·04	0·41 ±0·18
2	M	0·04 ±0·15	0·39 ±0·15	6	M	0·00 ±0·26*	0·12 ±0·11
3	M	0·11 ±0·12	0·19 ±0·14	7	F	0·13 ±0·14	0·23 ±0·15
4	M	0·23 ±0·06	0·28 ±0·12	*M*		0·13 ±0·12	0·28 ±0·14

Asterisks indicate the number of extra SVC settings used.

by the Walsh test ($p = \cdot 01$, one tail). This result was expected since it is very well known that, when *S* is stationary, two eyes give better constancy than one. As found previously for one eye, the display was perceptually ambiguous and was sometimes seen to advance or retreat as well as expanding and contracting. The addition of a second eye did not remove the ambiguity, and two Ss gave more varied binocular perceptions than monocular.

Experiment 2

The purpose of this experiment was to discover whether constancy is different for forward and backward movement when both eyes are used. To make sure that convergence was given adequately by the display, a visual fixation line was added to the circle. This was later found to be unnecessary (Exp. 3).

Method Twelve Ss were tested under our previous procedure, but using both eyes. Half were tested for forward movement, the other half for backward movement. Ss were instructed to fixate upon the vertical fixation line while making their judgements.

Results The results are shown in Table 25.2. Even when both eyes are used, forward movement gives significantly better size constancy than backward movement (Walsh test, $p = \cdot 01$, two tails). Nine of 12 Ss interpreted the display as advancing or retreating in space as they moved on the swing. One S saw only movement of the display and no size change, so that her results were calculated from the direction of the apparent movement instead of from the apparent size change (as described in the preceding paper).

TABLE 25.2

MEAN CONSTANCY SCORES ($\pm SD$) FOR FORWARD AND BACKWARD MOVEMENT
USING BOTH EYES

S	Sex	Forward	Backward	S	Sex	Forward	Backward
1	M	0·17±0·09	0·19±0·07	8	M	0·41±0·11	0·38±0·32*
2	M	0·41±0·09	0·40±0·09	9	M	0·43±0·12	0·28±0·10
3	M	0·24±0·20	0·11±0·15	10	M	0·26±0·16	0·04±0·09
4	M	0·38±0·11	0·19±0·19	11	M	0·32±0·15	0·17±0·11
5	M	0·13±0·11	0·16±0·07	12	M	0·30±0·12	0·26±0·05
6	M	0·16±0·12	0·01±0·19	*M*		0·31±0·12	0·19±0·11
7	F	0·37±0·15	0·22±0·33**				

Asterisks indicate the number of extra SVC settings used.

Experiment 3

To discover whether the addition of the vertical fixation line, presumably improving convergence, improved size constancy during movement of the observer using binocular viewing, 9 Ss were tested. Under the usual procedure, using both eyes, constancy was compared with and without the fixation line. Half the Ss were tested first with the line present, the other half without.

TABLE 25.3

MEAN CONSTANCY SCORES ($\pm$ SD) WITH AND WITHOUT A FIXATION LINE, USING BOTH EYES, AND SWINGING FORWARD

S	Sex	With line	No line	S	Sex	With line	No line
1	M	0·24 ± 0·13	0·12 ± 0·08	6	M	0·28 ± 0·18*	0·24 ± 0·12
2	M	0·34 ± 0·17	0·37 ± 0·18*	7	M	0·13 ± 0·16	0·19 ± 0·18
3	M	0·18 ± 0·16	0·20 ± 0·17	8	M	0·30 ± 0·14	0·28 ± 0·17
4	M	0·41 ± 0·10	0·38 ± 0·06	9	M	0·39 ± 0·15	0·45 ± 0·12
5	M	0·23 ± 0·09	0·21 ± 0·08	*M*		0·28 ± 0·15	0·24 ± 0·12

Asterisks indicate the number of extra SVC settings used.

In Table 25.3 the *M*s and *SD*s give no suggestion of a difference between the two conditions. Thus a fixation line seems unnecessary in using this technique for estimating constancy during movement.

Experiment 4

Method To discover whether the addition of proprioceptive information from the arms improved size constancy during movement, 16 Ss made judgements, using one eye only during forward movement. Two conditions were compared: one was the usual procedure of swinging passively (after starting the swing by pressing on the ground with the feet), while in the other procedure S swung himself while judging by holding the side ropes firmly and pulling and pushing on them. Half the Ss were tested first under each condition, and care was taken that the amplitude of swing was the same.

Results As shown in Table 25.4 size constancy was better with proprioception from the arms, the difference being significant (Wilcoxon test, $p = ·01$, two tails). Thus, proprioceptive information can add to visual information in the determination of size constancy during S's active movement. This result is of some interest in considering visual performance in driving, flying, or space travel for in such situations S is denied proprioceptive information from his movement, as, unlike walking or running, his limbs are carried with him. It also suggests that proprioceptive neural activity unrelated to velocity through space might give rise to visual errors, prejudicing judgement of speed and distance. In this experiment there was a slight indication of a sex

TABLE 25.4

MEAN CONSTANCY SCORES ($\pm SD$) FOR PASSIVE AND ACTIVE SWINGING, USING ONE EYE AND SWINGING FORWARD

S	Sex	Passive	Active	S	Sex	Passive	Active
1	F	0·08 ± 0·21*	0·00 ± 0·15	10	F	0·23 ± 0·20	0·32 ± 0·20*
2	M	0·20 ± 0·15	0·02 ± 0·05	11	M	0·28 ± 0·09	0·37 ± 0·08
3	M	0·30 ± 0·10	0·38 ± 0·10	12	F	0·14 ± 0·16	0·23 ± 0·08
4	M	0·15 ± 0·08	0·22 ± 0·09	13	M	0·15 ± 0·08	0·23 ± 0·07
5	F	0·07 ± 0·10	0·07 ± 0·20	14	M	0·08 ± 0·08	0·26 ± 0·12
6	M	0·00 ± 0·30*	0·22 ± 0·10	15	M	0·09 ± 0·12	0·19 ± 0·10
7	M	0·11 ± 0·20	0·27 ± 0·12	16	M	0·12 ± 0·09	0·23 ± 0·12
8	M	0·19 ± 0·12	0·34 ± 0·05	M		0·13 ± 0·12	0·23 ± 0·10
9	M	0·11 ± 0·32**	0·32 ± 0·08				

Asterisks indicate the number of extra SVC settings used.

difference in the use of proprioceptive information: the mean constancy index for the males was 0·25 and for the females, 0·16. This difference is not significant but agrees with the findings of Witkin (1949, 1952) who showed that, when postural and visual cues conflict, men make more use of postural cues than women.

[We may now look in more detail at the apparatus used for the simulated space experiments and some of the results. This work was undertaken by many people in co-operation. Jim Howe did a great deal of work building the control equipment of the 'railway' apparatus, and in testing subjects. Stephen Salter advised on engineering problems, and experimental work was carried out by Stuart Anstis and later by Richard Young and Freja Balchin. This is apart from Helen Ross, co-author of the two previous papers.

We tried to tackle this problem with a grant from the U.S. Air Force for building and setting up the equipment, in the Cambridge Psychological Laboratory. It was later moved to the Department of Machine Intelligence and Perception in the University of Edinburgh, to a hundred-foot brick tunnel specially built and financed by the university.

The following paper, previously unpublished, is based on progress reports for the U.S. Air Force.]

★   ★   ★

MEASURING VISUAL CONSTANCY DURING ACCELERATED (HARMONIC) MOTION IN SIMULATED SPACE CONDITIONS

Techniques for providing 'null' displays

CHANGES in the size of after-images in darkness are direct evidence for internal constancy scaling systems. These changes show that constancy is not a simple matter of the pattern of the retinal image, for it remains fixed. If we could measure apparent size changes during observer-movement, we would have a measure of constancy under these conditions. After-images themselves are not suitable for they cannot be physically controlled, so we must devise a suitable method for measurement.

In place of an after-image, we present a luminous object whose size (or shape) may be varied at the will of the experimenter. Its size is made to vary in a controlled manner related to the observer's movement.

The logic of this method of measuring constancy is as follows: a verbal report of expansion or contraction is unsatisfactory, for it is not quantified – but an observer finds no difficulty in stating reliably whether or not there is a change of some kind. The most accurate kinds of measurement in physics employ null techniques, where the measuring instrument is used as a detector rather than as a calibrated instrument embodying a scale. We employ here a kind of null method, in which the observer is used simply as a detector. The display presented to him is made to shrink as he approaches it, the rate of shrinkage being adjusted until it is reported as appearing unchanging. If there were no perceptual constancy scaling, change in apparent object size would be inversely proportional to distance, which would give a constancy index of zero. If constancy were perfect, the display would have to be kept fixed in size, giving a constancy index of 1·0. From the size change to be required to give the 'null' observation of no apparent change, we can calculate visual constancy during movement of the observer.

Apparatus design There are basically three ways of producing the changing display: (1) mechanical, (2) optical and (3) electronic. We have tested all three: they will be described in turn.

Techniques for controlling display size

1. *Mechanical techniques* There are two convenient ways of making a display which can be adjusted mechanically to give variations in size. This may be done (*a*) by forming a square aperture from a pair of sliding plates, each cut with a 90° V. When drawn apart the aperture increases, remaining a true square. (*b*) An iris diaphragm may be opened and closed.

Where the displays are to be viewed in darkness, a suitable light source for both of these is an electroluminescent panel, giving a maximum intrinsic intensity of about 2·5 ft. 1. These can be obtained in various colours; give virtually no heat (and so do not damage an iris or photographic transparency placed close to them). They are readily obtainable up to 10 in. × 8 in. They can be switched extremely rapidly, the switching being silent, and their intensity is very nearly proportional to applied voltage.

The special problem with a mechanical variable-mask system is the necessary linkage to the moving observer. Where the observer is being moved passively the vehicle carrying him can be connected to the display via a servo system, but this is somewhat elaborate. Direct mechanical connection via strings and pulleys is clumsy. We find that mechanical methods are inconvenient, and would only seem appropriate at very large sizes for use in out-of-door field studies.

2. *Optical techniques* Optical methods may be divided into:
(*a*) variable magnification projection systems, using zoom lenses, and (*b*) point source shadow systems.

(*a*) Zoom lenses are useful for complex displays (such as photographs of aircraft or landing strips) but they have the disadvantage of the mechanical systems mentioned above.

(*b*) A point source, casting the shadow of an object on a screen, has geometrical properties giving us a useful technique for measuring constancy during movement.

3. *Electronic techniques* The display is presented on a cathode ray tube face, and is generated by electronic oscillators. We use a circular lissajous figure, generated by a sine wave oscillator and a 90° phase shift network feeding the X and Y deflection plates. The display size is very simply controlled, by changing the signal amplitude. The circular trace is readily converted into an ellipse, of any eccentricity, by changing the amplitude on either the X or the Y plates. This is useful for measuring shape constancy.

If the screen of the C.R.T. is viewed directly, the display size is limited to about 10 inches. More serious, the edge of the tube face serves as an arbitrary reference when its presence is revealed by ambient light, and it may even be visible by the light from the trace. This is serious: if we change the size of the display to obtain a null measurement this change must not be referred to any background structure. To avoid the difficulty we project the lissajous display upon the back of a large translucent screen, the edges of which are either beyond the field of vision or are so far removed from the display that no effective reference is available. It is important to consider Weber's Law for length. In this connection: the smallest discriminable difference in length is directly proportional to the absolute length involved. If, therefore, the edge of a screen is far removed from the display the changes involved fall within the Weber constant, and so the edge of the screen cannot be used to give information of the display changes.

It is important to be able to modulate the intensity of the display, and to change the intensity in a manner related to its size. This is a simple matter with the C.R.T., as it can be z-modulated, and is also quite easily achieved with electroluminescent panels.

We find the electronic technique the most convenient, though it might not be suitable for high ambient light conditions. The mechanical techniques are clumsy but could be useful for large displays, outside the laboratory. The optical shadow technique is most useful where the observer is stationary.

MEASUREMENTS OF VISUAL CONSTANCY AND AWARENESS OF OBSERVER MOTION IN SIMULATED SPACE CONDITIONS

The large parallelogram swing (Fig. 26.1) is fitted with position monitoring potentiometers connected to a C.R.T. display, such that a generated circle is made to shrink as the subject approaches it, on the

FIG. 26.1 *'Awareness of movement' control mounted on the swinging chair. The subject tries to keep the sliding collar stationary as he swings – to give an electrical signal of his awareness of motion.*

swing, and to expand as he recedes from it. The amount of expansion and contraction is adjusted until it *appears* of constant size. From this 'null' setting, the subject's size constancy can be calculated.

A long linear potentiometer is fitted to the chair of the swing. A sliding collar is moved by the subject, who tries to keep it fixed, with respect to the ground. His success in this task is used as an index of how well he is 'aware' of his motion. This measure is related to his measured constancy (Fig. 26.1).

One pick-off potentiometer controls the amplitude of the signal which generates the lissajous display figure on the C.R.T. The second potentiometer provides a signal for giving repeatable and controlled complex movements of the swing's chair which is pushed by an assistant, from the back. This turns out to be easier and much quieter than electrical or hydraulic actuators, but it raises the problem of giving repeatable movements. This is solved by means of this second potentiometer, which deflects one trace of a double-beam monitor oscilloscope, viewed by the assistant pushing the chair. The other trace of the monitor 'scope is deflected by a function generator, arranged to give the required movements. The assistant has the task of so pushing the chair that the trace monitoring its movement coincides with the function generator. He thus has a simple tracking task. If he makes errors, they are recorded. The function generator is an Advance VLF Type SG 88 which produces a function determined by a rotating opaque mask which controls light reaching a photocell. The outline shape of the mask determines the function, which may be of any form and need not be mathematically simple.

The display can be switched on during either forward or backward movement, by means of a switch consisting of a sliding friction collar actuating a pair of contacts. This operates for any swing amplitude, without adjustment.

Recording equipment We record: (i) the motion of the swing, (ii) the setting of the display size variation, which is adjusted to give a null observation, (iii) the output of the VLF generator (to determine the assistant experimenter's tracking errors when pushing the subject) (iv) the subject's estimates of his movements.

Experiment 1: Recording the subject's judgements of his movement So far we have discussed the null method adopted for measuring constancy, and the techniques for moving the subject. It is however also important to get an indication of how the subject *believes* he is being moved. This, we find, raises quite surprising difficulties which will be discussed later. Basically, we try to get objective data by getting the subject to maintain a hand control at a constant position, with respect to the ground, while he is moving. We have tried two kinds of control: (*a*) a light-weight alloy arm suspended from a potentiometer mounted at the top of the swing structure. The subject holds the bottom of this arm with his right hand, and endeavours to keep it vertical while he swings. Deviations of the arm are recorded, and regarded as indicating errors in his appreciation of his movement. (*b*) As there is some danger of this hanging arm giving extraneous information of movement, since it tends to hang vertically and has some inertia, we abandoned this arrangement in favour of a specially made linear potentiometer mounted horizontally on the chair and carried with it. (This is shown in Fig. 26.1). The subject holds a collar which slides freely along the resistance winding (0·65 metres, in length) to give a positional signal, of his hand movements.

These signals are fed to a two channel pen recorder, and to a (12″) C.R.T., the swing position signal producing X-deflection; the 'subjective position' control giving Y-deflection. In the case of a simple harmonic swing movement, with precise following by the subject, this gives a straight line inclined at 45°. An amplitude error by the subject produces an ellipse, the eccentricity of which indicates the amplitude error. A phase error – e.g. a delay in responding to reversal of motion at the end of the swing cycle – produces a rotation of the major axis of the generated ellipse. A (35 mm. Exacta) camera is held open so that the generated lissajous figure produces a photographic record, for later analysis. This arrangement makes it possible to average the signals over several (in practice, five) cycles. The twin channel pen recorder gives an independent record useful for analysing non-systematic errors, which do not show up well with this photographic system.

We find that this double system of recording is satisfactory for the simple case of harmonic movement, but less so when the movement is random. With random movement the photographic oscilloscope records are virtually meaningless, and the information on the pen record is difficult to interpret. We are confident of our results only where the movement is harmonic; but this is a special case, and we would not expect these results to generalize to complex or random movements.

Result The variance in phase and amplitude were found to be extremely high on three subjects; while the fourth gave more consistent results, showing phase errors between $+5°$ and $+10°$ for low frequencies, zero at 0·3 c.p.s. and negative (phase lag) at higher frequencies. This preliminary experiment showed that untrained subjects find this task extremely difficult: but this is itself a result of some significance.

Experiment 2 The lever operated by the subject for indicating his perception of motion was replaced by the linear potentiometer shown in Fig. 26.1. This was mounted on the chair itself, so that it swung with the subject, thus any friction could not be a source of information as was possible with vertical arm control in the earlier arrangement. As in the earlier system, the subject was required to compensate for his movements, by keeping the slider of the linear potentiometer fixed in space, to the best of his ability.

TABLE 26.1

MOVEMENT SENSE PHASE ANGLES, FOR VARIOUS VISUAL CONDITIONS, FOR HARMONIC OBSERVER MOTION

Subject			Conditions				Means
	L	A	B	C	D	E	
1	− 9	− 21	− 20	− 13	− 19	− 19	− 17.2
2	− 11	− 29	− 15	− 16	− 22	− 14	− 17.8
3	− 16	− 16	− 15	− 13	− 10	− 16	− 14.3
4	− 19	− 16	− 14	− 20	− 15	− 13	− 16.2
5	− 26	− 19	− 23	− 12	− 16	− 18	19.0
6	− 12	− 13	− 14	− 9	− 17	− 21	− 14.3
7	− 14	− 17	− 16	− 21	− 24	− 10	− 17.0
8	− 15	− 18	− 20	− 23	X	− 13	− 17.8
9	− 9	− 23	− 18	− 23	− 24	− 18	− 19.2
10	− 10	− 12	− 10	− 16	− 10	− 17	− 12.5
11	− 7	− 10	− 13	− 18	− 13	− 9	− 11.7
12	− 14	− 14	− 13	− 12	− 11	− 15	− 13.2
	− 13.5	− 17.3	− 15.9	− 16.5	− 16.4	− 15.2	− 15.85

Conditions

	Ambient light	Lissajous display
L	Normal room lighting	Nil
A	Darkness	Nil
B	Darkness	Constant size circle
C	Darkness	Constant *apparent* size circle
D	Darkness	Constant retinal size of circle
E	Darkness.	Reversed D.

There is a general phase lag, averaging about 15.85° with extremes from −7° to −29°. There is very high variance, both between subjects and between conditions. Evidently this is a difficult task, even with considerable visual guidance information. (This is too complicated to show as a graph). There is evidence of improvement with added visual movement information.

The conditions were the same as the first experiment except that: (i) the slider control replaced the original lever; (ii) the sweep frequency generator was not used, as the high variance suggested that we should get more data at a constant swing frequency. The frequency adopted was the natural period of the swing: 0·3 c.p.s.

There were 30 trials for each subject, and five of the conditions were randomized within each block of five trials. (The brightness of the oscilloscope display was adjusted to keep the circle easily visible, but the screen was not sufficiently bright to act as a reference object. The intensity was reduced during each session as the subject became dark-adapted.)

Results

1. The constancy measurements obtained were extremely close to those found in the experiments reported above (Gregory and Ross 1964a, b [Nos. 24, 25]).

2. Large inter-subject differences were found for the movement-awareness measures. Each subject was reasonably consistent, but there were great differences between subjects on the amplitude measurement. Considering now the effect of varying visual movement information: amplitude remained surprisingly constant for each subject under the various conditions, though again the subjects were very different from each other. This is shown in Table 26.1. The phase measures show large differences, both between subjects and between conditions.

3. A highly significant improvement occurred during the course of each session, even when the subjects were not given knowledge of results.

The mean phase errors for all subjects ($N = 10$) for each condition of visual movement information were as follows:

Condition	L	A	B	C	D	E
Median ph. error	$+13\cdot0°$	$+16\cdot5°$	$+15.0°$	$+16\cdot0°$	$+16\cdot5°$	$+15\cdot5°$

The mean amplitude ratio is shown for the same ten subjects under the same conditions.

Condition	L	A	B	C	D	E
Median AR.	0·780	0·6555	0·605	0·615	0·625	0·690

It is of some interest to consider the relationship between the constancy index and the amplitude ratios. These were correlated with the Kendal 'T' rank correlation test between the constancy indices and amplitude ratios for each condition on all subjects. The results are as follows:

Condition	L	A	B	C	D	E
Correlation Coefft.	−0·65	−0·43	−0·43	−0.36	−0·47	−0.41
Significance level (2 tail)	0·88%	8·4%	8·4%	15%	5·9%	9·7%

We may conclude that the task is meaningful, and that we get results of some consistency.

Difficulties to be overcome

1. The 'apparent motion' control in this form limits the maximum amplitude to the effective length of the subject's arm. This means that the technique can only be employed for rather small amplitude movement of the swing.

2. There are difficulties in interpretation. A gradual drift in the mean position of the control may not always indicate a positional shift in the subject's awareness of his position in space, for (in electronic terms) the arm position may be A.C. coupled to the rest of the nervous system, or there may be drift in its indicated position to the C.N.S. This means that although the electronic equipment is error-free, there is always the link from the arms to the brain to be considered, and this is a weak link. We are faced with the problem of how best to interpret the data, given low frequency drift components beyond our control.

MEASUREMENT OF VISUAL CONSTANCY DURING LINEAR OBSERVER MOTION

To give constant velocity motion to an observer over a reasonable distance and duration it is necessary to use some kind of wheeled trolley rather than the swinging chair used for the harmonic motion experiments. For linear constant velocity motion, we have built an electric railway running on a track 20 metres in length (later extended) with a gauge of two foot. The maximum speed of the trolley is 10 m.p.h. but we restrict it in practice to a slow walking speed. (Fig. 26.2).

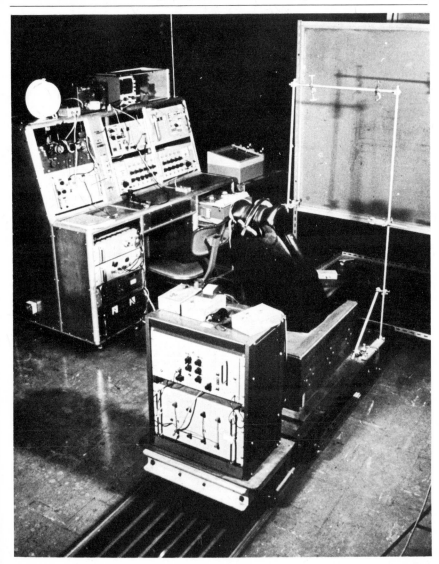

FIG. 26.2 *General view of the 'railway apparatus' space environment simulator. The control console is back left; the large back-projection display screen, back right and the trolley front. Its chair is facing the screen; its control electronics is in the rack behind the chair.*

Control system

The trolley is generally controlled from the console. There are the following facilities:

1. Manual control by the experimenter, from the console; via an eight-channel radio control link.

2. Automatically from servo at console; through the radio link.

3. Manual control by the moving observer; from the trolley.

4. Automatic control from sweeping switch driven by the trolley.

Methods 2 and 4 allow pre-set movements to be programmed for entirely automatic operation, over selected regions of the track.

Experimenter and observer communicate with a speech link; all speech is tape recorded.

The carriage position is indicated by a following-servo. The servo system works from a potentiometer mechanically driven from the carriage, connected to three of six conductor strips to unbalance a servo amplifier, whose output supplies a 1/10 h.p. D.C. reversing motor, which drives the following:

1. A carriage position signal potentiometer for the null display.

2. Sweeping stud switches for programming carriage movements automatically. Also for switching null display for selected regions of track.

3. A recording pen.

The carriage position signal (1 above) serves to change the size of the display, in conjunction with a pair of ganged potentiometers with digital read-out of their setting. These are set to control the size variation of the display with trolley position. This read-out gives the constancy index – when the size variation is adjusted to give a 'null' observation. The size variation is adjusted either (1) from the console, by the experimenter, or (2) from the moving trolley, by the observer. In addition, both this setting and the train position are continuously indicated, on a two-channel pen recorder.

Normally, the size variation control is left at one setting for a run, but it is known, from several experiments where sizes are matched at different static distances, that the perceptual constancy function over distance is not linear. But we have built in a linear function with this arrangement, and so we should not expect to find any one null setting which will hold precisely over the whole range of distance of the observer. Ideally, we should be able to change the function until it matches precisely the perceptual constancy function for any distance. This might be done in two ways: First we might use the present arrangement to obtain a null reading over a small section of track, and this we do, by switching on the display for a selected region of track and obtaining null readings for each selected section. In this way we can obtain the whole function by smoothing the readings obtaining for each section. The second, and probably better method is to generate non-linear variation control functions. This we do using a multi-step sweeping switch with a chain of pre-set resistors to generate any monotonic function.

We have not succeeded in recording the observer's 'awareness' of his movement on the railway. This was done on the swing, with the moving arm or the sliding collar described above, but this direct approach is not possible when the movement is greater than the reach of the arm. This general method may however be extended, by substituting for the sliding collar a continuous belt, moved hand-over-hand and arranged to give a velocity signal. (This situation should not be too unfamiliar as it is the same, for example, as grasping a bannister rail while walking upstairs).

Display capabilities

The null-observation display This is essentially the same as used in the swing apparatus described above. The oscilloscope is not, however, viewed directly but is arranged to give an image on a large back-projection screen, as a much larger display is needed, for the greater distances involved. Also, in conditions of ambient light, when the screen is itself visible, a large screen is necessary to avoid 'edge reference' effects.

Velocity-indicating displays It is important to investigate the limiting case of zero visual information. This is achieved by blacking out the corridor entirely, with black curtains. The train thus runs through a black tunnel, into which marker lights or projected displays may be added. (Marker lights along the sides are provided by small bulbs attached to the wall by magnets placed over the curtains).

The observer is moved at low velocity over a comparatively short distance, but we may need to simulate vastly greater velocities and distances. This is not too difficult, for reference lights can be placed optically at any distance, up to (or even beyond!) infinity using collimating systems. Further, it is possible to produce any relative velocities, using screens having constant spaced slots, generating moiré fringes which travel with or against the observer at any relative velocity.

The null display and the velocity indicating displays can be given any apparent distance, by controlling the convergence angle of the eyes, using small-angle prisms. Further, the displays may be presented as stereo projections, in which case not only the convergence angle of the eyes but also retinal disparity may be controlled – though motion parallax is absent, as for very distant objects.

EXPERIMENTS ON PERCEPTION AT CONSTANT VELOCITY IN SIMULATED SPACE CONDITIONS

Experiment 1: Zero visual information

Observations were made while the electrically driven trolley was run backwards and when it was run forwards, carrying the subject passively away from and towards the oscilloscope display. Each one-way run took about 30 seconds. The experiment was conducted in complete darkness, except for the C.R.T. display, which was a circle projected from the C.R.T. on to a large (4 ft. × 4 ft.) back-projection screen. The average size of the projected circle was 6 in. It was made to increase in size with increase in observer distance, and vice versa, to measure constancy by the null technique.

Results (i) There was no evidence of any constancy, (constancy index = zero). (ii) The variance was extremely high. (The variance was so high that any precise estimate of constancy is difficult to make; but there was no evidence of a constancy greater than 0.)

The large variance in this situation, although a nuisance in preventing us giving a precise constancy estimate, is itself a result of some practical importance, showing that the moving observer is *most unreliable* under these conditions – which are essentially the conditions of night flying and space travel.

Experiment 2: Zero visual information, with verbal information of distance

The subject was informed, through the speech link, of his distance – e.g. '48'——————42'——————36'——————30'——————' at intervals of 6 ft.

Result No change from the result of Experiment 1.

Experiment 3: Dim ambient lighting

(The lighting showed the general features of the experimental room).

Result (i) Constancy ranged from 0·6–0·9.
(ii) Variance was less where constancy was highest. This result is markedly different from the case of zero visual movement information.

Experiment 4: Zero ambient light: one dim source 2' above the null display circle, viewed binocularly

Result There was a marked reduction in variance: the mean standard deviation being 0·1. The constancy index averaged 0·5.

Conclusions These experiments show that the null method of measuring constancy during observer movement is feasible for this simulated space situation, using this null measurement technique. We obtain the kind of increase in constancy index to be expected with increase in movement information. Further, it appears that movement information of several kinds (e.g. proprioception, and acceleration forces) gives marked increase in visual constancy. This last point is not too surprising, for it is known from electrophysiological studies that there are direct connections (in the cat) from the labyrinths to the visual cortex. If the non-visual signals were inappropriate, we should however expect them to produce perhaps serious visual illusions especially in the visually non-redundant situation of space.

Proposed instrumental aid for astronauts' perception of distance

Our experiments on measuring size constancy during observer-movement in simulated space conditions show that we must expect poor human performance in the rendezvous situation. Learning through prolonged experience of space conditions is not likely to be of help, for the trouble is due simply to lack of available depth-information. It therefore seems important to consider the possibility of augmenting the available visual information with some kind of instrumental aid. We suggest an instrument to *help human vision* rather than instruments to *replace* it.

Since the trouble is primarily over-estimation of distance, it seems clear that we should consider the possibility of a miniature radar range detector feeding information to the human observer. The manner of presentation of the range information is important. If possible, the instrument should do more than provide scale readings for slow 'intellectual' judgments, but should provide continuous information in such a form that it can *serve vision directly*. Visual perception is lost without minimal adequate spatial references. The problem is to provide range information which the brain can accept as a reference for continuous visual information-processing.

Could the visual constancy scaling system come to accept a wholly artificial instrument-produced standard – such as an audible tone whose frequency would be a function of distance? The next experiments set out, not entirely successfully, to find this out. A positive answer might be of both theoretical and practical importance.

AN ATTEMPT TO IMPROVE VISUAL SIZE CONSTANCY DURING OBSERVER MOTION IN SIMULATED SPACE CONDITIONS BY ADDING (INSTRUMENTALLY GIVEN) SOUND-RANGE INFORMATION

From the results of the previous experiments on measuring size constancy during observer movement in simulated space conditions, we would expect poor performance when estimates of size, distance or relative velocity have to be made by astronauts, because there is insufficient visual information in space, compared with the conditions of high redundancy of visual information normally found on earth. Long periods of training or exposure in an environment with a scarcity of visual cues will hardly result in significant improvement in performance. We have suggested that the astronaut's visual information might be *supplemented* artificially to enable him to attain reliability – this would appear to be preferable to replacing him with a computer.

The best method of doing this is not at all obvious at this stage, nor do we in fact know whether it is possible to do this in any simple way. The rendez-vous of space vehicles has been very successfully solved by using radar and a small computer to guide the craft to within a hundred feet of each other. However, when astronauts are moving around freely in space by themselves, such a solution may not be practical.

The ideal instrument for this purpose should provide continuous information to the visual system directly, and should not require interpreting as, for example, in reading a compass.

The purpose of the present work was to determine whether an auditory tone which changes in pitch with change of distance is *directly* acceptable to the visual system for setting the internal size constancy scaling mechanism which gives perception of size and distance for moving observers.

To determine whether the auditory cue was influencing the observers' visual perception, their size constancy was measured during movement in darkness; repeated measurements gave an objective indication of any changes in the constancy index during the experiment. This method was used in all the experiments reported below.

By far the most difficult feature, and, as it turned out, the central problem, was the design of a task-situation which would enable the observer both to learn what information was given by the auditory cue and to practise using it. On this account the experimental design and the equipment was modified on several occasions.

The variable-pitch sound was derived from a voltage-controlled oscillator and associated circuitry. A signal from the potentiometer monitoring the swing position is taken to a D.C. differential amplifier. The output of this amplifier controls the frequency of a multivibrator, by determining the constant-current charging the cross-connecting capacitors. This arrangement gives substantially linear control of the audio frequency, over a 30:1 frequency range.

In the experiment, a linear sweep between 480 cycles and 1190 cycles was used. There is no special significance in this linear relationship between pitch and distance.

The audio signal was supplied to the observer by headphones.

Procedure

Constancy was measured, with the null technique, under three conditions:

(*a*) With sound-ranging signals; in normal ambient light.
(*b*) With the sound-ranging signals; in the dark.
(*c*) Without the sound-ranging signals; in the dark.

It was hoped that the sound signals (varying pitch) with distance as signalled visually in the first condition, would become associated with visual distance. (Earlier experiments had shown that this association was difficult to achieve, using specific tasks to be carried out during a training period).

Instructions were standardized as follows:

'The circle projected on the screen will change size as you swing backwards and forwards. It will either expand as you move towards it and shrink as you move away, or vice versa. We will ask you to decide whether it is bigger when you are closest to the screen or when you are furthest away. Remember that what matters is the actual size of the circle on the screen.

'We will give you five complete swings and then stop you and ask you. Try to make a definite decision, but if it is the same size in both positions then say so.

'The sound in the earphones rises in pitch the nearer you are to the screen, and falls the farther you are from it, so it can tell you your distance from the screen. So concentrate on listening to the sound and use it to help you see how far away you are.'

Results and discussion

Constancy with sound tends to be higher; but the observers reported that they already knew how they were moving, and so didn't find the sound of much assistance. They found it extremely difficult to ignore the normal acceleration cues in favour of the artificial one.

Further experiments were carried out, especially with the observer stationary and the display in motion, to avoid his acceleration cues of motion; and various training procedures were tested. Unfortunately these experiments had to be terminated before completion owing to our move from Cambridge to Edinburgh. They have not yet been resuscitated: possibly they suggest questions worth answering by further work. The results using accelerated motion on the swing apparatus were suggestive – but it is now clear that to find out whether such artificial range-information can directly mediate Constancy Scaling requires linear motion – as in the 'railway' apparatus. This was not available at the time, but these experiments continue.

27 Seeing in depth

[We now discuss, in general terms and with experimental data, the notion that the classical visual distortion illusions are intimately connected with processes giving size constancy under normal conditions. The papers which follow this one develop the theory of appropriate constancy scaling into the beginning of a formal theory of these distortion illusions.

It is important to realize not only that there are thirty or more theories of the illusions in the literature of perception, but that they occupy various logical levels. A theory which supposes that angles upset Hubel and Wiesel line orientation detectors is on a different logical level from the theory to be described here. Consider a computer: if a fault occurs in the circuitry, an output error may result. The error could also be due to a fault in the programme, or to the programme being inappropriate to the problem in hand. The logic of 'hardware' faults and 'software' errors are very different. They seem to correspond to 'physiological' and to 'psychological' disturbance.]

★   ★   ★

EYES are biological early warning systems. By giving information of events distant in space they serve to probe the immediate future, allowing brains to transcend simple reflexes and control strategic behaviour. Without information of distant objects there can be no anticipation of danger, no organized attack, no knowledge of the world. Indeed, the development of brains must have depended on seeing in depth.

The brain has a most difficult task interpreting retinal information from distant objects. The retinal image has lost a dimension: somehow the brain must construct depth from the projection of three dimensions reduced to two. For near objects the different views of the two eyes are used to compute depth, but the base line between the eyes is too small for distances beyond 50 ft. or so, when we are effectively one-eyed. With a single eye we generally see the world more or less accurately in three dimensions. For distant objects we use many 'clues' to depth, with a subtlety in the best traditions of the sleuth. With increasing distance, outlines look more blurred and fine detail is lost, objects look blue from increasing atmospheric haze, and more distant objects are in part hidden by those nearer the observer. These are some of the available clues to depth.

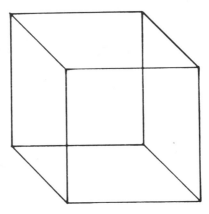

FIG. 27.1 *Necker cube.*

One can see why perception of depth is so difficult by thinking about pictures. Although a picture is itself two-dimensional, it represents objects lying in three dimensions. But this is strictly impossible, and so pictures are essentially ambiguous in depth. Consider a drawing of a simple ellipse: Is the object represented distant and large, or small and near? Is it an elliptical object, or a circle tilted at an angle? The two-dimensional drawing could represent any of an infinite set of objects. Add shading, perspective – or an indication that it is a wheel – then we see one specific object. Visual ambiguity in depth is seen dramatically in figures which could equally well lie in more than one orientation. For example, Fig. 27.1: a flat drawing of a skeleton cube. A given face is seen first as the front, then the back. The alternative 'hypotheses' are entertained perceptually in turn, and we never do see the figure as a unique unchanging object.

Pictures are not only ambiguous; they are also paradoxical. A picture is seen to be lying flat on its paper or canvas, and yet is also seen in three dimensions as indicated by its perspective and other depth cues. It is paradoxical in being seen as both flat and in depth at the same time. Conflicting cues to depth can produce 'impossible objects'. Fig. 27.2 cannot be an object lying in space. Fig. 27.3 cannot even be seen. In both cases, the trouble is over the third dimension.

Why should the eye accept a picture as representing objects lying in a space different from its own? It does so because a picture is essentially like a retinal image – both are flat projections of three-dimensional space. Pictures give simplified images, and very likely distorted in various ways, but the brain is so familiar with the problem of adding the third dimension from information given by the flat retinal image that we might expect it to cope with pictures.

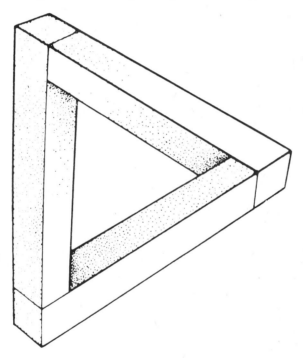

FIG. 27.2 *An impossible figure. This cannot represent any possible physical object, for it has conflicting depth 'cues'.*

But there is an important difference between pictures and retinal images. Both are ambiguous, but retinal images do not lie perceptually in both two and three dimensions. We do not 'see' the flatness of the retina, or its texture: they are not signalled to the brain. Thus the brain has a more difficult task dealing with a picture than with normal objects. The textured background imposes a highly artificial problem to the visual system which it cannot completely solve. It is indeed unfortunate that experiments in perception have largely used figures drawn on paper. It is only when the double reality of the picture and what it represents is being explicitly investigated that pictures should be used in visual experiments.

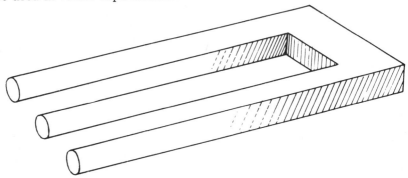

FIG. 27.3 *This figure cannot even be seen. Again the difficulty is over the third dimension.*

It is, however, possible to produce pictures which, like retinal images, have no information of their flatness. This we may do by avoiding all background texture, and viewing with a single eye. When Fig. 27.1 is shown in this way – luminous, glowing in the dark – it appears as a truly three-dimensional cube. It still reverses in depth – it is still ambiguous – but it is no longer paradoxical in depth. The luminous figure looks different in another way – the apparently further face always looks larger than the apparently nearer face, whichever this may be. We see this distortion most dramatically in a truly three-dimensional skeleton cube, made of wire and coated with luminous paint to make it glow in the dark. The true cube also reverses in depth, and when it reverses it changes shape – the apparent front appearing too small. It becomes a truncated pyramid. Also, it rotates in the most odd way when the observer moves round it, as the physical parallax shift between the front and back is attributed to the perceptually reversed front and back.

Why should the luminous cube change shape when reversed in visual depth? This is answered by asking a silly-sounding question – why does a cube normally look like a cube? This needs some explanation, for since the back face is further away, it must give a smaller image to the retina. But it does not look smaller – it looks the same size as the front. Although all objects give smaller retinal images as they recede from the eye, this geometrical shrinking is generally compensated by the brain, to give 'size constancy'. Size constancy was known to Descartes in the seventeenth century, and has been investigated intensively since, notably by R. H. Thouless in the thirties. It serves to give immediate recognition that a distant bottle is pint or half-pint, or whether it is a cat or a tiger about to spring. There are various theories about constancy (Ittelson, 1951; Epstein, Park and Casey 1961), but I believe it to be produced by an active scaling process in the brain, either set according to the apparent distance of viewed objects or set directly by various depth cues. We may call the underlying processes 'constancy scaling'.

When we see the skeleton wire cube distorted, when reversed in depth, we see our constancy scaling at work. But it is working backwards. For it is working according to the apparent and not the true depth of the object. Although constancy scaling normally corrects for the shrinking of retinal images with distance, reversal of depth makes the normally useful compensation distort visual space. The cube looks more distorted than it would if there were no constancy scaling correcting for the shrinking of the image with distance. These distortions occur whenever depth reverses in non-paradoxical figures. It could happen in real conditions, such as landing aircraft, or in space flight, and the consequences might be serious.

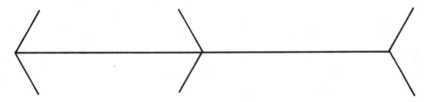

FIG. 27.4 *The Müller-Lyer arrow illusion. Outgoing fins expand the shaft joining them, the ingoing shrink it. The fins can be regarded as perspective lines of corners. When shown with no textured background (luminous) they look like true corners. The perspective depth appears to produce the illusion by triggering primary constancy scaling.*

The 'geometrical illusions'

We know, then, that visual space is distorted when depth is seen wrongly. Can this somehow explain the distortions of the well-known 'illusion figures'? Fig. 27.4 shows the most familiar example: the outgoing arrow heads expand the line (or the space) between them, while the ingoing heads shrink it. Now these 'arrow heads' can be thought of as perspective drawings of corners lying in depth. They are the same shape as the retinal images of real corners (Tausch, 1954). With the outgoing arrow heads the vertical line would be distant, the heads representing, for example, the lines of the ceiling and walls of the inside corner of a room. The ingoing heads are perspective drawings of an outside corner, say, of a building or box, where the joining line would be near.

If the perspective features of retinal images do indeed serve to set constancy scaling, then when these features are present in flat pictures we must expect them to produce distortions of visual space. Constancy scaling corrects for shrinking of the retinal image with increasing distance, but pictures present perspective depth features with no change in distance to compensate, since they are physically flat, and so the scaling must be inappropriate. We must expect objects indicated as further away to be systematically expanded (Gregory, 1963*b*) [No. 28]. This is just what happens, apparently for all the illusion figures, with people familiar with corners and parallel lines.

It has been known for sixty years that people who live in environments largely free of right angular corners and parallel lines – such as the Zulus, who live in a 'circular culture' of round huts – do not suffer these distortion-illusions (Segall, Campbell and Herskovits 1963). Miss Jean Wallace and I found that a man of middle age, who recovered his sight by corneal graft after being blind since early infancy, was hardly subject to the illusions [p. 117]. His perception of depth was also most odd. It seems that early experience of perspective features is important: apparently we learn to use perspective for setting constancy scaling.

Can we demonstrate experimentally a close connexion between depth and distortion illusions? There are several hints in the literature of such an origin of the illusions (Tausch, 1954; Teuber, 1960), but there is a difficulty. It is always assumed that size constancy works simply according to apparent distance (Ittelson, 1951) (which is indeed true for the luminous cubes), but if this were always the case it could not produce distortions in figures seen as flat. But the illusion figures are generally seen as lying flat on their paper backgrounds, so how can we invoke constancy to account for these distortions?

Measuring depth in pictures

The apparatus is shown in Fig. 27.5. The illusion figure is presented as a back-illuminated transparency. Light from it is polarized, and cross-polarized at one eye. Both eyes, however, view a small dim movable light which is optically introduced into the figure with a part-reflecting mirror. Now this light may be adjusted in distance, until it matches the apparent distance of any selected part of the figure seen with a single eye. The figure's depth is given by its perspective features, but the light's distance is given by convergence of the two eyes. Positions of the light are recorded on the graph paper at the top of the apparatus, and so we plot visual space in three dimensions, using the two eyes as a range-finder to measure the effect of perspective

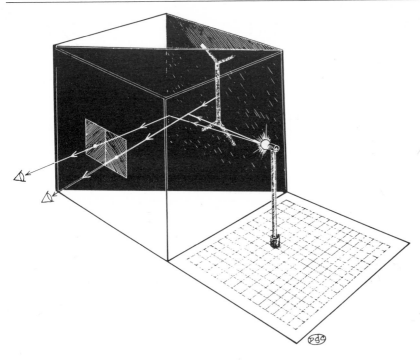

FIG. 27.5 *Apparatus for measuring visual depth in pictures. The picture (for example, an illusion figure) is back-illuminated, to avoid background texture. It is seen monocularly, the light being polarized, and cross-polarized at one eye. The movable reference light is seen binocularly and placed in the apparent positions of selected parts of the picture.*

on a single eye. Fig. 27.6 shows how the arrow illusion is related to its apparent depth, as measured with this technique. The similarity of the distortion and depth functions, for various angles of the fins, demonstrates the close relationship we should expect – if indeed perspective features can set constancy scaling directly – to produce illusions when the perspective is inappropriate to true distance.

Depth optics

Can we improve instruments, or devise new instruments, for extending the eye's ability to see in depth?

The microscope is a direct extension of the eye, extending its ability to see the very small by effectively making it see objects extremely near. But when used at high magnification, its depth of focus is so small that structures lying only a few microns further or nearer the plane of sharpest focus are degenerated to be unrecognizable. It cannot provide the separated views to the two eyes to give stereoscopic depth. This limitation, however, can be overcome

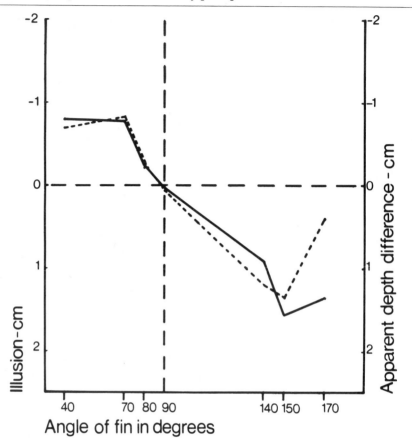

FIG. 27.6 *Full line shows extent of Müller-Lyer arrow illusion (measured by adjusting a 'neutral' line to apparent equality) for a range of fin angles. Figures presented without background texture, to a single eye. The depth (broken line) is the difference in apparent distance between the shaft and ends of the fins.*

(Gregory 1960, 1961*a* [No. 41]) by vibrating the objective lens of the microscope so that the plane of sharp focus scans rapidly up and down through the specimen, extracting the depth information with each scan. But if this were presented on a plane we would see confusion, for we would be compressing three into two dimensions. Somehow the information must be reconstituted into three-dimensional visual space. This can be done by projecting the image on to a screen kept vibrating in phase with the scan through the specimen. The image on the vibrating screen then changes systematically as it moves to and from the observer, and builds in the volume swept by the screen a 'solid image', magnified in depth. We can see, for example, brain cells magnified a thousand times in three dimensions. In practice the vibrating screen introduces difficulties, but it can be replaced by a rotating helical screen; or a screen avoided altogether, by sweeping the pair of images in opposition across the eyes, in a way the observer's brain accepts as signalling depth.

Could we devise a way of drawing pictures in three dimensions? Do artists have to be for ever limited to flat planes on paper? The problem here is to produce a pair of lines, one for each eye, produced under the control of the artist, so that correct stereoscopic depth is given by the horizontal separation of the lines. We have recently built just such a device. The depth artist holds a stylus, bearing a small bright light which is imaged on a pair of Thorn electroluminescent image-retaining panels. As he draws with the light, in three dimensions, glowing lines are presented to each eye and fused by the brain into a single picture in depth. He sees and creates in a three-dimensional world, where artist and scientist meet.

28 Distortion of visual space as inappropriate constancy scaling

[Here is the original source in which the 'Inappropriate Constancy Scaling' theory of distortion illusions was formally stated. It should be noted that the distinction made between 'primary' and 'secondary' scaling is vital for the theory. Unfortunately this has been ignored by several commentators, with confusing results. I would now describe primary constancy as scale-setting 'upwards', from sensory cues or data such as perspective convergence at the retina; and secondary scaling as scale-setting 'downwards', from assumptions of distance and shape stored in the brain from experience of familiar objects. This is developed in Gregory (1968a) [No. 30], in *The Intelligent Eye* (1970a), and most recently in Gregory and Gombrich (eds.) (1973).]

* * *

DISTORTIONS of visual space associated with certain simple patterns have been investigated since the beginning of experimental psychology (Boring, 1942), and many theories have been proposed (Woodworth, 1938), but so far none, in my opinion, has been satisfactory in explaining these so-called 'geometrical' illusions. Figs. 28.1, 2 and 3 show representative illusions of the kind we are considering.

The traditional theories fall into three classes: (1) That certain shapes produce, or tend to produce, abnormal eye movements. (2) That some kind of central 'confusion' is produced by certain shapes, particularly non-parallel lines and corners. (3) That the figures suggest depth by perspective, and that this 'suggestion' in some way distorts visual space.

The eye movement theories are difficult to support because the illusions occur undiminished when the retinal image is optically stabilized on the retina (Pritchard, 1958), or when the figures are viewed as after-images following illumination by a bright flash of light. Further, since distortions can occur in opposed directions at the same time (as with the Müller-Lyer figure (Fig. 28.1 *a*)) it is difficult to see how either overt or incipient eye movements could be involved. The various 'confusion' theories all suffer from vagueness, and they give us no idea as to why the distortions should occur in the observed directions, or only in certain kinds of figures. The perspective theory (Woodworth, 1938) is inadequate because it does not suggest why or how perspective should produce distortions in flat figures, but it does imply a generalization which seems to hold true of all the known illusion figures, and this gives a clue vital to understanding the origin of the illusions.

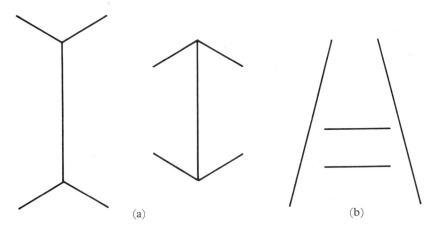

(a)   (b)

FIG. 28.1 (a) *the Müller-Lyer;* (b) *the Ponzo illusion.*

The illusion figures may be thought of as flat projections of typical views of objects lying in three-dimensional space. For example, the outward-going Müller-Lyer arrow figure is a typical projection of, say, the corner of a room – the fins representing the intersections of the walls with the ceiling and floor – while the in-going arrow is a typical projection of an outside corner of a house or a box, the converging lines receding into the distance. The following generalization seems to hold for all the illusion figures thought of in this way: *The parts of the figures corresponding to distant objects are expanded and the parts corresponding to nearer objects are reduced.* Thus in the Müller-Lyer figure the vertical line would be further away in the diverging case, and is expanded in the illusion, and vice versa, while in the Ponzo figure the upper horizontal line would be farther away and it also is expanded in the flat illusion figure.

Given that this generalization holds for all the illusions, why should these distortions occur?

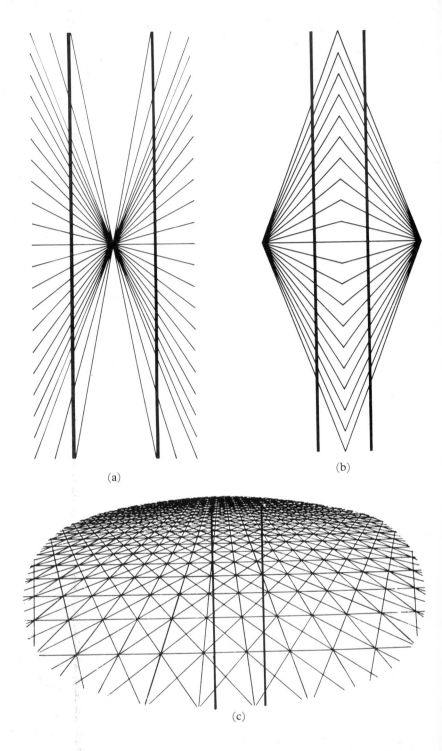

FIG. 28.2 (a) and (b) Alternative forms of the Hering illusion. The vertical lines are bowed outwards and inwards respectively. (c) An illusion showing how parallel lines indicating distance seem to diverge when presented on a texture gradient.

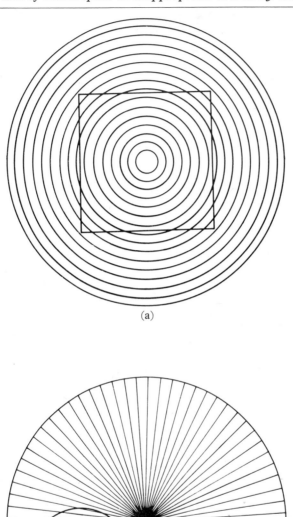

(a)

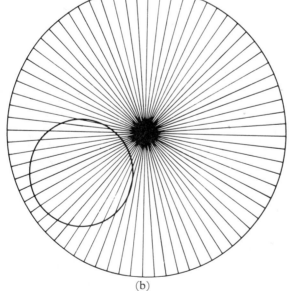

(b)

FIG. 28.3 *Further distortions to be expected on the distance hypothesis; the concentric circles and spokes set the constancy scaling by indicating depth.*

Do we know of any other perceptual phenomena involving systematic perceptual modification of the retinal image? There is a well-known set of phenomena which certainly does involve perceptual modification of retinal images – size constancy (Thouless, 1931, 1932*a*, *b*, Vernon, 1954). This is the tendency for objects to appear much the same size over a wide range of distance in spite of the changes of the retinal images associated with distance of the object. We may refer to the processes involved as constancy scaling. Now in constancy scaling we find known processes which not only could but also must produce distortion of visual space if the scaling were set inappropriately to the distance of an observed object. It is strange that apparently only one writer, Tausch, has considered constancy in connection with the geometrical illusions (Tausch, 1954).

We can see our own scaling system at work in the following demonstration of Emmert's law (Emmert, 1881). The after-image of a bright light is 'projected' on to a series of screens lying at various distances, or a single screen moved away or towards the observer. Although the effective retinal image is constant, the after-image perceived as lying on a screen looks larger the farther the screen is from the observer. Complete constancy would give a doubling in size for each doubling of distance, and the amount of scaling can be quantified under various conditions for stationary or moving screens. (Gregory, Wallace and Campbell 1959 [No. 22]; Anstis, Shopland and Gregory 1961 [No. 23].)

Clearly inappropriate constancy scaling would produce distortion of visual space, but why should this occur with the illusion figures which are in fact flat and are generally seen to be flat? It is generally assumed that constancy scaling depends simply on apparent distance (as Emmert's law might suggest); but if we are to suppose that constancy scaling can operate for figures clearly lying on a flat surface we must challenge this assumption, and suggest that visual features associated with distance can modify constancy scaling even when no depth is seen. If we are to suppose that the illusions are due to misplaced constancy scaling, we must suppose that the scaling can be set directly by depth features of flat figures, and that the scaling is not set simply as a function of apparent distance as is generally thought to be the case.

Perspective drawings and photographs are seen to depict objects as if they lay in three dimensions, and yet at the same time they appear flat, lying on the plane of the paper, and so they are perceptually paradoxical. The surface texture of the paper evidently prevents the perspective from making the objects appear truly three dimensional, for if we remove all texture and view with one eye, then perspective drawings can look as impressively in depth as the real world viewed with one eye.

We have presented the well-known illusion figures with no background texture – by making wire models coated in luminous paint so that they glow in the dark, or using back illuminated transparencies – and we find that, viewed with one eye, they look three dimensional, provided the angles are not marked exaggerations of perspective. The Müller-Lyer arrows, for example, look like corners and not like flat projections when presented as luminous figures in the dark, and those parts which appear most distant are the parts which are expanded in the illusions as normally presented on textured paper.

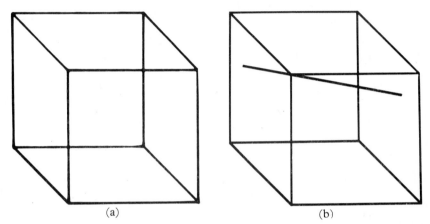

(a) (b)

FIG. 28.4 (a) *The Necker cube. This reverses in depth. When viewed as a self-luminous figure, the apparent front looks smaller, the back larger.* (b) *Humphrey's figure. The oblique line is seen as slightly bent, the direction of bending being determined by the angle against which it is placed, and not by the way the cube appears to lie in depth, when drawn on a textured background.*

Emmert's law may suggest that constancy scaling arises directly from apparent distance; but there is retinal information indicating the distance of each position of the screen, and possibly this might serve directly to set the scaling. However, the following demonstration shows conclusively that scaling can occur simply as a function of apparent depth and independently of retinal or other sensory information.

Fig. 28.4*a* shows the well-known Necker cube figure – a skeleton cube which reverses spontaneously in depth so that sometimes one face, sometimes another, appears the nearer. As shown on textured paper, it is paradoxical in the manner described here – it looks as if it were in depth and yet it is seen to be flat on the paper. By making a luminous model of this figure, and viewing it in the dark, we find that it still reverses but now it looks like a true three-dimensional figure, and it undergoes size changes – the apparently farther face looking somewhat larger than the nearer, showing that constancy scaling is now operating. Since the retinal image remains unchanged it follows that the scaling is set under these conditions as a simple function of apparent distance. This is shown most dramatically with a three-dimensional luminous cube. This looks like a true cube when seen correctly, but when perceptually reversed in depth it looks like a truncated pyramid, the apparently front face being the smaller.

It thus appears that there are two ways in which constancy scaling can be set. We may name these:

1. *Primary constancy scaling.* This is set by perspective or other features normally associated with distance. These features can be at variance with apparent distance in special cases, such as the illusion figures. (We call it 'primary' because it seems to be primitive, and to be mediated by neural systems situated early in the perceptual system).

2. *Secondary constancy scaling* is set simply by apparent distance, and this may be a function of previous knowledge and is not necessarily tied directly to visual information. Its existence is suggested but not proved by Emmert's law; but it is conclusively demonstrated with the ambiguous self-luminous objects which change their shape systematically according to which faces appear nearer or farther though there is no change in the retinal image. Errors in apparent distance should produce distortion of visual space via this secondary scaling system, and the well-known moon illusion may be an example.

Although the self-luminous figures do clearly demonstrate what we have called the secondary constancy sealing system, what clear evidence have we for the primary system, supposed to be set by typical depth cues even in the absence of depth perception? For our present purpose it is much more important to demonstrate the existence of primary than secondary scaling. To get evidence for primary scaling entirely independent of the illusions is very difficult, but the following is at least suggestive.

(*a*) It has been noticed by Professor George Humphrey (personal communication) that a straight line drawn across a corner of a Necker cube (Fig. 28.4*b*) appears bent. Now this is particularly interesting because the direction of bending is the same which ever way the cube appears to lie in depth. It is bent in the direction to be expected if constancy scaling is operating from the typical perspective interpretation of the angle against which the line lies.

(*b*) In primitive races living in houses without corners the geometrical illusions are reduced (Segall and Campbell 1962; Segall,

Campbell and Herskovits 1963). If learning is important, this would be expected.

(*c*) In a case of a man blind from the first few months of life, but gaining his sight after operation fifty years later, we have found that the illusions were largely absent, and his constancy appeared abnormal or absent although he could at that time, some weeks after the corneal graft operation, recognize common objects. This has been noted in other cases. (In fact, it was this observation which suggested to me this kind of theory of the illusions [p. 92].)

We should expect the different scaling systems to have somewhat different time-constants, and we are attempting to measure these to establish their separate existence quite apart from considerations of distortions of visual space.

It further may be suggested that figural after-effects – distortions similar to the geometrical illusions, but produced as a result of prolonged viewing of a suitable stimulus pattern and transferring to a second test pattern – may be due to the primary scaling being set by depth features present in the stimulus pattern, this scaling taking some time after lengthy fixation to become appropriate to the second test pattern, so the second pattern is distorted by scaling carried over from the earlier pattern. Preliminary experiments are providing strong evidence that figural after-effects can be thought of in this way, and such a theory would have advantages over present theories of the figural after-effects, which are *ad hoc*, involve dubious physiological speculation and fail to make useful predictions (Kohler and Wallach 1944; Osgood and Heyer 1951).

In attempting to give a general account of all illusions involving systematic distortions of visual space, either while viewing a figure or following on prolonged viewing, and relating the distortions to a known perceptual phenomenon – size constancy – we have not attempted to specify the neural processes involved, and we believe this to be impossible at this time. Recent work on recording from the visual regions of the cat's brain while presenting the eyes with moving or fixed patterns (Hubel and Wiesel 1962) gives promise that the underlying neural mechanisms may soon be revealed.

This work was supported by the U.S. Air Force under grant No. *AF–EOAR* 63–93 and monitored by the European Office, Office of Aerospace Research and also by the Medical Research Council.

29 Comments on the inappropriate constancy scaling theory of illusions and its implications

[This paper answers some criticisms of the illusion theory. I ignore papers which have, surprisingly, failed to understand the to me essential distinction made between 'primary' (or 'cue') scaling – set by available sensory data (e.g. perspective features) – and 'secondary' (or hypothesis) scaling – set by the selected 'perceptual hypothesis'. Concerning the interesting question of whether haptic (active) touch distortions are related to visual distortions, Frisby and Davies (1971) have recently found evidence that subjects with strong visual imagery show haptic illusions more than subjects with little or no visual imagery. It is possible that for people with marked visual imagery touch information of shape is treated as part of the – in their case mainly visual – perceptual hypotheses. There are implications here which remain to be worked out but it seems that size scaling may occur surprisingly early in the perceptual system.

It has recently been claimed by Paul Bach-y-Rita and his colleagues in San Francisco that touch patterns given by a mosaic of probes placed generally on the back and activated electrically, from scenes signalled by a television camera, allow remarkably complete perception through the skin. Objects in the field of the camera are experienced as 'out there' in external space, as in vision. The stages by which learning to 'see' haptically takes place are similar to the way in which the vision in S.B. developed after recovery from blindess by corneal grafts. The typical visual illusions are reported as occurring in this 'haptic vision'. But these experiments are still at an early stage.

It is an intriguing thought that haptic vision is just what we supposed the first visual perception to be (see p. 602), if touch pattern processing was taken over by the first primitive eyes. Could it be that this new television technique is repeating this ancient experiment – and may be successful now because it was successful then – hundreds of millions of years ago?]

★　　　★　　　★

IN the literature of perception no clear distinction is generally made between: (i) the *processes* leading to perceptual correction for changes in retinal image size with object distance, and (ii) the final *result* – near-invariance of perceptual size with object distance. Thus, J. J. Gibson is not at all concerned with brain mechanisms giving constancy, but regards it as determined by the surrounding pattern of the prevailing external world and to be fully describable in terms of texture gradients and the other pattern features he has done so much to investigate. But we must face the fact that the monocular depth cues are open to many interpretations, and it is difficult to believe that perception is wholly determined by them or can be understood without reference to brain processes involving probabilities. There are two particular situations which drive us away from Gibson's position: (1) depth-ambiguous figures, such as luminous Necker cubes, which change in shape following Emmert's Law with each reversal though the retinal pattern remains constant; (2) the limiting case of a single object having no visible background to determine its size or distance. Gibson does not consider the first of these, and says of the second that size and distance are indeterminate under these conditions. But the first shows dramatic and repeatable effects, not to be dismissed lightly, while for the second Gibson is forced by his position into statements empirically incorrect. He is forced to say that the moon, or an after-image viewed in darkness, have *no* perceptual size or distance. But they have a quite clear size and distance, which can indeed be measured. They may fluctuate, and may be wildly in error, but we never see an object or after image having *no* perceptual size or distance. Luminous figures viewed in darkness reveal that we accept hypothetical sizes and distances. Depth-ambiguous luminous figures change in step-functions, revealing alternative perceptual hypotheses – and perceptual constancy follows each hypothesis of distance. It is thus clear that constancy is not always tied to the external visual pattern. A 'stimulus' theory cannot be adequate, because it cannot describe the ambiguous figure case, or the limiting case of zero context information.

Gibson almost completely dismisses the distortion illusions, at times saying they do not exist. They are difficult to reconcile with a view of perception which regards percepts as determined by the pattern of the external world, without reference to brain processes which may be upset in certain situations. This leads us back to the distinction between (i) the processes leading to constancy and (ii) the size-distance invariance itself. We term the *processes* 'constancy size scaling' (or for short 'constancy scaling'), implying active brain processes, producing the size-distance invariance, to give *constancy*.

Considering now the scaling processes: the theory essentially involves two very different kinds of scaling, the first being tied to typical prevailing depth information, while the second is tied to the current perceptual hypothesis. Up to now I have called these 'primary' and 'secondary' scaling respectively, but it may be convenient to identify them by more explicit names. I suggest *'depth cue scaling'* and *'hypothesis scaling'* for the process giving constancy. Illusions occur when *either* of the scaling systems is set inappropriately to the prevailing three-dimensional external world. The standard visual illusions are to be attributed to *depth cue scaling* being set by perspective depth cues inappropriate to the flat figures. Other depth cues can give distortion when set inappropriately, such as incorrect convergences of the eyes through deviating prisms, or the 'wallpaper' effect when horizontally displaced repeated patterns are fused with resulting error in size. It is a matter for experiment to determine whether all depth cues can give distortion when set inappropriately to prevailing reality. From such experiments we can learn a great deal about the brain's scaling mechanisms.

Hypothesis scaling is very different. It is not always closely related to the prevailing retinal information, as we see from the depth-ambiguous figures, which change in size and shape with each perceptual reversal. Hypothesis scaling is subject to modification by the observer's 'set', by his pre-suppositions, and is more variable than is depth cue scaling. Perceptual hypotheses can be wildly wrong but they have the great biological value, in an uncertain world, of filling in gaps between available items of information – allowing usually appropriate behaviour to be maintained though there is no certain sensory information to control it. The favourite cannot always win; but runners-up do not generally lead to disaster. Illusions can normally be tolerated, but highly unusual conditions, such as space travel, may defeat the system when perceptual hypotheses run away from sensory control.

It is in the light of these general considerations that I now turn to consider the points made by Zanforlin, Virsu, Fellows and Over (1967).

Dr Zanforlin, in his first paragraph, says that I attribute the distortions to conflict of depth information from the figure and its background. This is not however quite correct, and the point is important both for understanding and for testing the theory. The relevant fact is that distortions are observed in the illusion figures whether or not they have a visible background. We cannot therefore attribute the distortions to conflict between depth features of the figure and its background. Experiments with luminous figures, having no visible background, show that: (1) the distortions persist though the background be removed; (2) the figures then generally appear to lie in three dimensions (though truly flat), according to their perspective features. They no longer lie in the queer paradoxical depth of pictures with backgrounds – where though depth is suggested the figure is seen as lying flat on its background and in (paradoxical) depth. (3) The distortions are affected by the non-paradoxical depth: apparent size of the figure as a whole, and of each feature, now obeying Emmert's Law. (This is seen most clearly with depth-ambiguous figures such as a luminous Necker cube, the apparently further face always appearing the larger, whichever this may be). (4) Depth-ambiguous illusion figures show both the residual illusions and size changes following Emmert's law upon reversal. (5) Necker cubes presented with a background do not change appreciably in shape with reversal in (paradoxical) depth.

The theory does not attribute the illusions to conflict between the figure's perspective depth features and its background; because the background is not necessary for the distortion. What the theory does assert is that the distortions occur in figures or objects having marked typical perspective features which are at variance with the *true shape* or *orientation* of the figure or object. For example: the converging lines of the Ponzo figure, or the arrow heads of the Müller-Lyer figure, mislead the perceptual constancy mechanism because these shapes are generally reliable perspective guides to the third dimension; but in these flat figures the eyes are misled because the perspective instead of being generated by the usual geometrical shrinking of the image with distance is present in the (flat) object itself.

This takes us to Zanforlin's doubt about my ability to define 'depth features', and his complaint that perspective representations can be ambiguous. I would go further and say that perspective is *always* ambiguous, and that it is this ambiguity which presents a major and continual problem to the perceptual system. We should think of this as a problem confronting any conceivable perceptual system allowed only two-dimensional representations of three-dimensional reality. The ambiguity results from the loss of a dimension at the eye, and perceptual theory should start with this basic situation. Ambiguity of depth is reduced as much as possible by the use made of the various 'depth cues' (investigated by Helmholtz, Ames, the Gibsons, and others), typical perspective shapes being used by late Renaissance artists to indicate the third dimension with fair success. Artists are, however, handicapped by the texture of their backgrounds, and it is amazing that we see any depth under these conditions and it may require special perceptual learning. It is important to note that a picture has a kind of double reality, and we cannot suppose that constancy scaling can be set correctly both for the picture as a flat object and for the objects it depicts in the quite different picture space. All figures are in this sense 'impossible objects', and the amazing thing is how well we handle them. Common sense is a fair guide to what is a 'typical' perspective projection, but one could take a set of photographs from normal viewpoints as a check. Obviously a square is not a typical perspective projection of a truncated cone viewed obliquely, and a view through opposite corners of a cube is not typical, or characteristic, either. Perhaps more important is what the perceptual system accepts as reliable perspective depth information. This is an empirical question open to experiment. Zanforlin's objection that we cannot establish depth features by presenting self-luminous figures in the dark (and measuring their effects quantitatively with the technique in which the two eyes are used as a range-finder for plotting monocular visual space) must not go without comment. He objects to the 'dubious predictions' of this technique, but surely he is pre-judging the issue without alternative evidence: and the measure of the power of a technique is the surprise of the results it can give. He should be clearer that the results are impossible, or that the technique is subject to serious artifacts, before denouncing it. A result of the technique (and not wholly surprising) is that for two identical shapes, one larger than the other, the larger is generally seen as nearer. It is absurd to argue *a priori* that the perceptual system must or should take a 50–50 per cent view of the situation – it is a matter for experiment to discover its strategy, and the technique allows us to discover how it deals with such ambiguous situations quantitatively and under any desired conditions. In fact, statistically, large images represent nearer objects and it turns out that the brain accepts this probability as a depth cue. As indeed we know from the many alley experiments (Ittelson and Kilpatrick 1952).

Perception of depth is not *completely* determined by texture or perspective. In impoverished environments the observer's pre-conceptions and his 'set' can be important. These 'internal' factors can be assessed from the depth measurements, and they are important for astronauts and others required to make perceptual judgement under impoverished conditions. The limiting case, of a single luminous object viewed in darkness, has been too little considered. It is remarkable that the moon is so constant in apparent size and distance when viewed in a clear sky giving no obvious depth information, and it evidently appears much the same size and distance to all observers – though of course we all see it quite wrongly! It seems that depth information serves to modify 'hypotheses', perhaps themselves derived from experience of many earlier situations accepted as relevant to the present conditions. Where there is little or no depth information, the prevailing 'perceptual hypothesis' may go unchecked, then size and distance vary wildly, especially in unfamiliar situations. Systematic illusions occur when the depth information is misleading through being atypical. The illusion figures give systematic distortion because they present perspective features which are typical of quite different objects, lying in three dimensions. Distortions are not however limited to flat objects – they are but one case; for any object can be so shaped that it displays misleading depth information which, it seems, can set constancy inappropriately to its true shape and so generate an illusion.

Dr Virsu's learned paper on contrast and confluxion does not need detailed comments. I find the notion rather vague, and would prefer to push what seems a more precise set of concepts – primary and secondary constancy scaling – to the limit before accepting them as incomplete, but certainly we do not have the evidence to assert that misplaced constancy is the *whole story* of illusions. Virsu could be correct; but if so the perceptual system is 'messier' than one might hope. Is there evidence to show this?

B. J. Fellows' experiment – showing that a line placed between the arrow heads of the Müller-Lyer figure but of insufficient length to reach either arrow may show a reversed illusion – strikes me as neat and perhaps important. I am not however clear why he argues with such confidence that 'these findings fail to support Gregory's inappropriate constancy scaling theory which would predict that the shorter lines would be subject to the same effects as the complete shaft of the Müller-Lyer figure'. Consider first what is well known about this illusion:

1. The Müller-Lyer illusion is unusual in that the figure *itself* is distorted, while generally it is imposed lines which are distorted. But here it is the separation of the arrows which is in error whether or not there is an intervening line.

2. The outward going arrows give expansion, and the inward ones shrinking *with respect to a neutral comparison line*. There can, then, be *expansion* or *shrinking* in the illusions.

3. The distortion is a change of *separation* between the arrow heads, and not of the *angles* of the figure, which is of theoretical importance.

Now given that the separation between the arrow heads is changed by the usual illusion (and this occurs in the absence of any line joining them) what 'should' happen to a short line placed between the heads? If the heads correspond perceptually to the retinal projection of corners, a shorter line could represent, in the case of the outgoing arrows, some object *nearer* the observer than the extreme of the (inside) corner. In the real world this would give a larger retinal image than when placed at the corner; so to give constancy it must be shrunk with respect to the corner – which is what Fellows finds in his experiment. (I would regard this figure as perceptually the same as the Ponzo illusion but, as it were, viewed end on. I would predict that the short line will be measured as perceptually nearer, with the depth-measuring technique[1]). No doubt there are other possibilities for interpreting this experiment which should be considered (what happens if the arrow heads, or neutral lines, are physically further or nearer the test line?) but to my mind the 'enclosing' effect argument is not attractive – unless by 'enclosing' one means the volume of 3-D space represented by the projection, and this is a very different notion.

Regarding the relevance of touch illusions to the illusions of vision (and especially Over's findings, which supplement those of Rudel and Teuber) I offer no comment at this stage. Haptic touch on the Müller-Lyer illusion is confounded by the poor touch acuity of the fingers, which tends to produce a similar effect for figures such as the visual Müller-Lyer though by quite different means. At present the whole question of the relation between touch and vision is too uncertain for us to say how relevant touch experiments are to a theory of visual illusions, but perhaps a close relationship would indicate that the touch and visual spaces are neurally related in the nervous system *after* visual primary constancy scaling has taken place. However this may be, the depth-ambiguity of retinal images implies that non-visual information (now or in the past) is needed to give meaning to retinal images in terms of external reality. It is essential for the development of the individual's visual perception (Gregory and Wallace 1963 [No. 3]), and for the development of the first effective eye-brain systems in evolution (Gregory, 1968c [No. 53]). But the relationship between touch and vision in illusion situations is at present largely mysterious, and it is unwise to make any specific statement at the present stage of knowledge.

---

[1] This prediction has since been confirmed when measurements of apparent depth were made in the figures for 16 subjects. This experiment, suggested by Fellows's results, was carried out in June 1967.

30 *Perceptual illusions and brain models*

[This paper develops the notion of perceptual hypotheses and also raises questions concerning the distinction to be made between 'analogue' and 'digital'. This is made in the context of the brain, and seems important if we are to be clear in how we use an engineering distinction. The point is: Should the distinction be regarded as one of engineering convenience (continuous or discontinuous mechanisms, or circuits) or should it be regarded as a deeper logical distinction? I incline to the latter view.]

★ ★ ★

AN adequate theory of visual perception must explain how the fleeting patterns of light upon the retinas give knowledge of surrounding objects. The problem of how the brain 'reads' reality from images is acute, because images represent directly but few, and biologically unimportant, characteristics of objects. What matters biologically are such things as whether an object is poisonous or food, hard or soft, heavy or light, sharp or blunt, friend or foe. These are not properties of images. The owner of the eye cannot eat or be eaten by its images, and yet his life depends upon interpreting them in terms of quite different characteristics of objects. It follows that eyes are of little biological value unless there is an adequate brain to interpret their images; which raises the evolutionary problem: how did the eye-brain combination arise? (cf. Gregory, 1968c [No. 53]). To read reality from images is to solve a problem: a running set of very difficult problems throughout active life. Errors are illusions. Certain situations present special difficulty, giving rise to systematic errors: can these serve as clues to how the brain generally solves the problem of what objects are represented by which images?

Illusions can occur in any of the sense modalities, and they can cross the senses. A powerful illusion crosses from the seen size of an object to its apparent weight, as judged by lifting. Small objects feel up to fifty per cent heavier than larger objects of the same scale weight. Thus weight is evidently not judged simply by the input from the arm but also by prior expectation set by the previous handling of weights. When the density is unexpectedly great or small we suffer a corresponding illusion of weight.

There are, however, illusions of quite different types. There are purely *optical* illusions, where light from the object to the eye is bent by reflection (mirrors) or by refraction (the bent-stick-in-water effect, and mirages). There are also what we may call *sensory* illusions. The

FIG. 30.1 *Spiral. When rotating anticlockwise it is seen to contract. If stopped after ten to twenty seconds viewing, a marked apparent expansion is observed. There is however no observed change in size. It seems that a specific velocity-detecting system has been adapted by the real movement.*

sense organs, the eyes, ears, touch and heat-sensitive nerve endings can all be upset, when they will transmit misleading information to the brain. They are upset by prolonged stimulation and by over-stimulation. For example, the 'waterfall effect' observed by Aristotle, is dramatically demonstrated by watching a rotating spiral (Fig. 30.1). If this is rotated on a turntable for ten or twenty seconds while the eyes are held at its centre, it will seem to contract or expand, depending on the direction of rotation. When stopped, there is a marked illusory movement in the opposite direction to the original movement. In the illusion, movement is seen but with no change of position.

Evidently a velocity detecting system has been adapted by prolonged stimulation to movement. As is well known, after-images occur after intense or prolonged stimulation of the retina by light: we see first a positive 'picture' which soon changes to a negative 'picture' which may persist for many minutes. This is due to local retinal adaptation, the brain receiving retinal signals essentially the same as for the normal image of an object but persisting beyond the physical stimulation of the retina. It is also possible for any sense organ to signal a quite wrong kind of stimulus. Pressure on the eye will send signals to the brain which are experienced as light; and electric current through the eye will produce the sensation of light, and through the ear sound. Fortunately, these sensory illusions seldom occur in normal conditions, though they are easily evoked in the laboratory.

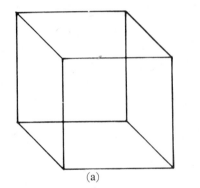
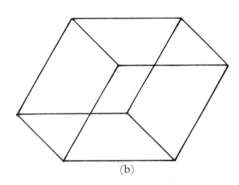

(a)   (b)

FIG. 30.2 (a) *Necker cube. This is the most famous of many depth-ambiguous figures. (When presented with background it changes in shape with each reversal, the apparent back being larger than the apparent front face.)* (b) *Necker rhomboid. This is the original form, presented by L. A. Necker in 1832.*

The types of illusions which concern us here are, however, entirely different from either optical or sensory illusions. We may call these *perceptual* illusions. They arise from misinterpretation by the brain of sensory information.

Several perceptual illusions were known to the ancient Greeks, but they have only been studied experimentally for just over a century. The first scientific description in modern times was a letter by a Swiss naturalist, L. A. Necker, to Sir David Brewster (Necker, 1832) describing how a rhomboid reverses in depth, sometimes one face appearing the nearer, sometimes another. Necker correctly noted that changes of eye fixation could induce this change in perception, but that it would occur quite spontaneously. This famous effect is generally illustrated with an isometric skeleton cube (Fig. 30.2*a*) rather than Necker's original figure (Fig. 30.2*b*). Perceptual reversals, or alternations (there can be several alternative perceptions) are not limited to vision. Repeated words, presented on an endless tape loop, give analogous auditory reversals (Warren and Gregory 1958 [No. 20]). A similar, even more striking effect, was noted by W. J. Sinsteden: that the rotating vanes of a windmill spontaneously reverse direction when it is not clear whether one is seeing the front or the back of the windmill (for references, see Boring, 1942). This effect is well shown by casting the shadow of a slowly rotating vane upon a screen, thus removing all information of which is the back and which the front. The shadow will also at times appear to expand and contract upon the plane of the screen. It is important to note that these effects are not perceptual distortions of the retinal image: they are alternative interpretations of the image, in terms of possible objects, and only one interpretation is correct.

The most puzzling visual illusions are systematic distortions of size or shape. These distortions occur in many quite simple figures; the distortions occurring in the same directions and to much the same extent in virtually all human observers and probably also in many animals. Their explanation presents a challenge which should be accepted, for a viable theory of normal perception must account for them and they could be important clues to basic perceptual processes.

The simplest distortion illusion was the first to be described: by the father of experimental psychology, Wilhelm Wundt (1832–1920), who was Hermann von Helmholtz's assistant at Heidelburg. Wundt described the 'horizontal–vertical' illusion – that a vertical line looks longer than the horizontal line of equal length. He attributed this distortion to asymmetry of the eye movement system. Although this has been invoked many times since to explain distortion illusions it must be ruled out, for the distortions occur in after-images, or in normal retinal images optically stabilized so as to remain stationary on the eye though it moves. In addition, distortions can occur in several directions at the same time, which could hardly be due to eye movements; and in any case it is difficult to see how curvature distortions could be related to eye movements. All the evidence points to the origin of the distortions being not in the eyes but in the brain.

Interest in the illusions became general upon the publication of several figures showing distortions which could produce errors in using optical instruments. This concerned physicists and astronomers a hundred years ago, when photographic and other ways of avoiding visual errors were not available. The first of the special distortion figures was the Poggendorff figure of 1860 (Fig. 30.3). This was followed by the Hering illusion (1861); its converse being devised by

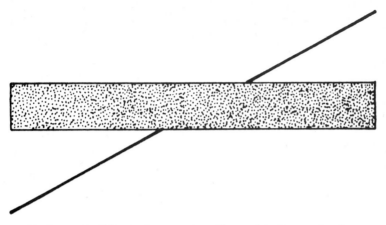

FIG. 30.3 *The Poggendorff illusion figure (1860). The straight line crossing the rectangle appears displaced.*

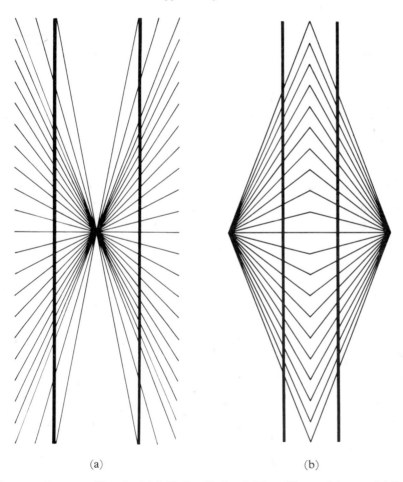

(a)   (b)

FIG. 30.4 *(same as Fig. 28.2)* (a) *Hering illusion (1861). The straight parallel lines appear bowed outwards.* (b) *Wundt's variant of the Hering illusion: the parallel lines appear bowed inwards (1896).*

Wundt much later, in 1896 (Thiéry 1896) (Fig. 30.4). The most famous illusion of all is the Müller-Lyer arrow figure (Fig. 30.5). This was devised by F. C. Müller-Lyer and was first presented in fifteen variants (Müller-Lyer, 1889). This figure is so simple, and the distortion so compelling that it was immediately accepted as the primary target for theory and experiment. All sorts of theories were advanced: Wundt's eye movement theory (in spite of its inadequacy); that the 'wings' of the arrow heads drew attention away from the ends of the central line, or 'arrow shaft', to make it expand or contract; that the heads induced a state of empathy in the observer (though the distortion seems far too constant for such an explanation), that the distortion is a special case of a supposed general principle that acute angles tend to be overestimated and obtuse angles underestimated.

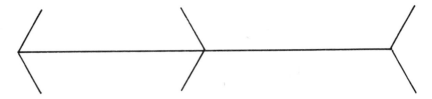

FIG. 30.5 *Müller-Lyer arrows figure (1889). The most famous illusion: the outward-going 'arrow heads' produce expansion of the 'shaft' and the inward-going heads contraction.*

This was, however, left unexplained, and it is not clear why it hould produce size changes without apparent changes of angle. All these theories had a common feature: they were attempts to explain the distortion in terms of the stimulus pattern without reference to its significance in terms of the perception of objects. There was, however, one quite different suggestion, made by A. Thiéry (1896) that the distortions are related to perspective depth features. Thiéry regarded the Müller-Lyer arrows as drawings of such objects as a saw-horse, seen in three dimensions, with the legs going away from the observer in the acute-angled figure and towards him in the obtuse-angled figure. This suggestion has seldom been considered until recently, though the 'perspective theory' was described by R. H. Woodworth in 1938: 'In the Müller-Lyer figure the obliques readily suggest perspective and if this is followed one of the vertical lines appears farther away and therefore objectively longer than the other'. This quotation brings out the immediate difficulties of developing an adequate theory along these lines, for the distortion occurs even when the perspective suggestion is not followed up, for the figure generally appears flat and yet distorted; and there is no hint given of a *modus operandi*, or brain mechanism responsible for the size changes. An adequate theory following Thiéry's suggestion that perspective is somehow important must show how distortion occurs though the figures appear flat. It should also indicate the kind of brain mechanisms responsible.

The idea that geometrical perspective – the converging of parallel lines with distance – has a bearing is at least borne out by the occurrence of these distortions in actual scenes. A simple example is the Ponzo illusion (Fig. 30.6). This is a skeleton drawing of typical perspective convergence of parallel lines with distance, as in the railway

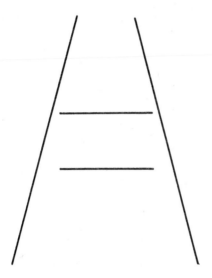

FIG. 30.6 *Ponzo figure. The upper of the parallel lines is expanded with respect to the lower.*

lines of Figure 30.7, (cf. Tausch, 1954). The upper superimposed rectangle, which would be more distant, is expanded. Similarly, the inside corner is expanded (Fig. 30.8*a*) and the outside corner shrunk (Fig. 30.8*b*) just as in the Müller-Lyer figures, which are like skeleton corners. In both cases, regions indicated by perspective as *distant* are *expanded*, while near regions are shrunk. The distortions are opposite to the normal shrinkings of the retinal image of objects with increased distance. Is this merely fortuitous, or is it a clue to the origin of the illusions? Before we come to grips with the problem of trying to develop an adequate perspective theory, it will be helpful to consider some curious features of ordinary pictures.

Pictures are the traditional material of perceptual research, but all pictures are highly artificial and present special problems to the

FIG. 30.7 *The Ponzo illusion is seen in this photograph of receding (railway) lines. Here the perspective significance of converging lines is obvious.*

perceptual brain. In a sense, all pictures are impossible: they have a double reality. They are seen both as patterns of lines, lying on a flat background and also as objects depicted in a quite different, three-dimensional, space. No actual object can be both two- and three-dimensional and yet pictures come close to it. Viewed as patterns they are seen as two-dimensional; viewed as representing objects they are seen in a quasi three-dimensional space. Pictures lying both in two and in three dimensions are paradoxical visual inputs. Pictures are also ambiguous, for the third dimension is never precisely defined. The Necker cube is an example where the depth ambiguity is so great that the brain never settles for one answer. But any perspective projection could represent an infinity of three dimensional shapes: so one would think that the perceptual system has an impossible task. Fortunately, the world of objects does not have infinite variety; there is usually a best bet, and we generally interpret our flat images more or less correctly in terms of the world of objects. The sheer difficulty of the problem of seeing the third dimension from the two dimensions of a picture – or the retinal images of normal objects – is brought out by special 'impossible pictures' and 'impossible objects', as we shall call them. They show just what happens when clearly incompatible distance information is presented to the eye. The impossible triangle (Fig. 30.9) (L. S. Penrose and R. Penrose 1958) cannot be seen as an object lying in normal three-dimensional space. It is, however, perfectly possible to make actual three dimensional objects – not mere pictures – which give the same perceptual confusion. Figure 30.10*a* shows an actual wooden object which, when viewed from one critical position, gives the same retinal image as the Penrose triangle (Fig. 30.9). It looks just as impossible – but it really exists. In fact, though one knows all about its true shape (Fig. 30.10*b*), it continues to look impossible from the critical viewing position (Fig. 30.10*a*).

Ordinary pictures are not so very different from obviously 'impossible' pictures. All pictures depicting depth are paradoxical, for we both see them as flat (which they really are) and in a kind of suggested depth which is not quite right. We are not tempted to touch objects depicted in a picture through or in front of its surface. What happens, then, if we remove the background – does the depth paradox of pictures remain?

To remove the background, in our experiments, we make the pictures luminous to glow in the dark. They are viewed with one eye in order to remove stereoscopic information that they are truly flat. They may be wire figures coated in luminous paint, or photographic transparencies back-illuminated with an electro-luminescent panel. In either case there is no visible background, so we can discover how

(a)

FIG. 30.8 (a) *The outward-going fins of the Müller-Lyer figure are seen here in flat projection of a photograph of the inside corner of a room.*

(b)

FIG. 30.8 (b) *The inward-going arrows are seen in the outside corner of the building. As in the Ponzo example, distance indicated by perspective is associated with illusory expansion.*

far the background is responsible for the depth paradox of pictures, including the illusion figures. Under these conditions the Müller-Lyer arrows generally look like true corners, according to their perspective. They generally appear indistinguishable from actual (luminous) corners. The figures are, however, not entirely stable; they sometimes reverse spontaneously in depth but generally they appear according to their perspective, and without the paradoxical depth of pictures with a background. The distortions are still present. The outward-going fins figure, looking like an inside corner, is expanded; while the in-going fins figure, looking like an outside corner, is shrunk as before – but now the paradox has disappeared.

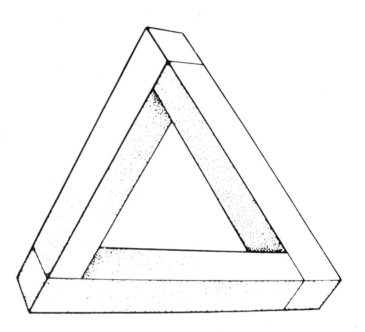

FIG. 30.9 *An impossible figure. This cannot be seen as a sensible three-dimensional figure – no appropriate 'perceptual model' is selected.*

The figures look like true corners: one can point out their depth as though they were normal three-dimensional objects.

Having removed the paradox it is possible to measure, by quite direct means, the apparent distances of any selected parts of the figures. This we do by using the two eyes to serve as a rangefinder for indicating the apparent depth of the figure as seen by one eye. The back-illuminated picture is placed behind a sheet of polaroid; one eye being prevented from seeing the picture with a crossed polarizing

(a)

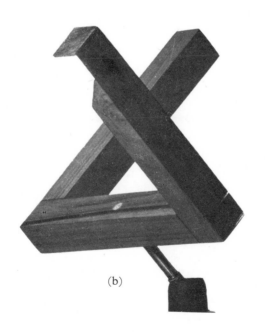

(b)

FIG. 30.10 (a) *An impossible object. From this critical viewpoint it appears impossible although it exists as a true three-dimensional structure. (b) The same object, but viewed from a non-critical position – the true structure is now evident.*

filter. Both eyes are however allowed to see one[1] or more small movable reference lights, which are optically introduced into the picture with a 45° part-reflecting mirror. The distance of these lights is given by stereoscopic vision (convergence angle of the eyes), and so by placing them at the seen distance of selected parts of the picture we can plot the visual space of the observer, in three dimensions. The apparatus is shown in Figure 30.11. Figure 30.12 shows the result of measuring depth (difference between the distance of the central line and the ends of the arrow heads) for various fin angles of the Müller-Lyer illusion figure. For comparison, the measured illusion for each angle for the same (20) subjects is plotted on the same graph. It is important to note that though the depth was measured with luminous figures, the illusion was measured (using an adjustable comparison line set to apparent equality) with the figures drawn on a normally textured background. So they appeared flat when the *illusion* was measured but as a true corner when the background was removed for measuring *depth*. This experiment shows that when the background is removed, depth very closely follows the illusion for the various fin angles. The similarity of these curves provides evidence of a remarkably close tie-up between the illusion as it occurs when depth is not seen with the depth which is seen when the background is removed. This suggests that Thiéry was essentially correct:[2] that perspective can somehow produce distortions. But what is odd is that perspective produces the distortion according to *indicated* perspective depth even when depth is not seen, because it is countermanded by the visible background.

The next step is to look for some perceptual mechanism which could produce this relation between perspective and apparent size. A candidate that should have been obvious many years ago is 'size constancy'. This was clearly described by René Descartes (1596–1650), in his *Dioptrics* of 1637.

'It is not the absolute size of images (in the eyes) that counts. Clearly they are a hundred times bigger (in area) when objects are

[1]There is no 'physical' reason why a luminous object viewed with a single eye should have any assignable distance. In fact even after-images have an apparent distance viewed in darkness (Gregory *et al.* 1959 [No. 22]). Luminous figures remain at remarkably constant apparent distance, for almost all observers, so that consistent measurements can be made with a single reference light. Presumably a fairly stable 'internal model' is called up, and this settles the apparent distance. This is true also for viewing the moon in a clear sky: it remains remarkably constant in size and distance, until near the horizon when it looks larger and nearer. Perspective and other information then seems to scale the 'model' and so change the size of the moon.

[2]Thiery's choice of a 'saw-horse' (a horizontal beam supported on legs forming triangles at each end) is a poor example for the legs are not at any specific angle, such as a right angle. He may not have seen that for perspective to serve as a depth cue, reliable assumptions about angles must be possible. The legs of a saw-horse can be at almost any angle; so it is not a good example of depth being given by perspective projection.

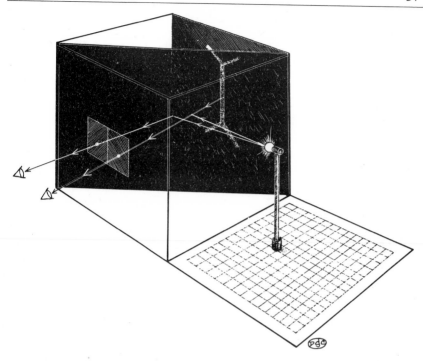

FIG. 30.11 *Pandora's Box. Apparatus for measuring subjective visual depth in pictures. The picture (in this case, an illusion figure) is back-illuminated with an electro-lumines-cent panel, to avoid background texture. In front of the picture there is a sheet of polaroid and in front of the eyes two sheets of polaroid at right angles; thus the picture can be seen by only one eye. The image of the reference lamp is reflected off a sheet of neutral density Perspex lying diagonally across the box and can be seen with both eyes. The real distance of the lamp, seen binocularly, is matched with the apparent distance of the picture, seen monocularly; and the positions are marked on the graph paper.*

very close than when they are ten times further away; but they do not make us see the objects a hundred times bigger; on the contrary, they seem almost the same size, at any rate as we are not deceived by too great a distance.'

We know from many experiments that Descartes is quite correct. But what happens when distance information, such as perspective, is present when there is no actual difference in distance to shrink the image in the eye? Could it be that perspective presented on a flat plane sets the brain's compensation for the normal shrinking of the images with distance – though in pictures there is no shrinking to compensate? If this happened, illusions *must* be given by perspective. We would then have the start of a reasonable theory of distortion illusions. Features indicated as distant would be expanded; which is just what we find, at least for the Müller-Lyer and the Ponzo figures.

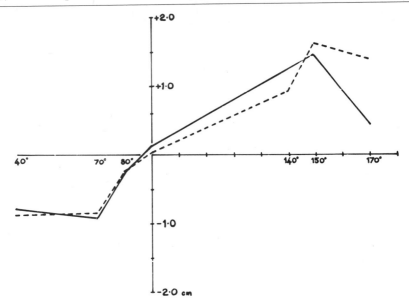

FIG. 30.12 *Müller-Lyer illusion and apparent depth, for various fin angles. The x axis represents the angle between the shaft and fins in the Müller-Lyer figure. (With fins at 90° the figure is a capital I, giving zero illusion and zero depth.) For angles greater than 90° the illusion is positive, for smaller angles negative. The illusion is measured by adjusting a line to the same apparent length for each angle of the illusion figure. The illusion is shown in the dotted line. It was presented on a normally textured background.*

The same observers were used to measure apparent depth for the same angles; the illusion being presented without background texture and monocularly to avoid competing depth information. The results in both cases are the means of three readings for each of twenty observers in all conditions. The figure was ten centimetres in length viewed from half a metre. Depth was measured with the 'Pandora's Box' technique, the comparison light-being set to the apparent distance of the shaft and the ends of the fins. Depth shown in the solid line.

The correlation between apparent depth and the length distortion is better than 0·9 (experiment by R. L. Gregory and Linda Townes, at M.I.T.).

It is likely that this approach to the problem was not developed until recently because although size constancy was very well known, it has always been assumed that it follows apparent distance in all circumstances. Also, it has not been sufficiently realized how very odd pictures are as visual inputs; but they are highly atypical and should be studied as a very special case, being both paradoxical and ambiguous.

'Size constancy' is traditionally identified with Emmert's Law, as illustrated by the apparent size of after-images. An after-image (preferably from an electronic flash) is 'projected' upon screens or walls lying at various distances. The after-image will appear almost twice as large with each doubling of distance, though the size of the retinal image from the flash of course remains constant. It is important to note, however, that there *is* a change in retinal stimulation for each wall or screen lying at a different distance, for *their* images will be different. It is therefore possible that Emmert's Law is due merely to the relative areas covered by the after-image and the screen, and not to visual information of distance changing the size of the after-image by internal scaling. This presents an experimental problem, which it is vital to solve.

There is a simple solution. We can use the ambiguous depth phenomenon of the Necker cube to establish whether Emmert's Law is due to central scaling by the brain, or is merely an effect of relative areas of stimulation of the retina by after-image and background. When we see a Necker cube drawn on paper reverse in depth, there is no appreciable size change. When presented on a textured background it lies in the paradoxical depth of all pictures with backgrounds. It does not change in size when it reverses in this quasi-depth. What happens, though, if we remove the background? The effect is dramatic, and entirely repeatable: whichever face appears most *distant* always appears the *larger*. The use of depth-ambiguous figures allows us to distinguish between what happens as a result of central brain size scaling mechanisms from what happens when the pattern of stimulation of the retina is changed. The answer is that at least part of 'size constancy', and of Emmert's Law, is due to a central size scaling mechanism following apparent distance, though the retinal stimulation is unchanged. But this is not the whole story.

Size is evidently set in two ways. (1) It can be set purely by apparent distance, but (2) it can also be set directly by visual depth features, such as perspective, even though depth is not seen because it is countermanded by the competing depth information of a visible background. When atypical depth features are present, size scaling is set inappropriately; to give a corresponding distortion illusion [cf. No. 27].

The size scaling set directly by depth features (giving systematic distortions when set inappropriately) we may call 'depth cue scaling'. It is remarkably consistent, and independent of the observer's perceptual 'set'. The other system is very different, being but indirectly related to the prevailing retinal information. It is evidently linked to the interpretation of the retinal image in terms of what object it represents. When it appears as a different object, the scaling changes at once to suit the alternative object. If we regard the seeing of an object as a hypothesis suggested (but never strictly proved) by the image, then we may call this system 'depth hypothesis scaling'. It changes with each change of hypothesis of what object is represented by the image. When the hypothesis is wrong we have an illusion, which may be dramatic.

We started by pointing out that visual perception must involve 'reading' from retinal images characteristics of objects not represented directly by the images in the eyes. Non-visual characteristics must already have been associated, by individual learning or through heredity, for objects to be recognized from their images. Illusions associated with misplaced size scaling provide evidence that features are selected for scaling according to early perceptual experience of the individual. This is suggested by anthropological data (Segall *et al.* 1966) and perhaps from the almost total absence of these illusions found in a case of adult recovery from infant blindness (Gregory and Wallace 1963)[1] [No. 3, p. 117].

Perception seems, then, to be a matter of 'looking up' stored information of objects, and how they behave in various situations. Such systems have great advantages.

Systems which control their output directly from currently available input information have serious limitations. In biological terms, these would be essentially reflex systems. Some of the advantages of using input information to select stored data for controlling behaviour, in situations which are not unique to the system, are as follows:

1. In typical situations they can achieve high performance with limited information transmission rate. It is estimated that human transmission rate is only about 15 bits/second (Miller, Bruner and Postman, 1954). They gain results because perception of objects – which are redundant – requires identification of only certain key features of each object.

---

[1] It seems possible that the curvature distortions given by radiating background lines (e.g. Hering's and Wundt's illusions, Fig. 30.4) should be attributed to mis-scaling from the spherical perspective of the images on the hemispherical surface of the retina to the effective linear perspective of perception. The distortions are in the right direction for such an interpretation, but precise experiments remain to be completed.

Errors in the prevailing model can be established independently of the standard distortion illusions, by introducing systematic movement. Most simply, a point light source is used to cast a shadow of a slowly rotating (1 rev./min.) skeleton object. The projected shadow, giving a two-dimensional projection of a rotating three-dimensional object, is observed. It is found that simple familiar objects will generally be correctly identified, as they rotate. The projections of unfamiliar objects, and especially random or irregular shapes will, however, continually change, the angles and lengths of lines of the projection changing as the object rotates, often appearing different each time the object comes round to the same position. By adding stereoscopic information (using a pair of horizontally separated point sources, cross-polarized to the eyes and a silver or ground-glass screen to prevent depolarization) we find that, on this criterion, the correct model is given more readily for unfamiliar or irregular figures: but stereoscopic information does *not* invariably select the correct model (Gregory, 1964b [No. 21]). We also use shadow projections for measuring perceptual constancy, especially during movement, as this allows null measures (Anstis, Shopland and Gregory, 1961 [No. 23]).

2. They are essentially predictive. In typical circumstances, reaction-time is cut to zero.

3. They can continue to function in the temporary absence of input; this increases reliability and allows trial selection of alternative inputs.

4. They can function appropriately to object-characteristics which are not signalled directly to the sensory system. This is generally true of vision, for the image is trivial unless used to 'read' non-optical characteristics of objects.

5. They give effective gain in signal/noise ratio, since not all aspects of the model have to be separately selected on the available data, when the model has redundancy. Provided the model is appropriate, very little input information can serve to give adequate perception and control.

There is, however, one disadvantage of 'internal model' look-up systems, which appears inevitably when the selected stored data are out of date or otherwise inappropriate. We may with some confidence attribute perceptual illusions to selection of an inappropriate model, or to mis-scaling of the most appropriate available model.

Selecting and scaling of models, and the illusions

The models must, to be reasonably economical, represent average or typical situations. There could hardly be a separate stored model for every position and orientation an object might occupy in surrounding space. It would be economical to store typical characteristics of objects and use current information to adjust the selected model to fit the prevailing situation. If this idea is correct, we can understand the nature of our 'depth cue' scaling – and why perspective features presented on a flat plane give the observed distortions. Inappropriate depth cues will scale the model inappropriately; to give a corresponding size distortion. This, I suggest, is the origin of the distortion illusions. They occur whenever a model is inappropriately scaled.

There will also be errors, possibly gross errors, when a wrong model is selected – mistaking an object for something very different, confusing a shadow with an object, seeing 'faces-in-the-fire', or even flying saucers. Each model seems to have a typical size associated with it, so mis-selection can appear as a size error. This occurs in the case of the luminous cubes, which change shape with each reversal though the sensory input is unchanged.

If this general account of perception as a 'look-up' system is correct, we should expect illusions to occur in any effective perceptual system faced with the same kind of problems. The illusions, on this theory, are not due to contingent limitations of the brain, but result from the necessarily imperfect solution adopted to the problem of reading from images information not directly present in the image. In considering the significance of experimental data and phenomena for understanding brain function, it seems very important to distinguish between effects which depend on the particular, contingent, characteristics of the brain and the much more general characteristics of any conceivable system faced with the same kinds of problem. Non-contingent characteristics can be regarded in terms of logical and engineering principles, and engineering criteria of efficiency can be employed (cf. Gregory, 1962*a* [No. 49]) to help decide between possible systems.

I have distinguished between: (*a*) selecting models according to sensory information, and (*b*) size-scaling models to fit the orientation and distance of external objects. I have also suggested that errors in either selecting or scaling give corresponding illusions. These systematic illusions are regarded as non-contingent, resulting from the basic limitations of the system adopted – probably the best available – by brains to solve the perceptual problem of reading reality from images. We should thus expect to find similar illusions in efficiently designed 'seeing machines' (Gregory 1967*c*).

Now let us consider an experimental situation designed to tell us something about the 'engineering' nature of brain models. We make use of the size/weight illusion, mentioned above, but we look for a change in discrimination as a function of scale distortion of weight.

Consider the following paradigm experiment. We have two sets of weights, such as tins filled with lead shot. Each set consists of say seven tins all of a certain size, while the other set has seven tins each of which is, say, twice the volume of the first set. Each set has a tin of weight, in grams, 85, 90, 95, 100, 105, 110, 115. The 100 gm. weight in each set is the standard, and the task is to compare the other weights in the same set with this standard, and try to distinguish them as heavier or lighter. (The tins are fitted with the same-sized handles for lifting, to keep the touch inputs constant except for weight). Is discrimination the same for the set of *apparently* heavier weights, which are in fact the same weights? The answer is that discrimination is *worse* for weights either apparently *heavier* or *lighter* than weights having a specific gravity of about one (Ross and Gregory 1970 [No. 13]). Why should this be so?

Suppose that sensory data are compared with the current internal model – as they must be to be useful. Now if the data are not only *compared* with it, but *balanced against it,* then we derive further advantages of employing internal models. We then have systems like

Wheatstone bridges, and these have useful properties. Bridge circuits are especially good (*a*) over a very large input intensity range and (*b*) with components subject to drift. Now it is striking how large an intensity range sensory systems cover ($1:10^5$ or even $1:10^6$), and the biological components are subject to far more drift than would be tolerated by engineers in our technology confronted with similar problems. Balanced bridge circuits seem a good engineering choice in the biological situation.

Consider a Wheatstone bridge in which the input signals provide one arm and the prevailing internal model the opposed arms against which the inputs are balanced. Now the internal arms are parts of the model – and will be set inappropriately in a scale-distortion illusion. In the size/weight illusion, visual information may be supposed to set a weight arm incorrectly. An engineer's bridge will give impaired discrimination either when the bridge is not balanced or when the ratio arms are not equal. The biological system gives just what a practical engineer's bridge would give – loss of discrimination associated with an error in balancing the bridge. This is perhaps some evidence that internal models form arms of bridge circuits. (There is no evidence for suggesting whether scale-distortion illusions result from unequal ratio arms or from imbalance of the supposed bridges. We propose to do further work, experimental and theoretical, to clear up this point).

Are brain models digital or analogue? It is possible to make an informed guess as to which system is adopted by the brain; in terms of speed of operation, types of errors and other characteristics typical of analogue or digital engineering systems (cf. Gregory, 1953*b* [No. 47]). The engineering distinction arises from the fact that in practice analogue systems work continuously but digital systems work in precisely defined discrete steps. This difference is immensely important to the kinds of circuits or mechanical systems used in practical computers. Discontinuous systems have higher reliability in the presence of 'noise' disturbance while analogue devices can have faster data transmission rates, though their precision is limited to around 0.1%. There is no limit in principle to the number of significant figures obtainable from a digital computer, if it has space enough and time.

Because of the clear engineering distinction between continuous and discontinuous systems, there is a temptation to define analogue in terms of continuous and digital in terms of discontinuous. But this will not do. We can imagine click stops fitted to a slide rule; this would make it discontinuous, but it would still be an analogue device. We must seek some deeper distinction.

The point is that both 'analogue' and 'digital' systems represent things by their internal states. The essential difference between them is not *how* they represent things, but rather in *what* they represent. The distinction is between representing events *directly* by the states of the system, and representing *symbolic accounts* of real (or hypothetical) events. Real events always occur in a continuum, but symbolic systems are always discontinuous. The continuous/discontinuous computer distinction reflects, we may suggest, this difference between representing the world of objects directly and representing symbolic systems. (Even the continuous functions of differential calculus have to be handled as though they were discretely stepped).

A continuous computing device can work without going through the steps of an analytical or mathematical procedure. A digital device, on the other hand, has to work through the steps of an appropriate mathematical or logical system. This means that continuous computers functioning directly from input variables necessarily lack power of analysis, but they can work as fast as the changes in their inputs – and so are ideal for real-time computing systems, provided high accuracy is not required. The perceptual brain must work in real time, and it does not need the accuracy or the analytical power of a digital system, following the symbolic steps of a mathematical treatment of the situation.

It is most implausible to suppose that the brain of a child contains mathematical analyses of physical situations. When a child builds a house of toy bricks, balancing them to make walls and towers, we cannot suppose that the structural problems are solved by employing analytical mathematical techniques, involving concepts such as centre of gravity and coefficient of friction of masses. It is far better to make the lesser claim for children and animals: that they behave appropriately to objects by using analogues of sensed object-properties, without involving mathematical analyses of the properties of objects and their interactions. Perceptual learning surely cannot require the learning of mathematics. It is far more plausible to suppose that it involves the building of quite simple analogues of relevant properties of objects: relevant so far as they concern the behaviour of the animal or the child.

This and other considerations force us to question the traditional distinction between 'analogue' and 'digital'. The discontinuous/continuous distinction will not serve. It is a matter of distinguishing between computing systems which solve problems by going through the steps of a formal argument, or mathematical analysis, from systems which solve problems without 'knowing' logic or mathematics – by following the input variables and reading off solutions with a look-up system of internal functions. We need a new terminology for this distinction.

To name the first type of computer, we can go back to Charles Babbage's Analytical Engine, of about 1840. Systems employing formal or mathematical analysis we may call '*Analytical computers*'. In practice these will be discontinuous, the steps representing the steps of the analytical argument, or mathematics. But this is not its defining characteristic, which is that it works by following an analysis of the prevailing problem or situation. A convenient term for computers which arrive at solutions by look-up systems of internal syntheses of past data – 'models' reflecting aspects of reality – is more difficult to find. We propose the term: '*Synthetical computers*'. It is hoped that these terms – analytical and synthetical computers – may be helpful.

It is reasonable to suppose that the invention of logic and mathematics has conferred much of the power humans have compared with other animals for many kinds of problem solving. We have *synthetical* brains which use, with the aid of explicit symbols, *analytical* techniques. It is interesting that even the most advanced analytical techniques are useless for some physical problems – predicting the weather, the tides, economic trends, for example – and then we have to rely on inductively derived models and crude synthetical techniques. Almost always simplifications and corrections have to be used when analytical techniques are applied to the real world; so it is not entirely surprising that synthetical brains are so successful. Indeed, we do not know how to programme an analytical computer to process optical information for performing tasks that would be simple for a child. Surely the child does not do it this way.

The brain must work in real time, but it need not work according to analytical descriptions of the physical world, if all it requires are quite crude synthetical analogues of input–output functions, selected by distinguishing features of objects. The perceptual brain reflects the redundancy of the external world: when it does so correctly we see aspects of reality without illusion. A wrong model – or the right model wrongly scaled – gives corresponding illusions. These can serve as clues to the way sensory information is handled by the brain, to give perception and behaviour.

31 *Illusion and depth measurements in right-angular and parallel line figures*

[I end this treatment of illusions with a very general question: Do these illusion figures directly upset brain mechanisms, such as orientation or feature detectors, or do they occur as a result of misplaced strategies? I have argued throughout that the systematic distortions arise especially when generally useful and reliable assumptions, adopted for interpreting two dimensional retinal images in terms of the three dimensional world of objects, are inappropriate – and so are systematically misleading. More specifically, we have argued that it is perspective convergence of parallel lines which is the main assumption which, when inappropriate, as when the lines are presented on a flat plane, leads to distortion. Perspective is usually associated with non-right-angles and non-parallel lines. It is however sometimes suggested that it is angles *per se* which upset the brain – not the significance they may have for indicating distance. This we may call a 'hardware' theory: it can be couched in physiological concepts, without any reference to the brain's strategies for handling sensory data in terms of the world of objects. How can we decide between these conceptually very different ways of looking at illusions? Fortunately there are indicators of distance present even in simple line figures which do not involve angles other than right-angles, or lines which are not parallel. Further, some of these figures are well-established distortion illusions. To suppose that the angles of, say, the Müller-Lyer illusion upset orientation detectors to produce shifts of the lines of the figure is perhaps in any case implausible; but it is impossible to suppose that this kind of thing occurs with right-angles or parallel lines, since the stimulation is symmetrical.

Mrs Carolyn Millar (née Cumming), who was my assistant from 1966 to 1970, has measured depth in the horizontal/vertical illusion, and also in a rotated L-figure. The experimental details and results follow. An improved form of the depth measuring apparatus (Fig. 31.1, 31.2) was used for measuring depth in the horizontal/vertical illusion,

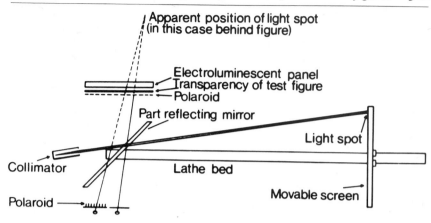

FIG. 31.1 *Diagram of research version of Pandora's Box. The reference light is projected by a collimator – placed at equal distance as the eye from the figure – on to a moving screen. This avoids lateral or vertical shift with change in distance.*

FIG. 31.2 *Photograph of research version of Pandora's Box.*

the rotated L-figure, and for a new figure consisting of a pair of vertical parallel lines one higher than the other. An illusion was predicted for this and confirmed, with the predicted depth correlation.]

★   ★   ★

THE HORIZONTAL/VERTICAL ILLUSION

THIS well-known illusion figure is simply a horizontal line with a vertical line dropping to bisect the horizontal. The vertical appears longer than the horizontal, though both are in fact of equal length. This illusion is of particular interest to us, because on our theory it does have a plausible interpretation although it has no angles other than right angles, and so could hardly be explained in terms of lateral inhibition effects or confusion of Hubel and Wiesel-type angle detectors. That it could be regarded and perhaps be treated by the visual system as a perspective figure, was pointed out by R. H. Woodworth (1938). The vertical line might be taken as representing an object lying along the ground, and so perhaps very much longer than an object represented by the horizontal line. There are in fact no objects as tall as the length of horizontal objects, (roads, rivers, etc.) and so, on a probability basis, a vertical line is likely to represent a greater length than a horizontal line. If this probability were accepted by the cognitive system, we could include this figure into our general account. Constancy is supposed to be given by active size-scaling processes in the visual system, the scaling generally being appropriate to familiar classes of objects.

Since the depth significance of a vertical line is ill-defined, by comparison with the explicit perspective significance of converging lines (Ponzo illusion) and corners (Müller-Lyer illusion), we should expect greater variance and perhaps a smaller over-all distortion. Both these expectations appear to be fulfilled in our results. Further, we should expect a smaller illusion if the vertical is placed not at the centre of the horizontal, but near or at one end of it: this also is the case. Finger and Spelt (1947) and Kunnapas (1955) have found a distortion of 8–10% for the inverted T, and only 3–5% for the L form.

In addition to investigating apparent depth in the T and L forms of the illusion, we also measured the apparent distances of two vertical lines of equal length; one line being *above* the other. One reason for adopting this display was to give our subjects a very simple figure for testing the depth measuring technique; but this figure is of special interest for the enquiry, for generally a *raised* vertical line would represent a more *distant* object. We would thus predict a new, and otherwise surprising, illusion from our theory – that the raised line should appear long (though presented on a textured background), and more distant (when presented with no visible background) than the lower line of equal length. These effects would seem difficult to explain on other theories, without invoking quite arbitrary assumptions.

Method

Subjects Twenty undergraduates, 11 female and 9 male, were used as *S*s. All *S*s did both parts of the experiment; half of them were randomly assigned to do the illusion measurement first and the other half did the depth measurements first.

Measurement of the illusion

Apparatus The electro-luminescent panel in the depth measuring apparatus (p. 381) was also used to display the illusion figures. The *S* sat facing the panel, half a metre from it, with the polaroid filters removed so that he saw the illusion figures with both eyes.

The illusion figures were etched out of an opaque plastic sheet, 120 mm × 180 mm, leaving a sharp outline of the figure on the transparent backing of the sheet. The horizontals in the inverted T (⊥) and L (L) were 50 mm long and the verticals were etched 80 mm long and reduced as required by masking. In the vertical bars figure, the left vertical line, which was the variable, was 80 mm (reduced by masking) and the right vertical (the standard) was 50 mm. The width of all lines was 3 mm. The figures subtended an angle of 5° 40' at the eye.

The figures were slotted into a steel plate which stood vertically in front of the electro-luminescent panel and was held on to it magnetically. The figures then appeared as luminous, but there was enough ambient light in the room for them to be seen as clearly on the background of the opaque plastic sheet, whose texture was similar to that of paper. Grooves in the sides of the steel mounting plate held a masking sheet which the experimenter, *E*, could move up and down over the figure to mask off lengths of the vertical line. A millimetre scale was fixed at one side of the plate so that the length of line masked off could be read. The scale was hinged so that it flapped back out of sight of *S* while he was making his judgements.

Procedure The order of presentation of the three figures was randomized.

For the ⊥ and ∟ figures, the *S*'s instructions were that the *E* would
vary the length of the vertical line, and the *S* was to judge when it
appeared to be the same length as the horizontal line. For the displaced verticals figure, *S* was told that the vertical on the left would be
varied in length and he was to judge when it was the same length as
the right hand line.

E began with the vertical either much longer (2 runs) or shorter
(2 runs) than the horizontal and then decreased or increased the
length slowly and continuously until *S* made the judgment of
'equal' by telling *E* to stop. *S* then closed his eyes while the scale was
read. Four judgements were made in this way for each of the three
figures.

Measurement of apparent depth

Three figures were made in the same way as for the illusion figures.
The vertical and horizontal lines were both 50 mm long and 3 mm
thick for the ⊥ and ∟ figures. The two displaced verticals were also
50 mm and 3 mm, and the upward displacement of one was 15 mm
from the base of the other.

The figures were viewed by the subjects at a distance of half a
metre, with cross-polarization to the left eye so that the figures were
seen only by the right eye.

The room was in darkness, and the panel brightness was set such
that the figure was only just clearly visible. Under these conditions,
the *S* could not see the background texture of the figures at all – they
appeared luminous against blackness.

Procedure The stereoscopically viewed light spot was introduced
into the ⊥ and ∟ figures at one of three points; (i) just beside the
top of the vertical (1 mm to the right of it); (ii) just above the end of the
right hand horizontal, or (iii) inside the right hand corner of the
vertical-horizontal intersection. For the | | figure, the spot was placed
beside the top of each line in turn, (1 mm to the right of each). The
order of presentation of the positions was randomized in each case.

At the start of the session, the *S* was shown the light spot moving
in depth, as it was driven by the motor, and they practised controlling
it, being instructed to move the reference spot until it appeared to be
in the same plane as the part of the figure in which it was positioned.
There was no time limit. Four judgements were made. After each
judgement, *E* switched off the panel illumination, noted the distance

reading on the counter, and then reset the position of the reference to a variable position either clearly nearer than or further than the display. Two consecutive trials were started from each starting position.

Results For each *S*, the means were calculated for the four *length* judgements of the first two figures and the four *depth* judgements for each point in these figures.

The size of the measured depth (difference between the measured distances of the top of the vertical and the end of the horizontal, without regard to its direction) was found for each *S*, and this was correlated, using Spearman's Rho, with the size of the illusion shown by that *S*.

TABLE 31.1
LENGTH DISTORTIONS FOR HORIZONTAL/VERTICAL ILLUSIONS (mm.)

Figures	a b / c d	e f g
Mean error (in mm)	(ab–cd) 3·79	(ef–fg) 1·64
% distortion	7·6	3·3
S.D.	3·5	2·3
No. of *S* showing illusion (N = 20)	18 — 20	17 — 20

TABLE 31.2
APPARENT DISTANCE OF SELECTED POINTS IN HORIZONTAL/VERTICAL ILLUSIONS (mm.)

.A / .B .C	A	B	C
	501·3	500·1	550·5
S.D.	9·3	14·8	8·0
.D / .E .F	D	E	F
	507·9	499·6	501·7
S.D.	17·2	12.4	9·3

Viewing distance of figure = 500 mm.

TABLE 31.3

MEASURES OF DEPTH IRRESPECTIVE OF SIGN, AND NUMBERS OF SUBJECTS ADOPTING EACH DEPTH SIGN FOR HORIZONTAL/VERTICAL FIGURES

Figures	Depths irrespective of sign (mm)		Depth signs: no. of S's for each	
	Means	Medians	A near	A distant
⌐.A .B .C	8·5	6·3	10	10
			D near	D distant
⌐.D .E .F	15·7	10·5	7	13

Spearman's Rho correlations Correlation of the size of the illusion with the apparent distance (depth) between the vertical and the horizontal lines of the ⊥ and ∟ figures, and between the two verticals for the | | figure, with the prediction that any correlation would be in a positive direction.

⊥ rho $= +0·4$ Significant at the 5% level, 1 tailed
∟ rho $= +0·1$ Not significant
| | rho $= +0·4$ Significant at the 5% level, 1 tailed

Conclusion

In the inverted T form of the horizontal-vertical illusion, a 7·6% illusion was found which was significantly positively correlated, $p > 0·05$, with the apparent distance difference found between the ends of the horizontal and the vertical lines.

The *direction* of the depth was virtually equally distributed between those Ss who saw the top of the vertical as being further away than the end of the horizontal, and those who saw the top of the vertical as being nearer. With regard to the depth of the horizontal and vertical intersection, exactly half the Ss saw this as nearer to them than the top of the vertical and half saw it as further; i.e. the vertical line appeared as tilted in depth either towards or away from the S.

This evidence supports the notion that the vertical line of the figure is taken as representing a foreshortened view of a line tilted in the vertical plane. The direction of tilt from the horizontal is ambiguous in the absence of defining cues from perspective if it could equally well correspond to 'ground' or 'sky'. The addition of further information, given by a line drawn perpendicular to the vertical and parallel to the horizontal – $\perp$, eliminates the illusion, and fixes the depth of the top and bottom of the vertical line at the same depth as the horizontal. We have shown this in a previous experiment (with the Müller-Lyer illusion, when the angles of the fins are 90°, which exactly corresponds to the $\perp$ figure) when we found no depth and no illusion.

Our results agree with those of Finger and Spelt (1947) and Kunnapas (1955) in showing that the L version of the vertical-horizontal illusion is considerably smaller than the inverted T. The illusion was $3\cdot3\%$, and the range between Ss was small, so it is perhaps not surprising that in this figure no significant correlation was found between individual S's size of illusion and apparent depth. The variance of the judgements of depth at the tip of the vertical was particularly high compared with the same position in the inverted T figure. This could be because the addition of the other horizontal component in the latter figure had some effect in reducing uncertainty about the range of possible depth positions of the vertical line in space.

The figure consisting of two vertical displaced lines is very interesting in showing a consistent illusion of over-estimation of the upwardly displaced line, averaging $6\cdot2\%$ and found in nineteen out of twenty subjects. This is nearly as large as the inverted T form of the horizontal-vertical illusion, but has not been reported in the literature as far as we know. Further, the size of the illusion is positively correlated ($p < \cdot05$) with the apparent distance between the two vertical lines. This depth was found to occur in either direction equally; 50% of Ss saw the upwardly displaced line as nearer, and 50% saw it as further away than the other line. This does not predict which of the lines would be over-estimated in length in the illusion. For this it seems that we would need to know more about what effect different amounts of upward displacement of one line have on the illusion, and whether this affects the apparent tilt of the lines, which was not measured in this experiment. The figure is useful in suggesting that an illusion can be produced by depth cues given only by the position in space relative to an assumed horizon of the components, in the absence of directional perspective features. It would be of interest to follow up how different apparent viewpoints affect an illusion like the 'displaced verticals'.

CORRELATION BETWEEN DISTORTION AND APPARENT DEPTH IN A ROTATED L-FIGURE

Avery and Day (1969) measured distortion encountered in the L-figure for various angles of rotation of the figure. They measured the distortion for each 15° of rotation, from 0° to 90°, by setting the originally vertical line to apparent equality with the other (originally horizontal) line of the L.

We had measured the apparent depth-tilt of a single line presented with various orientations from vertical (MRC Progress Report, 1968), and so we have now correlated our depth measures with Avery and Day's illusion-distortion measures, for each 15° rotation. The result is the extremely high positive correlation of 0·998.

The figures are as follows:

TABLE 31.4

Orientation to vertical	0°	15°	30°	45°	60°	75°	90°	
Length distortion, mm	2·4	1·2	−0·5	−1·9	−3·3	−4·5	−5·2	N = 98
Difference in distance mm	7·0	4·0	−0·5	−4·0	−9·0	−10·0	−10·0	N = 36

The sign change takes place at about 30° for both the illusion, measured by Avery and Day, and our measures of apparent depth of a line, for the various orientations.

Conclusion

Our previous data on figures having marked perspective features, (Müller-Lyer, Ponzo, etc.) showed correlations of the order of 0·9 or more between linear distortion and apparent depth. It remains possible that this should not be interpreted as evidence of a deep connection between depth and linear scale as our theory suggests, but rather that certain angles upset the primary shape detecting systems, and it is these angles occurring in perspective figures which produce the distortions, rather than their depth significance.

The fact that we obtain significant (though lower) correlations with figures containing only right angles or parallel lines seems to be good evidence against this interpretation; and in favour of the supposed tie-up between depth features and linear size scaling. The reduction in the correlation co-efficient in these conditions is hardly surprising, for a vertical or raised line must, at best, be a highly ambiguous cue to depth and so we should expect relatively large variances in these depth measurements. What is remarkable is to find a significant correlation in conditions which are highly 'reduced' for depth cues and, to the best of our knowledge, contain no features which could directly upset orientation or line detectors.

32 *The curious eye of* Copilia

[We now take up a quite different topic, a topic concerned with the early evolution of vision.

The nineteenth-century zoologist Exner reported in 1891 the structure of a copepod living in the bay of Naples, having what turned out to be a most curious eye – possibly a single channel scanning eye, like a simple mechanical television camera, feeding information of spatial structure down a single neural channel in time. Professor J. Z. Young pointed out to me that several compound eyes – especially the eye of *Daphnia* – are in the kind of 'continual lively motion' reported by Exner for *Copilia*. So, in short, we decided upon an expedition. This consisted, apart from myself, of Helen Ross and Neville Moray, who though a psychologist (at that time at Sheffield, now in Canada) had a background in zoology.

We had no drawings to go on (though in fact there are early drawings of *Copilia*) and so we did not know just what to expect. We examined a gallon of water a day, drop by drop, with three microscopes until, though fascinated by what we did see, we began to despair of finding *Copilia*. Then suddenly there she was! Incredibly beautiful: perfectly transparent – so no veil hid the secrets of her eyes.

This brief investigation led to five years of work, still to be described, on compound eyes of varying complexity and characteristics. This is the work of my students, Stephen Young (now a lecturer in zoology at Imperial College) and Tony Downing who is my colleague. They have developed techniques for studying the vision and behaviour of these creatures. We went on a second expedition in the summer of 1972 – and found *Copilia* even more fascinating as we came to know her better.]

★   ★   ★

EXNER (1891) described the visual apparatus of the copepod *Copilia*, which he examined at Naples in the 1880s. Exner's

390

account is discussed by Wilkie (1953), which directed our attention to this eye.

According to Exner, each of the lateral eyes of *Copilia* has a pair of lenses. The anterior lenses are large, and exceptionally widely separated. The posterior lens of each eye lies a great distance behind the anterior lens – half-way along the extraordinarily transparent body of the animal – so that it is not at first obvious that it has any connection with the eye. The most striking feature reported by Exner is that this second posterior lens was in continual and lively motion, apparently moving across the image plane of the anterior lens. From his description, it appears that there is no retina but rather a single functional receptor unit, transmitting its information to the central brain down a single pathway.

With what we now know about transmitting spatial information by conversion into a time-series by scanning, as in television, it seemed possible that Exner was describing an organism the eye of which works on a principle now very familiar to the engineer. We decided to try to find and examine this animal. This was made possible through the kindness and enthusiasm of Prof. J. Z. Young, and the generous co-operation of the Director and Staff of the Stazione Zoologica di Napoli.

The animals were collected from hauls made at a depth of about 200 m in the Bay of Naples. We succeeded in finding 9 living specimens of *Copilia*, in the course of examining some 14 plankton hauls. Of the nine, eight were female and one male.

Exner's description we found to be accurate with regard to the female specimens, the males being very different. Using high-quality optical microscopes (bright-ground, dark-ground and phase contrast Leitz equipment) we found that the internal structure, muscles, ligaments and the nervous system could easily be observed in the living unstained specimen. In particular, the oscillatory movement of the posterior lens and receptor, as reported by Exner, was readily observable.

The following remarks apply only to the female.

Copilia quadrata is about 3 mm in total length including the long tail; about 1 mm in width, and about 1 mm in depth through the maximum thickness of the body. The diameter of the anterior lens is about 0·15 mm. The posterior lens is situated about 0·65 mm behind the first, the two being joined by a delicate cone-shaped membrane. The posterior lens, lying deep in the animal, is clearly seen in Fig. 32.1, which shows the whole of the body but not the tail. The lens is attached to a heavily pigmented bow-shaped, orange-coloured structure which contains the photosensitive elements. The

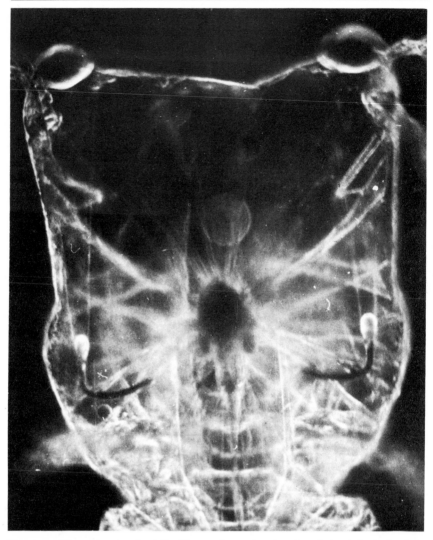

FIG. 32.1 *Photomicrograph of* Copilia quadrata *showing the whole of the body, from above, but not the tail. The anterior lenses are seen somewhat out of focus; the posterior lenses and the opaque pigment (orange) of the photoreceptors are seen in sharp focus. These 'scan', apparently across the image planes of the anterior lenses. The specimen is living and unstained.*

optic nerve is clearly seen in the living animal leaving the medial side of this bow-shaped structure, passing thence to the supracesophageal ganglion. It seems that the whole structure is essentially the same as a single ommatidium of a conventional compound eye, except that the distance between the corneal lens and the crystalline cone is vastly increased. The detailed structure of the 'rhabdom' of this 'ommati-

dium' has been described by Vaissière (1961), whose observations
both with optical and electron microscopy show the microstructure

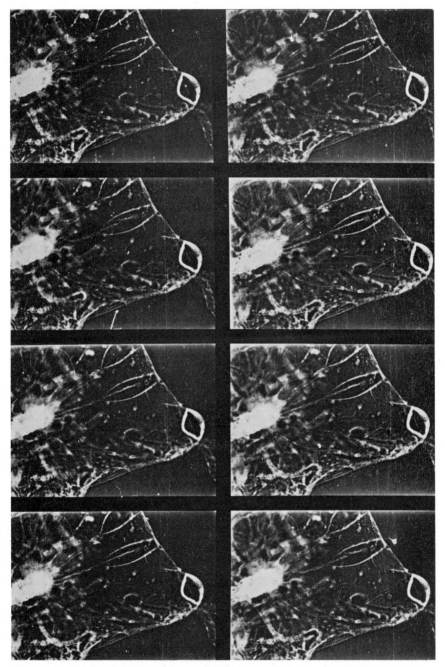

FIG. 32.2 *A series of eight consecutive ciné-frames of the living animal, during one scan. Photographed at 16 frames/sec.*

to be very similar to the conventional compound eye. There seem to be the usual cluster of receptor cells, generally believed to function as a single unit.

The anterior ('corneal') lens is rigidly fixed in the strong transparent carapace of the animal. The posterior lens ('the crystalline cone') is suspended in a dynamic system of ligaments and muscles which produce movements of the crystalline cone and its attached photoreceptor across what we assume to be the image plane of the corneal lens, but we were unable to get direct optical evidence for this. The oscillatory movement is 'sawtooth' in form, the receptors moving rapidly towards each other, separating comparatively slowly. The resting state (particularly noticeable in dying animals) is with the receptors farthest apart, when the optical axes of the two eyes are parallel. The axes never converge, and so the 'scanning' (as we are inclined to regard it) can scarcely be associated with range-finder distance vision. The maximum amplitude of the scan is about four times the diameter of the crystalline cone. The scan appeared unrelated to movements of other body structures, which were easy to observe simultaneously. We were able to confirm the independence of the movement of the eye parts by examination of cinematograph film of living specimens. This autonomy seems strong evidence for regarding the movement as scanning. We found the frequency to be very variable (though Exner reports it as constant), but the variability may have been related to the condition of the specimens, which we were unable to keep alive for more than about 12 h. The maximum observed frequency was about 15 scans per sec. in *Copilia quadrata*, though there appear to be species differences, which will be described in a subsequent report. A single scan is shown in the series of consecutive ciné frames in Fig. 32.2. We were unable to produce systematic variations in the scan by subjecting the animals to visual stimuli, although there were frequent spontaneous variations in amplitude and in frequency. Even violent changes in illumination (occluding the microscope lamp) produced no related changes in scanning, though the animals would try to avoid too bright a light. We regret that we did not use a red filter while examining them, as the animals are probably insensitive to red light. The maximum intensity they would encounter at the depth we found them is about that of moonlight, but we examined them with many times this intensity.

At this stage we can only speculate as to the place of this eye in the evolutionary sequence. Is it an unsuccessful 'experiment'? Is it a precursor of the compound eye – multiple ommatidia developing to overcome the limited information channel capacity of a neural path? This most curious of eyes seems an ideal target for a microelectrode.

PART TWO INSTRUMENTS

33 *A multi-channel printing chronograph*

[Instruments, tools and gadgets of all kinds demonstrate the power and the limitations of physical principles when combined in all manner of ways. To the psychologist and the physiologist they have the quite special importance of revealing our own powers and limitations. Consider counting, with the aid of one's fingers or an abacus. The simple fact that fingers or beads aid the brain shows at once that brains do not work like fingers or beads when counting. Similarly, screwdrivers are useful just because fingers are not like screwdrivers. (If we knew that Martians needed screwdrivers, or abacuses, or computers, we would at once know a lot about Martians. If we knew that they did *not* require screwdrivers, abacuses or computers, for tasks we understand, we would also know a lot about them, and how they must differ from us). By measuring just how much aid is given by tools or instruments, we might make quite surprising inferences about hidden processes. (This argument I developed in *The Intelligent Eye*.)

When thinking about neural sensory or control systems as embodying engineering principles, it seems essential to understand these principles generally before they can be recognized and appreciated in their biological setting. Instrument design principles are important for understanding many aspects of perception. But we cannot expect present-day technology to hold all the keys: we must be prepared for new combinations, and new principles – we must be prepared to invent in order to understand.

It is sometimes thought that when, say, it is suggested that there are 'neural servo-systems' this is intended as an *analogy* to engineering servo-systems. This view is, I think, profoundly wrong. The point is that there are physical and design principles which cut across, and are common to, engineering and biology. In this sense we are all 'gadgets'.

Instruments of many kinds are of course essential for controlling experiments and recording data. Most of the devices and gadgets described here were designed to be useful, for my own or other people's experiments. I can make no claim to be a 'successful' inventor: but trying to make one's ideas come alive by working is the most exciting thing I know.

The story of the first gadget began in 1952, when I was seconded to the Navy for a year, to work at the Royal Naval Physiological Laboratory on problems of escaping from submarines, following the *Affray* submarine disaster in which all lives were lost. The main problem was to establish how long a trapped crew could afford to wait before starting their escape, while surface vessels were searching for them. If the crew escaped before their stricken ship was found, they could be scattered and lost. It took about ten hours for the entire crew to escape, one man at a time, through the gun tower escape chamber. The escape procedure involved a complex series of operations for each man, and a mistake could incapacitate or kill the man in the chamber, blocking escape for the remaining crew. How long was it safe to postpone the escape, before lack of oxygen made the probability of such a mistake a hazard to the remaining crew, as conditions worsened? It became clear that a technical problem was how to record the behaviour of the submariners over long periods, in conditions of worsening atmosphere. It was soon obvious that human recorders, including myself, were too unreliable. This was especially

FIG. 33.1 *The original printing digital recorder Thoth, as used for the submarine escape experiments.*

FIG. 33.2 *The recorder outside the pressure chamber during the submarine escape experiments.*

so in these experiments, as we were subject to the same conditions as the submariners: unless we peered at them through the windows of the pressure chamber used for the experiments – which was not popular. Even in normal conditions, it is too easy to make mistakes when recording data over long periods, and here it would have been impossible to avoid errors.

At that time the standard, and virtually the only, automatic data recorder was the polygraph. Although it can be useful it has serious defects: especially that times must be derived from tedious length measurements from the record strip, which pours out of the machine even when there are no events to record. Miles of ink tracks would have to be measured in these experiments, and the probability of introducing errors in identifying and measuring the tracks would have been great. Some kind of automatic recorder was clearly essential but none suitable existed. So I decided to build one.

The first version, built for the submarine escape experiments, did not have the printing counter described here and used in the later versions. The original machine recorded time with a cycling letter code, provided by a 'uniselector' sweeping switch, driven in 0·5 second steps and wired to actuate six of the printing solenoids, to indicate time in a repeating sequence of letter combinations, printed only when a signal occurred, and at the end of each timing cycle. The printing counter for recording time was added later: its development took several years. The original machine was conceived and built in three weeks of the hardest work I can remember. I called it Thoth:

FIG. 33.3 *The inside of the pressure chamber, showing the dummy escape gear, fitted with contacts to operate the recorder.*

the Egyptian ibis-headed God – the scribe of the Gods, and the recorder of the goods and ills of men.

Figure 33.1 shows the appearance of the first Thoth, as it was used for the submarine escape experiments. It was placed outside the large pressure chamber (Fig. 33.2) in which the experiments were conducted in conditions of high carbon dioxide and low oxygen. Figure 33.3 shows the dummy escape gear, inside the pressure chamber. Electrical contacts signalled the submariners' performance with the controls to Thoth the recorder.

The following is a brief description of the next stage in the development of Thoth. This first (far too large) printing counter is now added to the channel printing system, so that time could be printed numerically.]

★   ★   ★

EXPERIMENTAL psychologists have always been concerned with the recording and timing of events. The most commonly used recording device is the Polygraph, which is a multi-channel development of the Astronomer's Chronograph. For its original use of recording star transits, the Chronograph was convenient and simple, but when the

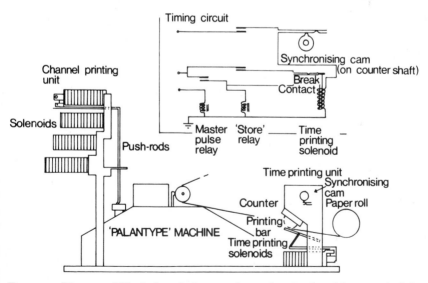

FIG. 33.4 *Diagram of Thoth the printing recorder, as first developed for numerical time printing.*

psychologist extends its use to measure, for example, multiple-choice reaction times, he uses several channels for comparatively long periods, which results in yards of record from which perhaps several hundred measurements have to be taken to derive the times of the recorded events. This limits the number of variables which it is practical to consider. Further, mistakes are apt to arise when reading the records through confusing the channels. It is also expensive in paper to operate at high speeds, and is not reliable since the pens are apt to become blocked. The device to be described avoids these objections.

The recorder has the following characteristics. There are 29 separate channels. Each channel is identified by a letter of the alphabet, or other symbol, which is printed upon the arrival of a signal on $2\frac{1}{2}$-inch record paper. Time is recorded in printed numerals which may be read directly from the record. The recording paper is stationary except when a signal arrives, when, after printing, it moves 3/16ths inch to allow the next signals to be printed.

Design

The main component of the recorder is the 'Palantype' shorthand machine. This is a manually operated machine similar to a portable typewriter, but differing in essential respects. In particular, any number of its 29 keys may be depressed together; they will then all print simultaneously, the characters being ranged across the paper in a line. There is no carriage as in a typewriter; when the keys are released the paper tape is fed on so that the next line can be printed below the first.

The 'Palantype' is ideal for the printing unit. Since any number of the keys can be pressed simultaneously a simple circuit can be used; if a normal typewriter were used it would be necessary to provide storage so that signals arriving together would be printed in sequence. This would be inconvenient and is avoided by arranging each channel to be independent throughout.

Time is also printed on the record paper; this is done with a printing counter driven at constant speed and made to print whenever a signal is received. The four numerals which are printed give a direct record of the time of each recorded event on any of the 29 channels to the nearest 0·1 second. Carter *et al.* (1951) used a similar short-hand machine as a recorder. They used it manually, with a constant speed paper drive and a time-marker as in the Polygraph. Welford (1952), using an electronic circuit and punched tape, codes the time to avoid continuous paper drive.

Construction

The Channel Recorder   The 'Palantype' machine – which records the channels though not the time of each occurrence – need not itself be modified. It is only necessary to screw it down to a baseboard. Above the keyboard 29 solenoids are mounted and so arranged that each will press a key when energized. (The solenoids used are 1 inch in diameter; they are mounted over the keys, in four rows, by bolting to a framework. This is made from strip brass; the strips supporting the solenoids are bent to conform to the plan of the keyboard, which is V-shaped. The construction is shown in Fig. 33.4. The solenoids are obtained from ex-Government Stores and are known as 'Cantilever Solenoids, 24 volt'. The levers with which they are furnished are used to actuate vertically mounted push rods which rest on the 'Palantype' keys.)

It is not sufficient simply to energize the printing solenoids from the incoming signals to be recorded; they must be energized with standard length pulses of about 0·01 second duration. There are several possible ways of providing such pulses – the method adopted was suggested by Dr Alfred Leonard, and has proved simple and reliable. Make-before-break relays are used (e.g. ex-Government, Ref. No. P. 27442 or P. 27710). One of these relays is placed in each solenoid circuit, the two sets of relay contacts being wired in series. Each relay is energized by signals on its channel; as it closes, a pulse is produced which energizes its printing solenoid for the desired 0·01 second. This pulse length is adjusted for each channel with a 1,000 Ω pre-set resistance in each circuit, and also with a master control in a metered 12-volt supply. (This supply need not be stabilized, but it should have at least a 4 amp. rating to prevent a serious drop in voltage when several signals are received together; a voltage tolerance of 20 per cent. is permissible).

In addition to providing pulses for the printing solenoids, the make-before-break relays also serve to isolate the current required for the printing solenoids (which are run at 40 volts) from the external recording circuit.

Time Recorder   This is built round a printing counter (series 428, supplied by English Numbering Machines Ltd.). It has type-face numerals and is designed to be driven continuously; it is geared so that one revolution of the drive shaft shifts the first counter wheel one numeral.

To record time to the nearest 0·1 second the counter is driven at 600 revs./minute. It is mounted immediately behind the 'Palantype' and arranged to print on the underside of the record paper; this is drawn over the counter by the 'Palantype's' paper feed whenever a signal is received.

A printed record of the counter is obtained by arranging for a printing bar to strike the paper on to the type wheels; a $\frac{1}{2}$-inch typewriter ribbon between the counter and the paper enables a reasonably clear impression to be obtained. The times are printed on the back of the record at a constant distance from their corresponding channel records; these are related with the aid of two slots in a simple reading desk, the times being read from underneath with a mirror mounted under the desk looking through one of the slots. To allow the numerals to be read directly in the mirror the type-face used is not inverted as is usual.

Before this system will work, certain precautions must be taken. The solenoid operating the printing bar must be supplied with a 0·01 second pulse whenever a signal is received on any of the recorder channels, and this pulse must be synchronized with the counter so that the striker only prints when a numeral on the high speed counter wheel is opposite the striker, otherwise this figure will be illegible. (The other figures look after themselves since they shift intermittently, but the first wheel is driven continuously from the drive shaft). The solution adopted is to feed the printing bar's solenoid through a contact which is closed once, by a cam for 0·01 second, for each revolution of the drive shaft. This allows the mechanism to print only when a numeral is opposite the striker. But a further problem remains: if a signal arrives when the synchronizing contact is open, it may be missed, but this must not happen. The problem is solved by storing the information that a signal has arrived by making it energize a relay with a holding-down circuit. This remains energized and the solenoid is energized when the synchronizing contact closes, which will be within 0·1 second after the signal arrives. When the time is printed, the holding-down circuit is broken so that the striker cannot print again until another signal arrives. If more than one signal arrives within the minimum discriminating time of 0·1 second the time will, of course, only be printed once; the characters denoting the channels on which the signals were received will lie in line across the paper and the time printed will apply to them all. A discontinuous counter drive used with this circuit makes the synchronizing less critical.

This method of recording time could be used independently of the rest of the recorder. It would then constitute a printing chronograph giving a time record which can be read directly. The rest of the recorder might be regarded as a means of extending the capacity of the printing chronograph from 1 to 29 channels.

A portable recorder

It is hoped to develop a portable recorder. In place of the shaft-driven counter a ratchet counter will be used; the intermittent drive gives a better printing/dead-time ratio, and allows a clock-controlled solenoid to be used for driving the counter. This is compact and can be at least as accurate as a normal stop-watch. The number of channels will be reduced to about six; they will be printed with plungers mounted close to the counter and will be arranged so that they can be worked manually, with buttons, or from solenoids.

Summary of performance characteristics

1. It records time to the nearest 0·1 second on 29 independent channels.
2. The channels are identified by printed characters.
3. Time is recorded in numerals and read directly.
4. The record paper is stationary except when a signal is recorded when it moves on 3/16ths inch.
5. The minimum permissible duration of input signal is 0·03 second.
6. The maximum repetition rate on each channel is five signals per second.

34 *A printing chronograph for recording data*

[Thoth was useful, but as an instrument too crude, and too dependent on critical adjustments. The problems of recording time reliably from a continuously driven printing counter turned out to be extraordinarily difficult. Not only were small high speed printing counters not then available, but it was difficult (*a*) to prevent printing occurring when the numbers on the count wheels are changing, which requires high precision synchronizing, (*b*) to perform the printing operation in the short time available while the wheels remain stationary, (*c*) not to lose event signals arriving during the 'dead' time while the count wheels are changing. These conditions have to be satisfied for signals arriving on any number of channels at any times.

The uses of this type of event recorder are discussed in the following extract from a lecture written at that time (1954).]

★   ★   ★

DATA recorders generally employ a continuous feed for the record paper, with some system for marking the paper when an event occurs, so that the time of occurrence of each event can be read by measuring intervals along the record paper. The continuous drive provides the time-base in a simple manner, but if small time intervals are to be discriminated a high drive speed is required, giving high running cost and requiring large storage space if records are to be kept over long periods. The machine to be described is rather more complicated than polygraph recorders of this kind, but it provides a convenient record, and the record paper is stationary in the absence of input signals so that running costs are low while the time and labour needed to read the record are also reduced. The machine employs standard electro-mechanical components, and servicing is possible without special knowledge of electronics. The machine is readily portable.

The time-base is digital and is provided by a cyclometer counter

406

fitted with type face. This is driven at a constant rate, with a small synchronous motor, the rate depending upon the time discrimination required. A count rate of either one or ten per second is entirely feasible with available small printing counters, and it may be possible to achieve a count rate of 100 c.p.s., giving a time discrimination of 0·01 second, with the latest nylon wheel counters. At present the best time-discrimination is to the nearest 0·1 second, the count rate being 10 c.p.s.

The cyclometer time-base alone would serve to indicate the times of occurrence of one type of event if signals were used to initiate a printing solenoid so that the numbers uppermost on the counter were printed whenever the event occurred. In this machine the counter is made to record the time of occurrence of signals arriving on many channels, these being indicated with appropriate letter symbols. The final record looks something like this:

```
1011    a
1138    b
2990    ab
3421      c
7955          ef
9532    a c   f
0000                  ★
1228    b
```

The following features may be noted:

1. The numbers indicate time of occurrence of signals arriving on each channel indicated by the letter symbols.
2. Time intervals may be determined by subtracting the earlier from the later time, the units being determined by the count rate used.
3. The record is closely packed, the paper being stationary except immediately after a print, when it moves a small fixed amount ready for the next print, whenever the next signal arrives.
4. Any number of channels may print together. This is an important feature; it leads to a simple circuit, since there is no problem of signals piling up waiting to be printed, and combinations of letter symbols can often be used to extend the number of effective channels.
5. The seventh line of the sample record: '0000   ★' shows what happens when the counter completes a cycle, returning to '0000'. This is indicated by the automatic printing of an asterisk in conjunction with the time print of '0000'. In the

absence of any input signals, the machine will print '0000 ＊'
at a constant interval, this depending upon the count rate used
and the number of wheels on the counter.

The machine is designed so that printing cannot take place while
the counter wheels are changing. This is done by sensing the position
of the counter drive shaft and providing a pulse to initiate printing
only when the counter wheels are stationary. If a signal arrives when
the counter wheels are rotating, it is stored by a self holding relay in
its channel circuit until the count wheels have stopped at their next
printing position. Printing then takes place, and the holding circuits
on each channel relay are momentarily broken, to prevent the machine
from printing again each time a pulse arrives from the counter's
sensing system. We normally wish to print only the moment of arrival
of a signal, though its end can also be printed, with another channel
symbol.

Extension of design principles to recording variable functions

The machine as described is limited to the recording of times of
discrete events. It is, however, clear that we may also record in digital
form the values assumed by variables. This may be done by substituting for the channel symbols one or more printing counters similar
to that used here for recording time. In place of the constant speed
drive, we arrange for the value of the variables, (or some suitable
multiple or function) to be represented by the new counters. A printed
record of time and the values of the variables may be obtained
whenever desired, perhaps when a variable input changes by some
predetermined amount. This arrangement has important advantages
over the standard analogue instruments used for recording for
example, temperatures and pressures in industry or meteorology, for
the record is not redundant if printing only takes place when the
variable changes by a significant amount. Time discrimination can
be better than that obtainable with feasible paper speeds on analogue
recorders used over long periods of time.

35 *Master patent specification for printing chronograph*

[Now began a long saga: perhaps a saga without foresight. It was clear that discontinuous event records have very real advantages over continuous devices, such as polygraphs, for many applications including studies of human and animal behaviour. They could also be useful in industry. A friend suggested approaching a firm, at that time called Nucleonic and Radiological Developments. I also approached the National Research Development Corporation (N.R.D.C.), then newly set up to help private inventors to put their ideas into practical form and introduce them to suitable firms: sometimes offering financial help for development. In this case, N.R.D.C. did not offer financial help but they did advise me to go ahead. I made a second prototype. This sat in a cupboard of the Nucleonics firm for eighteen months; when the company suffered a kind of fission – splitting up in several directions. One of the directors, Mr John Russell, started a small firm, Russell Electronics, in East Molesey. He took with him a talented engineer, Jack Sutton, who transformed Thoth from a clumsy bench model to a neat portable instrument. Reliability was not as high as we would have liked, but nevertheless it was useful and the only instrument of its kind. About sixty were sold, to various countries. Then, just as our hard work seemed justified, the small firm of Russell Electronics was bought up by a curious consortium – the Pena Group. This consisted of a band of financiers of many nationalities, who seemed to have been cast up on various beaches by the war. My favourite character was an ebullient Russian, who had worked on the Paris docks, and now collected paintings. I remember this large man, sitting behind his desk in his Regency-striped office in Wimpole Street, with a rare collection of secretaries and five different coloured telephones; the microphone of his pocket tape recorder strapped to his wrist, in case inspiration should dictate what he should dictate to his secretary of the day. Ushered in, I waited until, after shouting a different language down each of the coloured telephones, he raised his enormous fists to thump his desk with a cheerful bellow: 'I like being a tycoon!' We then went out to a lunch costing my weekly salary.

The group grew and grew. They bought up fifty-one companies, with a total value of 4·5 million pounds. They bought up a first-rate firm making crystal pick ups, and the largest firm in the country manufacturing projection T.V. They tried to get into transistor radios, at the beginning when circuits were few and the new components seemed like magic. Here one began to see that all was not well. The tycoon flew to Germany, with his wrist microphone, to order transistors for the new radio. He bought 20,000 transistors of a totally useless sort as he did not realize there were different *kinds* of transistors. After all – they all *looked* much alike. This cost tens of thousands of pounds. Shortly after, he found that the local bye-laws did not allow offices in Wimpole Street, so he had to move to less salubrious quarters.

Russell Electronics, with Thoth, became part of the Pena Group, which set up in a factory near Southampton. Thoth was just being produced in the new factory when disaster struck. The year was 1958. There was a small American recession which forced the group to borrow a quarter of a million pounds from a city merchant bank. This proved insufficient. Faces went grey, voices hoarse then silent. The comedy was over. The Group, and the merchant bank, died.

The Thoth patents, being assets of the Group, were claimed by the creditors. Fortunately, I was able to show that as they had paid no royalties they had broken their agreement, and so forfeited their rights to the patents which were returned to me without question. John Russell tried to extract his firm, but failing, he retired. I approached several instrument companies without success, until finally Thoth was taken up by the Cambridge Instrument Company. I conceived the highest respect for this remarkable company. Founded by one of Charles Darwin's sons, it has from its start had the tradition of not only developing its own ideas but also taking up ideas from outside, especially from the University. In this sense it is the fore-runner of the many successful research and development firms surrounding M.I.T. in Boston, U.S.A.

The Cambridge Instrument Company took immense trouble, carrying out extensive redesign during a difficult period when the works were being rebuilt. This made it necessary for the working drawings to be farmed out, which led to unforeseeable complications. Finally the new model was complete. For various reasons it was not produced in quantity; but there are still some around, timing and recording events in the world, according to a distant dream.

We certainly learned a lot. Perhaps other people did too. A Japanese firm is now making a printing event recorder, which is available in this country. This machine discriminates time to the nearest one second: ours gave time to the nearest tenth of a second, otherwise the records seem identical.

I now include the first complete Patent Specification (1 June, 1960). This was drawn up by my patent agents, Boult Wade & Tennant. I have come to admire and respect the skills and integrity of patent agents. They are unsung heroes of many small dramas.]

★   ★   ★

THE invention relates to a device (herein referred to as a printing chronograph) for recording the occurrence of events (e.g. operations of control members, or process changes) and the times at which they occur.

The invention provides a printing chronograph which comprises means for printing at any particular time, symbols representing that time, at least two independently operable printing members for printing symbols representing different events, a corresponding number of solenoid operated means for conditioning for printing operation any of the event symbol printing members, solenoid operated means for taking simultaneously printing impressions from the time printing symbols and from a conditioned event symbol printing member, and means for producing on the occurrence of an event an electrical impulse of fixed short duration independent of the length of the event and effective to cause operation of the conditioning means of a symbol printing member representing that event and also to cause operation of the solenoid operated printing impression taking means, and means for deconditioning the conditioned symbol after the impression taking operation.

The invention further provides a printing chronograph which comprises means for printing, at any particular time, a symbol (or group of symbols) representing that time, solenoid operated means responsive to electrical impulses for operating, or conditioning for operation, means for printing symbols (or groups of symbols) representing events, as they occur, and means for producing a single short electrical impulse capable of effecting (directly or indirectly) operation of the solenoid means on the occurrence of an event of longer duration than the impulse, comprising switch means operable (manually or automatically) on the occurrence of the event to close a direct current electric circuit containing the solenoid or a relay controlling energisation of the solenoid, a capacitor, and a resistor constituting a leak around the capacitor where-by closing of the switch causes a short capacitor-charging surge or impulse sufficient to energise the solenoid or relay, said impulse being arranged also to effect operation of the time printing means.

In one form of the invention the time printing means comprise a counter with type faces, a motor (e.g. of the synchronous type) for driving the counter at a constant rate and means operable (directly or indirectly) by an impulse produced as aforesaid for printing an impression from the counter reading. There may be an intermittent drive to the counter (e.g. the drive may include a Geneva motion) and the impression making means may be operable only when the counter is stationary. The impression making means may comprise a solenoid in a circuit controlled by a switch operable in synchronism with the counter to close the circuit only when the counter is stationary, said circuit also being controlled by the impulses so that printing is only effected when an impulse has been received and the counter is stationary.

According to a preferred form of the invention the impulses operate a relay which, when energised, closes a self-holding circuit for the relay which remains closed until the next operation of the time printing means, and effects energization of the solenoid for the printing of the event symbol. The relay may also constitute the impulse control for the circuit for the impression making means as aforesaid.

The chronograph may have several independently operable means for printing 'event' symbols and independent means for producing impulses to effect operation of such printing means, whereby the occurrences of different events may be isolated and recorded either separately or, if they occur simultaneously, at the same time. Such independent recording means are herein referred to as 'channels'.

When the time recording means include a counter as above described which is of the kind which, after it has attained the maximum reading for which it is designed, automatically returns to zero (or some other starting point) and starts a fresh count, it may be desirable to record such a fresh start. For this purpose the attainment of the maximum reading (or the starting of a fresh count) may be regarded as an 'event' and a separate channel may be provided and allocated to the recording of such events.

It is a preferred feature of the invention that the records are made on a continuous strip of record material (e.g. paper) and the strip is advanced a step at a time only after the printing of an 'event' symbol and the accompanying time symbol. The chronograph may accordingly include means for advancing a record strip in this way.

It is an advantage of the multi-channel form of the invention that each event, however long it may last, produces only one short impulse which effects the recording operation and the mechanism is then free for operation by another channel.

The 'events' may be recorded as they occur by manual operation of switch means to produce an electrical signal or such signals may be produced automatically by variations in such phenomena as light, sound, heat, capacity, inductance and radioactivity.

As an example of how the invention may be carried into effect, a specific construction of a multi-channel printing chronograph embodying the above and other features, will now be described with reference to the accompanying drawings [see pp. 429–32], which are to a large extent diagrammatic and in which:—

Fig. 35.1(1) is a perspective view of the chronograph;

Fig. 35.1(2) is a plan view of the chronograph with one part of the cover removed and another part folded back;

Fig. 35.1(3) is a section on the line 3–3 in Fig. 35.1(2), but showing the above-mentioned portion of the cover in its folded over, operative position;

Fig. 35.1(4) is an under plan of the counter and of the symbol printing means;

Fig. 35.1(5) is an end view, in the direction 5–5 in Fig. 35.1(4), showing the arrangement of the solenoids for operating the symbol printing means;

Fig. 35.1(6) is a plan view showing the means for driving the counter and a rotary switch;

Fig. 35.1(7) is a section on the line 7–7 in Fig. 35.1(2);

Fig. 35.1(8) is a section on the line 8–8 in Fig. 35.1(2);

Fig. 35.1(9) is a view in the direction 9–9 in Fig. 35.1(2);

Fig. 35.1(10) is a view in the direction 10–10 in Fig. 35.1(2);

Fig. 35.1(11) is a plan view of the mechanism shown in Fig. 35.1(10);

Fig. 35.1(12) is a detail view in the direction of the arrow 12 in Fig. 35.1(11);

Fig. 35.1(13) shows a switch operated by the counter;

Fig. 35.1(14) shows a portion of a record strip produced by the machine;

Fig. 35.1(15) is a circuit diagram of the machine; and

Fig. 35.1(16) is a circuit diagram of a 'slave' machine.

The chronograph forming the subject of this example has time printing means and seven channels by which records of events may be made, six of the channels being allocated to events external to the chronograph and one to internal events.

The machine comprises a base 20 carrying means for supporting a reel of paper 21 and guides 22, 23 for leading the paper over a presser bar 24 and then over a table 25 to a pair of sprocket wheels 26 which make feeding engagement in marginal perforations 27 in the paper. The paper is guided in engagement with the sprocket wheels by turned down edges 29 of the portion 30 of the cover which is shown folded back about the hinge line 31 in Fig. 35.1(3). The presser bar 24 is arranged for up and down movement by means of a solenoid 34 which is secured to the base 20, the upward movements being effected by energization of the solenoid. The return movements are effected by a spring within the solenoid in co-operation with a spring 35. These return movements are arranged, as later described, to operate a pawl and ratchet device to rotate the sprocket wheels 26 to advance the paper strip in steps of about $\frac{1}{4}$ inch.

Extending transversely across the upper face of the paper 21 above the presser bar 24 there is an ink ribbon 36. This ribbon extends between a pair of reels 37, 38 over four guide rollers 40 as seen in Fig. 35.1(9). The ribbon is progressively advanced during the operation of the machine by means later described.

Mounted above the ribbon at one side of the paper strip there is a four figure mechanical counter 44. This counter is driven by a synchronous electric motor 45, a gear train 46, 47 and a Geneva motion 48, the gear ratios and arrangement of the Geneva motion being such that the counter advances step by step one unit each $0 \cdot 1$ second. The train 46 however incorporates a speed change by which, if desired, the rate of advance of the counter may be reduced to one unit every second.

The figures of the counter have type faces and are aligned across the paper. The arrangement is that upward movement of the presser bar 24 presses the paper 21 and intervening ink ribbon 36 against the lowermost row of figures and so prints the figures on the paper, the figures representing time in tenths of a second (or seconds if the alternative gear is engaged) from a datum.

Rotatable with the driving member of the Geneva motion there is a rotary switch or commutator 50 which completes a circuit only during the idle periods when the counter is stationary. This switch has adjacent one end a set of four contacts, a single contact adjacent the other end and a central slip ring portion, which are engaged by three brushes 51, 52, 53. The brush 51 co-operates with the set of four contacts and is intended for use when the unit-per-second gear is engaged so as to make four contacts per second. The brush 53 co-operates with the single contact and is for use when the one unit per one-tenth of a second gear is engaged. In each case contact is made for about one-thirtieth of a second. The brush 52 and the central slip-ring provide a common return connection.

The rotary switch controls the energization of the coil RLG of a relay which has self-holding contacts RLG/5 and contact RLG/1 in the circuit of the presser bar solenoid 34, the solenoid being supplied with direct currect through a rectifier 56.

There is also a switch 60 (see Figs. 35.1(6), (13) and (15)) which is operated by the counter when it reaches its maximum reading (9999) and is returning to zero. The 'thousands' wheel 61 of the counter has a cam 62 which, as the zero turns to the bottom, rocks a lever 63 momentarily to close the contacts 60.

For the seven channels there are relays RL (A to F and H) and 'event' solenoids CS (1 to 6) and M.S.1 respectively which, when energized, control the printing on the paper of symbols (letters *a* to *f* and an asterisk) in line with the counter figures. The symbols are in the form of type carried on square bars 66 coupled by arms 67 to the armatures 68 of the solenoids. Springs 69 urge the bars towards the solenoids. When a solenoid is energised its bar is projected away therefrom to engage its end with a stop 70, e.g. as in the case of the bar 66*a* in Fig. 35.1(4). When a bar is so projected the type symbol (71) carried thereby lies on top of the ink ribbon 36 over the paper above the presser bar 24 and in alignment with the counter figures. Upward movement of the presser bar 24 then operates to print the symbol as well as the counter reading. The symbol bar is backed-up by a cross-member 72 which, by engagement with a flat face of the bar, also prevents rotation thereof. When the solenoid is de-energised the spring withdraws the symbol from the printing position.

Associated with the presser bar there are two so-called micro-switches 75, 76, both of which are normally closed but are opened just before the bar reaches the top of its upward movement. To effect the opening of the switches there is a cranked lever 78 pivoted at 79 on a pillar secured to the base 20 and arranged for engagement at its free end by an adjustable screw 80 when the armature 81 of the solenoid 34 has nearly reached its innermost position. The lever then operates the plungers 82 of the switches.

The machine is arranged for operation from alternating current mains 84 and includes a full-wave rectifier 85 and a low tension transformer 86.

The circuit arrangements and the operation of the machine will now be described.

The seven channels have similar circuits (see Fig. 35.1(15)) as follows, the seven circuits being in parallel. For the six eternal channels there are channel operating switches (CB1 to CB6) in the form of push buttons carried on a stand 90 (Fig. 35.1(1)) having a lead to a plug and socket connection 91 in the casing beneath the out-coming paper strip 21. There are also, in parallel with the switches CB, sockets SK2 for insertion of remote switches for alternative use. Ganged changeover switches (SW1*a* to SW1*f*) are provided for selection of switches CB and the sockets SK2, the switches SW1 having three positions in which, respectively, only switches CB are in circuit, both the switches and the sockets are in circuit, and only the sockets are in circuit. In the case of the 'internal' channel the above-mentioned switch 60 which is operated by the counter when it reaches its maximum reading, and the switch SW2a later described both constitute channel operating switches. The switches CB and/or the remote switches (depending on setting of switches SW1) may be used to effect a record through the appropriate channel of an external 'event' and the switches 60 and SW2a may be used to effect a record of an internal event. Each channel operating switch is in a circuit supplied by the rectifier 85 and containing the coil of one of the channel relays RL (A to F and H), a capacitor C (1 to 7) and a resistor R (1 to 7) shunted around the capacitor to constitute a leak. The capacitor has a value such that on closing the channel operating switch there is a charging impulse or surge sufficient to energize the relay RL and lasting for a period insufficient to overlap two consecutive periods in which the rotary switch 50 is closed (otherwise a single 'event' might be recorded twice).

Each of the channel relays RLA to RLF has four sets of contacts all of which are closed on energization of the relay coil. Relay RLH has only three sets of contacts. One of these sets (RLA/1 to RLF/1 and RLH/1) of each relay is in a circuit, supplied by the rectifier, containing the relay coil and in parallel with the capacitor C (1 to 7). The circuit also contains the micro-switch 75 operated by the presser bar solenoid 34. The arrangement operates as a holding circuit retaining the relay coil energized and the contacts closed after the end of the impulse until the printing means have been brought into operation when the coil is de-energized by opening of switch 75. Another of the sets of contacts (RLA/2 to RLF/2 and RLH/2) is in a circuit, supplied by the transformer 86, containing the 'event' solenoids CS (1 to 6) or MS1 whereby the solenoid is energized during the time that the relay coil is energized. The third set of contacts (RLA/3 to RLF/3 and RLH/3) is in a circuit, supplied from the mains, containing the presser bar operating solenoid 34 and the contact RLG1 of the relay RLG. The fourth set of contacts (RLA4 to RLF4) are connected to an external socket SK6 into which there may be plugged leads to a set of electrically operated visual counters so that there is available visual records of the number of times the solenoids are energized.

The operation is as follows. The six external channels are appropriated to external 'events' and on the occurrence of an event the switch CB or a remote switch plugged into socket SK2, appropriate to the event is closed manually or automatically. This causes an impulse which energizes the corresponding channel relay RL (A to F) thereby closing the holding circuit, the circuit for the 'event' solenoid and the circuit of the presser bar solenoid. The last circuit however is not completed unless or until the rotary switch is closed and the relay RLG controlled thereby is energized. When that happens the presser bar is operated to print the time and the symbol appropriate to the event. Just before the limit of the upward stroke of the presser bar the switch 75 is opened, which releases the energized channel relay and the switch 76 is opened which releases relay RLG. The final part of the upward printing stroke is effected by the momentum of the parts and the residual magnetism of the solenoid. During the return stroke of the presser bar the paper and ink ribbon are both advanced. The seventh channel operates in similar manner to print a symbol (i.e. an asterisk) when the counter reaches 9999, the closing of the counter operated switch 60 being equivalent to the closing of an external 'event' switch. Operation of switch SW2a produces a similar result.

The circuit through contacts RLG5 acts as a holding circuit for relay RLG and ensures that printing will be effected even if the rotary switch 50 opens before completion of the upward movement of the printing bar by solenoid 34. The holding circuit is broken by the opening of switch 76 just before the end of the upward movement.

Fig. 35.1(14) represents a typical section of a paper record produced by the machine.

It should be appreciated that the several channels can operate independently or together according to the incidence of 'events', that the fact of an event occurring during the changing of the counter figures is 'stored' until the counter is stationary and the time is then printed and that no record is made and no paper is fed except on the occurrence of an 'event' whereby a compact record is obtained. Furthermore even if one channel is occupied by an event of long duration only one record is made and there is no interference with the operation of other channels.

In some cases where it is desired to increase the number of different events which can be recorded, additional 'events' switches may be provided and arranged to operate two (or more) channels simultaneously according to a code, the result being that one event prints two (or more) symbols. Alternatively, or in addition, supplementary or slave machines having additional channels (but not necessarily time printing means) may be added to the machine described above. Furthermore the number of external channels in the machine itself may be varied.

Fig. 35.1(16) shows a circuit diagram for a slave machine without time printing means. It will be observed that the arrangement is similar to that of the master machine described above but is simplified by the omission of the time printing means. The slave machine has its own paper and ribbon feeding means which operate in synchronism with the master machine. An event recorded on either machine advances the paper for both and records the time on the master record strip.

The master machine described above is provided with sockets SK3 and SK4 for connection of one or two slave machines by plugging in slave plugs SP.

It is desirable that the beginning of a series of recordings should be indicated on the master-record strip and also, when provided, on the slave strips. For this purpose there is provided in the master machine a manually operable set of ganged switches SW2*a*, SW2*b* and SW2*c*. Switch SW2*a* is in parallel with switch 60 of the master and the switches SW2*b* and SW2*c* take the place of switch 60 in the slave machines so that operation of the switches SW2 at the beginning of a series effects, on the master record, the printing of the counter reading and an asterisk and, on the slave records, the printing of an asterisk.

The relay RLG has contacts RLG2 and RLG3 which, on energization of the relay coil through the rotary switch and a channel relay complete the printing solenoid circuits of the slave units so that an event recorded on any unit causes, as already mentioned, the advance of all the paper strips and the printing of the counter reading on the master.

The means for feeding the paper strips and the ink ribbon will now be described in more detail.

The presser bar 24 is carried on a bell crank lever 100 which is rocked by the solenoid 34 and is secured to a rock-shaft 101. The movements of this shaft are employed to feed both the paper and the ribbon, the feeding movements being derived from the return, idle, stroke of the presser bar.

To feed the paper, the shaft 101 carries an arm 102 which is hooked to engage behind (on the left as seen in Fig. 35.1(7)) an upright 103 pivoted at 104 to the base 20. This upright is urged by spring 105 up to a stop 106. At its upper end the upright carries a pawl 107 which engages a ratchet wheel 108 on the shaft of the paper feeding sprocket wheels 26. Accordingly movements of the upright to the left operate to rotate the sprocket wheels and to advance the paper, in steps, by one quarter of an inch each step. A spring blade 109 prevents return movements of the wheel 108.

To advance the tape there is an arm 120 fixed to the shaft 101 and carrying at its lower end a hooked pawl 121 which is pressed upwardly into engagement with a ratchet wheel 122 by a spring 123. Accordingly the idle movements of the shaft 101 rotate the wheel 122 anticlockwise (Fig. 35.1(8)) one tooth at a time. A pawl 124 loose on shaft 101 prevents return movement of the ratchet wheel. The wheel is splined to a shaft 126 which is supported in bearings for axial sliding movement (see especially Figs. 35.1(10) and (11)). Secured to the shaft there are a pair of bevel gears 128, 129 which are alternatively engageable with bevel gears 130, 131 on spindles supported for rotation by bulkhead 132, the spindles carrying at the rear of the bulkhead the ribbon reels 37, 38. Accordingly one or other of these reels is intermittently rotated by the operation of solenoid 34 depending upon which pair of bevel gears is engaged. To effect the axial movements of the gears 128, 129 and shaft 126 there is a bar 139 guided on the bulkhead for manual sliding movement and having a blade 140 between the gears. The inner, right hand end (Fig. 35.1(11)) of the bar 139 passes through a slot in a locking bar 141 which passes through the bulkhead. The bar 139 has a cam 142 which, as the bar is moved, draws the bar 141 through the bulkhead. On the other side of the bulkhead the bar 141 is guided for movement over the spindle 144 of the reel of paper 21. The spindle is supported in a fork in an upright pedestal 145 and, normally, the bar 141 overlies the spindle and retains it in the fork as seen in Fig. 35.1(12). When the bar 141 is withdrawn by the cam a latch 148 engages a notch 149 in the bar and holds the bar withdrawn so that the spindle may be removed. The latch 148 has a tail 150 which rises above the bottom of the fork when the latch is engaged in the notch. Accordingly pressure applied to the latch during replacement of the spindle releases the bar 141 which returns, by spring action, over the spindle.

The length of paper in a reel and the length of tape together with the rate of advance of each are so chosen that the tape is advanced nearly its full length during the printing of a reel of paper. The operation of inserting a new reel of paper involves withdrawal of the bar 141 to release the spindle 144, by movement of the bar 140, which has the effect of changing over the drive to the tape reels so that replacement of the paper automatically results in reversal of the tape movement.

The machine may be modified to record changes in variables. For example the value of a variable at any time may be represented by the reading of a reversible counter which is aligned with the time counter and any change in the reversible counter may operate as an 'event' switch to effect a printing of both counter readings.

The invention is not restricted to the details of the above example. For instance, an electro-magnetic counter operated by pulses of suitable length at ten pulses per second (generated by a spring clock or a valve circuit) may be used in place of the purely mechanical counter described. Again counters for the events recorded on each channel may be used as the printing members, whereby the total number of events in any particular period is automatically made available by comparison between the figures printed at the beginning and end of the period.

The printing means employed in the construction described above are the subject of my co-pending Application No. 6809/57 (Serial No. 836,113) and are claimed therein. Similarly the paper feeding mechanism described above is the subject of my co-pending Application No. 6796/57 (Serial No. 836,112) and is claimed therein.

What I claim is :—

1. A printed chronograph which comprises means for printing at any particular time, symbols representing that time, at least two independently operable printing members for printing symbols representing different events, a corresponding number of solenoid operated means for conditioning for printing operation any of the event symbol printing members, solenoid operated means for taking simultaneously printing impressions from the time printing symbols and from a conditioned event symbol printing member, and means for producing on the occurrence of an event an electrical impulse of fixed short duration independent of the length of the event and effective to cause operation of the conditioning means of a symbol printing member representing that event and also to cause operation of the solenoid operated printing impression taking means, and means for de-conditioning the conditioned symbol after the impression taking operation.

2. A printing chronograph which comprises means for printing, at any particular time, a symbol (or group of symbols) representing that time, solenoid-operated means responsive to electrical impulses for operating, or conditioning for operation, means for printing symbols (or groups of symbols) representing events, as they occur, and means for producing a single short electrical impulse capable of effecting (directly or indirectly) operation of the solenoid means on the occurrence of an event of longer duration than the pulse, comprising switch means operable (manually or automatically) on the occurrence of the event to close a direct current electric circuit containing the solenoid or a relay controlling energization of the solenoid, a capacitor, and a resistor constituting a leak around the capacitor whereby closing of the switch causes a short capacitor-

charging surge or impulse sufficient to energize the solenoid or relay, said impulse being arranged also to effect operation of the time printing means.

3. A printing chronograph as claimed in Claim 2 in which the time printing means comprise a counter with type faces, a motor (e.g. of the synchronous type) for driving the counter at a constant rate and means operable (directly or indirectly) by an impulse produced as aforesaid for printing an impression from the counter reading.

4. A printing chronograph as claimed in Claim 3 in which there is an intermittent drive to the counter and the impression printing means are operable only when the counter is stationary.

5. A printing chronograph as claimed in Claim 4 in which the drive comprises a Geneva motion.

6. A printing chronograph as claimed in Claim 4 or Claim 5 in which the impression making means comprise a solenoid in a circuit controlled by a switch operable in synchronism with the counter to close the circuit only when the counter is stationary, said circuit also being controlled by the impulses so that printing is only effected when an impulse has been produced and the counter is stationary.

7. A printing chronograph as claimed in Claim 6 in which the switch operable in synchronism with the counter comprises a constantly rotating commutator or rotary switch.

8. A printing chronograph as claimed in Claim 7 in which the commutator has sections with different numbers of segments arranged for alternative use.

9. A printing chronograph as claimed in any one of Claims 2 to 8 in which the impulses operate a relay which, when energized, closes a self-holding circuit for the relay which remains closed until the next operation of the time printing means, and effects energization of the solenoid for the printing of the event symbol.

10. A printing chronograph as claimed in Claim 9 as dependent upon Claim 6 in which the relay also constitutes the impulse control for the circuit for the impression making means as aforesaid.

11. A printing chronograph as claimed in any one of the preceding claims having several independently operable means for printing 'event' symbols and independent means for producing impulses to effect operation of such printing means, whereby the occurrences of different events may be isolated and recorded either separately or, if they occur simultaneously, at the same time.

12. A printing chronograph as claimed in any one of the preceding claims and including means for recording, as an event, the return to zero or other starting point of the counter.

13. A printing chronograph as claimed in any one of the preceding

claims in which the records are made on a continuous strip of record material (e.g. paper) and the strip is advanced a step at a time only after the printing of an 'event' symbol and the accompanying time symbol and means are included for advancing a record strip in this way.

14. A printing chronograph as claimed in any one of the preceding claims and including means for effecting as an internal 'event' printing of the counter reading at the beginning of a series of recordings.

15. A printing chronograph as claimed in any one of the preceding claims and including means for varying the speed at which the counter is driven.

16. A printing chronograph as claimed in any one of the preceding claims having in combination therewith at least one slave unit having printing means and means responsive to an electric impulse (corresponding to the occurrence of a different event to be recorded) to operate (or condition for operation) the printing means to record that impulse on strip record material separate from that of the master chronograph, and means in the combination for advancing the several strip materials a step after each master or slave printing operation and for effecting printing of the counter reading on the master strip at the same time as each such printing operation.

17. A printing chronograph as claimed in any one of the preceding claims having in combination therewith at least one visual counter recording the number of impulses corresponding to events or selected events.

[The problem of sensing the position of the first count wheel was first tackled with a brush contact, (described not quite accurately as a 'commutator'). This gave trouble, so the next step was to break a beam of light to a miniature photo-cell, once every revolution of the first print wheel. It was a great improvement, but the lamp had a finite life. When the machine was taken up by the Cambridge Instrument Company, their Mr King designed a beautiful system: he used an oscillator with a rotating aluminium vane which interrupted the positive feed back loop of the oscillator, ten times per second and for exactly the right duration, to provide the synchronizing signal for allowing printing to occur only when the count wheels were correctly placed. Virtually immortal transistors were protected by potting. The result was a truly elegant and completely reliable solution to a problem that had bothered us for years.

I give the last specification as an example of how long it can take to sort out technical problems; how one can be held up and sometimes defeated. Here the final solution had to wait upon development of technology – solid state components which were not available when

Thoth was born. At the beginning, small high speed printing counters, or suitable synchronous motors for driving them, were not available either. The original dream, for such it was, depended on the coming reality of other people's dreams of what became transistors, and high speed printing counters that would work fast and reliably enough to solve their problems. For a time the dream of Thoth matched technical reality. Inevitably technology moved on, to make Thoth no longer its living promise of gleaming steel and wire; but half dead dusty memories, ticking away like old men counting time in dark corners. What remains are the concepts embodied in the machine. Machines die and have to change at least a little at each generation; but they, like us, embody ideas inherited from their ancestors, ideas which may live on, in dreams made real by future technology.]

PROVISIONAL SPECIFICATION

A New or Improved Recording Device

I, RICHARD LANGTON GREGORY, M.A., a British Subject, of The Psychology Laboratory, Downing Place, Cambridge, Cambridgeshire, do hereby declare this invention to be described in the following statement:

The invention relates to a recorder (herein referred to as a printing chronograph) for recording the occurrence of events (e.g. operations of control members, or process changes) and the times at which they occur.

The invention provides a printing chronograph which comprises a 'counter' and means for driving the counter at a constant speed whereby a time base is provided, the counter being capable of producing a printed record of the total at any time, means responsive to an electrical impulse (corresponding to the occurrence of an event to be recorded) to operate (or condition for operation) printing means to record that impulse on strip record material and also to print, in alignment with the record, the counter reading, and means for advancing the strip material a step after each printing operation.

The invention further provides a printing chronograph which comprises means for printing, at any particular time, a symbol (or group of symbols) representing that time, solenoid-operated means responsive to electrical impulses for operating, or conditioning for operation, means for printing symbols (or groups of symbols) representing events, as they occur, and means for producing a single short electrical impulse capable of effecting (directly or indirectly) operation of the solenoid means on the occurrence of an event of longer duration than the pulse, comprising switch means operable (manually or automatically) on the occurrence of the event to close a direct current electric circuit containing the solenoid or a relay controlling energization of the solenoid, a capacitor, and a resistor constituting a leak around the capacitor whereby closing of the switch causes a short capacitor-charging surge or impulse sufficient to energize the solenoid or relay, said impulse being arranged also to effect operation of the time printing means.

In one form of the invention the time printing means comprise a counter with type faces, a motor (e.g. of the synchronous type) for driving the counter at a constant rate and means operable (directly or indirectly) by an impulse produced as aforesaid for printing an impression from the counter reading. There may be an intermittent drive to the counter (e.g. the drive may include a Geneva motion) and the impression making means may be operable only when the counter is stationary. The impression making means may comprise a solenoid in a circuit controlled by a switch operable in synchronism with the counter to close the circuit only when the counter is stationary, said circuit also being controlled by the impulses so that printing is only effected when an impulse has been received and the counter is stationary.

According to a preferred form of the invention the impulses operate a relay which, when energized, closes a self-holding circuit for the relay which remains closed until the next operation of the time printing means, and effects energization of the solenoid for the printing of the event symbol. The relay may also constitute the impulse control for the circuit for the impression making means as aforesaid.

The chronograph may have several independently operable means for printing 'event' symbols and independent means for producing impulses to effect operation of such printing means, whereby the occurrences of different events may be isolated and recorded either separately or, if they occur simultaneously, at the same time. Such independent recording means are herein referred to as 'channels'.

When the time recording means include a counter as above described which is of the kind which, after it has attained the maximum reading for which it is designed, automatically returns to zero (or some other starting point) and starts a fresh count, it may be desirable to record such a fresh start. For this purpose the attainment of the maximum reading (or the starting of a fresh count) may be regarded as an 'event' and a separate channel may be provided and allocated to the recording of such events.

It is a preferred feature of the invention that the records are made on a continuous strip of record material (e.g. paper) and the strip is advanced a step at a time only after the printing of an 'event' symbol and the accompanying time symbol. The chronograph may accordingly include means for advancing a record strip in this way.

It is an advantage of the multi-channel form of the invention that each event, however long it may last, produces only one short impulse which effects the recording operation and the mechanism is then free for operation by another channel.

As an example of how the invention may be carried into effect, a specific construction of a multi-channel printing chronograph embodying the above and other features will now be described.

The chronograph forming the subject of this example has time printing means and four channels by which records of events may be made, three of the channels being allocated to events external to the chronograph and one to internal events. Additional channels may be added if desired, as later described.

The machine comprises a frame having means for supporting a reel of paper and guides for leading the paper over a presser bar and then to a pair of feed rolls. The presser bar is arranged for up and down movements by means of a solenoid, the upward movements being effected by energization of the solenoid. The return movements are effected by spring means and these movements are arranged to operate a pawl and ratchet device to rotate the feed rolls to advance the paper by a strip of about $\frac{1}{4}$ inch.

Extending transversely across the upper face of the paper above the presser bar is an ink ribbon. This ribbon extends between a pair of reels beneath the paper, over guide rollers. A pawl and ratchet device operable by the return movements of the presser bar operates to rotate one or other of the reels slowly to advance the ribbon over the paper. This drive is diverted from one reel to the other when the end of the ribbon has been reached to reverse the motion. The change is effected by engagement of an eyelet on the ribbon with the pawl to swing it from a ratchet on one reel to a ratchet on the other.

Mounted above the ribbon at one side of the paper is a four figure mechanical counter. This counter is driven by a synchronous motor through a Geneva motion and reduction gear to advance one unit at a time each 0·1 second. The figures of the counter have type faces and are aligned across the paper. The arrangement is that upward movement of the presser bar presses the paper and intervening ink ribbon against the lowermost row of figures and so prints the figures on the paper, the figures representing time in tenths of a second from a datum.

Rotatable with the driving member of the Geneva motion there is a rotary switch which completes a circuit only during the idle period when the counter is stationary. This switch controls the energization of the coil of a relay which has contacts in the circuit of the presser bar solenoid.

There is also a pair of contacts operable by the counter when it reaches its maximum reading (9999) and is returning to zero.

For each of the four channels there is a relay and an 'event' solenoid which, when energized, controls the printing on the papers of a symbol (e.g. a letter) in line with the counter figures. Each relay has three sets of contacts all of which are closed on energization of the relay coil. The contacts and coils are in circuits later described.

Associated with the presser bar there is a switch which is opened as the bar makes its return movement.

The machine is arranged for operation from alternating current mains and includes a full-wave rectifier and a low tension transformer.

The circuit arrangements and the operation of the machine will now be described.

Each of the four channels has a circuit as follows, the four circuits being in parallel. There is a channel operating switch (or two or more switches arranged for alternative operation) which, in the case of the 'internal' channel is the above-mentioned switch operated by the counter when it reaches its maximum reading and in the case of the other three channels is either a manually operable push-button switch or is arranged for remote operation by the 'event' to be recorded. The switch is in a circuit supplied by the rectifier and containing ue coil of one of the channel relays, a capacitor and a resistor shunted around the capacitor to constitute a leak. The capacitor has a value such that on closing the switch there is a charging impulse or surge sufficient to energize the relay and lasting for a period longer than the period of opening of the rotary switch (otherwise an event occurring during that period might not be recorded) but not long enough to overlap two consecutive periods in which the switch is closed (otherwise an event might be recorded twice).

As already stated each of the channel relays has three sets of contacts. One of these sets of each relay is in a circuit, supplied by the rectifier, containing the relay coil and in parallel with the capacitor. The circuit also contains the above-mentioned switch operated by the return of the presser bar. The arrangement operates as a holding circuit retaining the relay coil energized and the contacts closed after the end of the impulse until the printing operation has been effected when the coil is de-energized by the opening of the presser bar operated switch. Another of the sets is in a circuit, supplied by the transformer, containing the 'event' solenoid whereby the solenoid is energized during the time that the relay coil is energised. The third set of contacts is in a circuit, supplied from the mains, containing the presser bar operating solenoid and the contacts of the relay controlled by the rotary switch aforesaid.

The operation is as follows. The three external channels are appropriated to 'events' and on the occurrence of an event, the switch of the appropriate channel is closed. This causes an impulse which energizes the channel relay, thereby closing the holding circuit, the circuit for the 'event' solenoid and the circuit of the presser bar solenoid. The last circuit however is not completed until the rotary switch closes and the relay controlled thereby is energised. When that happens the presser bar is operated to print the time and during its return stroke (which occurs on the opening of the rotary switch) it operates the switch which it controls to release the relay and also feeds the paper and ink ribbon. The fourth channel operates in similar manner to print a symbol when the counter reaches 9999, the closing of the counter operated switch being equivalent to the closing of an external 'event' switch.

It should be appreciated that the several channels can operate independently or together according to the incidence of 'events', that the fact of an event occurring during the changing of the counter figures is 'stored' until the counter is stationary and the time is then printed and that no record is made and no paper is fed except on the occurrence of an 'event' whereby a compact record is obtained. Furthermore even if one channel is occupied by an event of long duration only one record is made and there is no interference with the operation of other channels.

In some cases where it is desired to increase the number of different events which can be recorded, arrangements may be made whereby certain events operate two (or more) channels according to a code, the result being that one event prints two (or more) symbols. Alternatively or in addition, supplementary machines, having additional channels, (but not necessarily time printing means) may be added to the machine described above. Furthermore the number of external channels in the machine itself may be increased (say to six).

The machine may be modified to record changes in variables. For example the value of a variable at any time may be represented by the reading of a reversible counter which is aligned with the time counter and any change in the reversible counter may operate as an 'event' switch to effect a printing of both counter readings.

The invention is not restricted to the details of the above example. For instance, an electro-magnetic counter operated by pulses of suitable length at ten pulses per second (generated by a spring clock or a valve circuit) may be used in place of the purely mechanical counter described. Again counters for the events recorded on each channel may be used as the printing members, whereby the total number of events in any particular period is automatically made available by comparison between the figures printed at the beginning and end of the period.

The invention relates to a device (herein referred to as a printing chronograph) for recording the occurrence of events (e.g. operations of control members, or pressure changes) and the times at which they occur. The invention is an improvement in, or modification of, that forming the subject of Patent No. 836111.

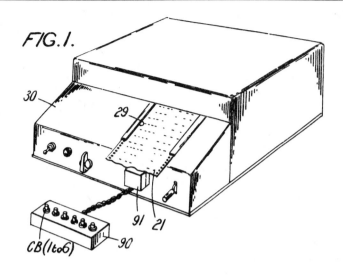

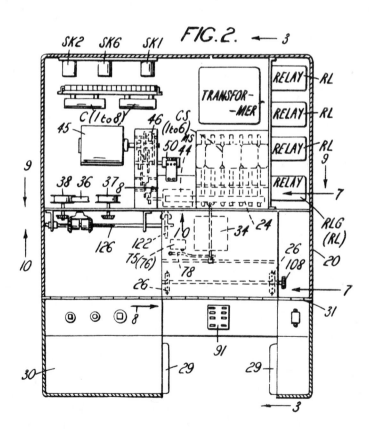

FIG. 35.1 *Illustrations for patent specification for printing chronograph (Thoth).*

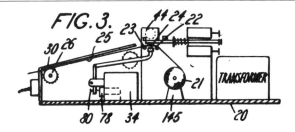

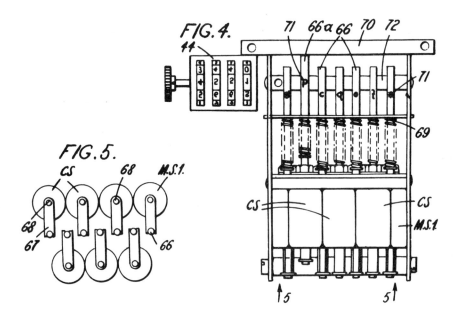

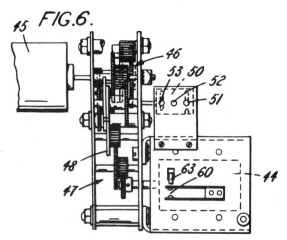

FIG. 35.1 (cont.)

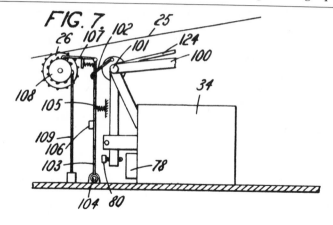

FIG. 7.

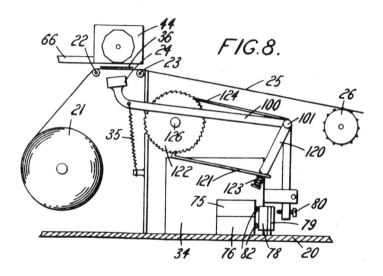

FIG.8.

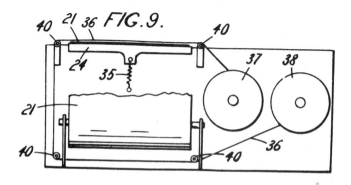

FIG.9.

FIG. 35.1 (cont.)

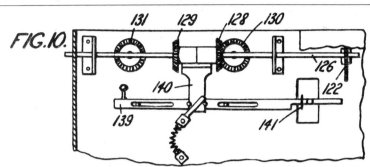

FIG.10.

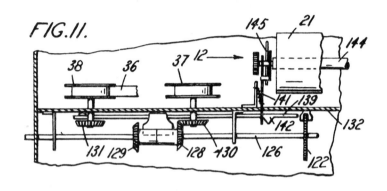

FIG.11.

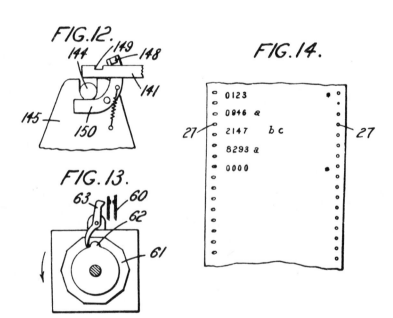

FIG.12.

FIG.14.

FIG.13.

Fig. 35.1 (cont.)

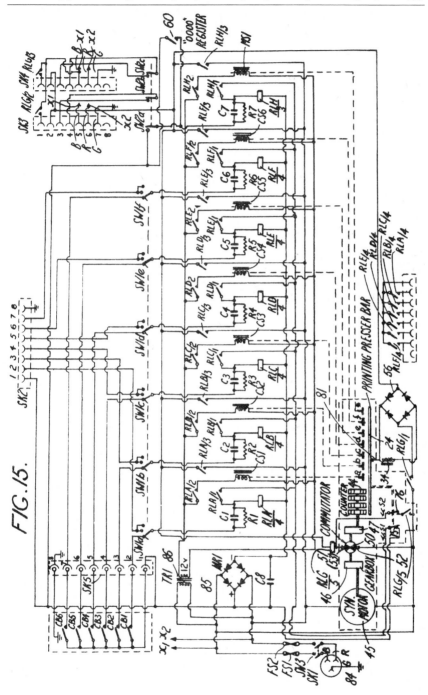

FIG. 35.1 (cont.)

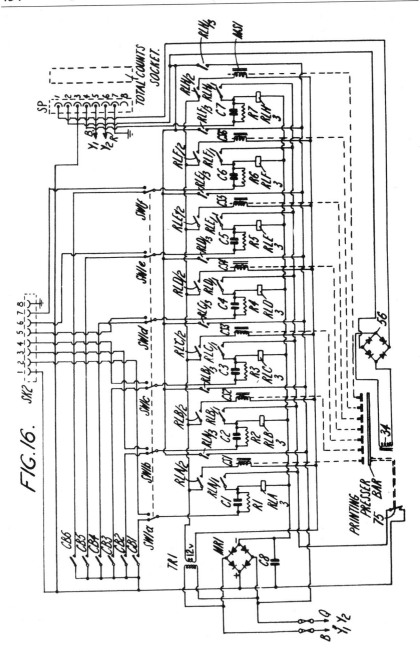

FIG. 35.1 (cont.)

36 Patent specification for 'Little Brother'

[Some years later, about 1966, we designed and built an 'eye' for Thoth. This consisted of a plate camera body, with miniature photo-cells placed at the focal plane and held in place with magnets. The cells could be placed, say, at the image of the choice points of a maze, so that the choices of the animal learning the maze would be printed, with the letter symbols and time prints of Thoth. The electronic eye, with Thoth, is shown over a rat maze in Fig. 36.1.

Thoth's eye could be placed well away from animals and did not affect them. It could be used for nesting behaviour in birds (if necessary with a telephoto lens) or for pedestrian behaviour at a street crossing or for a very different scale, down a microscope. It had the flexibility of camera, telescope and microscope optics, and could be operated in infra-red light to work, if necessary, secretly. Thoth and his eye 'Little Brother', might have been the basis of a comprehensive recording system, for kinds of data which even now are not handled well by electronic instruments or punched tape machines.

The circuit for Little Brother was designed by Stephen Salter and Brian Gaines. I give the Complete Specification (no. 25889/63) of 28 June 1963.]

★ ★ ★

THIS invention relates to devices for emitting signals in dependence on the occurrence of an event or events, more especially but not exclusively for use with machines for recording the occurrence and time of occurrence of the event or events.

According to this invention there is provided a signal emitting device comprising a lens (or the equivalent) and carrier means for carrying photo-electric cells at various positions or stations in or

FIG. 36.1 *'Little Brother' suspended over a rat-learning experiment, with printing recorder, 'Thoth', on the right.*

adjacent the focal plane of the lens, so that the cells can emit respective signals in dependence on the brightness of the parts of the image cast towards them by the lens.

According to a feature of the invention, the device comprises also viewing means for enabling an observer to see the image formed by the lens at said focal plane. In preferred arrangements the viewing means is such as to enable the observer to see the positions of the stations in relation to the various parts of the image.

In preferred constructions the cells can be placed in an infinite number of positions on the carrier, but in other constructions, a plurality of stations are provided each occupied by or adapted to receive a photo-electric cell. In the latter constructions, it is not essential that there is a photo-electric cell at each of the stations. In yet another aspect of the invention there are fewer cells than stations and there are at least some cells which can be moved from one station to another, as may be required. Alternatively it is possible, although less desirable, to provide a cell at each station and means for recording the response from only some of the cells.

According to another feature of the invention the carrier means comprises a member which is fixed relative to the lens, and magnetic means by which the cells are adjustably supported on said member.

In one such construction the member disposed in fixed relation to the lens is magnetizable, and arms are provided for carrying the respective cells, the magnetic means comprising magnets connected to the respective arms and mounted on said member, and the arrangement being such that the cells can be moved about in or adjacent the focal plane of the lens but are held in any desired position by the magnets.

The invention also provides the combination with a device as set forth in the second paragraph of this specification or statement of a recording machine, which records changes of at least a predetermined magnitude or rate in the response from individual cells and, simultaneously, a signal indicating on a time scale the time at which each change occurs.

Some embodiments of the invention will now be described by way of example with reference to the accompanying drawings [see pp. 438–9], in which:

Fig. 36.2(1) illustrates one form of the device.

Fig. 36.2(2) shows the circuit diagram of a suitable amplifier for use with each photo-electric cell to form part of, say, a recording machine.

Fig. 36.2(3) shows a circuit including a relay for operation by a signal from the amplifier, and

Fig. 36.2(4) shows a modified form of the device illustrated in Fig. 36.2(1).

The device comprises as shown in Fig. 36.2(1) a closed box 100 having a lens 101 mounted in one wall, the opposite wall of the box being constituted by a thin sheet of iron 102 which forms a carrier plate for a plurality of photo-electric cells 103 disposed within the box.

The photo-electric cells 103 are pin-like and have a diameter of 0·08″. Each cell has a square-shaped base 104 made of a magnetic material and the base of the cell is placed against the iron side of the box so that the cell projects towards the lens. Each of the cells is held in position by a corresponding small permanent magnet 105 disposed against the outside face of the iron side of the box. Thus, by moving one of the permanent magnets the corresponding cell can be moved also. A ground glass screen 106 is mounted within the box parallel to the iron side and is so disposed that it lies in or substantially in the focal plane of the lens. The size of the box is such that tips of the cells are very close to but do not touch the screen, so that the diffusing effect of the screen is minimised.

The output leads of each cell are in circuit with an individual amplifier, and the amplified signal obtained on occurrence of an event which produces a response from the cell initiates operation of a high-speed relay. The relay in turn actuates operation of a recording machine or other device, for example a recording machine of the kind described in Patent No. 836,111 or in Patent Application No. 42714/60 for recording the occurrence and time of occurrence of the event.

In these recording machines, the electrical response of each photo-electric cell to the occurrence of an event is arranged to produce an electrical impulse of fixed short duration independent of the length of the event, and this pulse actuates the printing of letters, figures or other symbols indicating the occurrence of an event and identifying

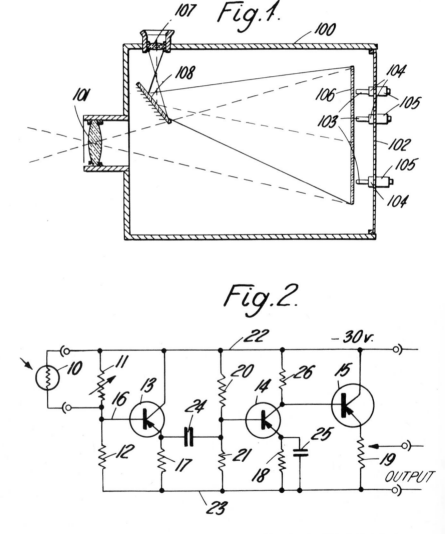

FIG. 36.2 *Illustrations for patent specification for 'Little Brother'.*

Fig.3.

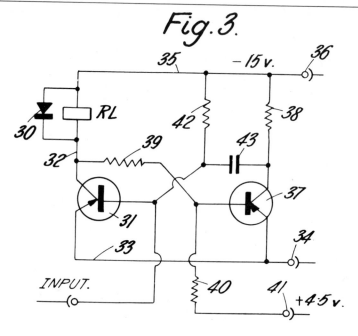

INPUT.

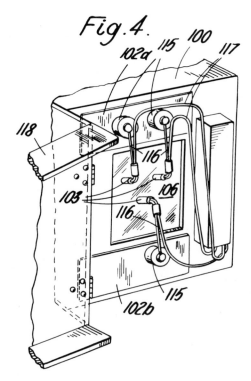

Fig.4.

FIG. 36.2 (cont.)

the cell which detected it and the time at which the event occurred.

To enable the observer to decide where to place the cells there is provided an arrangement of an eyepiece 107 and a mirror 108 enabling the observer to see the image cast by the lens on the ground glass screen and the positional relationship between the various parts of the image and the cells and to adjust the lens to bring the image into correct focus. The eyepiece is arranged so that the line of sight is generally at right angles to the optical axis of the lens and the mirror 108 is disposed just below the eyepiece and is set so that it reflects into the eyepiece the image cast by the lens on the ground glass screen.

If the observer wishes to obtain a record of the occasions upon which an event occurs in a particular part of the scene surveyed by the lens 101, he ascertains by looking through the eyepiece 107 upon which part of the screen 106 the image of the said part of the scene will fall. The event must of course be of such a nature as to produce a response in the photo-electric cell. He then moves one of the cells 103 into alignment with the said part of the scene by appropriate movement of its external magnet 105. As viewed through the eyepiece the position of the cell is indicated by a shadow which it casts on the screen. If the event occurs in the selected part or one of the selected parts of the scene surveyed by the lens, each of the photo-electric cell or cells in the corresponding position or positions will transmit a pulse to the recording machine so that a permanent record can be obtained of the fact that an event occurred and the time of occurrence of the event. After the occurrence has been registered in the recording machine, the machine is automatically re-set so as to be ready for the occurrence of the next event.

The box may if desired be designed to enable the ground glass screen to be removed through the side of the box.

A photographic exposure meter may be fitted to determine the optimum aperture of the lens giving the image.

Where the apparatus is used to provide a record of successes or errors of an animal, for example of a rat running through a maze, an experimenter can, by using the eyepiece, decide which route through the maze should be open and can place the photo-electric cells in the appropriate stations to survey the animal's progress.

If desired, the internal surface of the iron side of the box may be coated with glue at the commencement of an experiment and the cells may be appropriately placed, so that when the glue dries the cells are held fast.

In an alternative arrangement the iron side of the box is replaced by a set of parallel rods defining a plane at rightangles to the optical axis of the lens. The cells are carried on the rods by clamps, the arrangement being such that the cells can be placed in an infinite number of positions in the plane.

In the modification shown in Fig. 36.2(4), the iron side 102 of the box is replaced by two iron sheets 102a, 102b disposed one adjacent each of two opposite edges of the ground glass screen 106. A number of magnets 115, one for each cell, are disposed on the iron sheets 102a, 102b and each magnet has secured to it one part of an L-shaped arm 116, the other part of which projects towards the back of the screen 106 and carries the cell 103 at its end. The leads 117 connecting the cells to the amplifiers comprise flexible screened cables which extend along and are secured to the arm 116. The magnets 115 can be moved to place the cells where they are required to be and serve then to hold the cells firmly in the selected positions. A light-tight hinged lid 118 is provided for covering over the screen 106, sheets 102a, 102b the magnets 115 and cells 103. Only three cells are shown in Fig. 36.2(4) but it will be understood that more cells may be provided if desired.

In yet another arrangement the side of the box opposite the lens is a carrier plate provided with a matrix of holes in each of which a photo-electric cell can be positioned. The number of cells is fewer than the number of holes and a ground glass screen disposed in front of the carrier enables the cells to be positioned in the selected stations formed by the holes in the carrier plate.

By providing for adjustment of the position of the carrier for the cells towards and away from the lens, adjustment of the position of the cells in three dimensions may be obtained.

The outputs of the photo-electric cells may be fed into individual transistor circuits giving an amplified signal which is transmitted to the recorder. The signal may be arranged to operate, say, a switch, if required. For the latter purposes, high speed mechanical relays may be employed. One suitable arrangement is shown by way of example in Fig. 36.2(2).

Referring to Fig. 36.2(2) the terminals of the photo-electric cell 10 are connected in parallel with a resistance 11, and a resistance 12 is connected in series with resistance 11. Three transistors 13, 14 and 15 are connected in parallel with each other and resistances 11 and 12 between lines 22 and 23. The base of transistor 13 is connected by a line 16 to a point between resistors 11 and 12. The emitters of transistors 13, 14 and 15 have respectively in series with them resistances 17, 18 and 19. Two resistances 20, 21 are connected between lines 22, 23 in parallel with the resistors 11 and 12, and a capacitor 24 is connected between the emitter of transistor 13 and a point in the line between resistances 20 and 21. A second capacitor

25 is connected in parallel with resistance 18. The base of transistor 14 is connected to a point between resistances 20 and 21, and the base of transistor 15 is connected to the collector of transistor 14. The collector of transistor 14 is also connected to line 22 through a resistance 26. In this arrangement line 22 is maintained at a potential of −30V and the output terminals of the amplifier are respectively connected to line 23 and a tapping point on resistance 19.

In Fig. 36.2(3) the high-speed relay which is to be actuated by the response of the photo-electric cell to the occurrence of an event is indicated at RL and has a rectifier 30 connected in parallel with it. The output of the amplifier is connected to the base of a transistor 31, the collector of which is connected through a line 32 to the relay. The emitter of transistor 31 is connected by a line 33 to a terminal 34 which is maintained at zero potential. Relay RL is also connected by a line 35 to a terminal 36 which in this instance is maintained at a potential of −15V. A second transistor 37 has its emitter connected to line 33 and has its collector connected to line 35 through a resistance 38. The base of transistor 37 is connected through a resistor 39 to line 32 and is connected through a resistor 40 to a terminal 41 which in this arrangement is maintained at a potential of 4.5V. A resistance 42 is connected between line 35 and the base of transistor 31. A capacitor 43 is connected between the base of transistor 31 and the collector of transistor 37.

The relay actuating circuit provides a circuit by means of which an electric pulse received from the photo-electric cell via the amplifier causes the relay RL to be actuated even if the pulse lasts only a few micro-seconds. In effect the circuit produces a lengthened pulse to actuate the relay, the duration of this pulse being sufficient to hold the contacts of the relay closed for at least 0·1 second.

The following table shows the type or value of each of the components in the circuits shown in Figs. 36.2(2) and (3).

Component	Type or Value
Photo-electric cell 10	ORP 60
Resistance 11	2M
Resistor 12	470K
Transistor 13	OC 75
Transistor 14	OC 75
Transistor 15	OC 71
Resistor 17	10K
Resistor 18	1.2K
Resistor 19	15K

Resistor 20	270K
Resistor 21	12K
Capacitor 24	50 mf
Capacitor 25	16 mf
Resistor 26	15K
Transistor 31	OC 72
Transistor 37	OC 72
Resistor 38	1K
Resistor 39	39K
Resistor 40	68K
Resistor 42	47K
Capacitor 43	16 mf

The device thus gives a record which can be used immediately, for example for correction of errors of operation of a machine or other device being surveyed through the lens.

The device can also be used for giving a digital output from an analogue display such as a voltmeter or an oscilloscope and can do this without interfering in any way with the existing analogue device.

What we claim is :—

1. A signal emitting device comprising a lens (or the equivalent) and carrier means for carrying photo-electric cells at various stations in or adjacent the focal plane of the lens, so that the cells can emit respective signals in dependence on the brightness of the parts of the image cast towards them by the lens.

2. A device as claimed in claim 1, wherein there is provided viewing means for enabling an observer to see the image formed by the lens at said focal plane.

3. A device as claimed in claim 2, wherein the viewing means is such as to enable the observer to see the positions of the stations in relation to the various parts of the image.

4. A device as claimed in any of claims 1 to 3, wherein the cells can be placed in an infinite number of positions on the carrier.

5. A device as claimed in any of claims 1 to 3, wherein a plurality of stations are provided each occupied by or adapted to receive a photo-electric cell.

6. A device as claimed in claim 5, wherein there are fewer cells than stations and there are at least some cells which can be moved from one station to another.

7. A device as claimed in any of claims 1 to 6, wherein the carrier means comprises a member which is fixed relative to the lens, and magnetic means by which the cells are adjustably supported on said member.

8. A device as claimed in claim 7, wherein the member disposed in fixed relation to the lens, is magnetizable, wherein the carrier means comprises also arms for carrying the respective cells, and wherein the magnetic means comprises magnets connected to the respective arms and mounted on said member, the arrangement being such that the cells can be moved about in or adjacent the focal plane of the lens but are held in any desired position by the magnets.

9. A device as claimed in claim 7, wherein said member comprises a plate member disposed parallel to the focal plane but displaced therefrom to the side remote from the lens, wherein each cell is mounted on a magnetic base disposed against the face of the plate member nearer the lens and wherein the magnetic means comprises a magnet disposed on the other face of the plate member opposite each cell to hold the base for the cell in any selected position on the plate member.

10. A device as claimed in any of claims 1 to 6, wherein the carrier means comprises a carrier plate or honeycomb structure, and the stations are provided by apertures in the carrier plate or honeycomb structure.

11. A device as claimed in any of claims 1 to 6, wherein the carrier means comprises a set of parallel rods defining a plane at rightangles to the optical axis of the lens and clamps by means of which the cells are supported from the rods.

12. A device as claimed in any of claims 1 to 11, wherein a ground glass screen or a half-silvered mirror is disposed substantially in the focal plane of the lens and the photo-electric cells are disposed adjacent the screen on the side of the screen further from the lens.

13. The combination with a device as claimed in any of claims 1 to 12 of a recording machine, which records changes of at least a predetermined magnitude or rate in the response from individual cells and, simultaneously, a signal indicating on a time scale the time at which each change occurs.

14. A signal emitting device substantially as hereinbefore described with reference to and as illustrated in Fig. 36.2(1) or in Fig. 36.2(1) as modified by Fig. 36.2(4) of the drawings.

15. The combination with a signal emitting device of a recording machine substantially as hereinbefore described with reference to and as illustrated in Figs. 36.2(1) to (3) or in Figs. 36.2(1) to (3) as modified by Fig. 36.2(4), of the drawings.

37 *A device for giving a histogram of time-intervals*

[Experience soon showed that the 'reflex' optical version of Little Brother is not necessary: it is quite easy to position the photocells – preferably held by magnets – from the image as visible at the back of the ground glass screen. Here I would like to put in a plea for magnets – they are not used nearly enough. For example, surely they could be used on optical benches, and for many other temporary holding operations.

The next device is presented somewhat out of sequence but it is a data recording device and so is appropriate at this point. My colleague in this was Tim Eiloart, at that time working with me on the Department of Scientific and Industrial Research grant in my laboratory. He is a remarkable man. With his father, Bushy Eiloart, and two friends he attempted to cross the Atlantic in a balloon. In mid Atlantic the balloon *Small World* unexpectedly rose to great heights, in spite of its drag rope. Losing too much gas, it deposited its crew of four upon the ocean. Fortunately they had no mere wicker gondola; but a small boat capable, though with difficulty, of sailing. Though their radio transmitter had failed they at length did cross the Atlantic. In spite of sailing the second half they broke the world record for the longest ever balloon journey. Tim worked with me only for a short time; he went on to found his own firm, Cambridge Consultants, and has developed rare powers as an entrepreneur.

The concept embodied in the Histogram recorder is diverting, though it never really got anywhere in this form. It was developed in a different and far more elaborate form (see Fig. 37.1) by my colleague Stephen Salter. It was taken up, in still different guise, by a small firm who sold their version to a large firm which now manufactures it. But the present 'it' is so different from the original that I would not wish to claim credit for the perhaps over-mutated grandchild.]

★   ★   ★

446

FIG. 37.1 *The ball-dropping histogram recorder, developed and built by Stephen Salter.*
(This worked with a linear potentiometer servocontrol system, so is considerably different
from the original belt device).

IN human and animal behaviour studies it is often necessary to measure a large number of time-intervals – for example, stimulus-response times – and to find the mean and variance of the distribution of intervals for the various conditions of the experiment. At present this is either extremely laborious or it involves elaborate and expensive punch tape and computer techniques. The device to be described is designed to give the statistical distribution of time-intervals in a very simple manner. The distribution is built up during the experiments, and the mean and variance may be determined without the use of arithmetic. A photographic record of the distribution may be obtained without the use of a camera.

The histogram is built up by dropping ball-bearings into a row of equally spaced holes in a transparent strip of 'Perspex'. At the beginning of each interval to be included, a ball is made to travel at constant speed across the holes, which thus indicate time-intervals. At the end of each interval a ball is dropped into the hole lying immediately below it. The mechanical problem to be solved is how to accelerate a ball very rapidly from rest, to carry it at constant speed, and finally to drop it exactly when required.

It seemed important to try to limit the moving parts requiring acceleration to the ball itself, and this has been accomplished (Fig. 37.2). An endless belt, driven at constant speed, lies above the row of holes, and a long narrow electromagnet lies immediately above the belt. At the start of an interval to be included in the distribution, a ball is projected on to the under-side of the belt with a solenoid actuator; it sticks to the underside of the belt, being held by the magnet above it, and it runs along with the belt until the magnet current is cut, at the end of the time-interval. This system is found to work extremely well. It is possible to avoid any slip of the ball on the belt during the period of acceleration by projecting the ball at such an angle that its horizontal velocity equals the velocity of the belt. This angle may be adjusted for the various belt speeds used to give suitable time-scales for the histogram. For situations where the variance is small in relation to the time-interval, a fixed known delay

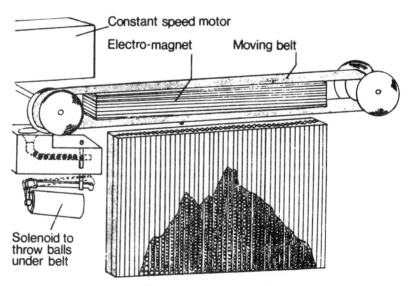

FIG. 37.2 *Histogram recorder. A ball is held by the magnetic field to the underside of the moving belt.*

may be introduced, and a suitable belt-speed used so that the display shows the whole of the variance with adequate spread.

A photographic record may be made at any time, by placing sensitive paper behind the display and exposing with a flash of light, when a shadowgraph of the columns of balls may be obtained.

Where a histogram is required for several conditions, one motor and gear box (the most expensive parts) may be used to drive a series of belts each producing a histogram under the required conditions. Alternatively, a series of the 'Perspex' strips with holes may be placed one at a time, in suitable order, under a single belt and magnet.

The method is not limited to recording time-intervals. With modifications, it may be used to record the number of events occurring in time. An example would be the number of vehicles passing a check point against time of day. For this purpose, either the hopper of balls or the 'Perspex' display is made to move at a constant (generally slow) speed. Whenever an event occurs to be included, a ball is released, and thus a histogram is built up against a linear time-base which may be in terms of minutes, hours or even days.

The method is not limited to time-intervals. For example, in psycho-physical experiments involving judgements of length, or intensity of light or sound, positions of a wedge or angles of rotation of a shaft can be represented by dropping a ball into a slot, the supply of balls being shifted across the display either mechanically or with M motors to link the wedge or shaft to the recording device. It can be used for any such purpose where the serial order of judgements is not required. Similarly, it might be used for industrial process control, to give the distribution of sizes or weights of machined parts.

The device is in the prototype stage, but the essential principle has been tested and found to work satisfactorily. It should be possible to find the mean of a distribution by balancing the display, and the variance by finding its moment of inertia.

38 *An optical micro-stimulator for the human retina*

[The following example of an optical device was designed for experiments that came to nothing. I include it to illustrate how one can sometimes adapt what exists to attain something new. Improvising can be vital, especially in a laboratory short of machining facilities or workshop time.]

★   ★   ★

As is well known, the application of micro-electrode techniques has provided new and suggestive data on the electrical activity of the retina. The data are so complex, however, that the functional significance of much of the activity as unknown.

In order to relate the electrical activity to photic stimuli it has been necessary to record from small areas of the retina and; in some cases, to stimulate small areas with light of carefully controlled intensity and wave-length. These special conditions of stimulation have raised problems of interpretation and have increased the importance of basic perceptual experiments using small spots of light. The study of perceptual phenomena associated with micro-stimulation might help to make it possible to interpret in detail the physiological records of retinal activity, and then to relate this activity to information used by the brain.

The instrument to be described is simple and versatile. It costs little and can be made by a mechanic without special experience of optical instruments. It is hoped that it may be adaptable enough for class demonstrations and sufficiently accurate at least for preliminary research of these problems.

450

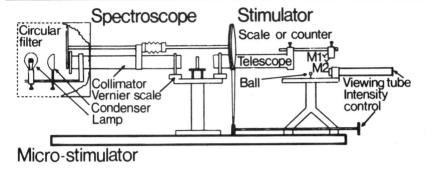

Fig. 38.1 *An optical device for stimulating the eye with small areas of controlled intensity and colour. It was built round an existing spectroscope.*

Design

In order to reduce construction to a minimum the instrument is built round a conventional table spectroscope. This may be antique but should be of a heavy design and fitted with an accurate vernier scale. It is not necessary to damage the spectroscope, for the various attachments to the tubes may be mounted with clips made of spring brass and locked with tightening screws.

Normally table spectroscopes are so arranged that the collimator tube is fixed to the prism table while the telescope is free to swing, but for our purpose it is convenient to keep the emergent beam at a constant angle for all values of λ. This is achieved by simply screwing the collimator into the telescope ring mounting, and vice versa; the threads of the two tubes are usually identical. λ is now varied by swinging the collimator, to which a slow motion drive should be fitted. Once the instrument is calibrated, λ may be determined from the vernier scale, but, if a prism is used, the relation between the scale reading and the wave-length will not be simple, because a prism does not give a 'normal spectrum'. The prism should therefore be removed and a small replica grating substituted. λ is now determined by $\lambda = d \sin \theta$, where d is grating space (which for Rowland's machine is $1{\cdot}693 \times 10^{-4}$ cm).

A lamp house is mounted on the end of the collimator tube; a suitable light source is a 6-volt car headlamp. Intensity must not be varied by varying the voltage, for this would change the spectral luminosity curve of the source, but by a neutral wedge filter which may be mounted on a shaft running along the collimator tube; the shaft is then rotated by the subject or the experimenter. The angle of rotation of this shaft is linearly related to intensity and may be measured on a scale attached to the drive end or, better, by means of a cyclometer counter geared to the shaft to provide a sensitive indicator of the angle. (A counter is more easily read at low levels of illumination; this is most important since readings must be taken quickly and fatigue avoided).

We can now produce a beam of light of variable and controlled wavelength and intensity. We must use this to produce small fields suitable for retinal stimulation. Extremely small fields are usually produced with a microscope used backwards, a comparatively large field being reduced twenty to one hundred times (Hartridge, 1950). The present instrument avoids the use of reducing lenses, which are expensive and liable to systematic chromatic effects.

The small fields are obtained by reflecting the light from small steel balls. Ball bearings are used; they are very accurately figured and are made to a tolerance of 0·0001 inch diameter. The size of the field is determined by the diameter of the ball and the viewing distance. The angular separation between fields may be controlled by employing a ball bearing for each field and adjusting the distance between them with feeler gauges. For very small angles one ball may be used, this being lit by two beams and the angle between the beams being determined. Continuous adjustment of angular separation is possible by rotating the mounting holding the ball bearings with respect to the subject's viewing tube.

It is possible to keep the wavelength of each field the same, both being varied together with the collimator adjustment, or to keep a constant difference in λ between the fields as the spectrum is swept by the collimator. d λ is dependent on the setting of the surface-silvered mirrors m1 and m2. In order to vary d λ continuously, one of the plane mirrors may be rotated in a controlled manner, or the ball-bearing mounting may be rotated with respect to the plane mirrors.

If the instrument is used to study interaction effects it is useful to be able to cut out each field. This may be done quite simply by mounting small vanes on relays, which may be electrically operated with keys by subject or experimenter.

Calibration

It is only necessary to calibrate on one spectral line since the collimator scale accurately follows a simple law. A sodium lamp, such as is used in street lighting, is used. The method is first to set the collimator vernier scale to the calculated value for the calibration line used (where d is 1.693×10^{-4}, and λ is 5889, the scale should be set to 20° 28': see Jenkins and White 1950). The plane mirror m1 should then be rotated until the orange sodium line falls onto the ball-bearing serving as spherical mirror and is seen with maximum intensity at the viewing tube. Any desired d λ between the two fields is now determined by setting the collimator scale to give the required difference and adjusting m2 in order to allow the line to fall on its spherical mirror; in this way the second field with the required difference in wavelength from the first is provided. It is thus possible to study interaction effects between small fields where these are of different colour. It is hoped that this technique might provide some information on the physiological basis of colour vision.

The stimulus variables which may be controlled are:

1. One, two or perhaps more stimulus spots, or fields, are provided (*a*) simultaneously, (*b*) in turn.
2. The intensity of the field is controlled, and at least relative measures up to 5 per cent. accuracy are possible. (Independent control of each field intensity is not described, but might be attained with a further calibrated filter interposed after m1 or m2. Shutters to produce flicker may also be incorporated).
3. The difference in wavelength between the fields (*a*) may be continuously varied, or (*b*) may be held constant at any value while the visual spectrum is swept by the collimator.
4. Angular separation between fields may be set to any given small value, or continuously varied.

39 *A single-flash rotary disk optical shutter*

[The next instrument is a high-speed optical shutter. It was originally used in the 'neural noise' experiments described in the Experiments section (No. 8). It is useful, as it can work over a large range, can give very short flashes (or exposure times), and can be extremely accurate.]

★   ★   ★

Iᴛ is often necessary, for example, for physiological and psychological experiments on vision, to provide short flashes of light of controlled duration. In some circumstances this presents a problem for which there is no ready solution. A pendulum shutter is at best clumsy, photographic shutters are sometimes employed, but even the most expensive are not sufficiently accurate for any but the crudest work. Not only are photographic shutters subject to a high degree of variance, but they tend to become faster with repeated exposures, introducing systematic changes very difficult to correct, and they are affected by temperature changes which is particularly serious when used in conjunction with a projection system where the heat may be considerable. In practice, flashes as short as 1 m. sec. are often required for visual research.

It is sometimes possible to avoid the use of shutters altogether by switching the light source itself, but this is not generally permissible. It is usually unsatisfactory where the light source is a filament lamp because of the low rate of rise and fall in intensity when switched, though filament lamps are often the most convenient source in other respects. Where the beam is split, it may be necessary to have a shutter in the system to affect only one beam (Fig. 39.1)

454

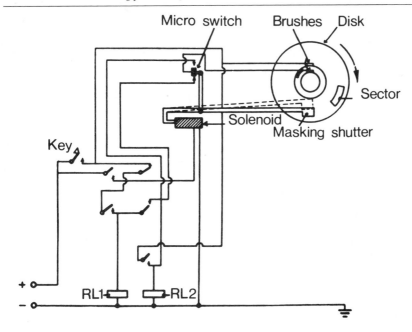

FIG. 39.1 *Diagram of arrangement for rotary disk optical shutter.*

Design

The shutter utilizes the well-known principle of the rotating disk with a peripheral sector. The disk is arranged to interrupt the light beam except for the sector at its periphery. To achieve as nearly as possible a square-wave flash the angular velocity of the sector should be high. This is particularly important if the optical aperture is large where the shutter cuts the beam. In practice a disk diameter of about ten inches is convenient.

The problem is to adapt this familiar arrangement to provide single flashes at the will of the operator. This is accomplished here with a solenoid-operated 'masking' shutter arranged to interrupt the beam except when a flash is required. It is so arranged that the masking shutter starts to open immediately *after* the sector in the continuously rotating disk has passed the light beam, which is therefore occluded by the disk for the maximum time before the sector returns. The masking shutter thus has the maximum possible time to open before the sector reaches the beam, which now results in a flash. The masking shutter then starts to close immediately the sector has passed the beam – i.e. immediately after the flash – and so it has also the maximum possible time to close before the sector again returns to the beam. Thus the flash duration is entirely determined by the disk with its sector, and the masking shutter can be comparatively crude. In fact, it is simply an aluminium flap operated by a solenoid and returned with a spring. The only problem is to synchronize this solenoid with the disk so that when a flash is required it is always energized and de-energized immediately after the sector has left the beam. A possible disadvantage of the system is that there is a slight variable delay between the operation of the shutter and the resulting flash, but this does not generally matter, especially as it is possible to record the time interval between the flash and the result (such as the observer's response) simply by adding a contact for the time recorder to the shaft of the disk.

The design problem is to synchronize the masking shutter with the disk so that one, and only one, complete flash is produced whenever the key is closed. It is most important that flashes are never cut short by the masking shutter failing completely to open or close in time for the sector's arrival at the beam.

The synchronizing circuit

When the key is closed, no circuit is completed until the commutator on the disk's drive shaft is 'made'. The synchronizing pulse from the commutator energizes $RL1$ which holds, the holding circuit being through the micro-switch operated mechanically by the masking shutter, and a 'break' contact on $RL2$ (see figure). The commutator is arranged to give a synchronizing pulse of just sufficient length to close $RL2$ when the disk is rotating at its maximum speed. The closing of $RL1$ energizes the solenoid, raising the masking shutter. While the masking shutter is opening, the sector is approaching the optical path: the solenoid remains energized until the commutator closes again, giving a second synchronizing pulse. But this time the micro-switch has been changed over by the mechanical movement of the masking shutter: the result is that the second synchronizing pulse energizes $RL2$, which holds. The closing of $RL2$ prevents the solenoid from being energized by further pulses, although the key may be held down. For high disk speeds this is an essential precaution against unwanted multiple flashes. When the key is raised, the holding circuit to $RL2$ is broken, and so the circuit re-sets.

There is a complication in that the key might be closed while the commutator is closed. When this occurs the synchronizing pulse will be cut short and may not be long enough to close $RL1$. When this occurs, the circuit remains inoperative until the next synchronizing pulse arrives, and this time it must be a complete pulse. It is important to note that the masking shutter has to be fully open before the sector reaches the optical path even when the beginning of the synchronizing pulse is lost, provided there is sufficient to close *RL*1. Thus the synchronizing should be set from the *end* of the pulse. Since there is some delay in the closing of *RL*1, the commutator should be advanced slightly.

The disk drive

A number of methods have been tried for driving the disk. Where it is necessary to vary its speed a Velodyne or a synchronous motor driven by a variable frequency oscillator may be used.

For the production of 1 m. sec. flashes, a shaft speed of 3000 r.p.m. is convenient. This flash duration will then be obtained with a 17° sector, providing the masking shutter can open fully within about 0·03 and close within the same time. Shorter flashes may be obtained by reducing the sector angle, though its width should be several times the width of the light beam if reasonably 'square' flashes are to be obtained.

Very long flashes may, of course, be obtained by stopping the disk so that light passes through the sector, and using the masking shutter as a simple solenoid-operated shutter. The lower limit to the obtainable flash lengths is set by the masking shutter. It should be possible to produce very short flashes by introducing a second disk, also with a sector, geared to the first so that the two sectors coincide, say, every ten revolutions of the first 'master' disk. The minimum flash length would then be reduced by a factor of ten.

[The 'solid-image microscope' is an idea that captivates, though whether it will ever be an instrument generally used is far from certain. I remember vividly how the idea struck. I was reading a paper, by the great experimentalist G. von Békésy, on movements of the bones of the middle ear, transmitting vibrations from the tympanum to the oval window of the cochlea. He was describing the difficulty: that the vibrations are of very small amplitude compared with the sizes of the bones – so when sufficient magnification was used to show up the vibrations the bones were not all in focus. The depth of field of microscopes is necessarily very small at high magnifications: this makes stereo microscopy impossible for magnifications much over × 100, and the appreciation of three-dimensional structures difficult and sometimes impossible at high magnifications.

While reading the paper of Békésy's late at night, I had a vivid mental image of a vibrating lens. I 'saw' the thin plane of focus of the lens sweeping up and down through the structure, to extract information in depth by an optical scanning. As I thought about it, it became clear that the depth of field of the lens should be as *small* as possible, to give high resolution in the Z-axis. It also became clear – and this turned out to be the main difficulty – that the image as well as the object would require scanning in depth; first to extract information of depth and secondly to reconstruct it into three-dimensional visual space.

The idea led to a long series of experiments, the earliest being undertaken with my respected friend, Peter Donaldson, who at that time was Technical Officer to the Physiological Laboratory at Cambridge. Peter Donaldson is that rare being, a truly first-rate engineer (not a mere gadgeteer such as myself) who though quiet and careful, has a hidden spark of the unorthodox. Much later, he joined Professor Giles Brindley, to implant electronic devices into the brains of blind people to give them at least rudimentary sight.

Although the solid-image microscope met considerable acclaim it is still not manufactured. One of the difficulties was that microscope firms did not want to get involved with moving parts, while general instrument firms did not want to get involved with microscopes. Since then, most of the English microscope manufacturers have been bought up by general instrument firms – rough justice!

The earlier versions were built with much help from Peter Donaldson, Bill Matthews and John Nosworthy. The later versions were built by Stephen Salter, who put a lot of work and inventive ability into this project.]

★   ★   ★

ALL knowledge is based upon information received by the senses, and all control is ultimately dependent upon movements of limbs. Instruments and tools are extensions of senses and limbs – whether telescopes or microscopes, hammers or cars. As science and technology advance, our senses and limbs become inadequate, and so civilization depends upon devices to increase the input information, and the output precision and power of bodies, themselves unchanged since long before civilized life began. Given instruments and tools, man is a species far removed from any other. Rather than dehumanizing man, technology de-apes him.

As instrument design advances we gain information previously denied us. The sense organs are transducers lying between the world and the central nervous system; instruments are transducers between the world and the senses, and they must be suitably matched to both, their design considerations bridging physics and sensory physiology. Most instruments are in fact extensions of the eye, which in man is the most efficient sense organ, the ear running in second place. The eye may be thought of as several largely independent sensory systems in one organ; for it provides information concerning brightness, colour, movement and form in three spatial dimensions. Now when we extend the functions of the eye by the addition of an instrument, some of these channels are generally sacrificed for technical reasons, and so though improving the matching of the eye to some selected features of the world, we may impair its matching to the brain by cutting out some of the normally functional neural channels, and the resulting perception can be misleading. A case in point, and the case with which we are concerned, is loss of stereoscopic vision in the microscope.

None of the usual cues to depth were available to the early microscopists. They were denied stereoscopic vision – which depends upon disparate images upon the two retinas resulting from slightly different view points – and they could not view objects from different positions by moving the head. The first attempt to provide binocular vision with a microscope was surprisingly early, being made by a French Capuchin friar, le Père Cherubin, this pre-dating any experimental work on stereoscopic vision by nearly two hundred years. He wrote, in 1677, 'Some years ago I resolved to effect what I had long before premeditated, to make a microscope to see the smallest objects with the two eyes conjointly; and this project has succeeded even beyond my expectations; with advantages above the single instrument so extraordinary and so surprising, that every intelligent person to whom I have shown the effect has assured me that inquiring philosophers will be highly pleased with the communication'. This was apparently quite forgotten until Wheatstone's invention of the stereoscope, introduced in 1838. Wheatstone asked both Ross and Powell to construct a stereoscopic microscope, but this was not done, the first instrument of modern times being that of an American, J. L. Riddell, built about 1850 and greatly improved by F. H. Wenham in 1853. Wenham realized that a high power objective derives different views from its central and marginal rays, and succeeded in deriving two disparate images from a single objective, by dividing the exit rays and producing appropriate right and left images for the two eyes corresponding to the different view points. This is the basis of all modern high power stereoscopic microscopes.

Binocular stereoscopic microscopes are used a great deal, but suffer from the essential limitation that it is not possible to produce an image of a thick section at high magnification with the structure in focus throughout the depth of the section. In other words, lenses giving large useful magnification must have but a small depth of field. Thus although the appearance of depth can be given in this way, the method can be used only over a very small range in depth in the object. The experimental microscope to be described does, at least in principle, beat this essential limitation in lenses as they are normally employed.

The general principle of the 'solid-image' microscope

The depth of field of high power microscope objectives is extremely small, the resolution in depth being comparable to the resolution in the image plane. What we do is to accept this, and to use this feature of high power lenses to extract information in depth by scanning the thin plane of sharp focus through the specimen.

As we know from the cinema, if a series of pictures is presented in rapid succession, they fuse. It might thus be thought that if a series of pictures were obtained corresponding to successive layers and presented in rapid succession, we would see the entire three dimensional structure, and that this would be the simple answer to the problem of the limited depth of focus of objectives; but this is not so, for we should see only a muddle of pictures lying upon each other like a series of photographs (though related photographs) taken upon a single film. This then is not the full answer. But now imagine the series of pictures as photographic transparencies placed in order, one behind the next, to form a cube of pictures through which we could look. Would we not have a solid, if layered, photograph in three dimensions? And could we not walk round it and see it from various positions? Would not the structure change by parallax as we change our view point, like a real object lying in space? If this would work, we should have put to advantage the limited depth of focus of microscope objectives, by using the thin plane of sharp focus to obtain separate pictures of the structure at various depths, to give a single 'solid' picture occupying three-dimensional space. Thick specimens could be used, for since the plane of focus moves through the specimen it can, and indeed must, be many times the depth of the plane of focus of the objective. The thinner the plane of focus the better the resolution in depth, and so the original optical limitation has been put to use.

It is in practice a nuisance to have to take a series of photographs, and it is difficult to arrange them so that there are no serious errors of registration between the planes; it would thus be better to provide a solid picture immediately, without the photographic intermediary.

Suppose we project the image obtained by the microscope's objective upon a screen, so that we may see it just as we look at a slide projected on a screen. Suppose now that we move the objective lens up and down, not slowly but fast, the focal plane running regularly up and down through the specimen many times a second. The result would be a blurred muddle – just as a set of photographs lying upon each other in two dimensions would be a muddle – but if, somehow, we could present the image corresponding to each depth at its correct distance from the observer, then we should obtain an image without confusion, and it would be a three-dimensional 'solid' image. This may be done simply by vibrating the screen back and forth, in synchrony with the scan of the focal plane through the specimen. As the screen moves away from the observer, the picture upon it changes to correspond with each new structure revealed in the depth of the specimen by the scan of the plane of focus. The observer may view the solid image lying in the volume swept by the vibrating screen from any frontal position, when he will see the structure change by parallax as though it were a real object: he will see a magnified model of the object lying in a luminous block of space.

We have built just such an instrument, and with it we can obtain 'solid' pictures which do show structure lying in depth. The rough surface of a slide looks like a miniature mountain range; the organs inside an insect may be seen in their relative positions. In place of a fly entombed in amber we have a fly in a block of light, and our fly need not be dead.

Design problems

It is of primary importance for acceptable resolution in depth that the plane of focus of the objective lens be as thin as possible for each point in the object to be represented in its correct position in depth in the image space. It is thus of first importance to examine the theoretical resolution obtainable in depth with microscope objectives.

The depth of field decreases as the aperture of the lens increases – which is fortunate for we also need high aperture to obtain good resolution in the normal image plane if high magnification is to be used, as was established theoretically by Abbé at the end of the nineteenth century. The depth of field, *df*, is determined by the allowed difference in path length from the centre and the periphery of the lens as the distance of the object is changed. Some criterion is needed to assign a value to the allowable difference, and Rayleigh's criterion of one quarter of a wavelength of light is generally accepted; *df* is then given by

$$df = \frac{\text{Allowed difference in path length } (\lambda/4)}{n. \, sin^2 \ U/2}$$

where *U* is the angle made by the marginal rays with the axis in the object space, and *n* is the refractive index of the medium on the object side of the lens. Taking the wavelength of light as 0·0005 mm the depth of field of lenses of various apertures may be calculated (Table 40.1).

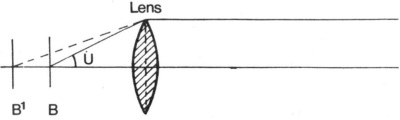

Fig. 40.1 *Geometry of the depth of field in lenses, showing the changing angle, U, and the central and peripheral rays.*

TABLE 40.1
CALCULATED FIGURES GIVING DEPTH OF FIELD FOR VARIOUS VALUES OF
NUMERICAL APERTURE

	Numerical aperture	Depth of field (mm)
Working in air	0·25	0·0079
	0·50	0·0019
	0·75	0·0008
Oil immersion	1·00	0·0007
	1·25	0·0004

It will be seen that the depth of field is very small for high apertures, and smaller working in air than oil immersed for equivalent apertures. Thus resolution in depth (which we may term the Z-axis) can be quite high – but we must make a correction if we are not to be misled into undue optimism. Rayleigh's criterion is generally taken for just acceptable loss of resolution, but we should demand more than this, for we wish to know when a point will be *invisible*, rather than just detectably fuzzy. For this reason the effective depth of field should probably be increased in each case by a factor of about ten, and we should thus expect resolution in depth to be considerably worse than resolution in the normal image plan. In practice, we should not require resolution in the Z-axis of the same order as the other axes, for it is only necessary to locate the position on the Z-axis of structures identified in the normal plane, and so this inevitable loss in the Z-axis might be acceptable. It does mean, however, that we can hardly expect image quality to be maintained for angles of view far round the side of the image.

In order to ensure that the objective is being used at its fullest aperture, it is essential to provide it with light from a high aperture sub-stage condenser. In practice the adjustment of this condenser is critical, but no special optics are required.

The choice of objective lens is difficult, for we need not only a large aperture but also a large working distance in order to scan the focal plane deep down into the specimen without coming up against the front surface of the lens. Now in practice high aperture lenses have very small working distances, and this is a major difficulty. Objectives having very long working distances have been made, but not with apertures greater than about N.A. 0·65, and this is not high enough to give acceptable resolution in the Z-axis. It is essential to obtain a specially designed lens for our final solid-image microscope.

It is necessary to accomplish the following operations, and all with high precision: (*1*) the focal plane must be scanned up and down through the specimen object, at a rate of at least 30 scans per second; (*2*)the screen must be vibrated at the same rate and in phase with the

FIG. 40.2 *Early tuning fork system for a vibrating-screen version of the solid-image microscope. The 50 cycle tuning fork was kept in continuous vibration with a solenoid mounted between its tangs.*

object scan, but with considerably greater amplitude. In fact the amplitude should be greater than the object scan by the magnification used.

We have tried nearly a dozen ways of obtaining the above mechanical movements. We have used tuned forks, a reciprocating engine – the screen being mounted on the piston – and various kinds of non-tuned vibrating elements, including loudspeaker cones. We have used only sinusoidal scans, the mechanical problem of producing precise linear saw-tooth movements of the objective at the rate required being probably greater than is justified by any advantages over sinusoidal movement (Fig. 40.2).

Experiment shows that tuned systems are not satisfactory, though it has taken a year for this conclusion to become clear. They have the advantage that relatively large amplitudes can be obtained with low power – we were able to get a screen amplitude of nearly 1-inch with an expenditure in power of about 10 watts, while the same amplitude in a non-tuned system required 200–300 watts – this is a serious consideration since the phase has to be controlled, which is difficult and expensive at high powers. However, timed mechanical systems drift in phase with slight temperature changes, and we never succeeded in making a stable arrangement of this kind.

It is not too difficult to impart precise sinusoidal movement of the small amplitude required (a few thousandths of an inch) to the objective lens. The best way we have found so far is to use standard moving coil vibrator units, manufactured for testing components against sustained vibration and metal fatigue. We drive a pair of these from an amplifier fed by a 50 cycles variable phase signal, the lens being mounted in the centre of a beam which vibrates up and down. The screen is more difficult in that the amplitude must be much greater, though the required precision is rather less. To use a non-tuned vibrator unit here is prohibitively expensive, and tuned systems we have ruled out as being too susceptible to spontaneous shifts in phase. We therefore need some new way to obtain the image scan.

It is possible to avoid vibrating the screen physically. This may be done by using a rotating disk of suitable design, and projecting the image on a sector of the disk which changes its position with respect to the observer as the disk rotates.

The simplest arrangement is to use a flat disk rotated on a shaft fixed to its centre but not quite normal to the plane of the disk. This is a 'swash plate', and an image projected on a sector will move backwards and forwards as the disk revolves, but it will also change in shape, appearing as a solid wedge. (In practice half the disk is painted black to give a scan only in one direction, and for the other

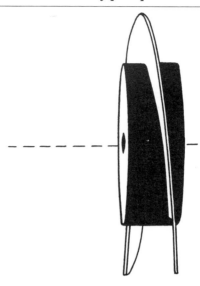

FIG. 40.3 *Diagram of a helical screen. It may be seen how the position of a given sector changes as the screen as a whole rotates round its axis.*

systems the light is chopped off on the return scan to avoid mis-registration of the images derived from the up and down scans, which are generally not quite identical in form. In addition, for sinusoidal scans it is essential to modulate the light source in order to increase the brightness as the velocity increases, otherwise all that is seen is a sandwich consisting of two pictures back and front, with nothing much in between where the screen velocity is high. This is done by using a high pressure mercury arc fed at 50 cycles.)

An arrangement preferable to the flat but tilted disk, though far more difficult to make to the required precision, is a plane helix. This has the great advantage that the picture is not distorted, and this represents the best means of producing the object scan we have so far devised, the helical disk being driven by a synchronous motor locked to the mains and rotating at 3000 r.p.m., half the helix being blacked out, to give 50 one-way scans per second (Fig. 40.3).

A rotating screen of this kind can give a linear scan, though it is difficult to impart this kind of movement to the objective. A reason-able arrangement seems to be to move the objective sinusoidally while the screen gives a linear scan, but to chop the light at the ends of the scan and use the middle only, which is substantially linear. The object and image scans can be brought into synchrony simply by rotating the body of the motor driving the screen until they are in phase. We thus have a very simple arrangement in which amplifiers and phase shifts circuits are avoided entirely, and it is stable and free from mechanical troubles.

Finally, it is almost certainly possible, though we have not yet done it, to avoid the screen altogether and give solid pictures by scanning, but viewed directly with a stereoscopic pair of eye pieces. This could be done by providing the object scan as described, but in place of a vibrating or rotating screen giving a real image, the virtual images provided by the eye piece lenses would be oscillated slightly from side to side in phase with the object scan. This would be optically equivalent to viewing the image on a vibrating screen, and would have the advantage that images sufficiently bright could be obtained with dark ground or phase contrast lighting, which is not the case with projection upon a screen. We might also expect an improvement in image quality, though it would not be a simple matter to view the image from various positions.

Applications of the solid image microscope to science and industry

By adopting the trick of scanning the focal plane through the specimen and catching the changing image upon a vibrating screen we have, it may be claimed, beaten an essential limitation of microscopes – their inability to render visible structure lying in thick sections. Whether the trick of optical scanning in depth will prove useful it is too early to say – all we can claim is that images can be produced in this way which do provide information in depth, and these may be obtained from thick sections of suitable kinds.

The experimental microscopes we have so far built rely on standard lenses, and little further progress is possible without a scaled up lens to give a larger working distance at high aperture. The instrument can be of little practical use until this is available. The images so far obtained are quite good for simple structures, arrangements of small particles such as dust, possibly nuclear tracks in thick blocks of emulsion, and arrangements of fibres. Small particles are seen clearly lying as dots in the image volume, and they may be moved through the luminous block at will by shifting what would normally be the focusing control. There is thus no doubt that the instrument as it stands does give genuine resolution in depth, and that the effect is not merely some kind of illusion.

The contrast is generally rather poor. We are greatly troubled by this, and it is likely always to prove a limiting factor. Contrast may be improved in some cases with oblique or dark ground lighting, but projection then becomes difficult or impossible, which would limit us to direct viewing. In fact, direct viewing, avoiding the screen in place of vibrating elements in the eye pieces, may in any case have advantages.

The quality of image at present obtained is sufficiently good, at a magnification of about three hundred, to show the relative positions of the hairs on the proboscis of insects, and the relative positions of their internal organs, but at this magnification the job would generally be better done with a standard stereoscopic instrument, and we cannot as yet use higher magnifications. Nuclear particle tracks are seen quite well, possibly better than with standard instruments. The principal troubles are the lack of working distance in available objectives which are otherwise suitable, and lack of image contrast even with apparently optimum lighting. The working distance problem waits upon a suitable lens; the impairment in image quality due to lack of contrast might be minimized in the following way, and there are other possibilities.

Consider the apparatus in any of the forms described, but in addition suppose we provide short bright pulses of light at some point in the scan. This would produce a bright layer lying in the block at a position depending upon the position of the pulses along the scan. This bright layer would have high contrast, and it could be moved at will along the Z-axis, simply by retarding or advancing the light pulse with respect to the scan. By maintaining some light during the rest of the scan, the structure seen in the normal image plane in the bright layer could be related to structure seen more dimly lying in front and behind this chosen layer. The relative brightness of the rest of the block could readily be controlled, and if the control setting the position of the bright layer on the Z-axis were calibrated, measurements in depth could be made quite simply. The brightening can be achieved electrically or mechanically. We are inclined to regard this as an important addition, and it should prove useful not only in improving contrast, by allowing a trading of contrast against detail in depth, but also for making accurate estimates of the position of structures in the Z-axis.

The most striking images so far produced are of rough surfaces. Now it happens that the study of rough surfaces is of some importance for industrial control and research into the properties of surfaces and lubricants. It might well prove a useful technique for examining wear, and it could almost certainly be used to advantage for the study of small particles, such as dust and smog, and for nuclear tracks in photographic emulsion.

The images given by arrangements of fibres are quite striking and suggest applications in the fabrics industries, and for such problems as the best bonding materials for brake linings, where it is at present difficult to examine the fibre structure. In medicine, it could be used for tracing the paths of small nerve fibres in muscle (a matter of clinical importance in diagnosing the causes of muscular atrophy) and, if the image can be considerably improved, for studying the connections of the cells of the brain, which is at present very difficult since they are not arranged in thin planes. In general, it could be used for perhaps any application where at present microscopists are tempted to use serial sectioning, and it would have great advantages over serial sectioning which not only is laborious but in some substances impossible, and difficult for any complex structures where the registration between the sections must be maintained.

A further type of possible use is in micro-surgery, a technique used for removing and introducing parts of cells in genetic research, and no doubt applicable for the production of micro-miniature electronic components. It would also be useful for the study of living cells, or groups of cells, for example for studying the effects of radiation.

Man-made electronic components are beginning to approach in scale the components of the nervous system, and many problems and techniques in engineering and biology meet and share common answers. The optical scanning microscope giving a solid image was conceived in terms of biological need, but it might well serve engineers studying micro-structure and producing minute parts. At this stage its uses must be speculative, but we may at least hope that it will in time throw some light in dark places, and make fewer microscopic caverns measureless to man.

41 *The solid-image microscope: a more technical description*

[Next we have a somewhat more technical description of the instrument at the same stage of development, together with its first form to see the light.]

★   ★   ★

WHEN a microscopist wishes to look into the depth of a thick section, or inspect a crack in a specimen of metal, he moves the body of the microscope up or down, using the fine focus control. This shifts the plane of sharp focus – which at high powers is only about one micron in thickness – through the specimen, revealing the structure at successive layers. Because the depth of focus of high-power microscope objectives is so small, it is not possible to see structures lying at different depths at the same time, and this can be a serious limitation in any standard optical microscope. Sometimes a set of thin sections may be cut, each giving the structure at a given depth – this being known as 'serial sectioning' – but this technique is difficult and time-consuming, and is possible only with suitable materials. It does not allow simultaneous examination of thick specimens in depth.

We have attempted to increase the depth of focus of objective lenses, and also to produce the image in a solid block of light, by introducing moving parts into a standard optical microscope. The method involves two essential processes: (1) the focal plane of the objective lens is scanned up and down through the specimen very rapidly, at a rate above the critical fusion frequency of the eye; (2) the image corresponding to each depth through the object is presented at its appropriate distance from the observer's eyes, so that we produce a solid image in space. This is done by projecting the series of pictures produced by the *object scan* described upon a screen vibrating in synchrony with it, thus giving the *image scan* by which a solid picture is built up. The rate of scan chosen is fifty vibrations per second, sufficiently high to avoid flicker, and convenient because the 50 c/s mains can be used to provide the signals for maintaining the two vibrating systems.

In fact, although we used a vibrating screen for the image scan for the early experiments, we now use a specially machined helical disc, driven by a synchronous motor to give 50 rotations per second. In addition, the light is chopped, except for about 80 per cent. of the scan in one direction. This has several advantages, the chief one being that any asymmetry in the wave form of the up- and the down-going scans cannot produce misregistration of the resulting pictures, since one of these pictures is entirely removed. The helical disk producing the image scan of the optical system is shown with the rest of the optical system below. The object scan is produced by mounting the

FIG. 41.1 *Helical screen version of the solid-image microscope. The rotating helical screen is above a standard microscope; the specimen is mounted on a vibrating beam.*

objective lens on a beam which is vibrated up and down over a small amplitude by a pair of electromagnetic vibrator units. This beam is also shown in Fig. 41.1.

We lose a lot of light using projection with a screen of this kind and

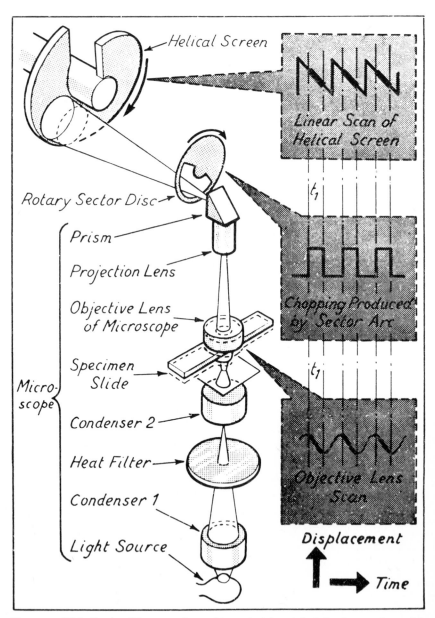

FIG. 41.2 *This diagram illustrates the working principles of the helical screen form of the solid-image microscope developed at Cambridge. The objective lens is mounted on a vibrating beam.*

this makes examination of opaque objects by reflected light almost impossible, which is a pity, because there are several potential applications in metallurgy. There are two ways in which this might be improved: (a) we might use a translucent screen having the same form, machining it out of Perspex and sand-blasting the front to give a suitable highly directional surface, the image then being viewed from behind the screen; or (b) by a radical redesign we might avoid the screen altogether, and use direct viewing. One might make an effective solid image by shifting the virtual images provided in a normal stereoscopic pair of eye pieces in synchrony with the object

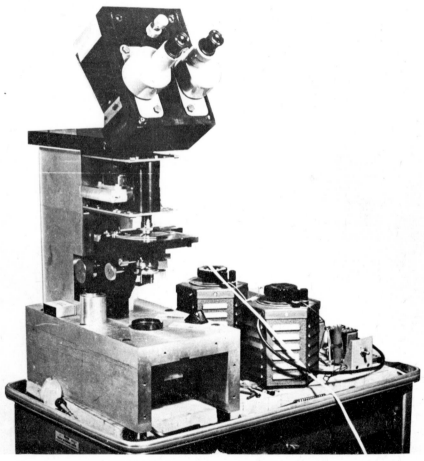

FIG. 41.3 *Oscillating prisms version of the solid-image microscope – built by Stephen Salter. The objective lens (centre) is mounted on a leaf-spring parallelogram, made to vibrate vertically with a moving coil actuator (hidden). Behind the eye pieces are a pair of oscillating prisms (hidden) which give changing separation of the images, synchronized with the object-scan.*

scan. In fact, we have done some experiments on both these possibilities, and at present the first seems to be a great improvement, while the second has not yet been successful.

There appear to be many industrial and research applications. We are able to see thick sections of brain tissue, suitably stained to reveal the nerve cells and their interconnecting processes, very well. The cell bodies lie in the block of light and their processes are seen clearly in depth, while without the scanning the processes appear broken and are readily lost, as only a thin plane is in constant focus. Similarly, nuclear tracks in photographic emulsion can be observed to advantage, though here the contrast is not so good. We hope that the scheme may be used for such industrial purposes as examining natural and artificial fibres, brake-linings, and the structure of rocks and metals, including the effects of wear and fatigue.

We have demonstrated that the principle is useful. It remains to make the instrument in a marketable form, and if this is successful to make it commercially available. The device is quite simple and involves no special difficulties in construction or use, and so we may hope that it will become a useful instrument.

42 *Patent specification for a heterochromatic photometer*

[This photometer might be a solution to an old problem: how to measure the visually effective intensity of lights of various colours. Normal comparison instruments cannot be used efficiently when the unknown light is of different colour from the internal standard, for it is then difficult to judge when the two fields are of equal intensity.

The idea arose from a chance observation: that if two sets of stripes move in opposite directions across each other, at the same speed, then if one set of moving stripes is illuminated at a higher intensity than the other, movement will be observed – *in the direction of the brighter stripes*. When the sets of stripes are of nearly equal brightness then no drift of movement is observed, but rather a strange and distinctive 'jazzing effect'. All this is *independent* of the *colours* of the sets of moving stripes; and so it would seem possible to use this as the basis of a visual photometer suitable for coloured lights. It has not been fully tested, and is not produced as an instrument. I am much indebted to the National Research Development Corporation for the drawings in the following Specification (53663/65 17 Dec. 1965), as they transform a crude bench test arrangement into a practical instrument.]

★   ★   ★

THIS invention relates to visual photometers of the kind in which there are arranged to be presented to the eye of an observer two fields of light whose brightnesses are respectively dependent on the intensities of two light sources to be compared, adjusting means being provided for equalising the brightnesses of the two fields.

In known photometers of this kind, the two fields are presented either simultaneously in neighbouring positions or (in the flicker photometer) alternately in the same position. The first arrangement is normally satisfactory if the two fields are of the same colour but if they are of different colours it is very difficult for the observer to judge when the brightnesses are equal. For heterochromatic photometry it

475

is therefore usual to employ the second arrangement, but even then it is not easy to make the necessary judgements, and there is consequently considerable variance in the results obtained.

It is therefore an object of the present invention to provide a visual photometer of the kind specified which is particularly suitable for use in heterochromatic photometry.

According to the invention, in such a photometer the two fields are arranged to be presented simultaneously in the same position, and means are provided for superimposing on the two fields respectively two similar dark patterns of striated appearance which individually would appear to the observer to move transverse to the striations with substantially equal velocities in opposite senses.

With such an arrangement it is found that when the brightnesses of the two fields are unequal, a coherent movement is perceived in a sense corresponding to the movement of the pattern superimposed on the brighter fields, but when the two fields are equal in brightness a shimmering or 'jazzy' effect is perceived without any sense of coherent movement. It is thus relatively easy for the observer to judge equality of brightness between the two fields; this is so whether or not the fields are of the same colour, which is explainable on the basis that the brightness differences are effectively coded into a movement signal which is perceived by the eye independently of colour. Because of the high sensitivity of the eye to movement, very small differences in brightness are detectable and the instrument is useful in cases where very low intensities are involved; in this connection it may be noted that by employing an appropriate viewing technique a user of the instrument may take advantage of the relatively high sensitivity to movement possessed by regions of the retina offset from the fovea. A further advantage is that the eye does not adapt to movement in the way in which it adapts to different brightnesses of mismatched static fields.

The moving patterns superimposed on the two fields may readily be provided by arranging that in forming each field light from the relevant source passes through a moving transparent member engraved with an appropriate opaque pattern. It will normally be convenient to use the same transparent member in respect of both fields, the necessary opposed senses of movement for the patterns superimposed on the two fields being achieved by appropriate choice of the parts of the transparent member which correspond to the two fields and appropriate design of the optical system used to superimpose the two fields as seen by the observer. In such a case the transparent member may conveniently be a disk arranged to rotate in its own plane about its centre, the two fields corresponding to two similar regions in the plane of the disk which are diametrically opposed with respect to the centre of the disk. The opaque pattern engraved on the disk may take the form of either a set of equally spaced radii of the disk or a series of turns of a spiral of constant pitch concentric with the disk; in the former case rotary motions will be perceived, while in the latter case apparent radial motions will be perceived. In order to avoid undue loss of light the engraved radii or spiral should be relatively fine so that only a small proportion (say about a tenth) of each field is obscured by the moving pattern.

One arrangement in accordance with the invention will now be described by way of example, with reference to the accompanying drawings [see p. 479], in which:—

Fig. 42.1(1) is a sectional side elevation of a portable visual photometer; and

Fig. 42.1(2) is an end elevation of the photometer, partly in section on the line II–II in Fig. 42.1(1).

Referring to the drawings, the components of the photometer are mounted within a casing 1, a projecting part of which is formed so as to constitute a handle 2. Within the main body of the casing 1 is disposed a transparent disk 3 engraved with an opaque pattern 4 in the form of about ten turns of a spiral of constant pitch concentric with the disk 3. The disk 3 is journalled in a bearing 5 for rotation in its own plane about its centre, the disk being arranged to be driven from an electric motor 6 via a bevel gear 7.

Two diametrically opposed circular regions 8 and 9 of the disk 3 are arranged to be illuminated respectively by light from an external source (not shown) which is to be investigated and by light from an internal source constituted by a replaceable electric lamp 10. The light from the external source is arranged to reach the region 8 via an objective lens 11, which is adjustable in position by means of a rack and pinion 12 so that a relatively sharp image may be formed on the region 8. Light from the lamp 10 is formed into a substantially parallel beam by means of a reflector 13 and a lens 14, this beam passing through a variable attenuator 15 before impinging upon the region 9, the attenuator 15 comprising a pair of opposed neutral density wedge filters 16 and 17 which are movable simultaneously in opposite senses by means of a worm mechanism 18 operable by a micrometer head 19.

Parts of the regions 8 and 9 of the disk 3, defined respectively by rectangular apertures 20 and 21 formed in a mask 22, are arranged to be viewed simultaneously by an observer; for this purpose, the instrument is provided with a Ramsden eyepiece 23 which is adjustable longitudinally so that the pattern 4 may be brought accurately into focus, the two fields defined by the apertures 20 and 21 being superimposed, as viewed through the eyepiece 23, by means of a system comprising an optical mixing cube 24 and a 45° prism 25 arranged to reflect light passing through the aperture 21 at right angles into the mixing cube 24. The mixing cube 24 is preferably such as to have a relatively high transmission/reflection ratio, so as not to reduce appreciably the brightness of the field derived from the external light source; if necessary, compensation for the different path lengths between the region 8 and 9 and the eyepiece 23 may be provided by inserting a transparent plate 26 between the aperture 20 and the mixing cube 24.

The motor 6 and lamp 10 are respectively arranged to be energised by means of separate batteries 27 and 28 housed in the handle 2, the latter being provided with a screw cap 29 to enable replacement of the batteries 27 and 28 to be effected. Thus the motor 6 is connectable to the battery 27 via a first pair of contacts of a three-position switch 30 adapted to be operated by a trigger 31 mounted in the handle 2, and the lamp 10 is connectable, in series with a variable resistor 32, across the battery 28 via a second pair of contacts of the switch 30, the resistor 32 being adjustable by means of a shaft 33 which is accessible through an aperture 34 in the casing 1. The switch 30 also has a third pair of contacts which is operable to complete a calibration circuit comprising a photo-voltaic cell 35, which is arranged to 'view' the lamp 10 through an aperture 36 in the reflector 13, and a voltmeter 37 whose indicator is viewable through a window 38 in the casing 1. The arrangement of the switch 30 is such that in its first position all three pairs of contacts are open so that the instrument is inoperative, in its second position the first and second pairs of contacts are closed while the third pair of contacts remain open so that the motor 6 and lamp 10 are energized but the calibration circuit is inoperative, and in its third position the first pair of contacts is open and the second and third pairs of contacts are closed so that only the lamp 10 is energized and the calibration circuit is operative.

Thus, with the switch 30 in its third position the instrument may be calibrated, with the attenuator 15 at a given setting, by adjusting the resistor 32 until a given reading is obtained from the voltmeter 37; the provision of the calibration circuit is, of course, necessary to take account of changes which may occur due to ageing of the battery 28 and the lamp 10. For normal operation of the instrument the switch 30 is set in its second position, so that the disk 3 is rotated. Each of the two rectangular fields of light presented to the eye of the observer, whose brightnesses are respectively dependent upon the intensities of the lamp 10 and the external light source under investigation, will

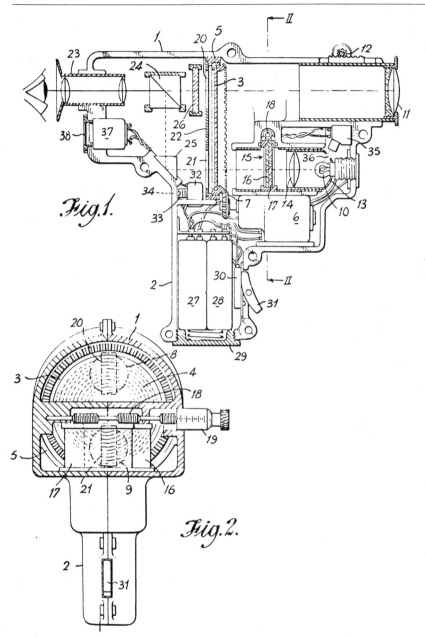

FIG. 42.1 *Illustrations to patent specification for a heterochromatic photometer.*

then have superimposed on it a pattern of curved dark lines extending generally across the width of the rectangle (each of which corresponds to part of one of the turns of the spiral pattern 4), which individually would appear to the observer to move parallel to the length of the rectangle, the movement being in opposite senses for the two fields by virtue of the disposition of the apertures 20 and 21 relative to the centre of the disk 3 and the design of the optical system comprising the mixing cube 24 and prism 25. To determine the intensity of the external light source the setting of the attenuator 15 is varied by means of the micrometer head 19 until the brightnesses of the two fields are equal, as judged by the absence of perception of systematic movement; the intensity of the external light source may then be deduced from the micrometer reading. It will be appreciated that when the instrument is orientated as shown in the drawings, that is with the handle 2 pointing vertically downwards, the apparent movement perceived when the brightnesses of the two fields are unequal will be in a vertical direction; this substantially avoids the possibility of any biasing of the observations by virtue of systematic movement of the eye, such as might occur if the apparent movement were in a horizontal direction. The precise speed of rotation of the disk 3 is not at all critical in obtaining satisfactory results, a suitable range of speeds for the arrangement described above being 5–20 revolutions per second. Variations of the speed which may occur, for example due to ageing of the battery 27, are unimportant since they will give rise to equal changes (in opposite senses) in the movement of the patterns superimposed on the two fields.

In a modification of the arrangement described above the variable attenuator 15 may be replaced by a plurality of variable attenuators arranged in series, one being infinitely variable to provide a fine adjustment and the others being variable in steps on a decimal scale to provide coarse adjustment.

What I claim is :—

1. A visual photometer of the kind specified, in which the two fields are arranged to be presented simultaneously in the same position, and means are provided for superimposing on the two fields respectively two similar dark patterns of striated appearance which individually would appear to the observer to move transverse to the striations with substantially equal velocities in opposite senses.

2. A photometer according to Claim 1, wherein said patterns are provided by arranging that in forming each field light from the relevant source passes through a movable transparent member engraved with an opaque pattern.

3. A photometer according to Claim 2, wherein the same transparent member is used in respect of both fields.

4. A photometer according to Claim 3, wherein the transparent member is a disk rotatable in its own plane about its centre.

5. A photometer according to Claim 4, wherein the opaque pattern engraved on the disk is in the form of a set of equally spaced radii of the disk.

6. A photometer according to Claim 4, wherein the opaque pattern engraved on the disk is in the form of a series of turns of a spiral of constant pitch concentric with the disk, the two fields corresponding to two similar rectangular regions in the plane of the disk which are diametrically opposed with respect to the centre of the disk and whose widths are bisected by the relevant diameter.

7. A visual photometer of the kind specified, substantially as hereinbefore described with reference to the accompanying drawings.

43 Patent specification for apparatus for visual researches (Pandora's Box)

[I shall illustrate something of the development of 'Pandora's Box', because it is useful in its earliest and in later forms. It is intended for teaching and for research on several problems of perception. It can be used for (a) Measuring apparent depth of features in pictures; (b) Differential intensity thresholds (with or without Weber's Law 'built in') with (i) separately controlled areas of background and test fields (ii) separately controlled durations of background and test fields; (c) As a tachistoscope (for back-illuminated transparencies only); (d) As a stereoscope, with separate control of the duration and intensity of the two eye fields; (e) For static (or with additions, dynamic) noise masking of pictures.

Since this allows a wide variety of experiments – with surprises – I call it 'Pandora's Box'. The first models I built with my technician, Bill Matthews, at Cambridge.

Pandora's box started out as an apparatus for investigating distortion illusions in terms of the apparent distance of selected features of illusion figures (see No. 27). It rapidly evolved into a general-purpose gadget, for my undergraduate Practical Class on human perception. It has been taken up by A. I. M. Electronics, Cambridge with the help of N.R.D.C. It was designed for production by Mr David Redgrave, and is now used in many university departments in this country and in America and Australia.

The essential idea for measuring depth, indicated by the 'indirect' cues of monocular vision, especially perspective, is to use the two eyes together as a 'range-finder'. The perceptual space of an observer can be plotted. The effect of any of the monocular clues to depth can be measured objectively.

The description will be taken from the Provisional Specification 'Improvements in or Relating to Optical Apparatus' filed 2 March 1965. The instrument as developed by A.I.M. Electronics is shown in Fig. 43.1.]

★   ★   ★

482

FIG. 43.1 *Pandora's Box – photograph of commercially available version produced by A.I.M. Electronics. Lower section contains timing circuits for use as tachistoscope.*

THE invention relates to optical apparatus, and is more particularly concerned with optical apparatus which can be used for comparing the ability of an observer to judge the apparent distance away from him of objects which are viewed by the observer with binocular vision (i.e. with both eyes) and with monocular vision (i.e. with one eye only) respectively.

The invention provides, in one of its aspects, optical apparatus which comprises displaying means for displaying to an observer a first object so that the observer can view it with binocular vision, and a second object so that the observer can view it only with monocular vision, and means for adjusting the relative positions (or apparent relative positions) of the two objects in a direction (or apparent direction) towards and away from the observer, until the two objects appear to the observer to be at the same distance from him.

The displaying means is preferably such that the two objects are apparently superimposed, to which end one of the objects is preferably displayed as an image reflected in a beam-combiner or other partially-reflecting device.

More particularly, the invention is concerned with optical apparatus for measuring the apparent distance away from an observer of an object viewed with monocular vision. Such an 'object' may be part of an apparently three-dimensional representation (which representation may be three-dimensional or flat) of a three-dimensional scene or display which has real or apparent perspective, texture, or other indication of real or apparent distance away from the observer in different parts of the scene or display (hereinafter referred to as 'an apparently three-dimensional representation of the kind described').

Thus the invention provides, in another of its aspects, optical apparatus for measuring the apparent distance from an observer of a selected part of a three-dimensional representation of the kind described viewed by the observer with monocular vision, which apparatus comprises means for displaying to the observer the three-dimensional representation or an image thereof so that it is viewed by the observer with monocular vision, means for displaying to the observer a reference object or image thereof so that it is viewed by the observer with binocular vision, means for adjusting relatively to each other the apparent positions away from the observer of the representation or image thereof and reference object or image thereof, until the latter appears to the observer to be the same distance away from him as the selected part of the representation, and means for providing a measure of the apparent distance away from the observer of the reference object or image thereof.

Preferably the displaying means is such that the reference object or image thereof is apparently superimposed upon, or is closely laterally adjacent to, the said selected part of the representation. To this end, the three-dimensional representation may be viewed by transmission through a partially reflecting mirror in which the reference object is viewed by reflection.

Preferably the level of illumination of at least the three-dimensional representation may be adjusted. The three-dimensional representation is preferably provided in the form of a transilluminated transparency. In order that the three-dimensional representation is seen by one eye only of the observer, two polarizing means may be provided, one optically between the representation and the positions of both of the observer's eyes, and the other optically between the said representation and the positions of the other eye of the observer, the polarizing means being mutually disposed so that no light from the representation reaches the position of the said other eye. In this case, the partially reflecting mirror is positioned optically between the said one polarizing means and the position of the observer's eyes.

The invention includes optical apparatus as aforesaid in which the level of illumination of one of the objects is adjustable, and there is provided means for suddenly apparently superimposing on the said one of the objects another illuminated object, the apparatus also including means for adjusting the level of illumination of the said one object and also the difference in the levels of illumination of the said one of the objects and the said other object so that the ratio of the said difference to the said level of illumination of the said one of the objects is constant. The objects are preferably provided by, or illuminated by, electro-luminescent panels. The means for adjusting the level of illumination of the panels preferably comprises a first voltage varying device arranged to vary the voltages applied to both of the panels whilst leaving the ratio between them unchanged, and a second voltage varying device arranged to vary the ratio between the voltages applied to the two panels. This facilitates use of the apparatus for experiments on the Weber-Fechner law applied to illumination levels.

One embodiment of the invention will now be described by way of example and with reference to the accompanying schematic drawings [see pp. 486–7], in which:—

Fig. 43.2(1) shows in plan view a dual-purpose apparatus arranged for the comparison of binocular and monocular vision;

Fig. 43.2(2) shows in plan view the same apparatus arranged for experiments concerned with the comparison of levels of illumination; and

Fig. 43.2(3) is a circuit diagram of electrical means for adjusting illumination levels, used in conjunction with the apparatus when arranged as in Fig. 43.2(2).

The apparatus of this example is built into a box or cabinet. A first electro-luminescent panel 11 is positioned inside the rear wall of the box. A second electro-luminescent panel 12 is mounted inside the right-hand wall of the box, which wall is hinged at 19 at its rear edge. Each panel is about ten inches square. A beam-combiner or partial reflector is provided in the form of a semi-silvered mirror 18 positioned diagonally across the box from front left to rear right, at 45° to the rear wall. In the front wall of the box are provided two viewing apertures so that an observer looking through them into the box has his left and right eyes at the positions 13 and 14 respectively. It will be apparent that the observer will view the panel 11 by transmission through the mirror 18 and the panel 12 (or other object on the right hand side of the mirror) by reflection in the mirror (provided that levels of illumination of the two objects are appropriate).

The two electro-luminescent panels 11, 12 are energized from the

A.C. mains through two voltage varying devices in the form of variable transformers of the type sold under the Registered Trade Mark 'VARIAC'. The first transformer 24 has its primary connected to the mains and its secondary connected to the primary of the second transformer 23 and also to the panel 12. The second transformer 23 has its secondary connected to the panel 11. It will be apparent that adjustment of the transformer 23 will adjust the ratio between the voltages applied to the panels 11 and 12 (and thus the ratio between one of them, and their difference), and that adjustment of the

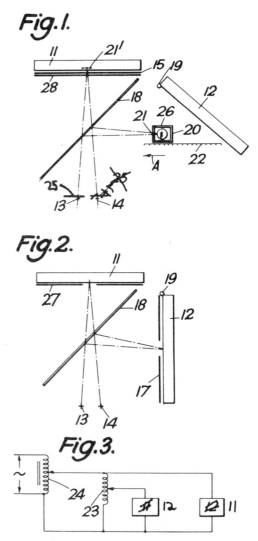

FIG. 43.2 *Illustrations for patent specification of Pandora's Box.*

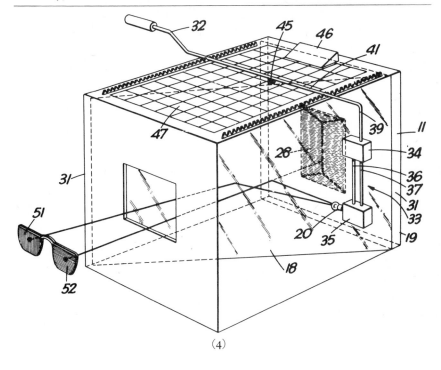

(4)

Fig.5.

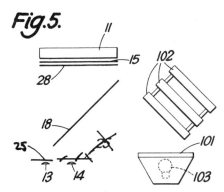

Fig.6.

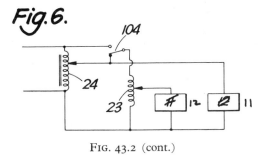

FIG. 43.2 (cont.)

transformer 24 will alter the respective voltages applied to the two panels without affecting their ratio, and consequently without affecting the ratio between one of them, and their difference. In this example, each panel is such that the intensity of light which it emits is proportional to the applied voltage. Thus the levels of illumination of the two panels can easily be altered whilst following the Weber-Fechner law, i.e. that the ratio of the difference in levels of illumination of the panels 11, 12 to the level of illumination of the panel 12 remains constant.

When the apparatus is used, as shown in Fig. 43.2(1), to compare the binocular and monocular vision of an observer, the panel 12 is swung out of the way and a reference object in the form of a translucent disk 21 illuminated from behind by an electric bulb 20 mounted in a tube 26 which shields unwanted light from the bulb. The tube and bulb are supported by rods so that the position of the disk 21 can be adjusted in a horizontal direction towards and away from the mirror 18 at 45 degrees thereto and perpendicular to the line of forward vision of the observer. This direction is indicated by the arrow A in Fig. 43.2(1). Since the observer sees an image of the disk 21 reflected in the mirror 18 apparently in a position 21' at or about the position occupied by the panel 11, movement of the disk as aforesaid moves the image 21' towards and away from the observer. The rods supporting the tube 26 are also arranged so that the disk 21 can be adjusted in a plane perpendicular to the aforesaid direction A.

Immediately in front of the panel 11 is placed an apparently three-dimensional representation 15 of a three-dimensional scene which has real or apparent perspective, texture or other indication of real or apparent distance away from the observer in different parts of the scene or display. The representation is provided in the form of an eight inch by ten inch high contrast photographic transparency, which is transilluminated by the panel 11. The advantage of this back illumination is that it tends to reduce or avoid the apparent texture of the face of a normal opaque photographic print or diagram, which may countermand the indication of apparent depth indicated by perspective or other features in the representation.

Immediately in front of the transparency 11 is placed a sheet 28 of polarizing material (e.g. such as is available under the Registered Trade Mark 'Polaroid') which covers the whole transparency. Over the aperture defining the right-hand eye position 14 is placed another smaller sheet 25 of this material. The planes of polarization of these two sheets are mutually perpendicular, so that the observer's right eye cannot see the representation 15, whilst he sees the image 21' with both eyes and apparently superimposed upon the representation 15.

To use the apparatus in this arrangement, the panel 12 is switched off and the panel 11 and the bulb 20 switched on. The observer looks through the eye apertures so that his eyes occupy the positions 13, 14, and he views the representations 15 with his right eye only and the reference image 21' with both eyes. He adjusts the disk 21 in the plane perpendicular to the direction A until the image 21' of the illuminated disk appears to be superimposed upon, or to lie immediately adjacent to, a selected part of the scene represented by the representation. The observer then adjusts the position of the disk 21 in the direction A, until the image 21' appears to him to lie the same distance away from him as the selected part of the scene. This distance may be read off (e.g. from a calibrated scale 22 along which the disk is movable) and noted. By repeating this process for successive adjacent parts of the representation, a three-dimensional plot of apparent visual space may be obtained.

To use the apparatus for experiments in connection with differential illumination intensities, as illustrated in Fig. 43.2(2), the reference object tube 26 and its lamp 20, and the scale 22, is removed, the side door swung shut so that the panel 12 is perpendicular to the panel 11. To the observer, the image of illuminated surface of panel 12 is superimposed upon the illuminated panel 11, so that the intensities of illumination are apparently added. Masks 27 and 17 respectively may be placed in front of the panels 11 and 12 to vary the shape of the illuminated fields seen by the observer. If complicated shapes are required, the masks may be made photographically. These masks are such that the illuminated fields they define are apparently superimposed. As previously described, the panels 11 and 12 are energized so that their intensities of illumination (I_{11}, I_{12}) may be altered in unison by the transformer 24 whilst retaining unaltered the ratio between their difference $(I_{12}-I_{11})$ and the level of illumination (I_{11}) of the panel 11. Further, the ratio I_{11}/I_{12}, and consequently the ratio $(I_{12}-I_{11})/I_{12}$, can easily be adjusted by the transformer 23. Consequently the validity of the Weber-Fechner law [$\Delta I/I =$ constant, where ΔI is the minimum detectable change in I] for the human eye can easily be tested by adjusting the transformer 24, whilst switching panel 11 on and off. Further, any departure from this law can easily be determined by adjusting transformer 23, and noting the voltages applied to the two panels. These experiments can be carried out over a wide range of levels of illumination. This is important for many research problems, including estimates of internal neurological noise, which appears to be largely responsible for the breakdown of the Weber-Fechner law at low intensities. This is a fundamental problem, which can be investigated most conveniently with this apparatus.

Further, the apparatus shown in Fig. 43.2(2) may be used for investigating flicker phenomena. The panel 12 may be driven by square wave electrical pulses from a suitable external source. Again, the area and shape of the field seen may be selected by means of masks. It is also possible to select which panel flickers, and at what frequency. Further, one panel may be kept at constant brightness while the other is made to flicker, so that the percentage modulation of flicker can be controlled. This is of great theoretical interest in revealing the bandwidth characteristics of the human visual system. It is possible to provide independent flicker to the two eyes, by providing polarizers in front of each panel and over each eye aperture, with their planes of polarization suitably aligned.

Further, the use of polarizers in this manner enables the apparatus to be used as a stereoscope having an exceptionally wide field of view. This makes possible many experiments in stereoscopic vision, especially as it is readily converted into a pseudoscope, in which the eyes are effectively reversed, simply by interchanging the planes of polarization of the polarizers at the eye apertures.

Fig. 43.2(4) is a further view of the apparatus, showing the apparatus in position inside a box or cabinet.

The second electro-luminescent panel 12 for investigating differential thresholds is not shown. This panel is mounted inside the wall (also not shown) which is hinged at 19 to the edge of the rear wall of the cabinet 31 to form a door. This door when opened allows access to the apparatus.

The light assembly 33 comprises two terminal blocks 34, 35 of the well-known kind referred to as 'chocolate boxes', and two rails 36, 37. The two rails 36, 37 are supported by the block 34 and carry the current to the lamp. The current supply to the block 34 is not shown. The rails 36, 37 serve as guide rails along which the block 35 can slide to adjust the position of the bulb in the vertical plane.

The light assembly 33 is supported at the down turned end 39 of the rod assembly 41 which is pivotably mounted on top of the cabinet. The other end of the rod assembly 41 is formed into a crank 32 which can be rotated to swing the light assembly round to permit the door or wall (not shown) to be shut to enable the second electro-luminescent panel 12 to be brought into position. The blocks 34, 35 act as counter balance weights which ensure that the light bulb always lies in the vertical plane through, or parallel to, the vertical plane through the horizontal central part of 45 of the rod assembly 41.

The clip 46 is for holding graph paper 47 securely in position on top of the box.

The integer at 45 comprises a wire loop or washer secured to the central part of the rod assembly and through which the tip of a pencil can be applied to mark the graph paper at a position corresponding with the position of the bulb in a horizontal plane.

The invention is not restricted to the details of the foregoing example. For instance, the semi-silvered mirror 18 may be replaced by a sheet of plate glass.

In fact 'neutral density' perspex is used; this avoids double reflection while being cheap, robust and easily cleaned without damage.

44 *Patent specification for 3-D drawing machine*

[The realization that drawings, whatever their manner of projection, from isometric to geometrical perspective, are essentially incapable of representing unusual structures without danger of serious error, leads to the thought: Could we design a machine for conferring the advantages of stereoscopic vision to drawings? Can we design and build a simple and inexpensive 3-D drawing machine? The following patent account shows that the answer is 'yes'. The design is shown most clearly in the following drawing (Fig. 44.1).

This device allows one to draw freely in 3-D. The drawing is however visible to but one person at a time. We are at present working on a version for making the 3-D drawings 'public' – allowing twenty or more people to view them at once, as they are drawn.

3-D drawing might be useful to architects and engineers, to medical students studying anatomy and as a general 'thinking tool'. It might also make an interesting toy for children – and perhaps could help children to understand and invent structures of the future.

It nearly became available, as a toy for children and adults, in 1966 while I was spending six months as a visiting professor to New York University, and living in Greenwich Village. Somehow, the millionaire owner of a large toy-making firm situated thirty miles outside the city came to hear of the device and invited me over to his house. The result was a fascinating vignette of what to a European is so extraordinary about American life – the warm enthusiasm of so many people with the power to get things done.

Within a day or two I was offered all facilities for building a version of the 3-D drawing machine, at the toy factory, which turned out to be impressively equipped and with an excellent model shop. I was not only given the full use of the model shop with any help required from its extremely helpful staff; but I was also given a large room next to the Technical Director's office. The room was equipped with a large drawing board with a red top. For the fun of it (and just to test out the situation) I at once made it clear that I would have preferred a green topped board – and instantly two men were summoned to remove the offending board and bring in a green one! All this with humour, and a sense that what we were engaged upon really mattered – that it was important to produce the device as a toy. I hope that it will still come about. We have now made several better versions.

Each morning, several days a week, I was collected by the delightful Technical Director from my Greenwich Village apartment and driven to the toy factory. Gradually the toy version came into existence as a prototype. In two or three weeks it was finished, and it worked. We in the model shop were delighted: it was made very simply, with a cardboard outer skin, but we showed that a simple and cheap version could be produced. Then the day of truth came – the impending visit from the owner of the toy factory. Everything depended on his word.

The morning of The Visit was brilliantly sunny, and as it turned out most unfortunately the model shop had no blinds, curtains or 'drapes'. The sun poured in – so bright that one could see nothing in our precious box. We moved it as far as possible from the light and hoped for the best. The door opened; the boss and an unknown but clearly respected friend approached our creation, and moved it to the window, the better to see it in a good light. But alas: the light killed its faint inner pictures so that, I suppose, it looked no more than a cardboard box with lenses and levers. Its magic was lost, and as a toy it never saw the light.]

★   ★   ★

THE present invention relates to devices for drawing in three dimensions.

A device for drawing in three dimensions has been proposed, in which two separate images of a point source of light are produced on an electro-luminescent panel. When the point source of light is moved along a path in space, two glowing images of the path are formed upon the panel. The images represent the path of the light as seen from differing viewpoints, and changes in the separation of corresponding parts of the images are related to movements in depth, as in normal depth perception.

The two images are viewed through a stereoscopic eyepiece in which each image is presented to its corresponding eye and they are fused together by the brain and interpreted as a single three-dimensional image.

However, in constructing such a device, difficulties have been experienced in the correct representation of perspective and move-ments in depth, that is, in directions towards and away from an operator using the device. Both these effects are of great importance to the human brain in its interpretation of a three-dimensional image.

It is an object of the present invention to provide an improved device for drawing in three dimensions.

According to the present invention there is provided a device for drawing in three dimensions, the device including a luminescent image-retaining means having a surface viewable by an operator of the device, a projection system for forming at said surface a pair of separated images of a light source, the projection system comprising a mirror so situated as to face said surface and a pair of projection lenses disposed between the mirror and said surface, and a stereoscopic viewing means enabling the operator to view said images in such a manner as to observe an upright three-dimensional representation produced by movements of the light source.

According to the present invention in another aspect, there is provided a device for producing a three-dimensional representation of an object, comprising a reference means attached to a linkage to which a source of light is also attached, the linkage being such that movements of the reference means cause related movements of the source of light, and image-retaining means having a surface viewable by an operator using the device, a mirror having its reflecting surface facing the image-retaining means, a pair of projection lenses disposed between the mirror and said surface and so arranged as to form two separated images of the source of light upon the image-retaining means, and a stereoscopic viewing means enabling the operator to view said images in such a manner as to observe an upright three-dimensional representation of the object.

The device may include means for projecting further stereoscopic images upon the luminescent image-retaining means to enable drawings to be made with reference to another structure.

Provision may also be made for drawing from more than one view-point by including a plurality of projection systems and luminescent image-retaining means that view the source of light from differing directions.

The invention will be described, by way of example, with reference to the accompanying diagrammatic drawings [see opposite], in which:

Fig. 44.1(1) shows a view in elevation of an embodiment of the invention;

Fig. 44.1(2) shows a plan view of the embodiment of Fig. 44.1(1); and Fig. 44.1(3) shows a plan view of another embodiment of the invention.

Referring to Figs. 44.1(1) and (2), a light pen 1 is freely movable within an enclosure 2 which has an orifice through which a hand of the

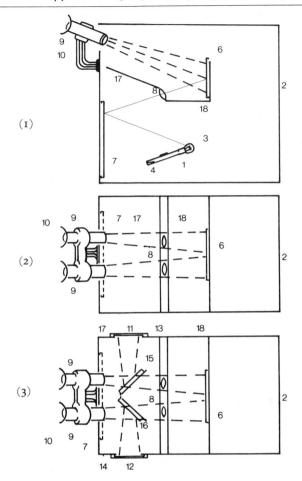

FIG. 44.1 *Diagrams of the 3-D drawing machine. The 'drawing light' is held in the hand and moved freely in the space of the lower part of the machine. It is imaged by a horizontally separated pair of lenses (the 'projection lenses') to form a pair of images on the 'image retaining panel' at the back. As the light is moved, these images move correspondingly – and change in horizontal separation with changing distance of the light – to form correct stereo pairs of drawings on the storage panel. The drawings are viewed independently by each eye, through the 'telescopes' forming the eye pieces. (The telescopes are inverting, to compensate the image inversion of the projection lenses. The mirror is to give correct direction to the depth (z-) axis).*

operator can be inserted to manipulate the light pen 1. The light pen 1 comprises a small light source 3, such as a microscope lamp mounted upon a stylus 4 which incorporates a source of electric power (not shown) and a switch 5, by means of which the brightness of the source 2 can be varied.

Mounted vertically within the enclosure 2 is an electroluminescent image-retaining panel 6, of a type manufactured by Thorn Electrical Industries Ltd. The panel 6 is powered by a source of uni-directional voltage (not shown), and has the properties that when it has been irradiated by light, the intensity of which is greater than a threshold value, it continues to emit light for a considerable period of time, as long as the uni-directional voltage is maintained across the panel 6, but if the voltage is removed the emission of light ceases. These two properties enable a line of a drawing to be terminated by reducing the intensity of the light source 3 below the threshold level, and also allow the complete drawing to be erased.

Facing the panel 6 is a plane mirror 7 which is so situated that a pair of projection lenses 8, which form two images of the light source 3 upon the panel 6, view the light source 3 by light reflected from the mirror 7. The provision of the mirror 7 ensures that the length of the optical path from the light source 3 to the projection lenses 8 is sufficient for the light source 3 to remain in focus throughout its possible movement in depth.

The projection lenses 8 are horizontally separated about the same distance apart as the human eye, and form two images of the light source 3 upon the panel 6. Movement of the light pen 1 in a plane parallel to that of the mirror 7 produces corresponding movements, in opposite senses, of the images on the panel 6, thus resulting in the formation of two glowing lines on the panel 6 (assuming the intensity of the light source 3 is above the threshold) which represent the path of the light pen 1 as seen from slightly differing viewpoints; movements of the light pen 1 in the direction perpendicular to the plane of the mirror 7 cause the separation of the images to change.

The projection lenses 8 are so arranged that the light source 3 is in sharpest focus when it is furthest from the operator, the thickness of the line thus decreasing with increasing depth and introducing correct perspective into the line thickness.

Each of the two images is observed by its corresponding telescope 9 of a stereoscope 10, the axes of the telescopes 9 being set to have a slight degree of convergence, sufficient to enable the images to be observed comfortably. The telescopes 9 are of a wide-field inverting type and correct for the inversion of the images caused by the projection lenses 8.

The telescopes 9 are magnifying in nature so as to utilise to the full the resolution of the panel 6 to make full use of the relatively small picture area of the panel 6. This area is restricted to reduce the necessary focal length of the projection lenses 8 so as to increase the depth of field of the projection lenses 8. Screens 17 and 18 prevent light from reaching the panel 6 directly from the light source 3.

The projection lenses 8 have their optical axes inclined upwards at some 20° to the horizontal, and the telescopes 9 have their optical axes inclined downwards at the same angle. This symmetrical arrangement of the projection lenses 8 and the telescopes 9 is necessary because the panel 6 is not transparent and must be excited and observed from the same side. Although the excitation and observation of the panel from the same side could be achieved by the use of semi-silvered mirrors, such a procedure would involve a decrease in the brightness of the image avoided by the described arrangement.

While using a relatively simple optical and geometrical layout, the device described above is such as to satisfy the requirements for relatively accurate representation of depth. In particular, movements of the light pen 1 by the operator in the direction perpendicular to the plane of the mirror 7 are accompanied by changes of the correct sense in the separation of the two images, and also given correct perspective by variation of the length of image lines representing a given displacement of the light pen 1 in planes parallel to the plane of the mirror 7.

Dimensions used in the construction of the above described embodiment are as follows:—

External dimensions of enclosure 2	$18'' \times 18'' \times 18''$
Size of panel 6	$6'' \times 4''$
Separation of projection lenses 8	$2''$
Focal length and aperture of projection lenses 8	75 m.m.; f16
Size of mirror 7	$13'' \times 9''$
Mirror-lens spacing	$5\frac{1}{2}''$
Panel-lens spacing	$4\frac{1}{4}''$
Separation of telescopes 9	$2''$ to $3''$
Magnification of telescopes 9	$\times 4$
Eyepieces of telescopes 9	Ramsden 50 m.m focal length aperture f2.8
Light source 3	15 watts, 6 volts.

Fig. 44.1(3) shows a plan view of an embodiment in which provision is made for introducing an existing pair of stereo photographs or drawings into the viewing optical system in order that 3-dimensional drawings may be made inside other drawings or photographs. They may also be made within a 3-dimensional reference system. This facility makes it possible to test design modification by drawing upon images of an extant structure, or to draw 3-dimensional graphs. Parts of the embodiment that are similar to those of previous embodiments have similar reference numbers. The added stereoscopic images of the existing structure, or the reference systems, are introduced by means of transparencies which are illuminated by standard electro-

luminescent lamps, the brightness of which may be varied by means of a variable alternating voltage power supply. These lamps and their power supply are not shown in the figure. The transparencies 11 and 12 are mounted in holders 13 and 14 which are attached to the enclosure 2 by means of magnets, also not shown. This form of mounting enables the holders 13 and 14 to be adjusted to give correct coincidence and fusion of the added stereoscopic images. Light passing through the transparencies 11 and 12 is reflected into the viewing system by means of two partially reflecting mirrors 15 and 16 that are placed at approximately 45 degrees between the telescopes 9 and the panel 6. The mirrors 16 and 17 have a reflectance of about 10%. The path length between the telescopes 9 and the transparencies 11 and 12 are made precisely equal to the path lengths between the telescopes 9 and the panel 6, so that both sets of images are in sharp focus at one setting of the telescopes 9.

As the panel 6 emits a yellow light and the electro-luminescent lamps emit a green light, the two pictures presented to the operator of the device are readily distinguishable.

Provision may be made for drawing simultaneously from a number of viewpoints by duplicating the optical system so that further pairs of projection lenses similar to the projection lenses 8 view the light pen 1 from other angles. Each of these further pairs of projection lenses would require its own panel similar to the panel 6, but unless it is desired to view the drawing from more than one angle before it is completed it is not necessary to provide each panel with its own viewing telescopes. Provision may be made for viewing the panels successively with a suitable stereoscope after the drawing has been finished, or alternatively photographs may be taken to give a permanent record, or to provide slides for projection.

In another embodiment of the invention, which is not illustrated, provision is made for making an accurate 3-dimensional drawing of an existing structure or model. A reference pointer is attached to a parallelogram linkage to which the light source 3 is also attached. The reference pointer is situated outside the enclosure 2, but the linkage projects into it. Thus the reference pointer may be moved over the edges of an object and the source of light 3 will trace out a path within the enclosure similar to that followed by the reference pointer. Preferably however, the reference pointer is replaced by a reference light source, and a semi-silvered mirror is interposed between the object to be drawn and the end of the linkage carrying the reference source. The reference source is seen reflected from the mirror; it is visually behind the mirror and therefore may be placed upon any part of the object, and the virtual image may be traced to

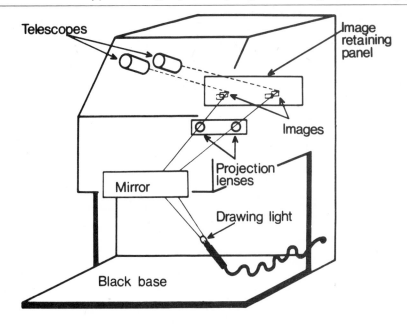

FIG. 44.2 *Later version of the 3-D drawing machine.*

FIG. 44.3 *Viewing the 3-D drawing machine.*

give an exact three-dimensional copy of the object. This arrangement has the advantage that there is no mechanical arm or stylus which might prevent the reference pointer from being placed on some desired feature of the object, as, for example, may occur if the object is hollow. The described arrangement however suffers from the disadvantage that movements in depth are reversed because as the reference light is moved away from the operator its virtual image approaches the part-reflecting mirror from behind it. If desired, this reversal may be avoided by placing a plane mirror immediately in front of the operator and facing the semi-silvered mirror, which then 'sees' the virtual image of the plane mirror, thus causing a second reversal of movements in depth. Alternatively the linkage may be such as to give the required reversal.

Additionally, in any of the embodiments described, the projection lenses 8 may be so moved by linkage attached to the light pen 1 that the light source 3 is maintained in focus throughout its range of movement, and the light from the light pen 1 may be collimated and so give an infinite depth of focus to the projection lenses 8. In this latter case, a linkage would be required to ensure that the light from the collimator is continually aimed at the projection lenses 8.

45 *A technique for minimizing the effects of atmospheric disturbance on photographic telescopes*

[The story behind this idea is, perhaps, of interest in showing how a question can suggest another more interesting question, leading with luck to something unexpected. The question concerned stereoscopic vision, but it led by three or four steps and a few minutes of thought in a darkroom, to the possibility of something quite different – a telescope camera for getting improved pictures of the moon, the planets and the stars. My father, C. C. L. Gregory, was a professional astronomer, and I had been brought up with telescopes and so with the problem of 'seeing' – the problem of the disturbance of telescopic images by atmospheric turbulence. This is beautifully described by Newton (*Opticks*, 1704) who was pessimistic about any cure. Indeed he said that a cure was simply impossible. But even Newton was not always right in his strictures: he declared that chromatic fringes would for ever beset images given by lenses; not at all foreseeing the invention of achromatic combinations of flint and crown glass lenses (generally attributed to John Dollond; suggested by Chester Moor Hall in 1729 and demonstrated by Samuel Klingen-Steirna in 1758). Newton describes the problem, and the supposed impossibility of cure, in the following passage in *Opticks*:

> If the Theory of making Telescopes could at length be fully brought into Practice, yet there would be certain Bounds beyond which Telescopes could not perform. For the Air through which we look upon the Stars, is in a perpetual Tremor; as may be seen by the tremulous Motion of Shadows cast from high Towers, and by the twinkling of the fix'd Stars. But these Stars do not twinkle when viewed through Telescopes which have large apertures. For the Rays of Light which pass through divers parts of the aperture, tremble each of them apart, and by means of their various and sometimes contrary Tremors, fall at one and the same time upon different points in the bottom of the Eye, and their trembling Motions are too quick and confused to be perceived severally. And all these illuminated Points

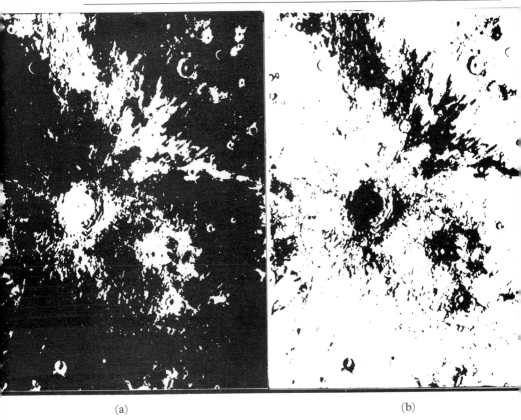

(a)   (b)

constitute one broad lucid Point, composed of those many
trembling Points confusedly and insensibly mixed with one
another by very short and swift Tremors, and thereby cause
the Star to appear broader than it is, and without any trembling
of the whole. Long Telescopes may cause Objects to appear
brighter and larger than short ones can do, but they cannot be
so formed as to take away that confusion of the Rays which
arises from the Tremors of the Atmosphere. The only Remedy
is a most serene and quiet Air, such as may perhaps be found
on the tops of the highest Mountains above the grosser Clouds.

The insights of genius can blind later generations. Sometimes, we
must turn away to see afresh. It is possible that this passage, no
doubt read by students of optics ever since it was written, helped to
inhibit seeing this as a problem to be considered.

I was led to a possible solution, before realizing there was a problem
that might be solved. It was a very different question which led to
this: the question 'Does the brain reject most of the information
from retinal images when "computing" depth from disparity
differences between corresponding points from the two eyes?'

(c)

FIG. 45.1 *A negative/positive pair of photographs and a difference picture. (a) is a positive, (b) the corresponding negative, and (c) is a difference picture. The positive (representing the image) and the negative (representing the Master Negative in the camera) are placed in contact to form a 'sandwich', which is opaque where the positive and negative coincide – as happens when the image features are undisturbed.*

This suggested the experimental question: 'What would a picture of the *difference* between stereo pairs look like?' To answer this, I made a photographic pair, and printed one as a positive and the other as a negative transparency. It was a simple matter, in the darkroom, to make a 'sandwich' of these, and place the sandwich pair of photographs in the enlarger. If the pictures were identical – but one a positive and the other a negative – then they should cancel each other. Virtually no light should get through. Any discrepancy (such as generated by stereoscopic disparities) should allow light to pass. The result should be a *difference picture*, in which only the discrepancies would appear. This worked much as expected. Large areas cancelled themselves out, and outlines representing stereo differences remained. It was while adjusting the negative/positive sandwich in the enlarger that I noticed the effect that suggested the possibility of automatically rejecting disturbances. When the photographic sandwich was most closely registered, the total light falling upon the enlarger easel was markedly less than when they were misplaced. When the negative registered most closely with the positive, cancellation was greatest, so the least amount of light got through the sandwich to the enlarger easel. It seemed clear that one might make a device for automatically matching something with its own negative. 'But,' I then thought 'suppose it is not a "thing" but an image – a fluctuating image – which is matched against itself.' If (and this was the crucial point) a photograph of an object was taken through the turbulence of the atmosphere – then surely the *disturbance* could be rejected. Surely telescopic pictures could be improved. It would be necessary to take a long exposure photograph of the object (the moon) through the disturbance; project the image of the moon through its own photographic negative, then detect the amount of light getting through the negative. When the light was most occluded, the image would be most highly correlated with its *average* self. In these moments its disturbance must be least – so if a second photograph were built up during these moments, this second, sampled photograph should be less disturbed than the original photograph. Having arrived at that point, I began to have such doubts that I almost rejected it out of hand. The thought: 'Wouldn't it be pulling oneself up by one's own shoe laces?' dominated, and almost killed the idea stone dead as it was born. But a few minutes more in the silent darkness convinced

FIG. 45.2 *First bench test apparatus to test the idea of running cross-correlation sampling, for improving telescope images.*

me that this would not be pulling one's self up by one's own shoe laces: for the object was continuously available for supplying more information. This chain of thought took perhaps twenty minutes. I rushed out of the darkroom in great excitement, and more or less collided with my Professor's wife. I explained that I had a great idea, and would she like to look at a demonstration? She looked at me sadly, and went on her way.

What happens is most clearly seen by making a negative/positive sandwich, and observing the changing difference picture with varying displacements. Local discrepancies can be introduced by deforming the 'sandwich' slightly with pressure from a finger. Fig. 45.1 shows a negative and its corresponding positive, and a difference picture obtained from this pair, showing partial cancellation. One may think of this dynamically to visualize the working of the sampling camera striving to defeat the confounding ever-changing air.

We collected all sorts of bits and pieces (including my gramophone amplifier) to set up a bench test experiment to try the idea out. (Fig. 45.2). So far as possible we used available equipment, but we had to make a 'sampling shutter', capable of operating on demand from electrical pulses, given by mismatch signals from the photo-cell behind the Master Negative. Bill Matthews and I built the first sampling shutter (later improved by Stephen Salter) using a pair of electro-magnetic vibrator units. These were mounted opposed to each other, carrying thin squares of metal, each a half-square. When drawn apart a square hole was revealed, allowing light to pass;

FIG. 45.3 *First sampling shutter. This consists of a pair of electro-magnetic actuators (at right and left) which draw apart a pair of half squares (hidden behind front element of lens), when a close match between image and negative is signalled from photocell.*

when drawn together the hole closed, preventing light reaching the second camera during sampling. This shutter is shown in Fig. 45.3.

We built this first apparatus in six weeks. It worked! For slowly oscillating images (moved with an oscillating Perspex plate in the light path) or later with random disturbance given by an agitated water bath, which proved a good simulator of atmospheric disturbance, we obtained very noticeable improvement with the sampling technique.

The following brief paper, which appeared in *Nature*, first described the idea, and the initial bench tests with the first crude apparatus. This led to our getting support, and help from many people, allowing us to build and test an instrument suitable for trials on telescopes. Would it – will it – reveal new secrets?]

★   ★   ★

I T is well known that images in astronomical telescopes are shifted and degenerated by atmospheric disturbance. This becomes extremely important with large apertures and high magnifications: the disturbances prevent the detailed photographs which would be expected from the theoretical resolving power of large instruments. The disturbances take several forms: (1) The image may be shifted as a whole, in any direction, with varying frequency and amplitude. (2) Parts of the image may move in different directions simultaneously. (3) The image may be degenerated, especially with large aperture instruments, when the effective wave-length of the disturbance is less than the diameter of the objective. This produces a 'milkiness' of the image. This is quite different from the effect of shift when seen visually, though it may appear similar in a long-exposure photograph when the shifts produce blurring of contours and loss of fine detail.

It seems that visual observation can be preferable to photographic recording in lunar and planetary work, because the effects of the shifts of images can to some extent be avoided by visually sampling those moments when the agitation of the images is least marked. The purpose of the technique described here is to enable photographic telescopes to select moments of quiescence to build up a correctly exposed photograph.

It is clear from the kinds of disturbances encountered that any attempt to compensate the disturbances by introducing equal and opposite movements of the image on the plate will be unsatisfactory, when movements can occur in several directions in different parts of the image. Further, to get a servo-system to perform this task it would be necessary to feed it with information of the direction and velocity of the shifts, which is extremely difficult, while the servo itself would be subject to some over-shoot and tremor.

The technique under investigation is to take, first of all, a long-exposure photograph of the (atmospherically disturbed) image. The resulting photograph is statistically correct, in the sense that the major features will fall near the centre of intensity gradients produced by the random disturbance of the image. But, although the position of the contours will be nearly correct, fine detail is lost, hence the problem. This long-exposure photograph is processed, and the resulting negative is placed in its original position in the optical system, so that the fluctuating image now lies on the transparent negative. The image is now almost entirely cancelled by its negative. It is, however, most completely cancelled when the image most nearly corresponds to the negative. As the image is displaced, by the atmospheric or other disturbances, there is an increase in intensity. This is detected by a single photoelectric cell which covers the entire image plane, and so receives plenty of light. We can thus detect the presence of any shift of the image – though not the direction of shift – from increase in the output of the cell. The output rises with any discrepancy of the image from the statistically correct 'master' negative – not only shifts but also loss of focus and the 'milkiness' produced by regions of different refractive index smaller than the aperture of the instrument. (This last point I have established by means of a ripple tank.)

Having attained a signal indicating disturbance from the statistically correct image, it is a simple matter to use the signal to produce a second photograph free of disturbance. This may be done by using a second camera which shares the image with the first, by means of a beam splitter. This second camera is fitted with an electrically operated shutter which opens only when the output from the photo-cell is near its minimum value, corresponding to a close fit of the fluctuating image with the master negative.

In this way we separate informational integration from the integration of energy needed to expose the final picture, which is built up from many short exposures occurring whenever the image is close to the 'master'.

The preliminary experiments are limited to simulation of atmospheric disturbance, by placing an oscillating 'Perspex' sheet between the object and the optical system, and a ripple tank.

The beam splitter is a half-silvered mirror placed at 45°, so that the second camera (an 'Exacta' 35-mm. single-lens reflex) is provided with the same image as the large camera carrying the master negative and the photo-cell. The second camera is fitted with a specially made shutter, consisting of a pair of electromagnetic vibrator units (Advance type VI) which drive a pair of metal vanes shaped to form

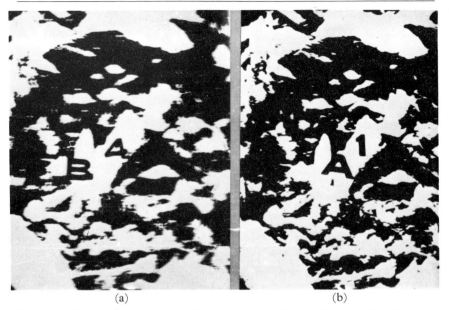

(a)   (b)

FIG. 45.4 *First improved picture.* (a) *not sampled;* (b) *sampled. The disturbance is given by an oscillating perspex plate, using the first apparatus, as shown in Fig. 45.2.*

a square opening, increasing in size as the vanes are withdrawn by the opposed vibrator units. The circuit consists of an oscillator (400 c/s) allowing a.c. amplification from a bridge which is unbalanced by the photo-cell changing in resistance with increasing light, when the image loses register with the master. The amplified output is rectified, and used to energize the vibrator units to close the shutter.

An example of how a shifting image is improved is shown in Figs. 45.4a and b. Fig. 45.4a was obtained from a long exposure of the Moon model while the 'Perspex' plate was oscillating about a vertical axis, to produce horizontal disturbance. The degeneration along the horizontal axis is very apparent. Fig. 45.4b shows the improvement obtained – the optical conditions being identical – when the shutter system is switched on. Some degeneration on the horizontal axis can still be seen: this may be further reduced by increasing the gain of the amplifier.

The improvement shown is given by a shutter open/closed ratio of about 6:1. This may be increased by increasing the gain in the present arrangement, or by introducing a gate, working the shutter as an all-or-none device. It is important to note that the improvement is from a blurred master negative identical with Fig. 45.4a since it was taken through the disturbance.

We are now simulating atmospheric disturbance with a layer of

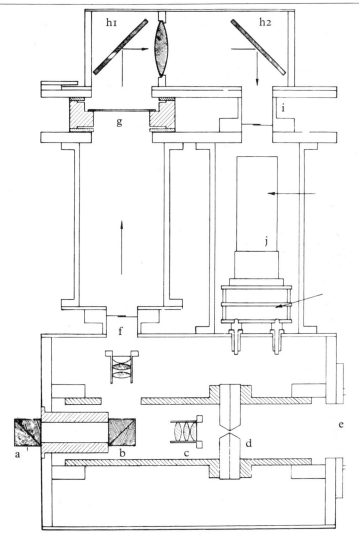

FIG. 45.5 *Layout of second sampling camera. This is a side elevation of the sampling camera showing all main optical and mechanical features, except the final-picture camera which is mounted at* (e).

(a) Mounting flange, *for fixing camera to a telescope.*

(b) Mixing cube, *50% of light to the master plate* (f), *and 50% to the final-picture camera* (e), *(not shown) via the sampling shutter,* (d).

(c) Secondary lens, *imaging telescope objective at :*

(d) *the* sampling shutter, *shown in Fig. 45.7, allowing, when open, light to reach :*

(e) *the final picture camera (not shown).*

(f) *is a manually operated* photographic shutter *for exposing :*

(g) *the* master plate, *whose holder is shown in Fig. 45.6.*

(h) *While sampling, light passes through the shutter* (f) *and the master plate* (g) *via mirrors* h_1 *and* h_2 *to :*

(j) *the* photomultiplier *which provides signals to the analogue computer, to actuate the sampling shutter* (d), *when the image most closely matches the master negative when the photomultiplier current is near a minimum : indicating that the fluctuating image is most nearly undisturbed – and so is the best representation of the object.*

FIG. 45.6 *Master Negative slide holder and locating system. The Master Negative plate is in the back square hole (top front) which is revealed when the mirror assembly (top), which sends light to the photomultiplier in further tube, (bottom) is slid back, as in this picture. The double dark slide is shown withdrawn, as when the plate is being exposed or when sampling is taking place. (The mirror assembly would however be slid forward over the Master Negative.)*

water agitated by an electromagnetic vibrator, driven from a low-frequency noise source. The resulting disturbances appear very similar to those experienced with an astronomical telescope. It remains to discover the efficiency of the technique under these more realistic conditions. It might then be directed to the Moon and the planets.

It was clear that to get further, we would have to embark on a major instrument design and building project: we would have to stretch our abilities and resources to the limit. It would take an unpredictable amount of time, money and effort to build an adequate instrument to make use of the idea effectively on a telescope. Also, we were hardly in the right kind of department – was this anything to do with psychology? (Actually, I now think that relating real-time data to a stored average may be extremely relevant to psychology; but I did not realise this at the time.) Would building a telescope camera be acceptable in the context of experimental psychology? Here we were particularly fortunate to be in the University of Cambridge, for Cambridge has a long and well-justified tradition of tolerating individual foibles. The head of the department, Professor Oliver

Zangwill, was tolerant, and the department of astronomy gave every encouragement and help – allowing us the sole use of a telescope for a year. This was the much loved century-old Thorrowgood refractor, in the care of Dr David Dewhurst, who was especially concerned with our project. The telescope is small, only eight inches in aperture; but it is sturdily built and well able to take the weight of our apparatus. We added a ring of red safe lights in the dome and replaced the nineteenth-century weight-driven drive clock with a synchronous motor driven from an accurate oscillator and – the fact is – we had an awful lot of fun and excitement in that little dome with its old brass telescope. Lastly money – we were given a generous grant from the Paul Fund of the Royal Society. This Fund exists to support the development of novel apparatus likely to be of scientific importance but of limited financial interest. It was a great day when all this came through, and we were able to plan our instrument for making more effective use of telescopes for probing the sky.

The sampling camera was built by Stephen Salter, a dedicated

FIG. 45.7 *Second sampling shutter, designed and made by Stephen Salter, using a pair of electromagnetic actuators (at ends) to deflect a pair of steel strips (feeler gauges) each having a small hole at its end: the holes coincide to allow light through when actuated by a sampling signal. (The feeler gauges are mounted with phosphor bronze pivot strips, in a mechanical matching transformer arrangement to give maximal efficiency.)*

FIG. 45.8 *Second sampling camera, on bench test. The randomly agitated water bath for simulating atmospheric disturbance is to the right with a pair of 90° prisms for passing the light from the object (off picture to the right) vertically through the water. The sampling camera is shown with its side plates removed, but otherwise complete, with the final-picture camera (partly hidden) at extreme left.*

engineer who applied all his skill. A darkroom was set up in the Thorrowgood dome by Philip Clark, who did trojan work organising temperature baths and fixing up a high speed processing service for the master plates. All through that incredibly wet summer of 1966 we strived to get improved pictures through gaps in the clouds.

The apparatus may be seen in the following figures. The general design of the sampling camera is shown in Fig. 45.5 and details such as the master plate location system (Fig. 45.6), the high speed on-demand sampling shutter, which presented the greatest difficulties. The problem here was to provide on-demand exposures down to about one milli-second, and this by mechanical means is quite surprisingly difficult. (Photographic shutters 'cheat' by employing pre-wound springs providing stored energy, so that they are not truly on-demand; or focal plane blinds whose moving slits give short exposures to each part of the film, though the entire exposure is quite long). We were helped by the fact that the image forming light in a telescope crosses near the final image, to make a small cross-sectional disk, which may be occluded with a small aperture shutter. The size of this disk depends on the optics of the telescope, but is generally only about one tenth of an inch in diameter. By placing our shutter exactly at this position of minimum required aperture it proved possible to get sample exposures down to just over one millisecond, with electromagnetic actuators suitably matched to thin steel blades. The arrangement, designed and built by Stephen Salter, is shown in Fig. 45.7. There may be no gain with a faster shutter (except for work on the sun) for there must be sufficient time to collect enough quanta for a reliable correlation estimate. We would however like to try switched image-intensifiers, as non-mechanical shutters. It would also be nice to avoid photographic processing for the Master Negative, by some kind of electronic image storage.

The camera can be seen on bench test in Fig. 45.8. A result, shown as a comparison pair of sampled and non-sampled pictures is shown in Fig. 45.9. The bench test improvement is really dramatic.

We obtained encouraging if not really conclusive results on the Cambridge telescope (Fig. 45.10) getting the kind of improvement apparent in Fig. 45.12 though this could have been due to chance improvements of the conditions between the sampled and unsampled pictures. We had enormous difficulty with the tracking of the

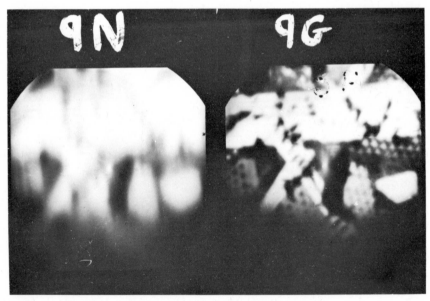

FIG. 45.9 *Example of disturbed picture improvement by sampling. Both pictures are taken through the same disturbance (randomly agitated water) but 9G is sampled while 9N is a normal exposure. The unsampled, 9N picture is the same as the Master Negative used for obtaining 9G by sampling. So this gives a fair idea of the amount of improvement obtained on bench test. (Unfortunately there are technical problems which have, so far, prevented comparable improvement on telescopes. I believe these difficulties will be overcome.)*

FIG. 45.10 *The 8″ Thorrowgood refractor at the Cambridge observatory, with the author. This was the first telescope used for trials. It is over a hundred years old, but an excellent instrument of its class.*

telescope: we could only hope to get results when it was tracking the object (planet or moon) almost within the resolution of the telescope over a sampling period of about 30 minutes. This turned out to be extraordinarily difficult, with any telescope we have met, and has led to the building of a photo-electrically guided tracking corrector, which is now (Feb. 1972) being tested.

The first telescope trials on large instruments started with a joint working party of the American National Academy of Science and

FIG. 45.11 *The New Mexico telescope with the sampling camera and Stephen Salter (wearing arctic clothes) at the Newtonian focus. (It was very frightening up there!)*

(a)

FIG. 45.12 *Unsampled* (a) *and sampled* (b) *pictures of the moon taken with the 8″ Thorrowgood refractor at Cambridge. There is a marked improvement, though less dramatic than improvement obtained with the same equipment on bench test (see Fig. 45.9). (It is possible for 'improvement' to be due to chance improvement in the seeing conditions between the two exposures, though these were taken within minutes of each other). Seeing conditions are so variable and cloud cover so frequent in the British Isles*

(b)

that we prefer to use bench tests, with repeatable controlled disturbances, for finding the optimum sampling strategy, master plate density and minimum acceptable object intensities. Also, the problem of sufficiently accurate tracking is avoided while effects of known tracking errors can be established. This has led to the building of a photo-electrically guided tracking corrector, which is being (1972) bench tested in preparation for telescope trials.

the U.S. Air Force, held over six weeks at the Witney Mansion at Cape Cod. This was a memorable time, with experts in optics, meteorology, mathematics and physics gathered to explore possible ways of improving images. It led to an invitation to try our apparatus out on the satellite tracking station, on a mountain in New Mexico. Fig. 45.11 shows the sampling camera, with Stephen Salter in arctic dress, on the telescope. The expedition was largely unsatisfactory, though we learned a lot. We then worked on the 61 inch reflector of the Lunar and Planetary Laboratory, Tucson, Arizona, through the kindness of its Director, Professor Gerard Kuyper. This also was a fascinating experience, and was more rewarding scientifically. But we were still troubled by tracking problems – which we hope will soon be resolved. So the present state of affairs is that we have a method and an instrument which works; provided its image is not allowed to drift systematically from its position of average register with its Master Negative reference. When this happens, the auto-correlation system breaks down and is useless. It is however perfectly possible to prevent this happening – and then we may get a new view from Earth of the stars.

PART THREE PHILOSOPHY

46 *A speculative account of brain function in terms of probability and induction*

[The first paper in this Part, on philosophy and speculation, was essentially written while I was an undergraduate reading psychology at Cambridge in 1949–50. At that time psychology was an Arts subject at Cambridge, in the Faculty of Moral Sciences, which also included philosophy, logic and ethics. I read these subjects for Part I of the Tripos, and Part II Psychology, under Professor Sir Frederic Bartlett. One of the last acts of Professor Bartlett before his retirement was to move psychology into the Natural Sciences. This rationalized his own emphasis on experiment and had an important later effect on the subject in Cambridge and throughout the country, even though psychology is still sometimes to be found in Arts Faculties. In my view psychology in Universities should be primarily experimental; but there are plenty of questions for which philosophy still has the only word. For philosophy, I had the privilege of attending 'supervisions' with Bertrand Russell, at the very end of his career in Cambridge, as well as his Part II Lectures on Non-demonstrable Inference, which were the basis of *Human Knowledge : Its Scope and Limits* (1948), a book which I regard as deserving a more important place than is usually accorded it in Russell's works. (I treasure a copy which he signed for me, after an argument on Keynes' theory of probability). This first paper probably owes a lot to Russell's influence, and to *Human Knowledge*. In any case, I believe strongly that problems should be considered as generally as possible before they are tackled experimentally. Also I am sure that one should not be ashamed or afraid of speculation. It is as possible grounds for speculation that observations take on significance, and experiments are conceived.

Looking back, I feel that this first paper stated much of what I have been trying to set out ever since, however unsuccessfully. The hint about learning (or at least Pavlovian conditioning) being essentially a matter of working through Mill's requirements for developing inductive generalizations from instances, given other events which could be confused with these instances, still seems important. It has still not been worked out; I suspect because although induction is accepted as important it tends to be discussed in terms of more or less specific brain mechanisms. In philosophical language, learning theories tend to confuse the contingent with the necessary, so that fundamental issues become blurred and lost.

We have experimented only ineffectively with this notion; rearing fish in a random environment, to see whether later learning would be made slower or impossible after a period when prediction required very large samples of events. Pavlov found that conditioning was difficult to achieve in his dogs unless the ambient conditions were kept constant. On this inductive generalization view this must be expected. One-trial learning would also be expected to be rare – for in a 'noisy' environment a single instance is not sufficient for reliable prediction. We tried to control the 'noise' level of the environment, in fish, but most unfortunately they died of a virus. There is a crucial issue here – the same that haunts the problem of distortion illusions – namely, Should we think in terms of the brain's *physiological* limitations, or in terms of the *strategy* it adopts? To take this case: Would an ideal *brain* (or computer) exhibit the same slow learning if confronted with a 'noisy' world? If so, the explanation of the form of actual learning curves is not to be found within physiology. (Similarly, if the distortion illusions (see pp. 346–9) are due to scale-setting strategies, which are inappropriate in certain conditions, then the concepts required for explaining the distortions are not found in physiology; though the strategy is mediated by physiological mechanisms. The same holds for computers; although the mathematical and logical steps are carried out with engineering components and nowhere are engineering concepts violated, it remains true that we cannot understand what is going on in engineering terms alone. To understand the computer we must understand the logic and the assumptions lying behind the computer's programmes. Engineering limitations will however set restraints, which might produce errors by not carrying through the programme faithfully. Errors, distortions, or this case of slow learning in brains, all have the same two very different kinds of explanation – necessary or contingent. This is far too little regarded in psychology, though it is surely a major problem how to decide whether an 'effect' is due to a physiological cause or to consequences of the brain's 'programmes'.]

★   ★   ★

I T is the foundation of empiricism that no pure deduction can tell us anything new about the world. Deductions are, of course, extremely useful but they cannot provide facts without empirical premisses.

Deduction involves operating with symbols according to prescribed rules. It is thus dependent on some sort of formal language; this might be English, or the cardinal numbers, or algebra, or some special calculus having more or less wide application. Deductive conclusions are obtained from premises whose truth is irrelevant to the validity of the argument – by a series of allowed operations on the symbols of the language. Logical fallacies are transgressions of the rules of the language. It is like a game having rigid rules. There can be any number of different games – or logical systems – but some are more useful than others.

This empiricist position that deduction is dependent on formal symbolic language is at once relevant to psychology, for it seems incompatible with the view that primitive thinking is in this strict sense deductive.

Inductions, on the other hand, are based on repetitions of events. The statement 'All swans are white' is inductive. It means more than that all swans so far observed have been white, for it also means that all swans though unobserved are white, and also that all swans yet unborn will be white. It is a generalization which goes beyond the evidence; it is an extrapolation, and it is not necessarily true.

All generalized knowledge of the world – such as expectations of events and laws of nature – are inductively derived even though they may be formulated in a deductive system.

Inductions are ultimately based on Induction by Simple Enumeration (like belief in the sun rising tomorrow because it has risen so often in the past) but there is more to it than this. Some inductions are good and some bad, and the precise conditions for good inductions are not agreed upon. But all are ultimately derived from observed relative frequencies of events.

Induction cannot be reduced to deduction or justified by deduction. They are essentially different. Roughly speaking, induction provides the empirical premises which may be formulated in a deductive language system which can then provide conclusions deductively related – according to the rules of the system – to the original premises. This system is a more or less satisfactory model of part of the world.

We may now give some specific objections to regarding the calculating machine as a fit model of brain function. We will then consider it in terms of a hypothetical Induction Machine.

Some objections to computer models of brain function
Computers function with mechanical and electrical analogues of logical deductive steps. The objections we shall make to the use of

computer analogues of brain function turn mainly upon the fact that they are deductive and thus, as we shall argue, inappropriate in essential respects.

1. Deduction is applicable only within formal systems, or where the number of alternative possibilities has already been determined. The former is highly sophisticated and involves a language with rules for operating on the symbols. The latter is less sophisticated – at least where the number of possible choices is small, but in any case the possibilities must be themselves inductively derived from experience.

2. Calculating machines must be fed with just the necessary information. But a most vital part of all problem solving is the selection of relevant (or helpful) features of the total situation. A machine which could do this might well be built, but the criteria of selection – if these also are not to be 'programmed' by the operator – must be 'learned' and the machine will then be, in part, an inductive machine; for the selection of information would have to be done by use of criteria arrived at through inductive procedures.

3. Perhaps most conclusions and decisions made by men and animals cannot be deductively derived. A conclusion is deductive only if its contradictory is logically incompatible with its premisses; but how often is this the case?

The contradictories of people's conclusions are seldom *logically* impossible. Most conclusions are assessments of what is most probable on the available evidence, but this sort of conclusion cannot be given by computing machines.

A computer can, of course, sometimes give an answer expressed as a probability; for example, it can work out a probability such as the chances of throwing double-six with two dice. But this answer, though it is expressed as a probability, is deductively derived from the (deductive) mathematical theory of probability, there being a theorem which states that separate probabilities should be multiplied to get the total probability of the several things happening. Unfortunately the theory of probability cannot itself serve as a model for induction because to apply it we need to know the number of alternative possibilities and the probability functions relating these, and this involves inductive generalizations about the world.

4. We are considering the logical steps necessary to get to conclusions from premisses. Now logically to justify an answer we must show that each deductive step is valid, but it does not follow from this that each conclusion was originally reached through deductive steps. This is true even within logical systems such as mathematics. For example, the binomial theorem can be derived, and might have been

discovered, by induction, but it must be *proved*, deductively. Formal proof is for most decisions unnecessary and in perhaps most cases impossible.

5. Thought does not seem to go through deductive steps in a logical order. This occurs only when there is great familiarity with the problem, as in arithmetic. Thought goes neatly through the steps only when familiarity has bred contempt.

Inductive method as a model of brain function

The relevance of explicit formulations of inductive methods to the study of brain mechanisms should be obvious to an empiricist because, as R. A. Fisher points out in *The Design of Experiments*, they can provide the only way we know of getting knowledge about the world. We must agree that the brain does this, and that this is its most vital function.

We will now attempt to describe some of the more important problems in psychology in terms of inductive method. In order to avoid the use of the special symbolisms employed by logicians we will imagine an Induction Machine. Such a machine would almost certainly have certain features; these will, on our analogy, become tentative psychological statements about brain function. They will be described as three 'Principles'. For clarity we will first make the general analogy more explicit.

STATEMENT OF ANALOGY

(1) *The brain is like a scientist looking for regularities upon which to base predictions.* All generalizations in science are based on inductive procedures of enquiry. This is true however formal an explanatory system may become. (It also seems to be true that science is in many respects an extension of common sense; as Bertrand Russell puts it, science is common sense grown less common and more sensible).

With co-operative effort and specialized techniques science does very much what the higher animals and man have to do in order to survive; only science does it more systematically.

On this analogy brain function is to be regarded in terms of classifying events on various criteria, and basing predictions on the relative frequencies of the classified events. Information, we will say, is stored largely in the form of inductively derived classes, and these may be related by probability functions based on class inclusion.

This manner of storing information is economical because each event does not need to be separately stored; what is stored for each event is the effect of this event, or experience, on the system of generalisations already built up. This is, it is suggested, the basis of learning. It will be described more fully later.

(2) *The brain is an induction machine continually making decisions.* Roughly speaking, it is continually trying out the best bet. To do this it must assess (a) What is most likely to happen, (or which possibility is most likely to be true), (b) Which likely possibility will be most rewarding. Thus two probability judgements are involved for each decision which is made, as is the case in betting. The result and the reward must both be considered.

The process of making decisions on changing information to accomplish changing ends might be described as a stochastic process. Each decision will change the probabilities for the next decision where these form a 'connected series'.

(3) *The decision mechanism is limited in capacity, both in regard to speed of making reliable decisions and number of decisions made simultaneously.* We postulate a maximum decision rate. Within limits, reliability of decisions will increase with extra time allowed. The 'device' will work in steps tending to give the best judgement on the available evidence.

(4) *It must assess its own best time to stop working on each decision.* A deduction machine must stop when it reaches the answer. But an inductive machine could not do this, because there is no one best answer. The induction machine might never stop.

For the machine to stop making a decision and give an answer, some predetermined value of the assessed reliability of the answer, at that stage of its development, must have been reached. This value must itself depend on the assessed importance of this decision in comparison with the importance of starting upon another.

This suggests experiments to determine the parameters of the decision mechanism. The time which is required to make decisions in various circumstances might be determined experimentally, and their reliabilities might also be assessed. It is important to note that an induction machine might always find a better answer by searching for more data, though this is not the case with a deduction machine. But since the capacity of the induction machine is limited there must be an optimum time to be taken for each decision and this will depend on the importance of the reliability of the decision, on the amount of relevant information to be considered, on the number of rival conclusions from which a selection must be made, and on the importance of the next decision, which is kept waiting. These variables which would determine the optimum decision-time of an 'ideal' induction machine might be experimentally determined for human and animal subjects, given an acceptable measure of reliability of decisions, and of importance of decisions.

(5) *The serial order of decisions is partly pre-determined.* We should expect an ideal machine to anticipate decisions which are likely to be needed in the immediate future and to allot sufficient time for each in its turn.

APPLICATION OF ANALOGY TO PSYCHOLOGY

The brain as a betting machine

The above principles, and the analogy of the brain functioning as a scientist in basing predictions on observed regularities, will now be used as a language for describing some typical psychological problems. It will be useful in so far as it helps to relate the various phenomena by permitting them to be described in common terms, and in so far as this description suggests new experiments.

Perception We will describe perception as a continually changing hypothesis of the world, which is tested by sensory data and stored generalizations based on past experience. We are saying that a perception of an object is similar to an hypothesis in science. It is an organization of data from many sources; the essential law of the organization being that the hypothesis is likely to be useful. It seems that perceptual hypotheses are developed to be generally useful, but also that they may be modified by particular circumstances.

It is illuminating to consider the Ambiguous Figure illusions in this connection. Here we have two alternative perceptual experiences with but one stimulus object. The jump from the one perceptual experience to the other represents, on our theory, the putting up of alternative hypotheses for testing, both hypotheses having equal probability on the evidence. First one then the other hypothesis is accepted, no decision being possible because there is no evidence available to decide between them.

We may now consider how perceptual hypotheses might be built up and selected. The perceptual decision mechanism must continually make probability judgements. The stimuli, or messages, from the sense organs, must be interpreted largely according to generalizations of previous experience. That some such interpretation of sensory data takes place is quite clear for it is at least certain that we do not experience the retinal image. Perception is based on no more than clues from the special senses, as such effects as the constancy phenomena and the filling in of the blind spot illustrate. We may say that where there are alternative likely interpretations of the sensory data that alternative with the highest probability will be accepted, but we should consider on what evidence the probabilities of the interpretations will be assessed.

The evidence for the selection will be, perhaps, from such information as: (1) Observed and stored regularities giving certain expectations. The illusions of conjurors are largely based on such expectations; temporal gaps must be almost continually filled in; for example, we are seldom aware of blinking. (2) More sophisticated beliefs about the world. For example whether a white object is seen as a ghost or a sheet might depend on such factors as belief in the supernatural, or the likelihood of a practical joke, or whether the day is Monday.

But this is only half the story. The probability of the present perceptual hypothesis must be itself checked against the incoming data, and can at any moment be entirely superseded by a fresh hypothesis. This will occur when the present perceptual hypothesis is highly improbable upon the acceptable interpretation of the sensory data; a new hypothesis in conformity with this interpretation will then be accepted.

We may account for the stability of perceptual forms by suggesting that there is something akin to statistical significance which must be exceeded by the rival interpretation and the rival hypothesis before they are allowed to supersede the present perceptual hypothesis.

The phenomena discussed by the Gestalt school can be interpreted by referring to our Second Principle. Gestalt writers point out, in effect, that certain simple perceptual forms tend to have preference. Now this preference for these simple forms might well be a way of saving decision-time by a preliminary acceptance of a first approximation. The first approximations, or preliminary hypotheses, are very often checked by further sensory information (interpreted sensory stimuli) but this is not always the case and we then have an example of Gestalt Configuration. This occurs either when there is no evidence available to develop the perceptual hypothesis, as in the case of the simple diagram, rows of dots etc. used to illustrate the phenomena – or when perceptual conditions are poor, as at night – or when there is available information but it cannot be used. This latter might occur when there is insufficient time, or when the organism is affected by fatigue or by drugs.

We might expect that where there are rival hypotheses between which a decision might be made on sensory data, these data might be specially selected. This suggests experiments on the selection of information; for example eye-movements might be recorded where there are plausible alternative hypotheses. We might expect of that part of the stimulus field scanning which is likely to provide information crucial to the decision to be made between the rival hypothesis.

The importance of symbols to perception, which is stressed by Professor Bartlett in *Remembering*, is particularly interesting. Symbols denote classes; to give an 'abstract' diagram a name might be expected to call up the generalizations associated with that name, and this will provide the perceptual mechanism with stored hypotheses (or schema?) which will form part of the perception of the stimulus object.

Symbols, recognition and 'set' modify perceptions, we suggest, by initiating different perceptual hypotheses and by calling up generalizations which are related by probability functions to the symbol or the object recognized (or wrongly recognized), and to the goal of the current behaviour.

The Nativist-Empiricist controversy in perception seems to resolve itself into the problem of the origin of the classes from which hypotheses are built. If these are all generalizations then pure Empiricism is the whole story; but if some events are given systematically antecedent probabilities, widely different from chance, then it might well seem that some decisions are not based on inductively derived classes and perception and behaviour will consequently appear Nativistic. It might be that some generalizations are phylogenetically developed and stored in the race by a resulting modification of structure, which is inherited just like a normal anatomical feature.

Learning The first point we would stress about learning is the importance of not being misled by inappropriate experiments. This point, is, of course, stressed by Professor Bartlett in his early rejection of nonsense syllables as fit material for learning experiments, and also in his continual insistence upon the importance of experimental situations being as realistic and life-like as possible consistent with the degree of control required to obtain specific information from the experiment. The importance attached to combining applied with theoretical work is perhaps related to this insistence that to discover the basic functional mechanisms the organism must, at least sometimes, be observed in natural conditions.

Most if not all Theories of Learning take the form of abstracting features which are common to many 'learning' situations. These common features are then defined and relations between them are described, perhaps mathematically. This type of procedure has worked very well in physics, but has the obvious danger in psychology that if unusual situations are used the special adaptations of the organism to these situations may not be recognized as such. When this occurs, for example, in a learning experiment, it may be impossible to say what information the experiment provides about learning. Some implications of this point may become clear in a moment.

Let us consider any learning or conditioning experiment where there is a series of repeated events or stimuli. Now on our induction machine model we would expect the later events in the series to influence the organism less than the first events. Consider the development of a generalization built from the series, perhaps of the form, 'Bell always followed by food'. Now when this generalization has attained an adequate reliability through sufficient repetitions, it will not pay the organism to go on increasing the reliability. This must almost certainly be true because if all the terms in a long series of repetitions were given equal weight the capacity of the brain would have to be virtually infinite. For example, if with every step one took when walking the normally accepted generalization 'The ground is solid' were improved, (and also an indefinitely large number of other generalizations: 'It does not hurt', 'My leg does not fall off', etc.) storage space would be used up with every step that was taken when walking; and there would be no advantage once the generalization was sufficiently strong to permit walking with confidence. Thus the typical falling off in learning curves takes on a rather new significance.

What does become important when a generalization is being formed, or is already formed, is an exceptional instance. Our model suggests that exceptions should provide important information on learning because it is by noting exceptions and the special conditions associated with them that new generalized knowledge is gained and linked with what is already accepted.

We have now reached the point at which the principles of inductive logic and statistical inference might be applied in detail to the problem of learning. A few suggestions will be risked.

Inductive logic is based on three of J. S. Mill's Inductive Principles. These are simply descriptions of how the factors which are relevant are separated from those which are irrelevant when a generalization is attempted. As a matter of fact Mill did not formulate his principles with quite this intention; he was attempting to reduce induction to deduction by providing a general premiss; the attempt failed and it is now believed that any such attempt is bound to fail. His description of induction is, nevertheless, regarded as essentially correct once certain confusions are removed. The three essential Principles are: The Method of Agreement, the Method of Difference, and the Method of Concomitant Variation. The last is essentially the statistical principle of correlation; we will for the moment confine our discussion to the first two.

The importance of these Principles, or Methods, in considering learning is, we suggest, two-fold, First, they provide a clear description of the only way we know of gaining new knowledge; and secondly, an induction machine which used them rigorously would be economical in the amount of experience (number of instances) required to make a reliable generalization. These considerations make it likely that, in learning, generalizations are developed essentially according to the model of the Confirmation Tables for the Methods of Agreement and Difference. Table 46.1 and Table 46.2 show how the Tables may be formulated.

TABLE 46.1
A CONFIRMATION TABLE FOR THE METHOD OF AGREEMENT

$A \rightarrow B_1 \ \& \ C_1 \ \& \ D_1 \ \& \ K_1$ . . . . .
$A \rightarrow B_2 \ \& \ C_2 \ \& \ D_2 \ \& \ M_2$ . . . . .
$A \rightarrow B_3 \ \& \ C_3 \ \& \ M_3 \ \& \ P_3$ . . . . .
$A \rightarrow B_4 \ \& \ K_4 \ \& \ L_4 \ \& \ P_4$ . . . . .
(Indefinite number of confirmatory and no
disconfirmatory instances).

– – – – – – – – – – – – – – – – –

Every case of A *no matter what else is the case*
is also a case of B.

TABLE 46.2
A CONFIRMATION TABLE FOR THE METHOD OF DIFFERENCE

$A \rightarrow B \ \& \ C \ \& \ D \ \& \ E \ \&$

$\bar{B} \rightarrow \bar{A} \ \& \ C \ \& \ D \ \& \ E \ \&$

– – – – – – – – – – –

Every case of A is also a case of B.

The Method of Agreement attempts to show that A *by itself* leads to the occurrence of B. The different conditions, (presence or absence of the factors, C, D, E, etc.) make no difference to the A-B connection in the Confirmation Table shown in Table 46.1.

The Method of Difference shows that A is a necessary condition of B when it shows that not-B leads to not-A when other factors are held constant.

For a good generalization of the form A→B both the Method of Agreement and the Method of Difference need to be used. The Method of Concomitant Variation is simply a statement of the principle that if A varies in a manner related to variations in B then there is an A-B connection. This is best discussed in statistical language in terms of correlation and significance.

The relevance of the Confirmation Tables to Learning may now be discussed. The first point is that there is, of course, a distinction between *finding out* that A is connected with B and *having to remember* the connection. It is the distinction between being told something which one is to remember, and finding something out which then may or may not be remembered. But psychologically the distinction is not a clear one because the appropriateness of the moment of recall must be determined inductively even where the Confirmation Table is made minimal by the connection between A and B having been given verbally or in some other way. There seems to be at least nearly always an element of *finding out* in a learning situation and this element introduces terms into the confirmation table; that is, it involves the organism in discovering just what it is which has to be learned.

It is frequently pointed out in the literature of induction that the methods of Agreement and Difference are implicit in the primitive Induction by Simple Enumeration, providing the conditions vary. This is readily seen; if A→B is found to hold on many occasions the generalization is strengthened by the exclusion of irrelevant factors although these are not separately noted, simply because they are in turn present or absent at the various occurrences of A→B. They may be assumed to vary although their presences and absences are not noted. This raises a fundamental experimental issue: Does the organism rely entirely on chance differences between conditions at each repetition of the related events to strengthen the generalization, or are these differences recorded and themselves generalized?

This question seems relevant to the problem of Transfer of Training. It might be interesting to determine experimentally just how generalizations are built up. Learning curves might be related to the number of conditions which are being 'attended to' using the Confirmation Tables for the necessary mathematical model. Behaviour in exceptional instances might be related to subsidiary generalizations developed from the conditions accepted in the Confirmation Table. The variables which have been investigated in relation to Transfer, such as the effect of teaching general principles, might be related to the selection of the conditions of factors included in a confirmation table which, we suggest, is worked through during learning.

Behaviour and personality

We may describe personality (there seems no better word) in terms of the parameters of the decision device of our induction machine. Moods will be short-term changes in the parameters. The personality will be not simply the average values of the parameters of an individual but rather the values which are assumed under various circumstances.

Such terms as 'optimist', 'pessimist', 'generous', 'mean', etc., may be analysed in terms of the values the parameters of the decision device assume in various social and other circumstances.

The general picture is of gambling on probabilities: the reward for which each bet is made is itself seldom or never certain, that it *is* a reward is itself a gamble.

Long-term changes in personality may be the result of coming to accept different odds. This may be general in the whole field of experience, when the individual might be called 'cynical' or 'rash', or it might be more specific when he might be described as, say, 'careful over money'. Not only must the chance of a given gain be considered, but also the importance of the possible loss, and this will depend on the available capital and the limit below which the individual will not allow his capital to fall. This limit might vary with age, perhaps being partly determined by generalized success or failure.

To develop this picture we should again particularly consider the Second Principle: the limited capacity of the decision device. We may then describe 'irrational' beliefs or 'prejudices', and this it is most important to do if we are to escape from a quite inadequate account of behaviour. Prejudices we may represent as systematic refusal to consider data which are relevant to certain kinds of decision. Now this refusal might well be useful (since the decision device is limited in its capacity) because if all relevant data were used for each important decision, too much time would be required for each decision. Prejudices might well be important for the business of 'getting on with it'. A Philosopher would probably make a poor General; because speed is vital in making decisions in battle, whereas speed is sacrificed in academic dispute where it is important to consider all possibilities, though many of these will have a low antecedent probability and are better ignored by the man of action.

The importance of formal languages and clearly formulated definitions and procedures is largely in saving decision-time, by organizing information so that it can be used efficiently and communicated to others, thus allowing co-operative work in building up generalizations and testing hypotheses. It is here that deduction becomes important in thinking.

The original thinker bets on outsiders. He considers many

hypotheses having low antecedent probabilities and doubts many hypotheses having high probability, and in so doing he sacrifices decision-time. Gains will be few in comparison with the number of bets, but a win will carry a high reward. The reward will be large, partly because few other individuals are likely to make the same bet.

Persuasion represents a change in the parameters of the decision mechanism, which is produced in an interesting manner. Verbal or written information which is emotionally toned tends to produce rapid decisions and agreement with the majority of the group. Now this might represent a primitive type of decision associated with emergency. Accuracy is sacrificed to speed and agreement with the majority, both of which are important in emergencies in primitive conditions. The emotive language of the political speaker, and the use of exclamation marks by advertizers, are significant in this respect.

SUGGESTED EXPERIMENTS

We may now indicate the form some experiments might take to give quantitative values to be interpreted according to our picture of a Decision Mechanism acting on inductively derived generalizations based on frequencies.

Learning as systematic modification of the null hypothesis

Consider an apparatus consisting of a number of small windows – say four – in each of which is an unique symbol which may be lit by a separate lamp. The symbols – say A, B, C and D – are arranged to be lit one at a time in a complex sequence, their frequencies in general being different. The subject's task is to guess which letter will next appear.

The subject has the *a priori* knowledge that there are four letters; i.e. he knows N. But he knows nothing of their relative frequencies and therefore he should assign a probability of $p = \frac{1}{4}$ to each letter. The Null Hypothesis is that for each letter $p = \frac{1}{4}$. (A 'preference' would be a significant deviation from $p_1 = p_2 = p_3 = p_4$. This could be determined by arranging the frequencies to be equal, and noting whether the decisions are distributed equally between the N choices).

Now learning might be regarded as an abandoning of the Null Hypothesis (in the special case where there is no *a priori* information about relative frequencies) in favour of a set of probability functions which reflect observed frequencies in the external world. This suggested apparatus might be used to glean information on the processes involved in this process. In separate trials the relative frequencies of the alternatives might be arranged to be different; it may then be possible to determine how different these must be before a new pattern of response is initiated. This could be interpreted as a measure of the criterion of 'significance' which the organism adopts, or demands, in this situation.

The time taken to make each choice might be taken as a measure of the subject's degree of belief in the correctness of his choice. This must however be used with care for doubtless other factors affect the time taken, but it might provide a relative measure in a standard situation.

The use of probability judgements for quantifying preference scales

It was suggested some years ago by Ramsey, and it is taken as an explicit assumption, although never experimentally demonstrated, by Von Neumann, that people make probability judgements in such a manner that the 'odds' they are prepared to accept will in general reflect their preferences. If this is indeed true it might be of great importance as a possible method of quantifying Preference and Attitude scales.

Suppose an individual has ranked in order of preference three mutually exclusive choices, (e.g. three types of ice cream any one of which he may have). These are ranked in a preference order such that A > B > C. The problem is to compare the degree of preference of A to B with that of B to C. The suggested method is to ask the individual to accept, or refuse, a bet such that he may either have B or a 50%–50% chance of A; or B or a 50%–50% chance of C. If he accepts the bet on these terms his preference for A to B must – it is said – be equal to his preference for B to C.

This might not only be tested experimentally, (perhaps by seeing whether consistent judgements are made, and also perhaps by comparing the results obtained with other scales such as the Weber-Fechner scale by choosing questions where such comparison is possible), but it might be further developed, if it is possible to use relations other than the 50%–50% relation, into a powerful tool for quantifying preferences.

The relation between eye-movements and hypothesis formation

It might be interesting to record eye movements during object recognition, in order to relate eye movements to visual hypothesis formation. We might expect eye-movements to be related to expectation of the position of sources of information important in deciding between rival hypotheses. Somewhat ambiguous stimulus fields might be used, and the perceptual process might be slowed down by making the conditions difficult.

47 *On physical model explanations in psychology*

[This paper (published in 1953, but written two or three years later than the previous one) looks at Gestalt theory in terms of machine analogies of brain function, to ask: Is the brain digital or analogue?]

★   ★   ★

MUCH current theoretical work in psychology takes the form of looking for appropriate physical models with which to describe, by analogy, the findings of experiment and observation. The 'problem of consciousness' is shelved, or regarded as a logically different sort of question from those the experimentalist can hope to answer with his techniques. The experimentalist asks instead what sort of mechanism could perform the tasks undertaken by the central nervous system. He considers the ordered activity of the organism in performing a skill, and the changes in performances during the learning of skills, and he considers perception and learning and nervous organization in terms of practical or theoretically possible machines.

Perhaps the best-known examples of this way of thinking in psychology are the computer and the servo-mechanism analogies. The former was suggested by the feats of the large electronic calculating machines capable of producing numerical solutions to problems requiring perhaps years of work by a mathematician unaided by machines. The latter analogy was suggested during the war, when for example, automatic gun-aiming devices were developed which caused guns to follow moving targets in a manner which seemed similar to eye-hand co-ordination. The servo-mechanism analogy has proved useful both in interpreting the physiological mechanisms responsible for controlled movement, and for the design of machines such as aeroplanes which must be accurately controlled by men. The man is himself regarded as part of the total servo-loop, his parameters are determined (for example the phase angle of the error for various

537

input frequencies), and these are accepted as part of the data to be considered when designing the control systems of aircraft.

The explicit use of such analogies is limited to the last decade in psychological writing, but the wisdom of regarding the mind as in some sense a machine has been debated at least since the work of Pavlov. J. B. Watson's attempt (1919 and 1925) to describe behaviour in terms of the conditioned reflex was criticized at the time by writers, particularly those of the Gestalt school, as being too mechanistic.

Psychological theories are traditionally divided into two classes, namely 'atomistic' theories and 'field' theories. The atomists stem from Scottish analytical philosophy, from the attempt to describe experience in terms of complexes of simple elements, while field theories stem from German metaphysics, and its insistence on the doctrine (so important to the Kantian theory of knowledge) of 'internal relations'. It seems important to indicate the origins of these dichotomous approaches if only to suggest the relevance of epistemological considerations to the study of brain function. The experimental psychologist is perhaps apt to ignore the point that his theory of how the brain works must be commensurable with his theory (if any) of how it is *possible* to gain knowledge of the world.

If the relevance of epistemology to the study of brain function be accepted, then some of the difference between the Atomists (or Associationists) and Field theorists (or Gestalt writers) may be discussed by the philosopher as well as by the psychologist.

J. Z. Young makes the point, in *Doubt and Certainty in Science*, that it is convenient to talk about brain function in terms of machine analogies because we are familiar with machines. Our language is developed to talk about machines and the properties and behaviour of common objects; we find great difficulty in talking about anything else. This suggests that the psychologists who have not explicitly used machine analogies may well have done so implicitly. I suggest that this is true of the Gestalt school.

Consider the emphasis placed by the Gestalt writers on the 'Principle of Good Configuration' or 'Good Gestalten'. The point which is most stressed by the Gestalt school is the importance of direction in thinking, and in activity and in the processes leading to perception. This directive-tendency is described in terms of the tendency of the physical Gestalten (situated in the brain) to assume states of maximum stability.

Köhler, in his essay 'Physical Gestalten' (1920), discusses the physicist's equilibrium, and dynamic states of physical systems; and he holds that the directive-tendencies of thought and perception are to be regarded as manifestations of the physicist's laws of the tendency of physical systems to adopt equilibrium states. At the same time Köhler objects to talking about 'mechanism' when discussing brain function; he does not want to reduce his physical Gestalten to simpler elements.

The Gestalt school's objection to 'mechanical' models is, perhaps, responsible for masking the surely indisputable fact that the postulated physical Gestalten – with the physical laws supposed to describe their properties – constitute a machine analogy of brain function. It seems that the Field theorists are not averse to mechanical analogies, but they choose larger units than do the Associationists. The often-quoted phrase: 'The whole is more than the sum of the parts', with which Gestalt writers sum up their objection to the Associationist's analysis of, for example, the perceptual field, clearly indicates their point of view. The status of their objection is another matter and depends upon the philosophical analysis of the phrase, the whole is greater than the sum of the parts; and in particular upon whether it be regarded as a fact about the world that essentially new properties emerge upon the combination of elements or whether, on the other hand, this 'newness' is not rather surprising but in principle predictable. In other words, is emergence a fact about the world (and thus of ontological status), or is it epistemological – the result of our ignorance about how to analyse wholes into parts so that the whole is completely described? I do not propose to dwell or to make any decision on this point, but it is important to make the problem explicit if we are to avoid confusion in our attempt to compare Field with Atomistic theories.[1]

We have said, then, that both the Atomists and the Field theorists adopt physical analogues as explanatory concepts for psychology. Perhaps the recognition that they are both machine analogies makes comparison more fruitful. An essential difference between them is the size of the units chosen, and thus the function of the unit elements in the brain mechanism, which both regard as obeying physical laws which in some sense underlie psychology. The Gestalt writers might prefer to think of some psychological phenomena 'emerging' from the physical states, this emergence being in principle unexplainable in simpler terms, but they certainly use the physicist's laws describing equilibrium states as explanatory concepts for their Field theory.

The atomists also use physical laws for explanations of psychological findings. As we have said their units are smaller; they talk of

---

[1] For a discussion on Emergent Properties see C. D. Broad, 1925.

'switches' and 'connections', for example, in their postulated brain mechanisms. Their procedure is to consider which machines (actually or theoretically possible) behave in a manner similar to some isolated feature of the organism's behaviour, such as, for example, learning or perception. They then suggest that there are in the brain physiological correlates of the switches, relays or whatever comprises the machine.

In the case of thinking, the Atomists compare the organism with computers, particularly to large electronic machines such as the E.D.S.A.C. The processes taking place in the organism are supposed to be similar to those taking place in the machine; the neurones, or groups of them, are supposed to function like the basic 'flip-flop' circuits. As in the Gestalt physical analogy we have stable states, but here these correspond to the store of each bit of information which is being operated on, perhaps according to logical rules, by the interrelated activity of the switches.

Now it is well known that computing machines are classified into two groups: analogue machines, and digital machines. The former work by providing a continuously variable physical analogue of the function under consideration; the most common example is the slide-rule. A further example is the mechanical integrator. Digital machines work in small steps each representing a unit logical step. Physically, these steps may be represented by the teeth on gear wheels, as in the desk computer, or by the stable states of such circuits as the 'flip-flop'.

It is the contention of this paper that the Field theories of brain function bear the same relation to the Atomist theories as the analogue computing machines bear to the digital machines. If this be accepted, it seems possible to discuss the rival types of theory in terms of the advantages and disadvantages of the two types of machines as they are used for various purposes. To pursue this theme in detail would require more technical knowledge of these machines than the writer possesses, but we may suggest the chief advantages of the two types.

The digital machine has the following advantages:

1. Flexibility. (It will solve any problem which does not require logical operations which are not built in. Further limitations may be imposed by the finite 'storage' of any physical machine).

2. Accuracy. (Provided the machine does not actually make a false step the answer will be correct; analogue machines are subject to random error throughout. Further, their accuracy is dependent on the precision of their construction; this is not true of digital machines).

The analogue machine has the following advantages:

1. Speed. (Though their range of function is limited they are fast – hence their use for bomb aiming).

2. Simplicity. (Typically they are comparatively simple, but this may be because they are normally designed for but one class of problem).

3. In some cases by changing the physical characteristics of the device it may be made to give solutions for various functions.

This list of advantages and disadvantages of the two types of machine may now be compared with the requirements of the brain mechanism. In general we may say that where speed is important the analogue machine is the best bet; but the choice must be influenced by the way in which the mechanism of learning is regarded. The Gestalt school stress the importance of innate tendencies in perception and thinking, while the Atomists stress past experience; the mechanism of learning and storage of information must be regarded as very different in the two theories.

For the Field theorists learning will constitute modifications in the physical characteristics of the analogue device. Information will be stored in a form akin to a collection of cams of various profiles, which may be substituted one for another. Anticipation, or 'set', might be a pre-selection of the appropriate analogue cam.

Learning for the Atomists will be similar to the building up of the libraries of punched tape found in large computing laboratories. These tapes are punched with the steps required for many types of problem; they are used to save time where similar problems have been solved before.

Enough has been said to indicate how the principles of computers may be taken over as languages to describe brain function. To the writer it seems important to call attention to the analogue-digital distinction, and its apparent correspondence in the Field *v.* Atomist controversy. Perhaps this suggests what to look for to make a decision on what is commonly regarded as a fundamental issue in psychological theory.

This way of thinking suggests that there is a *hiatus* in the Gestalt writers' use of the analogue machine as the paradigm of perception and thinking. The use made of the tendency to equilibrium of the physical Gestalten seems to involve the assumption that the spatial form of the physical Gestalten bears approximately a one-to-one relation with (in the case of perception) the object in the stimulus field. For example, the physical Gestalten related to a perceived circle is supposed to be itself circular in form. If this one-to-one relation is not supposed then the Gestalt thesis that the psychological phenomena of 'closure', etc., can be attributed to the physical properties of the Gestalten is not tenable. There is no obvious reason why the brain should elect to represent a circle with a circular neural modification.

The mathematical techniques of information theory, the notion of the capacity of information channels, and criteria such as economy in the use of neurones, suggest that sensory and other information are likely to be *coded* in some manner. If this is so then the Gestalt thesis that 'closure' and 'directive-tendencies' can be explained by the physical properties of Gestalten breaks down. If we do not know the code (or the manner in which the transducer works) then we can say nothing whatever about the physical properties of the information store.

An objection to both types of theory, as they are commonly expounded, is that brain function is not explicitly related to the epistemological requirements for gaining knowledge.

An adequate account cannot limit brain function to deductive inference; to gain knowledge inductive generalization is necessary. Practical calculating machines must be fed with the relevant, and only the relevant, information. This is done by the human operator, but obviously he cannot be included in the analogy. Yet without him the machines will not even begin to produce an answer. We must imagine a machine capable of selecting its own information and devising its own operating rules: it must generalize and develop criteria of relevance. It must be an Inductive machine.

48 *The two psychologies*

[This paper is one of a series of contributions, 'The Impact of Biology', which appeared in the *Cambridge Review*. It looks rather critically at psychology as a science. I think I still agree with myself that 'it is a sickening fact that those parts of psychology which have made the most impact are those parts which have the least scientific credence'.]

★   ★   ★

THE impact of psychology comes less from the specific results of experiments than from realizing that scientific method can be applied to Man. The acceptance of scientific method as appropriate implies that we are not separate from Nature but are subject to the laws of physics – a view diametrically opposed to the ancient theological conception of Man as unique in the Universe, hovering somewhere between Matter and God. The Victorians were challenged by the idea that man is in origin and structure an animal; in this century, and through psychology, we realize the full implications of the Darwinian revolution. T. H. Huxley saw the implications very clearly: that man has an animal brain, and animals are akin to machines. But this was for a time lost in the amalgam of clinical intuition and religion put forward by psycho-analysts. Psychological theory goes in two directions: the relating of human to animal behaviour (as the Victorians related human to animal structure), and exploring the power of symbols. These approaches to the study of man may seem essentially opposed but yet incomplete in themselves. We are, however, beginning to see how they can link up.

Experimental psychology reveals relations between the structure of the brain and its function, which makes the understanding of human behaviour comparable to understanding machines. The approach is similar to that of the engineer – in both cases causal processes are sought. The brain is thought of as a vast computer, accepting, storing and handling information to give behaviour. The brain does not in fact seem to be very like actual man-made computers: it is primarily concerned with prediction, so that behaviour is a step ahead of reality. The main impact of the idea that the brain is a machine lies in the thought that we are controlled in our behaviour and experience by physical processes which can be understood in terms of physics and chemistry. This means that psychology has become truly a Natural Science, and can call upon the intellectual and technical tools of the other sciences to tackle its particular problems. This is not only philosophically important but directs the stream of research, and the requirements of teaching, into new channels.

The computer analogy has a further important consequence – it begins to close the gap between the physiological and psycho-analytic approaches. The point is that a computer is not to be thought of only as a complex set of circuits, but also as a system controlled by a 'programme'. The logic of a problem, and the steps required for its solution set by the programme, can be considered apart from the actual functioning of the circuits. In a computing laboratory we find engineers concerned with the machines, and mathematicians concerned with the symbols used by the machines. They need to communicate, but their skills and interest are different. This is paralleled by those who work with the brain and those who deal with the symbols of the mind. When something goes wrong, a cure may be found by changing the circuits or the symbols. Analysts try to provide cures by sorting out 'programming confusions,' while physiological psychologists directly affect the brain with drugs, surgery or shock, as though they were engineers, not programmers. Freudian psychology is entirely concerned with the power of symbols; but the brain can be physically deranged, and symbolism is most difficult to control or investigate scientifically, for symbols have long tentacles which cling desperately to otherwise unrelated facts. The task of sorting out conflicting structures of symbols, and reorganizing them by talking to patients, is quite different from the procedures of experimental psychology where the emphasis is on establishing behaviour norms, measuring abilities, and discovering relations between behaviour and processes going on in the nervous system. Psycho-analysis sometimes looks too much like magic; but it does deal with symbols handled by the brain and not with the brain itself, so we should not expect sensible-sounding statements like those concerning familiar objects.

Psycho-analysts may seem like witch doctors, but we owe them a great debt. Whatever the merits of psycho-analytic therapy, we must be grateful for its impact and attack on the traditional theological attitude to punishment and guilt. Since Freud, it is difficult to justify retributive punishment, and punishment for corrective purposes now needs to be justified on its proved effects. The abandoning of the theological conception of punishment, though humane, has led to its own difficulties, for though punishment is difficult to defend it is the easiest kind of behaviour control to apply. We have not yet recovered from this particular impact, which strikes at the root of jurisprudence. Even more important is the liberation of physical and mental disease from sin and guilt. We no longer think of the mentally or physically ill as stricken somehow for their own or other people's edification, but recognize clearly that disease is a misfortune that must be fought openly with all the weapons available, whether or not it has 'psychological' origins.

Psychology is sometimes thought of as sinister. In so far as psychology teaches how behaviour can be controlled it *is* sinister, for this power like others can be misapplied. But as with other forms of power, greater understanding brings safeguards. For psychology to be more than an observational science, methods of controlling behaviour must be developed, if only for experimental purposes, and once discovered they may be used for good or ill. The power of fear, guilt and reward have been recognized from ancient times, and organized society depends upon their use, but more recently operant conditioning has led to precise 'shaping' of behaviour, and in this we have a subtle tool for studying behaviour by modifying it. It may also prove an important tool in teaching.

Psychology could have its most immediate impact in education, but strangely little serious effort has been devoted to educational psychology. True, psychologists have devised many kinds of performance and aptitude tests, and animals and human experiments on learning form a vast literature; but the tests do not command the universal respect accorded the measuring scales and instruments of the physical sciences, while it is quite remarkable how little we know of the learning process itself. Experiments on nonsense syllables and other meaningless material give nice lawful results, but in general true-to-life situations do not. The result is that laboratory studies are not readily applied to the class room. The new teaching machines are useful tools for presenting material to be learned in a controlled way, and the designing of their programmes is throwing up the question of what are the essential features of human learning, and in a form which may be answered by their use. In the last decade elaborate learning theories were developed, these being structures of axioms and predictions, with certain critical experiments. They had the same logical form as geometry, but the earth proves easier to measure than the mind, and these theories are now generally discarded in favour of simpler statements backed by far more data. But learning remains an enigma: we are ignorant of the changes which take place in the nervous system to store and generalize experience. Until this is understood in physical terms, there is unlikely to be sufficient understanding to make a real impact on education by speeding up the process of learning, or increasing the power of thought by developing symbols to match the characteristics of the brain.

Language marks off man from other animals, and experimental psychology and psycho-analysis meet over the study of language – as indeed does philosophy. It is an important question how far our extraordinary intellectual ability is due to language, and how far we owe language to our superior brain.

Psychology has made many practical contributions. The measurement of skill is vital, especially where lives depend on pilots and drivers. The design of synthetic trainers rests in large measure on psychological experiments to determine the important features of the real situation to be incorporated. Again, measures of performance under conditions of stress or boredom set limits to what can be expected of factory workers, or astronauts. Indeed space travel sets a host of new problems to the psychologist; he must discover how far the nervous system, which has evolved from the beginning of life, can be relied upon to work reliably in alien worlds.

It is a sickening fact that those parts of psychology which have made the greatest impact are those parts which have the least scientific credence. The achievements of experimental psychology in relating behaviour to brain function, in showing the kinds of information systems providing perception of the world and our reactions to it, are substantial. The semi-mystical intuitions of the psycho-analysts have changed profoundly our conception of Man and Society. It is not the results of controlled experiments but vague and ambiguous pronouncements, having no clear foundation of evidence, which have made an impact raising more than a ripple.

49 *The brain as an engineering problem*

[The following paper represents a breakaway not only from Gestalt thinking, but also from some rather generally accepted neurological doctrines. The title implies that it is *engineering* rather than the more general *physical* analogies which are likely to be appropriate for thinking about brain function. Engineering implies design. Once we know that a system is designed we can consider its efficiency, and how one part serves another part to perform its role. This reflects the extreme importance of the Darwinian revolution in biological thought; for since Darwin, 'purpose' and 'function' can be applied in biology without evoking metaphysics. The same is not, however, true for the physical sciences, except for engineering; which makes engineering – *applied* physics – of special interest to biologists.]

★　　　★　　　★

The brain serves to cool the blood
Aristotle

The brain is like an oven, hot and dry,
Which bakes all sorts of fancies, low and high
The Duchess of Newcastle

BIOLOGISTS generally refer to the activity of living organisms as 'behaviour'. When talking about machines, engineers tend to use the word 'performance'. To interchange these words is to raise a smile, perhaps an appreciative smile, but the speaker risks being labelled quixotic. It does appear, however, that the terms 'behaviour' and 'performance' are interchanged much more now than in the past, the reason almost certainly being the influence of cybernetic ideas,

547

which have unified certain aspects of biology and engineering. Some biologists even go so far as to regard their subject as essentially a branch of engineering, and some engineers use examples from biology, such as living servo-systems, to illustrate their principles. The activity of organisms is most often referred to as 'performance' when their efficiency is being considered. Thus play-activity is called 'behaviour', while a skilled worker's activity may be called 'performance'. This change is interesting, for it brings out the influence of the engineering way of thinking upon even lay thought about human and animal activity.

It is worth stressing that physical principles have not always been accepted as appropriate to biology. Aristotle did not make any basic distinction between the living and the non-living, but a sharp distinction was drawn by Kant in the *Kritik der Urtheilskraft* (1790). Perhaps Kant was so influenced by the patent inadequacy of Descartes' attempts to describe organisms in terms of his Natural Philosophy that he was led to say that the behaviour of living systems cannot be governed by causal principles applicable to the physical world. To Kant, living systems are somehow outside the dictates of the laws of nature, and this has been held by some biologists since – certainly as recently as E. S. Russell (1946), who regards 'directiveness' as a special property of living organisms. The influence of Kant's teaching upon biology has been profound and (to the cybernetically inclined) disastrous. Historically, it has led to the creation of special entities to distinguish the living from the non-living, such as Driesch's Entelechy, Bergson's *élan vital* and the Emergent Properties of the Gestalt school of psychology.[1]

We do indeed think of inanimate matter as somehow different from animate matter. If we did not, these words would have no special meaning, for no distinction would be implied. The point is this: is it useful to describe, or to explain, this difference by postulating some *special factor* which is held to be present in animate and absent in inanimate matter? To biologists looking for general explanatory concepts, after the manner of the physical sciences, such postulated special factors must appear harmful. These factors do not enable us to relate phenomena; they do not provide any sort of picture; they do not enable predictions to be made. The trouble with Entelechy, *élan vital* and the rest is that they do not help us to understand. Such terms give a sacrosanct air of life, which may be pleasing, but which

[1]Köhler, in his book *Die physischen Gestalten* (1920), takes a different view from that of most Gestalt writers. He does not suppose that organisms are unique in this respect, but rather that Emergence is to be found in many physical systems. Some philosophers have also taken this view. It leads to the difficulty that 'emergence' is used so generally that it points to nothing special. This point is considered in Gregory, 1953*b* [No. 47].

tends to warn off further enquiry. The Gestaltist's plea for the special nature of 'organic unities' is effectively a warning against attempts at further analysis, the doctrine being that it is *in principle impossible* to analyse the whole in such a manner that its activity can be completely described by the causal relations between the parts. It is, however, just this sort of analysis which is the goal of exploration in the physical sciences. Further, it is important to note the *in principle impossible* here: it is not the complexity of the task which is held to make analysis impossible, but rather the claim that the organic world is such that analysis into parts is doomed to failure, however complete our knowledge of it may be. Curiously, this is regarded by some as an exciting and interesting discovery about living systems. This is an attitude puzzling to those who believe that useful explanations in science should take the form of analysis into simpler elements. Now it *could* be that there is something irreducible about living systems which defies such analysis, but surely we have no right to claim this until the traditional types of explanation have failed for a very long time, and certainly not now while exciting advances are being made in the biological sciences. If we seek the types of explanation found in the physical sciences, *élan vital*, or the concept of Emergence, will appear as doctrines of despair. To postulate such special unanalysable factors is to make a philosophy of pessimism. To say that *x* is an Emergent Property is to put *x* into the limbo of the unknown and shut the door upon it, while warning others against peeping through the keyhole.

To regard the brain as a problem in engineering is to look for possible solutions in terms of engineering principles to the questions set by biological enquiry. This chapter is concerned not with answers to specific questions – such questions perhaps as: How are memories stored? How does the eye guide the hand? What are dreams made of? But rather will it attempt to discuss some of the difficulties in taking over engineering methods into biology, and some implications of this approach for the study of the central nervous system.

An alternative to the Kantian doctrine is to say that living systems are *machines*. The cybernetic view is often put in this way, but it has objections. If we use the term 'machine' to include living organisms, it loses its major classificatory use. Further, the term 'machine' is very difficult to define in general terms. We might call a given system a machine though it has no predictable output, displays goal-seeking behaviour, and is in fact indistinguishable in its behaviour from at least simple living systems. If we mean merely that it is man-made, then the distinction is trivial. We cannot get away with an ostensive definition of 'machine' (pointing to all existing machines), for we must allow the possibility of future new kinds of machine, and these could not be included. If animate systems are called 'machines', at least two important things might be meant: (1) that their functioning could be described in terms of known physical principles, or (2) that their functioning could be described, if not in terms of principles known at present, at least in terms of principles which *could* be known to us. This is to say that living organisms are in fact so constituted that we could in principle understand them as engineers or physicists understand their systems. It appears that to call an animal a machine is to indicate that its manner of functioning is not *essentially* different from machines which might be designed or made by men. To deny that animals are machines is, it would appear, to suppose that they *are* essentially different. Those who take the former view feel that existing or possible machines performing similar functions may provide clues as to how animals work, and in particular how their central nervous systems are organized. Those who hold that animals are not machines refuse to accept that this could ever give the whole story. Both types of biologist might well agree that we should go as far as we can in looking for analogies, while being careful not to oversimplify or to accept similarities in a naïve manner.

THE USE OF ENGINEERING CRITERIA FOR DECIDING BETWEEN MODELS OF BRAIN FUNCTION

When a biologist or engineer considers what sort of system might be responsible for producing a given function, he may run up against one of two difficulties: (1) that there does not seem to be *any* known type of system capable of just the observed functions under the given conditions, or (2) that there is a *large number* of possible mechanisms, any of which might provide the required functions. We cannot say anything here about the first contingency, except of course that further observation, experiment or thought might suggest possible mechanisms, but we can say something about the second. It is worth thinking about this, for the principles available for deciding which of various alternative types of mechanism are appropriate are just the principles we need for verifying cybernetic hypotheses. Without such principles we can do no more than guess.

Consider an engineer in a position of doubt about how an unfamiliar machine works. We may take an actual example of a dramatic kind: consider the problem of discovering the manner of function of the control mechanism of an enemy's secret weapon, such as the V1 rockets during the last war. The engineer could make use of the following considerations. First, it was clear that the rocket had been made recently by men in Germany. This knowledge that they were man-made was clearly enormously important, though probably never explicitly stated. Martian rockets would offer many more alternatives, including the high probability of principles quite unknown to us. As it was, new principles were unlikely, though possible. Secondly, examination of rockets which failed to explode revealed many already familiar components such as motors, condensers, valves etc., and a great deal was already known about these. Thirdly, it would seem certain that the rockets must have been designed as efficiently as possible. Now how far does the biologist examining brain function share these assets?

1. Since living organisms are not designed and made by men, any number of new principles might be expected, as in the imaginary case of Martian rockets. As an example, it is now believed that feed-back loops are important in organisms, but these were not known to the engineer until Clerk Maxwell's work in the last century, and there could always be further more or less fundamental principles involved which are so far unknown to engineers.

2. Examination of the brain reveals many identifiable 'components', such as Betz cells and amacrine cells, but the functional properties and circuit potentialities of cells are not as well understood as the functional properties of electronic or mechanical components – and even these have their surprises.

3. Efficiency is a difficult criterion to apply to biological systems for a logical reason: it cannot be assessed without some idea of purpose. It is, however, important to note that the notion of efficiency (and also that of purpose) does not imply specific design for a known end. Thus it might be said that a screw-driver makes a good paint scraper, though it was not designed for that purpose. For something to be said to be efficient, it must be efficient for a stated end though not necessarily for a designed end. Thus if it said that some postulated brain mechanism is more efficient than some other mechanism, we must know what end these mechanisms are supposed to serve, and we must know how to assess relative efficiency towards this end. We may ask, for example, 'how efficient is the eye?' and its efficiency may be measured. Thus its acuity and its sensitivity may be measured and expressed in appropriate units. The difficulty arises when we do not know what to measure through not knowing the functional significance of the structure or system involved. Clearly we could not talk about the efficiency of the eye if we did not know that it subserved vision. If a system is found to be highly efficient, in general but few possi-

bilities are left open when it comes to guessing how it works – not many engineering tricks would be good enough.

When an engineer talks about efficiency he may mean a number of things; he may simply mean that it works well, or that its fuel consumption is low, or that the capital or running cost is low, or a number of other things. If the biologist is to make a reasonable guess at which type of mechanism is responsible for a given type of function, and he wants to use efficiency criteria, he must be clear which criteria it is appropriate to take over, and this raises a number of difficulties. Let us, for the fun of the thing, consider a few engineering efficiency criteria in the context of biology.

(a) Thermal efficiency

This may be used for power systems. The efficiency E of a heat engine is given by $E = W/JQ$, where W is the useful work done by the machine when a quantity of heat, JQ mechanical units, is supplied to it. Since no machine can create energy, W cannot be greater than JQ, so that no engine can have an efficiency greater than 100%.

Now, knowing the total thermal efficiency of a given machine, and knowing the expected efficiency of the type of system by which it is supposed to function, it is clear that if the actual efficiency is higher than predicted, then the hypothesis is false and some other explanation must be sought. If, on the other hand, it is too low some cause for the loss may always be postulated. It follows that where the predicted efficiency is high, more possible solutions are ruled out as too inefficient to be likely, and so the criterion is more useful. This criterion might be used in biology to test a hypothesis about, say, conversion of chemical energy into mechanical energy in muscle. It is hardly applicable to the brain because its thermal properties do not seem important to us, though they did to Aristotle when he regarded its function as cooling the blood.

(b) Information efficiency

Information rate may be defined by the rate of transmission of information defined by binary choices, or 'bits'. The Hartley-Shannon Law, which is basic here, states that

$$C = W \log_2 (1 + S/N),$$

where C is the channel capacity, W the band width, S the average signal power, N the average noise power. Some communication systems are more efficient than others. In particular, a change in the manner of coding the information might make a large difference to the efficiency of the system. Now this does appear to be directly applicable to neurological systems, which is one reason why quantitative estimates of information rate for human subjects, as made by Hick (1952) and Crossman (1953) among others, are of great importance here. The most efficient type of coding is important once we think of the nervous system as handling information and as subject to the same limitations as a man-made system. This criterion has in fact been applied to test between different possible codes adopted by neurones in transmitting information. MacKay and McCulloch (1952) decided, tentatively, in favour of pulse interval modulation for peripheral nerve fibres on this basis.

(c) Capital cost

This is difficult to assess. We might at least say that where general, or some specific, nutriment is in short supply, cells may be 'expensive'. Further, weight may be at a premium, which will limit the permissible number of cells. Also, it might be the case that increase in the number of cells would impose an informational strain on the available information coded in the gametes.

(d) Running cost

Not much can be said about this, beyond the obvious point that if food is scarce it will be an 'expensive' commodity.

(e) Simplicity

This is difficult. The engineer favours the 'neat' solution to a problem, and he dislikes certain 'complicated' types of mechanism. This may be in part due to the aesthetic appeal of simplicity, but simple mechanisms perhaps also tend to be cheaper and more reliable, though not necessarily so. Carburettors for petrol engines have in fact become more and more elaborate, with gain in running economy and overall reliability. Have we any reason to suppose that we should find in nature the 'simplest' way of going about engineering problems? Certainly nature is handicapped by lack of many materials and techniques indispensable to the engineer. It is striking, for example, that flight with flapping wings is for an engineer more complicated, and in every way inferior to, flight with fixed wings, though the former is found in nature. But then nature has not got a suitable engine to provide forward drive independently of the wings, and nature has not got true bearings, or the wheel. This case is far removed from neurology, but neurology also provides examples. A familiar one is that of the retina, which is 'inside out'. The light has to pass through layers of blood vessels, ganglia and supporting cells before it reaches the receptors. This optically shocking arrangement appears to be dictated by embryological, or perhaps basically developmental, considerations. Considerations of this kind make the use of the criterion of simplicity difficult and dangerous to apply.

(f) Length of life

Some types of machine outlive others. There are many reasons for this – choice of materials, friction between moving parts and many more. This criterion for deciding between rival designs can hardly be applied at present to the living machine because of its self-repairing properties.

We conclude that some engineering design criteria can be applied to biological systems in order to ascertain which, among many possible types of mechanism, is the most likely to be operating in any particular case. Efficiency criteria, particularly thermal and information efficiency, seem to be the ones most readily applied in the biological context, but in some cases other criteria might also be used. If this way of linking behaviour study with neurology is adopted, then rather precise 'engineering-type' data will be required. It is unfortunate that it appears difficult to apply the other criteria commonly used by engineers. As a result, cybernetic writing easily becomes science fiction, where the supposed theories and me   nism may be limited in variety only by the imagination of their in entors. This is unfortunate for a vitally important approach to biology.

LOCALIZATION OF CEREBRAL FUNCTION

What is meant by saying that some feature of behaviour is localized in a part of the brain? It cannot mean that the behaviour itself is to be found in the brain, or that a region of the brain can be sufficient for any behaviour. The intended meaning is that some necessary, though not sufficient, condition for this behaviour is localized in a specific region of the brain.

The evidence for localization is mainly from studies of ablation and stimulation of regions of the brain. If, for example, when a point on the occipital cortex is stimulated, flashes of light are reported by the patient, it is generally held that this region of the cortex must be important for vision. If an area in the left frontal lobe is damaged and speech is found to be disturbed, it may seem that we have found something causally necessary for speech. But have we?

This area may be *necessary* for speech (i.e. if it is removed, speech may disappear) but so also are a number of other parts of the organism, for example the vocal cords, the lungs and the mouth. There is nothing special about the brain here. It may be that the 'speech area' is concerned only with speech, but if so it is not unique in this respect either: if we except coughing, the vocal cords have no other function but to subserve vocalization. Now we may say that the vocal cords are *causally necessary* for speech, and also that the 'speech area' is somehow *causally necessary*, but it is not clear in the second case just what the causal functions are, though we do understand the causal role of the vocal cords. There is an important point here: we may say that *A* is the cause of *B* if *A* is found inductively to be a necessary condition for *B*, and the evidence may be purely inductive for this type of causal argument. No understanding of the mechanisms involved is required to assert the causal relation between *A* and *B*. But we may also say that *A* causes *B* on *deductive* grounds, when we understand (or think we understand) the mechanism by which *A* produces, or causes, *B*.

Once we distinguish these two types of argument from physical structure and function to causal relationship, we should ask which sort of causal argument is being used in discussions about brain function. Take the case of the speech area. It would appear that the reason why this region of the brain is held to be associated with speech is that speech is found to be defective or absent when the region is damaged. This is clearly an inductive argument, and it does not presuppose or imply any knowledge of how the speech area works, or what causal part it plays in the production of speech. Again, we know fairly clearly the causal role of the vocal cords, but not that of the 'speech area'.

Consider now the word 'function'. We may say that it is the *function* of the vocal cords to vibrate in certain ways, producing pulses of air which resonate in cavities . . . we see the causal role of the vocal cords and we come to understand the mechanism of speech production. And now what about the word 'localization'? What is it to say that a *function is localized*? The question is: How can we say that a function is localized until we know what the function (of a given bit of brain tissue) is? To say this we need to know in some detail how the system works. It seems that before we can talk usefully about localization of function we must have some idea of *how* the system works.

It might be interesting to consider how an electronics engineer deals with, and represents, specific functions in a complex device. He uses three types of diagram to represent an electronic machine. These are *(a) blue prints*, showing the physical locations in space of

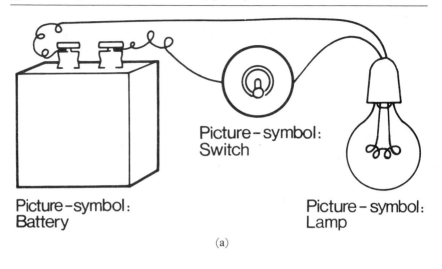

Picture-symbol:
Switch

Picture-symbol:
Battery

Picture-symbol:
Lamp

(a)

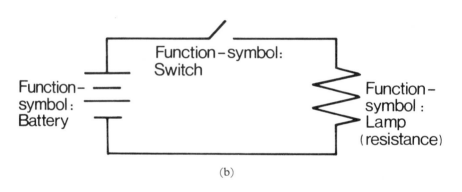

Function-symbol:
Switch

Function-
symbol:
Battery

Function-
symbol:
Lamp
(resistance)

(b)

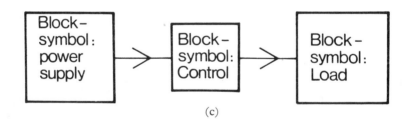

Block-
symbol:
power
supply

Block-
symbol:
Control

Block-
symbol:
Load

(c)

FIGURE 49.1

(a) *Shows a simple blue print type of diagram. Pictorial representation of components are linked with paths of conductivity (wires), also shown pictorially. This may be compared with histological descriptions of the brain.*

(b) *Shows a circuit diagram. The symbols show conventional functional properties of the components. This may be compared with the physiological descriptions of the brain.*

(c) *Shows a block diagram. The blocks show the functional units of the system, indicating the causal processes in terms of the flow of power or information. This may be compared with cybernetic descriptions of the brain.*

the components, with their sizes and shapes. These drawings will give dimensions and describe the structure, so to say the cyto-architecture, of the machine. *(b) Circuit diagrams*, in which each component is shown in diagrammatic form with its connections (usually paths of perfect conductivity) with other components having idealized properties. *(c) Block diagrams*, in which there are a number of boxes connected together with flow lines, each box being labelled with its 'function'. Thus one might be labelled 'Radio frequency amplifier', another 'mixer' and so on. Now what knowledge of the system is conveyed by *(a)*, *(b)* and *(c)*? And what knowledge, therefore, must the man who designs the diagrams have of the system? *(a)* requires a knowledge of the look of the thing; *(b)* implies information about certain selected properties of the 'components' of the system. (A capacitor in series marked 0·1 μf., for instance, conveys a great deal of information about what will happen for various conditions – for example, that direct current will be blocked while high frequencies will hardly be affected, except for a phase shift.) But the general effect of these changes produced by a component will not be apparent except in terms of *(c)*, the block or function diagram. The condenser may then turn out to be part of an oscillator, and then its purpose within that functional section of the device could be stated. For example it might provide feed-back between anode and grid of a valve. Now when a trained engineer looks at a circuit he can very often see almost at a glance what it will do and how it does it. With an unfamiliar circuit this might be difficult, but he could probably predict its function and performance given the circuit valves and a slide rule. To do this he will make use of a number of generalizations, or Laws, such as the conditions for obtaining oscillation, or linear amplification or whatever it is. The point is that *(c)* implies these general principles while *(b)* does not. Only a skilled engineer could design or work out a block diagram, but anyone who can recognize components by their appearance could draw a circuit diagram. The question for neurology is: Do we want diagrams of structure of the 'circuit' with component characteristics, or functional block diagrams? I would suggest that only the last describe how a system works. They are comparatively simple, but alone convey (and imply for their drawing) a knowledge of the function of the system.

The neurologist can discover the properties of *his* components, the neurones; he may discover how the components are wired up. Can he discover the causal mechanisms involved? Can he find out where they are situated in the brain?

There seems to be a widespread hope that, by ablation and stimulation of parts of the brain, functional regions may be discovered, these being logically the same as the boxes in a block diagram. Is this a reasonable hope?

ABLATION AND STIMULATION AS TECHNIQUES FOR DISCOVERING FUNCTIONAL REGIONS OF THE BRAIN

Suppose we ablated or stimulated various parts of a complex man-made device, say a television receiving set. And suppose we had no prior knowledge of the manner of function of the type of device or machine involved. Could we by these means discover its manner of working?

In the first place, and most important, to remove a part of a machine, even a discrete component, is not in general to remove a necessary condition for some feature of the output. If a part is removed from a complex machine, we do not in general find that simple elements or units are now missing from the output. It should be noted here that the functional processes taking place in the components, or groups of components, of a machine are generally quite different from anything in the output. Thus we do not see the spark is a car engine represented in its output – we see wheels turning and the car moving: no spark. If a component is removed almost anything may happen: a radio set may emit piercing whistles or deep growls, a television set may produce curious patterns, a car engine may back-fire, or blow up or simply stop. To understand the *reason* for these 'behavioural' changes we must know at least the basic principles of radio, or television, or car engines, or whatever it is, and also some of the details of the particular design. Of course, if we already know about radio, or engines, then these abnormal manifestations may well lead to correct diagnosis of a fault: the difficulty is to reverse the procedure.

Consider a television set which has, of course, two quite distinct outputs – sound and vision. Some 'ablations', or 'extirpations', may quickly reveal which parts are *necessary* for each output, and also which parts are *common* to the two outputs. In the case of the brain, there is a large number of inputs and outputs: the limb movements, the face with its various expressions, the voice, and so on. It may be a fairly simple matter to discover regions of the brain which are necessary for these various outputs, and in general they will lie near the peripheral output of the system. The inputs, the senses and their projection areas, we might also expect to locate in this way without undue difficulty. What I suspect *is* difficult, indeed impossible, is to locate functional regions of the system. It seems to me that this conclusion is forced upon us by considering the possibility of isolating elements of a complex output in a single channel in the case of man-made machines. In a serial system the various identifiable elements of the output are not separately represented by discrete parts of the system. Damage to a part may indeed introduce quite new factors into the situation, and these could only be comprehensible when we are provided with a model indicating the function of the parts. If the brain consisted of a series of independent parallel elements with separate output terminals for each, like a piano, it might be possible to identify behavioural elements with particular parts of the system, as the various notes of the piano might be regarded as being 'localized' in the piano; but where output is the result of a number of causally necessary operations taking place in a series, then this is not possible. The removal, or the activation, of a single stage in a series might have almost any effect on the output of a machine, and so presumably also for the brain. To deduce the function of a part from the effect upon the output of removing or stimulating this part we must know at least in general terms how the machine works. The point here, perhaps, is not so much that the piano is a parallel rather than a serial system, but that it is a set of largely independent machines in one box. Where they do interact, as in the pedal systems, then one 'ablation' may affect all the notes. Parts of the brain could be independent.

The effects of removing or modifying, say, the line scan time-base of a television receiver would be incomprehensible if we did not know the engineering principles involved. Further, it seems unlikely that we should discover the necessary principles from scratch simply by pulling bits out of television sets, or stimulating bits with various voltages and wave forms. The data derived in this way might well lead to hypotheses once we knew something of the problem in engineering terms.

But we should, in some systems, be able to map projection areas and delimit pathways, and this is a good deal. Analogy with familiar physical systems strongly suggests that to go further these studies should be used to test rival hypotheses of brain function, rather than to attempt to isolate functional regions. This brings us back to the idea of physical model explanations, with ablation and stimulation studies as one way of trying to decide between rival models. We are left with the difficulties besetting this approach: in particular, the brain might work on some novel principle, and then its true manner of function would never come up for testing by any experimental technique. It would clearly require a most highly sophisticated set of techniques to discover a quite new principle in the living brain, but this is conceivable. Perhaps the principle of scanning, or heterodyning, could be discovered by these techniques, even in a jelly.

It is a common finding that with electronic equipment several very different faults may produce much the same 'symptom'. For example, anything which produces a change in the supply voltage will first affect the part of the system most susceptible to supply changes, and so anything affecting the supply will tend to produce the same fault. To aggravate the position, faults affecting the supply voltage are not limited to the power pack supplying the voltage to the various parts of the system, but may be in any of these parts, increasing or decreasing the load and so affecting all the other parts in greater or lesser degree. Thus the removal of any of several widely spaced resistors may cause a radio set to emit howls, but it does not follow that howls are immediately associated with these resistors, or indeed that the causal relation is anything but the most indirect. In particular, we should not say that the function of the resistors in the normal circuit is to inhibit howling. Neurophysiologists, when faced with a comparable situation, have postulated 'suppressor regions'.

Although the effect of a particular type of ablation may be specific and repeatable, it does not follow that the causal connection is simple, or even that the region of the brain affected would, if we knew more, be regarded as functionally important for the output – such as memory or speech – which is observed to be upset. It could be the case that some important part of the mechanism subserving the behaviour is upset by the damage although it is most indirectly related, and it is just this which makes the discovery of a fault in a complex machine so difficult.

We may consider one or two further points. Since learning is important in at least the mammalian nervous system, it is clear that where animals and men have had different past experiences their brains are likely to be in some ways different. What is 'stored' must at any rate vary between individuals of the same species. It is known that for man surgical removal of some areas of the brain, e.g. the frontal lobe, may pass almost unnoticed in some individuals, while in others it produces serious defect of function. This might perhaps be due to the different importance of specific causal mechanisms in individuals employing different 'strategies', or possibly to the unequal importance of various pieces of stored information. In any case we should expect, and do in fact find, individual differences. This is a complicating factor in interpreting ablation studies which would hardly concern an engineer using man-made machines, except indeed for certain electronic computers.

A further point that might be made is this: Suppose we ablate or stimulate some part of the brain, and lose or evoke something in behaviour, then it is not clear – even quite apart from previous considerations – that this region is the seat of the behaviour in question. Might it not lie along a 'trunk line' or 'association pathway'? A cut telephone line might affect communication over a wide area, principally behind the region of damage. This has at least two important implications: first, unless the region is known not to lie on a 'cable' the region cannot be identified with a brain 'centre' responsible for some aspect of behaviour, since the 'centre' responsible but cut off might lie anywhere from this region along the trunk line. This is further complicated by the consideration that it might be cut off in some conditions but not in others: it might conceivably depend upon whether the animal is motivated in a particular way, receiving information from a particular 'store', or countless other possibilities, whether this block will matter; and the same is true of damage to, or stimulation of, a 'centre', even if this word is taken as meaningful. In many machines it might be possible to remove large parts without any effect except under certain working conditions.

There are two points here: (1) damage might produce, so to say, a shadow within which brain function is lost to regions of the brain on the 'other side' of the damage. If the better analogy is a short-circuited power line, the effect may extend both ways along the cable. (2) The damage may be important only under certain critical circumstances. It does not matter that a car's trafficators are not functional until the driver wishes to turn a corner in traffic – or that his brakes do not work until he tries to stop.

This view of what we mean by 'function' is important in considering brain 'centres'. These are supposed loci for particular types of behaviour: thus Hess has a 'sleep centre' for the cat, in the hypothalamus. This idea of 'centres' has been taken over by Ethology and is particularly important in Tinbergen's writings. But we may well feel worried about the concept of functional centres when we do not know what is going on, in functional terms, in the region concerned. The above considerations apply here *mutatis mutandis*. Why, if stimulation of a given region produces sleep, should this region be regarded as a 'sleep centre'? To take a facetious example: if a bang on the back of the head produces stars and a headache, is this a 'centre' for stars and headaches?

In summary:

1. It might be argued that 'localization of function' means that some feature of behaviour has certain vital (but not sufficient) causal mechanisms located in a given region of the brain. But before we know

how, in general terms, the brain works we cannot say what these supposed causal mechanisms are, and thus it is very difficult to say what we mean by 'localization of function'.

2. Stimulation and ablation experiments may give direct information about pathways and projection areas, but their interpretation would seem to be extremely difficult, on logical grounds, where a mechanism is one of many interrelated systems, for then changes in the output will not in general be simply the loss of the contribution normally made by the extirpated area. The system may now show quite different properties.

3. It would seem that ablation and stimulation data can only be interpreted given a model, or a 'block diagram', showing the functional organization of the brain in causal, or engineering, terms. Such data may be useful in suggesting or testing possible theoretical models.

4. These models are explanations in the engineering sense of 'explanation'.

CONCLUSION

It would be nice to say something more constructive about the use of engineering thinking in biology. Given that there are certain difficulties in taking over engineering ideas of design into biology, can we not still use engineering techniques and devices to make some better-than-random guesses about how the brain works?

We have throughout looked at the brain as an engineering problem in a general way: we have not considered any particular engineering techniques, or mechanisms, or machines which might throw light on biological function. We have mentioned radio sets and car engines when thinking about localization of brain function, yet it is at least clear that brains are very different from these. We could certainly think of machines more like brains – and this might be worth doing. What about computers? Obviously we should expect more similarities between computers and brains than between car engines and brains, for the inputs and outputs are similar for the one though not for the other. Now we might go further and ask: what *sort* of computer is most like the brain? There are many different types of practical computer. As is well known, they are divided into two main classes: analogue and digital. Each has certain advantages. The former are usually simpler in construction, they are fast, and are generally subject to rather large random errors. The best-known example is the slide rule. Their inputs and outputs are usually continuously variable, though this is not always so: a slide rule might be made with click stops and still be called analogue. The essential point is that the input variables are represented by the magnitude of some physical variable, such as a length or a voltage. Digital computers, on the other hand, are generally slower, and their answers tend to be either correct or wildly wrong. They work in discrete steps, and according to some fixed rules or calculus. The functional units (essentially switches) of a digital computer take up certain discrete semi-stable states according to a code. For some purposes the analogue type would be chosen by the engineer, and for others the digital type. Thus we may now ask: which would be the most suitable type of computer for a brain, an analogue or a digital computer? Or perhaps a mixture? To answer this question we may make a list of the relevant properties of the brain and try to decide which type of computer fits best [see No. 47]. Some of the difficulties we anticipated at the beginning: we found that engineering criteria are not easy to apply, and that some are indeed inappropriate. The basic efficiency criteria evidently may be applied, but they have their difficulties unless we know a good deal about the functional properties and efficiencies of the components of the brain. Thus it is not possible, for example, to say whether the brain works too fast to be a digital computer unless we know the rate at which the components can change their states, or count. If we also knew the minimum number of steps logically required to reach a given solution with the available data it would be possible to say whether the brain *could* work digitally.

Similar considerations apply to testing the hypothesis that the brain is an analogue machine. We may ask: is the brain too accurate for an analogue machine? We cannot answer this until we know how the 'templates' representing the variables work; we need to know more about the actual ironmongery available; 'ideal' considerations are not adequate here, we must know the properties of the components. If we invoke feed-back principles the brain might be an analogue device given rather variable templates – there are many such 'saving' possibilities. In fact this view that the brain is in essential respects analogue is perhaps borne out by the type of errors observed in control situations. The point is that engineering here supplies the hypotheses for testing, and also (up to a point) the manner of testing them, but to make these decisions it is important to know in detail the functional limitations of the components of the brain. It is also important to have 'engineering' performance data. Much experimental work in psychology is in fact undertaken for this purpose. It may well be vital for linking psychology with neurology, and we should use engineering concepts both to suggest appropriate experiments and to integrate and interpret the available data. For example, studies on tremor take on a new significance within the context of servo-theory, for all error-correcting servos are subject to 'hunting'.

A rather different approach, which we might do well to adopt, is the following: We might look for what we are virtually certain to find and then measure it. Two, rather different, examples must suffice. First, we believe that a system cannot itself gain knowledge without inductive generalization, and we know that this is impossible without probability estimates. This involves some form of counting, and some form of store for count rates or relative count rates. This at once suggests that the brain should be looked at as in part an inductive machine (e.g. Gregory, 1952*b* [No. 46]). Probably no one had actually built an inductive machine until Uttley (1954*a* and *b*) built his, specifically as a possible model of brain function, but the man-made induction machine follows standard engineering principles. To go to the next stage and ask whether the brain is the *same sort* of induction machine as Uttley's raises all sorts of difficulties, some of which we have already discussed. The point here is that we believe on *very general grounds* that probabilities must be important to achieve adapted behaviour, and so induction and probability mechanisms really must be found if we look for them.

The second example of this approach is the interesting though more specific problem of 'noise' in the nervous system. It is well known that all communication systems are ultimately limited by random noise, which tends to cause confusion between signals. It seems impossible that the nervous system can be an exception, and so it is hardly a discovery that there is 'noise' in nerve fibres, and in the brain. The assessment of the actual 'noise' level in the various parts of the nervous system (Gregory and Cane 1955 [No. 7]; Gregory, 1956; Barlow, 1956, 1957*a*) and of changes in 'noise' level due to ageing or brain damage [No. 8] may throw some light on neural function, if only by helping us to apply efficiency criteria to test between rival explanatory models. It is interesting in this connection that Granit (1955) has recently summarized the evidence for random firing of the optic nerve but has not interpreted this as a background 'noise' level against which visual signals must be discriminated, but rather regards it as necessary for keeping the higher centres active. Thus the same observation might be regarded as a necessary evil or a special and useful part of the mechanism. Here the very general properties of communication systems would lead us to the former interpretation, but without these general considerations there would have been no reason to suppose that random firing is not useful to the organism and, so to speak, part of the design. Given the engineering viewpoint, we should ask how the system is designed to *minimize* the effect of the background noise, and this is quite a different sort of question, leading to quite different experiments.

Information rates and noise levels will not in themselves tell us how the ear or the eye gives us useful information – how they work – but such measures are in conformity with the engineer's insistence upon knowing the performance limits, and the reasons for the limits, of his systems. Experimental psychology is currently, and for practical reasons, concerned with the limits of human ability in many directions, e.g. in steering and guiding. These measures may be vital in deciding how the guiding or steering is done. In many cases it is only limits, such as sensory thresholds, which can be used to provide 'engineering' data from complex organisms. Now this idea of looking for properties which are found in all, or at least in most, engineering control systems, and then obtaining quantitative measurements of them under various operating conditions is rather different from the idea of thinking of a physical model as a possible 'analogy' to a behaviour mechanism and then testing this model with observation or experiment. Before we attempt seriously to test specific models of brain function – types of memory store and the like – we might do well to make careful estimates of such things as neural 'noise' levels which we are virtually certain must be there to be found. Having done this, we may be in a stronger position to test specific hypotheses, for we should be able to apply engineering criteria with sufficient rigour to make some hypotheses highly improbable, while others might be shown to be quite possibly true.

These considerations have some relevance to the progress of experimental psychology. If we have no idea of the sort of system we are dealing with, controlled experiment becomes impossible, for we cannot know what to control. On the other hand, a too fixed and particular model tends to blinker the mental eye, making us blind to surprising results and ideas without which advance is impossible.

50 *Models and localization of function in the central nervous system*

[Some apparent logical difficulties of inferring normal brain function from behaviour changes resulting from ablation of limited regions of brain are next taken up – in a paper which has annoyed some people a good deal! I still think that my criticisms are justified against direct inferences from results of ablation to supposed brain function but in this paper I overstressed the problem. Ablation experiments can be used to suggest or test hypotheses – but it is particularly difficult to state the necessary assumptions in this situation because our general hypotheses for brain function are so inadequate.

The general question is raised: what sort of explanations are appropriate for biology? Teleology is rejected, while explanation in terms of conceptual models of the engineering kind is accepted. It is argued, however, that the engineering approach does not rid us of the necessity for making decisions on the purpose of observed structures or behaviour. Engineers generally know the design ends of their devices, but we have to guess the functional significance of biological systems. Certain difficulties are discussed. These considerations lead to the problem of distinguishing between 'accidental' and 'functionally important' features of biological systems. The criteria for distinguishing between these would seem to require conceptual models.

Localization of function is discussed in general terms. The use of the words 'localization' and 'function' is discussed, and a comparison is drawn between removing or stimulating parts of machines and brains. It is argued that the performance changes associated with removing parts of machines cannot be understood except in terms of functional models of the machine. The same would seem true for the central nervous system. In the case of independent parallel systems, such as telephone installations, much might be learned given only the crudest 'anatomical' model, and this is largely true of the peripheral nervous system. In the case of the cortex, this approach is likely to be misleading, especially if it is a tightly coupled system, for then removal of part of the system will either have little effect, except in certain conditions, or will introduce new functional features, for we now have a different system. These new features can only be understood, and only have significance, in terms of a functional model. It is concluded that ablation and stimulation of the brain may, and indeed do, bring out interesting facts, but that these must be interpreted in terms of models, for without a model we cannot say what is localized.]

★   ★   ★

WHEN a biologist considers the fundamental question: 'What *is* an explanation of behaviour?' he may have a sense of conflict, even of paradox. Biology seems to be a science in its own right, or set of sciences having common aims, and so it should have its own language and explanatory concepts; yet when any specifically biological concept is suggested and used as an explanatory concept it seems to be unsatisfactory and even mystical. There are many biological concepts of this kind: Purpose, Drive, *élan vital*, Entelechy, Gestalten.[1] Physicists and engineers seem, on the other hand, to have clearly defined concepts having great power within biology. Why should this be? Is it that biology is not sufficiently advanced as an explanatory science to have developed its conceptual systems sufficiently far? Or is it that biologists should not look for *special* concepts, uniquely applicable to living systems? This latter view implies that biologists should think of living systems as being examples of physical or engineering systems, in which case engineering language should be applicable for description and explanation in biology.

If an engineer is presented with a piece of equipment about which he knows very little, he will at least know that it was designed by men, for some purpose he could comprehend. He is unlikely to find any quite new techniques involved in its design or construction. The 'black box' situation is artificial in engineering: the boxes an engineer sees are not as black as all that. In the case where the box *is* sealed (perhaps as a game, or a test or in war) he still has a lot of information about it if he only knows that it was made for human beings by

---

[1] Some biological concepts have been given 'engineering' definitions; for example Drive and Purpose. Whether they still cover the cases required by biologists is an important question. Perhaps Survival of the Fittest is a specifically biological idea, and in a sense an explanatory concept, though it does not attempt to explain the functioning of an organism but only how it came to be 'designed'. Although the idea started as a biological theory, it may be extended to other cases, in economics for example, and it may be expressed in non-biological, largely statistical, language.

human beings. Biological systems are not designed by humans, and the purpose of many of their characteristics may be highly obscure. Thus, in important respects, the engineer is not on his home ground when he advises the biologist.

Biologists are shy of the notion of purpose; in particular, they reject teleological explanations as 'unscientific'. It is not clear, however, that classification of biological structure and function in terms of purpose should, or can, be avoided. At first sight engineering analogies may seem to do this, but this is not so. To take an example of A. Uttley's, it is a discovery, and a most important one, that the heart is a pump. It would be impossible to understand it without recognizing this. Biological systems are adapted, through genetic experience, to serve ends which we might, or might not, discern. We have to discover what this end is before we can think up what sort of system it is, or assess its efficiency. We can see what the purpose of a piston or a boiler is, once we understand steam engines, and we can see the functional purpose of the heart, or the eye. Why, then, do we not find purpose in inanimate nature? It is poetic, and most misleading, to say, for example, that the purpose of rain is to water flowers, and yet one might say that a purpose of rootlets is to suck up moisture. Is this because rootlets are alive, but rain is inanimate? Rain does not fall especially upon flowers, but flowers do take advantage of what rain there is, by specially adapted structures. Only living things and machines are adapted, in this sense, to take advantage of their environment, and only they display purpose. To state a purpose is, evidently, to specify what a thing is adapted or designed to do; and we only find adaptation, or design, in organisms and machines.

If one supposed, say, a car engine to be a hair drier, the exhaust pipe would have an obvious use – but the rotating shaft would not. It would seem to be a very poorly designed hair drier: noisy, smelly, dirty and inefficient – with a most annoying rotating shaft. The noise, and smell and the heat will however appear 'accidental' once the shaft output is recognized as such, and quite different estimates of its efficiency will be made. It is often difficult to decide whether an observed feature is functionally important or merely accidental. Any physical system will for example have some colour; but generally this is unimportant to its function. It requires a knowledge of function to classify observed features into 'essential' and 'accidental' properties: without hypotheses of function this classification is impossible. The engineer's insights into the functional significance of observed features would thus seem of the greatest importance to the classification of biological observations and findings. Biologists have tended to make this distinction implicitly, as may be shown by looking at their choice of words. Let us consider an example of this. *Fatigue* indicates loss of efficiency after prolonged use; *Adaptation* suggests that a change which might be identical, and might occur under exactly the same conditions as fatigue, is useful. Thus, 'the retina has recovered from *fatigue*' and 'the retina has become *adapted*', may refer to the same facts, and yet these sentences have different meanings for they imply different decisions on the significance of the facts. A useful feature in a machine might be regarded as having been specially designed to that end. Useful biological features tend to be regarded as the 'essential' features of the system given by specially adapted mechanisms.

The decision between 'functionally important' and 'accidental' is often difficult to make in biology. Consider the continual small tremors of the eyeball. Are these useful, or do they represent a failure of precise control? Do they serve to aid vision, perhaps by preventing retinal fatigue at contours, by producing re-stimulation of the retinal cells? If the tremor can be shown to be useful in this respect (and this is an empirical question open to experimental test) would it be supposed that there are special mechanisms evolved to produce the tremor, as there are mechanisms which have evolved to give accommodation changes, and colour vision? Would it be worth looking for such special mechanisms? If we found a bit of the brain which seemed to serve no function but to induce tremor in the eye, would we be more inclined to think that tremor has been specially developed? If we took this course, perhaps we should look at earlier eyes, for the tremor mechanism might *have* been useful though *now* it might not be. Suppose in fact the tremor *is* accidental, perhaps mere noise in the system; a biologist might still do well to study its effect on vision, but its status would affect his way of thinking about the visual system as a whole. It might affect the choice of explanatory model we would develop. The engineer may be able to help here by suggesting what special features of the phenomenon to look for to make the decision between 'essential' and 'accidental'. Thus hunting might be distinguished, by statistical or other criteria, from noise. This sort of suggestion would seem to be of the greatest benefit to biologists. The engineer can help not only in suggesting models, but perhaps even more important, by suggesting what to look for to develop criteria for deciding between 'accidental' and specially adapted or 'essential' features.

Within the field of behaviour, probably the most important decision of this kind is whether the slowness of learning is specially adapted or is a limitation of the brain mechanism. One-trial learning is rather rare; why is this? If we knew what takes place in the brain during learning, then we could probably say whether or not this is a weakness of the design of the system, or whether it is specially built in according to genetic experience. Without this knowledge of the mechanisms subserving learning we can only ask: would one-trial learning be, on the whole, an advantage? If we decide that it would be a good thing, then it will appear a weakness of 'design', or inadequacy of the materials of the brain, that it is so rare. This is a shaky argument, but it is frequently used in biology for lack of anything better. In fact, we can point to advantages in *not* having one-trial learning; for unreliable inductive generalizations are less likely to occur. It is notable that Pavlov required a silent laboratory, with nothing untoward occurring during his Conditioning experiments: distractions made the process longer.[1] We might suggest that slow learning is generally useful. We may then be tempted to think that the brain could have provided fast learning, but that it would have been inappropriate. If so, certain types of engineering models may be ruled out. The biologist's assessment of the utility of the things he observes may affect the choice of 'engineering' model. The engineer might well question the biologist, and ask whether there are *any* cases where, for example, very fast learning does occur. If he can find such cases, the possible limits of the system will have been extended. This might open up further possibilities, or rule out others. 'Imprinting' is interesting in this connection, for here very fast learning does occur, and it is plainly useful, for it occurs in a restricted environment in which what is learned is unlikely to be inappropriate.

ON HOW AN ENGINEER MIGHT LOOK AT THE NOTION OF LOCALIZATION OF CORTICAL FUNCTION

What neurologists mean by 'localization of function'

It is often suggested by neurologists that some functions are localized in more or less specific regions of the central nervous system. Thus it may be suggested that speech, or some particular feature of speech behaviour, is localized in Broca's area, in the left frontal lobe. Or it may be said that the pre-frontal gyrus is a 'motor area'. It is not always clear what neurologists mean by saying that a function is localized in a specified region of the brain. If this is not clear, any test or experiment

---

[1]This is a signal/noise situation. The irrelevant events constitute noise which has to be ignored as far as possible if responses are to be appropriate. This is a very general problem for organisms making decisions on sensory or other data.

involving behaviour is made difficult, and discussion is likely to be confused. I shall now try to examine the language used to describe localization of function. We may then see whether the techniques used by engineers for establishing and describing function might be helpful in relating behaviour with neural systems.

If we consider the phrase: 'localization of (cortical) function', we can be puzzled by the use both of 'localization' and of 'function'. The neurologist generally means, evidently, that *a given region (of the brain) is especially associated with some particular type of behaviour.* This seems to be clear from the contexts in which the phrase is used – mainly ablation and stimulation experiments in which behaviour changes are correlated with brain damage or stimulation. This idea that a given area, or region, of the brain is particularly associated with certain behavioural functions goes back at least to the phrenologists. They spoke of a 'bump of intelligence' where, in some sense, intelligence was supposed to reside. The bigger the 'bump' the greater was the intelligence supposed to be.

'*Localization*'

At first sight, at least, it may seem that the neurologist speaks of regions of the brain in the same way that the geographer speaks of regions of the Earth. Thus: 'The Sahara is a region in Africa' and, 'the striate area is a region of the occipital lobes', are similar sorts of statement. A desert ends when the sand becomes soil: the striate area ends when the cell structure changes in a recognizable way. Suppose now that there is no visible dividing line to delimit regions of the brain: How could we specify such regions? The same thing happens in geography, and the analogy may prove helpful. In *physical* geography natural features, such as seas or continents, are bounded by shores. In *economic* geography, countries or trading areas may not be so bounded: they are essentially *functional* areas. These make sense only in terms of functional activity in customs, economics, etc. These things cannot be observed, like shore lines, by simply looking. A further point – countries may usually be fairly compact, for reasons of transport and communication, but this may not be so. Thus in a sense the British Empire might be said to be (or to have been) one country, though scattered across the world. The bits were linked by connections which could be described as 'functional', but they could not be observed as 'structure' in any single way.

The distinction between physical and economic geography holds for the neurology of the brain. A region may be isolated, and, named, either (a) by virtue of its special *structure*, or (b) by virtue of its special *function*. Do these always coincide?

'Function'

In normal speech, to specify an object's function is to say what causal part it plays in the attainment of some end. It would seem that an object's function may be specified in two quite distinct ways, and the difference between these is important. Consider, say, a rheostat, used as a dimmer to control the brightness of a lamp. The resistor may be referred to in terms of its property of changing the current in the circuit, or simply as a dimmer. The word can only be used in the first way within the context of electrical theory; it is essentially a *technical* sense of the word. The same component may also be referred to quite non-technically, as: 'the thing which dims the lamp'. Here no special knowledge is required beyond the generalization that when the knob is turned the lamp dims. The grounds for using the word 'function' are quite different in the two cases, depending upon whether it is used to designate an essentially *inductively* derived generalization that A produces B (turning the knob has always dimmed the lamp, and so it is a dimmer) or whether it denotes a *deductive* inference within a theory: (added resistance reduces the current flowing in a circuit; the reduced current gives less power . . . therefore the lamp must dim). If the current was not reduced, it could not possibly be a variable resistance. It should be noted that we may be mistaken in calling a given object a resistance, but if it is a resistance then it must have certain functional properties, in a given system. Now it is clear that this second, deductive, use of the word can only be used within a theoretical system or model. The burning question is: has the neurologist got such theoretical systems or models, to enable him to use 'functional' in this technical way?

It seems that the word 'function' is generally used in neurology in the non-theory laden, (inductive), sense. If it is said: 'speech is localized in Broca's area', or: 'the function of Broca's area is to (with the vocal chords and many other things) produce speech', then we are using an inductive type of argument. The evidence for the induction is based largely on speech defects which are observed with lesions in this region of the brain. Broca's area is said to be a speech centre, without a notion of just *what* it does or *how* it does it. Again, it may be said that the striate area is 'used' for vision, but we may not know what processes are going on in this region during visual perception.[1]

[1]The neurologist's concern with cortical function is the extreme case; it would be interesting to consider questions of localization of function in simple cases. There are, however, comparatively simple examples to be found in the brain: thus certain regions can be described as 'chemo-receptors', serving to monitor the blood concentration of CO_2. The signals from these regions have a direct action on respiration. I do not question that some areas have specific functions, but to state what their function is we must have a model of the system within which

It often happens that, with man-made machines, we can recognize the various components for what they do. We may see that there are, for example, motors, resistances, levers or bearings in the machine. Once the components are identified as functional units, then deductive inference is possible. Of course we may always be wrong at the identification stage of the process: a resistance may be mistaken for a condenser, and then the premiss for the argument will be wrong. But the argument is still deductive though the conclusion may then be wrong. Now if nerve cells varied in form in more different ways, each type having corresponding functional properties, then the neurologist would be in the position of the engineer in having readily identifiable components from which he might infer the function of the circuit. Unfortunately, the neurologist is perhaps never in this position, for the brain is too like porridge. This means that this way is generally not open, for we cannot usually, at least at present, identify and recognize function from appearance, by looking at cells and their connections.

If any changes take place upon the removal of part of the brain, the changes are either (*a*) *loss* of some feature of behaviour, or diminution or worsening of some skills, or (*b*) introduction of some *new* behavioural features. Now it is often argued that if some part of behaviour is lost, or diminished in efficiency, then in some sense this behaviour, or rather the causal mechanisms necessary for this behaviour, is localized in the affected region. But does this follow? We may assume that the association is no chance association, but a causal one, and still seriously doubt whether before the advent of the lesion the region in question contained causally necessary mechanisms for the affected behaviour. To illustrate this, we can take an example from radio engineering. If a main smoothing condenser breaks down (shorting the H.T. to earth through a low resistance), the set may stop working, or work in a peculiar manner. The local oscillator may stop, although the rest of the system may continue working normally. Would we then say that the condenser was functionally important for the radio's oscillator, but not for the rest? If so, we would surely be wrong. Its purpose in the system is to smooth the ripple for the whole system, but it happens that this part of the system is more sensitive to reduction in supply voltage than

they play their part. To name an area as a 'chemo-receptor' is to give it a (sensory) function. It might be recognized as such either (*a*) by the recognition of distinctive properties (like recognizing a rose, or a friend) or (*b*) by recognizing its place in a system. (*a*) requires prior knowledge of such components or parts, (*b*) requires a knowledge of the rest of the system in functional terms. In either case, to specify the function of part of a system we must know something of *what* it does and *how* it does it. This is true of the simplest, as well as the most complex, types of system.

the rest. Suppose that when the condenser breaks down, the set emits piercing howls. Do we argue that the normal function of the condenser is to inhibit howling? Surely not. The condenser's abnormally low resistance has changed the system, and the new system may exhibit new properties – in this case howling.

There *are* physical systems where removal of a part removes a specific feature of the output. Thus consider a piano: if a string, a hammer or a key is removed but one note is lost, and the rest may play as before. A piano is largely an arrangement of independent parallel systems, each with its own input (a key) and output (a string). Here functional localization is a simple matter – a piano tuner soon knows where to look for any trouble. This is not in general true of machines, where loss of a part may produce the most bizarre symptoms. Only by understanding the principles involved, and the causal functions of the parts, can the trouble be explained. Further, even where there are parallel semi-independent systems, a fault in a part serving the various parallel systems may have a selective effect on them, and this can be confusing. Thus, reduced air pressure on an organ might affect some pipes a great deal and others not at all.

Arguments from stimulation

If a part is stimulated and something happens, such as a muscle twitching, or the patient reporting a cloud of balloons floating over his head, what can be inferred? The considerations here are similar to the above. We now have a different system, which might have quite new properties.

The functional 'centres' of Hess, and of the ethologists, are interesting. If stimulation of the given region produces a sequence of movements similar to, or identical to a normal behaviour pattern then, it is suggested, this region is the locus or 'centre' of this behaviour pattern. But there are difficulties in this idea of a localized functional centre. The word 'centre' here suggests that the causal neural processes leading to the behaviour pattern are located in space, closely packed, and even that there are not other causal mechanisms in the same region. But, just as many races may live in the same country, (perhaps talking the same language and perhaps not), so causal mechanisms subserving different end results could well reside entangled. They may not be grouped neatly, but might perfectly well be strung about in tenuous filaments, very difficult to find, identify, or stimulate in a controlled manner. Perhaps most important, why should the stimulation by some arbitrary 'signal' leading to familiar behaviour patterns, be regarded as more interesting than bizarre behaviour? Surely all it could mean is that some preorganized set of sequences has been set off, leading to familiar behaviour; but this happens with lights shone in the eye, or sounds applied to the ear, yet no one wants to say that the 'centres' are in the eye or the ear, except in very special cases. Indeed, it would be surprising if stimulation of the cortex did *not* sometimes produce behaviour sequences, but it would not follow that the region stimulated contained the mechanisms responsible for the activity in any direct sense. Certainly it must have something to do with the activity, but it may be far removed both spatially and causally. One might even suspect that if a complete normal behaviour pattern is elicited with an artificial stimulus, then the stimulated area is rather less likely to be directly responsible than if the behaviour patterns are bizarre, for the stimulus might be expected to produce disruption of normal function if introduced in the middle of a causal mechanism, even if the stimulus is the correct trigger for the mechanism.

'Localization of function' takes on further difficulties when we go from innate to learned mechanisms, for here each individual will differ according to what is 'stored' and also, perhaps, according to different developed 'strategies'. If the arguments (or at any rate the conclusions) suggested here are substantially correct, the changes produced by ablation or stimulation should be interpreted in terms of the changes to be expected in systems of various kinds.

In a tightly coupled system, it is impossible to specify a flow of information, or to say where any particular function is localized, for there is interaction throughout the system. Its performance may change when bits are removed or stimulated, but the changes can only be understood in terms of the functional organization of the whole system. In short, we need a model to interpret the changes, and this is where the engineer should be able to help. The changes in behaviour associated with lesions might however be important evidence for suggesting and testing models: and the models should serve to explain the effects of stimulation or ablation.

Modern neurology started when large telephone exchanges were first being built. The 'telephone exchange analogy' has no doubt been useful in the study of the peripheral nervous system, but it is extremely misleading for tightly coupled systems, as the brain would seem to be. The input and output regions of the brain – the 'projection areas' – would be expected to be revealed fairly simply by suitable lesions or direct stimulation, for no doubt they lie in telephone-like pathways, as for the peripheral nerves, though even here there tend to be some cross connections which complicate the picture. The problem becomes acute where the nervous system is analysing or computing, for here the system cannot be like a telephone exchange. Histological examination suggests more or less random networks in large parts of the cortex (Scholl, 1957). Such systems are only beginning to be studied. Lashley's 'Equipotentiality' (that any part of the cortex is equivalent functionally to any other part, certain areas excepted) which he established for the rat brain (Lashley, 1929, 1950) would be expected for such a system. If part of a tightly coupled system is destroyed there is generally very little effect on its performance, except when it is pushed to its limits, for it is now a smaller system. This is just what Lashley found. It is interesting that Uttley's conditional probability computer consists in part of random circuits; some destruction here would not have any devastating effect on the function of this machine (Uttley, 1955).

The behavioural effects of brain damage are of vital importance to the brain surgeon quite apart from their interpretations. They also provide fascinating data for insights into the function of the normal brain but only, I submit, if we look at the changes in the light of conceptual models of brain function. We only come to understand fully how car engines and radio sets work, even after reading about them, by noting their eccentricities and their ailments. We see why a certain 'symptom' is produced when we know how the normal system works, and we come to understand more fully how it works when we see and think about the symptoms of overheating, weak mixture, or whatever it may be. We could not possibly say what a plug in a car engine does simply by noting what happens when we remove it, unless we understand the general principles of internal combustion engines – we must have a model. The biologist has no 'Maker's manual', or any clear idea of what the purpose of many of the 'devices' he studies may be. He must guess the purpose, and put up for testing likely looking hypotheses of how it may function. In both these tasks, he should receive valuable help from the sympathetic engineer.

DISCUSSION

Mr J. T. Allanson: I want to take up two points which are not central to Mr Gregory's argument. The first one is in relation to the systems which he has described as tightly coupled. Since this paper is largely concerned with the problem of what may be learned from engineering situations and engineering methods of analysis, I think it is relevant to point out that in many fields of engineering, tightly coupled systems do not obey two of the generalizations which are made in this paper. In the theory of electrical networks, for instance, it is possible to define quite precisely what one means by systems which are tightly coupled. By and large, such systems cannot satisfy at the same time, the generalization on page 574 of possessing bizarre behaviour when part of the system is destroyed, and the generalization on page 576 that if part of the tightly coupled system is destroyed there is generally very little effect.

I am doubtful if any system at all can satisfy both of these generalizations at one and the same time. If there is generally very little effect, I do not see how one can say that the effect is bizarre. I suggest that this phrase (highly-coupled systems) is not a particularly useful description or way of looking at the brain at all.

The second point centres on page 576. Mr Gregory says if we take Dr Uttley's probability computer and remove some of the circuits it would not have a devastating effect on the function of the machine. I think this depends entirely on the original state of the computer.

If there is a certain superfluity in the connections it is perfectly true. If one takes the connections as described for the precise version of the computer, in which they are not made at random, but there is *one* AB unit and *one* BC unit and so on, a removal of a percentage of these connections would result in bizarre effects rather than in a very slight modification without significance.

Dr A. J. Angyan: I was very glad to read Mr Gregory's paper, and think I can agree with all his main points. I, too, shall try to demonstrate a model which is intended to be a representation of some kind of localization of function in the nervous system.

I would like to know how Mr Gregory differentiates between 'essential' and 'accidental' features when making a model. Are, for example, the 'essential' features of a nerve cell not 'accidental' when describing the learning process of the organism in the more general sense, as compared with these terms when used to describe the anatomical and electrophysiological properties of the cell?

Dr W. S. McCulloch: I am one of those unfortunate men who began his study of neurophysiology in the days when practically everything had to be deduced from the effects of lesions. Eilhard von Domarus in his famous Ph.D. thesis at Yale poked fun at us – I mean at neurophysiologists thus:

Clinicians correlated the loss of specific responses with the destruction of particular portions of the nervous system and supposed the function lost to be that of the tissue lost, instead of realizing that all they knew was that the remaining functions were functions of the remaining structure. We might caricature this by saying that stereoscopic vision was the function of the right eye because a man who lost his right eye lost stereoscopic vision. The notion of inhibition, or neural shock, prevented a clear conception of what they did actually know. Now return to the caricature.

Suppose that we had seen patients who had lost stereoscopic vision by loss of the right eye and attributed that function to that eye, and then had a patient who had lost a left eye; we might now explain his loss of stereoscopic vision by supposing that the destruction of his left eye, by *inhibitorische Fernwirkung*, prevented his right eye from functioning stereoscopically. And, as if this had not been enough, the gratuitous hypothesis of the vicarious assumption of function obfuscated all issues. We have discovered that the right eye gave stereoscopic vision and the left eye plain vision; but in our patient who had lost his left eye the right eye vicariously assumed the function of plain vision. This completes the caricature.

In other words, the argument from lesions, unless we are careful, leads us into utter rubbish, and the great difficulty is that we have been compelled to think of new ways of defining functions. I have been trying to define functions in new ways because I am interested in the functional organization of the brain; but all that I can say is, that the function of any component is to be excited by those things which can excite it, and to be inhibited by those things which can inhibit it, and perhaps to drift a little in its properties with use. When we try to say more or speak of the function of a whole tissue or a whole area, we are very apt to talk nonsense.

Dr D. M. MacKay: I wonder whether we may not go too far in running away from the idea of localized function. I have in mind the rather analogous case of a human community, to which much that Mr Gregory has said of the brain would seem to apply. The economist attributes a function to each man as a cog in the machine; but he also distinguishes functions such as that of an industry. The man is sharply localizable; the industry need not be, but often is – witness the power of strategic bombing.

I feel that this analogy can be useful and stimulating towards a more balanced view on the vexed question of 'function'. No economist pictures the country as parcelled into discrete 'areas'; but he gains great flexibility of thinking by the ability to picture more or less discrete entities with definite functions such as the cotton industry, the electronics industry, and so forth. I see no reason why evidence from comparative anatomy, from developmental studies, and above all from the action of drugs which are function-specific, should not give us valid functional maps (not necessarily having any simple geographical interpretation) with the same power to catalyse our thinking about cerebral organization.

Dr J. A. V. Bates: I think Mr Gregory has brought out a useful point in stressing that there may be confusion in the use of the word 'function'. For many years people have pointed this out – soon after Broca published his observations on brain lesions affecting speech in 1861, Hughlings Jackson and Wundt were saying that to localize the parts of the brain which destroy speech and to localize the function of speech are two different things. So if this has been the obstacle to clear thinking that Mr Gregory or Dr McCulloch have made it out to be, I would say that there is no excuse. But I think the difficulty lies elsewhere, and in Mr Gregory's terminology it is this: that if you have any complex organization, there will be systems within it which are to be considered tightly coupled, and systems which are to be considered loosely coupled; if we study the effects of brain lesions how are we to know which sort of system we are dealing with? Probably the degree of coupling in sub-systems in a complex organ like the brain shows a hierarchy of grades, just as it does in the radio set which Mr Gregory uses in analogy; if the set goes silent because a resistor has gone 'open-circuit', he is correct to point out that it would be ridiculous to say the function of that resistor was to produce sound, but with the same set, if the same defect is found to be due to some change in the loudspeaker cone, it would not be ridiculous to say that the function of the loud-speaker cone was to produce the sound. We know that in the brain one can hit on examples of extremely tight coupling in this sense. For example, if one interferes with certain tracts in the brain stem and gets anaesthesia, one is not amiss in assigning to those tracts a particular function in conduction of impulses which give rise to the sensation of pain. Other types of lesion produce altered sensation through inter-ference with loosely coupled systems and one characteristic of such systems which the neurologist recognizes is that such defects tend to recover. But one essential difficulty in studying brain function by means of lesions lies in deciding which sort of system you are dealing with. It would be instructive to learn if engineering has produced any general rules or theorems on this subject which could be of value in this type of investigation.

Dr H. B. Barlow: I agree, of course, with a lot of what Mr Gregory has said, but I am distressed by the general tenor of it, for this reason. Suppose nobody had ever done any ablation experiments, then after hearing his talk one would say, 'Here are some experiments I need not do at all'. But obviously a very great deal of valuable information about the brain has been obtained by ablation experiments. The fact that one can be confused by the results is true of any experiments. There are some cases, after all, where you do get quite clear-cut results. For example, if you hold a blind-folded cat so that the tops of its front paws touch the edge of a table, then it will lift them up and place them on the table. Now if a small region at the frontal pole of the cat's cortex is removed, then this placing reaction (on the contralateral side) is no longer performed: but if the whole of the cerebral cortex except this small region is ablated, then the placing reaction is retained.

When you can get clear experimental results like this, the experiments are surely worth doing, even if the interpretation is not as simple as appears at first sight.

Sir Frederic Bartlett, Chairman: There are two questions which I should like to ask Mr Gregory to answer. Towards the end of his paper, on the last page, he says that if one is considering a biological system which is computing, or working in an analytical sort of way, we have to consider that system as containing a number of very large parts, and we have to have recourse to a notion something like, at any rate, that of Lashley's notion of equi-potentiality, where any part, within limits, has the same properties in response as any other part. So far as I can see, Lashley himself arrived at this principle through a very long inductive process, and I would like to know from Mr Gregory if he considers that the distinction that he has drawn between the use in this field of an inductive process and a deductive process really does amount to very much – whether, in fact, one has not got to use the experimental approach in order to get at any of these general properties of large systems.

The second question that I want to ask I can put very simply indeed. He says it is interesting that Dr Uttley's conditional probability computer consists in part of random circuits. Does this mean that any model which has to be constructed and is useful to help in dealing with the central nervous system is all right so long as it contains a number of random circuits?

Finally, I wish he would say, for my information and for others, what sort of valuable help he wants from the sympathetic engineer.

Mr Gregory (in reply): I do not know whether I can at all adequately deal with the points raised, but thank you very much for them. The first point raised by Mr Allanson brings to light something pretty silly on my part. I did not wish to say that with a tightly coupled system one would *at the same time* get a bizarre change and no change at all when parts are removed. I think there is some confusion in my paper on this point. I should have said, perhaps, that (a) where the system is tightly coupled there would be only small output changes except when the system was being pushed to its limits, and (b) where there are serial processes without feed-back loops there will in general be rather large and bizarre changes in the output. I think that Mr Allanson is correct in his second point – concerning removal of some of the circuits in Dr Uttley's probability computer. It is perhaps interesting to note that in general lesions are more serious in adult than in young animals or people: could it be that there are fewer superfluous connections in the adult organism?

I think I do not fully understand Dr Angyan's query about

'accidental' and 'essential' features of nerve cells. It seems to me that we might mean by 'essential' those features which are of causal importance to the functioning of the system, while 'accidental' are those features which are not causally important. A model should be helpful in indicating and emphasizing the 'essential' features of the system in this sense.

Dr McCulloch seems to me to have put the main argument far more clearly than I have succeeded in doing. I am grateful for this support. It may well be that some of the early neurologists were less confused than many modern neurologists seem to be on this matter. Hughlings Jackson, for example, said very much the same sort of thing, though not in the context of engineering models of brain function.

I agree with Dr MacKay that analogy with localized functions in human communities is useful. I have tried to develop this line of thought in *The brain as an engineering problem* [No. 49]. I think with him that the important point is that functional maps in general do not have simple geographical interpretations, either in communities, industry or machines. This is partly why simply looking at a system and removing 'parts' is not sufficient for gaining an understanding of the manner of function of the organism.

I do not altogether follow Dr Bates' first point. Perhaps the difficulty lies with the undue emphasis which I placed on 'tightly coupled' systems. One might say that the sound comes from the loudspeaker cone, but I think that this is because it is the output terminal of the system. I tried to emphasize that in my view one *can* localize input and output terminals, and parallel paths, quite simply.

Dr Bates seems to be using the term 'tightly coupled' in a sense different from the way I was using it. Perhaps he means what might be called 'closely matched'. I meant not closely matched, but rather a system of servo loops tending to give stability to the system as a whole. I do not agree with Dr Bates that interference with certain tracts of the brain stem with anaesthesia would necessarily imply that those tracts function to conduct impulses normally giving rise to pain. There may well be further considerations which together with this observation would lead to such a conclusion, but in itself it is surely not sufficient grounds for the conclusion. All we could say is that when these tracts are anaesthetized the system does not give rise to pain. It remains a question *why* it does not give rise to pain. One possible answer is that the tracts were conducting impulses representing pain information. But this is not the only possibility, and so it does not follow that they were in any direct manner important to giving rise to pain.

In respect to Dr Barlow's point: the last thing I wanted to suggest was that ablation experiments are a waste of time. I tried to make this clear at the end of the paper. I was, however, concerned to point out that their interpretation seems almost impossible (except in a few special cases) *in the absence of some functional model,* however tentative this may be. It seems to me that we can seldom say anything directly about what a given region does by observing changes in behaviour after ablation. The exception is where there are parallel paths, and this is the case for the visual projection areas, if they are visual projection areas.

Sir Frederic Bartlett points out that Lashley arrived at his principle of equipotentiality by lengthy inductive processes. It seems to me that this is so if we take the term 'equipotentiality' to refer to the observed behaviour changes with various amounts of ablation, but not if we take it to refer to supposed properties of the neural structure responsible for the behaviour. To infer something about the function of the brain from observed behaviour does not seem to me to be an induction from the data. It seems to be a hypothesis which may be suggested by the data, but which cannot be *inferred* from it, either inductively or deductively. It is not always clear whether writers on equipotentiality are using the term as a short-hand label for the inductive generalizations, which Lashley made, or whether they are using it as an explanatory concept to refer to a supposed property of the brain: namely that any part is functionally equivalent to any other part. If it is a label then it is, so it seems to me, an *induction*, but if it refers to the brain then it is a hypothesis about the neural systems involved, and it is an attempt at *explanation.* I think we should be very careful to make it clear when such a term is being used as a label and when it is being used to denote an explanatory concept.

To suggest that the brain is a system which might on general grounds be expected to display impairment only when pushed near its limits, is to make any special postulate unnecessary. It thus seems to me that defenders of equipotentiality as an explanation of the facts should show that the brain is not such a system. Until this is done, any special postulate for the system is unnecessary. It is also a poor explanation, because it does not relate the case of the brain to other systems whose functional principles are known to us, but even suggests that in this particular it is unique, which may inhibit the development of explanatory models in terms of known systems.

I fear that I have raised (or fished up?) a red herring in putting emphasis on random circuits in this context.

Dr Bates has largely answered the query as to what sort of help the sympathetic engineer might provide. He points out that an essential difficulty in studying brain function by means of lesions is to know which sort of system we are dealing with. It seems to me that the engineer can be of great help in suggesting just what to look for, and what sort of experiment to perform, in order to discover what kind of system it is. For example, once we know about servos and their properties under various conditions, we know that studies on tremor are likely to be important, and careful experiments are then carried out which would be thought silly, or even mad, in the absence of the alternative models suggested by analogy with other control systems. Again, in the context of engineer's systems Lashley's ablation results seem to have a simple explanation. In the absence of engineering knowledge special principles tend to be invoked by psychologists and physiologists. Since these do not have application beyond the biological examples considered, they have little explanatory power, and are often merely alternative labels for what needs explanation. An example of this would be Bergson's *élan vital*, which is utterly useless as an explanation, because it does not compare the unknown with anything else. It is no more than a label, but such labels can have a fascination. They tend to quell further questions which might lead to new experiments, and explanation in general terms.

51 *Köhler's perception*

[Apart from the following paper, book reviews have not been included in this volume, but Köhler's final (posthumously produced) lectures, *The Task of Gestalt Psychology*, represent the last words of the original Gestalt school, and so a review of these lectures may be of interest. Page references are to the lectures. (This review adds some comments to No. 47.)]

★   ★   ★

WOLFGANG Köhler, who died in June 1967, was the last remaining member of the original Gestalt school of psychology. Köhler was born in Estonia of German parents and was brought up in Germany, to become by 1921 the director of the Institute of Psychology in the University of Berlin. He resigned in 1935, after defying Hitler and all his works, to settle in the United States. He grafted a German tradition on to the very different stem of American empiricism, at that time flowering with J. B. Watson's behaviourism. Gestalt psychology was a strange graft, generally appearing more alien than symbiotic; but the contrasting colours of the two blooms emphasized their special features.

Köhler's main works are: *The Mentality of Apes* (1917), in which he described 'insightful' behaviour, solutions occurring suddenly rather than by overt trial-and-error; *Gestalt Psychology* (1929); *Dynamics of Psychology* (1940); and many papers, originally appearing in *Psychologische Forschung*, mainly concerned with problems of perception. The present book is a series of four lectures – delivered at Princeton in 1966 – posthumously edited by Solomon Asch, Mary Henle, and Edwin Newman, and introduced with a useful historical essay by Carroll C. Pratt. The lectures discuss the early contributions of Gestalt psychology to perception, physical analogies for describing brain function, and experiments on d-c cortical recording, and include a delightful description of the classical observations of the 'genius' chimpanzee Sultan and the active but less 'insightful' Rana engaged in reaching bananas from movable boxes. This study was undertaken over 50 years ago and has been discussed by psychologists ever since. It takes on a fresh significance now that 'intelligent' machines begin to have similar ability: what is it to build 'insight' into a machine? Are psychological theories adequate to tell us?

In these lectures Köhler seldom goes back on his earlier statements or adds anything significantly new. Rather, he surveys with some satisfaction past achievements of the school of which he was so eminent a member. But is there cause for satisfaction? What remains of importance from the vast wordage of Gestalt writings? Certainly Köhler's observations of chimpanzee problem-solving are a foundation stone of ethology. The Gestalt rejection of mosaics of stimuli or sensations (not always clearly distinguished by Köhler) and the emphasis on interactive perceptual effects involving large units, was demonstrated by simple experiments with patterns of dots. We would not, however, now accept that the significance of these effects was correctly appreciated by those who pointed them out.

Perhaps the Gestaltists' works suffered somewhat from pollution by a stifling metaphysics; at any rate the Gestalt rejection of analysis, or explanation in terms of logically simpler concepts or defined underlying mechanisms, makes their theories no more than occasionally suggestive. Worse, it is far too easy to raise serious difficulties, questions which they should surely have raised themselves and attempted to answer. Here Köhler's last lectures are disappointing, for no veils are lifted. Köhler's isomorphic brain fields, for example, are suspect on logical grounds, quite apart from Lashley's famous experiment with the implanted gold wires (not mentioned in these lectures) which should have distorted the fields but apparently did not. If we suppose that a circle is represented as a circular brain trace, then – apart from the difficulties of how the rest of the nervous system has access to this trace without having to see it with an inner eye, leading to infinite regress – are we supposed to believe that the brain trace of a traffic light changes from red to green? How are touch and temperature and music represented? These are supposed to obey Gestalt interactive laws, but can the Gestalt kind of representation possibly apply to them? If shape, why not music in the brain? Again, to argue that physically intermittent movement which appears the same as continuous movement (phi) 'clearly proves' (p. 39) the existence of such interacting processes is to omit the strong possibility that velocity is coded early in the visual system (as we now know it is in the retina of frog and rabbit) and transmitted as velocity signals which continue unimpaired through small gaps in time or space. Some tolerance to intermittency is all that is logically required (though there may be more to the matter), and yet phi is a foundation observation of Gestalt theory, supposed to *demonstrate* isomorphic traces. Another such is autokinetic movement. This apparent movement of a stationary light is supposed to demonstrate directly the presence of internal and shifting reference frames. The argument is that since all movement is relative but nothing external moves in the autokinetic situation, there must be something internal – reference frames – which moves. But this is to ignore the vital distinction between veridical and disturbed observation. A neural system transmitting velocity information would be expected to transmit false velocity signals, giving an *appearance* of movement though all is stationary, if its calibration is upset. Surely by regarding the senses as transducers and as instruments for making decisions on data, at least such mistakes can be avoided.

An emphasis on innate principles permeates all Gestalt writing. The kind of evidence accepted as establishing the primary importance of innateness in perception would hardly be accepted now but is repeated in these lectures. Köhler presents figures that 'contain' other, familiar figures which however are not recognized. He argues that the difficulty in seeing the figures proves that 'past experience cannot be the main factor responsible for the appearance of objects in visual fields' (p. 52).

Clearly there is something important here, though we may question its relevance to the innate-versus-learning controversy. Köhler goes on: '. . . one should not simply call [such objects] "wholes". Surely they *are* wholes rather than mere regions within a general mosaic of local sensations. But we should always add an adjective, namely "segregated" or "detached" wholes. For . . . objects appear in the visual field only if their boundaries are visually preserved.' He goes on to say that the processes which make 'unitary' objects 'emerge' were insufficiently emphasized in early Gestalt psychology. This extraction of objects now assumes the greatest importance in the very difficult problem of making intelligent machines accept raw data from the surrounding world without having to be fed only with what is relevant. It turns out that certain typical characteristics of objects, such as closure of contours, have to be provided, or programmed in, before seeing machines can identify objects from backgrounds. Exceptional situations (including such complications as shadows) can fool the machine, as they can fool us, though we are at present more subtle. The old illusions and the newer 'impossible figures' take on profound importance in this context, for they reveal the assumptions that are

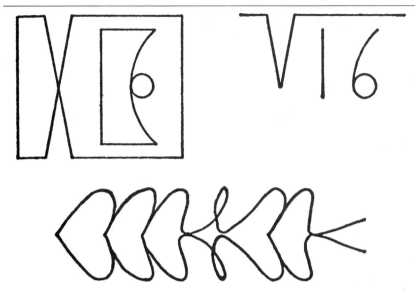

FIG. 51.1 *Figures used by Köhler which he claims demonstrate that 'the principles according to which visual objects are established differ from the processes which the empiristic explanations, the explanation of learning, makes one expect'* (The Task of Gestalt Psychology, *p. 51*). *The figure at the upper left seems 'not at all familiar. But it contains one part with which we are all well acquainted', shown at upper right. The lower figure consists of a common word resting on its mirror image.*

accepted to make the problem generally tractable. The same line of thought allows us to reconsider the basic Gestalt emphasis on perception as being of 'wholes'. It turns out that a computer program attempting to extract particular shapes by a rigorous point-to-point analysis is far too slow. Rather, it seems necessary to fit what may be termed partial templates to key features – to establish with just sufficient precision the presence or absence of features used for object identification. Once they are identified, redundancy in space and in time reduces the information needed to maintain perception of the ever-changing positions and orientations of objects. Without such simplifying assumptions, cartoons would be meaningless to us; indeed it is surprising how little attention cartoons have received as experimental material for revealing just what is necessary for recognition of familiar objects.

The Gestalt school grew from German metaphysics and always resisted the precise analysis of empirical science. It may however be that Köhler, Wertheimer, and the rest saw from their simple introspective experiments with lines and dots key features of the brain's perceptual programs, which we are beginning to build into machines that are inadequate when designed according to the rigorous empiricism that was their first inspiration. If the truth is that Gestalt theory reflects the brain's partial analysis of data, we may use insights of Gestalt theory to solve problems of artificial intelligence, to design seeing machines by making them similarly nonrigorous if detailed analysis takes too much time. This is far removed from the aims and hopes of the original Gestalt school, but it is more than possible that Köhler would approve of the application of his insights to problems in physics and engineering – instead of, as so often in psychology, the other way round.

52 *On how so little information controls so much behaviour*

[We move now to cognitive aspects of brain function. The following was presented at a conference on Theoretical Biology organized by Professor C. H. Waddington, held at the lovely Villa Serbelloni on Lake Como. This was an extraordinary series of conferences – very possibly heralding an important new subject, largely of Professor Waddington's invention. 'Wad' has a range and power of mind to be envied: extending through much of science, to art, to effective social concern such as how to build towns fit to live in.

I gave much the same paper at a NATO meeting in Thessalonika, Greece, organized by Alan Welford. Professor Welford began and edited the journal *Ergonomics*, where this paper also appears. It takes up a theme started in an early paper (No. 46) and developed in *The Intelligent Eye*, namely that behaviour is controlled in higher animals and man by what may be called 'hypotheses' selected by sensory data. The brain's perceptual hypotheses may continue through gaps in sensory data, and may provide data beyond what is available to make behaviour appropriate to non-sensed features of objects. It seems a safe prediction that engineers will soon latch on to the power of internally stored hypotheses, to develop what would surely be biological machines.

The essential notion is implicit in Berkeley's *A New Theory of Vision* (1709); though he did not regard perception as an active process analogous to – indeed a kind of – thinking; for to Berkeley, as to the other British Empiricists, perception is passive, though it involves combinations of sensory data. It is an interesting speculation: What would have happened to Empiricist philosophy if perception had been regarded as actively created hypotheses, subject to error as thoughts and opinions are subject to error?

The brilliant Cambridge psychologist, Kenneth Craik, who was tragically killed in an accident in 1946, seems to have been the first to state clearly that the nervous system may symbolize reality. In his *The Nature of Explanation* (1943) he says (p. 61): 'If the organism carries a "small-scale model" of external reality and of its own possible actions within its head, it is able to carry out various alternatives, conclude which is the best of them, react to future situations before they arise, utilize the knowledge of past events in dealing with the present and the future, and in every way react in a fuller, safer, and more competent manner to the emergencies which face it.' It is odd that it has taken so long for the importance of this to be realized – and to be developed into cognitive psychology and machine intelligence.

Part of the trouble has been in seeing how to experiment on the internal structure of the brain's symbolic 'models', or 'hypotheses' as I prefer to call them. The new school of linguistics headed by Noam Chomsky has given a boost here, but it is still seductively easy to believe that we will only get repeatable and significant results in the laboratory if the nervous system works by direct stimulus-response links. That so little attention has been paid to the kinds of things Craik was saying, nearly thirty years ago, reminds one of the first words of Wittgenstein's preface to the *Tractatus* (1922): 'This book will perhaps only be understood by those who have themselves already thought the thoughts which are expressed in it – or similar thoughts.' I believe that I had to think up 'perceptual hypotheses' before I understood what Craik was saying before I was a student. Had he lived, anything written here would have been unnecessary.]

*　　　*　　　*

PERHAPS the most fundamental question in the whole field of experimental psychology is: How far is behaviour controlled by currently available sensory information and how far by information already stored in the central nervous system? Considering the origin of neurally stored information, we believe that this has only two origins: (1) ancestral disasters, changing neural structure according to the principles and processes of other phylogenetic changes occurring by natural selection; (2) previous sensory experience of the individual, stored as 'memory'. We may call these two ways of gaining stored information phylogenetic and ontogenetic learning respectively.

It is important to distinguish two quite different kinds of stored information. We learn *skills* and *events*. Some skills (e.g. walking, swimming, fighting) may be inherited (though often showing as behaviour only after sufficient maturation) and so are examples of gaining information phylogenetically; while learning or storing *particular* events is always ontogenetic. For examples of inherited skills, babies walk without special training at about fifteen months, and as Coghill (1929) showed, salamanders kept from all movement by anaesthesia will nevertheless swim normally as soon as allowed, once the neural connections of the spinal cord (visible in the living animal) are complete. For examples of learned skills we may take games such as tennis, piano playing and chess. We may be able to recall the odd particular games or concerts, but as skills it is not individual past events which are stored, but rather appropriate behaviour and strategies which give more or less complete success in later similar situations. Evidently crucial generalized features of the original situation are stored and used when appropriate. But sometimes stored features are used when inappropriate: then we have an example of 'negative transfer of training' – for example playing table tennis with the straight arm movements appropriate to tennis. This serves as a handicap.

It is an open question just how far individual events are stored as such, and how far they have to be 'constructed' for recall (cf. Bartlett 1932). What is certain is that information gained phylogenetically is always of the general 'skill' kind. We are not able to recall individual events experienced by our ancestors.

We know quite a lot about the stages by which skills are learned by individuals. I would like to suggest that this can provide clues to the nature of how behaviour is controlled by sensory information. It suggests that control is not direct, except in the special cases of reflexes, but is via internal neural models of reality. These internal models are essential for skills – including perception of the external world.

The learning of skills. It has been clear ever since the experiments of Blodgett (1929) that 'latent' learning occurs – that is, some information storage which does not at once show itself in behaviour nevertheless occurs during the early stages of developing a skill. We find two features of learning curves characteristic of ontogenetic skill learning: first, in learning discriminations – which seem vital to 'map the ground' in the first stages of learning – learning curves are positively accelerated; there being at first no progress, then later progress appears at an increasing rate. Experiments have shown that the animal (generally a rat) is responding to other, and it turns out irrelevant, features of the situation. Secondly, learning curves of skill show marked 'plateaux', during which no progress is observed but each plateau is followed by a sudden jump in performance, associated with a different strategy. In learning Morse code, typing, or the piano, increase in speed of performance occurs in steps as the input is handled in larger and larger units. Thus in typing, while each letter remains a unit, speed is limited to about two letters per second; but later, letter groups up to whole words and finally groups of words become the neural units. Speed is then far greater than is possible with the maximum decision rate of about 0·5 sec per decision possible for the human neural system. Lashley has described the process for piano playing:

> The finger strokes of a musician may reach sixteen per second in passages which call for a definite and changing order of successive finger movements. The succession of movements is too quick even for visual reaction time. In rapid sight reading it is impossible to read the individual notes of an arpeggio. The notes must be seen in groups, and it is actually easier to read chords simultaneously and to translate them into temporal sequence than to read successive notes in an arpeggio as usually written.

This grouping of what is at first discrete inputs is however done at the cost of complete flexibility. Unusual combinations of inputs may be missed, or accepted as though they were in a more usual order, with consequent errors. Random music is very difficult to play and random letters very difficult to type.

A system which makes use of the redundancy, in space and time, of the real world has the following advantages.

1. It can achieve high performance with limited information transmission rate. (It is estimated that human transmission rate is only about 12 bits/second.) The gain results because perception of objects – which are always redundant – requires identification of only certain key features of each object. Some kind of search strategy for these features would save a great deal of processing time for object recognition. (This is open to experimental investigation and has implications to pattern recognition, which is *not* the same as object recognition, which is perhaps an artificial concept.)

2. It is essentially predictive. In suitable circumstances it can cut reaction time to zero. (Experimental situations for demonstrating reaction time are somewhat artificial, seldom occurring during actual skills, such as driving, typing, piano playing, etc.)

3. It can continue to function in the temporary absence of any input, e.g. turning the music page, blinking, or sneezing while driving.

Loss of input is very different from loss of output control (e.g. the steering wheel coming off), and this difference seems important for investigating these internal selected groupings, or as we call them 'models', of reality.

4. It can continue to function when the input changes in kind. Thus in maze learning, rats can continue to run a maze once learned though each sensory input in turn is denied it – vision, smell, kinaesthetics, etc.

(There is an important implication here for interpretations of brain ablation experiments, for so-called 'mass action' might appear though each sensory and corresponding learning system were precisely located in the brain, for the other specific systems might take over after destruction. The fact that rats can swim a flooded maze after learning to run it dry is particularly striking, for evidently it is *not* primarily patterns of motor movements which are learned. This is important evidence for cognitive learning at the level of the rat, and we believe that it gets even more important higher up the phylogenetic scale.)

5. It can extract signals from 'noise'. If the internal models are highly redundant, they can be called up with minimal sensory information. This means that the models can enormously improve the effective signal/noise ratio of sensory systems.

6. Provided a particular situation is similar to the situations for which a 'model' was developed, behaviour will generally be appropriate. This, in the language of experimental psychology, is 'positive transfer of training'.

We come now, however, to *disadvantages* of conceivable systems (including robots) in which behaviour is based on internal models.

1. When the current situation is sufficiently similar to past situations which have been selected and combined to give an internal model, but the current situation differs in crucial respects, then the system will be *systematically misled by its model*. This is 'negative transfer'.

2. Internal model systems will be essentially conservative – showing inertial drag to change – for internal models must reflect the past rather than the present. (This implies that rapid change of environment or social groups is biologically dangerous, and of course it favours young members of such groups.)

Further implications of internal models. Since no model can be complete, and few if any are entirely accurate in what they represent, biological or computer systems employing internal models can always be fooled. They are fooled when characteristics which they accept for selecting a model occur in atypical situations. It is always possible that a wildly wrong model may be selected when this happens. It will happen most often when only a few selection characteristics are demanded or are available to the system. We know from many learning and perceptual experiments that there are great individual differences in what kinds of features are demanded. (In general 'brighter' individual animals, such as rats, demand where possible non-visual features while the dimmer brethren are largely content with visual features. This is curious in the case of the rat, which is generally regarded as rather a 'non-visual' animal.)

A model may be selected on purely visual data, but once selected it is generally used for non-visual predictions. Thus, in driving a car, the road surface is 'read off' the retinal image: what matters is whether the road is slippery. Slipperiness, though not a property of images, can be read from the retinal image.

In general, the eye's images are only biologically important in so far as non-optical features can be read from the internal models they select. Images are merely patches of light – which cannot be eaten or be dangerous – but they serve as symbols for selecting internal models which include non-visual features vital to survival. It is this reading of object characteristics from images that *is* visual perception.

Gross errors may occur when a wrong model is selected. Errors of scale can also occur; and these, I believe, are the familiar perceptual distortion illusions. These illusions are interesting because they can tell us something of how internal models are made to fit the precise state of affairs in the outside world [Nos. 3, 27, 28, 30].

We cannot suppose that there are as many internal models as there are perceptible objects *of all sizes, distances, and positions in space*. But it is important for the models to represent the current sizes, distances, and positions of external objects if they are to mediate appropriate behaviour. To solve this problem we may suppose that the models are flexible. They can be adjusted to fit reality. They are adjusted by 'size scaling' visual features – such as perspective convergence of lines – though not always appropriately.

In the absence of any available scale-setting data, perception is determined by average sizes and distances. These are modified by 'scale-setting' sensory information when available. When scale-setting information is inappropriate to the prevailing reality, then perception is systematically distorted. On this view we can use distortion illusions as quite basic research tools. In the Müller-Lyer, Hering, or Orbison visual illusions, typical perspective depth features are presented on a flat plane. Features which would be distant if these figures were truly three-dimensional are expanded in the flat illusion figures. Thus expansion is normally appropriate – since it is object size and not retinal image size which is biologically important – but here the system is misled by the scaling information and systematic distortions occur. By studying these distortions we can discover experimentally just how flexible the internal models are; what sorts of information are used to give object scale, and also something of how internal models are built by perceptual learning.

Biologically important features of the world must be read from available sensory information. To be useful, visual features must be related to the weight, hardness, and chemical properties of objects which have to be handled or eaten. Now it is well known that a small object of the same weight as a larger object feels up to fifty per cent heavier. This is the 'size-weight' illusion. Vision selects a model calling up appropriate muscle power for lifting the weight, but when the internal model is inappropriate the power called up is inappropriate – and we suffer an illusion corresponding to the error.

The weight setting adopted by the nervous system in the absence of information of the size of the weight corresponds to a density of one – about the average density of common objects.

It is interesting that scale distortion illusions are (a) similar in different individuals from the same culture, but differ somewhat in different cultures when the available characteristic features are different, and (b) are very slow to change in adults. (On the other hand, systematic changing of *all* inputs, with e.g. distortion glasses, does produce rapid appropriate adaptation in adult humans.)

In a case of adult recovery from infant blindness we found (Gregory and Wallace 1963 [No. 3], newly available inputs were only accepted when they could be directly related to previous touch experience. In our present terms, vision was only possible after the corneal grafts when visual data could select *already available* internal models, based on earlier touch experience. Building new models was very slow, taking a year or more. The use of vision for size-scaling occurred within a few months, the initial distortions being very great in situations where touch or other information had not previously been brought to bear – as when looking at the ground from a high window, when the ground appeared almost within touch range though actually forty feet below. The normal systematic distortion illusions did not occur: I suppose that there was no 'negative transfer' of perceptual learning where there had been no opportunity for learning of the normal size-scaling features, such as perspective.

Sensory discrimination and the appropriateness of models. I have distinguished between (a) selecting models according to sensory information, and (b) size-scaling models to fit the orientation, size, and distance of external objects.

Now let us consider an experimental situation which may tell us something about the 'engineering' nature of the models in the brain. The experimental question is: What happens to sensory *discrimination* when there is a scale distortion?

Consider the following paradigm experiment. We have two sets of weights, such as tins filled with lead shot. Each set consists of say seven tins all of a certain size, while the other set has seven tins each of which is, say, twice the volume of the first set. Each set has a tin of weight, in grams, 85, 90, 95, 100, 105, 110, 115. The 100 gram weight in each set is the standard, and the task is to compare the other weights in the same set with this standard and try to distinguish them as heavier or lighter. The tins are fitted with the same size handles for lifting to keep the touch inputs constant except for weight. Is the discrimination the same for the set of *apparently* heavier weights but which are in fact the same weights? The answer is that discrimination is *worse* for weights either apparently *heavier* or *lighter* than weights having a specific gravity of about one (Gregory and Ross 1967 [No. 12]). Why should this be so?

Suppose that sensory data are compared with the current internal model – as they must be to be useful. Now if it is not only *compared* with it, but *balanced against it*, then we derive further advantages of employing internal models. We then have systems like Wheatstone bridges, and these have useful properties. Bridge circuits are especially good (a) over a very large input intensity range and (b) with components subject to drift. Now it is striking how large an intensity range sensory systems cover ($1:10^5$ or even $1:10^6$), and the biological components are subject to far more drift than would be tolerated by engineers in our technology confronted with similar problems. So balanced bridge circuits seem a good engineering choice in the biological situation.

Consider a Wheatstone bridge in which the input signals provide one arm, and the prevailing internal model the opposed arm against which the input is balanced. Now the internal arm is part of the model – and will be set wrongly in a scale distortion illusion. In the size/weight illusion, visual information has set the weight arm wrongly. This means that the bridge will not balance. The illusion is the misbalance of the bridge. Now an engineer's bridge which is not balanced suffers in its ability to discriminate changes in its input, for it is no longer a null system but relies on scale readings of the galvanometer or other misbalance detector. Thus the supposed biological system gives just what a practical engineer's bridge would give – loss of intensity discrimination associated with an error in balancing the bridge. This is some evidence that internal models form arms of bridge circuits in the brain.

Speculations on mental events – normal and abnormal. On this general view, perception is not directly of sensory information but rather of the internal models selected by sensory information. Indeed, the current perception *is* the prevailing set of models.

There are well-known situations in which the sensory information calls up two or more incompatible internal models with equal probability. The best-known example is the spontaneously reversing Necker cube. The available information is insufficient to decide between rival internal models, and each comes to the fore in turn. It is interesting that in this case the addition of tactile information –

provided by holding in the hand a luminous cube viewed in darkness –
does not serve to abolish visual reversals, though it does reduce their
rate of occurrence (Shopland and Gregory 1964 [No. 19]). Evidently
the visual internal model system is largely autonomous, though it is
partly under the control of other senses. Visual size and distance can
be set by other senses, especially touch. It is also worth noting that size
scaling follows not only currently available sensory information, but
also changes in the internal model. Thus, a luminous cube appears as a
cube when seen correctly – though the further face is smaller at the
retina – but as a truncated pyramid when depth-reversed. Here there
is no change at all in the sensory input, only in the internal model, so
the scale changes *with the model*, though the sensory information
remains constant.

Generally, the internal model is reasonably complete and appropriate, but a wrong model may always be selected, and even if
appropriate it may be wrongly scaled. We know from perceptual
experiments in situations where only minimal information is available
that both selection and scaling can be quite wrong. So it is a small step
to say that in the absence of any sensory information entirely wild
models might be called up. This could be the case in dreaming, and in
drug or fatigue-induced hallucinations. Hallucinogenic drugs might
call up internal models either by increasing cortical noise or by
reducing the threshold criteria for acceptance of the stored models.

Abnormal conditions such as schizophrenia might be caused by
inappropriate models being built in the first place, or by wrong selection criteria being employed. Greater knowledge of the processes and
conditions for perceptual learning might have implications for
psychiatry. If the models *are* our internal world, we should find out
more about them.

Implications for the design of robots. Devices which respond to
sources of information are commonplace. There is no difficulty in
arranging for a door to open itself when someone breaks a beam of
light to a photocell. But such devices do not 'see' or 'perceive' in the
sense that we do. Similarly, our reflex blink to a sudden bright light is
not 'seeing', 'perceiving', or 'observing'.

Theories of perception (especially the Gestalt theory) lay far too
much stress on sensory characteristics, giving insufficient weight to
the vital point about perception: perception is geared to *objects*, for it
is objects which are biologically important. Objects are dangerous or
useful, food or disaster; but retinal images, and vibrations of the
tympanum, are of no importance except to indicate the identity of
external objects. The patterns of sensory activity are but symbols
from which reality may be read. This involves far more than the recog-

nition of patterns. Pattern recognition is only an early stage of perception, for objects are more than patterns, and it is objects that matter. Objects have all manner of vitally important properties which are seldom sensed, so current sensory information cannot be adequate for dealing with objects.

On this theory, perception allows behaviour to be appropriate to the hidden properties of objects, when the internal models sufficiently reflect their properties. This is very like the notion of a medical syndrome – a few spots may indicate the past, present, and future course of a disease, together with an appropriate strategy for dealing with it. Once recognized, the syndrome – or perceived objects – may be accepted for guiding the most complex behaviour with but little current information.

The special feature of perception is that it does not mediate behaviour directly from current sensory information, but always via internal models of reality – which themselves reflect the redundancy in space and in time of the external world. This is where perception differs from devices such as photocells actuating doors, or biological reflexes, for these give control directly from the inputs. They do not use the current information to call up appropriate models, giving information drawn from the past of the hidden features of the present situation. The past is usually a reliable guide, and our memory contains vastly more information than can be transmitted in reasonable time by the sensory channels even when the relevant information is available – which is rarely the case.

One might be tempted to think that objects, as perceived, are no more than statistical groupings of sensed events – syndromes of sensation. But to say this is to miss a vital point. Sensed events are categorized also in terms of the use made of them. A book, for example, is seen as a single object. This is because we handle the collection of pages as one object. Sensory inputs are grouped according to the repertoire of behavioural skills of the owner of the perceptual system.

One man's object may be another's pattern – or be nothing but randomness.

This brings out the kind of difficulty we have in imagining the perceptual world of animals, or even people whose interests are very different from our own. It also has implications for designers of robots – machines to see and act on what they see. If they are to respond to objects via internal models – and all the biological advantages will apply to the machine – then its models must be appropriate to *its* sensory inputs and to *its* repertoire of actions. These will differ greatly from ours. But could we communicate with a robot having internal models very different from our own? We should expect the same extreme difficulty that we have in trying to communicate with other animals or with schizophrenics. Even though we design and build our own robot, and know exactly how its circuits function, communication could be impossible when its internal models are not ours.

The status of perceptual brain models. We suppose that perceptual models are aggregates of data about objects, and about how objects behave and interact in various circumstances. Perceptual models bear a resemblance to hypotheses in science. We may think of sensory data suggesting, testing, and sometimes modifying perceptual models in much the same way that scientific data suggest, test, and modify theory and hypothesis in science. A precise comparison of perceptual processes with the logic and method of scientific inquiry could be highly rewarding.[1]

We are concerned here with not only the logical but also the biological and the engineering status of brain models. Whatever they are, one thing is quite clear – they are not isomorphic pictures of external shapes. The Gestalt theory misses the point here, for all sorts of information about objects must be stored but pictures can only represent specific shapes and colours. Shape and colour have only indirect significance: what matters is whether the object is useful, a threat, or food. It is non-optical properties that are important. When we look at a picture, we can read all kinds of significance beyond mere shape and colour. The picture serves to evoke our internal models, which have been developed by handling objects, so that non-optical features have become associated. Similarly the pictures in the eye, the retinal images, only have significance when related to non-optical properties of objects. Without such correlations all pictures, including retinal images, would be meaningless – mere patterns. The artist by presenting selected visual features plays games with our internal brain models, and may quite drastically change them by evoking new associations. It is clear that the brain models cannot be logically at all like pictures, for though pictures can evoke models, their appropriateness is in terms of objects, not pictures, which in themselves are utterly trivial.

The computer engineer will ask: are these supposed brain models digital or analogue? This distinction is important to the engineer, because analogue and digital systems have very different design features and advantages and disadvantages for various purposes. Indeed, it is possible to make an informed guess as to which system is adopted by the brain in terms of speed of operation, types of errors, and other

---

[1] This project was planned by Norwood Russell Hanson and myself, but tragically Russ Hanson was killed in a plane crash.

characteristics typical of analogue or digital engineering systems (cf. Gregory, 1953*b* [No. 47]). The engineering distinction arises from the fact that in practice analogue systems work continuously but digital systems work in precisely defined discrete steps. This difference is immensely important to the kinds of circuits or mechanical systems used, and vital practical implications follow. Discontinuous systems can have much higher reliability in the presence of 'noise' disturbance. Analogue devices can have much faster data transmission rates, but their precision is limited to around 0·1%. There is no limit in principle to the number of significant figures obtainable from a digital computer, if it has space enough and time.

Because of the clear engineering distinction between continuous and discontinuous systems, there is a temptation to define analogue in terms of continuous, and digital in terms of discontinuous. But this will not do. We can imagine click stops fitted to a slide rule: this would make it discontinuous, but it would still be an analogue device. We must seek some deeper distinction.

The point, surely, is that analogue and digital systems both represent things, and so in both cases their internal states represent something else. The essential difference between them is not in their engineering, but rather that they represent logically different kinds of things. The distinction is between *actual events in the world*, which occur continuously, and *symbolic representations of events*, which are always discontinuous. (Even the continuous functions of differential calculus have to be handled as though they were discrete steps.)

A continuous computing device can work without going through the steps of an analytical or mathematical procedure. A digital device, on the other hand, has to work through the steps of an appropriate mathematical or logical system. This means that continuous computers functioning directly from input variables necessarily lack power of analysis, but they can work as fast as the changes in their inputs – and so are ideal for real-time computing systems provided high accuracy is not required. The perceptual brain must work in real time, and it does not need the accuracy or the analytical power of a digital system following the symbolic steps of a mathematical treatment of the situation. Perceptual motor performance only has an accuracy of around one per cent. It seems that a continuous analogue system is appropriate for perceptual data processing. This holds both for actual brains and future robots.

Perceptual learning involves not the development of software programmes for programming a digital system according to mathematical analyses of the behaviour of objects, but rather by developing quite crude continuous analogues of the organism's input-output functions, in the presence of recognized objects. From the point of view of the perceptual computer, objects represent transfer functions between the organism's input and output in various situations. Behaviour is given by selecting the appropriate transfer functions, which are stored in the perceptual model elicited by the recognized object.

To build a seeing machine, we must provide more than an 'eye' and a computer. It must have limbs, or the equivalent, to discover non-optical properties of objects for its eyes' images to take on significance in terms of objects and not merely patterns. The computer must work in real time. It need not work according to analytical symbolic descriptions of the physical world – all it requires are quite crude analogues of input-output functions selected by distinguishing features of objects. These collections of transfer functions give appropriate behaviour through predictions, made possible by the redundancy of the world of objects. Ultimately the perceptual brain models reflect the redundancy of the external world – when they do so correctly we see aspects of reality without illusion.

53 *The evolution of eyes and brains – a hen-and-egg problem*

[The next paper, though speculative, follows directly from the final paper of the Experiments section, No. 32, *The curious eye of* Copilia. This investigation directly suggested the following speculation of the origin of visual perception in evolution. There are several predictions, of what should be found, some of which we are engaged in testing in the laboratory.]

★   ★   ★

IT is a truism, but nevertheless true, that all new knowledge comes through the senses. This at once suggests an intimate link between the evolutionary development of brains and eyes. Somehow, brains and eyes developed by the random steps forming the evolutionary ladder, according to the dictates of survival-value at each rung. Once started, there was no question of 'back to the drawing board', for once the thing began ceaseless competition forced it to go on, with little opportunity for experiments on the side. The development of perceptual mechanisms took place under the kind of restraints we find in hard-pressed industry, rather than in the unhurried speculation of the ivory tower, where fantasy blooms and even hopeless experiments may prosper for lack of competition.

The restraints imposed upon the development of perception by natural selection are some help in trying to guess how eyes and brains came into being. Unfortunately, the fossil record is almost useless, for the crucial steps took place long before the incunabula of the rocks begins. We may, however, look at existing primitive forms, and try to put them into sequence according to various criteria. We shall not here attempt any detailed account, but rather try to outline how the principal forms of eye could have come about, and consider the hen-and-egg problem of the relation between eyes and brains through

602

evolution, to give perception. Which came first, the brain or the eye? How could either develop without the other?

THE ORIGIN OF SIMPLE EYES

By a 'simple' eye is meant an eye which has but a single optical system (generally a lens, though it could be a pinhole) serving many photoreceptors. This may be contrasted with the 'compound' eyes found in arthropods, such as insects, which have up to many thousand individual optical systems, each with its own photoreceptor. Clearly both kinds of eye have to have appropriate neural systems to handle the information the eyes provide. We start, then, with a hen-and-egg problem, for it is very difficult to imagine how an eye could develop unless there were some suitable neural system already present. But also, why should there be a 'visual' neural system before there was an eye? If we can find some kind of an answer to this, we may be able to go on to consider why there should be the two great classes of eye – 'simple' and 'compound'.

The surface skin of all primitive creatures, even the single-celled, is sensitive to light, which may give negative or positive phototropisms in the simplest creatures. Evidently the first skin pigments absorbed light (and heat), and started off as crude insensitive photoreceptors. (Photopigments probably developed to accept solar energy, as in plants.) (See Walls 1963.)

Animals live in a world of objects, some edible, some dangerous, some protecting (such as crevices in rock), with many objects irrelevant to survival. Now objects have many characteristics beyond shape and colour – which alone are represented by optical images – and it is these *other* characteristics which are biologically important. One cannot be attacked and eaten by an image (hence, indeed, the purely vicarious pleasures of the cinema) and neither can one eat images. It follows that information given by eyes is only of indirect use to living creatures. To make use of it, a good deal of computing is required. Other senses, especially touch and smell, do however give information which is of immediate use to the survival of primitive creatures. We may with some confidence assume that it is these senses which were first developed.

Now touch receptors on the skin can signal pattern and movement, so it is reasonable to suppose that the touch neural system was taken over and used for primitive 'shadow vision'. Indeed, primitive creatures will not distinguish between moving shadows falling on their skins and actual contact with moving objects. It would seem that the same nervous system served both touch and the first crude vision.

It is rather easy to imagine gradual improvement in light-sensitivity; certain cells becoming specialized photoreceptors, developing in regions where they would be most useful in detecting danger, or crevices for shelter. The ends of the animal were favoured with the first true eyes, which were gradually deepening pits lined with specialized light-sensitive cells. The pits served to increase the contrast of shadows, by reducing ambient light. They were like the shafts dug in the ground by ancient astronomers to see stars in the daytime. Plato describes how Thales fell down such a pit, being so eager to know what was going on in the heavens that he could not see in front of his own feet, and being rallied by 'a clever and pretty maidservant from Thrace'. Thales should have covered his pit to prevent such accidents, and it seems that the eye pits of primitive creatures did develop covers – transparent windows – preventing blockage by alien bodies (not astronomers however, but rather particles of floating food and grains of sand). These windows, it is supposed, gradually thickened towards their centers, as this increased intensity where it was most useful – at the bottom of the eye pits, where ambient light was already at a minimum. This process would gradually evolve a lens giving, finally, true image formation. There must then have been the biggest jolt since life began, for the ancient touch neural system suddenly had its inputs reversed, with the optical reversals of the lens (or pinhole). This required extensive neural reorganization, which we see today in the weird crossings of the vertebrate nervous system.

It is not difficult to see why, for mobile creatures, even a primitive eye should have such advantage over touch that it transformed the entire nervous system. The essential point is that touch is inevitably limited to signalling the presence of objects in actual contact with the creature, while even the crudest shadow vision gives some information of *distant* events. Now information of objects distant in space gives warning of the future; and this is the crucial advantage of all distance receptors. Provided there is a brain capable of handling the information, behaviour can be far more elaborate, and subtly adapted to changing conditions, when the future can be guessed from the present. Touch always arrives too late – and it gives no warning, no computing time – to devise a strategy to deal with the situation. Eyes are early warning systems, allowing brains to transcend mere reflexes, to give strategic behaviour. In this sense, surely, the development of the brain must have had to wait upon the image-forming eye.

We may suppose, then, that the simple eye with its single lens and host of densely spaced photoreceptors, developed from the skin. We may also suppose that the visual brain developed from the ancient

touch nervous system, to go beyond reflexes to give strategy behaviour.

It is not too difficult to imagine the simple eye developing from the
gradually deepening pits, covered by protecting windows which became lenses through central thickening. It is, however, more difficult
to conceive how the compound eye came about. How could many
identical optical systems arise by natural selection, when a single one
would be useless?

THE ORIGIN OF COMPOUND EYES

Each unit, or ommatidium, of a compound eye consists of three basic
elements. There is first the *corneal lens*, then a second lens, the *cone
lens*, and finally the photoreceptor or *rhabdomere*. Compound eyes are
found in the first fossils, in trilobites from the lower Cambrian rocks
of around 600 million years ago. They appear essentially the same as
modern insect eyes. But since there is no earlier fossil record, we must
guess at the first stages as well as we can, using existing creatures as
living examples of what occurred in the distant past, however uncertain the order may be. There is a special difficulty about the compound eye, for what could be the intermediary steps giving rise to
many separate and identical elements, each complete with lens and
photoreceptor? It is difficult enough to imagine how the simple eye
developed – but several hundred, all at once? And yet a single photoreceptor with a lens all its own would seem quite pointless. Or is it?

Let us have a slight digression, and return to the problem after
considering the role of touch in a little more detail. It is here, I suggest, that we find a clue to the problem of the development of compound eyes.

We have supposed that the simple eye took over existing touch
neural mechanisms, and we will later point out that there are quite
basic reasons for supposing that touch was necessary for the first eyes.
The same reasons hold for the compound eye. Now, there are two
kinds of touch, involving entirely different neural mechanisms:
passive touch and *active touch*.

Passive touch is the reception of patterns by contact with areas of
skin. Active touch is very different: it requires exploratory movements of a limb or probe. The movements of the probe are signalled
to the nervous system either by monitoring of commands, or by
proprioceptive feedback. There are vital differences between active
and passive touch, the main ones being: (1) Passive touch gives information only of structures lying on the two-dimensional surface of

the skin; while active touch can give information of the third dimension. (2) Considering the neural systems involved, passive touch is mediated by a *large number of parallel neural channels* sending simultaneous pattern information to the nervous system; while active touch is essentially *single-channel*. It signals structure in three dimensions, but spread out in time as the probe explores external space. The nervous mechanisms responsible for passive touch require a large number of nerve fibres transmitting in parallel simultaneously, while active touch requires essentially but a single channel, transmitting information of the limb position as it traces structure in time. Not only the peripheral but also the central neural systems mediating these two kinds of touch must be very different. Now I shall suggest that the *compound* eye originally fed its information into this second touch neural system: the system mediating *active* touch. I shall suggest that the modern compound eye is a multiplication of single units, which originally were moving photic probes, seeking out structure and signalling down a single channel through time – as in a moving limb exploring structure by active touch.

Is there an actual example, in a living creature which we can examine, of such a single-unit eye working as a moving photic probe? Indeed there is. The author – thanks to the kindness of Professor J. Z. Young and the Marine Biology Laboratory, Naples – with his colleagues Dr Neville Moray and Miss Helen Ross, had the opportunity to find and examine just such an eye (Gregory *et al.*, 1964 [No. 32]). The clue to its existence came from a paper by Exner (1891) in which he reported a small copepod, *Copilia*, living in the waters of the bay of Naples. He described it as having a pair of strange eyes, like telescopes, with two lenses; the second 'eyepiece' lens being deep in the body, and in 'continual lively motion'. Following the description, we set out to find and describe this unique creature of the deep, with an eye truly fit to 'see Naples and die'. But we hoped that some, at least, would still be alive. In fact, after almost despairing, we did find *Copilia*. In a month we found seven female specimens and one male: it is the females which I will now describe.

Copilia quadrata is a strange and beautiful creature. The female is four to five millimetres in length, one millimetre in width, and entirely transparent, there being no colouring except for orange pigment surrounding the single photoreceptors of each eye. She is exceedingly difficult to see with the naked eye because she is so transparent; and almost impossible to pick out from among the other planktonic creatures among which she lives. We found her by dragging the sea with a fine net and examining single drops of water, one at a time, with low power microscopes. This is a tedious and lengthy task. Under the microscope *Copilia* is truly a wonderful sight, with every internal structure clearly visible in the living creature. The entire structure of the eyes, even the optic nerve, can be seen clearly with a microscope of medium power.

There are two separate eyes, far removed from each other, at either side of the creature, whose shape is unusual for a copepod, being very wide at its anterior. There are two huge lenses (looking like automobile headlights) placed far apart in front. Each eye has two lenses: the large anterior lens, of beautiful shape, and a second smaller lens shaped like a pear, situated deep inside the transparent body of the creature. Almost half her total volume is taken up by the two eyes. Attached to the second, posterior, lens is a long orange-pigmented structure which extends back from the posterior lens and curves inward, but does not touch its fellow of the other eye. The posterior lens is situated at the image plane of the large anterior lens, and it moves with a 'sawtooth' scan, horizontally across the image plane of the first lens. The scanning rate varies from about one scan per two seconds to about five scans per second. Each scan has a sawtooth wave form, and the eyes are exactly synchronized; the second lens and photoreceptor of each approaching and receding precisely together. The resting position is with the optical units away from each other, near the tough transparent outer cuticle of the creature; from which position they rapidly approach each other, and then slowly separate across the image of their respective anterior lenses (Fig. 53.1).

The optic nerve is clearly visible; it arises from about halfway down the pigmented photoreceptor and enters the brain, which is located at the centre of the creature. *Copilia* is a filter-feeder, with very simple mouth parts, feeding like a whale. There is almost certainly sexual reproduction, requiring recognition of the male – who, typically of the copepodia, is dull by comparison with the female and comparatively passive. We do not really know just what use *Copilia* makes of her eyes, but what does seem clear is that each eye is a single optical unit, working by temporal scanning, like a simple television camera. It is, indeed, a single-channel optic probe. Detailed examination of the structure of the eye reveals something very interesting. Each of the elements of the eye is extremely similar to corresponding elements of a single ommatidium of a modern compound eye. The spacing between the anterior and posterior lenses is however quite different: distant in *Copilia* but almost touching in arthropods. But the lenses themselves, and especially the single 'rod' photoreceptors, are almost identical. It is possible that *Copilia* is a surviving form of a prototype single-channel scanning eye, from which the compound eye developed by multiplication of the elements, to give finally mosaic vision. It seems

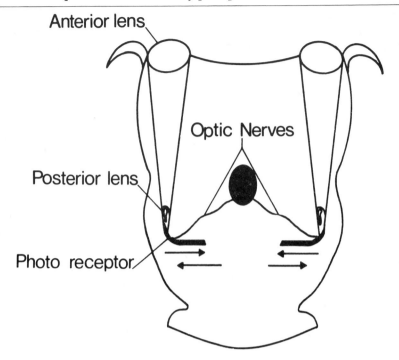

FIG. 53.1 *A schematic drawing of the copepod* Copilia quadrata. *Each eye has two lenses: a large anterior lens and a second smaller lens deep in the body, with an attached photoreceptor and single optic nerve fibre to the central brain. The second lens and photoreceptor are in continual movement across the image plane of the first lens. This seems to be a scanning eye: a mechanical television camera.*

easier to suppose this than that a hundred or a thousand units sprang up together. But why should the prototype single-element scanning eye give way to its multiple development – the 'modern' compound eye? The answer to this seems fairly clear. There is a basic engineering limitation of all scanning systems: namely, that the amount of information they can transmit is limited by the information capacity of the channel. Now the channel capacity of any nerve fibre found in nature is extremely low, compared with electronic channels. At best, the maximum frequency response approaches only 1000 pulses per second; while, for comparison, to transmit 625-line television pictures we need about a 6-million-cycle band width. Even granting that sophisticated perceptual systems save channel capacity by various tricks, a vast discrepancy remains. Now if a scanning eye were duplicated, the elements could send down information simultaneously. This would be rather like exploring a structure with two fingers at once. We may then add three fingers, four fingers . . . a thousand fingers. Finally, there is no need to sweep the hand of a thousand fingers – or the eye of a thousand optical units – across the structure, for the entire pattern can be signalled by simultaneous transmission down the many *static* channels. We may suppose, then, that although the compound eye started by using the single channel, and the temporal information-processing of active touch, it ended by developing many static parallel channels, to become finally like the simple eye based upon the passive touch neural system. Interestingly enough, we still can find compound eyes which have too few elements to have entirely abandoned scanning (or active exploration) by each photic probe. In *Daphnia* we find a compound eye of about 20 elements (actually 22), and this eye is in continuous oscillatory movement. Here we seem to see an eye which is halfway up the sequence between the single-channel scanning eye of *Copilia* and the fully developed static compound eye, containing enough elements to match the optical acuity of each element. In *Daphnia* there are but few units, and it seems that the deficiency is made up by oscillatory scanning, very like the unique single-unit eye of *Copilia*.

We have outlined, in general terms, a possible sequence of events leading to simple and to compound eyes. Each, we suppose, took over and developed for its own use the primordial neural mechanisms mediating touch. The *simple* eye taking over the *passive* touch system; the prototype scanning unit, later forming *compound* eyes by multiplication, taking over *active* touch neural mechanisms. By supposing that in each case already existing touch mechanisms were taken over for vision, we escape the hen-and-egg problem of which came first. This is some justification for the assumption that touch came first, but now we should examine other and deeper reasons for this assumption. We will jump a hundred million years or so.

It is important to note that our argument here will attempt to be general, covering not only actual nervous systems and eyes as evolved on earth, including our own, but also any conceivable perceiving machine made by man, or any life form presented with the same problems to be found on other worlds than earth.

THE ORIGIN OF VISUAL PERCEPTION

What are the essential differences between perception in primitive creatures and in man? It is generally believed that primitive perception is largely a matter of reflex neural mechanisms, activated by more or less specific 'stimuli', though affected by certain internal states of readiness, or need. Perceptual learning is certainly minimal in primitive creatures; and so we must suppose that these special visual patterns have taken on significance through ancestral disasters, just as in the development and inheritance of more obvious structural characteristics through natural selection. Some insects do show visual learning – bees, for example, learn key features of the terrain around their nests for navigation – but this ability becomes infinitely greater in mammals and especially the primates. Now what is clear is that perception, as it developed phylogenetically, became less and less tied to specific visual patterns, so that finally a large variety of patterns elicited the same behaviour. We may say that perception becomes geared to responding to *objects*, no matter how they are presented to the senses. Retinal images become indicators, symbols, of the presence and position of objects lying in three-dimensional space. The point is: we perceive far more than is actually sensed in each moment of perception. We 'see' that a table is hard, and a chair safe to sit upon. We 'see', from a smile, that a person is pleased. Now all this goes far beyond the given sensory data, and yet it is generally correct. This ability of the human perceptual system to go beyond immediate data is brought out most dramatically by considering cartoons. A few lines convey an entire story, with the personality of each person and his mood. It is astonishing that this is so. It is useful to think of perceptions as *hypotheses*, based upon, but not limited by, current sensory data.

No one would want to argue that an insect or lower vertebrate would appreciate a cartoon. (Though this does suggest experiments, and is indeed the basis of the ethologist's studies of 'releaser stimuli', where isolated and sketchy features can initiate complex behaviour as in the full visual situation.) The point is that when visual information leads to behaviour appropriate to nonvisual features – indicated but not given directly by the retinal image – such as the hardness, or solidity, of a table, though the image is not hard or solid, then the retinal image is acting as a *sign of things beyond itself*. Images are thus symbols: like words in a language. Like any other symbols, there must be a process of initial learning by association. We may gain some clues here by considering the learning of languages, and here it is useful to use Russell's distinction between, 'knowledge by acquaintance' and 'knowledge by description' (Russell, 1940). It is necessary for a repeated event (e.g. a speech sound) to become a symbol, to be linked to other events to give it meaning. All knowledge by description is ultimately dependent upon knowledge by acquaintance, for otherwise symbols are in a logical vacuum. Retinal images as symbols must be given meaning by association with other sensory experience.

We may take a comparatively simple example. Retinal images are but flat projections of a three-dimensional world, and yet they give perception of three dimensions. If we consider this problem quite generally – as in designing a perceiving machine – we find that there must be direct and nonvisual information of the third dimension for images to become symbols of the extra, third, dimension. What other information can there be? The obvious candidate is touch. It appears that any conceivable perceiving device relying on two-dimensional images without adequate extra optical aids (e.g. stereopsis) must use, at some stage, touch information if it is to see in three dimensions.

Dependence upon early touch experience for visual perception in man is supported by evidence from cases of recovery from congenital and early blindness (Gregory and Wallace 1963 [No. 3]), and in kittens from the work of Held and Hein (1963). Now what is true for development of perception in the individual, should also be true for the development of primitive vision through evolution, in so far as primitive creatures judge distances from their retinal images. (This suggests a host of experiments. Perhaps the Held and Hein experiment with active and passive kittens was a little too severe in its conditions – what would happen if limb movements are systematically disturbed? Would this upset later visual perception *systematically*?)

If we now go on to ask why it should be *active* movements which are as important as appears to be the case, we are on less sure ground, for one might design a perceiving machine to gain its correlations between direct contact with the world and its ambiguous retinal images either by passive or by active movements. We will, however, hazard the guess that in primitive sea-living creatures without skeletal limbs, command signals would be more reliable than proprioceptive feedback and that limb position was first given by monitoring of command signals and not by feedback. Octopus tentacles do not possess proprioception: perhaps without rigid skeleton or joints it would be too difficult to provide. Creatures immersed in water have approximately zero effective weight, so command signals would be expected to produce predictable movement in any direction. It may be that feedback control is only important for creatures living in a gravity environment, when the same command will give very different movements in different directions. If it is the case that proprioception is a late development in nervous systems, then perhaps we have a clue as to why *active* appear to be more important than *passive* movements for perceptual learning in man.

(It would be interesting to compare the octopus, weightless through floating in the sea, with a human astronaut in zero gravity. Does he return to a primitive preference for command signals for controlled movement? Is it possible that without gravity, he may be better than on earth at precise manual tasks, through not requiring feedback from his limb positions? This might make an interesting space experiment.)

CONCLUSION

All this is, of course, speculative. But in science, as in the stock market, speculation can lead to important gains provided we are lucky. Insights into the evolutionary sequences by which perception came into being do not, and cannot, tell us directly what goes on or how it works, but they may provide some guiding principles for planning experiments. The brain is so complicated that any guides, however uncertain, are better than none. There are three guides used implicitly in this sketchy account: (1) a possible evolutionary sequence, especially of the development of the two great classes of eyes; (2) limitations imposed by engineering considerations; (3) limitations imposed by logical considerations. Examples of engineering limitations would be the maximum band width of actual nerve fibres which would inevitably limit the performance (and therefore the development) of any biological scanning-type eye. If such an eye is to develop it has to change its manner of function. Other limitations are imposed by the maximum resolution possible for a given optical aperture, and there are many others which must be borne in mind as we come to explore more central neural mechanisms. Computer design considerations may not give the answers here, but they certainly can tell us what is *not* feasible, for brains of given size and complexity.

By *logical* considerations, I mean that there are always certain really basic requirements for any *conceivable* system to function. Thus it seems a logical necessity that certain patterns or objects should be accepted as surrogates of other objects or situations for them to have meaning – to be symbols. Once perception develops to the stage where the retinal image conveys more than is given directly – more than shape from one viewpoint, and colour – then it is logically necessary to suppose that there must have been (in the past of the animal or its ancestry) direct experience of nonvisual features by other senses, for these features to be 'read' by the brain from retinal images. For example, if hardness is 'read' optically, then the visual indications of hardness must have been established through touch associated with these optical characteristics of the image. We should think of perceptual learning as involving this sort of association between the senses as a logical necessity, for any visual system to perceive non-optical features in the world of objects (cf. *The Intelligent Eye*). This is a logical point, in the sense that any conceivable biological man-made perceiving device must have this non-visual information for its 'retinal' images to be symbols of non-optical characteristics. It is also necessary for optical characteristics which are not present in a given image, such as the third dimension from single stationary two-dimensional images. How far this extra information is given by modification through natural selection – phylogenetic learning – and how far through individual perceptual learning is a matter for experiment, but there are good reasons for believing that only associations having marked survival value over long periods of time will be inherited. All the rest must be learned by the individual with each new generation.

Sensory information is used, once rich associations have been built up, to suggest and test visual hypotheses of prevailing external reality. Sensory information no longer determines behaviour by reflexes, and we live not strictly according to the present state of external affairs but rather according to the probable future and what we want to do about it. The eye, by making prediction possible, allowed the brain to develop. The developed brain entertains many possibilities only some of which are true. I hope this theory is one of them.

54 *The speaking eye*

[The following appeared at the time of publication of *The Intelligent Eye* (1970) and describes some of the themes of that book. The discussion starts by distinguishing between perception of objects and perception of *pictures* of objects. It is argued that these are surprisingly different, and that some unfortunate confusion has arisen in perceptual research through the use of pictures as test material, when pictures are, in an important sense, paradoxical – through being both objects in their own right and simultaneously representing quite other objects of different scale and in a different space. It is suggested that the specifically human capacities to draw and appreciate pictures, and to write speak and understand language, are perhaps linked in no accidental way but represent an almost unitary skill; a skill unique to human beings. This raises many questions: What is special – unique – about the human brain? Does the use of symbols confer these special powers to brains (or machines) representing the states, and following the moves of symbolic 'games'? Has symbolic thought and expression developed from the brain's perceptual 'computer' – concerned long before language with interpreting sensory data in terms of external object situations? Why have only human brains (and computers?) this special power to handle language?]

★   ★   ★

Because the eye is physically so like a camera, and because in general we are so used to seeing things without conscious effort, it is difficult to appreciate the enormously complicated processes that must be going on in the brain for vision to be possible. When we 'see' a cup, for instance, a curved image of the cup in perspective is projected onto the retina at the back of the eye and stimulates nerve cells there. What obviously does not happen next is that this effect is transmitted to the part of the brain connected with vision to activate there, a region shaped and coloured like the cup. And yet somehow the

614

patterns of light and colour at the retina are interpreted, so that the brain 'perceives' a solid object existing in external space. More than that, the brain also 'knows', for example, that the eye's view of the rim of the cup as an ellipse would become a circle if the eye were moved over it, and it 'knows', or anticipates, what the cup would feel like, and what sensations one would get if one tried to move it. This is a unique property of the brain, and as yet there has been small success in designing machinery that can emulate it.

Just what goes on in the brain is beginning to become clear, particularly from the work of two American physiologists, D. H. Hubel and T. N. Wiesel. By electrical recordings from individual cells in the parts of a cat's brain concerned with vision, they discovered that patterns at the eye are 'described' by what might be called the internal language of perception. In their experiments, a fine wire electrode was placed on a brain cell while the eye was stimulated with moving or stationary lines, or with shapes of various kinds. It was found that a given cell gave a signal only when the eye was stimulated with a certain shape, or with movement in a given direction. Apparently optical patterns at the eye are broken down into elements and described by combinations of features selected by these cells and the nerves connected with them. In much the same way as we might describe an object or a scene in words, so these activated cells present to the brain mechanisms further up the line, features which identify the object as a circle, a house or whatever. It turns out that the visual brain is organized in many functional layers. As the message that started at the retina passes through these layers, more and more features of the seen object – its colour, characteristics signalled by the other senses, and perhaps associated memory information – are added to the initial pattern as described by its lines of various slopes, its curves and parts which move.

The continual task of translating images on the retina into 'perceptions' of objects involves the brain in an extraordinarily difficult problem-solving activity. Generally we are not aware of it as being any kind of a problem, but there are shapes or objects that do present difficult, even impossible, problems. These can make us aware of alternative solutions, only one of which can fit reality. Language, as we all know, can produce sentences where the meaning is unclear or confusing; similarly, there are visual uncertainties, ambiguities and even paradoxes when things look logically impossible. The fact that a pattern on the retina may be seen at one moment as one thing and the next moment as another, shows how we 'search' for an adequate answer – we try different explanations in the hope of recognizing the correct one. In cases when there is more than one likely answer, the brain cannot make up its mind! What we see may change to something else, and back again, forever.

The 'impossible' wooden triangle shown on page 369 really exists, and yet, when looked at directly from one point, it looks quite wrong. It looks flat when it is really three-dimensional, and it has each corner in an impossible relation to the others. Evidently the usually reliable assumptions adopted for solving the continual problem 'What object is casting this image in the eye?' are here misleading – and yet the assumptions are so firmly held that we are driven to a conclusion that we know is ridiculous. We see that the 'perceptual' answer to this problem is wrong, and yet we cannot change it. If this is true of how we see, is it true of how we think? If we faced our beliefs squarely, would they be just as paradoxical?

The ability to perceive objects occurred late in the evolution of brains. In the simpler creatures there were no more than reflex responses to certain stimuli. Most of what was within visual range was filtered out by the eye and not signalled to the brain. These creatures reacted to any shadow as a sign of danger, or turned away from light. Even we, as highly evolved creatures, respond directly to stimuli when we are startled; as by a sudden noise or flash of light, or when hurt by a blow, or a hot object. We do not pause to identify the origin of the light, the blow or the burn; we respond purely to the physical stimulus, in a quite primitive way, avoiding hurt or danger as quickly as possible.

What we call perception in man and the higher animals is a far more subtle matter, for it is concerned with objects and not determined by mere stimuli. Perceptions are guesses – hypotheses – as to what object has produced the stimulation of the nerves. When we 'see' things, what we see – what is present in the mind – are hypotheses of what object, or kind of object, stimulated the eye. One might indeed think of perceptual hypotheses as the earliest form of belief. By developing elaborate internal descriptions of objects the brain escaped the tyranny of reflexes: decisions no longer depended directly on data available to the centres at that particular moment. The available sensory data could be used far more effectively, because the information could be expanded in terms of what had been learned in the past. The fact that there are perceptual illusions of many kinds, however, does seem to show that our perceptual hypotheses are only barely adequate. In unusual or specially misleading situations they can let us down badly.

The average human brain is more than twice as heavy as the brain of the gorilla, the largest of the other primate brains, but our ability to use pictures and languages can hardly be due to overall brain size.

There is a rare kind of human dwarfism (Tom Thumb was affected by it) in which the adult is as little as 23 inches in height, and yet has normal proportions. The brains of these dwarfs are correspondingly smaller than normal human brains – and are smaller than the brains of many apes. Even so, these human dwarfs can understand language and speak quite well. This suggests that the ability to use language depends on the presence of some crucial structure in the brain, rather than on brain size as a whole. We have a good idea of what is important from the work of an American neurologist, Norman Geshwind, who found that the human brain is uniquely rich in pathways linking the senses of vision, hearing and touch. Now in order to develop and use words or pictures, sounds must be associated with the appearance and feel of external objects. These associations must also be related to emotional states, associated with primitive regions of the brain, and to memory. It seems that the brains of monkeys simply lack the number of association pathways between the senses that are required to use symbols. Once brains developed, in evolutionary history, the ability to use symbols, these symbols turned out to be incredibly powerful tools. Given language, and rules of logic and mathematics, we can solve problems that our nearest biological relations cannot begin to grasp. What is so remarkable is that human thought is so powerful though our brains are essentially similar to other brains. It seems that symbols confer decisive power: once appropriate rules for using them are known, the way we use our brains is radically different from what we may call 'biological thought'. Man, with tools and symbolic languages, stepped, at this moment in evolution, out of the world of mere biological reality, to become unique.

Pictures are most odd. They have, perceptually, a kind of double reality: they exist as objects in their own right – and at the same time they represent quite other objects, in a different space and a different time. In this, pictures are like written sentences, which are both marks on paper and representatives of quite different things. This double reality is common to all symbols, and it presents a problem that only the human brain can solve. An ape seeing a banana may eat it, or throw it in fun at his mate; but seeing a banana as a banana is quite different from seeing a picture of a banana. We do not mistake the picture for a banana – we do not try to eat it – and yet we see it as representing a banana. The picture *means* a banana, though it is clearly not one. Also, the picture is flat, and yet we know that the banana it represents is a three-dimensional object. The picture looks both flat and, in a way, three-dimensional – which is impossible for any object. Pictures are paradoxical, impossible, and yet by accepting them we became unique in nature.

FIG. 54.1 *Egyptian figure drawings did not represent depth. What they seem to have done is to 'assemble' a human body, for example, from component bits. The pictures were later used as abstract symbols.*

It seems that it was the artists of the Cromagnon cave men, of 20,000 years ago, who made the great breakthrough, from seeing objects merely as objects to accepting certain objects as meaning something else. This breakthrough was surely the first vital step to symbolic language, to the use of numbers and, eventually, organized scientific hypotheses and theories.

The first known drawings were cartoons; a few well-chosen lines evoking a stricken animal or a hunting scene. It was many thousands of years before artists represented objects naturalistically in a fair semblance of the three-dimensional space that objects inhabit. The Egyptians, for example, did not succeed in showing sloping surfaces accurately in their technical drawings. They could not draw the top of a table, or a draught board, as viewed from the side so that the state of play could be seen. People were represented as combinations of typical views, the whole being anatomically impossible, and yet this 'identikit' of views serves well enough as a pictorial language. Why was realistic drawing so difficult for the Egyptians, and why did it take so long to achieve?

Objects were probably not represented in the perspective of retinal images and photographs until the Italian Renaissance. The first strict perspective drawings were made by the designer of the dome of Florence cathedral, Brunelleschi (1377–1446). It seems that the needs of architecture demanded a scientific solution to the problem of representing three-dimensional objects as realistically as possible on the flat surface of a picture, and that artists were aided by such scientific developments as the *camera obscura*, which optically projected objects on to a flat surface. Leonardo da Vinci describes mechanical methods for solving the problem, which seems to have been beyond the unaided eye of the artist.

The first written languages were pictures arranged to tell a story. We can see in the development of Egyptian hieroglyphics how pictures became adapted to represent simple abstract ideas and eventually logical relations. For instance, it is impossible to convey directly in a picture the notion of 'not' or 'none' – the notion is obviously not to be conveyed by omitting the picture of the object. The Egyptians succeeded in expressing 'no' by representing a typical human gesture as a formal symbol – the arms thrown wide apart. This is probably the origin of our negative sign ' – '. To understand the 'spread-out arms' symbol, it must be seen as more than a pattern or a picture; it is an instruction to think in a certain way, to take a particular step of thought and action.

Familiar objects were represented by the Egyptians with simple drawings we can often recognize. For example the Sun, as one might expect, was represented by a circle. Later this same sign took on further and more abstract meanings; it came to signify not only the disk of the Sun but also 'time', and 'life'. With the development of several abstract meanings, the signs became confusing and ambiguous. The Egyptians could have adopted more and more signs, but in fact they did something more interesting: they used some existing signs as determinatives, to show which kind of meaning was intended. To indicate that the intended meaning was too abstract to be seen in a picture, they added the drawing of a papyrus scroll, rolled tightly and tied up with a bow. Thus the reader was warned to use his imagination – to go beyond what could be pictured directly.

As symbols escaped the semblance of objects, and became less like pictures, so they became more powerful. In the development of the determinatives, and of the signs for logical operations, we see how the power of symbols and formal languages as tools developed, drawing men inexorably away from their biological origins. It was, surely, the artists who took the first crucial step; to *see*, and to select and make objects as representing something else; something existing in a different space and time or not existing at all. This used the eye in quite a new way. It was this new use of the eye and the ear to understand symbols which free the brain from immediate reality; and by introducing the strange power of formal symbols it made science possible.

The strangest thing about symbols is that they do not depend upon brains. They can confer the power of symbolic thought to machines. The first recorded mechanical thinking was done with pebbles, laid out to represent numbers (hence *calculi*, the Greek for pebbles, and so 'calculate'). As it turned out, the simple abacus had certain powers greater than the human brain. It is disturbing that a score of beads on strings can transform the brain's power to solve problems. Even more disturbing is the fact that the abacus can easily be mechanized, with gear wheels, and once the mechanics are set up all the human has to do is turn the handle – or switch on the motor – or let the machine sort out how to tackle the problem. The science-fiction fear of the machine taking over, in fact happened long ago, with the invention of formal symbols and mechanical aids to thought. Most profoundly, it was language which changed how we think – and perhaps largely determines what we think about.

As with other tools, language tends to be used most for what it is well suited. It is surprisingly easy to make machines accept symbols and obey rules, to solve certain kinds of problems with superhuman efficiency. It is however, extremely difficult to make machines perform many skills which have been carried out apparently without effort by living creatures for hundreds of millions of years. The development of 'intelligent machines' is quite the reverse of biological evolution; for machines can handle symbols, but cannot perceive the world. In several laboratories attempts are being made to feed computers with optical information, from television cameras, and to teach the machine to recognize surrounding objects; but it turns out to be an extraordinarily difficult problem. Perhaps it is necessary to build into the machine something of the internal language of brains to make it possible. In this way, working backwards, we may make machines quite like organisms.

Now that computers are so obviously a power to be reckoned with, they stir up strong loyalties and antagonisms, which spill over to our attitudes towards symbols and reality, art and science. There is a division between people who accept analytical thinking as a way of life, finding beauty in precise formal statements, and those who react violently against symbolic languages of all kinds, seeking instead the most intense sensory stimulation, through drugs and through music that may be ear-damaging in its intensity.

Does rejection of debate and precise expression represent a fear of 'mechanical' thinking – of becoming de-humanized by the power of symbols? If so, this is a process which started many thousands of years ago and surely cannot be halted without a return to the jungle. If the machine does move the abacus beads, it is we who ask the questions – and we alone who can appreciate the answers, with our unique abacus of brain-cell 'beads'.

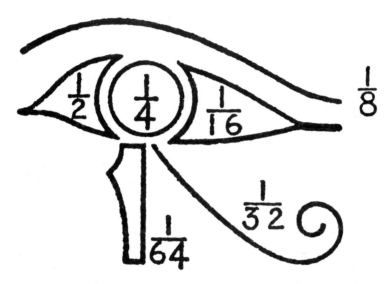

FIG. 54.2 *The sun-eye of the Egyptian god Horus. Fractions were represented by parts of the torn eye of the god – put together again by the god of wisdom: Thoth. Was this the beginning of digital arithmetic?*

55 *The grammar of vision*

[The relationship between perception and language – and especially whether language developed from perception – is taken up again in the following radio talk which raises the possibility that Chomsky's Deep Structure has its origin in the classification of sensory data in terms of the external world.]

★   ★   ★

WHEN we are up against a problem we sometimes have a flash of insight, or a feeling of illumination. 'I *see* the answer,' we say. Or if we are not so bright, we may complain that the situation is 'as clear as mud'. More poetically, I see 'as through a glass darkly'. Now these are all visual analogies for what is essentially an intellectual process: understanding, or the lack of it. Indeed it is difficult to avoid such visual terms when talking about thinking. It now looks as though our use of these visual metaphors is no accident: seeing, thinking and language are inextricably tied up in the brain – so much so that the brain deals with language and vision in much the same ways. If this is so there may be far-reaching consequences both for linguistics and for the study of processes in the brain.

The links between thought, language and vision are not immediately obvious. After all, animals other than man can see but they cannot speak. There is no doubt that animals communicate to each other with cries of warning or entreaty. Cats call to each other, all too vehemently; and even the humble firefly will flash to his mate signals more brilliant than any diamond. But these are not languages in the sense that new situations or concepts can be communicated. Granted that when a dog responds appropriately to the human words, 'Fido – bone', we must suppose that a relation between the sound of the word 'bone' in English, and the object bone, as it is sensed by the nose and eyes of the dog, is established by learning. This could not be an innate response, simply because there is no long ancestral history of the sound of the word 'bone', in English. But animals do not have structured languages, with grammars.

Animals seem to respond to each other's cries and gestures much as they respond to any natural events that give warning of danger, or show the way to food or shelter. Take cows lying down in a field before it rains. Evidently, cows are capable of seeing the sudden formation of cloud and darkening of the sky, possibly much as we do. Whether cows have to learn that these signs mean it is going to rain, or whether they are born with the knowledge already built into their nervous systems is an open question. It is always much harder to determine that something is innate than to be certain that it has to be learned. For example, if we wanted to find out whether each cow has to learn for itself that clouds mean rain, we should have to compare the behaviour of cows living protected from the weather with cows subject to clouds and rain. If we found that the weather-protected cows tended to lie down before rain, then we would infer that weather lore is innate in cows. If the protected animals did not seem to read the signs, then we might decide that this ability is not built into the nervous system; or, if it was built in, the ability was lost through lack of use because the cows were protected.

Inherited associations take thousands of generations to develop because they do so by the slow tortuous processes of natural selection. Perhaps cows tended to die off from the ill-effects of damp fields for so long that those with a glimmering of ability to predict the coming of rain tended to live longer and have more progeny. Such an ability would develop in the same kind of way that a thicker or more water-proof skin would develop, to keep out the damp. It is worth adding that the ability to read the signs, to predict the probable future, has enormous advantages – because danger may be avoided before it occurs.

What has the case of the cow predicting the weather got to do with perception and language? It illustrates that there is no clear distinction between seeing objects straightforwardly as they are – grass to be eaten, or water to be drunk – and using objects and events as signs of something else, even though that 'something else' may be very different from the perceived object it represents or predicts. Rain is very different from the cloud: but evidently differences of appearance present no great problem. It is hard to think of greater differences than the sound of the word 'bone' and the look, feel, taste and smell of the bone itself; yet those great sensory differences obviously do not prevent dogs from recognizing a bone from its smell, its appearance, or the sound of the word 'bone' in our language.

The various characteristics of objects sensed by the nose, the eyes, the tongue and so on are very different in kind from each other. Yet somehow they are brought together by the brain and accepted as various aspects of the same object. This ability is vital for perceiving objects, whether you are an animal or a man. What is odd about associating a word with an object is that, because the word is imposed by a particular language, it is a recent association – recent on any evolutionary time-scale, that is. Moreover, although words are recent, and differ between languages, it is extraordinarily difficult to see an object without thinking of its name. One of the things about abstract paintings that disturbs people to the point of anger is that there are no appropriate names for the shapes on the canvas.

Just because words differ between languages, and because languages are so recent and change so rapidly, it is quite clear that our knowledge of the names of things cannot be innate – it cannot be built into the nervous system. Words and names cannot be inherited. So it has generally been accepted that although much of perception may be innate, all aspects of language must be learned. But, and it is an important 'but', one of the challenges of the new linguistics, led by Noam Chomsky, is a denial that children have to learn all of human language from scratch.

At first sight such a denial seems absurd, if only because babies born in England come to speak English, and those on the Continent French or Italian or whatever. There is no recorded case of a mix-up here, so you might expect we had every reason to believe that languages *are* learned from scratch. Chomsky will not disagree with this. What he does say is that there is far more to language than naming objects. Human languages have a grammatical structure, and it is this structure which is inherited. At first sight, again, this makes no sense. After all, different languages have different grammars, as every schoolboy knows to his cost. But Chomsky is not referring to the specific rules of the grammar of each language – what he calls the 'surface structure' of sentences. He is talking about something more basic. He believes that all languages have a common 'deep structure', from which sentences having acceptable surface structure can be derived, in any natural human language. It is this deep structure which he regards as innate, inherited, and unique to human beings. Here Chomsky seems to have unearthed a fact about language which is so familiar that it took a genius to see it. The thing he pointed out was that we can understand a sentence we have never heard before in our lives, and which may not be associated with any previous event in our experience.

Unique sentences can be understood provided they obey grammatical rules. They must obey the surface-structure rules of the parti-

The point I am driving at is
common for an invention deve
used to solve a quite differen
history of the development fo
most surprised at the apparen
seen as an entirely new bloom
centrated effort to get to the m
dreds of years of development
ing, chemistry and electronics
Now the question arises: di
development of our brain?
millions of years, of somethin
which we finally cashed in on fo
that Chomsky's deep structure
rather something else – devel
some other end.

Let us suppose that the stru
from the way animals came to
The brain must translate the f
the eye for the animal to percei
and retinal system actively cl
that retinal images can be in
characteristics of the physical
survival – because the pattern
are themselves useless. It is obj
or useful, to be handled accorc
ordinary thing is how we, an
retinal images hidden feature
states. We only have to see ou
to know that the rest of her is
up and get breakfast.

There are important similar
about the nature of language.
makes sense of patterns nev
recognize objects from strange
familiar objects fairly well. Tl
tions, because perception is be
rules. The artist can quite eas
seen as objects, and are recogni
which the stairs are always go
devised by L. S. and R. Pen
Escher. We have recently pr
impossible from certain positio

cular language, and these rules in turn obey, for any language, according to Chomsky, the deep structure. The underlying deep structure allows the same thought to be expressed with a variety of surface structures. For example, the same thought is expressed with the sentence, 'the ball is kicked by David', as 'David kicked the ball'. Both these surface structures are generated by the deep structure of language; both are equally acceptable.

But the deep structure is even more powerful than that, because we can recognize that a sentence is grammatically correct even though it is clearly false, or even nonsense. The sentence, 'the cat jumped over the mat', which is quite likely true, and the obviously false 'the mat jumped over the cat', are equally good sentences. Neither violates any grammatical rule. Then there is Chomsky's now famous example of a nonsense sentence: 'Colourless green ideas sleep furiously'. It means nothing, but it is a sentence. And you will have recognized it as a sentence. For if we rearrange the same words we get something we cannot accept as a sentence: 'Furiously sleep ideas green colourless'. Both these arrangements of the same words make nonsense, yet we recognize one as a sentence in English while the other is totally rejected. The simple fact that we can accept unique sentences as sentences shows that our language involves something more than associating events and objects with words or sequences of words. Human language is very different from the case of the dog and his bone: so much so that the task of learning a language from scratch would be impossibly difficult. Now it happens that many psychologists have said the same sort of thing about babies coming to perceive the world of objects with their eyes and other senses. The speed with which babies come to associate the properties of objects, and go on to learn how to predict hidden properties and future events, would be impossible unless some of the structure of the world were inherited – somehow innately built into the nervous system.

To a biologist, Chomsky seems a bit too unconcerned about the origins of his deep structure. He says it is innate, built into the brains of human babies – and leaves it at that. But to the biologist, this presents the problem: how could this unique structuring arise in a mere few thousand years, when other adaptive biological changes are so slow? Our attitude to such a problem has entirely reversed in the course of a century. The Victorians were emotionally upset by the notion that we developed from the lower animals. Today we find it intellectually upsetting to discover a structure in us arising apparently from nowhere, without time for it to have developed by the slow processes of natural selection. The problem here is acute because – on the biological time-scale – structured grammatical language is so

recent. Man is perha
million years ago, eve
such a radical change
probably started a mer

If Chomsky is not w
After all, if innovator:
get off the ground. B
question: what, if any,
tures of perception th
the deep structure of l
thing like the gramma

To answer this ques
of how our human a
thinking. We must sor
of language but also ou
language used as a te
power? Or is it that
animals? In other wor
superior brain? If we
it is useful to draw an
have machinery for ex
are incredibly more e
surprise us because th
invention is applied to
the original design, dra
This is true not only
formation. Long befor
a vital tool for count
precision and speed.
history. With a few be
arithmetic, the brain'
fold: a clear example
system of symbols and

The power of the
symbols, is so great th
work like an abacus
abacus and arithmeti
way. The question is:
to work in a quite nev
would be interesting
birth would be as han
without pencil and
equivalents.

a box or a knife or a fruit we set up a chain of possibilities and predictions, which are organized by what we may call the 'grammar of vision'. Impossible pictures and objects seem to violate the grammar of vision, much as 'furiously sleep ideas green colourless' violates the structure of our language. Much as we read meaning from a printed page in terms of our previous experience of the world, so we read from retinal images the external world of objects and events.

The suggestion is that Chomsky's deep structure of language has its roots in the brain's rules for ordering retinal patterns in terms of objects. More specifically, what I am suggesting is that human language has its roots in a take-over operation, in which man cashed in on the long development through which animals became able to classify objects to read reality from their eyes. If you like, words are the beads of our internal abacus designed for seeing.

Now how much do we know about what goes on in the brain during perception? When communicating with language, we use certain sounds or marks on paper as symbols, and these are organized according to the rules of the language. Does the brain adopt some kind of internal and private set of symbols and grammar for organizing sensory patterns into perception of objects? If so, can physiology tell us what these internal symbols are like?

Over the last ten years, physiologists have discovered that certain patterns at the eye produce activity in specific cells of the brain. For example, a line moving bodily in one direction will cause firing of certain cells, while movement in some other direction will not affect these cells, but will affect others. The American physiologists D. Hubel and T. N. Wiesel have identified a number of features of retinal patterns selected for the internal language of the brain. What emerges from these studies is very different from the old notion that the brain traffics in pictures, like a picture history book. What does emerge is that objects are not pictured, but rather described by selected features of the retinal patterns as represented by the firing of individual brain cells. Very recently Hubel and Wiesel have found how the brain – which of course exists in the same three spatial dimensions as other objects – can represent the many non-spatial dimensions of objects as well. This has always been a great problem for theories which supposed that the brain carries some kind of a picture of a viewed object. Perhaps a circular object might be pictured with a circular brain trace: but how could colour, hardness, temperature or sound be so represented? It is absurd to suppose that when we watch a traffic light turn green, part of our brain turns green to represent it. What is needed is some kind of internal descriptive language. We are beginning to understand this brain language.

cular language, and these rules in turn obey, for any language, according to Chomsky, the deep structure. The underlying deep structure allows the same thought to be expressed with a variety of surface structures. For example, the same thought is expressed with the sentence, 'the ball is kicked by David', as 'David kicked the ball'. Both these surface structures are generated by the deep structure of language; both are equally acceptable.

But the deep structure is even more powerful than that, because we can recognize that a sentence is grammatically correct even though it is clearly false, or even nonsense. The sentence, 'the cat jumped over the mat', which is quite likely true, and the obviously false 'the mat jumped over the cat', are equally good sentences. Neither violates any grammatical rule. Then there is Chomsky's now famous example of a nonsense sentence: 'Colourless green ideas sleep furiously'. It means nothing, but it is a sentence. And you will have recognized it as a sentence. For if we rearrange the same words we get something we cannot accept as a sentence: 'Furiously sleep ideas green colourless'. Both these arrangements of the same words make nonsense, yet we recognize one as a sentence in English while the other is totally rejected. The simple fact that we can accept unique sentences as sentences shows that our language involves something more than associating events and objects with words or sequences of words. Human language is very different from the case of the dog and his bone: so much so that the task of learning a language from scratch would be impossibly difficult. Now it happens that many psychologists have said the same sort of thing about babies coming to perceive the world of objects with their eyes and other senses. The speed with which babies come to associate the properties of objects, and go on to learn how to predict hidden properties and future events, would be impossible unless some of the structure of the world were inherited – somehow innately built into the nervous system.

To a biologist, Chomsky seems a bit too unconcerned about the origins of his deep structure. He says it is innate, built into the brains of human babies – and leaves it at that. But to the biologist, this presents the problem: how could this unique structuring arise in a mere few thousand years, when other adaptive biological changes are so slow? Our attitude to such a problem has entirely reversed in the course of a century. The Victorians were emotionally upset by the notion that we developed from the lower animals. Today we find it intellectually upsetting to discover a structure in us arising apparently from nowhere, without time for it to have developed by the slow processes of natural selection. The problem here is acute because – on the biological time-scale – structured grammatical language is so recent. Man is perhaps a million years old. If language started a million years ago, even this would seem to be too short a time for such a radical change in brain structure and function, yet language probably started a mere 20,000 years ago, at the start of social living.

If Chomsky is not worried about this, I suppose he may be excused. After all, if innovators worried about every detail they would never get off the ground. But recent research is aimed at answering this question: what, if any, is the connection between the inherited structures of perception that we use to interpret events in the world, and the deep structure of languages? Is there a grammar of vision, something like the grammar of a language?

To answer this question, we first have to consider the wider problem of how our human ancestors so rapidly developed the power of thinking. We must somehow explain not only the rapid development of language but also our unique power to solve abstract problems. Is it language used as a tool for thinking which gives our brains such power? Or is it that our brains are so superior to those of other animals? In other words, is language the reason for, or a product of, a superior brain? If we want to consider language as a tool for thought, it is useful to draw an analogy from the tools of technology. Once we have machinery for extending the power and precision of muscles we are incredibly more efficient; and we are efficient in ways that often surprise us because they were not anticipated. Then again, once an invention is applied to a new set of problems, outside the intention of the original design, dramatic improvement may occur quite suddenly. This is true not only of power tools but also of aids for handling information. Long before the modern computer, the simple abacus was a vital tool for counting and for solving arithmetic problems with precision and speed. Indeed, it has an important though unsung history. With a few beads on strings, and the rules for counting and for arithmetic, the brain's power to calculate was increased a thousand-fold: a clear example of mental ability being vastly increased with a system of symbols and the following of rules which any fool can use.

The power of the abacus, and of arithmetical rules and written symbols, is so great that we may infer that the unaided brain does not work like an abacus when solving such problems. Evidently, the abacus and arithmetic rules allow the brain to work in a quite new way. The question is: does spoken language similarly allow the brain to work in a quite new way, giving our brains their unique power? It would be interesting to think that children denied language from birth would be as handicapped in their thinking as we are doing sums without pencil and paper, or without an abacus or its modern equivalents.

The point I am driving at is this. In the history of technology it is common for an invention developed for one kind of problem to be used to solve a quite different problem. If we did not know the history of the development for the original purpose, we would be most surprised at the apparent sudden flowering of what would be seen as an entirely new bloom. For example, the ten years of concentrated effort to get to the moon depended for success upon hundreds of years of development in mathematics, astronomy, engineering, chemistry and electronics undertaken for quite different ends. Now the question arises: did something similar happen in the development of our brain? Was there slow development, over millions of years, of something originally serving some other use – which we finally cashed in on for our language? If so, we may suppose that Chomsky's deep structure did not originally serve language; but rather something else – developed millions of years ago, to serve some other end.

Let us suppose that the structure of language has been taken over from the way animals came to structure the world in order to see it. The brain must translate the fleeting and ever-changing patterns at the eye for the animal to perceive external objects. The animal's brain and retinal system actively classify patterns of light and shade so that retinal images can be interpreted, or 'read', in terms of the characteristics of the physical world. This capability is essential to survival – because the patterns of light and shade of retinal images are themselves useless. It is objects, not images, which are dangerous or useful, to be handled according to their potentialities. The extraordinary thing is how we, and the higher animals, can read from retinal images hidden features of objects and predict their future states. We only have to see our wife's foot sticking out of the bed, to know that the rest of her is there too, and is probably going to get up and get breakfast.

There are important similarities here to what Chomsky has to say about the nature of language. In particular, the perceptual system makes sense of patterns never previously encountered. We can recognize objects from strange points of view and can deal with unfamiliar objects fairly well. There are, however, interesting limitations, because perception is beaten by patterns which violate certain rules. The artist can quite easily produce pictures which cannot be seen as objects, and are recognized as impossible: circular staircases in which the stairs are always going up, the sort of impossible pictures devised by L. S. and R. Penrose and by the Dutch artist M. C. Escher. We have recently produced actual objects which appear impossible from certain positions. Once we classify something as, say, a box or a knife or a fruit we set up a chain of possibilities and predictions, which are organized by what we may call the 'grammar of vision'. Impossible pictures and objects seem to violate the grammar of vision, much as 'furiously sleep ideas green colourless' violates the structure of our language. Much as we read meaning from a printed page in terms of our previous experience of the world, so we read from retinal images the external world of objects and events.

The suggestion is that Chomsky's deep structure of language has its roots in the brain's rules for ordering retinal patterns in terms of objects. More specifically, what I am suggesting is that human language has its roots in a take-over operation, in which man cashed in on the long development through which animals became able to classify objects to read reality from their eyes. If you like, words are the beads of our internal abacus designed for seeing.

Now how much do we know about what goes on in the brain during perception? When communicating with language, we use certain sounds or marks on paper as symbols, and these are organized according to the rules of the language. Does the brain adopt some kind of internal and private set of symbols and grammar for organizing sensory patterns into perception of objects? If so, can physiology tell us what these internal symbols are like?

Over the last ten years, physiologists have discovered that certain patterns at the eye produce activity in specific cells of the brain. For example, a line moving bodily in one direction will cause firing of certain cells, while movement in some other direction will not affect these cells, but will affect others. The American physiologists D. Hubel and T. N. Wiesel have identified a number of features of retinal patterns selected for the internal language of the brain. What emerges from these studies is very different from the old notion that the brain traffics in pictures, like a picture history book. What does emerge is that objects are not pictured, but rather described by selected features of the retinal patterns as represented by the firing of individual brain cells. Very recently Hubel and Wiesel have found how the brain – which of course exists in the same three spatial dimensions as other objects – can represent the many non-spatial dimensions of objects as well. This has always been a great problem for theories which supposed that the brain carries some kind of a picture of a viewed object. Perhaps a circular object might be pictured with a circular brain trace: but how could colour, hardness, temperature or sound be so represented? It is absurd to suppose that when we watch a traffic light turn green, part of our brain turns green to represent it. What is needed is some kind of internal descriptive language. We are beginning to understand this brain language.

It has been known for a long time that the so-called striate area at the back of the brain is especially involved with vision. It is called the striate area because of its distinctive parallel layers of cells. Now what Hubel and Wiesel have found is that cells at the deeper layers represent more abstract characteristics of retinal patterns, and further, that there are many functional 'columns', though these are not normally visible, which represent the addition of more and more descriptive information of the patterns represented at the surface. Down the columns more and more characteristics seem to be added to the first description of mere spatial position and shape until, presumably, an adequate description of perceived objects is built up, much like a sentence describing the same object. From this work we begin to understand the words of the language of perception, but it is far from clear how they are put together. In other words, the mechanism of the grammar underlying the perceptual sentences is still hidden from us.

The position now is that linguistics is giving insights concerning the importance of generative grammars; electrophysiology is giving evidence of the physical nature of the brain symbols of perception and to some extent how they are organized; and studies of the phenomena of human and animal perception show its efficiency and its limitations under special conditions. Meanwhile, work is going on in several laboratories in programming computers to accept visual patterns from artificial eyes, so that machines may come to recognize objects – to see, in fact. The most successful attempts work by selecting certain features of the patterns of light falling on the artificial eye, and using these in an organized 'language', with a kind of grammar. It may well be that until we develop a successful artificial eye that can really see like this, the surprisingly difficult problem of translating languages by machine will not be solved. It may be that language and vision are indeed based on common ground and that the basic problems of both must be solved together.

One thing is certain. Once these basic problems are solved, we shall be able to make intelligent machines: machines that will learn about the world as babies do, and come to make decisions on their own account – decisions appropriate to the external world sensed by their artificial eyes and ears, and communicated by speech to match the deep structure of our brains. In that case, if we are right that the deep structure of language has its origins in the organization of visual patterns, we would be in a position to reverse Biblical authority, and say: 'In the beginning was the grammar of vision – in the end came the word.'

56 *Social implications of intelligent machines*

[Finally, we point to the future, with a talk I delivered to the Machine Intelligence Workshop in Edinburgh. It was intended to be provocative, and to hint at what might be the nature of intelligence.]

★   ★   ★

THIS paper is designed to have a high coefficient of fiction. This should not be taken to mean that it will necessarily be false; but rather that it will play with possible realities. It will indeed be argued that playing with possible realities is the essence of intelligence; and that machines will not be intelligent until they are designed to function not by direct control from events, but rather from a continual running internal fiction of the world of events.

What do we mean by intelligence? There is no agreed definition; and psychologists are apt to confuse processes leading to intelligent solutions with what it is to say that a solution is intelligent. But it is confusing to equate, say, good memory or concentration, or any such, with intelligence – even if these characteristics are necessary for deriving intelligent solutions. It is confusing because we should be clear about what it is to say that one *solution* is intelligent, another not, irrespective of how the solution is obtained. To judge that a solution is intelligent we do, however, have to know what data and what previous solutions were available, or we will be in danger of attributing intelligence to something that merely copies. Clearly a necessary criterion of intelligence is novelty. Novelty alone, however, is not enough, for what is novel may be arbitrary, or downright misleading. Evidently, to be appropriate is also a necessary condition for intelligence. I shall suppose that these two criteria are sufficient for defining intelligence. I shall proceed to define an intelligent act, or an intelligent solution as *any act, or solution, which has appropriate novelty.* This definition should allow intelligence to be quantified, and measured.

Whether it is a man or a machine which is responsible for an

630

example of appropriate novelty, that man or that machine will be called intelligent. It is perhaps not quite clear how far appropriateness can be quantified; but certainly novelty can be quantified – in terms of prior probability. That man or that machine which succeeds in producing appropriate solutions having the lowest prior probabilities, will be declared the most intelligent man or the most intelligent machine. Others will be graded according to the lesser novelties of their solutions; while any 'solutions' which are not appropriate will be ruled as non-intelligent. Appropriate novel solutions might, of course, occur by chance, but this will be exceedingly unlikely to happen for a given man or a given machine on many occasions; and so if it does occur on many occasions we may be sure that that particular man or particular machine is indeed intelligent – and so is likely to produce further appropriate novel solutions.

We may now ask: How did intelligence develop in organic evolution? It is clear that early organisms do not show intelligence, according to our definition, for though their actions are often appropriate, they are seldom novel. Behaviour of simple life forms is essentially reflex, actions being initiated by rather specific stimuli. Whether a given reflex is exhibited may depend on the hormonal or other state of the organism, and what is elicited may be a complex series of actions, forming behaviour patterns; but reflex behaviour can be described fairly adequately in terms of the setting of conditional circuits – so that an input directly triggers an output response. This may be appropriate but will not be novel – and so it will not be intelligent.

Stimulus/response, or other direct-control-of-output-by-input systems, have essential limitations. It is in terms of overcoming these limitations that we see the development of intelligence in evolution. The first limitation of systems controlled directly by inputs is that they are lost when their inputs fail. Mechanical systems, such as cars, are lost when their control wheels come off, and a sophisticated servo-follower is lost when it loses its information link with its target. In general, machines stop, or their output becomes inappropriate when their inputs fail: but this is not true of the higher organisms, in spite of the fact that the problem is acute for organisms because the flow of sensory data is extraordinarily unreliable. Also, very often what is available is strictly inappropriate to guide the task in hand. Organisms keep going through gaps in the flow of sensory data quite remarkably well. They also succeed in behaving appropriately to characteristics of objects which are not monitored by their senses. For example, we generally pick up the cool end of a soldering iron, without having to monitor the heat we avoid. Now what does this imply? The ability to behave appropriately during data-gaps implies quite directly that we are not merely reflex-response systems, as some psychologists have supposed. Since we are able to bridge data-gaps by effective assumptions of what is going on, it follows that *behaviour is controlled by assumptions of the state of the world*. I shall call such assumptions of external states *fictions*. When used to predict future states they might be described as *hypotheses*. The brain's fictions may closely correspond to aspects of reality: the term 'fiction' should not be taken to imply that they are false – any more than all literary fiction is quite false. Just as a story is based on past experience, and may largely correspond with the present or the future, so the brain's fictions may be appropriate, and so useful.

The special power of brain fiction is that it frees behaviour from the tyranny of immediate sensory control. It seems reasonable to guess that it first developed to bridge gaps in sensory data, and that the first brain fiction was no more than simple extrapolations of observed trends: to bridge the unsensed present by projecting the past into the future. This does require the tacit assumption that nothing drastic will happen during the gap, and it is bound to fail if conditions change too much. A failed prediction of this kind may be novel but it will not be appropriate, and so it should not be regarded as intelligent. Data-gap filling, although useful and a necessary step toward intelligence, is not itself intelligent because it is not able to generate appropriate novelty.

We may describe data-gap bridging as *cognitive inertia*. It is important not only for what it led to in evolution, but also for greatly increasing performance reliability when the available input of data is intermittent, as it generally is for organisms.

We have already hinted at what seems to have been the second important step in the evolution of intelligence: the ability to read hidden features of the world from what little is given by the senses. One example is avoiding the hot end of the soldering iron; another is accepting an ice cream, on the evidence of the retinal image which itself is not cold, heavy, sweet, or edible. These characteristics are read from the retinal image; much as we read from a book, say, that a lighthouse stands on a cliff. We should say that the image of the ice cream has selected a *fictional account*, stored in the brain, of ice creams and what they can do, and what the brain's owner can do to them. Behaviour is but distantly controlled by the retinal image: it is controlled by the brain's fictional account of ice creams, cliffs and lighthouses – by a host of objects and situations drawn from the past. Brains then have the possibility of generating appropriate novelty; for they have but to present items of stored fiction to each other, or to sensed situations, and they may discover appropriately novel solutions.

The discovery may appear, from the outside, as a unique creation.

To produce intelligent machines, we might repeat this supposed development of organisms – to produce machines controlled not by direct information from the world but rather by their own fictions. We can however hardly expect that the machines' fictions will be like ours: but this is only a small part of the problem of predicting their effect on human society. First we should consider the social effects of *non*-intelligent machines; particularly whether we can predict their effects on us.

SOCIAL EFFECTS OF NON-INTELLIGENT MACHINES

Up to now, almost all machines have been passive slaves controlled as we wish by inputs from the world or by human commands. A train is guided directly by its track, and power tools cut according to instructions. Instruments, such as rulers and sextants, give readings directly of selected features of the world. There is however one machine, invented in its modern form six hundred years ago, which is fundamentally different. This machine is not under continuous, but only very occasional, control or interference from outside. It has a kind of inner secret life and the answers it gives are, when appropriate, most useful. I refer to the clock. Clocks do not record time directly. Indeed, we do not know what it would be to record time directly. A clock works by 'living' an inner fictional time; which we can read from the gestures of its hands on its inter-face.

A clock is the extreme case of a system which is useful because of its inertia. By plodding on regardless, and not responding to particular events, it can mirror the average change of things and in this it is useful. If a clock departs from what it is set to represent it becomes inappropriate, misleading without striking analogies. We should say that a clock is never intelligent: for just when it is appropriate it is not novel; and when it is novel then it is no longer appropriate.

Clocks show us that inertia, though useful for filling data-gaps with fiction which might be appropriate and useful, is nevertheless not adequate for intelligent machinery. We may however say that the early clock-makers paralleled the first crucial step in organic evolution towards intelligence – they made the first machines to work by fiction.

Clocks have had quite large social effects, but not especially because they function by inertia. They do strike us with a special awe, as subtly different from other machines, but there are many machines which have had more effect on human life. The inventions of the plough, the lathe, and a thousand others must have had more social effect than clocks. Most inventions are to some extent anticipated and few have the startling implications of machine intelligence yet all important inventions seem to catch us unawares, to produce unpredicted results. Perhaps it is science fiction writers who have the best record for accurate prediction; but they are more often wrong than right. Jules Verne was the most accurate in his predictions, but even he saw no engines beyond beam engines. His future floating island, for example, had no radio but had to plug into undersea telegraph lines, existing in his time. Space travel seemed impossible to professional astronomers before the 1939 war; and the Chief Engineer of the BBC declared firmly that television was theoretically impossible, at about the time it was demonstrated by John Logie Baird.

The history of inventions sometimes makes one wonder how far we are intelligent, and how far we are merely inertial even at peaks of imaginative creation. An excellent source of cases is Samuel Smiles' *Lives of the Engineers* (1861), which gives fascinating details of the difficulties and hang-ups of inventors. As an example of what appears to be inertial thinking, we may take the first stages of the design of railway engines. Several inventors had difficulty in imagining that it would be possible to apply power to wheels to make a vehicle move. Even Trevithick, in his master patent of 1813, stated that 'the driving wheels should be made rough, by the projection of bolts or crossgrooves, so that adhesion to the road might be secured'. In the same year a Mr Brunton, of the Butterley Works, Derbyshire, patented his Mechanical Traveller, 'to go *upon legs*, working alternatively like a horse'. Unfortunately the boiler burst on its first and only trial. In 1814 Thomas Tindall designed a locomotive in which 'the power of the engine is to be assisted by a *horizontal windmill*; and the four pushers, or legs, are to be caused to come successively in contact with the ground, and impel the carriage'. The point is that wheels on vehicles up to that time had been passive, as carts and carriages were pulled by animals. The notion of powered wheels was novel, and evidently difficult to grasp even after it had been suggested, as it was not part of the brain fiction of the time.

To us, looking back at this, steam horses look like a clear symptom of cognitive inertia rather than intelligence. A rather different example of cognitive inertia is the transfer of ideas from bird to human flight. At first the dynamic wings of birds were copied by inventors, leading to several flapping human deaths.

From the social history of inventions it is clear that important effects arise from completely unnoticed origins. An interesting example is how the use and limitation of horse-drawn buses and trams led rather directly to the building of houses of poorer people in the growing towns in valleys, rather than on hills, though the valleys were difficult to drain and so were unhealthy for large numbers. The hills remained the preserve of the rich largely because public vehicles, with their heavy loads, over-taxed the strength of horses, while privately-owned vehicles carrying only a few passengers were not too heavy. This situation continued until engined buses could manage hills (when in any case the drainage problem was solved) and now we can all go to work from the heights. This was not predicted or planned. But what of intelligent machines? If the social effects of horse buses and petrol engines cannot be anticipated, what hope have we for the impact of intelligent machines? How can we hope to overcome our cognitive inertia – to use our intelligence to guess correctly for such a novelty?

SOCIAL EFFECTS OF INTELLIGENT MACHINES

The only hope we seem to have for predicting the effects of intelligent machines is that intelligence already exists. Let us start by assuming that our intelligent machines will be metal men with similar intelligence and with inner fictions that are similar to ours. Further, we will suppose that in their construction they will be typical electro-mechanical machines.

Such machines would have, at the very least, the advantages of brave men dressed in asbestos armour; eating little or nothing, and with a tranquilliser so effective that they can sleep for centuries, to be awakened when they reach distant planets, or to teach our descendants intimate history. These metal men would be of great help in war and in all kinds of dangerous and boring industrial jobs. It seems all too clear however, from our reaction to people with different origins and only slightly different looks, that even if the brains of the metal men were essentially like ours we would hardly accept them into the human club. At best, they would be another and very odd race, which we would have every excuse to exclude from human ethical restraints – as we would have no reason to believe them capable of experiencing pain. This is, of course, a science fiction theme but it should not be quite dismissed on that account. Science fiction can be regarded as the first probings of the imagination; the first attempt to consider a problem, if not solve it. Indeed, the ancient cosmologies were just this. We no longer believe that the earth stands on an elephant; but the very asking of the question led to appropriate observations, and formulated theories giving precise predictions. The important point is that neither primitive cosmologies nor science fiction are safe guides to prediction. This is clear from their contradictory variety. We could write a plausible science fiction story in which the metal men are accepted by human society; but with the result that men lose their confidence, because the flesh is so obviously weaker than metal. We could write another story, in which the women become so fixated upon the metal men that the human race dies out for lack of gene pairings – or even that the genes get polluted with iron filings! In still another story we might invent, human work and decisions are taken over, until men give up all serious things to play only games. The final game is the destruction of the metal men – leading to the end of the human race, as men have forgotten how to live at all like animals. Now the point of these stories is that all are possible fictions. Although referring to possible futures, they are however no more than games, with familiar ideas as counters. But can the future be described at all adequately in terms of present-day facts? The limitation of this kind of primitive – inertial – prediction is that essentially novel possibilities are excluded. It is therefore non-intelligent. It is just this which is the weakness of history, used for prediction.

Surely we cannot predict the effect of intelligent machines on this basis. Is it possible to base predictions on anything more likely to succeed than stories limited by cognitive inertia? Surely physical science makes at least some kinds of prediction possible: can the methods of science help us to predict the social effects of intelligent machines?

To take an early example of prediction by the methods of the physical sciences, we may consider the prediction of eclipses. Solar eclipses have been predicted, with fair accuracy, for perhaps four thousand years. Presumably it was noted that eclipses occur only at full moon, and under certain other conditions occurring in cycles, allowing prediction once these cycles had been mastered. In fact the heuristic programme required for prediction of *all* eclipses at any place on earth is extremely complicated and complete accuracy was not attained until a conceptual model of the solar system was developed. Prediction was then not in terms of the solar system as observed, but in terms of the conceptual fictional model. It was only when the observations became secondary to the model that prediction became adequate. Further, it was possible to predict not only eclipses but a host of other phenomena. It became also possible to introduce quite new factors, space ships, into the situation – and to touch the moon.

It is particularly interesting that as prediction became more reliable, and the planets were seen to move along fictionally defined orbits, the notion that they are intelligent, or are pushed along by intelligent beings, was dropped. This is compatible with our definition of intelligence, for as we develop the power to predict so there is less novelty in the events predicted. Scientific theories destroy the appearance of intelligence in things as prediction becomes possible. This is true for biology as it is for physics. This does however lead to a paradox for sociology.

Sociologists are concerned to predict the effect of changes on future society. But is prediction *in principle* possible when intelligence is involved? If intelligence is the production of novelty, prediction might seem to be strictly impossible. However this may be, it seems that the present trouble about social prediction is simply that there are no adequate theoretical models of societies. This means that politicians are almost powerless to predict, plan, or control except with incredible errors. We find ourselves in just this position in trying to assess the implications of future intelligence. We are in the position of the early astronomers, with no model of the solar system.

In these circumstances the best we can do is to write fiction from our past; and hope that the story we like best turns out to be true. Without a theoretical model of society we can do no more than adopt inertial procedures, and accept that our predictions are virtually certain to be neither appropriate nor novel.

The vital point about intelligent machines is that once they are trusted they will take decisions, and these decisions will directly affect us. In a sense present-day technology makes decisions – certainly it sets up situations beyond our power to predict or prevent. Intelligent machines will be a fundamentally different case when we ask for their opinions. Perhaps the most important questions here concern the ethics of responsibility. Suppose a mechanized judge (programmed with the law, and the relevant data of the case) condemns a man to punishment. Now suppose that, after the punishment is inflicted, the mechanical judge is found to be in error – what would our attitude be? We might assume that the machine went wrong – that some electronic malfunction was responsible for the error. We might then blame the designer or the maintenance staff – at least if they were human – but surely not the judge-machine; any more than we blame our car when the battery is flat. Suppose that it was clear that the machine's components did not fail – but rather that the machine had to balance probabilities, and on this occasion the most likely candidate happened to be innocent. This is bound to happen for human judges, and it is also bound to happen for machine judges, for it is not always the most probable which occurs. Indeed if it did there would be no useful concept of probability. Would we blame the machine for the im-probable event happening to occur? We might – rationally we should not. We might, because we do tend to blame people when this happens. But is our blame rational? I think it is not.

Of course to blame or censure a judge for an error may serve to sharpen his future judgement, and no doubt a similar procedure could be appropriate for machine judges. This would however be called optimizing the machine's procedures, rather than punishing or censuring it. Possibly, as this becomes the general practice for dealing with machines which come up with incorrect answers, our notion of punishment and of blame may change – and in becoming adapted to the machine we might ourselves become more humane.

If machines are to make decisions on human affairs, then certainly they will have to be programmed (or will have to discover for themselves) a great deal about the behaviour, aspirations, and fears of human beings. More profound: in order to design human-like intelligent machines, we will have to make psychology a far more effective science. There are indeed already signs that the study of machine intelligence is affecting experimental psychology. Here we come back to the inner fiction, the brain's symbolic models, describing features of the external world. It is surely vitally important to go beyond stimulus-response psychology, and to accept clearly that the prevailing sensory input is but a small part of what determines human behaviour. It is surely the detailed studies of cognitive structures which will be the effective description of man. It is these structures, no doubt partly reflected in the structure of language, which will be the essential design descriptions for intelligent machines.

PERSONAL RELATIONS WITH INTELLIGENT MACHINES

We may be correct in concluding that it is impossible to predict the effects of the introduction of a new feature into society, but we should still ask: Is it possible to predict the 'psychological' relation between people and intelligent machines?

Unfortunately, we seem to be forced to the view that just as an adequate theoretical model is necessary for predicting effects of a novel feature into society, so a detailed model is required to predict individual reactions. The fact is that we know so little about people that historians show almost no agreement even over which past events should be regarded as causally related to later events, or to later individual or social attitudes. If the past cannot be interpreted in this way – when the range of possibilities is limited by what is known to have happened – what hope have we to predict the future, when the possibilities are limited only by logical considerations? Unfortunately we must adopt the inertial procedure, arguing on the basis that we do know what it is like to deal with intelligent organisms, especially other people having roughly similar fictions, hoping the case of intelligent machines is not strictly novel. There are surely some considerations which apply both to other people and to intelligent machines of human capability.

This brings us to our final consideration, which is: What happens when the internal fiction of the machine is very different from human brain-fiction? This will surely generally be the case, for even if we understood human brain-fiction in detail, which certainly we do not at present, it seems most unlikely that the kind of software developed through evolution for survival in past conditions would be optimal for machines designed specifically to solve problems – even if they are *our* current problems. Human emotion may be important for selecting immediate priorities, in terms mainly of survival and reproduction, but the selection of data and aims set by emotional states would surely be inappropriate for machines having very different survival and reproduction problems. Human prejudice is useful in saving thinking time: clearly it would be intolerable to have to consider all relevant possibilities. No doubt pre-selections of possibilities, which we might as well call 'prejudice', would have to be accepted by machines also, but there seems no reason why their prejudices should agree in any detail with ours. The trouble is that if they do not, communication is certain to be extremely difficult. Just as it is very difficult to communicate across prejudice (or opinion) barriers between people, so it will be equally difficult or impossible with machines. The power of philosophical discussion is, surely, to make explicit underlying assumptions in human arguments: if the software of machine arguments is totally exposed, and the machines are pitted against us in debate, then we can expect exciting and perhaps too challenging clarification of our thinking. This will be an extension of the effect that computers are already having on our understanding of logic and mathematical procedures. The hope is that intelligent machines may reveal where we are arbitrary and non-rigorous in our use of language having semantic content, much as existing computers show up inconsistencies in formal orderings of symbols apart from what meaning we may attach to the symbols.

Apart from the sheer difficulty of reproducing human brain-fiction it is most unlikely that it would be worth while; except that it may be essential if we are to communicate directly with the machines. One can imagine a class of machines which works quite mysteriously, with non-human fiction, to give us answers without justifications we could understand. Some people might come to trust such machines, much as they trust cars though they have no idea how the steering wheel is connected to the front wheels. But would it be possible to phrase questions appropriately to such machines? It seems more likely that these alien machines would be outside direct human control, but would feed themselves with raw data through their own sensory systems, and be left to find answers to problems we may but vaguely understand. These machines would form a separate race of hidden intelligence; which could come up with devastating novelty, which we might be hard pressed to find appropriate. We might find it difficult to accept the decisions of very intelligent machines as appropriate, and so as intelligent.

There is a related point here of importance: an issue which is already with us as computers are used to store and handle personal and confidential details of individuals. Quite apart from the intelligence of the computers, or lack of it, we tend to feel threatened by this impersonally-stored mass of data, which can be retrieved at a moment's notice by anonymous bureaucrats. If the bureaucrats were machines, we might feel much the same. The worry is the threat to personal liberty implied by the ready availability of facts about ourselves. On the other hand, it might be admitted that administrative decisions would be more effective, and perhaps more just, if adequate facts were available. There is a conflict of opinion here, though no logical conflict for both opinions could be right. We may expect a loss of individual freedom, at least to get away with minor transgressions, while perhaps attaining more rational government.

How far personal information should be collected and made available for computer handling can only be judged in terms of a preferred fiction of the future – what sort of world we wish to leave to our descendants. Here we reach a curious ethical question.

It is clear that people living at various times and in different societies have somewhat different moral standards and preferences. Further, people generally accept the moral standards and preferences of their own society; at any rate if these do not change too rapidly. Since we tend on the whole to accept our own society, what right have we to inhibit present developments, on the grounds that our values will continue to be held by later generations? In fact, we may assume that changes made now will become more acceptable as time goes on. Indeed value judgments may represent no more than cases of extreme, though not complete, moral inertia. To take an example of this kind of situation, consider the Victorian attitude to the telephone. For many years it was regarded as an intrusion into the privacy of the home, for it was every middle class man's right to be 'not at home' to visitors, and the principle was violated by the telephone. The Victorians might have banned the development of telephone exchanges handling private numbers, and so inhibited at least for several years the general use of telephones. Now although this would have seemed a good idea to them, does it now seem a good idea to us? To generalize this question: Are there technical developments which were foreseen and which we now wish had been suppressed for social reasons? There may be a few, but generally we seem to adapt to and accept the results of technical innovation. At present we do not in any case know how to suppress technical innovations; and so we have to hope that people will adapt to their social effects, or will invent adequate counter measures. This has worked quite well for the results of artificial power and non-intelligent machines. We can only hope that the introduction of intelligence to machines will not result in situations beyond human ability to accept or to counteract. At least we should be able to harness the power of the intelligent machines to tackle their threat to humanity, as now we use machines to counteract ill-effects of other machines.

Although ethical notions change, with time and across societies, no doubt some notions and restraints are shared. These could be programmed into the intelligent machines, and in this way they could be made to 'see' our morality. But as human morality changes, should the morality of the machines be made to follow? Should we build human ethical, and other, intertias into machines? It would certainly be intolerable for us to be judged by values accepted in past times; so presumably we should wish the machines to follow our social mores as they change, rather than (like ideal clocks) be perfectly inertial, in the hope of representing ultimate values.

Turning from the 'seeing' of situations and events in terms of ethical values; there are deep problems over what it would be to say that machines 'see' the common physical objects we take for granted. Here is the most difficult question of all: In what sense can a machine share our world?

This question might be phrased in our terms as: How far can machines share our fiction? It has been argued in other places by the author that perceiving the world involves a kind of *non-formal* intelligence; an intelligence not dependent upon language, but perhaps providing the origin of language. It seems likely that perceptual intelligence has to be non-rigorous, not strictly analytical, in order to come up with useful solutions – perceptions – in real-time. We can expect the same from seeing machines; but the assumptions they will adopt, to make the problems of perceiving objects from images tractable, will no doubt be different from our simplifying assumptions. If so they will, in an important sense, see a different world, because their fiction will be different. We will be able to understand the machine's behaviour to its world, only as we partly understand the behaviour of animals different from ourselves. It may be difficult to work in close cooperation with such machines. Intelligent machines will have impenetrable fictions, engaged in rather mysterious ways even on the tasks which we set for them. In the long run this may be to our advantage, for it will remain true that we are special and so not directly challenged by the machines. No athlete is worried by the fact that horses run faster than any men, and mathematicians are not bothered by the computer's superior ability at arithmetic; presumably because horses and computers are sufficiently different from us. On this basis a world with intelligent machines could be not only interesting but compatible with human happiness; providing the machines are very different from us – or carefully programmed to show due tact to their masters.

BIBLIOGRAPHY

Adrian, E. D. (1928) *The Basis of Sensation.* London.

Adrian, E. D. (1932) *The Mechanism of Nervous Action.* London.

Aguilar, M. and W. S. Stiles (1954) Saturation of the rod mechanism of the retina at high levels of stimulation. *Optica Acta* 1, 59.

Ames, A. (1946) Some demonstrations concerned with the origin and nature of our sensations. *Laboratory Manual,* Dartmouth Eye Institute.

Anderson, E. E. and F. W. Weymouth (1923) Visual perception and the retinal mosaic. *Amer. J. Physiol.* 64, 561.

Anstis, S. M., C. D. Shopland and R. L. Gregory (1961) Measuring visual constancy for stationary or moving objects. *Nature,* Lond., 191, 416. [No. 23]

Anstis, S. M., R. L. Gregory, N. de M. Rudolf and D. M. MacKay (1963) Influence of stroboscopic illumination on the after-effect of seen movement. *Nature,* Lond., 199, 99. [No. 18]

Anstis, S. M. and R. L. Gregory (1965) The after-effect of seen motion: the role of retinal stimulation and of eye movements. *Quart. J. exp. Psychol.* 17, part 2, 173. [No. 17]

Aubert, H. (1887) Die Bewegungsempfindung. *Pflug. Arch. ges. Physiol.* 40, 459.

Avery, G. C. and R. H. Day (1969) Basis of the horizontal-vertical illusion. *J. exp. Psychol.* 81, 376.

Bach-y-Rita, P., C. C. Collins, B. W. White, F. Saunders, L. Scaddon and R. Blomberg (1969) Vision substitution by tactile image projection. *Nature,* Lond., 221, 963.

Barlow, H. B. (1952) Eye movements during fixation. *J. Physiol.* 116, 290.

Barlow, H. B. (1953) Action potentials from the frog's retina. *J. Physiol.* 119, 58.

Barlow, H. B. (1956) Retinal noise and absolute threshold. *J. opt. Soc. Amer.* 46, 634.

Barlow, H. B. (1957a) Increment thresholds at low intensities considered as signal/noise discrimination. *J. Physiol.* 136, 469.

Barlow, H. B. (1957b) Purkinje shift and retinal noise. *Nature,* Lond., 179, 255.

Barlow, H. B. (1963) Slippage of contact lenses and other artifacts in relation to fading and regeneration of supposedly stable retinal images. *Quart. J. exp. Psychol.* 15, 36.

Barlow, H. B., R. Fitzhugh and S. W. Kuffler (1954) Resting discharge and dark adaptation in the cat. *J. Physiol.* 125, 28P.

Barlow, H. B., R. Fitzhugh and S. W. Kuffler (1957) Change of organization in the receptive fields of the cat's retina during dark adaptation. *J. Physiol.* 137, 338.

Bartlett, Sir F. (1932) *Remembering*. London.

Bartley, S. H. (1941) *Vision: A Study of its Basis*. London.

Battersby, W. S., R. L. Kahn, M. Pollock and M. B. Bender (1956) Effects of visual, vestibular and somato-sensorimotor defects on auto-kinetic perception. *J. exp. Psychol.* 52, 398.

Békésy, G. von (1929) Zur Theorie des Horens. *Physik. Z.* 30, 721.

Békésy, G. von (1956) Simplified model to demonstrate the energy flow and formation of travelling waves similar to those found in the cochlea. *Proc. Nat. Acad. of Science* 42, 12, 930.

Békésy, G. von (1957) The ear. *Sci. Amer.* 197, 66. Also in J. L. McGaugh, N. M. Weinberger and R. E. Whelan (eds.) (1966), *Psychobiology: Readings from Scientific American*. San Francisco.

Bell, D. A. (1953) *Information Theory*. London.

Blodgett, H. C. (1929) The effect of the introduction of reward upon maze performance of rats. *Univ. Calif. Publ. Psychol.* 4, 113.

Boring, E. G. (1942) *Sensation and Perception in the History of Experimental Psychology*. New York.

Bouman, M. A. and H. A. van der Velden (1947) The two quanta explanation of the threshold values of visual acuity of the visual angle and the time of observation. *J. opt. Soc. Amer.* 37, 908.

Bower, T. G. R. (1971) The object world of the infant. *Sci. Amer.* 225, 4.

Brindley, G. S. (1953) The effects on colour vision of adaptation to very bright lights. *J. Physiol.* 122, 332.

Brindley, G. S. (1954) The summation areas of human colour receptive mechanisms at increment threshold. *J. Physiol.* 124, 400.

Brindley, G. S. (1957) Human colour vision. In J. A. V. Butter and B. Kats (eds.), *Progress in Biophysics*, vol. 8. London.

Brindley, G. S. and P. A. Merton (1960) The absence of position sense in the human eye. *J. Physiol.* 152, 127.

Brindley, G. S. and W. S. Lewin (1968) The sensations produced by electrical stimulation of the visual cortex. *J. Physiol.* 196, Reprinted in T. D. Sterling *et al.* (eds.) (1971), *Visual Prosthesis*, London and New York.

Broad, C. D. (1925) *Mind and its Place in Nature*. London.

Brown, J. F. (1931) The visual perception of velocity. *Psychol. Forsch.* 14, 199.

Brown, R. H. (1961) Visual sensitivity to differences in velocity. *Psychol. Bull.* 58, 89.

Burton, D. and G. Ettlinger (1960) Cross-modal transfer of training in monkeys. *Nature*, Lond., 186, 1071.

Cane, V. R. and R. L. Gregory (1957) Noise and the visual threshold. *Nature*, Lond., 180, 1403.

Carpenter, A. (1948) The rate of blinking during prolonged visual search. *J. exp. Psychol.* 38, 587.

Carr, H. A. (1910) The autokinetic sensation. *Psychol. Rev.* 17, 42.

Carr, H. A. (1935) *An Introduction to Space Perception.* London.

Carter, L., W. Haythorn, B. Meirowitz and J. Lanzetta (1951) A note on a new technique of interaction recording. *J. Abnormal and Social Psychol.* 46, 2.

Charpentier, A. (1886) Sur une illusion visuelle. *Comptes-rendus de l'Acad. des Sciences* 102, 1155.

Clay, H. M. (1954) Changes of performance with age in similar tasks of varying complexity. *Brit. J. Psychol.* 45, 7.

Coghill, G. E. (1929) *Anatomy and the Problem of Behaviour.* London.

Cooper, S., P. M. Daniel and D. Whitteridge (1953) Nerve impulses in the brain stem of the goat: short latencies obtained by stretching the extrinsic eye muscles and the jaw muscles. *J. Physiol.* 120, 471.

Cooper, S., P. M. Daniel and D. Whitteridge (1955) Muscle spindles and other sensory endings in the extrinsic eye muscles: the physiology and anatomy of these receptors and of their connexions with the brain stem. *Brain* 78, 564.

Cornsweet, T. N. (1956) Determination of the stimuli for involuntary drifts and saccadic eye movements. *J. opt. Soc. Amer.* 46, 987.

Covell, W. P. (1952) The ear. In E. V. Cowdry, *Problems of Ageing: Biological and Medical Aspects,* 3rd ed. A. I. Lansing, Baltimore.

Craik, K. J. W. (1938) The effect of adaptation on differential brightness discrimination. *J. Physiol.* 92, 406.

Craik, K. J. W. and O. L. Zangwill (1939) Observations relating to the thresholds of a small figure within the contour of a closed-line figure. *Brit. J. Psychol.* 30, 139.

Crawford, B. M. and W. N. Kama (1961) Remote handling of mass. Wright-Patterson Air Force Base (U.S.A.F. A.S.D. Tech. Rep. 61–627).

Crossman, E. R. F. W. (1953) Entropy and choice time: the effect of frequency unbalance on choice response. *Quart. J. exp. Psychol.* 5, 41.

Dandy, W. E. (1933*a*) Menière's disease: diagnosis and treatment. *Amer. J. Surg.* 20, 693.

Dandy, W. E. (1933*b*) Treatment of Menière's disease by section of only the vestibular portion of the acoustic nerve. *Bull. Johns Hopkins Hosp.* 53, 52.

Dandy, W. E. (1935) The treatment of bilaterial Menière's disease and pseudo-Menière's disease. *Acta neuropath. in hon. L. Prinsepp.* 9, 10.

Davis, H. (1951) Psychophysiology of hearing and deafness. In S. S. Stevens (ed.), *Handbook of Experimental Psychology,* New York.

Descartes, R. (1637) *Philosophical Writings,* trans. N. K. Smith, London 1952.

Deutsch, J. A. (1951) A preliminary report on a new auditory after-effect. *Quart. J. exp. Psychol.* 3, 43.

Dinnerstein, D. (1965) Intermanual effects of anchors on zones of maximal sensitivity in weight discrimination. *Amer. J. Psychol.* 78, 66.

Ditchburn, R. W. and B. L. Ginsborg (1952) Vision with a stabilized retinal image. *Nature,* Lond., 170, 36.

Dix, M. B., C. S. Hallpike and J. D. Hood (1948) Observations upon the loudness recruitment phenomenon. *Proc. Roy. Soc. Med.* 41, 516.

Dodge, R. (1903) Five types of eye movement in the horizontal meridian plane of the field of regard. *Amer. J. Physiol.* 8, 307.

Dodwell, P. C., L. G. Standing and H. Thio (1969) Are thresholds reduced by illusions? An attempt at replication. *Quart. J. exp. Psychol.* 21, 127.

Drew, G. C. (1950) Variations in reflex blink-rate during visual-motor tasks. *Quart. J. exp. Psychol.* 3, 73.

Duke-Elder, W. S. (1938) *Textbook of Ophthalmology.* Vol. 1, 2nd ed., London.

Duncker, K. (1912) Induced motion. In W. E. Ellis (ed.) (1938), *A Source Book of Gestalt Psychology*, London.

Duncker, K. (1929) Über induziente Bewegung. *Psychol. Forsch.* 12, 180.

Egan, J. P., F. R. Clark and E. C. Carterette (1956) On the transmission and confirmation of messages in noise. *J. acoust. Soc. Amer.* 28, no. 4, 536.

Emmert, E. (1881) Grossen verhalnisse der Nachbidder. *Klin. Mb. Augenheilk* 19, 443.

Epstein, W., J. Park and A. Casey (1961) The current state of the size-distance hypothesis. *Psychol. Bull.* 58, 491.

Ettlinger, G. (1960) Cross-modal transfer in monkeys. *Behaviour* 16, 56.

Exner, S. (1891) *Die physiologie der facettirten Augen von Krebsen und Insecten.* Leipzig and Vienna.

Exner, S. (1886) Über autokinetische Empfindungen. *Z. Psychol.* 12, 313.

Fantz, R. L. (1961) The origin of form perception. *Sci. Amer.* 204, no. 5, 66.

Fechner, G. T. (1860) *Elements der Psychophysik.* Leipzig.

Fellows, B. J. (1967) Reversal of the Müller-Lyer illusion with changes in the length of inter-fins lines. *Quart. J. exp. Psychol.* 19, 208.

Fernberger, S. W. (1931) Instructions and the psychophysical limen. *Amer. J. Psychol.* 43, 361.

Ferree, C. E., G. Rand and E. F. Lewis (1935) Age as an important factor in the amount of light needed by the eye. *Arch. Opthal.* 13, 212.

Finger, F. W. and D. K. Spelt (1947) The illustration of the horizontal-vertical illusion. *J. exp. Psychol.* 37, 243.

Finney, D. J. (1952) *Probit Analysis.* London.

Fitzhugh, R. (1957) The statistical detection of threshold signals in the retina. *J. gen. Physiol.* 40, 925.

Fletcher, H. (1929) *Speech and Hearing.* New York.

Fletcher, H. (1938) Loudness, masking and their relation to the hearing process and the problem of noise measurement. *J. acoust. Soc. Amer.* 9, 275.

Frisby, J. P. and I. R. L. Davies (1971) Is the haptic Müller-Lyer a visual phenomenon? *Nature*, Lond., 221, 463.

Fry, G. A. and S. H. Bartley (1935) The effect of one border in the visual field upon the threshold of another. *Amer. J. Physiol.* 112, 414.

Fulton, J. F. (1955) *A Textbook of Physiology.* 17th ed., Philadelphia.

Geschwind, N. (1964) The development of the brain and the evolution of language. In C. I. J. M. Stuart (ed.), *Report of the 15th Annual R.T.M. on Linguistics and Language*. Monograph Series no. 17.

Galambos, R. and H. Davis (1944) Inhibition of activity in single auditory nerve fibres by acoustic stimulation. *J. Neurophysiol.* 7, 287.

Garner, W. R. and H. W. Hake (1951) The amount of information in absolute judgments. *Psychol. Rev.* 58, 446.

Gibson, J. J. (1950) *The Perception of the Visual World*. Boston.

Glen, J. S. (1940) Ocular movements in reversibility of perspective. *J. gen. Psychol.* 23, 243.

Goldstein, K. (1932) Restitution in injuries to the brain cortex. *Arch. Neurol. Psych.* 27, 736.

Graham, C. H. and R. Margaria (1935) Area and the intensity-time relation in the peripheral retina. *Amer. J. Physiol.* 113, 299.

Graham, C. H. and C. Cook (1937) Visual acuity as a function of intensity and exposure-time. *Amer. J. Psychol.* 49, 654.

Granit, R. (1947) *Sensory Mechanisms of the Retina*. London.

Granit, R. (1955) *Receptors and Sensory Perception*. Yale.

Gregory, R. L. (1952a) Variations in blink rate during non-visual tasks. *Quart. J. exp. Psychol.* 4, part 4, 165. [No. 5]

Gregory, R. L. (1952b) (unpublished) A speculative account of brain function in terms of probability and induction. M.R.C.A.P.U., Cambridge. [No. 46]

Gregory, R. L. (1953a) A multi-channel printing chronograph. *Quart. J. exp. Psychol.* 5, 33. [No. 33]

Gregory, R. L. (1953b) On physical model explanations in psychology. *Brit. J. of Philosophy of Science* 4, 192. [No. 47]

Gregory, R. L. (1953c) An optical micro-stimulator for the human retina. *Quart. J. exp. Psychol.* 5, part 3, 136. [No. 38]

Gregory, R. L. (1955a) A note on summation time of the eye indicated by signal/noise discrimination. *Quart. J. exp. Psychol.* 7, part 3, 147. [No. 10]

Gregory, R. L. (1955b) Colour anomaly, the Rayleigh equation and selective adaptation. *Nature, Lond.*, 176, 172. [No. 6]

Gregory, R. L. (1956) An experimental treatment of vision as an information source and noisy channel. In C. Cherry (ed.), *Information Theory, 3rd London Symposium*. London.

Gregory, R. L. (1957a) A single-flash rotary disk optical shutter. *J. of Scientific Instruments* 34, 463. [No. 39]

Gregory, R. L. (1957b) Increase in neurological noise as a factor in ageing. In *4th Congress of the International Association of Gerontology*, Fidenza.

Gregory, R. L. (1958a) Eye movements and the stability of the visual world. *Nature, Lond.*, 182, 1214. [No. 14]

Gregory, R. L. (1958b) Models and the localization of function in the central nervous system. In National Physical Laboratory, Symposium no. 10, *Mechanization of Thought Processes*, vol. 2, H.M.S. [No. 50]

Gregory, R. L. (1959) A blue filter technique for detecting eye movements during the autokinetic effect. *Quart. J. exp. Psychol.* 11, 113. [No. 15]

Gregory, R. L. (1960) The solid-image microscope: a more technical description. *Research* 13, 422. [No. 41]

Gregory, R. L. (1961*a*) The solid-image microscope. *Research and Development* 1, 101. [No. 40]

Gregory, R. L. (1961*b*) The brain as an engineering problem. In W. H. Thorpe and O. L. Zangwill (eds.), *Current Problems in Animal Behaviour*, London. [No. 49]

Gregory, R. L. (1962*a*) The brain – an engineering problem. *Discovery* 23, 22.

Gregory, R. L. (1962*b*) Visual illusions in space. *New Scientist* 15, 446.

Gregory, R. L. (1963*a*) Sensory processes. In G. Humphrey (ed.), *Psychology through Experiment*, London. [No. 1]

Gregory, R. L. (1963*b*) Distortion of visual space as inappropriate constancy scaling. *Nature*, Lond., 199, 678. [No. 28]

Gregory, R. L. (1964*a*) Human perception. *Brit. Med. Bull.* 20, part 1, 21. [No. 2]

Gregory, R. L. (1964*b*) Stereoscopic shadow images. *Nature*, Lond., 203, 1407. [No. 21]

Gregory, R. L. (1964*c*) The two psychologies. *Cambridge Review* 85, 379. [No. 48]

Gregory, R. L. (1964*d*) A technique for minimizing the effects of atmospheric disturbance on photographic telescopes. *Nature*, Lond., 203, 274. [No. 45]

Gregory, R. L. (1965*a*) Seeing in depth. *Proc. Roy. Inst.* 40, 311. [No. 27]

Gregory, R. L. (1965*b*) Seeing in depth. *Nature*, Lond., 207, 16.

Gregory, R. L. (1966*a*) *Eye and Brain*. London.

Gregory, R. L. (1966*b*) Visual illusions. In B. Foss (ed.), *New Horizons in Psychology*, Harmondsworth.

Gregory, R. L. (1967*a*) Comments on the inappropriate constancy scaling theory of illusions and its implications. *Quart. J. exp. Psychol.* 19, 3. [No. 29]

Gregory, R. L. (1967*b*) Origin of eyes and brains. *Nature*, Lond., 213, 369.

Gregory, R. L. (1967*c*) Will seeing machines have illusions? In N. L. Collins and D. Michie (eds.), *Machine Intelligence* 1, Edinburgh.

Gregory, R. L. (1967*d*) First progress report on development of a telescope camera to give real-time sampling for minimizing atmospheric image disturbance. Unpublished.

Gregory, R. L. (1967*e*) Early telescope tests of the real-time sampling technique for minimizing image disturbance. Supplementary paper 3, in S. P. Morgan (ed.), *Restoration of Atmospherically Degraded Images*, U.S.A.F. and National Academy of Sciences.

Gregory, R. L. (1968*a*) Perceptual illusions and brain models. *Proc. Roy. Soc.* 171, 279. [No. 30]

Gregory, R. L. (1968*b*) On how so little information controls so much behaviour. Bionics Research Report 1, Dept. of Machine Intelligence and Perception, Edinburgh University. In C. H. Waddington (ed.), *Towards a Theoretical Biology* 2, Edinburgh 1969. Also in A. T. Welford and L. Houssiadas (eds.), *Contemporary Problems in Perception*, London 1970. [No. 52]

Gregory, R. L. (1968*c*) The evolution of eyes and brains – a hen-and-egg problem. In S. J. Freedman (ed.), *The Neuro-psychology of Spatially Orientated Behaviour*, Illinois. [No. 53]

Gregory, R. L. (1968*d*) Information processing in biological and artificial brains. In A.G.A.R.D. Conference 44: *Principles and Practice of Bionics*.

Gregory, R. L. (1970*a*) *The Intelligent Eye*. London.

Gregory, R. L. (1970*b*) Köhler's perception. *Science* 168, 712. [No. 51]

Gregory, R. L. (1970*c*) The speaking eye. *Sunday Times Magazine*, 26 April 1970, 26. [No. 54]

Gregory, R. L. (1971*a*) The grammar of vision. *Listener* 83, 242. [No. 55]

Gregory, R. L. (1971*b*) The social implications of intelligent machines. In B. Meltzer and D. Michie (eds.), *Machine Intelligence* 6, Edinburgh. [No. 56]

Gregory, R. L. and V. Cane (1955) A statistical information theory of visual thresholds. *Nature*, Lond., 176, 1272. [No. 7]

Gregory, R. L., V. Cane and J. G. Wallace (1956) Increase in 'neurological noise' as a factor in sensory impairment associated with ageing. Unpublished thesis submitted to C.I.B.A. foundation. [No. 8]

Gregory, R. L. and V. Cane (1958) A theory of visual thresholds. *Nature*, Lond., 181, 1487.

Gregory, R. L. and J. G. Wallace (1958) A theory of nerve deafness. *Lancet* 1, 83. [No. 9]

Gregory, R. L., J. G. Wallace and F. W. Campbell (1959) Changes in the size and shape of visual after-images observed in complete darkness during changes of position in space. *Quart. J. exp. Psychol.* 11, part 1, 54. [No. 22]

Gregory, R. L. and T. M. B. Eiloart (1962) A device for giving a histogram of time-intervals. *Nature*, Lond., 1893, 605. [No. 37]

Gregory, R. L. and J. G. Wallace (1963) Recovery from early blindness: a case study. *Monogr. Supp.* 2, *Quart. J. exp. Psychol.* Cambridge. [No. 3]

Gregory, R. L. and O. L. Zangwill (1963) The origin of the autokinetic effect. *Quart. J. exp. Psychol.* 15, 252. [No. 16]

Gregory, R. L., H. E. Ross and N. Moray (1964) The curious eye of *Copilia*. *Nature*, Lond., 201, 1166. [No. 32]

Gregory, R. L. and H. E. Ross (1964*a*) Visual constancy during movement: 1. Effects of S's forward and backward movement on size constancy. *Percept. Motor Skills* 18, 3. [No. 24]

Gregory, R. L. and H. E. Ross (1964*b*) Visual constancy during movement: 2. Size constancy using one or both eyes or proprioceptive information. *Percept. Motor Skills* 18, 23. [No. 25]

Gregory, R. L. and H. E. Ross (1967) Arm weight, adaptation and weight discrimination. *Percept. Motor Skills* 24, 1127. [No. 12]

Gregory, R. L. and C. Miller (1970) Illusion and depth measurements in right-angular and parallel line figures. Unpublished. [No. 31]

Gregory, R. L. and E. H. Gombrich (eds.) (1973) *Illusion in Nature and Art*, London.

Guild, S. R. (1932) Correlations of histological observations and the acuity of hearing. *Acta Oto-Laryngol.* 17, 207.

Guilford, J. P. and K. M. Dallenbach (1928) A study of the autokinetic sensation. *Amer. J. Psychol.* 40, 83.

Guilford, J. P. (1936) *Psychometric Methods*. New York.

Guzman, A. (1971) Analysis of curved line drawings using content and global information. In B. Meltzer and D. Michie (eds.), *Machine Intelligence* 6, Edinburgh.

Hartline, H. K. (1934) Intensity and duration in the excitation of single photoreceptor units. *J. cell. comp. Physiol.* 5, 229.

Hartline, H. K. (1938) The response of single optic nerve fibres of the vertebrate to illumination of the retina. *Amer. J. Physiol.* 121, 400.

Hartline, H. K. (1940a) The nerve messages in the fibres of the visual pathway. *J. opt. Soc. Amer.* 30, 239.

Hartline, H. K. (1940b) The receptive field of the optic nerve fibres. *Amer. J. Physiol.* 130, 690.

Hartline, H. K. (1940c) The effects of spatial summation in the retina on the excitation of the fibres in the optic nerve. *Amer. J. Physiol.* 130, 700.

Hartline, H. K. and C. H. Graham (1932) Nerve impulses from single receptors in the eye. *J. cell. comp. Physiol.* 1, 277.

Hartridge, H. (1950) *Recent Advances in the Physiology of Vision*. London.

Head, H. and G. Holmes (1911) Sensory disturbances from cerebral lesions. *Brain* 34, 102.

Hebb, D. O. (1949) *The Organization of Behaviour: a Neuro-psychological Theory*. London.

Hecht, S. (1935) A theory of visual intensity discrimination. *J. gen. Physiol.* 18, 767.

Hecht, S. and E. U. Mintz (1939) The visibility of single lines at various illuminations and the retinal basis of visual resolution. *J. gen. Physiol.* 22, 593.

Hecht, S., S. Shlaer and M. H. Pirenne (1942) Energy quanta and vision. *J. gen. Physiol.* 25, 819.

Hecht, S., S. Ross and C. G. Mueller (1947) The visibility of lines and squares at high brightness. *J. opt. Soc. Amer.* 37, 500.

Held, R. (1955) Shifts in binaural localizations after prolonged exposures to atypical combinations of stimuli. *Amer. J. Psychol.* 68, 526.

Held, R. and A. V. Hein (1958) Adaptation of disarranged hand-eye coordination contingent upon reafferent stimulation. *Percept. Motor Skills* 8, 87.

Held, R. and A. V. Hein (1963) Movement-produced stimulation in the development of visually guided behaviour. *J. comp. Psychol.* 56, 872.

Helmholtz, H. L. F. von (1856–66) *Handbuch der Physiologischen Optik*. Hamburg and Leipzig. Trans. 1924 by J. P. C. Southall, *Physiological Optics*, Optical Society of America. Dover reprint 1962.

Hering, E. *Beitrage zur Physiologie*, vol. 1. Leipzig.

Hick, W. E. (1952) On the rate of gain of information. *Quart. J. exp. Psychol.* 4, 67.

Holmes, G. (1938) The cerebral integration of ocular movements. *Brit. Med. Journ.* 2, 107.

Holst, E. von. (1954) Relations between the central nervous system and the peripheral organs. *Brit. J. anim. Behav.* 2, 89.

Holway, A. H. and C. C. Pratt (1936) The Weber ratio for intensive discrimination. *Psychol. Rev.* 43, 322.

Holway, A. H., L. E. Goldring and M. J. Zigler (1938) On the discrimination of minimal differences in weight: 4. Kinaesthetic adaptation for exposure-intensity as variant. *J. exp. Psychol.* 23, 536.

Honeyman, W. M., N. C. Cooper and E. W. Rose (1946) The autokinetic illusion. Flying Personnel Research Committee, Rep. no. 664, Air Ministry, London.

Hood, J. D. (1950) Studies in auditory fatigue and adaptation. *Acta Oto-Laryngol.*, Supplement 92.

Hood, J. D. (1955) Auditory fatigue and adaptation in the differential diagnosis of end-organ disease. *Ann. Otol. Rhinol. Laryngol.* 64, 507.

Howarth, C. I. and M. G. Bulmer (1956) Non-random sequences in visual threshold experiments. *Quart. J. exp. Psychol.* 8, 163.

Howe, J. A. M. and R. L. Gregory (1968) Visual perception in simulated space conditions. *J. Brit. Interplanetary Soc.* 21, 209. [No. 26]

Hubel, D. H. and T. N. Wiesel (1962) Receptive fields, binocular interaction and functional architecture in the cat's visual cortex. *J. Physiol.* 160, 106.

Ittelson, W. H. (1951a) Size as a cue to distance. *Amer. J. Psychol.* 64, 54 and 188.

Ittelson, W. H. (1951b) The constancies in perceptual theory. *Psychol. Rev.* 58, 285.

Ittelson, W. H. (1952) *The Ames Demonstrations in Perception*, Princeton.

Ittelson, W. H. and F. P. Kilpatrick (1952) Experiments in perception. *Sci. Amer.* 185, 50.

Jonckheere, A. R. (1954) A test of significance for the relation between *m* rankings and *k* ranked categories. *Brit. J. stat. Psychol.* 7, 93.

Kanizsa, G. (1955) Margini quasi-percettivi in campi con stimolazione omogenea. *Rivista di psicologia* 49, 7.

Kant, I. (1770) *Kritik der Umtheilskraft*.

Kay, J. (1951) Learning of a serial task by different age groups. *Quart. J. exp. Psychol.* 3, 166.

Keidel, W. D., U. D. Keidel and M. E. Wigand (1961) Adaptation: loss or gain of sensory information? In W. A. Rosenblith (ed.), *Sensory Communication*, New York.

Kern, E. (1952) Der Bereich der Unterschiedsempfindlichkeit des Auges bei festgehaltenem Adaptationszustand. *Z. Biol.* 105, 237.

Kilpatrick, F. P. (1954) Two processes in perceptual learning. *J. exp. Psychol.* 47, 362.

Koffka, K. (1935) *Principles of Gestalt Psychology*. London.

Köhler, I. (1962) Experiments with goggles. *Sci. Amer.* 206, part 5, 62.

Köhler, W. (1917) *Mentality of Apes*. New York.

Köhler, W. (1920) *Die physischen Gestalten*. Trans. in W. E. Ellis (ed.), *Source Book of Gestalt Psychology*, London and New York 1938.

Köhler, W. (1929) *Gestalt Psychology*. New York.

Köhler, W. (1940) *Dynamics of Psychology*. New York.

Köhler, W. (1969) *The Task of Gestalt Psychology*. Princeton.

Köhler, W. and H. Wallach (1944) Figural after-effects: an investigation of visual processes. *Proc. Amer. phil. Soc.* 88, 4.

Kornmüller, A. E. (1930) Eine experimentelle Anästhesie der äusseren Augenmusklen am Menschen und ihre Auswirkungen. *J. Psychol. Neurol. Lpz.* 41, 354.

Koseleff, P. (1958) Studies in the perception of heaviness: II. *Acta Psychologica* 14, 109.

Krauskopf, J. (1954) Figural after-effects in auditory space. *Amer. J. Psychol.* 67, 278.

Kuffler, S. W. (1953) Discharge patterns and functional organization of mammalian retina. *J. Neurophysiol.* 16, 37.

Kuffler, S. W., R. Fitzhugh and H. B. Barlow (1957) Maintained activity in the cat's retina in light and darkness. *J. gen. Physiol.* 40, 683.

Kuhn, T. (1962) *The Structure of Scientific Revolutions.* Chicago.

Kunnapas, T. M. (1955) Influence of frame size on apparent length of a line. *J. exp. Psychol.* 50, 168.

Lashley, K. S. (1929) *Brain Mechanisms and Intelligence.* Chicago.

Lashley, K. S. (1950) *In Search of the Engram.* Symposia of the Society for Experimental Biology, IV. London.

Lawson, R. W. (1948) Blinking: its role in physical measurement. *Nature,* Lond., 161, 154.

Lee, D. N. (1969) Theory of the stereoscopic shadow-caster: an instrument for the study of binocular space perception. *Vision Research* 9, 1.

Leibowitz, H. W. (1955) The relation between the rate threshold for perception of movement and luminance for various durations of exposure. *J. exp. Psychol.* 49, 209.

Leonard, J. A. (1953) Advance information in sensorimotor skills. *Quart. J. exp. Psychol.* 5, 141.

Lettvin, J. Y., H. R. Maturana, W. S. McCulloch and W. H. Pitts (1959) What the frog's eye tells the frog's brain. *Proc. Inst. Radio Engrs.* 47, 1940. New York.

Licklider, J. C. R. (1946) Effects of amplitude distortion upon the intelligibility of speech. *J. acoust. Soc. Amer.* 18, 429.

Licklider, J. C. R. (1950) The intelligibility of amplitude-dichotomised, time-quantised speech waves. *J. acoust. Soc. Amer.* 22, 820.

Licklider, J. C. R. (1951) Basic correlates of the auditory stimulus. In S. S. Stevens (ed.), *Handbook of Experimental Psychology,* New York.

Locke, J. *An Essay Concerning Human Understanding.* 6th ed., London 1960.

Lowenfeld, V. (1952) *The Nature of Creative Activity.* Trans. O. A. Oeser, London.

Lowy, K. (1945) Some experimental evidence for peripheral auditory masking. *J. acoust. Soc. Amer.* 16, 197.

Luce, R. D. (1959) *Individual Choice Behaviour.* New York.

Luckiesh, M. and F. K. Moss (1942) *Reading as a Visual Task.* Princeton.

Lythgoe, R. J. (1938) Some observations on the rotating pendulum. *Nature,* Lond., 141, 474.

Mach, E. (1886) *The Analysis of Sensations.* Trans. of 5th ed., New York 1959.

MacKay, D. M. (1958) Perceptual stability of a stroboscopically lit visual field containing self-luminous objects. *Nature,* Lond., 181, 507.

MacKay, D. M. (1959) A 'solid-image' microscope. *Nature*, Lond., 183, 246.

MacKay, D. M. (1961) Interactive processes in visual perception. In W. A. Rosenblith (ed.), *Sensory Communication*, London.

MacKay, D. M. and W. S. McCulloch (1952) The limiting information capacity of a neuronal link. *Bull. Math. Biophysics* 14, 12.

Mackworth, N. H. (1950) *Researches on the Measurement of Human Performance*, Medical Research Council, Special Report Series, no. 268. London.

Marler, P. (1955) Characteristics of some animal calls. *Nature*, Lond., 176, 6.

Matthews, B. H. C. (1931) The response of a single end organ. *J. Physiol.* 71, 64.

Merton, P. A. (1961) The accuracy of directing the eyes and the hand in the dark. *J. Physiol.* 156, 555.

Miller, G. A. (1951) *Language and Communication*. New York.

Miller, G. A., J. S. Bruner and L. Postman (1954) Familiarity of letter sequences and tachistoscopic identification. *J. genet. Psychol.* 50, 129.

Morgan, C. T. and E. Stellar (1950) *Physiological Psychology*. New York.

Müller-Lyer, F. C. (1889) Optische Urtheilstauschungen. *Arch. Physiol.*, Suppl. Bd. 263.

Müller-Lyer, F. C. (1896) Uber Kontrast und Konfluxion. *Z. Psychol.* 9, 1; 10, 421.

Munson, W. A. and J. E. Karlin (1954) Measurement of human channel transmission characteristics. *J. acoust. Soc. Amer.* 26, 542.

Myers, C. S. (1925) *Textbook of Experimental Psychology*. 3rd ed., London.

Necker, L. A. (1832) Observations on some remarkable phenomena seen in Switzerland: and an optical phenomenon which occurs on viewing of a crystal or geometrical solid. *Phil. Mag.* 1 (3 ser.) 329.

Neff, W. D. (1947) The effects of partial section of the auditory nerve. *J. comp. Physiol. Psychol.* 40, 203.

Osgood, C. E. (1953) *Method and Theory in Experimental Psychology*. London.

Osgood, C. E. and A. W. Heyer (1951) A new interpretation of figural after-effects. *Psychol. Rev.* 59, 98.

Oshima, M. *et al.* (1954) Changes in physical functions by age. Annual Report of the Institute for Science of Labour, Japan, no. 47.

Osterberg, G. (1935) Topography of the layer of rods and cones in the human retina. *Acta Ophthal. Suppl.* 61, 1.

Over, R. (1967) Intermanual transfer of practice decrements with a haptic illusion. *Quart. J. exp. Psychol.* 19, 215.

Penrose, L. S. and R. Penrose (1958) Impossible objects: a special type of illusion. *Brit. J. Psychol.* 49, 31.

Pickersgill, M. (1959) The determinants of perception of some aspects of visual movements, and their relation to certain personality variables and to brain injury. Ph.D. Thesis, University of Leeds.

Pirenne, M. H. (1948) *Vision and the Eye*. London.

Pirenne, M. H. and E. S. Denton (1952) Accuracy and sensitivity of the human eye. *Nature*, Lond., 170, 1039.

Poggendorff, J. C. (1860) Poggendorff did not publish his illusion of this date. He called F. Zollner's attention to it, and it was named for him by Burmester; see E. Burmester (1896), Beitrang zur Experimentallen Bestimmung geometrisch-optischen. *Z. Psychol.* 12, 355.

Polyak, S. I. (1941) *The Retina*. Chicago.

Ponder, E. and W. P. Kennedy (1928) On the act of blinking. *Quart. J. exp. Physiol.* 18, 89.

Poulton, E. C. (1952*a*) Perceptual anticipation in tracking with two pointer and one pointer displays. *Brit. J. Psychol.* 43, 222.

Poulton, E. C. (1952*b*) The basis of perceptual anticipation in tracking. *Brit. J. Psychol.* 43, 295.

Poulton, E. C. and R. L. Gregory (1952) Blinking during visual tracking. *Quart. J. exp. Psychol.* 4, part 2, 57. [No. 4]

Pritchard, R. M. (1958) Visual illusions viewed as stabilized retinal images. *Quart. J. exp. Psychol.* 10, part 2, 77.

Pritchard, R. M. (1961) A collimator stabilizing system for the retinal image. *Quart. J. exp. Psychol.* 13, 181.

Pritchard, R. M., W. Heron and D. O. Hebb (1960) Visual perception approached by the method of stabilized images. *Canad. J. Psychol* 14, 67.

Pulfrich, C. (1922) Die Stereoskopie im Dienste der isochromen und heterochromen Photometrie. *Naturwissenschaften* 10, 533.

Ranke, O. F. (1952) Die optische Simultanschwelle als Gegenbeweis gegen das Fechersche Gesetz. *Z. Biol.* 105, 224.

Ratliff, F. and L. A. Riggs (1950) Involuntary motions of the eye during monocular fixation. *J. exp. Psychol.* 40, 687.

Rees, D. W. and N. K. Copeland (1960) Discrimination of differences in mass of weightless objects. Wright-Patterson Air Force Base, Tech. Rep. 60–601.

Revesz, G. (1950) *Psychology and Art of the Blind*. Trans. H. A. Wolff. London.

Riesen, A. H. (1947) The development of perception in man and chimpanzee. *Science* 106, 107.

Riesen, A. H. (1950) Arrested vision. *Sci. Amer.* 183, part 1, 16.

Rose, A. J. (1942) The relative sensitivities of television pick-up tubes, photographic film and the human eye. *Proc. Inst. Radio Engrs.* 30, 293.

Rose, A. J. (1948) The sensitivity of the human eye on an absolute scale. *J. opt. Soc. Amer.* 38, 196.

Ross, H. E. (1964) Constant errors in weight judgments as a function of the size of the differential threshold. *Brit. J. Psychol.* 55, 133.

Ross, H. E. (1965) The effect of apparent versus physical stimulus magnitude upon sensory discrimination. Unpublished Ph.D. thesis, University of Cambridge.

Ross, H. E. (1969) When is a weight not illusory? *Quart. J. exp. Psychol.* 21, 346.

Ross, H. E. and R. L. Gregory (1964) Is the Weber fraction a function of physical or perceived input? *Quart. J. exp. Psychol.* 16, part 2, 116. [No. 11]

Ross, H. E. and R. L. Gregory (1970) Weight illusions and weight discrimination – a revised hypothesis. *Quart. J. exp. Psychol.* 22, 318. [No. 13]

Rudel, R. G. and H.-L. Teuber (1963) Decrement of visual and haptic Müller-Lyer illusion on repeated trials: a study of cross-modal transfer. *Quart. J. exp. Psychol.* 15, 125.

Rump, E. E. (1961) The relationship between perceived size and perceived distance. *Brit. J. Psychol.* 52, 111.

Rushton, W. H. (1952) Apparatus for analysing the light reflected from the eye of the cat. *J. Physiol.* 117, 47.

Rushton, W. H. (1953) Aspects of retinal physiology. Instituto de Biofisica, Rio de Janeiro.

Rushton, W. H. (1965) The rhodopsin density in the human rods. *J. Physiol.* 134, 30.

Rushton, W. H. and F. W. Campbell (1954) Measurement of rhodopsin in the living human eye. *Nature*, Lond., 174, 1096.

Rushton, W. H., F. W. Campbell, W. A. Hagins and G. S. Brindley (1955) The bleaching and regeneration of rhodopsin in the living eye of the albino rabbit and of man. *Optica Acta* 1, 183.

Russell, B. (1940) *Enquiry into Meaning and Truth*. London.

Scholl, D. A. (1957) *The Organization of the Cerebral Cortex*. London.

Seashore, C. E. (1896) Weber's Law in illusions. *Stud. Yale Psychol. Lab.* 4.

Segall, M. H. and D. T. Campbell (1962) *Cultural Differences in the Perception of Geometric Illusions*. Unpublished monograph, State University of Iowa and Northwestern University.

Segall, M. H., D. T. Campbell and M. J. Herskovits (1963) Cultural differences in the perception of geometric illusions. *Science* 139, 769.

Segall, M. H., D. T. Campbell and M. J. Herskovits (1966) *The Influence of Culture on Visual Perception*. New York.

Senden, M. von (1932) Trans. P. Heath. *Space and Sight: The Perception of Space and Shape in the Congenitally Blind Before and After Operation*. London 1960.

Shannon, C. E. (1949) A mathematical theory of communication. *Bell System Technical Journal* 27, 379 and 623.

Shannon, C. E. and W. Weaver (1949) *The Mathematical Theory of Communication*. Urbana, Ill.

Sherif, M. (1936) *The Psychology of Social Norms*. New York.

Sherrington, C. S. (1906) *The Integrative Action of the Nervous System*. London.

Shopland, C. and R. L. Gregory (1964) The effect of touch on a visually ambiguous three-dimensional figure. *Quart. J. exp. Psychol.* 16, part 1, 66. [No. 19]

Siegal, S. (1956) *Nonparametric Statistics for the Behavioural Sciences*. New York.

Simons, J. C. and M. S. Gardner (1963) Weightless man: a survey of sensations and performance while free-floating. Wright Patterson Air Force Base (U.S.A.F. Tech. Rep. AMRL-TDR-62-114).

Singleton, W. T. (1954) The change of movement timing with age. *Brit. J. Psychol.* 45, 166.

Sloan, L. L. and A. Altman (1954) Factors involved in several tests of binocular depth perception. *A.M.A. Arch. Ophthal.* 52, 524.

Smiles, S. (1861) *Lives of the Engineers.* London.

Smith, K. U. and W. M. Smith (1962) *Perception and Motion: An Analysis of Space-structured Behaviour.* Philadelphia.

Steinberg, J. C. and M. B. Gardner (1937) The dependence of hearing impairment on sound intensity. *J. acoust. Soc. Amer.* 9, 11.

Steindler, O. (1906) *Die Farbenempfindlichkeit des normalen und farblenblinden Auges.* Vienna.

Stratton, G. M. (1896) Some preliminary experiments on vision. *Psychol. Rev.* 3, 611.

Stratton, G. M. (1897a) Vision without inversion of the retinal image. *Psychol. Rev.* 4, 341.

Stratton, G. M. (1897b) Vision without inversion of the retinal image. *Psychol. Rev.* 4, 463.

Sutherland, N. S. (1961) The methods and findings of experiments on the visual discrimination of shape by animals. *Experimental Psychology Society Monograph*, no. 1.

Szafran, J. (1951) Changes with age and with exclusion of vision in performances at aiming tasks. *Quart. J. exp. Psychol.* 3, 111.

Tanner, W. P. and J. A. Swets (1954) A decision-making theory of visual detection. *Psychol. Rev.* 61, 401.

Tausch, R. (1954) Optische Tauschungen als artifizelle Effekte der Gestaltungsprozesse von Grossen und Formenkonstanz in der naturlichen Raunwahrehmung. *Psychol. Forsch.* 24, 299.

Teuber, H.-L. (1960) Perception. In Field *et al.* (eds.), *Handbook of Physiology,* Section 1: *Neurophysiology.* American Physiological Society, Washington.

Thiéry, A. (1896) Über geometrisch-optische Tauschungen. *Phil. Stud.* 12, 67.

Thouless, R. H. (1931) Phenomenal regression to the 'real' object: 1. *Brit. J. Psychol.* 21, 339.

Thouless, R. H. (1932a) Phenomenal regression to the 'real' object: 2. *Brit. J. Psychol.* 22, 1.

Thouless, R. H. (1932b) Individual differences in phenomenal regression. *Brit. J. Psychol.* 22, 216.

Travis, R. C. (1936) The latency and velocity of the eye in saccadic movements. *Psychol. Monog.* 47, part 2, 242.

Treisman, M. (1964) Noise and Weber's Law: the discrimination of brightness and other dimensions. *Psychol. Rev.* 71, 314.

Tussing, L. (1941) Perceptual fluctuations of illusions as a possible fatigue index. *J. exp. Psychol.* 29, 85.

Uttley, A. M. (1954) The classification of signals in the nervous system. *E.E.G. Clin. Neurophysiol.* 6, 479.

Uttley, A. M. (1955) *The Conditional Probability of Signals in the Nervous System.* Radar Research Establishment, Malvern, Memorandum no. 1109.

Vaissière, R. (1961) Morphologie et histologie comparées des yeux des crustacéens copépodes. *Arch. Zool. exp. et générale*, 100, Fasc. 1.

Valvo, A. (1971) Sight restoration after long-term blindness: the problems and behaviour patterns of visual rehabilitation. American Foundation for the Blind, New York.

Vernon, M. D. (1954) *A Further Study of Visual Perception.* London.

Vince, M. (1948) The intermittency of control movements and psychological refractory period. *Brit. J. Psychol.* 38, 149.

Virsu, V. (1967) Contrast and confluxion as components in geometric illusions. *Quart. J. exp. Psychol.* 19, 198.

Wallace, J. G. (1956) Some studies of perception in relation to age. *Brit. J. Psychol.* 47, 283.

Wallach, H., E. R. Newman and M. R. Rosenweig (1949) The precedence effect in sound localization. *Amer. J. Psychol.* 62, 315.

Walls, G. L. (1963) *The Vertebrate Eye and its Adaptive Radiation.* New York.

Walsh, E. G. (1957) *Physiology of the Nervous System.* London.

Warren, R. M. and Gregory, R. L. (1958) An auditory analogue of the visual reversible figure. *Amer. J. Psychol.* 71, 612. [No. 20]

Watson, J. B. (1919) *Psychology from the Standpoint of a Behaviourist.* London.

Watson, J. B. (1925) *Behaviourism.* London.

Welford, A. T. (1951) *Skill and Age: An Experimental Approach.* London.

Welford, N. (1952) An electronic digital recording machine – the SETAR. *J. Scientific Instruments* 29, 1.

Werner, H. and S. Wapner (1955) The Innsbruck studies on distorted visual fields in relation to an organismic theory of perception. *Psychol. Rev.* 62, 130.

Wertheimer, M. (1912) Experimentelle Untersuchungen über das Sehen von Bewegung. *Z. Psychol.* 61, 161.

Weston, H. C. (1949) On age and illumination in relation to visual performance. *Trans. Illumination Eng. Soc.* 14, 281.

Wever, E. G. (1949) *Theory of Hearing.* New York.

Wever, E. G. and C. W. Bray (1937) The perception of low tones and the resonance-volley theory. *J. Psychol.* 3, 101.

Wever, E. G. and M. Lawrence (1954) *Physiological Acoustics.* Princeton.

Wilkie, J. S. (1935) *The Science of Mind and Brain.* London.

Willmer, E. N. (1946) *Retinal Structure and Colour Vision.* London.

Willmer, E. N. (1950) The relationship between area and threshold for lights of different colours. *Quart. J. exp. Psychol.* 2, part 2, 53.

Witasek, S. (1899) Uber die Natur der geometrisch-optischen Tauschungen. *Z. Psychol. Physiol. Sinn.* 19, 81.

Witkin, H. A. (1952) Further studies of perception of the upright when the direction of the force acting on the body is changed. *J. exp. Psychol.* 43, 9.

Witkin, H. A. (1969) Sex differences in perception. *Trans. N.Y. Acad. Sci.* 12, 22.

Witkin, H. A., S. Wapner and T. Leventhal (1952) Sound localization with conflicting visual and auditory cues. *J. exp. Psychol.* 43, 58.

Wohlgemuth, A. (1911) On the after-effect of seen movement. *Brit. J. Psychol. Monog. Suppl.* no. 1.

Woodrow, H. (1933) Weight discrimination with a varying standard. *Amer. J. Psychol.* 45, 391.

Woodworth, R. S. (1938) *Experimental Psychology.* New York.

Woodworth, R. S. and H. Schlosberg (1955) *Experimental Psychology.* London.

Wright, W. D. (1934) The measurement and analysis of colour adaptation phenomena. *Proc. Roy. Soc. B* 115, 49.

Wright, W. D. (1936) The breakdown of a colour match with high intensities of adaptation. *J. Physiol.* 87, 23.

Wright, W. D. (1949) The present state of the trichromatic theory. *Documenta Ophthalmologica* 3, 10.

Young, J. Z. (1961) The failures of discrimination learning following the removal of the vertical lobes in *Octopus. Proc. Roy. Soc. B* 153, 18.

Young, T. (1802) On the theory of light and colours. *Philos. Trans.* 92, 20.

Young, T. (1807) *A Course of Lectures on Natural Philosophy.* London.

Zanforlin, M. (1967) Some observations on Gregory's theory of perceptual illusions. *Quart. J. exp. Psychol.* 19, 193.

Addenda

The following papers have appeared too recently to be included in the bibliography—many of them extend the topics of this book. In particular, (1) gives the depth of field of the 'solid image microscope', but without moving parts, by making use of chromatic aberration; (7) gives new data on cognitive contours.

1. Courtney-Pratt, J. S. and R. L. Gregory (1973) Microscope with enhanced depth of field and 3-D capacity. *Applied Optics* 12, 2509.

2. Gregory, R. L. (1973) The confounded eye. In R. L. Gregory and E. H. Gombrich (eds.), *Illusion in Nature and Art,* London.

3. Gregory, R. L. (1974a) Choosing a paradigm for perception. In E. Carterette and M. Friedman (eds.), *Handbook of Perception,* New York.

4. Gregory, R. L. (1974b) Paradigms of perception. In *Proceedings of the Royal Institution,* Applied Science, London.

5. Gregory, R. L. (1974c) Perceptions as hypotheses. In S. Brown (ed.), *Philosophy of Psychology,* London.

6. Gregory, R. L. (in press) Do we need a cognitive concept? In M. Gazzaniga and C. Blakemore (eds.), *Handbook of Psychobiology,* New York.

7. Harris, J. P. and R. L. Gregory (1973) Fusion and rivalry of illusory contours. *Perception* 2, no. 2, 235.

NAME INDEX

Abbé, E. 462
Adrian, E. D. 169
Aguilar, M. 166
Allanson, J. T. 576–7, 580
Ames, A. 56, 353
Anderson, E. E. 19, 181
Angyan, A. J. 577, 581
Anstis, S. 54, 276, 280, 281, 305, 346, 374 n.
Aristotle 548, 552
Asch, S. 584
Aubert, H. 263
Avery, G. C. 388

Babbage, C. 379
Bach-y-Rita, P. 67, 350
Baird, J. L. 634
Balchin, F. 316
Barlow, H. 8, 10, 13, 14, 23, 60, 62, 154, 160, 165, 166, 170, 172, 228, 237, 564, 570 n., 579–80, 581
Barnett, S. A. 436 (Fig.)
Bartlett, Sir F. 85, 130, 521, 529, 580, 582, 591
Bartley, S. H. 20, 187
Bates, J. A. V. 578, 581, 582
Battersby, W. S. 264, 270
Békésy, G. von 40, 41, 199, 239, 242, 458
Bell, D. A. 223
Bergson, H. 548, 583
Berkeley, G. 69, 226, 589
Blodgett, H. C. 591
Boring, E. G. 296, 342, 360
Bouman, M. A. 178
Bower, T. G. R. 292
Brandt, H. F. 535
Bray, C. W. 196, 218
Brewster, Sir D. 359

Brindley, G. S. 29, 31, 151, 155, 183, 272, 458
Broad, C. D. 539 n.
Broca, P. 578
Brown, J. F. 58
Brown, R. H. 58
Brunelleschi 619
Bruner, J. 374
Brunton (inventor of mechanical traveller) 634
Bulmer, M. G. 160–2, 164, 165, 166, 229
Burton, D. 66

Campbell, F. W. 179, 222, 296, 298, 304, 346
Campbell, D. T. 57, 66, 338, 348, 349, 374
Cane, V. 62, 154, 155, 157, 160, 161, 162, 164, 165, 166, 167, 168, 220, 228, 237, 564
Carpenter, A. 136, 144
Carr, H. A. 263, 264, 265, 270, 271, 273 n.
Carter, L. 402
Carterette, E. C. 43
Casey, A. 337
Charpentier, A. 263
Cherubin, P. 460
Chomsky, N. 622, 624
Clark, F. R. 43
Clark, P. 512
Clay, H. M. 209
Coghill, G. E. 590
Cook, C. 181
Cooper, S. 25, 257
Copeland, N. K. 239
Cornsweet, T. N. 58
Covell, W. P. 193 n.
Cowper, N. C. 263

GENERAL INDEX

Abacus, 626; its power suggests limitations of brain, 620

ablation studies, 63; and location of cerebral function, 554–62

acceleration forces, their effect on size constancy, 304–10

accommodation of lens of eye, 6; shown by Purkinje images, 6; affecting acuity, 18

'active' theories of perception, xviii, xix, xxiv

acuity, visual, 16–21, 171–4; impairment of, associated with ageing, 170–1, 174; related to intensity discrimination, 171–4

adaptation: in retinal receptors, 8; to intensity of light, 23–4, 222–7; to movement, 26, 255; and its effect on discrimination, 238–9; of eye/head system, suggested cause of autokinetic effect, 272–5; distinguished from fatigue, 569; to social change and technological innovation, 640–1

after-effect: of movement, 26; figural, used as test on patient having recovered sight, 99; figural, result of inappropriate setting of primary constancy scaling, 349

after-images, 359; and passive eye-movements, 25; and voluntary eye-movements, 25; used to study stability of visual world, 257; and autokinetic effect, 274; change of size of, with observer movement, 295–8

ageing, theory that it is related to raised neural noise, 167–215

ambiguity illusions: visual, effect of touch data on, 283–9; auditory, 290–1; as demonstrating selection of perceptual hypotheses, 360, 527, 615–16; see perceptual hypotheses

Ames room, 57, 97–8; used as test on patient having recovered sight, 98

analogue: and digital systems, distinction between redefined, 377–9, 599–601; system, brain as, 378–9, 563, 600–1; devices, characteristics of, 541, 562

aqueous humour, 6

A.R.I.D. (Automatic Rejection of Image Disturbance), 501–18; 502–5, 508–18 (Figs.)

association pathways, between different sense modalities, may be important for use of symbols, 617

atomism: as a psychological theory, 538–40; compared with Gestalt theory, 540

autokinetic effect, 27–8, 61–2, 260; detection of eye movements during, 261–2 (see eye movements); theory for, 263–75

Behaviour: and its relation to engineering 'performance', 547–8; whether controlled by sensory information or by stored hypotheses, 590–601

behaviourism: as a self-defeating philosophy, xv; limitations of, xvi; usefulness of, xvi

binocular vision, 11–12; and reduction of absolute threshold, 189–91; and measurement of monocular depth, 370 (see Pandora's Box)

blindness: recovery from, a case study, 65–129; recovery from, as a philosophical problem, 68–9; definition of and clinical tests for, 72–3

blind spot, 9–10